T0190495

Lecture Notes in Computer Science 12376

More information about this series at http://www.springer.com/series/7409

Klaus Miesenberger · Roberto Manduchi ·
Mario Covarrubias Rodriguez ·
Petr Peňáz (Eds.)

Computers Helping People with Special Needs

17th International Conference, ICCHP 2020
Lecco, Italy, September 9–11, 2020
Proceedings, Part I

 Springer

Editors
Klaus Miesenberger (iD)
Institute Integriert Studieren
JKU Linz
Linz, Austria

Mario Covarrubias Rodriguez (iD)
Dipartimento di Meccanica
Politecnico di Milano
Milan, Italy

Roberto Manduchi (iD)
Jack Baskin School of Engineering
UC Santa Cruz
Santa Cruz, CA, USA

Petr Peňáz
Support Centre for Students
with Special Needs
Masaryk University Brno
Brno, Czech Republic

ISSN 0302-9743   ISSN 1611-3349   (electronic)
Lecture Notes in Computer Science
ISBN 978-3-030-58795-6   ISBN 978-3-030-58796-3   (eBook)
https://doi.org/10.1007/978-3-030-58796-3

LNCS Sublibrary: SL3 – Information Systems and Applications, incl. Internet/Web, and HCI

Klaus Miesenberger · Roberto Manduchi ·
Mario Covarrubias Rodriguez ·
Petr Peňáz (Eds.)

Computers Helping People with Special Needs

17th International Conference, ICCHP 2020
Lecco, Italy, September 9–11, 2020
Proceedings, Part I

Springer

Editors
Klaus Miesenberger
Institute Integriert Studieren
JKU Linz
Linz, Austria

Roberto Manduchi
Jack Baskin School of Engineering
UC Santa Cruz
Santa Cruz, CA, USA

Mario Covarrubias Rodriguez
Dipartimento di Meccanica
Politecnico di Milano
Milan, Italy

Petr Peňáz
Support Centre for Students
with Special Needs
Masaryk University Brno
Brno, Czech Republic

ISSN 0302-9743   ISSN 1611-3349   (electronic)
Lecture Notes in Computer Science
ISBN 978-3-030-58795-6   ISBN 978-3-030-58796-3   (eBook)
https://doi.org/10.1007/978-3-030-58796-3

LNCS Sublibrary: SL3 – Information Systems and Applications, incl. Internet/Web, and HCI

Preface

Since its inception in 1989, ICCHP has evolved to become the largest European conference on accessibility and inclusion, and in particular on technical aspects such as eAccessibility and Assistive Technology. ICCHP addresses the many unnecessary barriers, physical or otherwise, that impede opportunities for work, education, and participation by people with disabilities.

It capitalizes on progress in all areas of technology that can contribute to remove these barriers. Artificial intelligence has certainly captured the lion's share of attention for technological trends in accessibility. Smartphone apps now read text, recognize objects, and automatically describe the content of pictures. Ever-improving speech understanding algorithms enable hand-free control of computers, appliances, or devices, with research ongoing on the recognition of dysarthric speech. Autonomous cars may in the near future provide individualized transportation to those who cannot drive, while exoskeleton systems will enable ambulation to people with paraplegia. Intelligent homes offer opportunities for independent living to those with reduced motion control. At the urban scale, mapping and localization systems are being deployed in public spaces to support orientation and wayfinding, or to identify safe paths to traverse for wheelchair users. It is encouraging that all major information technology companies have committed to including accessibility features in their products, and even started their own research labs in access technology.

Yet, sometimes innovation comes from the grassroots. Communities of makers have taken on the challenges of designing low-budget assistive technology, often involving people with disabilities in exciting co-design experiments. Crowdsourcing and micro-volunteering projects have evolved into accessibility platforms with thousands of contributors and users. The scope of ICCHP encompasses all of these technologies, with the common goal to build a more accessible, inclusive, and participative world.

In 2020, the proceedings of the 17th conference are delivered to you as a compendium of new and exciting scholarly and practical work going on in our field. ICCHP runs a highly competitive process for selecting the contributions for publication and presentation. The Program Committee, including 130 experts, guarantees that each paper is reviewed by at least 3 experts. 1 member of the panel of 15 conference chairs assesses the review results of each contribution to come to a final decision, which was made during online meetings held over 3 days. This two-phase selection procedure guarantees high scientific quality, making ICCHP unique to our field. 107 contributions were accepted and you will find them in the two-volume proceedings embedded in the structure of thematically grouped chapters. The concept of organizing Special Thematic Sessions again helped to structure the proceedings and the program in order to support a deep focus on highly desirable selected topics in the field as well as to bring new and interesting topics to the attention of the research community.

Due to the COVID-19 crisis, we decided to run the conference online only. Although we do hope that the situation becomes better, at the time of writing this preface, travel and contact opportunities were frequently changing. We needed predictable organization and plannable programs, which could only be made available online. Running the conference virtually was challenging but also an important experience in terms of interaction and communication, in particular for accessibility. We still managed to host a high-quality and fully accessible meeting for scientists, users, practitioners, educators, and policy makers. We strive to be able to provide new and innovative opportunities for exchange and cooperation. The Service and Practice Track, organized in addition to scientific presentations, supported a cross-domain exchange and cooperation. ICCHP aims to support young researchers, the next generation of experts in our field, and encourages them to contribute. ICCHP accepts the challenge to provide new and innovative online conference spaces, aiming at less formal discussions. This important factor, supporting the transfer of knowledge so needed in our endeavors, must not be lost when moving online.

Thank you for your attendance at ICCHP 2020 and we hope that you and your colleagues to be regular participants in its most important mission, also recognized through patronage of the United Nations Educational, Scientific and Cultural Organization (UNESCO). It is here that research, innovation, and practical endeavors in important topics of Assistive Technologies and eAccesibility can come together to be shared, explored, and discussed.

September 2020

Klaus Miesenberger
Roberto Manduchi
Mario Covarrubias Rodriguez
Petr Peňáz

Organization

ICCHP Committees

Our special thanks go to those who have contributed in putting this conference together:

General Chair

Roberto Manduchi   UC Santa Cruz, Jack Baskin School of Engineering, USA

Publishing Chairs

Miesenberger, K.	JKU Linz, Austria
Covarrubias Rodriguez, M.	Politecnico di Milano, Italy
Peňáz, P.	Masaryk University Brno, Czech Republic

Program Chairs

Archambault, D.	Université Paris 8, France
Buehler, C.	TU Dortmund, FTB, Germany
Coughlan, J.	Smith-Kettlewell Eye Research Institute, USA
Debevc, M.	University of Maribor, Slovenia
Fels, D.	Ryerson University, Canada
Kobayashi, M.	Tsukuba University of Technology, Japan
Kouroupetroglou, G.	National and Kapodistrian University of Athens, Greece
Murphy, H. J.	California State University, Northridge, USA
Pawluk, D.	Virginia Commonwealth University, USA
Suzuki, M.	Kyushu University, Japan
Weber, G.	Technische Universität Dresden, Germany
Zagler, W.	Vienna University of Technology, Austria

Young Researchers Consortium Chairs

Archambault, D.	Université Paris 8, France
Chen, W.	University of Bergen, Norway
Fels, D.	Ryerson University, Canada
Fitzpatrick, D.	Dublin City University, Ireland
Kobayashi, M.	Tsukuba University of Technology, Japan
Morandell, M.	Health University of Applied Sciences Tyrol, Austria

Pontelli, E.	New Mexico State University, USA
Prazak-Aram, B.	Austrian Institute of Technology, Austria
Scaccabarozzi, D.	Politecnico di Milano, Italy
Weber, G.	Technische Universität Dresden, Germany
Zimmermann, G.	Hochschule der Medien, Germany

Service and Practice Track Chairs

| Petz, A. | University of Linz, Austria |
| Pühretmair, F. | KI-I, Austria |

International Program Committee

Abascal, J.	Euskal Herriko Unibertsitatea, Spain
Abbott, C.	King's College London, UK
Abou-Zahra, S.	W3C Web Accessibility Initiative (WAI), Austria
Abu Doush, I.	American University of Kuwait, Kuwait
Andreoni, G.	Politecnico di Milano, Italy
Andrich, R.	Fondazione Don Carlo Gnocchi Onlus, Italy
Atkinson, M. T.	The Paciello Group, USA
Augstein, M.	University of Applied Sciences Upper Austria, Austria
Azevedo, L.	Instituto Superior Tecnico, Portugal
Banes, D.	David Banes Access and Inclusion Services, UK
Barroso, J.	University of Trás-os-Montes and Alto Douro, Portugal
Batusic, M.	Fabasoft, Austria
Bernareggi, C.	Universita degli Studi di Milano, Italy
Bernier, A.	BrailleNet, France
Bosse, I.	Technische Universität Dortmund, Germany
Bu, J.	Zhejiang University, China
Caruso, G.	Politecnico di Milano, Italy
Christensen, L. B.	Sensus, Denmark
Conway, V.	WebKitIT, Australia
Crombie, D.	Utrecht School of the Arts, The Netherlands
Darvishy, A.	Zurich University of Applied Sciences, Switzerland
Darzentas, J.	University of the Aegean, Greece
Debeljak, M.	University of Ljubljana, Slovenia
DeRuyter, F.	Duke University Medical Centre, USA
Diaz del Campo, R.	Antarq Tecnosoluciones, Mexico
Draffan, E. A.	University of Southampton, UK
Dupire, J.	CNAM, France
Emiliani, P. L.	Institute of Applied Physics Nello Carrara, Italy
Engelen, J.	Katholieke Universiteit Leuven, Belgium
Galinski, Ch.	InfoTerm, Austria
Gardner, J.	Oregon State University, USA
Hakkinen, M. T.	Educational Testing Service (ETS), USA
Hanson, V.	University of Dundee, UK

Haslwanter, T.	University of Applied Sciences Upper Austria, Austria
Heimgärtner, R.	Intercultural User Interface Consulting (IUIC), Germany
Höckner, K.	Hilfsgemeinschaft der Blinden und Sehschwachen, Austria
Inoue, T.	National Rehabilitation Center for Persons with Disabilities, Japan
Iversen, C. M.	U.S. Department of State, USA
Jitngernmadan, P.	Burapha University, Thailand
Kiswarday, V.	University of Primorska, Slovenia
Koumpis, A.	Berner Fachhochschule, Switzerland
Kozuh, I.	University of Maribor, Slovenia
Küng, J.	JKU Linz, Austria
Kunz, A.	ETH Zurich, Switzerland
Lee, S.	W3C Web Accessibility Initiative (WAI), UK
Lewis, C.	University of Colorado Boulder, USA
Lhotska, L.	Czech Technical University in Prague, Czech Republic
Macas, M.	Czech Technical University in Prague, Czech Republic
Magnusson, M.	Moscow State University, Russia
Mavrou, K.	European University Cyprus, Cyprus
McSorley, J.	Pearson, USA
Mihailidis, A.	University of Toronto, Canada
Mirri, S.	University of Bologna, Italy
Mohamad, Y.	Fraunhofer Institute for Applied IT, Germany
Moreira Silva Dantas, P.	Federal University Rio Grande do Norte, Brazil
Mrochen, I.	University of Silesia in Katowice, Poland
Müller-Putz, G.	TU Graz, Austria
Muratet, M.	INS HEA, France
Normie, L.	GeronTech - The Israeli Center for AT and Ageing, Israel
Nussbaum, G.	KI-I, Austria
Oswal, S.	University of Washington, USA
Paciello, M.	The Paciello Group, USA
Panek, P.	Vienna University of Technology, Austria
Paredes, H.	University of Trás-os-Montes and Alto Douro, Portugal
Petrie, H.	University of York, UK
Pissaloux, E.	Université Rouen, France
Rassmus-Groehn, K.	Lund University, Sweden
Raynal, M	University of Toulouse, France
Sanchez, J.	University of Chile, Chile
Sik Lányi, C.	University of Pannonia, Hungary
Simsik, D.	University of Kosice, Slovakia
Slavik, P.	Czech Technical University in Prague, Czech Republic
Sloan, D.	The Paciello Group, UK
Snaprud, M.	University of Agder, Norway
Stepankowa, O.	Czech Technical University in Prague, Czech Republic

Stephanidis, C.	University of Crete, FORTH-ICS, Greece
Stiefelhagen, R.	Karlsruhe Institute of Technology, Germany
Stoeger, B.	University of Linz, Austria
Tarabini, M.	Politecnico di Milano, Italy
Tauber, M.	University of Paderborn, Germany
Teixeira, A.	Universidade de Aveiro, Portugal
Teshima, Y.	Chiba Institute of Technology, Japan
Tjoa, A. M.	Vienna University of Technology, Austria
Truck, I.	Université Paris 8, France
Velazquez, R.	Panamerican University, Mexico
Vigo, M.	University of Manchester, UK
Vigouroux, N.	IRIT Toulouse, France
Wada, C.	Kyushu Institute of Technology, Japan
Wagner, G.	University of Applied Sciences Upper Austria, Austria
Waszkielewicz, A.	Foundation for Persons with Disabilities, Poland
Watanabe, T.	University of Niigata, Japan
Weber, H.	ITA, University of Kaiserslautern, Germany
White, J.	Educational Testing Service (ETS), USA
Yamaguchi, K.	Nihon University, Japan
Yeliz Yesilada	Middle East Technical University, Cyprus

Organization Committee

Andreoni, G.	Politecnico di Milano, Italy
Bieber, R.	Austrian Computer Society, Austria
Brunetti, V.	Politecnico di Milano, Italy
Bukovsky, T.	Masaryk University Brno, Czech Republic
Covarrubias Rodriguez, M.	Politecnico di Milano, Italy
Feichtenschlager, P.	JKU Linz, Austria
Heumader, P.	JKU Linz, Austria
Höckner, K.	Hilfsgemeinschaft der Blinden und Sehschwachen, Austria
Hrabovska, L.	Masaryk University Brno, Czech Republic
Koutny, R.	JKU Linz, Austria
Lepschy, C.	JKU Linz, Austria
Miesenberger, K.	JKU Linz, Austria
Murillo Morales, T.	JKU Linz, Austria
Ondra, S.	Masaryk University Brno, Czech Republic
Pavlíček, R.	Masaryk University Brno, Czech Republic
Peňáz, P.	Masaryk University Brno, Czech Republic
Petz, A.	JKU Linz, Austria
Salinas-Lopez, V.	JKU Linz, Austria
Scaccabarozzi, D.	Politecnico di Milano, Italy
Schult, C.	JKU Linz, Austria
Seyruck, W.	Austrian Computer Society, Austria
Stöger, B.	JKU Linz, Austria

Tarabini, M.	Politecnico di Milano, Italy
Válková, H.	Masaryk University Brno, Czech Republic
Verma, A.	JKU Linz, Austria
Wernerová, P.	Masaryk University Brno, Czech Republic

ICCHP Roland Wagner Award Committee

Dominique Burger	BrailleNet, France
Christian Buehler	TU Dortmund, FTB Vollmarstein, Germany
E. A. Draffan	University of Southampton, UK
Deborah Fels	Ryerson University, Canada
Klaus Höckner	Hilfsgemeinschaft der Blinden und Sehschwachen, Austria
Klaus Miesenberger	JKU Linz, Austria
Wolfgang Zagler	Vienna University of Technology, Austria

Once again, we thank all those who helped put the ICCHP 2020 conference together, thereby supporting the AT field and a better quality of life for people with disabilities. Special thanks go to all our supporter and sponsors, displayed at: https://www.icchp. org/sponsors-20.

Contents – Part I

**XR Accessibility – Learning from the Past, Addressing Real
User Needs and the Technical Architecture for Inclusive
Immersive Environments**

Serious and Fun Games

Large-Scale Web Accessibility Observatories

Accessible and Inclusive Digital Publishing

AT and Accessibility for Blind and Low Vision Users

Art Karshmer Lectures in Access to Mathematics, Science and Engineering

Tactile Graphics and Models for Blind People and Recognition of Shapes by Touch

Environmental Sensing Technologies for Visual Impairment

Contents – Part II

**ICT to Support Inclusive Education - Universal Learning
Design (ULD)**

Hearing Systems and Accessories for People with Hearing Loss

How to Improve Interaction with a Text Input System

Human Movement Analysis for the Design and Evaluation of Interactive Systems and Assistive Devices

Service and Care Provision in Assistive Environments

User Centred Design and User Participation in Inclusive R&D

User Centered Design and User Participation in Inclusive R&D

Introduction to the Special Thematic Session

Klaus Miesenberger[1]([⊠])(ID), Cordula Edler[2], Susanne Dirks[2](ID),
Christian Bühler[2], and Peter Heumader[1](ID)

[1] Institute Integriert Studieren, Johannes Kepler University,
Altenbergerstraße 69, Linz, Austria
{klaus.miesenberger,peter.heumader}@jku.at
[2] TU Dortmund University, 44227 Dortmund, Germany
cordula.edler@icloud.com,
{susanne.dirks,christian.buehler}@tu-dortmund.de

Abstract. This session reflects R&D on User Centered Design and Development and User Participation (in short UCD in the following) for/with people with disabilities. Better guidelines, methods, techniques and tools are needed to improve the quality of R&D and practice both in the domain of Assistive Technology (AT), eAccessibility and eInclusion itself but also for improving the quality of mainstream R&D through UCD and participation of people with disabilities. We analyze the state of the art, identify gaps and problems as well as discuss examples and new approaches presented in 5 papers. The introduction integrates the topic into the broader context of UCD in Information and Communication Technology (ICT) and Human-Computer Interaction (HCI) playing a major role for AT, eAccessibility and digital inclusion. We underline the need for ongoing and more intense R&D on UCD to improve quality and usability. By promoting this session in the ICCHP conference series we aim at establishing a comprehensive point of access to scientific work in this domain.

Keywords: User Centered Design · Participative research · People with disabilities · Accessibility · Assistive Technology

1 Introduction

UCD is recognized as important success factor for R&D to reach a high level of usability and good user experience (UX). It has a profound impact on the quality of products, processes and services. UCD thereby provides a very level of high return on investment (ROI) [1]. We can expect that this also holds true for the domain of AT and eAccessibility. A number of success stories underlines the potential [2]. But besides singular examples, considerable gaps are identified. Guidelines, methods, techniques, tools and practice for UCD in R&D still show problems in efficiency, effectiveness and usability. This relates to inclusion of people with disabilities in UCD for mainstream

© Springer Nature Switzerland AG 2020
K. Miesenberger et al. (Eds.): ICCHP 2020, LNCS 12376, pp. 3–9, 2020.
https://doi.org/10.1007/978-3-030-58796-3_1

R&D and application, but also for R&D in AT and eAccessibility itself. For example, only rather recently cognitive accessibility got taken up for WCAG [3].

UCD in practice is often an add-on to the R&D process, restricted to initial user requirements studies and final evaluation. Because of a lack of concepts and methods of cooperation with different user groups, UCD is often regarded as an additional burden in R&D projects, despite the proven benefits for usability and accessibility [4, 5]. Holistic approaches also facilitating participation of people with disabilities throughout the process, contribution to ideation, planning, decision making and leadership are not considered, as successful examples of UX based design would propose. R&D still tend to be more "about" then "with" people with disabilities what risks lower quality of output and restricted uptake. Recent studies provide evidence both on these gaps but on the other hand also on the benefits of UCD leading to increased quality of R&D [6].

This STSs intends to provide an open and creative platform for further evaluating and reflecting this state of the art and discussing new and innovative ideas and concepts. It intends to provoke and support more R&D. As an ICCHP series over the next years it should lead to a comprehensive point of access to scientific R&D.

2 ICT, HCI, Assistive Technology (AT) and Accessibility

UCD is the result of a fundamental paradigmatic shift taking place over less than a century. In 1933 the motto of the world exhibition in Chicago "A Century of Progress", was: "Science finds, Industry applies and Man conforms!" [7]. Only a few decades later, this has been turned around into "People Propose, Science Studies, Technology Conforms", as expressed by Donald A. Norman [8]. ICT and in particular the HCI in the second half of the 20th century have been playing a key role in this turnaround [e.g. 9]. More and more resources are invested to bridge the gap between the *conceptual models* of computing systems, and the *mental models* of the growing diversity of user in differing contexts and situations. Besides technical functionalities, overcoming the *"gulf of execution"* in terms of understanding what functionalities the interface provides and affords, and the *"gulf of evaluation"* in terms of understandability of the reactions/output becomes a challenge [10]. Four steps describe this development: [8]

- **Utility**: "It fulfils the task, provides **functionalities** needed."
- **Usability**: "I can use it, it's **easy, efficient, effective**."
- **Desirability:** "I like the style and **look&feel**."
- **Experience:** "It is part of my**self**/my lifestyle."

Each step requires and builds upon what was learned and achieved on the steps before. And with each step the complexity and interdisciplinary challenge increases. Statistics underline that more and more resources, even up to 50% in ICT projects, are invested in HCI and usability due to the high level of ROI [11]. UCD is a key answer to this increased need of addressing usability and a profound set of guidelines, principles, methods and tools for UCD gets available [e.g. 12, 13].

AT and accessibility can hook on this state of the art. Three qualities of ICT/HCI facilitate this progress and have enormous potential for people with disabilities [14]:

1. First, even if computing entered into a fast and ever accelerating development with more and more hard- and software, the basic *principles of HCI are considerably stable, standard, universal and sustainable*. Once learned, one can use the restricted number of elements (e.g. windows, icons, menus, pointer – WIMP, but also speech output, haptics, images, videos) and interactions (e.g. point&click, drag&drop, touch, gestures) in all situations and on the diversity of devices, what makes HCI a basic cultural technique. We change or devices and application faster and faster, but only because we can trust that the basic principles of interaction are still there. Only slight changes taking place as otherwise users would not follow. And this offers an enormous potential to AT, Accessibility and inclusion. The more digitization, the more systems and services integrate into the standard HCI. Instead of running behind the numerous interfaces with their particular and proprietary features, we can focus on one global standard [14]. There is strong evidence that this has been forming the base for the sustainable development of standards as WCAG [15].

2. Second, standard and stable HCI, when running in a digital virtual environment with more and better tools and techniques, is considerably *flexible and adaptable to the user*, their tasks and their environmental settings. We might use only a few operating systems with a similar look&feel and applications using the same features etc., but each personal interface is different, adapting to personal, tasks and environmental factors. And this holds also true for people with disabilities. As all other users, people with disabilities can expect that the HCI adapts and supports their AT and interaction preferences. And we can expect more form the upcoming user tracing and Artificial Intelligence (AI) trends. We see a lot of impact on mainstream as many features for adapting the HCI origin from AT and Accessibility R&D.

3. Third, this makes usability and *UCD a key factor for the success and progress* also for AT, eAccessibility and eInclusion. Systems are requested to react and adapt on the fly to users including those with disabilities, tasks and situations when computing becomes ubiquitous including things and processes in the environment (e.g. IoT).

3 AT/Accessibility/HCI/ICT and UCD

Progress can be seen for most groups of people disabilities. Studies underline that UCD is an indispensable aspect of R&D in accessibility, AT and digital inclusion [e.g. 16]. First approaches to and examples of targeted guidelines, methods, techniques and tools are at hand to reach a high level of usability for people with disabilities [15]. But the state of the art also underlines, that UCD is not taken up and widely used in a comprehensive manner due to lacking understanding of the benefit, lack of know-how and support for efficiently facilitating UCD. Also, the cost of UCD are not valued against its ROI. Therefore, UCD stays more an add-on than the guiding principle of R&D.

For people with cognitive disabilities in particular the situation is even worse. Considerable obstacles are reported relating to a lack of methods and tools for including the group due to communication issues [6, 17]. UCD here goes beyond adapting content, methods, techniques and tools in the UCD process. Cognitive disabilities demand for approaches of decoding, processing, understanding content and processes perceived and making it part of a mental structure to allow people becoming active and participating in UCD. This goes beyond standard sensory and physical accessibility issues [18]. It is underlined that R&D for this target group mostly works based on expert opinions and a mediated understanding of the user. The core demand of participation is much less reached for this group [17].

But also new and innovative R&D and experimenting on methods, technique and tools/ATs for UCD can be identified for people with disabilities also including those with cognitive disabilities. Participatory Action Research (PAR) [e.g. 19], which is well established in social and educational sciences, is considered and tested for inclusive R&D. Inclusive PAR (IPAR) [20] aims at adapting guidelines, methods, processes and tools for people with disabilities. IPAR involves people with disabilities in all steps of action research and therefore also addresses complex communication barriers. Combining IPAR with UCD, as proposed by Edler [21], provides a holistic approach for innovative and new R&D worth being discussed and explored.

This shows the broad domain of UCD in R&D. Guidelines, methods, techniques and tools are to be analyzed, evaluated and adapted for inclusive settings, new approaches are needed. This session as part of the ICCHP conference series addresses:

- UCD in inclusive and participatory R&D and design processes and settings, e.g. phases, timing, role & task allocation, room
- Accessible and supportive R&D and communication environments: respecting, expressing, discussing, influencing, noting, evaluating, understanding at same level
- New and adapted guidelines, methods, techniques and tools for inclusive and participatory R&D and design
- New approaches in supporting user tracking and understanding, also based on AI, supporting better UCD and user participation
- Impact, outcome of R&D based on UCD

4   Contributions to Inclusive R&D in Inclusive UCD

The contributions to this session integrate into this context and demonstrate the importance of progress in this domain. The critical reflection is done against the above-mentioned holistic participation of users in all steps of the process. From the numerous submissions received, five got accepted for this session. It is also to be mentioned that many of the scientific R&D presented at ICCHP and in other literature is worth to be reflected against this state of the art.

– The first paper discusses accessibility support for mobility by an app, in particular when doing a train journey by blind and low vision users. The problem is outlined by a service provider (Swiss Railways) and negative experiences expressed by disabled clients. Beyond the basic accessibility of the systems an emphasis is given to the user experience. The core UCD method used is a hackathon (action research), where in all cycles of the event end users are involved. During the cycles, observation is used for eliciting requirements, followed by a final survey. Important aspects of UCD are addressed, but not yet a holistic approach as discussed above. The problem definition enters directly into a UCD approach with strong user participation but user participation in the following phases is unclear, except the evaluation at the end.

– The second paper focusses on eliciting the requirements and expectations of older people from supportive robots. The approach is based on the review and analysis of the state of the art in this domain and provides evidence that the obvious potential fails in raising interest for integration into application and practice. This provides a fine example for user participation in requirements studies using interviews and coding the results (NIVO), but does not discuss the following R&D regarding UCD.

– The third paper presents the process of implementing a prototype for a visual/tangible environment for developing programming skills, in particular for children. The state-of-the-art analysis provides evidence that the manifold approaches and tools in this domain are inaccessible. In a usability study, including pre-training, accessibility, problems and challenges are identified using a training and an evaluation session. UCD is concentrated in these initial studies and a survey at the end.

– The fourth paper presents a new method for evaluating accessibility with/by people with disabilities. The consigliere evaluation method is proposed for situations where very specific domain knowledge is needed and no or very few users with disabilities can be found. To overcome this limitation in UCD, three people are to be employed to play three roles: the participant with disability (end user knowledge), the consigliere (domain knowledge) and the enforcer (domain accessibility expert). A case study for using the consigliere methodology is presented (university system management) employing 8 blind and visually handicapped users. The case study proves the concept of an innovative approach helping to overcome a key restriction in UCD with/for people with disabilities, what should meet with considerable interest for other domains and target groups.

– The final paper presents the IPAR-UCD method (Inclusive Participatory Action Research for User Centered Design). The method proposes to educate and involve people with disabilities, in this case people with cognitive disabilities, as co/peer-researchers. They take part in the whole process of R&D and influence/direct decision making in all phases. The method is developed and tested in the frame of a bigger R&D project. For the selected target group IPAR-UCD provides a fine example of a holistic UCD approach of interest for other domains and also target groups.

These examples show a broad and interesting mixture of approaches, where the first are more focused on examples of applying UCD to proof the scientific value of R&D. The methodological setting is mostly defined on base of restricted available resources and the pressure to deliver results underlining that there is still a need to improve the understanding for the contribution of UCD to R&D. Even if UCD is outlined as essential for R&D, the selection of the methodology is often not reflected and appropriate for the intended R&D. The last two papers are exceptional in this sense in terms of addressing UCD methods at a meta level. This invites to more research to increase the quality of AT and accessibility products and services. Monitoring and analyzing the methodological approaches in much more detail is needed to better understand if and how a more holistic and comprehensive UCD and participation of end users in all steps of R&D could be beneficial for procedures, results and uptake.

Acknowledgment. This session and this introduction has been facilitated in the frame of the Easy Reading project, which received funding from the European Union's Horizon 2020 research and innovation program under grant agreement No. 780529.

References

1. Nielsen, J., Berger, J.M., Gilutz, S., Whitenton, K.: Return on investment (ROI) for usability (2019). https://opus.bsz-bw.de/fhdo/frontdoor/deliver/index/docId/2166/file/ROI_for_Usability_4th_Edition.pdf. Accessed June 2020
2. Lumsden, J., Hakobyan, L., Leung, R., O'Sullivan, D.: Disabilities: assistive technology design. In: Encyclopedia of Computer Science and Technology. CRC Press (2017)
3. W3C/WAI: Cognitive and Learning Disabilities Accessibility Task Force (Coga TF) of the AG WG and APA WG. https://www.w3.org/WAI/GL/task-forces/coga/. Accessed June 2020
4. Dirks, S.: Empowering instead of hindering – challenges in participatory development of cognitively accessible software. In: Antona, M., Stephanidis, C. (eds.) HCII 2019. LNCS, vol. 11572, pp. 28–38. Springer, Cham (2019). https://doi.org/10.1007/978-3-030-23560-4_3
5. Dirks, S., Bühler, C.: Assistive technologies for people with cognitive impairments – which factors influence technology acceptance? In: Antona, M., Stephanidis, C. (eds.) UAHCI 2018. LNCS, vol. 10907, pp. 503–516. Springer, Cham (2018). https://doi.org/10.1007/978-3-319-92049-8_36
6. Miesenberger, K., Edler, C., Heumader, P., Petz, A.: Tools and applications for cognitive accessibility. In: Yesilada, Y., Harper, S. (eds.) Web Accessibility. HIS, pp. 523–546. Springer, London (2019). https://doi.org/10.1007/978-1-4471-7440-0_28
7. Wikipedia: A Century of Progress. https://de.wikipedia.org/wiki/A_Century_of_Progress. Accessed June 2020
8. Norman, D.A.: Things That Make Us Smart, Defending Human Attributes in the Age of the Machine. Addison-Wesley Publishing Company, Reading (1993)
9. Ko, A.J., Whitmire, E.: User Interface Software and Technology. https://faculty.washington.edu/ajko/books/uist/index.html. Accessed June 2020
10. Norman, D.: The Design of Everyday Things: Revised and Expanded Edition. Basic Books (AZ), New York (2013)
11. Csorny, L.: Careers in the growing field of information technology services. https://www.bls.gov/opub/btn/volume-2/careers-in-growing-field-of-information-technology-services.htm. Accessed June 2020
12. Usability.gov: Improving the User Experience – How To & Tools. https://www.usability.gov/how-to-and-tools/methods/project-team.html. Accessed June 2020
13. Martin, B., Hanington, B.M.: The Pocket Universal Methods of Design: 100 Ways to Research Complex Problems, Develop Innovative Ideas, and Design Effective Solutions. Rockport Publishers, Beverly (2018)
14. Miesenberger, K.: Best practice in design for all. In: Stephanidis (ed.) The Universal Access Handbook. CRC Press, Boca Raton (2009)
15. W3C: Web Content Accessibility Guidelines. https://www.w3.org/WAI/standards-guidelines/wcag/. Accessed June 2020

16. Weber, H., Edler, C.: Supporting the web experience of young people with learning disabilities. In: Miesenberger, K., Klaus, J., Zagler, W., Karshmer, A. (eds.) ICCHP 2010. LNCS, vol. 6179, pp. 649–656. Springer, Heidelberg (2010). https://doi.org/10.1007/978-3-642-14097-6_103
17. WebAim: Cognitive Disabilities - We Still Know Too Little, and We Do Even Less. http://webaim.org/articles/cognitive/cognitive_too_little. Accessed June 2020
18. Rumelhart, D.E.: Schemata: The building blocks of cognition. In: Theoretical Issues in Reading Comprehension, pp. 33–58. Routledge (2017)
19. Bergold, J.: Partizipative Forschung und Forschungsstrategien, eNewsletter Wegweiser Bürgergesellschaft (2013). https://www.buergergesellschaft.de/fileadmin/pdf/gastbeitrag_bergold_130510.pdf. Accessed June 2020
20. Ollerton, J.M.: IPAR, an inclusive disability research methodology with accessible analytical tools, Original practice development and research. Int. Pract. Dev. J. 2(2). Article 3. http://www.fons.org/library/journal/volume2-issue2/article3. Accessed June 2020
21. Edler, C.: e-Inclusion – Inklusive-Partizipative Forschung und Entwicklung, User-Centred Design und Empowerment, Dissertation, Pädagogischen Hochschule Ludwigsburg (2020, accepted)

My Train Talks to Me: Participatory Design of a Mobile App for Travellers with Visual Impairments

Beat Vollenwyder[1]([⊠])[ID], Esther Buchmüller[2], Christian Trachsel[2], Klaus Opwis[1], and Florian Brühlmann[1][ID]

[1] Center for Cognitive Psychology and Methodology, Department of Psychology, University of Basel, Basel, Switzerland
{beat.vollenwyder,klaus.opwis,florian.bruehlmann}@unibas.ch
[2] Swiss Federal Railways, Bern, Switzerland
{esther.buchmueller,christian.trachsel}@sbb.ch

Abstract. Travellers with visual impairments may face substantial information gaps on their journeys by public transport. For instance, information displayed in trains, as well as on departure boards in train stations and on platforms, are often not available in acoustic or tactile form. Digital technologies, such as smartphones or smartwatches, can provide an alternative means of access. However, these alternatives do not guarantee that the user experience is comparable in value, quality and efficiency. The present case study details a participatory design process, where travellers with visual impairments co-designed a mobile app. The goal was to tackle information gaps on journeys by public transport and to learn how participatory design can facilitate the provision of comparable experiences for users with disabilities. Travellers with visual impairments were involved in a collaborative process in all project phases, including problem identification, technical feasibility, proof of concept, design and development. Participatory design contributed to a thorough understanding of the user perspective and allowed the app to be optimised for the needs of travellers with visual impairments. Furthermore, co-design proved to be an effective method for fostering awareness and knowledge about digital accessibility at all organisational levels.

Keywords: User experience · Digital accessibility · Participatory design · People with visual impairments · Case study

1 Introduction

Beginning a journey, visiting your loved ones, or commuting daily to work: There are many reasons for boarding a train. People with visual impairments also share this daily travel routine. However, this group of travellers may face additional challenges on their journeys by public transport. In Switzerland, where the present case study was conducted, no immediate acoustic or tactile information

© The Author(s) 2020
K. Miesenberger et al. (Eds.): ICCHP 2020, LNCS 12376, pp. 10–18, 2020.
https://doi.org/10.1007/978-3-030-58796-3_2

is available to aid people when they board trains. Announcements in trains are usually made only a few minutes before departure, which can lead to stressful situations or even trips to the wrong destination. A similar dearth of information exists in train stations and on platforms. Currently, travellers with visual impairments have no direct means of accessing the information on departure boards listing the next available train connections. There are alternative means for obtaining this information; for instance, by querying the timetable provided in the mobile app of the Swiss Federal Railways. Nonetheless, such alternatives require extra effort, and the experience is hardly comparable to a quick glance at a departure board. As a consequence, this information gap may substantially limit a traveller's autonomy and comfort.

Information systems installed in trains, train stations and on platforms have long life cycles, making it more difficult to address information gaps that were not previously considered. Digital technologies, such as smartphones or smartwatches, can provide an alternative means of access. Although these personal devices are widely available and have become pervasive in everyday life, they still do not guarantee a comparable experience [1]. Comparable experience here refers to digital information and services that are comparable in value, quality and efficiency for each user [9]. For instance, the ease of the aforementioned quick glance at the departure board could be replicated for travellers with disabilities by equipping apps with device features such as geolocation and screen reader support, thereby providing an efficient alternative means for them to interact with local information. Thus, designing comparable experiences for as many people as possible requires more than the mere transfer of identical content and functionalities to other technologies.

1.1   Access to Experience

Power, Cairns and Barlet [7] describe three layers involved in achieving comparable experiences for users with disabilities. The authors refer to the work on digital accessibility that focuses on providing basic access to technologies as *First Wave Inclusion*. Basic access can be provided by offering alternative input modes (e.g., switch access that replaces interactions via touchscreen for users with limited dexterity in their hands) and by translating information into alternative output modalities (e.g., access by screen reader for users with visual impairments). While work on basic access remains vital for digital accessibility, recent work has broadened the perspective and moved away from the focus on mainly technical aspects [5,8].

Second Wave Inclusion shifts the perspective towards enabling users with disabilities to achieve their goals [7]. This leads to a more usability-oriented understanding of digital accessibility, including traditional criteria such as effectiveness, efficiency and satisfaction in a specified context of use [5]. The opinion that digital accessibility and usability are related concepts is regularly discussed in research [6] and is widely accepted by accessibility experts [12]. Further, the understanding that this relationship benefits the overall quality of a product was shown to be a main motivation for considering digital accessibility [10].

Based on the analyses of access and enablement covered in the two previous layers, *Third Wave Inclusion* focuses on understanding the subjective experiences of users with disabilities in an interactive system [7]. This perspective goes beyond performance-related criteria and includes aspects related to user experience such as affect, trust or aesthetics [1]. However, in the digital accessibility field, this more holistic perspective is rarely adopted [4], and only a few tools and techniques have been developed to capture the subjective experience of users with disabilities [7]. A frequently cited approach is *participatory design*, in which users with disabilities actively define and shape the design of a product [4]. Participatory design contrasts with traditional user-centred design methods that involve users but leave their design decisions to be made by a project team of specialised professionals.

In the present case study, we detail the development of a mobile app, which was co-designed by travellers with visual impairments. The project was conducted in collaboration with the Swiss Federal Railways and pursued the goal of identifying and closing crucial information gaps that hinder travellers with disabilities during their journeys by public transport. Rather than giving specific advice on how to implement an accessible app, this report aims at providing insights into a participatory design process and also inspiring similar activities in other projects.

2   Case Study

2.1   Problem Identification

In a first phase, we asked travellers with disabilities to provide us with their experiences regarding any information gaps that they confronted during journeys by public transport. For this purpose, we contacted the Advisory Board for Barrier-free Travel of the Swiss Federal Railways, which represents travellers with visual, hearing and motor impairments. The board consisted of one person with a central scotoma since childhood (m, 45), two people who have been almost blind since childhood (f, 42; m, 59), one person with severe hearing loss since early childhood (f, 51), one person with age-related hearing loss (m, 77), one person with cerebral palsy since birth (m, 42), a low vision optician (m, 62), an acoustician (m, 80) and an expert in the field of barrier-free public transport (m, 71).

In two workshops, we mapped a complete user journey, ranging from planning, arriving at the station, finding the platform, boarding the train, travelling to the destination, and orienting oneself after arrival. For each part of the user journey, the representatives of the advisory board introduced potential information gaps and rated these according to their severity. Later, these insights were enriched with observations from first-hand experiences on an exemplary journey. For instance, the representatives with visual impairments demonstrated their lack of information when boarding a train by giving the non-disabled project members simulation glasses so that they could experience this issue personally.

2.2   Technical Feasibility

Detailed problem descriptions derived from the user journeys were used as input for a *hackathon*. In a hackathon, teams of programmers and other specialists involved in software development collaborate intensively on a given project over a few days. One of the teams, including a blind programmer (m, 44), focused on information availability when boarding a train. With the development of an app using Bluetooth beacons and publicly available information from the Swiss public transport's open-data platform[1], the team was able to prove the app's technical feasibility and its compatibility with assistive technologies. A few weeks later, another team extended the prototype in a second hackathon with regard to information availability in train stations and on platforms. By using geofencing based on GPS positioning, it was possible to provide a digital version of the departure boards which showed the next available train connections at the current position.

2.3   Proof of Concept

We decided to further develop the ideas created in the technical feasibility phase for multiple reasons. First, the two aforementioned issues belonged to the most pressing information gaps for travellers with visual impairments. Second, the proposed solutions showed potential for being extended to travellers with other forms of disability; for example, by providing acoustic announcements in text form for people with hearing impairments. Third, another project involved installing Bluetooth beacons on a selection of train lines to test a different application, which allowed us to start our project immediately using existing infrastructure. A basic test app applying components built in the technical feasibility phase was distributed to a group of 34 interested travellers with visual impairments. The participants regularly travelled on specific train lines that were already equipped with Bluetooth beacons. They provided feedback via their communication channel of choice (e.g., via email, phone or voice messages). In addition, we conducted three exemplary journeys with a total of 10 travellers (6 women, 4 men; 5 blind, 5 with severe visual impairments) to discuss the app's functionalities and design in a real context. During the proof of concept phase, we collaboratively created first drafts for the final product design. For instance, the test app featured the concept of the master-detail pattern, providing a short overview of the travel information with an option to see more content. Participants deemed this concept as impractical in the present context, since it requires browsing through an often changing list and an additional click to look for further information. In collaboration with the participants, a concept using tab navigation at the bottom end of the app and reserved areas for the most important information was outlined. These reserved areas have a fixed position on the screen and enable quick access and orientation using a screen reader.

To decide whether to continue the project, the proof of concept phase was closed with a questionnaire answered by a total of 14 participants (age $M = 55.3$,

---

[1] https://opentransportdata.swiss/en.

$SD = 10.3$, range 30–71; 4 women, 10 men; 7 blind, 4 with severe visual impairments, 3 with light visual impairments). Participants used the test app with various combinations of assistive technologies, including screen reader and voice control ($N = 6$), screen reader, voice control and inverted colours (3), screen reader only (3), and screen magnification (1). They rated the overall impression of the test app positive ($M = 4.23$; $SD = 1.1$; $1 = worst\ rating$, $5 = best\ rating$). To gain further support for the project, we decided to use the test app to spread awareness of digital accessibility issues within the organisation. In 3 workshops, a total of 60 employees of the Swiss Federal Railways were invited to personally experience the addressed information gaps. Travellers with visual impairments were present during these workshops and shared their experiences in dealing with these issues.

2.4 Design

Based on the insights generated in the previous phases, we compiled a final conceptual design. The app was named SBB Inclusive (i.e., SBB stands for Schweizer Bundesbahnen, Swiss Federal Railways). Next, we asked four blind users (age $M = 46.7$, $SD = 14.4$, range 30–65; 1 woman, 3 men) to participate in a usability test, in which they solved typical tasks with an early prototype [3]. Often, such tests are carried out with pen and paper or wireframes, which cannot be accessed directly by users with visual impairments. A simple web prototype built using HTML and CSS proved to be an effective workaround. This allowed us to test the navigation structure, the order of the displayed elements, and the richness of information directly using a screen reader. Participants had the choice between using either a test device or their own personal device. This allowed them to participate in the test while using their own familiar settings, such as their personal screen reader speech rate. To refine the concept, we discussed findings with the participants immediately after each test session and collaboratively outlined design improvements.

Finally, we created a visual design for the app, taking the accessibility features of the operating systems into account. For instance, a specific screen layout was designed for large text settings, which allows for text resizing without loss of content or functionality. The evolution of the app during the design phase is presented in Fig. 1.

2.5 Development

An app version for iOS using SwiftUI and a version for Android using Flutter were created from scratch. We deemed both technologies as being optimally suited for building the intended features. Travellers with visual impairments who participated in the proof of concept phase were invited to upgrade their apps to the new app and were asked to give their feedback on the ongoing development using a built-in contact form. At the date of this publication, the new app was just made available for testing. Therefore, little feedback has been received so far; however, most of it expresses a positive first impression of the final version of the app. The public release of SBB Inclusive is planned for fall 2020.

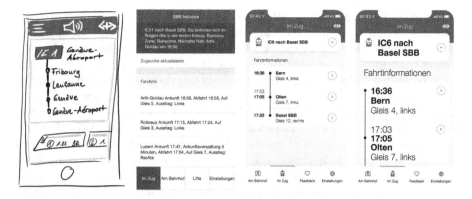

Fig. 1. Evolution of the app during the design phase. From left to right: first scribbles, HTML prototype, final design and final design with increased text size.

2.6 Future Development

With regard to future development, we plan to focus on additional information gaps that were revealed in the problem identification phase. Current ideas include developing features to display acoustic announcements in text form to travellers with hearing impairments, to monitor the status of elevators in train stations for travellers with physical impairments, and to provide information in reduced language complexity for travellers with cognitive and learning disabilities.

3 Discussion

Travellers with visual impairments participated in all phases of the present case study. The co-design process allowed us to obtain a thorough understanding of information gaps during journeys by public transport from a user's perspective. Especially, the workshops with representatives from the advisory board in the problem identification phase and the exemplary journeys in the proof of concept phase proved to be helpful for this purpose. These occasions also created a space for collaboratively drafting ideas, which led to the conceptual design used in the final product. In the present case study, participatory design allowed us to attain a level of quality which would arguably not have been achieved with traditional user-centred design methods.

Further, the shared understanding provided a solid basis for the development phase of the app, which required continuous design decisions that had to be in line with user needs. For this mainly technical phase, it would have been a major advantage to have a person with visual impairment as a fixed member of the development team [4]. This was partly the case during the technical feasibility phase and proved vitally important for the iterative testing of solutions, for integrating resources from first-hand experiences into the product, and for receiving hints on how similar functionalities are solved in other apps. Future projects should extend participation to all project phases and staff a more diverse development team. At the same time, close involvement of a broad user group should be maintained. Such a setup allows for a balance between the expertise of a project team and the perspectives of unbiased users.

Another insight from the present case study was the importance of the impact that participatory design has on stakeholders within the organisation. Recommendations to involve users with disabilities in the development process in order to foster awareness at all organisational levels were put into practice effectively [10]. In particular, the proof of concept phase with its workshops which allowed participants to personally experience the inconvenience caused by the information gaps proved to be an effective tool for promoting knowledge about digital accessibility within the organisation. Internal stakeholders who were initially somewhat indifferent to information gaps for travellers with disabilities soon saw the importance of these issues while collaborating with travellers with visual impairments. The involvement also contributed to a reduction in misconceptions regarding digital accessibility; for instance, the prevalent belief among stakeholders that aesthetics and technologically advanced products would be compromised by introducing accessible solutions [2]. An extension of the participatory design process to other groups of users with disabilities would benefit this promotional effect. Since the scope of digital accessibility often centres around users with visual impairments [11], such a step could broaden an organisation's awareness for various perspectives and motivate it to invest in providing comparable experiences for all user groups. Another benefit of involving internal stakeholders closely was the opportunity to exploit synergies with other projects. The possibility to reuse an existing technical infrastructure was crucial to obtaining the technical solution described in the present case study, as this allowed the project to start immediately and shortened the implementation time substantially. Perhaps, there will be further synergies in other contexts that can be used in a creative way to support digital accessibility.

4   Conclusion

In the present case study, a mobile app was co-designed by travellers with visual impairments to create a user experience that is comparable in value, quality and efficiency to that of non-disabled travellers. Participatory design contributed to a thorough understanding of the user perspective and allowed us to optimise the app to the needs of travellers with visual impairments. By extending the use of participatory design to all development phases and by staffing projects with a more diverse team, these observed benefits could be further employed in future projects. Interactions between travellers with visual impairments and the stakeholders within the organisation helped to spread accessibility awareness and knowledge at all organisational levels and triggered synergies with other projects. Future work should broaden the spectrum of disabilities considered to include as many people in as many situations as possible. We hope that our research will encourage project teams to benefit from a wide range of user perspectives in order to improve their work.

Acknowledgements. We sincerely thank all the people who participated in the development and testing of SBB Inclusive and are grateful to Hermione Miller-Moser for her editorial assistance on this paper. Research and development were supported by the Swiss Federal Railways.

References

1. Aizpurua, A., Harper, S., Vigo, M.: Exploring the relationship between web accessibility and user experience. Int. J. Hum. Comput. Stud. **91**, 13–23 (2016). https://doi.org/10.1016/j.ijhcs.2016.03.008
2. Ellcessor, E.: <ALT="Textbooks">: web accessibility myths as negotiated industrial lore. Crit. Stud. Media Commun. **31**(5), 448–463 (2014). https://doi.org/10.1080/15295036.2014.919660
3. Henry, S.L.: Just Ask: Integrating Accessibility Throughout Design. ET, Madison (2007)
4. Oswal, S.K.: Breaking the exclusionary boundary between user experience and access. In: the 37th ACM International Conference, pp. 1–8. ACM Press, New York (2019). https://doi.org/10.1145/3328020.3353957
5. Petrie, H., Kheir, O.: The relationship between accessibility and usability of websites. In: Proceedings of the SIGCHI Conference on Human Factors in Computing Systems, pp. 397–406. ACM, New York (2007). https://doi.org/10.1145/1240624.1240688
6. Petrie, H., Savva, A., Power, C.: Towards a unified definition of web accessibility. In: the 12th Web for All Conference, pp. 1–13. ACM Press, New York (2015). https://doi.org/10.1145/2745555.2746653
7. Power, C., Cairns, P., Barlet, M.: Inclusion in the third wave: access to experience. In: Filimowicz, M., Tzankova, V. (eds.) New Directions in Third Wave Human-Computer Interaction: Volume 1 - Technologies. HIS, pp. 163–181. Springer, Cham (2018). https://doi.org/10.1007/978-3-319-73356-2_10
8. Power, C., Freire, A., Petrie, H., Swallow, D.: Guidelines are only half of the story: accessibility problems encountered by blind users on the web. In: Proceedings of the SIGCHI Conference on Human Factors in Computing Systems, pp. 433–442. ACM, New York (2012). https://doi.org/10.1145/2207676.2207736
9. Swan, H., Pouncey, I., Pickering, H., Watson, L.: Inclusive design principles. https://inclusivedesignprinciples.org. Accessed 12 June 2020
10. Vollenwyder, B., Iten, G.H., Brühlmann, F., Opwis, K., Mekler, E.D.: Salient beliefs influencing the intention to consider web accessibility. Comput. Hum. Behav. **92**, 352–360 (2019). https://doi.org/10.1016/j.chb.2018.11.016
11. Vollenwyder, B., Opwis, K., Brühlmann, F.: How web professionals perceive web accessibility in practice: active roles, process phases and key disabilities. In: Computers Helping People with Special Needs. ICCHP 2020. LNCS, vol. 10897, pp. xx–yy. Springer, Cham (2020)
12. Yesilada, Y., Brajnik, G., Vigo, M., Harper, S.: Exploring perceptions of web accessibility: a survey approach. Behav. Inf. Technol. **34**(2), 119–134 (2014). https://doi.org/10.1080/0144929X.2013.848238

What Do Older People Actually Want from Their Robots?

Sanjit Samaddar[(⊠)] and Helen Petrie

Department of Computer Science, University of York, York, UK
{sanjit.samaddar,helen.petrie}@york.ac.uk

Abstract. There has been a lot of research concerning robots to support older people. However, there may be some areas of robots for older people that have not been as heavily researched or that is being missed. This study aimed to reassess if existing research is addressing the needs of 22 older people and asked them "without being concerned about any limitations, what would you want from a robot?" The study also showed them pictures of different robot types and asked them which type, if any, they would prefer. It was found that the older people have a lot of daily tasks and needs that are not addressed by current research. It was also found that older people were generally intimated by humanoid robots and are concerned about their privacy with voice agents but do not have a specific preference otherwise.

Keywords: Robots for older people · User needs · Robot preference

1 Introduction

There has been extensive research and development of robots, including robots to support older people. Robots have been developed that can help older people with many functions, including health care [1], medicine reminders [2], coaching for physical activity [3], and social interaction [4]. Robots can thus potentially provide many different kinds of support for older people to assist them in living more independently. However, even with extensive research and development, robots have yet to become prevalent in the homes of older people and much of the research is driven by technological developments rather than a careful consideration of user needs.

Therefore, the aims of this research are to investigate: the needs of older people and reassess if existing research on robots is addressing these needs the opinions of older people concerning different types of robots.

2 Related Work

The three areas of physical healthcare, cognitive support, and social interaction for older people have been researched in areas such as gerontology, psychology, and sociology. In line with this research, robots have been developed to help with these three areas. Examples in physical healthcare include an 'eHealth portal' with virtual and physical agents that would track health and other activity and provide users with

K. Miesenberger et al. (Eds.): ICCHP 2020, LNCS 12376, pp. 19–26, 2020.
https://doi.org/10.1007/978-3-030-58796-3_3

feedback and suggestion based on the tracked activity [5], or a robot platform that could analyse a video feed to detect heart rate and breathing rate and use additional sensors to alert family members if an extraordinary event occurred [6]. Robots have also been used as coaches for exercise, where the robot would demonstrate an exercise and would ask the user to follow along and also provide motivation as the exercises were performed [3].

Examples of cognitive support include a robot that provides mental games and tasks for a user to do and tailors the games to suit the user's level of cognitive ability [7]. Other robots combine both entertainment and cognitive stimulation by providing games such as bingo [8] or a card matching memory game [9]. Examples in social interaction include robotic pets and other robots that provide a means of social interaction designed to combat loneliness for older people. Robot pets provide companionship like a real pet but are more suited for older adults who may not be capable of taking care of a real pet's needs. Paro [10] is such a robot, a small, furry seal robot that reacts to touch, which has had a significant positive influence on older people's lives at a care home.

However, there is a limited amount of literature that has looked at other needs older adults may have. Petrie and Darzentas note that the understanding of the needs of older people in robotic research may be "somewhat superficial or stereotypic" [11, p. 34]. With advances in robotic technology and the different types of robots available, it is important to involve older users in the development of robot systems and investigate whether there are more areas in which older adults would like to be supported and where robots could help.

Some research has been conducted into comparing older people's attitudes to different types of robots and robots with other possible supportive devices. Heerink et al. [12] compared a virtual agent to a robot agent and compared older people's perception of how socially present they thought both types of agent were. They found that both agents were perceived to be socially presented regardless of their physical or virtual embodiment. However, it was found that the virtual agent was more likely to be used in the future by the participants. Fasola and Mataric [3] investigated the difference between a virtual and physical embodied robot as an exercise coach. They found there was a strong preference for the physical robot rather than the virtual embodiment amongst older users.

Research like this shows that there is some preference for robots over virtual agents, usually dependent on the task being performed. Almost all studies compare a virtual vs a physical robot but not different types of physical robots.

3 Method

A semi-structured interview approach was used, as it allows participants and researchers to explore ideas and opinions as they arise while also allowing the researchers to guide the participants to certain areas of interest. In the first part of the interview, participants were asked what they would want from a robot in their home.

They were not given any information about what kind of robot it would be, or what the capabilities the robot would have. When the participant had no more suggestions or was struggling to come up with more needs, the researcher went through the three key areas of current robot research and prompted the participant to discuss their ideas pertaining to each one. Finally, participants were presented with photographs of five different types of robots and other support agents (Fig. 1). Two variations of each type were shown so participants would not assume that each type only had one design. The five robot types presented were: large humanoid robots (Robovie and Pepper); voice agents (Amazon Alexa and Google Home); robot pets (Paro and Aibo); tabletop robots (Nabaztag and Elli-q); and virtual agents (tablet and smartphone). Participants were encouraged to give their first reactions to the examples and asked which one they would most want to use or not want to use.

24 participants took part in the study, average age 71 years, ranging from 66 to 82 years old. 12 were women and 12 were men. Almost all the participants were familiar with one of the voice agents but were generally not familiar with any of the other robots or other robotic technology. Two participants did not want to be recorded. Therefore, their data was not included in the coding and analysis.

All interviews were recorded, transcribed, and coded using NVIVO [13]. The transcriptions were analysed using thematic analysis [14]. Analysis was separated into the three separate sections: older people's own opinions of their needs, what they think of existing functions, and opinions on the five robots presented. Two coders analysed the data independently. Both coders then compared themes to find similarities and discuss any disagreements. A final set of themes was constructed factoring in input from both coders and their initial set of themes.

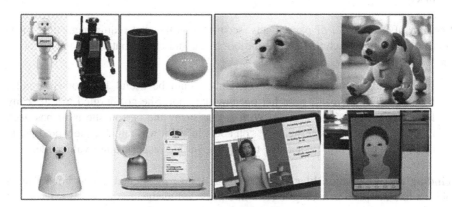

Fig. 1. The 5 different robot types presented to the participants.

4 Results

4.1 What Do Older People Want?

Forgetting Things. One of the most common themes, mentioned by 11 (50%) participants. Most of the participants mentioned forgetting day-to-day activities, rather than scheduled activities such as medication or meeting appointments.

> **P01:** I leave the gas on... or forget to lock the door and ... burning the toast ... I do that more often than anything. I burn toast. I also burn pans. You know, you are in the middle of cooking and you go to the computer or something and it all goes wrong on the computer, you get sidetracked and you burn the pans.

Dexterity Issues and Help with Mobility. The other most common issue, mentioned by 12 (55%) participants, was robots helping with tasks that require a certain amount of dexterity or strength.

> **P08:** I think they could help me with mobility. Getting out of bed, just something to lean on, if you could get it to come and get up with it. Or support you so you can do it yourself... One of the most important things is the physical assistance. With a bit of help, I know people with walkers and it's big and clumsy. So something with intelligence might be better

Help with Cooking. Help with cooking was mentioned by 8 (36%) participants.

> **P04:** ... if it could tell me recipes while I was cooking. If it was just speaking to me, I would have it say the list of ingredients and keep saying that until I've got it all in place.

Security. For 5 (23%) of participants, security was the first requirement they mentioned. Suggestions included having a robot that could check that doors and windows are locked.

> **P05:** I think it [security system] certainly would be useful for mother. Purely, because we don't really want her opening the door. She got burgled just after my father died, deception burglary. With a fear, being the person she is or has been mentally, somebody is at the door, "oh come in". If it was raining, she would invite them in. We just don't want that to happen. In that respect, quite vulnerable.

Finding and Fetching Objects. 4participants (18%) mentioned having robots fetch objects like the post or finding objects like keys and medication.

> **P01:** Well I have a friend, who is mostly bound to her chair, and she used to have a dog who got the newspaper in the morning. So that would be something useful. Or something to get the phone to her when it rings?

Games and Exercise. 3(14%) participants mentioned a robot helping with exercise or providing entertainment in the form of games.

P16: Another area I think would be good if you were sedentary… Could it … go through certain exercises with you? You know, do this, do that, wiggle your toes?

Other Themes. Participants were encouraged to adopt a 'blue-sky' thinking approach, so mentioned unusual needs, including having a robot monitor the boiler and press a reset button when required, and help with shopping for clothes for older people who have limited mobility and cannot leave their homes.

P06: Say an elder person who can't go to the shops to try clothes on. I don't know if there's a way that you can devote robotics so that you have models, their shape and size, to try clothes on that they can see… does that sound stupid? So that then they'll know more clearly that something's going to suit and fit them, and then they would order the product.

4.2   Existing Robot Functions

Physical Healthcare. Most participants (20, 91%), had no particular comment on robots helping with their healthcare.

Social Interaction with the Robot. 16 (73%) of participants had an opinion or reaction to the area of interacting with, and specifically talking to, a robot. All these participants thought it was a good idea but almost all of them mentioned it being good for older friends and family. Most did not see themselves conversing with a robot.

P07: Like, my mother watches TV, there is a film or something, she makes up her own story which is quite different to the storyline is on the television. So this will enable the older person to have a conversation on their own terms, and it could tell stories…

Cognitive Stimulation/Entertainment. While not as frequently discussed as conversation with a robot, 6 (27%) participants commented on cognitive stimulation and entertainment and expressed positive interest in using a robot for these needs.

P18: Well, I mean, you can already get an app, which I've got, it's called Social Chess.. So it's nothing robotic… but something visual on the screen showing the other person… That would be much better than if you were just playing against the computer making its moves, and you know it's going to win.

4.3   Opinions and Preference of Robot Type

When participants were shown the robot and agent types, they were encouraged to think out loud and voice their opinions on any and all robot types that they wanted. Participants were asked if they had a preferred type that they would want to use and one they would not use. Seven (32%) participants did not have a preference or said that they would be happy with any of the robots as long as they had functions that would be helpful. In some instances participants provided two types that they would not use. The most common preference was for the pet robot (27%) and the most common robot or agent type that participants did not want to use was the humanoid robot (41%).

P08: I think I would be a bit nervous of Robovie, it looks like it would exterminate you!

5 Discussion and Conclusions

The themes which emerged from the initial open discussion of what participants would like from a robot showed that what older people want only partly overlaps with the current emphasis in robot research. Overlapping areas include forgetting things, help with dexterity, fetching objects, and games and exercise. However, there are areas where robot research is currently missing needs that are important to older people. For example, participants emphasized forgetting day to day tasks, such as the process of cooking or running a bath. A robot that can monitor and provide feedback about these tasks would be more useful to older people compared to a robot that reminds them of regularly scheduled events such as medicine or doctor appointments.

Cooking and security are both themes that were important to the participants but compared to other areas are not given as much importance in the research. However, there are many mobile apps that provide cooking help and many security systems that exist to fulfill these needs. It might be that the participants are not aware of these other systems or are actually looking for more intelligent robotic solutions that can help them with cooking or securing their home. It could also be that these apps are not designed specifically for older people and do not consider how they would need to interact with the systems. In addition, having one intelligent agent that can provide all this functionality may be attractive in comparison to have a whole range of different systems to deal with.

It is very noteworthy that none of the participants mentioned physical healthcare or social interaction when given the opportunity to suggest ways in which robots could help them. These are areas which did not occur to the participants as areas that they wanted or needed help in. When physical healthcare was brought up, most did not have any comment or generally agreed that it could also be useful. In contrast, conversation and social interaction with the robots was extensively discussed by participants who generally thought it a good idea.

For cognitive stimulation and entertainment, an interesting point raised by the participants was connecting and playing with other people with that interaction being mediated by the robot. There is indeed research on both robots that mediate communication with other people and robots that play games with the user. A combination of these two functions would be very useful according to these participants.

In terms of which robot and agent types people would use or not use, although pet robots were the most frequently chosen as one people would use, participants did have differing views on these, with some saying that they were a great idea and some reporting finding a fake pet quite disconcerting. Five of the six participants who said they would most prefer the robot pets were female, and the three participants who said that they would not use the robot pets were male. This might reflect gender differences in terms of what older adults prefer, but requires further study with physical presence of the robots rather than pictures. The humanoid robots were the least liked, and were generally found to be intimidating and too large for home use. For the participants who did like the humanoid robots, it was because they felt these robots would be most likely to help with limited mobility and helping them with tasks such as getting out of bed. Functionality was more important than the appearance of the robot for these participants.

Finally, it is worth highlighting that 7 participants did not have a most preferred robot, but 20 of the participants had a least preferred one. Participants were particular about which type of robot they would not use, under any circumstances. However, they were less inclined to indicate a preference for a type that they would use. This suggests that outside of specific types of robots that they disliked, they might prioritise function over aesthetic.

This study investigated the needs of older people in relation to robots and provides some idea of what types of robot older people prefer. The open style of interview worked well, as participants could take time to explain exactly what they felt they need from robots and allowed us to find specific areas that might be currently lacking in existing research. Showing pictures of all the robots facilitated and encouraged discussion well. While not feasible for this study, having actual robots present during the study for the participants to interact with would have been ideal. In hindsight, providing different, less controversial voice agents that were not tied to well-known companies (which have had negative publicity about their security procedures) may have encouraged more discussion about that type of robot. However, the researchers wanted to study opinions about robots that were both publicly available and used in research, and all the robots in the study represented both those factors.

In conclusion, this study has shown that there are many aspects of older people's day to day lives in which robots could help. While existing research is addressing some of those aspects, it may be missing the possibly mundane and daily tasks that older people would find very beneficial to have help with. Needs such as being reminded that the hob is on or that they left the bath running, providing cooking instructions, intelligent security, and a method to play games with other older people is what the majority of the participants said they needed or would like. The study highlights these areas where existing research can adapt to further help older people.

Investigating the preference for robots provided interesting initial information about what types of robots older people prefer. It is clear that robots that look intimidating or robots that cause privacy concerns are not favoured by older people. Furthermore, the results highlighted a possible gender difference in preference for robot pets and virtual agents, with men preferring virtual agents and women preferring pet robots. We intend to conduct further research with a quantitative study which will investigate robot type preferences in more detail with participants interacting with actual robots.

Acknowledgements. We would like to thank all our participants for taking the time to participate in our study. Their feedback has been extremely valuable in our ongoing work with robots for older people.

References

1. Robinson, H., MacDonald, B., Broadbent, E.: The role of healthcare robots for older people at home: a review. Int. J. Soc. Robot. **6**(4), 575–591 (2014). https://doi.org/10.1007/s12369-014-0242-2
2. Broadbent, E., et al.: Robots in older people's homes to improve medication adherence and quality of life: a randomised cross-over trial. In: Beetz, M., Johnston, B., Williams, M.-A. (eds.) ICSR 2014. LNCS (LNAI), vol. 8755, pp. 64–73. Springer, Cham (2014). https://doi.org/10.1007/978-3-319-11973-1_7
3. Fasola, J., Matarić, M.J.: Socially assistive robot exercise coach: motivating older adults to engage in physical exercise. In: Desai, J., Dudek, G., Khatib, O., Kumar, V. (eds.) Experimental Robotics. STAR, vol. 88, pp. 463–479. Springer, Heidelberg (2013). https://doi.org/10.1007/978-3-319-00065-7_32
4. Bickmore, T.W., Caruso, L., Clough-Gorr, K., Heeren, T.: 'It's just like you talk to a friend' relational agents for older adults. Interact. Comput. **17**(6), 711–735 (2005)
5. Wang, D., Tan, A.H.: EHealthPortal: a social support hub for the active living of the elderly. In: ACM International Conference Proceeding Series, vol. Part F1306, pp. 19–25 (2017)
6. Hening, S., Cottrell, P., Teoderescu, M., Kurniawan, S., Mantey, P.: Assistive living robot: a remotely controlled robot for older persons living alone. In: Proceedings of the 6th International Conference on Pervasive Technologies Related to Assistive Environments, pp. 10:1–10:4 (2013)
7. Tapus, A., Vieru, A.-M.: Robot cognitive stimulation for the elderly. In: Ferrández Vicente, J.M., Álvarez Sánchez, J.R., de la Paz López, F., Toledo Moreo, F.J. (eds.) IWINAC 2013. LNCS, vol. 7930, pp. 94–102. Springer, Heidelberg (2013). https://doi.org/10.1007/978-3-642-38637-4_10
8. Li, J., Louie, W.Y.G., Mohamed, S., Despond, F., Nejat, G.: A user-study with Tangy the Bingo facilitating robot and long-term care residents. In: 2016 IEEE International Symposium on Robotics and Intelligent Sensors (IRIS), IRIS 2016, pp. 109–115 (2017)
9. Khosla, R., Chu, M.T.: Embodying care in matilda: an affective communication robot for emotional wellbeing of older people in Australian residential care facilities. ACM Trans. Manag. Inf. Syst. **4**(4), 1–33 (2013)
10. Wada, K., Shibata, T.: Living with seal robots; its sociopsychological and physiological influences on the elderly at a care house. Trans. Rob. **23**(5), 972–980 (2007)
11. Petrie, H., Darzentas, J.: Older people and robotic technologies in the home: perspectives from recent research literature. In: ACM International Conference Proceeding Series, vol. Part F1285, pp. 29–36 (2017)
12. Heerink, M., Kröse, B., Evers, V., Wielinga, B.: The influence of social presence on enjoyment and intention to use of a robot and screen agent by elderly users. Test, pp. 695–700 (2008)
13. QSRInternational, "NVIVO." https://www.qsrinternational.com/nvivo/what-is-nvivo. Accessed 29 Sept 2019
14. Braun, V., Clarke, V.: Using thematic analysis in psychology. Qual. Res. Psychol. **3**(2), 77–101 (2006)

Accessibility of Block-Based Introductory Programming Languages and a Tangible Programming Tool Prototype

Emmanuel Utreras and Enrico Pontelli[✉]

New Mexico State University, Las Cruces, NM 88003, USA
eutreras@nmsu.edu, epontell@cs.nmsu.edu

Abstract. Visual programming languages (VPLs) were designed to assist children in introductory programming courses. Unfortunately, despite the positive results in teaching, VPLs are believed to be inaccessible for children with visual impairments and low vision due to the dependency of visual graphics as both input and output methods. To identify the barriers that users with visual impairments and low vision face while using Block-based programming environments, as well as to acquire feedback regarding the design of a new tangible programming tool prototype, a usability study was conducted which involved nine adult participants with visual impairments and low vision. This paper presents the findings of this usability study and provides a list of features that are needed in order to make Block-based environments accessible. Furthermore, based on observations, interviews, and post-surveys this study demonstrates that our prototype can be used by users with visual impairments and low vision and provides a guideline for the design of tangible interfaces to teach programming concepts.

Keywords: Introductory programming · Low vision · User study · Visual impairment

1 Introduction

Learning *programming concepts* plays an important role in children's learning process. However, teaching programming to children is not an easy task due to the complexity of the courses and languages syntax. To remedy this problem, researchers have developed *visual programming languages (VPLs)* (e.g., Scratch, Alice, Lego NXT, App Inventor) which make use of an intuitive graphical syntax and fun projects to encourage children in learning to code. One of the commonly used approaches of VPLs is *Block-based programming,* which allows the user to build code by dragging, dropping, and connecting visual blocks. The blocks represent different program constructs, and the shape of the blocks facilitate the correct combination of such constructs in the construction of a program.

Supported by the National Science foundation 1914635, 1401639 and 1757207.

© Springer Nature Switzerland AG 2020
K. Miesenberger et al. (Eds.): ICCHP 2020, LNCS 12376, pp. 27–34, 2020.
https://doi.org/10.1007/978-3-030-58796-3_4

Typically, the execution of such programs result in some form of visual output, such as graphics, animations, or control of the movements of a robot.

Unfortunately, despite the positive results shown in the teaching field, VPLs are believed to be largely inaccessible for children with visual impairments (VI) and low vision (LV) due to the dependency on visual constructs in both the construction of the program as well as in the output of the execution. Additionally, most VPLs are incompatible with assistive technologies such as screen readers [5]. These issues might have a negative impact on the learning process of children with VI and LV.

To identify the barriers that users with VI and LV face while using VPLs, and more specifically block-based introductory programming languages, we present a usability study designed to address the following research questions:

- *RQ1: Can a VPL environment like Scratch[1] be accessible to users with VI and LV?*
- *RQ2: What are the barriers that users with VI and LV face using Scratch?*

These questions are aimed at informing the design of a novel teaching platform, a *tangible programming tool (TPT)* environment; our study includes the following questions about our first TPT prototype:

- *RQ3: Is our TPT prototype accessible for users with VI and LV?*
- *RQ4: What barriers do the participants face while using the TPT prototype?*

This study explores these questions by performing a usability study with nine participants with VI and LV. The study helps in identifying features that Scratch needs in order to be accessible. Furthermore, this study demonstrated that our TPT prototype can be used by users with VI and LV. In addition, the study provides guidelines for the design of tangible interfaces to teach programming to children with visual impairments.

2   Background

Block-based programming is an approach used by most educational VPLs. A block-based programming environment enables the construction of a program as the process of assembling visual blocks on the screen. Each block has a specific shape (like jigsaw puzzle pieces) and represents a specific programming constructs (e.g., conditional, loop). The shape of the block constrains how the block can be used in a program, thus facilitating the construction of programs that are "syntactically" correct.

VPLs have proven to be effective in the teaching field; indeed, there now exist a wide range of educational VPLs, focusing on a variety of application domains. The main objective of these environments is to aid students in introductory programming courses such as object-oriented programming [2] and data science [1,8]. *Scratch* [6] is a VPL environment designed for children in K-12 grades,

---

[1] We use Scratch as a representative block-based language, due to its popularity.

that became very popular due to its wide availability and the presence of a rich literature and collections of educational modules. Scratch allows students to build animated novels, 2D games, and music projects. Unlike Scratch, Lego NXT-G is a block-based environment whose programs are used to control a robot's movements instead of visual graphics.

The challenge of accessibility of teaching programming environments has been addressed by researchers. Blocks4All [7] is an environment that provides the visually impaired students with audio cues to connect the blocks. P-Cube [3] is a TPT that uses physical cubes to program a robot's movements. The robot provides audio feedback announcing its position. On the other hand, Torino [9] is a tangible tool that uses audio sounds and audio story as an output method, and enables collaboration between students with diverse VI and students with no VI.

3   Tangible Programming Tool

Although the purpose of this paper is to report the findings in the user study, we will briefly overview our prototype design. Our project aims to develop a TPT to aid children with VI and LV to learn basic programming concepts using music as an output method. To build our prototype we used modified Duplo Lego blocks (height $= 25.80$) and a Lego panel (8 rows $\times$ 9 columns). Each 2×2 block is modified with a 3.5 mm male audio jack connector which connects to a female audio jack placed in the Lego panel. Each Lego block represents a different instruction to build a program. For the identification of each block we used a 3D printed symbol on top and a Braille label in front. The Lego panel is divided into cells to facilitate the block's connection and the physical assembling of a program. The semantics of program is described in terms of music and the execution of a program is a melody.

4   Usability Study

4.1   Evaluation

The study consists of two parts. The **first part** is aimed at assessing the accessibility of *Scratch*, a block-based programming environment. The study consists of a training session, where the moderator teaches the participants how to use Scratch's interface and basic programming concepts, such as loops, conditional statements, and variables. A task completion section was implemented to evaluate the following features of the Scratch interface: (**1**) labels of the blocks (names of the blocks), (**2**) Directional arrows (rotational arrow symbols), (**3**) the indication of correct placement for a block connection (block's background changes to gray, simulating shadow), (**4**) parameter form (Scratch provides a geometric form to connect parameters), and (**5**) graphic feedback to debug code.

The tasks included different scenarios which present a problem to the participants and pre-built programs where they must complete or fix it. Each task had a time limit of five minutes. To evaluate Scratch environments we used success (completed with no help), partial success (completed with help regarding concepts), and failure (not able to complete) of the tasks. The tasks' order was set by using balanced latin square to eliminate bias in results. The screens were recorded in video format while time to complete the task was measured manually. Lastly, a post-survey was provided to participants to gauge their overall experience and ask for suggestions related to Scratch's environment. A screen reader (NonVisual Desktop Access) and screen magnifier were provided to the users.

In the **second part** of the study, the participants assessed a preliminary version of our TPT prototype, performed three different tasks, and were interviewed by the moderator.

The first step involved allowing the users the opportunity to explore the prototype. This provided us information regarding exploration techniques of the participants to identify and associate physical objects such as Lego blocks, panel, and audio jack connectors. It additionally gave us feedback on hardware's improvements that must be implemented. The second step involved completion of the following tasks:

(T1) *Lego panel connectors and cells' height* – The participants plugged and unplugged a block into cells with different heights (8.32 mm, 11.49 mm, 14.61 mm, 17.97 mm, 21.10 mm) and chose which height was easier to connect the block. The connection's correctness is important to read the blocks effectively. Otherwise, it will be difficult to debug a code where blocks are not in the right position.

(T2) *Block's location* – The participant located a Lego block placed in a specific cell and identified its location.

(T3) *3D printed block's symbols* – Before starting this task, the participants were taught about basic programming concepts (*variable, constant, loop, conditional, functions*). Once we were confident they understood the concepts, three symbols per concept were given to them. Participants chose the best symbol to represent each concept. Additionally, they were allowed to provide their symbol ideas.

Once tasks and interview sessions were completed, we showed them an example of our idea which uses tangible tools to create music as a code output. Lastly, a self-reported survey was provided for prototype evaluation and to collect their suggestions regarding the hardware and music output. Results have been collected in a video-audio format. The videos provide vital information regarding hand movements, block's location, and tactile exploration.

4.2 Participants

Nine adults (Female = 5, Male = 4) with an average age of 52.6 years and differing VI and LV levels participated in this study (see Table 1). The participants were recruited through the *Asociación Puertorriqueña de Ciegos* inc. and by email.

Table 1. Summary of participants of the usability study. The labels were assigned randomly and do not represent the order of evaluations.

Participants	Age	Gender	Programming experiences	Assistive technology
P1	74	M	No	Screen reader
P2	60	M	No	Screen reader and magnifier
P3	50	F	No	Screen reader
P4	25	F	No	Screen reader
P5	37	F	No	Screen reader
P6	no	F	No	None
P7	48	F	No	Screen reader
P8	54	M	No	Screen reader and magnifier
P9	53	M	Yes	Screen reader and magnifier

The study was performed in the facilities of the *Asociación Puertorriqueña de Ciegos* and library Antonio Roig located in Puerto Rico. Each participant completed the study individually. Eight participants used screen readers and three of them used magnifiers to access visual information. As Table 1 shows, participant six (P6) did not use assistive technology due to a lack of familiarity with computers. Eight participants had no experience in programming, while one was an experienced programmer. However, none of them had experience with Block-based programming or Scratch. Before the study, five participants had never heard about TPT, three knew about them but never tried, and one participant has used it.

5   Results

5.1   Part I

In the Scratch interface evaluation, only two participants were able to successfully complete the tasks. From now on we will refer to them as participant (a) and participant (b). To complete the study participant (a) used screen magnification while participant (b) used screen reader and screen magnification. As Table 2 shows both participants were able to complete all the tasks. Also, we can see that task three and four were the most time-consuming for both participants. Those tasks are related to blocks and parameter connections. Participant (a) suggested the use of a button or key to navigate through the interface since it was difficult to keep track of the mouse position while using screen magnifier. Additionally, participant (a) indicated that using sound when connecting a block will help the participant know when a block is connected. Participant (b) recommended keyboard shortcuts to facilitate the block's connections.

Table 2. Results of the first part of the user study. Success means that participants finished the task with no help, partial success that finished with help, and fail means that participant does not finish the task in five minutes.

Tasks	Participant (a)				Participant (b)			
	Time (s)	Success	Partial success	Fail	Time (s)	Success	Partial success	Fail
1	46	x			69	x		
2	47	x			35	x		
3	300		x		290		x	
4	285		x		285	x		
5	196		x		58	x		

The results of the post-survey shows that although it was difficult to connect the blocks, both participants liked the use of graphics as an output.

Based on observations, results, and post-survey of the first part we found the following:

A) *Focus Navigation:* A navigation button or keyboard shortcut should be added to move through Scratch's interface (Programming blocks, work-space, animation window). Participant (a) showed difficulty finding the mentioned sections in the interface while using a screen magnifier.

B) *Auditory Cues:* The Block-based environment of Scratch relies on text labels, symbols, and colors to identify blocks. The participants who could not complete this section claimed the incompatibility of screen readers with block labels and symbols and the absence of an alternative way to move blocks, such as a keyboard, as the main reasons for the failure.

C) *Keyboard Shortcuts:* The interface of Scratch depends on mouse or touch-pad devices to drag and drop the virtual blocks. Participant (b) suggested the use of keyboard shortcuts to move and connect the blocks.

D) *Connection Validation:* Scratch programming consists of connecting blocks to build a program. Audio feedback that indicates the right position of the connection would help users with VI and LV to know where to drop blocks.

5.2 Part II

All participants were able to successfully complete the first and second tasks, interview, and post-survey. The blocks used contain a 3.5 mm stereo audio jack inside, which requires precision to connect them. To facilitate the connections, Lego bricks were placed in the panel, which created cells and functioned as a frame. The results of the first task show that participants have difficulty connecting the blocks in cells with height of 8.32 mm and 11.49 mm. None of the participants choose the first two heights. Four participants choose 14.61 mm, two choose 17.97 mm, and three choose 21.10 mm. Two of the participants claimed that the highest cell was better, other participants commented that it was uncomfortable to disconnect the blocks due to the pressure on their fingers. Results of the second task show that using the rows and columns method is intuitive for the participants. Once they found the block, they proceed to start counting columns and rows to indicate its position automatically. The third task was a challenge for the participants, according to their reports during the interviews. However, they were excited with the 3D printed symbols. Symbol ideas were collected from people with no experience in programming. Two participants did not complete the task due to low touch sensitivity. They recommended that in addition to 3D symbols we could use different block sizes (heights) to identify them. Additionally, they recommend the use of buttons to enable multi-instruction in each block. Another participant commented that geometric figures are an easier and faster way to identify blocks. Results show that participants identify the programming concepts with the symbol of the first letter of its name (e.g., Loop (L), Variable (V), etc.). Furthermore complex symbols such as printed words, combined geometric figures in one block, or object symbols were time consuming and difficult to identify. The idea of using music as an output for the built code was accepted by the participants. For this step we used an environment called FoxDot [4] to present our idea of creating music with coding. All of the participants agreed or strongly agreed with using coding for music.

Based on results of tasks completion, post-survey, and interviews we created a guideline for the final design of our TPT:

A) *Lego Panel Design:* A Manhattan map design in a tangible tool prototype simplifies the movement around the panel. Counting the number of cells (horizontally and vertically), all participants were able to find a specific given coordinate. This feature is extremely important to provide good programming feedback to the users.

B) *Height of the Cell Divisions:* We found that a specific height is needed for two reasons: to act as a frame for the block connections as well as to highlight the cell divisions. Our results showed cell's height of 14.61 mm are preferred by the users.

C) *Connection Type:* As a result of the post-survey, four participants totally agreed with the statement that connecting and disconnecting blocks was an easy task. Four participants agreed with the statement and one voted neutral.

D) *Block Identification:* Using 3D printing in our blocks was a good approach and a challenge as well. The majority of the participants were very excited about using a 3D printed symbol to identify each block. However, it was also a challenge to find symbols that represent programming concepts. Our results showed that simple symbols (e.g., geometric figures) are better and enhance the identification speed.

E) *Music as Code Output:* Although the TPT was in a preliminary stage, we showed our idea of using music as an output method. Five participants agreed and 4 totally agreed to the recommendation of music as an output method from execution of a program.

6   Conclusion

Based on the results of the first part of the study, we can conclude that it is possible to make VPL accessible to users with VI and LV by including the following: focus navigation to move between interface sections; audio effects to indicate a valid connection; and compatibility of screen readers with block labels and symbols (e.g., directional arrows). Some of the barriers that participants faced while using Scratch included navigating between interface sections as well as getting feedback regarding valid positions to connect a block.

The second part of this study establishes guidelines for building a successful TPT and demonstrates that our prototype can be used by users with VI and LV. Some of the barriers that participants encountered while using our prototype include the identification of blocks with complex 3D symbols and connecting blocks in the Lego panel with low cell heights. The next step of this ongoing project is to implement participants' recommendations, including the music environment to build an efficient TPT.

References

1. Broll, B., et al.: A visual programming environment for learning distributed programming. In: Proceedings of the 2017 ACM SIGCSE Technical Symposium on Computer Science Education, pp. 81–86 (2017)
2. Cooper, S., Dann, W., Pausch, R.: Using Animated 3D Graphics to Prepare Novices for CS1 (2010). https://doi.org/10.1076/csed.13.1.3.13540, https://www.tandfonline.com/action/journalInformation?journalCode=ncse20
3. Kakehashi, S., Motoyoshi, T., Koyanagi, K., Ohshima, T., Kawakami, H.: P-CUBE: Block type programming tool for visual impairments. Proceedings - 2013 Conference on Technologies and Applications of Artificial Intelligence, TAAI 2013 pp. 294–299 (2013). https://doi.org/10.1109/TAAI.2013.65
4. Kirkbride, R.: FoxDot: live coding with Python and supercollider. In: Proceedings of the International Conference on Live Interfaces, pp. 194–198 (2016)
5. Ludi, S.: Position paper: towards making block-based programming accessible for blind users. In: Proceedings - 2015 IEEE Blocks and Beyond Workshop, Blocks and Beyond 2015, pp. 67–69. Institute of Electrical and Electronics Engineers Inc., December 2015. https://doi.org/10.1109/BLOCKS.2015.7369005
6. Maloney, J., Resnick, M., Rusk, N., Silverman, B., Eastmond, E.: The scratch programming language and environment. ACM Trans. Comput. Educ. (TOCE) **10**(4), 16 (2010)
7. Milne, L.R., Ladner, R.E.: Blocks4All: overcoming accessibility barriers to blocks programming for children with visual impairments. In: Conference on Human Factors in Computing Systems - Proceedings, April, vol. 2018. Association for Computing Machinery, April 2018. https://doi.org/10.1145/3173574.3173643
8. Rao, A., Bihani, A., Nair, M.: Milo: a visual programming environment for data science education. In: 2018 IEEE Symposium on Visual Languages and Human-Centric Computing (VL/HCC), pp. 211–215. IEEE (2018)
9. Thieme, A., Morrison, C., Villar, N., Grayson, M., Lindley, S.: Enabling collaboration in learning computer programing inclusive of children with vision impairments. In: Proceedings of the 2017 Conference on Designing Interactive Systems - DIS 2017, pp. 739–752 (2017). https://doi.org/10.1145/3064663.3064689, http://dl.acm.org/citation.cfm?doid=3064663.3064689

Consigliere Evaluation: Evaluating Complex Interactive Systems with Users with Disabilities

Helen Petrie[1]($\boxtimes$) , Sanjit Samaddar[1] , Christopher Power[2] ,
and Burak Merdenyan[1]

[1] Department of Computer Science, University of York, York YO10 5GH, UK
{helen.petrie, sanjit.samaddar,
burak.merdenyan}@york.ac.uk
[2] School of Mathematical and Computational Science, University of Prince
Edward Island, Charlottetown, PE C1A 4P3, Canada
cdspower@upei.ca

Abstract. Conducting accessibility evaluations with users with disabilities is an important part of developing accessible interactive systems. Conducting such evaluations of systems which require complex domain knowledge is often impossible, as disabled users do not exist or are very rare. This paper presents a user evaluation method to address this problem, consigliere evaluation. A consigliere evaluation has the disabled user as the main participant, but they are assisted by an advisor, or *consigliere*, who understands the complex domain; the consigliere is in turn, monitored by an accessibility expert, who acts as an *enforcer*. As in all user evaluations, the disabled participant undertakes a series of tasks. But in a consigliere evaluation, if the task requires some particular domain knowledge or skill, the role of the *consigliere* is to provide appropriate information. However, it is easy for the *consigliere*, who usually does not have knowledge of the accessibility domain, to provide information not specifically about the domain, but about how to do the task in general. So the role of the *enforcer*, who is an accessibility expert, is to ensure this does not happen, and also to provide assistance and explanation if accessibility issues arise that the disabled participant cannot solve. The paper illustrates the consigliere method with a case study, the evaluation of Skillsforge, an online system used by a number of universities to manage progress of postgraduate students. This system requires considerable domain knowledge of the terminology and progression requirements for these students. It is used by university administrative staff, academic staff who supervise postgraduate students or are involved in monitoring students and the students themselves. The case study illustrates how the consigliere evaluation method works and some of the things which need to be considered in conducting the evaluation appropriately.

Keywords: Evaluation methods · Disabled users · Complex systems · User evaluations

© Springer Nature Switzerland AG 2020
K. Miesenberger et al. (Eds.): ICCHP 2020, LNCS 12376, pp. 35–42, 2020.
https://doi.org/10.1007/978-3-030-58796-3_5

1 Introduction

Conducting accessibility evaluations with users with disabilities is an important part of developing accessible interactive systems. Conducting such evaluations when the use of the system requires specialist knowledge poses particular problems. For example, to evaluate the accessibility of banking systems which are only used by highly skilled bank employees requires the user to have an in-depth knowledge of banking procedures and terminology. Finding sufficient numbers of users with disabilities for a reliable user evaluation is often difficult, and finding users with disabilities who have very specific and specialised domain knowledge in such situations is often impossible.

In response to this problem, we have developed a user evaluation method, which we have called the consigliere evaluation method, after the Godfather films[1]. This paper will present the method and then discuss a case study of a recent evaluation conducted using the method in the evaluation of a new version of an interactive system to monitor the progress of research students at universities, to be used by university administrators, faculty members who supervise such students and the students themselves. The different views on the system used by the different user groups require different kinds of specialist knowledge about procedures and terminology within the institution in relation to research degrees and the students undertaking them.

2 Background

The most common approach to evaluating accessibility of interactive systems is to assess conformance to design guidelines. For web-based systems, the Web Content Accessibility Guidelines (WCAG) [1] are available. There are also accessibility guidelines and design patterns for other kinds of interactive systems, for example smartphone apps [2, 3], public access terminal such as automatic teller machines for banking and ticket machines for public transport [4], interactive voice systems [5] and games consoles [6]. Nonetheless, it is clear that developing interactive systems solely by following guidelines, while they are an important source of information and guidance, does not necessarily produce systems that are highly usable for disabled or older people [7, 8].

Evaluation by target users of a system remains the "gold standard" of evaluation techniques [9]. This is even more so in the case of the development of interactive systems for people with disabilities or older people, for a number of reasons [10], although see discussion in [11]. Finding people with disabilities who can take part in user evaluations can often be difficult, however can be achieved with determination and persistence [10, 12]. However, if one is evaluating a system that requires specialist domain skills or knowledge, it can become impossible. It can be a "chicken and egg" problem: people with disabilities may not be able to develop the specialist skills if they

---

[1] The use of this term in no way implies admiration for the mafia, but we were inspired by the Godfather film in which the consigliere whispers advice in the ear of the mafia boss.

cannot use the system, but if there are no disabled people with the necessary skills, how can the specialist system be developed accessibly?

In order to address this methodological gap, we have developed the consigliere evaluation method, in which disabled people are the main participants in the user evaluation, but are assisted by an advisor, or consigliere [13], who in turn, is monitored by an accessibility expert, who acts as an enforcer. The next section explains how the method works, and the following section presents a case study of how we have used it for the evaluation of a system that required specialist knowledge of university proce-dures for dealing with the administrative needs of students on research degrees.

3   The Consigliere Evaluation Method

A consigliere evaluation is similar to other user-based accessibility evaluations, in that participants are asked to do a number of tasks which are designed to assess the accessibility of the system. They may be asked to do this with a concurrent verbal protocol, this works well in consigliere evaluations. They may be asked to complete standardized or bespoke questions about the accessibility and their user experience after each task and at the end of a set of tasks. The difference in consigliere evaluation is that each evaluation session requires three people, who play different roles:

- The participant with disabilities – this will be someone from the target user group, who may be a user of assistive technology, if so a competent user of that tech-nology. However, they will not have any of the specialist domain knowledge required to use the system under evaluation
- The *consigliere* – this will be someone who has the specialist domain knowledge, most likely a non-disabled user of the technology or someone from the specialist domain of interest. They will probably not know anything about disability, acces-sibility or assistive technologies.
- The *enforcer* – this will be someone who is an expert in the accessibility of the kind of technology under evaluation, for example web accessibility, accessibility of Windows applications or mobile accessibility.

Before the session, the enforcer needs to brief the consigliere about how the session will work. The *consigliere* should provide the participant with the necessary specialist knowledge they need to interact with the system, this might be in terms of terminology and domain procedures. But they must not give any help in how to actually interact with the system to undertake the procedures and tasks. This may be hard for the *consigliere* because they have no knowledge of accessibility issues and they may inadvertently give messages that provide information to the participant about how to execute actions. So rather than saying "you now need to find function x" they might say "the link for function X is in the list headed Y". The *enforcer* may need to take the *consigliere* through some examples of things to do and not to do and how to word advice.

At the beginning of the session the participant also needs to be briefed about the nature of the evaluation. They should be reassured that they are not expected to understand the domain of the system, and that they can ask the *consigliere* for any help, although this will be moderated by the *enforcer*. During the evaluation session, it should be the participant who leads the dialogue – they should ask for advice whenever they feel they need it. The *consigliere* should only proactively offer advice when they think the participant has made a mistake due to a mis-understanding of domain knowledge.

During the session, particularly in the initial sessions, the *consigliere* should not offer advice without first checking with the *enforcer*. This may require a means of communication which the participant is not party to, for example hand gestures and messages on a notebook that the participant cannot see. This ensures that the *enforcer* can be sure that too much information is not communicated to the participant. The *enforcer* may also initiate support for the participant. Because the *consigliere* does not necessarily understand about accessibility issues, they may not realize whether the participant is having a problem due to a domain issue or an accessibility issue, so the *enforcer* may ask the *consigliere* to provide some domain knowledge. In addition, the *enforcer* can help when the participant gets stuck due to accessibility problems. Once a problem has been identified, there is no point leaving the participant to struggle with it, the *enforcer* can explain what the problem is and give assistance in getting over it.

This sounds very complicated, but with a little practice and cooperation, it becomes relatively easy and very interesting. It does mean that evaluation sessions, particularly the first ones, can take longer than usual, one needs to allow 25% to 50% longer. However, we have found that all parties involved find it a very rewarding and interesting experience. Participants learn something about a new domain, a new evaluation method and know they have contributed to the accessibility evaluation of an important system. *Consiglieres* (or *consiglieri*) learn a lot about accessibility and feel valued for their domain expertise. *Enforcers* learn about a new domain and often acquire more detailed accessibility information from the discussions with participants and *consiglieres*.

4 The Case Study: Consigliere Evaluation of Skillsforge

We recently used the consigliere evaluation method to assess the accessibility of a system used in a number of universities for the management of the progression and assessment of students doing postgraduate degrees, the Skillsforge system [13]. This system requires considerable domain knowledge of the terminology and progression requirements for these students. There are numerous processes which need to be logged in Skillsforge with different forms. This includes:

- Reporting on supervision meetings between students and supervisors (which need to be approved and signed by both student and supervisor, and if either edits the text, both need to sign off again);
- Scheduling and writing reports on Thesis Advisory Panel (TAP) meetings which consist of the student, supervisor and an independent Assessor (who also needs to be appointed and logged in the system);
- Logging that students have given seminars and submitted papers for publication (which need to be signed off by different people);

- Logging that students have submitted annual progress reports;
- Scheduling and writing reports on Progression meeting which consist of the student, the independent Assessor and a Progression Panel Chair (who also needs to be appointed and logged in the system);
- Appointing External Examiners for the examination of the thesis;
- Logging submission of the thesis.

As can be seen there are many different processes, with different people involved in particular processes. There are also different processes in each of the three or four years that a student is enrolled in their PhD so they cannot develop a rhythm of the processes, and students enroll at different times of the academic year, so supervisors find it difficult to develop a rhythm as well.

There are three separate main roles of users of the Skillsforge system:

- University administrators responsible for a group of students, in a department or unit. Typically, they need to ensure that all students are meeting the requirements for progression towards their degrees. They may need to monitor between 10 to 100 students.
- Supervisors, independent assessors and Progress Panel chairs. These are academic members of staff, they are responsible for one or more students they are supervising, plus one or more students for whom they are acting as independent assessor and Progress Panel chair. Thus, they may be responsible for one to several dozen students (the first author of this paper is responsible for 17 students as an academic)
- Research students. They are responsible to log their own progress and may use Skillsforge as a repository for documents for their PhD.

8 blind participants took part in the consigliere evaluation. They included 2 women and 6 men, aged 19 to 64. Some participants had been blind since birth, some had lost their sight at some later point in life. There was a mixture of users of different screenreaders, JAWS, NVDA and VoiceOver. All the screenreaders were used in the evaluation, as well as different browsers, including Chrome and Safari. Each participant evaluated all three roles in Skillsforge: university administrator, supervisor/independent assessor and PhD student. They completed 9 tasks, 3 tasks per role. Each evaluation session took between 90 min and 2 h.

The first, second and fourth author acted as the consigliere and enforcer in different parts of the evaluation. The first author is very experienced in the role of being a supervisor and independent assessor and the second and fourth authors were experienced at being PhD students. A member of the development team at Skillsforge also acted as consigliere, particularly for the university administrator role, which none of the authors were familiar with.

Here we illustrate some of the interesting situations which arose in these evaluations which highlight issues that need to be considered when conducting a consigliere evaluation:

Participant is confused about deadline numbers and why there is no deadline. The consigliere provides expert knowledge on the domain space without providing extra navigation help for the task. The consigliere provides domain expertise, and in turn the participant makes clear that even with the domain knowledge they would need a better heading.

P1: Deadline 2? Where is deadline 1?
Consigliere: Deadline 1 may have passed in this case [for this student] as of today's date Deadline 1 has already passed, so will not be available in the menu.
P1: Okay but I would expect a better heading then to explain what the deadline is for.

The *consigliere* should not give specific information that allows the participant to easily search for the solution to a task, sometimes this made things difficult. The *enforcer* decides when to help the participant. Here the *enforcer* has the knowledge to hint towards using different screenreader keywords, whereas the *consigliere* may have been tempted to ask the participant to search for "milestones".

Participant was told to find "upcoming deadlines" although in Skillsforge they are called "milestones". The phrasing of this task was intentionally chosen to avoid participants immediately using the search function and encourage them to navigate around the screen. In this instance the participant could not identify what was required:

P1: Ah yes, if I had known it was milestones I would have just searched for that after not finding anything on the page by tabbing through it.
Enforcer: Okay how about you look through the drop downs or headings?

In completing forms, the *consigliere* has to give detailed domain information about how fields should be completed in a form. The *consigliere* is explaining the process for a PhD student to request a leave of absence. However, he gave the information one form field at a time, means that participant could guess what type of form field to expect next. We then realised that we should give all the information at the beginning of the form, not necessarily in the order the participant will find them in the form, and tell the participant they can ask for the information to be repeated:

JAWS: Change summary stat, type edit text.
Consigliere: So here you can just say "requesting a leave of absence"
P1: Okay. (types into text field)
Consigliere: And I can tell you that this is a "long term temporary" type of absence
P1: So that's the next field then! (Participant managed to fill this field in very quickly because he had been cued as to what came next, this was too much support).

The participant is asked to log into the system. The *consigliere* does not say what edit fields are required or the nature of the input type. For example, he does not say "Could you please type in your email and password", as this would prompt participants to immediately use the form or edit shortcuts to find the sign in fields. However, in this case the participant explains that he would default to trying to find form fields anyway as the task is to sign in:

Consigliere: Please try logging in.
P4: One of the things with JAWS is that there is so much customization. So if I know I am looking for a form field to fill in, normally I would type 'F'... and that seems to have worked. A lot of this is once you have got some clues, you don't have to scramble around to find it.

5 Conclusions

We have presented a method to conduct accessibility evaluations with users of complex systems which require considerable domain knowledge. The consigliere evaluation method involves using two facilitators – a *consigliere* who provides domain knowledge and an *enforcer* who ensures that the *consigliere* does not provide too much information about interacting with the system and who also provides accessibility support for the participant and explanations to the *consigliere*. We have found this method very useful in conducting evaluations which have yielded much helpful information for developers of complex systems such as Skillsforge and an interesting and rewarding experience for the participants, the *consiglieres* and the *enforcers*.

Acknowledgements. We would like to thank the participants who took part in this evaluation, they helped us clarify the consigliere evaluation method. We would also like to thank Skillsforge for the opportunity to work with them and the Engineering and Physical Sciences Research Council (EPSRC) and the University of York for funding the research through the Innovation Voucher Programme.

References

1. World Wide Web Consortium – Web Accessibility Initiative (W3C WAI): Web Content accessibility Guidelines (WCAG) 2.1 (2018). https://www.w3.org/TR/WCAG21/. Accessed 12 Apr 2020
2. Android Developers. Make apps more accessible. https://developer.android.com/guide/topics/ui/accessibility/apps. Accessed 12 Apr 2020
3. Apple Human Interface Guidelines. Accessibility. https://developer.apple.com/design/human-interface-guidelines/accessibility/overview/introduction/. Accessed 12 Apr 2020
4. Centre for Excellence in Universal Design. Public access terminals, 1 July 2019 http://universaldesign.ie/technology-ict/irish-national-it-accessibility-guidelines/public-access-terminals/public-access-terminals.html. Accessed 12 Apr 2020
5. Centre for Excellence in Universal Design. Telecoms. http://universaldesign.ie/technology-ict/irish-national-it-accessibility-guidelines/telecoms/telecoms.html. Accessed 12 Apr 2020
6. AbleGamers. Design patterns for APX. https://accessible.games/accessible-player-experiences/design-patterns/. Accessed 12 Apr 2020
7. Sani, Z.H.A., Petrie, H.: User evaluation of an app for liquid monitoring by older adults. In: Antona, M., Stephanidis, C. (eds.) UAHCI 2017. LNCS, vol. 10279, pp. 86–97. Springer, Cham (2017). https://doi.org/10.1007/978-3-319-58700-4_8
8. Power, C., Freire, A., Petrie, H., Swallow, D.: Guidelines are only half the story: accessibility problems encountered by blind users on the web. In: Proceedings of the 30th International Conference on Human Factors in Computing (CHI 2012). ACM Press, New York (2012)
9. Petrie, H., Bevan, N.: The evaluation of accessibility, usability and user experience. In: Stephanidis, C. (ed.) The Universal Access Handbook. Taylor and Francis, London (2009)

10. Sears, A., Hanson, V.L.: Representing users in accessibility research. ACM Trans. Access. Comput. **4**(2), 7 (2012)
11. Aizpurua, A., Arrue, M., Harper, S., Vigo, M.: Are users the gold standard for accessibility evaluation? In: W4A: Proceedings of the 11th Web for All Conference (2014). Article 13
12. Power, C., Petrie, H.: Working with participants. In: Yesilada, Y., Harper, S. (eds.) Web Accessibility. HIS, pp. 153–168. Springer, London (2019). https://doi.org/10.1007/978-1-4471-7440-0_9
13. https://skillsforge.com/

IPAR-UCD – Inclusive Participation of Users with Cognitive Disabilities in Software Development

M. A. Cordula Edler[✉]

i n b u t, integrative Beratung und Unterstützung, Teckstrasse 23,
73119 Zell unter Aichelberg, Germany
cordula.edler@icloud.com

Abstract. This article presents a new inclusive research concept for research and development (R&D) IPAR-UCD. An adaptation for collaborative R&D with peer-researchers for cognitive accessibility is still missing. This inclusive research concept investigates and combines two methodological approaches: Inclusive Participatory Action Research, IPAR [1] and User-Centered Design, UCD. With this inclusive research and development method, a concept is presented that has already been successfully applied and further developed in the »Easy Reading« project (ER) itself, together with the target group [2, 14].

Keywords: Inclusive-Participatory · Action research and development · e-Inclusion · Accessibility · UCD · Cognitive disabilities

1 Introduction

About 15% of the world's population lives with some form of disability, of whom 2–4% experience significant difficulties in functioning. According to the World Health Organization, almost 200 million people worldwide have cognitive disabilities or learning difficulties. Most of them need special support. According to the WHO this number will increase due to population growth, medical progress, and aging processes [4]. The accessibility of assistive technologies, AT, has made significant progress, but not to the same extent for the target group of people with cognitive disabilities. For them, accessibility is still missing.

The use of new media and digital services for people with cognitive disabilities or learning difficulties, e.g. for using, reading, and understanding internet content, is difficult. Often this excludes them from social communication and makes them depend on support or services. Enabling them to use the web and web technologies and thus to develop further is of crucial importance for the individual and is also a human right.

It is essential for society and the economy that people with intellectual and cognitive disabilities are and stay as active as possible, and participate in society [3, 16, 17]. The growing potential for flexibility and adaptation of digital technologies has to be encouraged for this target group to bridge the digital divide. Therefore, understanding the requirements of the target group is a key aspect of software development to create products that are accepted, wished, and can be used by the target group [2].

K. Miesenberger et al. (Eds.): ICCHP 2020, LNCS 12376, pp. 43–50, 2020.
https://doi.org/10.1007/978-3-030-58796-3_6

The involvement of the affected target group in the development process, in the sense of user-centred design, must be an integral part of this [5]. Despite some progress, however, there are still many development phases in which users are not involved due to cost and time constraints. In many cases, this leads to limited usability and acceptance of the developed products.

2   State of the Art

In research on cognitive accessibility, the W3C describes the challenges faced by people with learning difficulties or cognitive disabilities when using web content/technologies [7]. Nevertheless, there is hardly any inclusive participation of this target group as researchers or experts in their own affairs.

Literature reviews have shown that no methodological approaches to the practice of inclusive participatory research and user-centred design have been documented [18, 19]. Methods and tools to support communication and interaction to adequately involve the target group are missing.

Only in the social sciences are there some inclusive research approaches to be found. "Inclusive Research with People with Learning Disabilities" by Walmsley, Johnson [8], and IPAR, an Inclusive Disability Research Methodology by Ollerton [1], mark the beginning. In particular, this research deals with people with cognitive disabilities and involves them actively as co-researchers or peer-researchers.

Until now, conventional research has mostly assumed that people with cognitive disabilities are not able to make independent decisions [15]. Often creativity, methods and tools to support communication and interaction to adequately involve the target group are missing. There is also a lack of access and support for the target group in developing digital media [6, 18].

2.1   Findings for Inclusive Participatory Research and Development from the Literature

My own literature review gave the following insights for inclusive participatory research and development and the concept.

- Inclusion of the target groups as peer-researchers requires a high degree of willingness and intuition on the part of the researchers and developers.
- The necessary resources like time, material, and also the payment of the peers must be considered [18].
- The research project must have a high level of accessibility. For this, the target group needs all information in easy and understandable language about the research (the content and aims of the research, further processing of the information, and explanation about anonymity) [22].
- Peer-researchers are expected to participate voluntarily and to show interest and a certain degree of personal responsibility.
- To meet the ethical requirements for research, informed consent in plain language and/or another format is necessary and at best also confirmed in writing [21].

- Transparency and traceability require not only the complete documentation of the research process, but also that the peer-researchers are mentioned by name as co-authors and that the results are available to them in is easier to understand language [8].
- Before the development of the process starts, a formal introduction/training in research skills for people with intellectual disabilities is necessary to enable them to contribute to research [23, 24].

3   IPAR and UCD Together as a New Concept

IPAR, first practiced by Ollerton, is an inclusive approach, and an alternative to Participatory Action Research (PAR) as presented by Kemmis [26]. Inclusive Participatory Action Research, IPAR, represents an alternative, inclusive, empirical research approach.

IPAR provides the framework for inclusive, participatory action research with people with cognitive disabilities. Ollerton [1] actively involves these people in research, either as co-researchers or as peer-researchers, to improve their quality of life. With Ollertons methods, people with cognitive disabilities were encouraged to define their needs in daily life and organize their lives themselves [15] or (re)design their things [12, 13].

To allow the target group to participate on an equal level, the creativity of the researcher is required. For IPAR Ollerton adapted and developed methods and tools from action research to meet the needs of the target group. These are simple instruments for data collection and analysis (see Part II. Concept) that are accessible (barrier-free) to people with different resources and qualifications. Peer-researchers can thus be involved in the whole research process, including the analysis/evaluation phases.

User-centred design and user experience design, UCD/UXD also include the potential users in the development process. That means: they deal with user-centred design processes, including the design of assistive technologies and accessibility. People with disabilities are also included as potential users in this research, with the exception of people with cognitive disabilities [5]. For this, there are important questions: Which type of services or support are useful and could help you? What is not useful for you and does not help you? What would you like to do? How would you improve it?

Traditional research and development for people with cognitive disabilities mainly uses methods such as proxy statements, interviews (which are very critical for this target group), and observations. These methods are not as time and cost-intensive, but often not adequate for the target group.

As you can see, IPAR [1] and UCD [9–11] have many parallels in the participation of the potential users but still have not been formally linked. Both can refer to a wide range of methods, techniques, and tools. These may be combined for inclusive research and development and adapted or simplified to the level of people with cognitive disabilities, so that the persons concerned or potential users could be involved in the development. This is worth a try and should be combined for inclusive research and development and adapted or simplified for people with cognitive disabilities.

3.1   IPAR and UCD and the Needs and Advantages of This Combination

There are several advantages with this link. IPAR-UCD and the collaboration with peer-researchers address their support needs:

- People with cognitive disabilities or people with learning difficulties are no longer the subject of research, but participate in research.
- Developers must respect them as users and develop applications that do not frustrate them.
- Peers must cooperate seriously. They have an important task in R&D.
- Recognition and acceptance enable good teamwork and trust.
- Methods are adapted and developed.
- Through an inclusive, user-centred design process software developers and designers more able to understand and to meet the needs of users with cognitive disabilities.

3.2   IPAR-UCD in Scientific Practice

When adapting this new concept, coordination between peers and developers on the one hand and quality criteria for qualitative research on the other have to be ensured.

- Adequacy of the research subject and the research process,
- Validity, reliability, and credibility of the data,
- Transparency and intersubjective traceability,
- Reflective subjectivity (principle of self-reflexivity) on the part of the researchers.

4   The »Easy Reading LAB« and IPAR-UCD

In the Project »Easy Reading« , together with the target group and with the help of the IPAR-UCD concept a software was engineered and designed as AT to support the cognitive accessibility of web content, e.g. reading texts. The finished software should be available free of charge for all those who need help on the internet.

The international development team of »Easy Reading LAB«, included scientists, as well as peer-researchers with cognitive disabilities and people with learning difficulties. They came from Austria, Sweden, and Germany, and were involved in all phases of the interdisciplinary project. A holistic approach to user-centred design was implemented and we involved the target group from the beginning as peer-researchers.

To be able to successfully design the intuitive use and take it into account during development, the needs and requirements of the users, as well as the context of the use of the tool, must be known. The first step was to investigate the difficulties of accessing, reading, and understanding web content.

The first step was to find out the user needs and requirements to develop the software and its services according to the needs (requirement analysis). During development, the peer-researchers tried out different forms of support and assistance. They told the developers what works well and what needs to be improved. The focus was not only on functionality but also on interaction design and the actual look and feel of the software.

In developing interaction design and information architecture, the physical, psychological, and emotional needs of the peer-researchers had to be taken into account. User Research and User-Centered Design, therefore, belong together. Due to the complexity, attempts were made to solve the design requirements in a multidisciplinary way, often focusing less on technical issues and more on creativity. However, the latter proved to be a particular challenge. The peer-researchers were primarily concerned with individual preferences in appearance and less with actual comprehensibility. However, standard design disciplines for product and communication design, as well as issues of ergonomics, information architecture, and usability research are important.

4.1   The New Challenges of IPAR-UCD in the Project

In the »Easy Reading« project, many decisions were made. The process clarified how cooperation should be structured. For example: what access the peer-researchers had to the current field of research? How did they define their role as researchers?

The challenge in the »Easy Reading« project was to identify their ideas on research and development in concrete terms and to include further proposals on the inclusive research agenda during the development process. The stepwise, often iterative procedure requires more time and personnel support than in standard research projects. It was also a challenge to develop inclusive attitudes, procedures, and methods so that the peer-researchers were perceived as fully-fledged members of the research team and that cross-border and cross-language cooperation was able to function.

5   Development and Improvement of the IPAR-UCD Concept

The method used here is "Design-Based Research" (DBR) [12, 13]. Development and further development of the proposed IPAR-UCD concept was based on this quality approach. This means: iterative designing and redesigning by those who are involved.

A preliminary concept was set up based on numerous experiences with the target group, and digital media as well as on the scientific background of media education research. After recruitment of peers and a workshop at the beginning of the »Easy Reading-LAB«, three groups started their work as peer-researchers in different places. The peer researchers were given an iPad as a personal tool, which they could use mainly for communication (e-mail, skype and observation). Most of the time they worked in their group with support, or in tandem (peer-researcher and assistant). The work with the developers took place on-site but also virtually. Focus groups were installed for discussion. Diaries and notes were used. New suggestions were developed again until everyone was satisfied with the result and could work with it.

For the IPAR-UCD methodology, individual steps of the research process, as well as the research instruments, were selected and tested together with the different participants and their individual skills. For this purpose, a mix of methods was used in order to give equal attention to each peer-researcher and to promote the empowerment and responsibility of the other co-researchers.

The working materials and research methods had to be simple and understandable. The research concept as well as all materials for the peer-researchers and methods for inclusive-participative design were selected and adapted, for instance:

- *Collaborative Method* - participatory group process for planning, implementation, and evaluation;
- *Focus Group* - Moderated group discussion with the peer-researchers;
- *Card Sorting* - Development of requirements and information architecture;
- Scenarios - Detailed description of a possible defined situation;
- *Visual Storytelling, Photo and Video Elicitation* - Visualization of interactions, scenarios and visions;
- *Cognitive Walk Through* - Plan and realize action steps;
- *Thinking Aloud Test* - Pronouncing your thoughts during testing

The quality criteria for the collection, analysis and interpretation of data have been clearly and comprehensibly defined and applied. The results and analyses of the qualitative data and their conclusions have been presented as far as possible in accessible form.

6   Experience with IPAR and UCD and Advantages of This Approach

This combination of IPAR and UCD as a first inclusive, design-based research concept enables the participation of people with cognitive disabilities as peer-researchers throughout the development process and support user-centred R&D.

The experiences in the research lab »Easy Reading« showed, at the beginning of a project, a workshop with all team members is essential. It is important to become familiar with the tasks, instruments, methods, inclusive work, and also to set a concrete timetable. Peer-researchers working in a group (focus group) or team was preferred in the »Easy Reading« project. For example, the peer-researchers carried out the adapted Cognitive Walkthrough in tandems. This gave them security, and it did not affect the result. Also, we noticed that methods that work from the beginning with visualization are more suitable than text-based or strongly language-oriented methods. In many cases, text-based methods need additional explanations and/or visualizations. Therefore, in a new research project, IPAR-UCD should first be adapted and refined together with the target group.

It has been shown that adequate attention and creativity on the part of researchers and developers and the adaptation and (further) development of usability methods and tools lead to inclusive participation of potential users as peer-researchers in user-centred R&D processes.

7 Conclusion

IPAR-UCD as a concept for inclusive research and development was used in the »Easy Reading« project for the first time. Further, it was modified in collaboration with the peer-researchers of the project. The »Easy Reading-LAB« demonstrates that people with cognitive disabilities can very well be involved as peer-researchers in the development of interactive digital media and services from the first design phase onwards. The research for »Easy Reading« should be done together with them.

For new applications, adapted methodology and tools are now available. They can be used in these contexts. This ensures that people with cognitive disabilities can participate in a research and development process that affects them, and that development can match their needs [1, 6, 14].

Different perspectives on inclusive-participatory research with people with cognitive disabilities have shown that this research approach IPAR-UCD also is also based on German law and on the precepts of UN-CRPD and as such feasible, normative, and ethically justifiable for research and development. Therefore IPAR-UCD can be referred to an alternative methodological approach for inclusive research and development (R&D) and human-computer interaction (HCI). In future, IPAR-UCD could fill a gap as a new qualitative research method in inclusive research.

References

1. Ollerton, J.M.: IPAR, an inclusive disability research methodology with accessible analytical tools . Int. Pract. Dev. J. **2**(2), 3 (2012). http://www.fons.org/library/journal/volume2-issue2/article3, Accessed 14 Feb 2019
2. Heumader, P., Edler, C., Miesenberger, K., Wolkerstorfer, S.: Requirements engineering for people with cognitive disabilities – exploring new ways for peer-researchers and developers to cooperate. In: Miesenberger, K., Kouroupetroglou, G. (eds.) ICCHP 2018. LNCS, vol. 10896, pp. 439–445. Springer, Cham (2018). https://doi.org/10.1007/978-3-319-94277-3_68
3. Vereinte Nationen: Konvention über die Rechte von Menschen mit Behinderung (2016) http://www.un.org/disabilities/convention/conventionfull.shtml. Accessed 14 Feb 2019
4. WHO: Factsheet on Persons with Disabilities. https://www.un.org/development/desa/disabilities/resources/factsheet-on-persons-with-disabilities.html. Accessed 14 Feb 2020
5. Istenic Starcic, A., Bagon, S.: ICT-supported learning for inclusion of people with special needs. Brit. J. Educ. Tech. **45**(2), 202–230 (2014)
6. Miesenberger, K., Edler, C., Heumader, P., Petz, A.: Tools and applications for cognitive accessibility. In: Yesilada, Y., Harper, S. (eds.) Web Accessibility. HIS, pp. 523–546. Springer, London (2019). https://doi.org/10.1007/978-1-4471-7440-0_28
7. W3C/WAI: Cognitive and Learning Disabilities Accessibility Task Force (Cognitive A11Y TF). https://www.w3.org/WAI/PF/cognitive-a11y-tf/. Accessed 14 Feb 2020
8. Walmsley, J., Johnson, K.: Inclusive Research with People with Learning Disabilities. Jessica Kingsley Publishers, London (2003)
9. Shneiderman, B.: Universal usability. Commun. ACM **43**(5) (2000)
10. Sarodnick, F., Brau, H.: Methoden der Usability Evaluation. Hogrefe, Freiburg (2016)
11. Nielsen, J.: Designing Web Usability: The Practice of Simplicity. New. Riders Publishing, Berkeley (1999)

12. Reimann G.: Innovation ohne Forschung? Ein Plädoyer für den Design Based Research Ansatz in der Lehr- und Lernforschung. Zeitschrift für Lernforschung. Beltz/Juventa, Frankfurt am Main (2005)
13. Reimann, G.: Design-Based Research am Beispiel hochschuldidaktischer Forschung, Redemanuskript (2016). https://gabi-reinmann.de/wp-content/uploads/2016/11/Vortrag_Berlin_Nov2016.pdf. Accessed 14 Feb 2019
14. Easy Reading, Keeping the user at the digital original. https://www.easyreading.eu/. Accessed 13 Apr 2020
15. Buchner, T., König, O., Schuppener, S.: Inklusive Forschung. Klinkhard, Heilbrunn (2016)
16. Hirschberg, M.: Behinderung im internationalen Diskurs. Springer, Frankfurt am Main (2009)
17. Hirschberg, M.: Menschenrechtsbasierte Datenerhebung, Deutsches Institut für Menschenrechte, vol. 19. Berlin Deutsches Institut Für Menschenrechte (2012)
18. Fasching, H., Biewer, G.: Wissenskonstruktionen mit Menschen mit intellektueller Beeinträchtigung in der Bildungswissenschaft (2014). https://doi.org/10.1007/s35834-014-0100-1. Last Accessed 07 Oct 2019
19. Cumming, T., Strnadová, I., Knox, M., Parmenter, T.: Mobile technology in inclusive research: tools of empowerment (2014). https://www.researchgate.net/publication/260553455_Mobile_technology_in_inclusive_research_Tools_of_empowerment. Accessed 08 Jan 2018
20. Kerkmann, F., Lewandowski, D.: Accessibility of Web Search Engines: Towards a Deeper Understanding of Barriers for People with Disabilities (2012). http://www.bui.fh-hamburg.de/fileadmin/user_upload/lewandowski/doc/Postgrad_Research_in_LIS_Article_preprint.pdf. Accessed 05 Jun 2020
21. Kremsner, G.: Macht und Gewalt in den Biographien von Menschen mit Lernschwierigkeiten, eine (forschungsethische) Herausforderung? In: Schuppener, S., et al.: Inklusion und Chancengleichheit. Klinkhard, Bad Heilbrunn (2014)
22. Goeke, S., Kubanski, D.: Menschen mit Behinderungen als GrenzgängerInnen im akademischen Raum. Forum Qual. Soc. Res. 13(1), 6 (2012). http://nbn-resolving.de/urn:nbn:de:0114-fqs120162. Accessed 06 Dec 2013
23. Strnadová, I., Walmsley, J.: Do co-researchers with intellectual disabilities have a voice? (2017). https://onlinelibrary.wiley.com/doi/abs/10.1111/jar.12378. Accessed 30 Mar 2020
24. Coons, K., Watson, S.: Conducting Research with Individuals Who Have Intellectual Disabilities. J. Dev. Disabil. (2013). http://www.oadd.org/docs/Pages_from_41016_JoDD_19-2_14-24_Coons__Watson.pdf. Accessed 08 Aug 2016

Artificial Intelligence, Accessible and Assistive Technologies

Artificial Intelligence, Accessible and Assistive Technologies

Introduction to the Special Thematic Session

E. A. Draffan[1(✉)] and Peter Heumader[2]

[1] Faculty of Physical Sciences and Engineering, University of Southampton,
Southampton, UK
ead@ecs.soton.ac.uk
[2] Institute Integriert Studieren, Johannes Kepler University, Linz, Austria
peter.heumader@jku.at

Abstract. Artificial intelligence (AI) has been around for at least 70 years, as have digital technologies and yet the hype around AI in recent years has begun to make some wary of its impact on their daily lives. However, in this special thematic session authors will be illustrating how increased speed of data crunching and the use of complex algorithms have boosted the potential for systems to be used in ways that can be helpful in unexpected ways, in particular when thinking about assistive technologies. The black box nature of AI may be alarming; with its apparent lack of transparency, but it has enormous potential to make digital content, services and systems more accessible and helpful for people with disabilities. The following series of papers related to these issues propose new and innovative ways of overcoming concerning issues with positive approaches to reducing barriers for those with disabilities.

Keywords: Artificial intelligence · Disabled · Machine learning · Natural language processing · Accessibility · Assistive technology

1 Introduction

The fact that it is possible for companies and organisations to collect ever-increasing amounts of data related to the digital lives of individuals as well as activities within our built environment has proven to be exciting as well as disturbing. Tailoring experiences both off and online sounds like a positive approach to making everyday life easier. Often this is the case, especially when shopping and ordering regularly required items if the process is considered a boring one. However, there are times when personalisation based on our online interactions crosses platforms and devices and affects our reading choices and understanding of what is available. Targeted advertisements for particular products that may be part of recent website browsing history can alarm those who do not understand the systems involved. The items offered may be unwanted and unhelpful, perhaps even causing distress where there are concerns around diversity, equity, and inclusion [1].

© Springer Nature Switzerland AG 2020
K. Miesenberger et al. (Eds.): ICCHP 2020, LNCS 12376, pp. 53–58, 2020.
https://doi.org/10.1007/978-3-030-58796-3_7

These issues have also been shown to be particularly worrying when it is found that personal customization requirements and individual preferences are overruled or data misrepresents minorities, including those with disabilities [2]. There have been examples of image recognition with biases [3] and chat bots that may not offer the expected help [4]. On the other hand, taking a positive stance, there are times when data can be used with algorithms that offer more accurate navigation around buildings for those who are blind and helpful text summarisation for those with cognitive impairments, when coping with complex information. Natural Language Processing (NLP) and prediction models are being used for language translation and speech recognition [5], not only helping those who speak another language, but also those with complex communication needs and specific learning difficulties such as dyslexia. Automatic video and audio transcripts and captions have improved and can offer accessibility for those who have hearing impairments. Accuracy remains an issue in some fields [6] and with some translations [7], but we can expect that scientists using AI with its machine learning, deep learning and neural networks, plus the right data and algorithms will eventually enable improvements in output.

Some of the challenges and positive aspects of AI in relation to access for those with disabilities are discussed under the following themes; improving access to digital content, recommender systems for enhancing access and navigation systems to aid wayfinding.

2   Improving Access to Digital Content

For many years, individuals have worked to make digital content accessible for those with physical, sensory and cognitive impairments. The process has required not only adaptations to online and uploaded documentation, but also skills in understanding the needs of assistive technology users. Individuals come with a range of skills and linguistic abilities and content that is online varies from that which is read for interest to essential information. There have been several reports offering guidelines for 'Easy Reading' [8] and these include the use of text simplification for those with intellectual disabilities. John Rochford is his paper on the subject has taken six of the most appropriate guidelines for his participants and adapted online text using those rules and neural machine translation as if the original English needed translating into simplified English [9]. This approach has huge potential, as it would allow the same to happen in other languages, although it is accepted that there are machine translation differences when compared to text simplification. Examples given included the fact that not all the words translate into easier words and many do not have a one to one correspondence.

This is also true when looking at symbol label to concept linking, as is mentioned by Ding et al. in their paper on AI and Global AAC Symbol Communication. Symbol labels often have to be 'cleaned' with removal of characters or word combinations to allow for more accurate sematic linking. This is achieved with the use of ConceptNet combined with Natural Language Processing (NLP) to build on the base from which the ISO standard (used by Blissymbolics) and a Concept Coding Framework can be used to increase interoperability between symbol sets [10]. Those with literacy skill difficulties and/or cognitive impairments and AAC users would benefit from the combination of text simplification and text to symbol translations for web content and yet without accessible websites this cannot occur.

There remains therefore the need for web accessibility checkers to help speed the process of ensuring ease of use and access to digital content. The addition of AI in the form of NLP and image recognition, as suggested by Draffan et al. in their paper allows for warnings and visual representations showing aspects of the web pages that cannot be checked automatically via the code. This includes overlaps on text enlargement or accuracy of alternative text for images that fail to represent what is actually in the picture.

Assistive Technology users depend on digital accessibility, but it is clear that barriers can be lowered further by adding additional AI enhanced personalization strategies to increase usability such as text simplification and text to symbol translations, which have both been mentioned in recent Web Content Accessibility Guidelines where the statements or success criteria for web accessibility checks originate[1].

3   Recommender Systems Enhanced by AI

Recommender systems make use of personalized, context-sensitive data or hybrid versions of this idea with the help of machine learning where they compare a person's preferences to another set of similar preferences. In the case of the "Easy to Read Methodology" (E2R), that is designed to provide guidelines for easier to read documents, the comparison is being made between the adaptations made to the text and the content in the guidelines. Mari Carmen Suárez-Figueroa suggests that the use of NLP and machine learning to perform the analysis and transformation of documents in a (semi)-automatic fashion will reduce the need for time consuming manual checks and allow for automated recommendations that will improve documents designed for those with cognitive impairments. This process could well support the work of John Rochford mentioned above and any digital accessibility checks are undertaken.

However, as a recommendation system it could also be used to guide users benefitting from the research carried out by Yu et al. on book recommendations for those with visual impairments. A filter as to whether a book had easy to read content. But, Yu et al. found that as users could not scan web pages when searching online libraries, they had to depend on listening to content read aloud in a linear fashion, which did not help as a filtering system for books of no interest. This meant their preferences were often missed and recommender or prediction models failed. Once again, the research plan included a context-aware recommendation algorithm. In this case, the strategy was based on fusion preferences (combining data from the user's behavior with content data) and user attention. Predictions were based on user's interests and the content of available books that matched these preferences, in order to reduce the number of random books found. The results of the research were successful in speeding up the finding of books of interest and once again showed how the use of AI can enhance outcomes.

---

[1]   https://www.w3.org/TR/WCAG21/.

The same principles also work in a learning situation where user behaviors are gathered. A user plays a game and when mistakes are made they may not move to the next level, but are asked to practice the tasks again. Then when they are successful they jump to another level and gain points and are motivated to continue playing. Karaton: An Example of AI integration within a Literacy app for Education has been designed with these ideas in mind using a decision tree based on expert knowledge around reading development. The Karaton mini-games aim to encourage children with poor literacy skills to keep challenging themselves. In the past teachers have adapted the games to suit individual skills. Their changes have been based on the data already collected. Now plans have been made to incorporate AI prediction models that will offer recommendations as to which mini-game to play next and feedback the results to the knowledge base. This will not only allow teachers to monitor progress but also enable machine learning to take place, continually improving the app's ability to provide accurate steps and motivational comments. Meaningful feedback is paramount with any recommendation system, as inaccurate or poorly defined results usually suggest inadequate validation, the user leaves a website if their search has been unsuccessful or gives up on a game.

4   Navigation Systems to Aid Wayfinding

Having discussed the use of AI for improving digital content and how recommendation systems can provide helpful feedback to users, the two final papers present the practical aspects of finding ones way around indoor premises with audio feedback in a 3D environment. Wayfinding outside for those who are blind or have visual impairments has been supported by the use of Global Positioning Systems (GPS) and smart phones with speech synthesis. However, these systems do not help in enclosed spaces and two alternative systems have been presented.

Haoye Chen proposes the use of an indoor semantic visual positioning system with the use of 3D reconstruction and semantic segmentation of RGB-D images captured from a pair of wearable smart glasses. The Red, Green, and Blue (RGB) bands of light caught by the camera with simultaneous depth (D) sensing provides machine learning-based 3D information with audio for those who cannot see. The user has more real time information about objects in the vicinity, with sound prompts to ensure avoidance tactics are possible. This can be reassuring when navigating in an unknown space, although these cameras may not work with all materials or in certain lighting conditions. Nevertheless, this system requires no previous fixtures or fittings such as location based Radio-Frequency Identification (RFID) tags or Bluetooth-based beacons that connect to smartphones.

Vinod Namboodiri points out that the planning for the placement of a GuideBeacon system is important, in order to ensure smooth navigation around an area, when a user locks onto the system. IBeaconMap provides an automated indoor space representation for Beacon-Based Wayfinding, through the use of floor plans and avoids expensive mapping of the areas used in the building. The provision of any real-time location specific information for those who are blind or anyone who is confused by the complex layout of a large indoor space is invaluable and the options available with the use of AI have enhanced access to the built environment in recent years.

5   Discussion and Conclusion

There have been enormous changes in the way developers have adapted their assistive and access technologies to encompass the use of AI. Although there remain concerns about the way data has been used, often with a bias that clearly has an impact on those with disabilities, the papers discussed in this special thematic session highlight the potentially constructive areas for its use. From AAC to web content and literacy skill support to wayfinding the research has shown that it is possible to innovate in ways that increase access to both digital and built environments. There may still be challenges in the way we evaluate the outcomes from AI systems and yet more prospects for future work. There may even be the concern that technology driven systems still do not have real conceptual understanding when issues arise about the barriers that remain. However, we have to keep removing those barriers with support from AI, accessible and assistive technologies.

References

1. Katyal, S.K.: Artificial intelligence, advertising, and disinformation. Adv. Soc. Q. **20**(4) (2019)
2. EDF report "Plug and Pray? A disability perspective on artificial intelligence, automated decision-making and emerging technologies" (2018). http://www.edf-feph.org/sites/default/files/edf-emerging-tech-report-accessible.pdf. Accessed 14 June 2020
3. Zimmermann, G., Brenner, P., Janssen, N.: AI bias in gender recognition of face images: study on the impact of the IBM AI fairness 360 toolkit. J. Tech. Disab. **31**(Special Issue: AAATE 2019 Conference - Global Challenges in Assistive Technology: Research, Policy & Practice. The 15th International Conference of the Association for the Advancement of Assistive Technology in Europe (AAATE)), 39 (2019). https://doi.org/10.3233/TAD-190001
4. Zumstein, D. Hundertmark, S.: Chatbots -an interactive technology for personalized communication, transactions and services. IADIS Int. J. WWW/Internet **15**(1) (2017)
5. Otter, D.W., Medina, J.R., Kalita, J.K.: A survey of the usages of deep learning for natural language processing. IEEE Trans. Neural Netw. Learn. Syst. (2020)
6. Liyanagunawardena, T.R.: Automatic transcription software: good enough for accessibility? A case study from built environment education. In: European Distance and E-Learning Network (EDEN) Conference Proceedings, no. 1, pp. 388–396. European Distance and E-Learning Network (2019)
7. Ciobanu, D., Secară, A.: Speech recognition and synthesis technologies in the translation workflow. In: The Routledge Handbook of Translation and Technology (2019)
8. IFLA: Guidelines for easy-to-read materials. International Federation of Library Association and Institutions IFLA Professional reports 120. Revision by Misako Nomura, Gyda Skat Nielsen and Bror Tronbacke (2010)

9. Wang, T., Chen, P., Rochford, J., Qiang, J.: Text simplification using neural machine translation: association for the advancement of artificial intelligence (AAAI). In: Thirtieth AAAI Conference on Artificial Intelligence, Phoenix, Arizona, USA (2016)
10. https://www.aaai.org/ocs/index.php/AAAI/AAAI16/paper/view/11944/12251. Accessed 14 June 2020
11. Lundälv, M., Derbring, S.: AAC vocabulary standardisation and harmonisation. In: Miesenberger, K., Karshmer, A., Penaz, P., Zagler, W. (eds.) ICCHP 2012. LNCS, vol. 7383, pp. 303–310. Springer, Heidelberg (2012). https://doi.org/10.1007/978-3-642-31534-3_46

AI and Global AAC Symbol Communication

Chaohai Ding[✉], E. A. Draffan, and Mike Wald

Web and Internet Science Group, School of Electronics and Computer Science,
University of Southampton, Southampton SO17 1BJ, UK
{c.ding,ead,mw}@ecs.soton.ac.uk

Abstract. Artificial Intelligence (AI) applications are usually built on large trained data models that can recognize and label images, provide speech output from text, process natural language for translation, and be of assistance to many individuals via the internet. For those who are non-verbal or have complex speech and language difficulties, AI has the potential to offer enhanced access to the wider world of communication that can be personalized to suit user needs. Examples include pictographic symbols to augment or provide an alternative to spoken language. However, when using AI models, data related to the use of freely available symbol sets is scarce. Moreover, the manipulation of the data available is difficult with limited annotation, making semantic and syntactic predictions and classification a challenge in multilingual situations. Harmonization between symbol sets has been hard to achieve; this paper aims to illustrate how AI can be used to improve the situation. The goal is to provide an improved automated mapping system between various symbol sets, with the potential to enhance access to more culturally sensitive multilingual symbols. Ultimately, it is hoped that the results can be used for better context sensitive symbol to text or text to symbol translations for speech generating devices and web content.

Keywords: Alternative and augmentative communication · Web accessibility · Complex communication needs · AI and inclusion

1 Introduction

According to the American Speech-Language-Hearing Association (ASHA), over 2 million people use alternative and augmentative methods of communication (AAC) in their daily lives. Generally, this is due to severe speech, language, reading and learning difficulties [6]. Depending on the type of difficulties encountered, different styled characters, images or pictographic symbols can be used to support other gestures or vocalizations. However, alternative forms of communication come with a learning curve that may be more challenging when compared to spoken language and literacy skills and yet they can leave the user without the range and variety of options for expression. Just choosing pictures often means users are restricted to simple forms of language and when they want to build

© Springer Nature Switzerland AG 2020
K. Miesenberger et al. (Eds.): ICCHP 2020, LNCS 12376, pp. 59–66, 2020.
https://doi.org/10.1007/978-3-030-58796-3_8

phrases and sentences, the availability of pictographic representations may also lack linguistic complexity and cultural sensitivity. AAC users also face a wide variety of barriers to accessing current web content when they are using symbols as their primary means of communication for both consuming and producing information. One of the main challenges is a lack of standardized interoperability between different symbol sets, or a mechanism for translating the concept represented in one symbol set from another symbol set without a high degree of misrepresentation. This paper will discuss ideas about how to leverage Artificial Intelligence (AI) techniques to enhance the interoperability of AAC symbols across different symbol sets and improve the access to a global and inclusive symbol repository with more culturally sensitive multilingual symbols for AAC users.

2   AAC and AI

Symbols are widely used in AAC systems to represent objects, actions, concepts, and emotions, which can include drawings, photographs, objects, facial expressions, gestures, auditory symbols, or orthography[1]. There are three different types of symbols communications following three language presentation methods that are commonly used in AAC:

- Alphabet system methods use traditional orthographies and rate enhancement techniques such as word or phrase prediction.
- Single meaning methods use each pictographic symbol to represent one word or one meaning.
- Multiple meaning methods combine pictographic symbols in various semantic sequences to form words or phrases based on the concept of multiple-meaning iconic encoding.

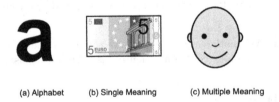

(a) Alphabet   (b) Single Meaning   (c) Multiple Meaning

Fig. 1. Three different kinds of symbols: (a) Alphabet: a; (b) Single Meaning: 5 euro banknote; (c) Multiple Meaning: smile, happy, glad or happy to do something

Multiple meaning methods sometimes known as 'semantic compaction', may be used to present more flexible and meaningful sentences for complex communication needs. The freely available ARASAAC pictographic symbol set[2] has examples (see Fig. 1) that illustrate the three language presentation methods.

---

[1] https://www.asha.org/PRPSpecificTopic.aspx?folderid=8589942773&section=Key-Issues#AAC_Populations.

[2] http://www.arasaac.org/.

2.1   Related Works

AI-based techniques have the potential to improve digital accessibility and the capability to accelerate progress in serving individuals with complex communication needs. Computerized text-based AAC devices often include some form of word prediction or sentence generation using a language model [3,9]. D. Jeffery Higginbotham et al. [4] explored the development of AI and Natural Language Processing (NLP) techniques for AAC, particularly in the areas of interface design and word prediction. They also discussed the future direction of how AI and NLP-enabled AAC systems could benefit AAC users such as context and genre based word prediction. S. Dudy et al. also proposed a method to generate language models for corpus-less symbol sets, which could generate synthesizing training data for machine learning [2]. S.C. Sennott et al. [7] discussed the implications, promises, and precautions of each component of the various AI techniques and what they could bring to AAC, namely knowledge representation, reasoning, natural language processing, machine learning, computer vision, and robotics. Annalu Waller [10] has shared insights and stories of how the combination of user-centered design, interdisciplinary research and the application of intelligent computing could provide a vision for future generations of AAC technologies. All of these works have encouraged further research into the advantages of AI techniques to create more intelligent and personalized AAC applications.

2.2   Challenges and Limitations

Current AAC systems offer a range of symbols that are often found on a grid layout with several categories considered representative of a person's spoken vocabulary and understanding. The choices may be based on the user's age, cognitive and language abilities, environment, cultural needs and context. The way they are accessed, their layout and editing features vary depending on the particular AAC system, but they invariably need to be sensitive to change. This potential to be customized and modified throughout the lifetime of an AAC system's use is essential [1]. There have been several attempts to support online social interactions with the harmonization of AAC symbol sets, so that users can communicate with other symbol users, each using their chosen symbol sets with text translations in various languages. In an effort to advance the situation, a Concept Coding Framework (CCF) was developed by Lundalv and Derbring [5] offering the mapping of different symbol sets. However, there were some limitations to the resulting output. The lack of freely available symbol sets made it difficult to provide personalized AAC at the time and even today it is felt that additional metadata is required to increase accuracy levels. Expense in terms of time is also a factor when designing personalized AAC symbol systems, so there is a need to develop methods that allow for the individualization of AAC symbol systems that are low cost and adaptable. The lack of interoperability between different symbol sets taking account of the range of cultures and languages around the world is also a real barrier for AAC users when text to symbol or symbol to text translation is required, not forgetting the need for text simplification and syntax changes.

3 Global Symbols

Global Symbols[3] is a project that has been developed to create and link freely available AAC symbol sets with different linguistically and culturally localised symbols to provide worldwide access to appropriate pictographic based communication. There are five primary symbol sets that have already been linked all with open or Creative Commons licenses namely:

- ARASAAC offers more than 10,000 pictographic symbols for individuals who may have autism, intellectual disabilities, language impairment or other spoken language difficulties.
- Blissymbolics[4] as a semantic graphical language made up of ideographic and pictographic symbols that can be combined to represent different meanings.
- Tawasol Symbols[5] with 700 Arabic localised symbols that can be used alongside the ARASAAC symbols.
- Mulberry Symbols[6] with scalable SVG graphic images designed for adults.
- Jellow Symbols[7] which has more than 1,000 symbols in English, Marathi and Hindi.

In order to link the symbol sets, ConceptNet [8] was used with additional metadata to provide descriptions and parts of speech. ConceptNet is a collection of interlinked descriptions of entities, objects or abstract concepts making up a 'knowledge graph' version of the Open Mind Common Sense project. ConceptNet, has been applied as the common knowledge base that semantically links to the symbol labels.

3.1 Key Results and Limitations

Initially, Global Symbols automatically linked the five aforementioned AAC symbol sets, providing a repository that can be searched or filtered using the available languages or a chosen symbol set. At present, the results of the mapping are approximately 77% successful, but many of the parts of speech have been skipped or are inaccurate. There are issues around multiple representations of symbols that fail to resolve concerns regarding different meanings for the same symbols, where tense is involved or some labels or glosses producing very different symbol concepts, even antonyms, which can be seen when filtering takes place. At present, symbol searching are totally dependent on the accuracy of the labels with limited metadata. Many of the inappropriate search results are due to the different label methodologies used by symbol sets; time has to be spent on cleaning data. It is felt that by using concept linking with improved Natural Language Processing (NLP) techniques, plus data tagging and image recognition

---

[3] https://globalsymbols.com/.
[4] http://www.blissymbolics.org/index.php/about-blissymbolics.
[5] http://madaportal.org/tawasol/en/home/.
[6] https://mulberrysymbols.org/.
[7] http://www.jellow.org/.

it would be possible to speed search processes, as well as provide more meaningful results across the symbol sets. This in turn, would provide those supporting AAC users with better access to a wider range of more appropriate symbols, as well as more accurate classification features.

4   Global Symbols 2.0

The next version of Global Symbols (GS2) aims to have a more inclusive and concept searchable series of AAC symbol sets compared with the first version. The proposal is to have advanced search and filtering approaches using AI techniques alongside the previous methods using ConceptNet. The present mapping strategies will not be discarded, but enhanced with the use of semantic embedding to find related symbols, using the pre-trained word-embedding model (ConceptNet Numberbatch [8]). In the future, this process will be combined with additional metadata and image recognition techniques to offer improved automatic clustering of AAC symbols.

4.1   Methodologies and Experiment

In both the first version of Global Symbols (GS1) and the second, label mapping has been the initial step to link symbols to concepts. In GS2 the proposed process integrates different strategies to improve the mapping of symbol labels to correct concepts in ConceptNet, which includes a label text preparation strategy, label-to-concept mapping strategy, and the Out-of-Vocabulary (OOV) strategy. It is a common issue that label text for individual symbols can contain various special characters, which affect the concept mapping process. Therefore, the proposed 'label text preparation' strategy will remove these characters and extract the text part to clean the label text.

The proposed OOV strategies for label-to-concept mapping process include: 1. find relevant concept entity matching the label text; 2. if no match and containing single word, delete last letter from the word with maximum twice; 3. if no match and containing multiple words, separate the words and go to step 1. After mapping the labels to the concept entities, word embedding model Numberbatch [8] is applied to find similar concept entities. Numberbatch provides a semantic embedding model that adjusts the values of existing word embeddings (GloVe, word2vec, OpenSubtitles 2016) by taking the ConceptNet knowledge graph into account. It also supports 78 languages, which will be helpful in the multilingual environment of the repository.

For this part of the experiment, 12,847 ARASAAC symbols were used, the special characters in the labels were removed using the strategies described above. Based on observation, some symbol labels could be divided into multiple concepts and OOV strategies were used to map symbol labels to concept entities that had been developed to solve this problem:

– Single Word Matching: (a) delete the last letter if OOV (b) if non-matched with maximum two letters deleted, then indicate non-matched.

– Multiple Words Matching: (a) delete the last letter if OOV (b) if non-matched with maximum two letters deleted, then divide the multiple words into multiple single-word; (c) process single word matching strategy

4.2   Results and Evaluation

There were 362,891 concept entities for the label-to-concept mapping process in the pre-trained word embedding model, 150,875 being in English. Although, 12,847 ARASAAC symbols were used in the current experiment, 13,173 text labels were generated based on the proposed label cleaning strategies. Of these, 3,520 symbol labels were not matched with any concept entity. An evaluation study was conducted using a sample result from the mapping of the symbols in both GS1 and GS2 based on 100 high frequency core words used for AAC[8]. The results were gathered via an online voting procedure sent out to 5 AAC experts and users with 1,172 symbols generated using the GS2 methodology and 784 symbols generated from the original system. GS1 resulted in a 45.4% exact match of symbol to core word, while, in new version of GS2, 48.03% matched the exact meaning. The pilot showed the symbols and the target core word with no labels, that made the exercise harder for the voters. In the second experiment using the 500 Core Words[9] it was possible to see not only the label matches achieved for both versions of GS, but also the next best match of any other semantically linked labels in GS2. The results showed that 47.24% of the labels matched in GS1 whereas 57.86% matched in GS2 and when the top most similar labels (scoring above 70%, but not antonyms) were considered the score rose to 85.47% for GS2 compared to 69.8% for GS1. Table 1 presents the example of top 10 similar symbols related to a search for **automobiles**. The similarity score for each symbol has been generated based on the ranking of semantic relatedness, which is calculated from the concept embedding model.

Finally, another experiment used the K-mean clustering method for automatic symbol categorization. Different K values were applied to explore how different symbols with similar semantic relatedness could be grouped together. The preliminary result (K = 100) showed a 85% accuracy compared with other K values from 50 to 100. Therefore, although label-based clustering can be used to categorize symbols into different groups, some symbols with the same label still produced questionable results. For example, when searching for a 'car' where the label or gloss is used, the result using the ARASAAC symbol set produced the symbol of a 'horse and cart' as well as several different types of car. This highlights the need for additional AI based approaches, in order to discriminate the items represented in these symbols. There were also several instances where the opposite of a word would appear in the similarity list for example 'she' for 'he' or 'her' for 'him', which could be removed using additional metadata from ConceptNet and WordNet.

---

[8] https://aaclanguagelab.com/resources/100-high-frequency-core-word-list.
[9] https://studylib.net/doc/6811573/core-word-comparison-for-language-building.

Table 1. Top 10 similar symbols related to automobiles in GS2

Score	Label	Concept	Symbol	Score	Label	Concept	Symbol
1.00	automobiles_1	'/c/en/automobiles'		0.74	vehicles_3	'/c/en/vehicles'	
1.00	automobiles_2	'/c/en/automobiles'		0.74	vehicles	'/c/en/vehicles'	
0.81	cars	'/c/en/cars'		0.74	vehicles_3	'/c/en/vehicles'	
0.81	cars_1	'/c/en/cars'		0.74	vehicles_2	'/c/en/vehicles'	
0.81	cars_2	'/c/en/cars'		0.74	vehicles_1	'/c/en/vehicles'	

5   Conclusion

Most speakers will have access to spoken and written language that fits their cultural, social and linguistic environment. This is rarely a reality for AAC symbol users and yet the use of machine learning using large amounts of data with NLP has allowed companies such as Google to provide automatic translations for over 104 languages despite their often complex linguistic and orthographic differences. These processes have provided text to speech, speech to text and captions to support understanding between communities. A multilingual standardized global symbols model could offer improved interoperability between symbols from different sets and has the potential to enhance communication and literacy skills for those with complex communication needs.

However, without the support of harmonisation across all AAC symbol sets there will always be a challenge for AAC users who wish to use their personalized language system when they collaborate and communicate with other symbol users online. The work of the W3C 'Personalization Semantic Explainer'[10] and Easy Reading EU project[11] teams have explored these technologies in order to support text to symbol representations of web-based content. So it is clear this is an important area of work, but the results of this recent use of AI models only produced a limited increase in successful symbol to concept matching. It was still not sufficiently accurate be considered a successful way of offering symbol set harmonisation. Therefore, the next step in this research will focus on how to combine semantic relatedness with an increase in linked metadata and image recognition to improve symbol mapping outcomes.

---

[10] https://www.w3.org/TR/personalization-semantics-1.0/.

[11] https://www.easyreading.eu/.

References

1. Beukelman, D.R., Mirenda, P.: Augmentative & Alternative Communication: Supporting Children and Adults with Complex Communication Needs. Paul H. Brookes Publishing, Baltimore (2013)
2. Dudy, S., Bedrick, S.: Compositional language modeling for icon-based augmentative and alternative communication. In: Proceedings of the Workshop on Deep Learning Approaches for Low-Resource NLP, pp. 25–32 (2018)
3. Garay-Vitoria, N., Abascal, J.: Text prediction systems: a survey. Univ. Access Inf. Soc. **4**(3), 188–203 (2006)
4. Higginbotham, D.J., Lesher, G.W., Moulton, B.J., Roark, B.: The application of natural language processing to augmentative and alternative communication. Assistive Technol. **24**(1), 14–24 (2012)
5. Lundälv, M., Derbring, S.: AAC vocabulary standardisation and harmonisation. In: Miesenberger, K., Karshmer, A., Penaz, P., Zagler, W. (eds.) ICCHP 2012. LNCS, vol. 7383, pp. 303–310. Springer, Heidelberg (2012). https://doi.org/10.1007/978-3-642-31534-3_46
6. Odom, S.L., Horner, R.H., Snell, M.E.: Handbook of Developmental Disabilities. Guilford press, New York (2009)
7. Sennott, S.C., Akagi, L., Lee, M., Rhodes, A.: AAC and artificial intelligence (AI). Top. Lang. Disord. **39**(4), 389–403 (2019)
8. Speer, R., Chin, J., Havasi, C.: Conceptnet 5.5: an open multilingual graph of general knowledge. In: Thirty-First AAAI Conference on Artificial Intelligence (2017)
9. Vertanen, K., Kristensson, P.O.: The imagination of crowds: conversational AAC language modeling using crowdsourcing and large data sources. In: Proceedings of the Conference on Empirical Methods in Natural Language Processing, pp. 700–711. Association for Computational Linguistics (2011)
10. Waller, A.: Telling tales: unlocking the potential of AAC technologies. Int. J. Lang. Commun. Disord. **54**(2), 159–169 (2019)

Can a Web Accessibility Checker Be Enhanced by the Use of AI?

E. A. Draffan$^{(\boxtimes)}$ ⓘ, Chaohai Ding, Mike Wald, Harry Everett,
Jason Barrett, Abhirami Sasikant, Calin Geangu,
and Russell Newman

WAIS, ECS, University of Southampton, Southampton, UK
{ead, cd8e10, mw}@ecs.soton.ac.uk

Abstract. There has been a proliferation of automatic web accessibility checkers over the years designed to make it easier to assess the barriers faced by those with disabilities when using online interfaces and content. The checkers are often based on tests that can be made on the underlying website code to see whether it complies with the W3C Web Content Accessibility Guidelines (WCAG). However, as the type of code needed for the development of sophisticated interactive web services and online applications becomes more complex, so the guidelines have had to be updated with the adoption of new success criteria or additional revisions to older criteria. In some instances, this has led to questions being raised about the reliability of the automatic accessibility checks and whether the use of Artificial Intelligence (AI) could be helpful. This paper explores the need to find new ways of addressing the requirements embodied in the WCAG success criteria, so that those reviewing websites can feel reassured that their advice (regarding some of the ways to reduce barriers to access) is helpful and overcomes issues around false positive or negatives. The methods used include image recognition and natural language processing working alongside a visual appraisal system, built into a web accessibility checker and reviewing process that takes a functional approach.

Keywords: Digital accessibility · Disability · Automatic checkers · Artificial intelligence

1 Introduction

Over the past twelve years, a Web2Access[1] system of 15 accessibility checks has been used as a functional review system for the accessibility of websites used for elearning by students, teachers and other academics. Anyone could access the reviews or add an evaluation that went some way to ensuring the online services listed highlighted possible barriers for people with disabilities. The checks were originally based on the W3C Web Content Accessibility Guidelines (WCAG) version 2.0 [1] and took the user on a journey through a website. They started at the login stage catching the issues that might arise with reCAPTCHAs and unlabelled forms. The reviewer then went on to test

---

[1] https://web2access.org.uk/.

© Springer Nature Switzerland AG 2020
K. Miesenberger et al. (Eds.): ICCHP 2020, LNCS 12376, pp. 67–73, 2020.
https://doi.org/10.1007/978-3-030-58796-3_9

for a lack of alternative text for images, style sheets that changed the navigation and then to the type of page that might require checks involving the use of keyboard only access, magnification and colour contrast levels. Other important interactive elements included in the review list were videos and audio accessibility, appropriate feedback from forms and access to tables, page integrity and text styles etc. to encompass the concept of readability. A recent experimental study of a Thai translation of Web2access showed that it could be used reliably by novice developers to predict the accessibility of websites where barriers existed for those with disabilities [2].

Updates to WCAG 2.1 with the addition of seventeen new success criteria [3] meant that the Web2Access review system had become outdated and it was time to follow others looking into the potential of AI as a method to support checks [4]. The original Web2Access tests required additional elements and the method for the reviews with a mix of automatic and manual checks needed to be overhauled. It was necessary to abide by the UK Government's guidance stating that web accessibility compliance must include the specific requirements mentioned in the WCAG 2.1 Success Criteria (SC) that are 'testable statements' at levels A and AA. This meant that the update to Web2Access needed to include five additional success criteria at Level A and seven at Level AA. Furthermore, in order to allow the reviewers the chance to evaluate more than one web page at a time the Web Accessibility Conformance Evaluation Methodology (WCAG-EM)[2] was included in the update. This enabled the team to produce an automated accessibility statement that could be added to a website as stipulated in the recent Public Sector Bodies (Websites and Mobile Applications) (No.2) Accessibility Regulations 2018 [5].

2   Method

Much of the original database design of Web2Access remained in place with individual tests having additional text added to incorporate the extra information required for the updated success criteria. Some of the tests were merged to allow for the new ones from WCAG 2.1. Particular attention was paid to the additional success criteria that included Orientation (SC1.3.4), Non-text Contrast (SC1.4.11), Text Spacing (SC1.4.12) and Label in Name (SC2.5.3) that is important when form filling as these were the tests that it was felt could be automated.

The web accessibility checker developed to assist with the reviews required a new build using an accessible React, a JavaScript interface[3] with additional ARIA attributes. The accordion design involved the participation of five accessibility experts at every stage. Each expert had over ten years' experience in the field, all used assistive technologies in their day-to-day work and were regularly evaluating the accessibility of digital content. As per user-centred design principles [6], their involvement was ongoing throughout the project, even when testing the outcomes of the checker and commenting on general concerns about the reliability of automated accessibility testing tools [7].

---

[2] https://www.w3.org/WAI/test-evaluate/conformance/wcag-em/.

[3] https://reactjs.org/.

Behind the interface that presented the results of multiple tests, the team implemented the use of the open source Pally[4] accessibility checker with the additional WCAG 2.1 checks. An innovative series of visual appraisal pages were integrated within the drop down results to allow the reviewer to see where issues might arise when the automated checking could have produced false positives or negatives. A false positive was considered an accessibility check that returned a mistake that did not actually exist or did not affect the use of the page and a false negative was one where there might have been an issue, but the automatic checker had not captured it. Algorithms were developed to offer the reviewer the chance to check the results of two particular issues that were arising. Where the success criteria required, for instance no overlaps when using text spacing, a visual representation was designed to outline areas where there were suspected issues. In terms of false negative concerns, the issue was mainly about the alternative text description being accepted, but by adding additional checks there appeared to be a mismatch between the content in the 'alt tag' and the actual image. Once again, a visual representation of the image was supplied, alongside the alternative description. The reviewer could then accept or reject the results of the automated tests. All the tests once completed remain available via the Web2Access database if public mode is chosen, or private to the registered reviewer carrying out the checks.

AI models were used when it came to evaluating the accuracy of the alternative text offered for images. Pre-trained neural networks model based on the MobileNet23 image classifier and the COCO-SSD24 model for object detection and classification provided a comparison between the actual image used and the alternative text provided. As mentioned, the output could be seen on the appropriate visual appraisal page, providing the reviewer with the opportunity to make a final decision should there be any doubt resulting from the automatic check.

As an addition to the completed work there remains the intention to use the work of Sen (2019) [8] and to explore further the issue related to hypertext links that fail to comply with the WCAG 2.1 Success Criterion 2.4.4 Link Purpose (In Context). This is possible by capturing groups of words, such as three words before and after the hyperlink from the source and then comparing this with a similar amount of words at start of the target page using word-embedding techniques. "A two-layer neural net that processes text by "vectorizing" words"[5] called word2vec [9] was chosen as this works with word association and Word Movers Distance (WMD) [10]. Sen hypothesised that if the WMD scores were low this should show that the target text and the link text would be helpful to users.

---

[4] https://pally.org/.

[5] https://pathmind.com/wiki/word2vec.

3 Results

The team never intended to evaluate the success or otherwise of the Pa11y automatic checker but to see whether it was feasible to use AI for some of the new WCAG 2.1 success criteria and would a visual appraisal system reduce the questions that might arise from possible false positives or negatives with some checks. A series of website reviews were performed on a sample taken from the top 500 sites, according to alexa.com[6]. No false positives or negatives were discovered when double checks were made for the checks of the top five sites; where five pages were selected from Google, YouTube, Tmall, Facebook or Qq. All the issues appeared to be relevant when manually checked, even those on the two Chinese sites (Tmall and Qq). Where results were negative, the code producing the fault appeared in the collapsible content under the various sections for each success criteria on the results page, once the checker had gone through all the pages selected (Fig. 1).

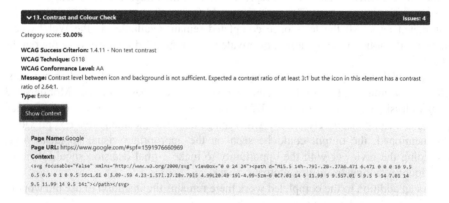

Fig. 1. Google home page issue with WCAG SC 1,4,11 - Non-text contrast

It was also possible to see the additional results for those success criteria using the visual appraisal system, where issues could be checked for accuracy, such as the accuracy of an alt attribute (tag) providing the alternative text description (Fig. 2).

Fig. 2. qq.com website where a Chinese logo was captured and checked for its alternative text (Beijing Xicheng District Mayor: Newly diagnosed cases have not been to Jilin yesterday.)

---

[6] https://www.alexa.com/topsites.

Concerning the contextual hyperlink detection task, a word2vec model was generated based on the contextual hyperlink and the description of target page, compared against other pre-trained word embedding models. The results for the model created on the generated dataset looked promising, but further work was needed to develop a specialised dataset, with the use of Natural Language Processing to improve matches. This result meant that the test could not be included in the final accessibility checker, before the evaluation of the project was completed, due to time constraints. The team agreed that without robust results, this test would also be a concern when outputting content to the accessibility statement (Fig. 3).

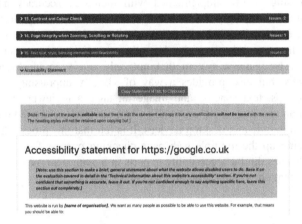

Fig. 3. Output to the accessibility statement that can be copied to a reviewer's website.

The five digital accessibility experts tested the application at various times during the design and implementation phases. As the project had to be completed in a few months from design phase to completion, the number of people able to finally evaluate the accessibility checker for usability purposes was low. However, Nielsen stated in 2000; "The best results come from testing [with] no more than 5 users and running as many small tests as you can afford" [11]. Constant feedback via weekly meetings and the use of Slack[7] for messaging, as part of an iterative process, resulted in several changes over the course of the project. All the experts were able to use the system and commented on the helpfulness of the visual appraisal pages as a way of confirming results from the automatic checker. It was noted how useful it was to have automatically captured images from the web pages showing where issues were arising. These can be helpful for the web developer as well as being able to feed issues into the automatically produced accessibility statement.

---

[7] https://slack.com/intl/en-gb/.

4   Conclusion

There were some limitations to this research in terms of time constraints, failure to access password protected sites in a secure manner and issues around model windows and contrast levels. Nevertheless, there are WCAG 2.1 Success Criteria that can respond to the use of AI despite the fact that there has been little use of machine learning techniques as a way of supporting web accessibility checks in the last few years. Abou-Zahra et al. commented that the "significant drawback of artificial intelligence for web accessibility at this time is a lack of accuracy and reliability" [3]. Ultimately, it is hoped that further use of machine learning, neural networks and natural language processing can be implemented with increased accuracy and reliability, especially when there are larger data sets available from accessibility checks. However, these need to be open and available in order to build useful corpora. At present models are dependent on external data sets that have the potential to skew results.

Nevertheless, by using a system that not only offers an increased number of automated checks, but also provides a way of visually appraising issues, such as orientation, overlaps, text spacing and image alt tags, a reviewer can be relatively reassured about an accurate result, especially when the tests are carried out on multiple browsers on both mobile and desktop devices. It is felt that this process has provided a means of speeding up the multiple web page checking process for any large organisation. It also enables digital accessibility experts in a team who may not be coders, to highlight issues that are arising with an increased evidence base.

References

1. W3C Web Content Accessibility Guidelines (WCAG). https://www.w3.org/WAI/standards-guidelines/wcag/. Accessed 15 Apr 2020
2. Wald, M., Angkananon, K.: Development and testing of a Thai website accessibility evaluation tool. Int. J. Electron. Commun. Eng. **10**(5) (2020)
3. W3C WCAG 2.1 What's new in WCAG 2.1. https://www.w3.org/WAI/standards-guidelines/wcag/new-in-21/. Accessed 15 Apr 2020
4. Abou-Zahra, S., Brewer, J., Cooper, M.: Artificial Intelligence (AI) for web accessibility: is conformance evaluation a way forward? In: Proceedings of the Internet of Accessible Things, pp. 1–4 (2018)
5. UK Government Legislation Public Sector Bodies (Websites and Mobile Applications) (No.2) Accessibility Regulations (2018). http://www.legislation.gov.uk/uksi/2018/852/contents/made. Accessed 15 Apr 2020
6. Norman, D.A., Draper, S.W.: User Centered System Design; New Perspectives on Human-Computer Interaction. L. Erlbaum Associates Inc., USA (1986)
7. Duran, M.: What we found when we tested tools on the world's least-accessible webpage (2017). https://accessibility.blog.gov.uk/2017/02/24/what-we-found-when-we-tested-tools-on-the-worlds-least-accessible-webpage/. Accessed 12 June 2020
8. Sen, S.: Artificial Intelligence and Web Accessibility (Unpublished Master's thesis) (2019). https://shaunaksen.github.io/AI-for-Web-Accessibility/. Accessed 15 Apr 2020

9. Mikolov, T., Chen, K., Corrado, G., Dean, J.: Efficient estimation of word representations in vector space. arXiv preprint arXiv:1301.3781 (2013)
10. Kusner, M., Sun, Y., Kolkin, N., Weinberger, K.: From word embeddings to document distances. In: International Conference on Machine Learning, pp. 957–966, June 2015
11. Nielsen, J.: Why you only need to test with 5 users (2000). https://www.nngroup.com/articles/why-you-only-need-to-test-with-5-users/. Accessed 15 Apr 2020

Towards the Assessment of Easy-to-Read Guidelines Using Artificial Intelligence Techniques

Mari Carmen Suárez-Figueroa[1]([⊠]) [ID], Edna Ruckhaus[1],
Jorge López-Guerrero[2], Isabel Cano[3], and Álvaro Cervera[3]

[1] Ontology Engineering Group (OEG), Universidad Politécnica de Madrid
(UPM), Madrid, Spain
{mcsuarez, eruckhaus}@fi.upm.es
[2] Universidad Politécnica de Madrid (UPM), Madrid, Spain
jorge.liglesias@alumnos.upm.es
[3] ACCEDES, Madrid, Spain
{icano, acervera}@accedes.es

Abstract. The Easy-to-Read (E2R) Methodology was created to improve the daily life of people with cognitive disabilities, who have difficulties in reading comprehension. The main goal of the E2R Methodology is to present clear and easily understood documents. This methodology includes a set of guidelines and recommendations that affect the writing of texts, the supporting images, the design and layout of documents, and the final editing format. Such guidelines are used in the manual processes of (a) adapting existing documents and (b) producing new materials. The process of adapting existing documents is cyclic and implies three activities: analysis, transformation, and validation. All these activities are human resource consuming, due to the need of involving people with cognitive disabilities as well as E2R experts. In order to alleviate such processes, we are currently investigating the development of methods, based on Artificial Intelligence (AI) techniques, to perform the analysis and transformation of documents in a (semi)-automatic fashion. In this paper we present our AI-based method for assessing a particular document with respect to the E2R guidelines as well as an initial implementation of such a method; our research on the transformation of documents is out of the scope of this paper. We carried out a comparative evaluation of the results obtained by our initial implementation against the results of the document analysis performed by people with cognitive disabilities.

Keywords: E2R methodology · Cognitive accessibility · Artificial intelligence

1 Introduction

People with cognitive disabilities have some problems related to reading comprehension, communication, and ability to respond to routine situations as well as to challenging scenarios. These obstacles become a daily barrier in the understanding, interaction, and use of products and services in different environments. To overcome

© Springer Nature Switzerland AG 2020
K. Miesenberger et al. (Eds.): ICCHP 2020, LNCS 12376, pp. 74–82, 2020.
https://doi.org/10.1007/978-3-030-58796-3_10

the aforementioned barriers and to improve the daily life of people with cognitive disabilities, a methodology called Easy-to-Read (E2R) [1, 2] was created. This methodology aims to present clear and easy to understand contents to different sectors of the population that include people with disabilities and people with limited language or reading proficiency, among others. The E2R Methodology provides guidelines for content, language, illustrations, as well as graphic layout in documents. The final aim is to have materials that are compliant with the E2R guidelines and recommendations, such as to use simple and short phrases, to avoid technicalities, abbreviations, acronyms, among others, to have an adequate typography, to include pictures that reinforce the message and clarify the content, and to select an editing format that is easy to use and convenient for the expected use of the material.

When a particular material needs to be adapted to the E2R Methodology, three key activities are performed as part of a cyclic process: (1) analysis of which E2R guidelines are fulfilled in the material, this can be seen as a kind of assessment activity; (2) transformation of the material by E2R experts based on the unsatisfied guidelines discovered during the previous assessment; and (3) validation of the transformed material by a professional team comprised by people with intellectual disabilities, called validators. The activities of analysis, transformation (or adaptation), and validation are complementary activities for achieving good quality and effective final materials in terms of cognitive accessibility. These activities are human resource consuming due to the need of involving people with cognitive disabilities as well as E2R experts.

In order to help in the labour-intensive and costly process of adapting materials to the E2R guidelines, and thus to facilitate the work of those who manually adapt documents, our research is currently focused on applying different AI-based methods and techniques to (semi)-automatically perform both the analysis and the transformation of documents. To the best of our knowledge, there is no significant research in the analysis of how E2R compliant is a document, a crucial point for achieving cognitive accessibility. Nevertheless, there is some work on transforming materials based on E2R guidelines: a text simplification system for Spanish [3] and a method for extending a grammar checker with E2R guidelines for English and German [4].

Specifically, in this paper we present our method for assessing how E2R compliant is a particular document written in Spanish; our research on the transformation of these documents is out of the scope of this paper. The proposed method is based on the use of AI techniques such as rule-based techniques, pattern recognition, and Natural Language Processing (NLP). This paper also presents an initial implementation of the proposed method: an E2R compliance tool called Easy-to-Read Advisor. Our method and the proof of concept are focused on educational presentations written in Spanish.

The rest of the paper is organized as follows: Sect. 2 is devoted to the state of the art on the E2R Methodology. In Sect. 3 we explain our research methodology; while Sect. 4 describes our contributions: a method and an initial implementation for assessing E2R compliance of documents. Section 5 presents the initial evaluation of our proposal. Finally, we show some conclusions and future work on this research.

2 State of the Art

The need of having understandable content and accessible information for people with learning difficulties has received increased attention in the last decade [5]. In this regard, the E2R Methodology is crucial for having more readable and understandable materials. The main goal of having materials that are easy-to-read is to present clear and easy to understand contents that are appropriate for different groups [1]. To achieve these documents, content, language, illustrations, as well as the graphic layout must be taken into consideration. The E2R Methodology provides guidelines, requirements, and recommendations for different aspects of a document [1]: writing of texts, supporting images, design and layout of documents, and the editing format. However, there is no general acceptance on the level of depth in E2R guidelines [6].

To know whether a document is compliant with the E2R Methodology there are two main manual techniques: (a) using checklists, as for example the one[1] created in the PUZZLE project and (b) involving groups of people who discuss the E2R requirements satisfied in a document. However, manual approaches are labour-intensive and costly. In order to decrease both time and resources spent for assessing E2R guidelines, semi-automatic tools, called validators, can be used. One example is the tool presented in [8], which is based on an approach to empirically evaluate E2R guidelines in German documents. Another example is VisRA [9], whose aim is to support the writer in the task of revising a German text with respect to E2R guidelines. To the best of our knowledge, there are no validators for Spanish documents. Nevertheless, research work on transforming Spanish texts using NLP techniques focused on text simplification has been performed [3]. It is worth mentioning that most of the approaches pays attention only to E2R guidelines related to writing aspects (spelling, grammar, vocabulary, and style), while aspects related to the design and layout of a document have not been considered. Our research work focuses on all E2R aspects as well as on both, analysis and transformation of documents.

3 Our Research Methodology

Our general research question is: Is it possible to use AI-based methods and techniques to facilitate the cognitive accessibility to educational materials? This question can be divided into two specific research questions: (1) Can we use AI-based methods and techniques to analyze whether an educational document conforms to the E2R Methodology? and (2) Can we use AI-based methods and techniques to transform an educational document to one compliant to the E2R Methodology? In this paper we present our initial contributions regarding the answer to the first question; therefore, it should be noted that the second question is out of the scope of this document.

Our research methodology includes the following six activities: the first activity was to acquire the knowledge related to the E2R Methodology. We used the catalogue of guidelines as a basis [7]. This catalogue is organized into the following categories:

---

[1] http://www.puzzle-project.eu/docs/EN/IO1/IO1_EtRLearningMaterial_Checklist.pdf.

(a) spelling, grammar, vocabulary, and style in the writing field, (b) images, typography, composition of text, and pagination in the design and layout field, (c) paper, binding, and printing in the production field, and (d) others.

The second activity was to select the collection of E2R guidelines to consider in our research. Since we decided to focus on educational materials in the form of sets of slides, the E2R conformance evaluation of the documents included both the writing field and the design and layout field. This implies a total of 69 E2R guidelines related to spelling aspects such as capital letters, punctuation, and dates or to grammar aspects like verbs, parts of the sentence, and complete sentences, among others. Examples of guidelines are 'to use the dot to divide sentences' and 'to avoid the use of the comma to divide phrases' related to the punctuation aspect; and 'sentences should always include the subject' related to parts of the sentence aspect.

Our third activity was to analyze and decide which AI techniques could be the most appropriate for the creation of a method for assessing the easy-to-read compliance in a document written in Spanish. We decided to use the following techniques:

- Since our goal is to create a diagnosis method, a rule-based approach can be applied. The background knowledge that establishes whether a particular document is compliant with a specific E2R guideline can be represented as problem-solving rules. The term rule in AI is defined as an "IF-THEN" structure that relates a set of given information or facts in the "IF part" to some action in the "THEN part", which means "IF Conditions happens THEN do Actions".
- Conditions in the "If statements" can be represented in a declarative way and can be expressed as patterns. In particular, we decided to create syntactic patterns taking as an inspiration Hearst patterns [10]. This implies that our proposal includes the use of pattern recognition techniques.
- Due to the fact that our method needs to analyze issues such as spelling, grammar, vocabulary, and style in the text included in the document, we consider also the need to use NLP techniques. In particular, techniques to perform parsing, morphological, and syntactic analysis.

The fourth activity was to create the method for assessing whether a particular material is compliant with the E2R Methodology and to implement such a method.

The fifth activity was to select a corpus of slides in Spanish and to create a gold standard. This gold standard consists of slides annotated with the guidelines fulfilled and not fulfilled by people with cognitive disabilities.

The sixth activity was to validate our proposal using a comparative evaluation using the gold standard and the same set of slides analyzed by the proof of concept.

4 Our Proposal for Assessing E2R Guidelines

This section presents our method for analyzing which E2R guidelines are not fulfilled in a document, and our proof of concept called Easy-to-Read Advisor[2].

---

[2] Available in September 2020 at "easy2read.oeg.fi.upm.es".

4.1   E2R Assessment Method

Our method for assessing whether a particular material is compliant with the E2R Methodology is composed of the following activities: (1) gather the document to be analyzed, (2) extract from the document the set of elements related with the writing, and the design and layout fields, (3) parse and analyse morphologically and syntactically the set of elements related with the writing field, (4) recognize patterns in each set of elements, (5) infer knowledge using the collection of rules, and (6) generate the report about the original document.

In more detail, the pattern recognition activity relies on a collection of general syntactic patterns, which aims to identify the relevant elements in a document. This collection has been created using Hearst patterns as inspiration and taking into account that for each of the E2R guidelines, at least one pattern is needed to represent the knowledge. The activity of inferring knowledge related to the original document implies the use of a production system that consists of a collection of rules that formalize the E2R guidelines, and an inference engine that implements the control strategy and applies the rules. The structure of the rules is the following: the "if part" is composed of one or more conditions related via the AND logical connector, while the "then part" is an action to report the compliance or non-compliance of the original document with respect to a particular E2R guideline. An example of a syntactic pattern and a rule associated to an E2R guideline is shown in Fig. 1.

E2R GUIDELINE: G1. To always use a font that is clear and easy to read. The list of suggested fonts are: Arial, Calibri, Candara, Corbel, Gill Sans, Helvética, Myriad, Segoe, Tahoma, Tiresias, and Verdana.
GENERAL SYNTACTIC PATTERN: P1[a]: Text hasTypeOfFont (ToF,)* (or|and) ToF
GENERAL RULE: IF T[b] ⊂ (Arial | Calibri | Candara | Corbel | Gill Sans | Helvética | Myriad | Segoe | Tahoma | Tiresias | Verdana) THEN to report that original document is compliant with G1

Fig. 1. Example of E2R guideline, syntactic pattern and rule ([a]*P1 in E2R Advisor:* *<TextElement style="font-family: (ToF,)* ToF"> Text </TexElement>,* [b]*T: set of font types extracted from the original document via our general syntactic patterns).*

4.2   Proof of Concept: Easy-to-Read Advisor

We have developed an E2R conformance checker, which is based on our E2R assessment method described in Sect. 4.1. This proof of concept is focused on the analysis of educational documents in the form of sets of slides written in Spanish; these slides have been created in HTML[3]. Easy-to-Read Advisor provides as output a report on the guidelines satisfied (marked in green) and the ones not satisfied (marked in red), as shown in Fig. 2.

Easy-to-Read Advisor extracts from each slide the collection of elements, tags and attributes related to the writing and the design and layout fields. Extracted elements, tags and attributes are matched with the catalogue of patterns. This initial prototype implements 22 E2R guidelines as patterns: ten of them are related to the design and layout field and twelve of them are related to the writing field, as shown in Table 1.

---

[3] SlideWiki platform (https://slidewiki.org/) can be used to create slides in HTML.

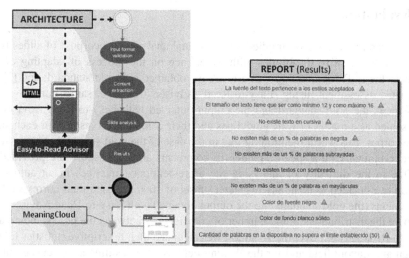

Fig. 2. Easy-to-Read Advisor: Architecture *(Easy-to-Read Advisor uses MeaningCloud* (https://www.meaningcloud.com/es) *to perform the parsing, morphological, and syntactic analysis of the Spanish text in each slide)* and Example of Report *(Report obtained for* "https://slidewiki.org/deck/108653-2/lectura-facil/slide/710658-10/").

Table 1. E2R guidelines implemented in Easy-to-Read Advisor

Design and layout field guidelines	Writing field guidelines
M1. The text font belongs to the accepted styles	T1. The size of the lines is correct
M2. The font size must be large enough	T2. Large numbers are expressed correctly
M3. Text avoids italics	T3. Text avoids the use of special characters
M4. Text includes moderately bold words	T4. Text avoids the use of ordinal characters
M5. Text includes moderately underlined words	T5. Text is made up of short sentences
M6. Text avoids typographic effects	T6. Dates are written in full
M7. Text uses capital letters according to the general rule	T7. The use of pronouns is correct
M8. The contrast between text and background is correct (focused on text color)	T8. Text avoids the use of Roman numbers
M9. The contrast between text and background is correct (focused on background)	T9. Text is written in the second person
M10. The amount of words in the text is correct	T10. Text avoids passive voice
	T11. Sentences have a subject
	T12. Text is made up of simple sentences

5   Evaluation

Our comparative evaluation implied: (1) a manual analysis of a corpus[4] of slides by a person with cognitive disabilities with experience on the process of adapting documents to the E2R Methodology; as a result we obtained our gold standard; and (2) an automatic assessment using Easy-to-Read Advisor over the same corpus. Each assessment, the gold standard and the output obtained with Easy-to-Read Advisor, is represented as a matrix of E2R guidelines and their compliance (yes/no) for each slide in the corpus; it is worth mentioning that in the case of the gold standard, when a slide is not compliant with a specific guideline, comments and suggestions are provided.

Due to the difficulty of analysing the aforementioned matrices in an automatic fashion, we decided to manually inspect a subset of 10 slides[5] and their corresponding assessments (the gold standard and the output obtained with Easy-to-Read Advisor). To compare the distributions of the number of coincidences between the gold standard and Easy-to-Read Advisor over the 10 slides, we calculated their descriptive statistics for the Design and Layout field and for the Writing field. No major differences between those fields arise other than the difference in medians, 7 vs. 8.5, and third quartiles, 7.75 vs. 9; being the results for the Writing field slightly higher than the results for the Design and Layout field. With these figures, we could say that Easy-to-Read Advisor (1) is analyzing the slides in a reasonably precise way, and (2) is identifying better the aspects related to the Writing field. Thus, Easy-to-Read Advisor should improve the way in which some guidelines are analyzed. In order to know which are those guidelines, we also analyzed the non-coincidences by computing: (a) the number of "Yes (gold standard) - No (Easy-to-Read Advisor)", which may indicate that the tool fails because the guideline is satisfied according to the gold standard (false negative) and (b) the number of "No (gold standard) - Yes (Easy-to-Read Advisor)", which could indicate that the tool fails because the guideline is not satisfied according to the gold standard (false positive). This analysis in the Design and Layout field shows that these non-coincidences between the gold standard and the tool represent 31% of the total number of comparisons. From these non-coincidences, 35.5% are "Yes-No" (false negative) and 64.5% are "No-Yes" (false positive). This same analysis in the Writing field shows that the gold standard and the tool disagree 33.4% of the time. All disagreements are due to false positives ("No-Yes"); there is no "Yes-No" disagreements. In addition, we calculated the number of non-coincidences between the gold standard and Easy-to-Read Advisor for each guideline. It can be observed that guidelines with the largest number of non-coincidences are T9 and M9, with 9 and 8 respectively; T1 and T5, with 7; and T11 and T12, with 6. In all these cases, except in the M9 guideline, the non-coincidence was due to a false positive. These figures imply that Easy-to-Read Advisor should be mainly improved with respect to false positive scenarios. In particular, we should focus our efforts on guidelines related to writing aspects such as using second person in texts and using a correct and simple grammatical structure ("Subject + Verb + Predicate.").

---

[4] This corpus is currently composed of 50 slides written in Spanish and created in SlideWiki.

[5] Slides available at "https://slidewiki.org/deck/91466-1/plan-de-formacion-datos-abiertos-ayto-de-zaragoza/deck/91466-1/". Slide 8 was not included in the corpus.

6 Conclusions and Future Work

In this paper, we present the initial results of our research on assessing E2R guidelines in a particular document. We propose a method for analyzing how easy-to-read compliant is a particular document. This method is independent on the format in which the material has been created. The method is based on rule-based techniques, pattern recognition, and NLP. We have also implemented a proof of concept of the method as an E2R conformance checker called Easy-to-Read Advisor. This checker is a specific implementation of the method and assesses which ER2 guidelines are satisfied in educational presentations written in Spanish.

We have performed a comparative evaluation between our gold standard and the results obtained by Easy-to-Read Advisor over a set of slides. The results indicate that on average over 70% of the guidelines in the checker are coincident with the gold standard. This evaluation provides us with clues to improve and refine Easy-to-Read Advisor. In addition, E2R experts validated this implementation; they provided positive comments and interesting suggestions for further work as well as remarked that to speeding up the E2R adaptation process is the potential of the tool.

Our plan is to improve Easy-to-Read Advisor (a) in the guidelines in which there was no coincidence with the gold standard, (b) with respect to the comments received, (c) and implementing the complete set of E2R guidelines.

Acknowledgements. This research work has been funded by the project Datos 4.0 (TIN2016-78011-C4-4-R) (Agencia Estatal de Investigación del MINECO y Fondos FEDER). We would like to thank Iván Martínez and Arminda Moreno for their comments, and Sandra Cartas and Álvaro Bermejo for their analysis of E2R guidelines.

References

1. IFLA: Guidelines for Easy-to-Read Materials. International Federation of Library Association and Institutions IFLA Professional Reports 120 (2010)
2. Norma UNE 153101:2018 EX Lectura Fácil. Pautas y recomendaciones para la elaboración de documentos (2018)
3. Bott, S., Saggion, H.: Automatic simplification of Spanish text for e-accessibility. In: Miesenberger, K., Karshmer, A., Penaz, P., Zagler, W. (eds.) ICCHP 2012. LNCS, vol. 7382, pp. 527–534. Springer, Heidelberg (2012). https://doi.org/10.1007/978-3-642-31522-0_79
4. Nietzio, A., Naber, D., Bühler, C.: Towards Techniques for Easy-to-Read Web Content. Procedia Comput. Sci. **27**, 343–349 (2014)
5. Matausch, K., Nietzio, A.: Easy-to-read and plain language: defining criteria and refining rules. In: Miesenberger, K., Petz, A., Matausch, K. (eds.) W3C WAI Symposium on Easy-to-Read on the Web (2012)
6. Leskela, L.: Guidelines or standards for Easy-to-read? In: Easy-to-Read on the Web. Symposium W3C. WAI 2012
7. Garcia Muñoz, O.: Lectura fácil: Métodos de redacción y evaluación 2012. Real Patronato sobre Discapacidad. M-34791-2012

8. Nietzio, A., Scheer, B., Bühler, C.: How long is a short sentence? – a linguistic approach to definition and validation of rules for easy-to-read material. In: Miesenberger, K., Karshmer, A., Penaz, P., Zagler, W. (eds.) ICCHP 2012. LNCS, vol. 7383, pp. 369–376. Springer, Heidelberg (2012). https://doi.org/10.1007/978-3-642-31534-3_55
9. Oelke, D., Spretke, D., Stoffel, A., Keim, D.: Visual readability analysis: how to make your writings easier to read. IEEE Trans. Visual. Comput. Graph. **18**(5), 662–674 (2012)
10. Hearst, M.A.: Automatic acquisition of hyponyms from large text corpora. In: Conference on Computational Linguistics (COLING 1992) (1992)

Research on Book Recommendation System for People with Visual Impairment Based on Fusion of Preference and User Attention

Zhi Yu[1,2,3]([✉]), Jiajun Bu[1,2,3], Sijie Li[1,2,3], Wei Wang[1,2,3],
Lizhen Tang[4], and Chuanwu Zhao[5]

[1] Zhejiang Provincial Key Laboratory of Service Robot, College of Computer
Science, Zhejiang University, Hangzhou, China
{yuzhirenzhe,bjj,21621177,wangwei_eagle}@zju.edu.cn
[2] Alibaba-Zhejiang University Joint Institute of Frontier Technologies,
Hangzhou, China
[3] Ningbo Research Institute, Zhejiang University, Ningbo, China
[4] China Braille Press, Beijing, China
eicatang_l@163.com
[5] Zhejiang Toman Intelligent Manufacturing Technology Co. LTD.,
Xinchang, China
zhaocw@zjtoman.com

Abstract. With the development of the Internet, the information explosion problem comes into being and it is challenging for users to search for the information they needed from e-books. Although the book recommendation system can help users find their focuses, it is not applicable for visually impaired users when using ordinary visual reading methods for knowledge acquisition. Therefore, a book recommendation system that suits their behavior habits is required. In order to provide accurate and effective book sets for users, we propose an algorithm based on fusing their preferences. For intelligently ranking the candidate book sets and help users find the right book quickly, we propose a context-aware algorithm based on users' attention. Meanwhile, we introduce an improved calculation method for users' attention to solving the problem of inaccurate prediction on users' current attention when their action history is cluttered. We use the self-attention to preserve the users' reading tendencies during the reading process, analyze users' personal features and book content features, and improve the accuracy of the recommendation by merging the feature space. Finally, the improved algorithm proposed and comparative experiments were employed on the dataset collecting from the China Blind Digital Library, and the effectiveness of the improvement is proved in each experimental comparison results.

Keywords: People with visual impairment · Digital book · Recommendation system · User attention

© Springer Nature Switzerland AG 2020
K. Miesenberger et al. (Eds.): ICCHP 2020, LNCS 12376, pp. 83–90, 2020.
https://doi.org/10.1007/978-3-030-58796-3_11

1 Introduction

With the rapid development of the Internet, massive amounts of data can be applied to analysis and research. The problem of how to choose useful and personalized information brings more challenges to the information service system. The recommendation system can effectively solve such problems, so it has rich practical applications in the fields of entertainment, content, e-commerce, and services. As a part of the content recommendation field, book recommendation is also being developed and improved. Many reading platforms have developed their own recommendation systems to serve them.

However, a large part of people still does not benefit from it. According to the statistics of the China Disabled Persons' Federation, as of the end of 2010, there are approximately 12.63 million people with visual disabilities in China, and this number continues to grow. For visually impaired users, because of their visual abilities, it is difficult to obtain information through normal visual channels, and can only rely on other sensory channels such as touch and hearing. Ordinary reading methods cannot meet their needs for knowledge acquisition. As developers and beneficiaries of the Internet, when enjoying the convenience and knowledge brought by massive data, we should also pay attention to these groups so that the visually impaired can also enjoy the information from the Internet.

Visually impaired people have different behaviors and methods when they browse the Internet: they are more willing to receive voice messages, often browse fixed websites, and often use the favorites function; at the same time, they have many challenges during browsing the webpages. For example, it is difficult to switch webpage windows, browse the entire webpage, and useless information greatly affects the browsing experience. When they want to acquire e-books in a huge amount of internet data, how to find what they are interested in quickly is an essential problem. Even because of visual defects, screening information is more difficult for them than sound people. Book recommendation systems in the market are recommended for the reading habits and interests of healthy people, which is not suitable for visually impaired people. Therefore, we need to set up a Braille book recommendation system for visually impaired people in accordance with their behavior habits.

We elaborate on the development of book recommendation systems and the problems encountered by visually impaired people when reading books, and propose a context-aware recommendation algorithm based on fusion preferences and user attention, which respectively solves the problems encountered in book recall and intelligent ranking Insufficient recalls and inaccurate rankings, and the algorithm was reasonably integrated into the accessible book recommendation system, and corresponding improvements were made to the characteristics of the visually impaired population. Experimental results on real datasets of the Chinese Braille Club library show that this method has outstanding advantages in terms of recommendation accuracy and intelligent ranking of recommendation lists.

2   Related Work

We give a general introduction to the related technologies used, mainly introduce the development of recommendation systems, and concepts of user attention mechanisms.

In 1990, with the development of computer algorithm development and application deployment, recommendation systems began to appear. In 1992, Goldberg [1] and others first proposed collaborative filtering. Two years later, the first automated recommendation system GroupLens [2] was proposed by the University of Minnesota and applied collaborative filtering technology to the recommendation. In 1997, the Recommendation System was first proposed and began to become a research area. Subsequently, the recommendation system gradually became a popular research direction due to the strong role of consumption guidance in e-commerce. Amazon applied the recommendation system to product recommendation as early as 1998 and launched collaborative filtering based on products. Through continuous improvement and Exploration, and finally reached a GMV contribution rate of 20% to 30% [3], illustrating the significant role of the recommendation system. After more than 20 years of accumulation and precipitation, the recommendation system has gradually formed a complete and comprehensive research system. At the algorithmic level, it is generally believed that there are three basic recommendation methods, namely content-based recommendation [4], user behavior-based recommendation [5], and hybrid recommendation.

The Encoder-Decoder based model is a variant of Recurrent Neural Network(RNN) [6, 7], where the Encoder encodes the input X into a fixed-length hidden vector C, and the Decoder decodes the hidden vector C to the target output Y, where the process from X to C and from C to Y is built with RNN. However, such models lack discrimination for the input sequence ABC, but all become the same hidden vector C. Therefore, in 2015, Kyunghyun Cho et al. [8] introduce the attention mechanism into the model to solve this problem. Attention is a mechanism used to change the calculation method of the hidden vector C, thereby improving the effectiveness of the Encoder-Decoder model.

Self-attention [9] is very different from the traditional attention mechanism. It is performed separately in the calculation of the encoder and decoder. The encoder and decoder each calculate the self-attention related to their input and output. The obtained result is only the dependency between its input and output. Finally, the self-attention of the encoder is added to the self-attention of the decoder, and finally, the attention of the entire model is obtained. The advantage of Self-attention is that it can directly calculate in parallel without resorting to the cyclic characteristics of RNN. It directly uses the attention model to model the sequence, and the model effect is better. Therefore, we chose self-attention as the attention in this article. Baseline algorithm of the force mechanism.

3 Recommendation Method

The recommendation algorithm based on fusion preferences proposed in this paper combines user behavior data and content data. The main idea is to obtain user preference vectors for books by mining user behaviors, user characteristics, and book characteristics, thereby recommending books of interest to users.

In terms of content calculation, due to a large amount of text data (such as abstracts, keywords, categories, tags, etc.) in the book recommendation system, we will focus on the text function, which is used to calculate the user's interest in books and books. Secondly, in order to retain the user's personalized preference interest expressed by the content data, we quantify the user's implicit feedback on the book based on the user's historical behavior record and behavior type and generate the user's behavior for the user's personalized preference expression vector. In order to retain the neighborhood preferences expressed by user behavior, we propose a novel co-occurrence book pair selection method that models users to read all co-occurrence book pairs in a book and extract relevant text from them based on the characteristics. Theme Similarity and text similarity can help a lot to find similar content books, while users reading behaviors on the similar content book are in common to some extent. We will predict multiple candidate book sets to keep the diversity of the results and sparse user preference matrix is used to present the user feature, we combine the user's preference with the content text's preference to facilitate user recommendation.

Our proposed context-aware recommendation algorithm based on user attention is divided into three parts: In the first part, we use a recurrent neural network RNN to mine the sequence information read by the user, train the user to read the book's probability model and then personalize the book for the user recommend. In the second part, we introduce the user self-attention model to further accurately describe the user's reading behaviors. In the third part, we use the feature space fusion attention mechanism to further simulate the user's real attention. By constructing different behavioral features in different feature spaces, we retain the part of global attention which is biased towards the feature space to accurately characterize user behavior attention. During the training part, we obtain the probability of each book in the candidate book set and recommend to each specified user with achieving intelligent book ranking and improving the ranking effect through model improvement.

4 Experiment

4.1 Dataset

The data set used in this paper is divided into two parts: reading records and book content information. The reading record collected data from the Chinese Braille Library for 830 days from April 2016 to August 2018. It contains 44375 reading records of 3282 books by 3368 visually impaired users, 7013 bookmark records and 1193 Articles are added to the collection record, which is extremely sparse. Since our records describe the user's reading, bookmarking, and favorite records, they are a data set consisting of the user's implicit feedback. Due to the inconvenience of visually impaired users, user operations are very difficult for them, so there is no explicit scoring mechanism. Each of our reading records contains a user unique identifier, a book unique identifier, a reading start timestamp, and a reading progress bar at the end of the reading. We have four types of display for the form of book contents: e-books, oral images, audiobooks, and e-braille, with a total of 8986 books. For each book, we collected the book's unique identifier, book display type, book title, author, keywords, book introduction, and book content type to extract the content features of the book.

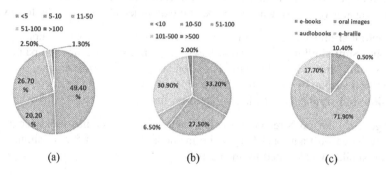

Fig. 1. Distribution of the number of books read by the user (a), distribution of the number of times the book was read (b), and the distribution of books read by visually impaired users (c)

Figure 1 shows the number of books read by the user (a) and the distribution of the number of times each book was read (b). It can be seen that nearly half of the users (49.4%) have read less than 5 books, and only a few users have read them. More than 50 books; most books (60.7%) have not been read more than 50 times, and only 2% of popular books. Figure 1 (c) shows the distribution of reading for various categories of books by visually impaired users. It can be seen that users prefer to listen to audio directly, and have fewer times to listen to oral images. It can be seen that our user behavior is extremely sparse, and most users lack a sufficiently long behavior sequence and enough user ratings, but since our proposed algorithm can perform sequence input without limiting the fixed length, it can effectively adapt to us At the same time, we use the updated user preference vector to augment user ratings, and can also handle the preference evaluation of sparse data. The behavior distribution of books is more saturated. More than two-thirds of the books have been read more than ten times, which can better calculate the similarity of books.

This article mainly studies book recommendations for this special group of visually impaired people. It is divided into two stages: recalling the Top-N recommendation set and intelligently ranking the recommendation set. During the recall phase, we calculated a recommendation list of length N for a given user 's reading history, so that the recommendation list contained as many books as the user would read. In the sorting stage, for a given user's reading context information and book collection, we calculate the prediction of whether each book in the collection will be read, so that the possibility of a book with a large prediction probability is read. Therefore, our main evaluation indicators are Mean Average Coverage (MAC) and AUC.

4.2   Experiment on Fusion of Preference

In this section, a comparative experiment will be performed to prove that the recommendation algorithm based on user fusion preferences has a good effect on the recommendation recall of Top-N. In the selection of comparison experiments, since this algorithm calculates the recommended recall set based on the improved similarity and recommendation vectors, as a baseline comparison, we introduce content-based collaborative filtering, and to explore four similarity calculation methods separately Under the recommendation results generated by the recommendation vector, we also conducted comparative experiments. The specific experimental scheme is as follows:

1. **BaseSimi similarity** calculation based on common co-occurrence pairs
2. **NormalSimi similarity** calculation based on common co-occurrence pairs
3. **StableSimi similarity** calculation based on stable co-occurrence pairs
4. **TextSimi similarity** calculation based on text similarity
5. **FusionSimi similarity** calculation based on fusion similarity.

To generate the top-N recommendation, method 1 ranks similar books according to similarity based on traditional ICF, while methods 2, 3, 4, and 5 rank similar books based on similarity calculated by themselves.

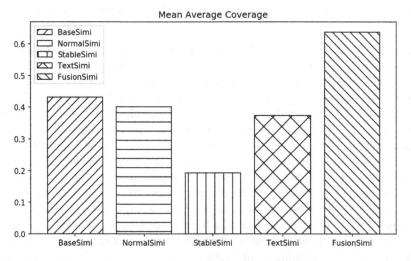

Fig. 2. MAC comparison between the proposed method and the comparative methods

As can be seen from Fig. 2, the coverage of FusionSimi is significantly higher than the other four solutions. This is because the similarity calculation of the fused features takes into account the user's strong association, weak association and book content association, especially the book content association. The collection of books it covers is very different from the collection covered by NormalSimi in order to be able to mine as many book associations as user behavior can't, thereby recalling books that most users might be interested in.

4.3   Experiment on Fusion Attention

In this section, comparative experiments will be performed to prove that context-aware recommendation algorithms based on feature space fusion attention have better performance in the ranking. In the choice of comparison experiments, because the algorithm uses contextual information to predict and improve the user's personalized book preferences, we use Bayesian personalized ranking algorithm BPR as the comparison experiment. For the ranking algorithm under the force mechanism, we also conducted comparative experiments on the RNN without any attention, with the self-attention (ARNN), or with the fusion-attention (FARNN).

Table 1. Time and AUC comparison between the proposed method and the comparative methods

Method	Time (s)	AUC
BPR	153.3	0.8798
RNN	4340.5	0.9035
ARNN	4132.2	0.9042
FARNN	377.7	0.9060

As can be seen from Table 1, the time complexity of BPR is the lowest. This is because BPR is calculated based on the Bayesian model. Compared to neural networks, it naturally saves time. Therefore, the model performance of BPR is worse than all RNN-based solutions. In the three neural networks of RNN, ARNN, and FARNN, it can be seen that FARNN greatly saves the training time of the recurrent neural network, and its AUC is also the highest among the three neural network models.

5   Conclusion

This paper proposes a context-aware recommendation algorithm based on fusion preferences and user attention. This algorithm solves many problems encountered in recommending books to visually impaired people and integrates into an accessible book recommendation system. To providing visually impaired users with accurate and effective books of interest, we propose a recommendation algorithm based on fusing preferences. To predict the preferences of the visually impaired when selecting books, we explore the user's behavior-based interests and content-based interests and combined these two features to predict the books that users want to read more accurately. To intelligently categorize collections so that users can quickly find books of interest when browsing sequentially, we propose a context-aware recommendation algorithm based on user attention to intelligently categorize collections. The experimental comparison results show the effectiveness and improvements of our method.

The current experiment is an offline experiment based on the Braille database dataset, so the recommendation level cannot be adjusted for real-time feedback from users. Next, we plan to optimize the recommendation method during training by applying an online recommendation algorithm based on user feedback.

Acknowledgments. This work is supported by Alibaba-Zhejiang University Joint Institute of Frontier Technologies, The National Key R&D Program of China (No. 2018YFC2002603, 2018YFB1403202), Zhejiang Provincial Natural Science Foundation of China (No. LZ13F020001), the National Natural Science Foundation of China (No. 61972349, 61173185, 61173186) and the National Key Technology R&D Program of China (No. 2012BAI34B01, 2014BAK15B02).

References

1. Goldberg, D., Nichols, D., Oki, B.M., et al.: Using collaborative filtering to weave an information tapestry. Commun. ACM **35**(12), 61–70 (1992)
2. John, R., Mitesh, S., Neophytos, I., et al.: GroupLens: an open architecture for collaborative filtering of netnews. In: ACM Conference on Computer Supported Cooperative Work. ACM (1994)
3. Linden, G., Smith, B., York, J.: Amazon.com recommendations: item-to-item collaborative filtering. IEEE Internet Comput. **7**(1), 76–80 (2003)
4. Pazzani, M.J., Billsus, D.: Content-Based Recommendation Systems. In: Brusilovsky, P., Kobsa, A., Nejdl, W. (eds.) The Adaptive Web. LNCS, vol. 4321, pp. 325–341. Springer, Heidelberg (2007). https://doi.org/10.1007/978-3-540-72079-9_10
5. Sarwar, B.M.: Item-based collaborative filtering recommendation algorithms. In: International Conference on World Wide Web. ACM (2001)
6. Sutskever, I., Vinyals, O., Le, Q.V.: Sequence to Sequence Learning with Neural Networks. (2014)
7. Cho, K., Van Merrienboer, B., Gulcehre, C., et al.: Learning phrase representations using RNN encoder-decoder for statistical machine translation. Computer Science (2014)
8. Cho, K., Courville, A., Bengio, Y.: Describing multimedia content using attention-based encoder-decoder networks. IEEE Trans. Multimed. **17**(11), 1875–1886 (2015)
9. Vaswani, A., Shazeer, N., Parmar, N., et al.: Attention is all you need. (2017)

Karaton: An Example of AI Integration Within a Literacy App

Hannes Hauwaert[1]([⊠]), Pol Ghesquière[2], Jacqueline Tordoir[2], and Jenny Thomson[3]

[1] Happs Development, Hoogstraat 10, 1600 Sint-Pieters-Leeuw, Belgium
hannes@karaton.be
[2] KU Leuven, Oude Markt 13, 3000 Leuven, Belgium
pol.ghesquiere@kuleuven.be
[3] University of Sheffield, Broomhall, Sheffield S10 2TG, UK

Abstract. Integrating AI into educational applications can have an enormous benefit for users (players/children) and educational professionals. The concept of customisation based on user preferences and abilities is not new. However, in this paper the abilities of the players of a literacy skill application are being collated and categorized, so that in the future they can automatically offer the next instructional level without external manual support. The app Karaton has been designed in such a way that there is a presumption of competence and no child should feel a failure or need to wait to be told that they can try a higher level. It has been found that this improves self-confidence and encourages independent literacy skills.

Keywords: Literacy app · Reading difficulties · Dyslexia · Artificial intelligence

1 Introduction

Oral language is considered to develop spontaneously and in an informal way. Learning to read, however, is highly dependent on explicit instruction. Formal instruction is needed to develop this academic skill. Becoming a fluent reader is one of the most important standards children need to achieve at primary school. In most cases, repeated practice makes sounding out of written words a very accurate, fast and automatic skill, enabling the reader to focus on the reading content, comprehend what is being portrayed and enjoy it. This is the basis for learning other academic subject matters (Dehaene 2009). For children with dyslexia (5–7% of the school population) becoming a fluent reader is very difficult. They need to practice much more and even then it can be hard for them to achieve the same reading proficiency level as their peers, making these children more at risk of encountering broader academic disadvantages (Snowling 2000). In these cases and where there are struggling readers who lack fluency skills for whatever reason, it is extremely important to introduce highly motivating opportunities to practice for example word decoding. Research has shown that reading achievement at primary school age is highly associated with socioeconomic status at middle adulthood, independently of relevant confounding variables (Ritchie and Bates 2013).

© Springer Nature Switzerland AG 2020
K. Miesenberger et al. (Eds.): ICCHP 2020, LNCS 12376, pp. 91–96, 2020.
https://doi.org/10.1007/978-3-030-58796-3_12

1.1 Development of Karaton

Karaton came into existence as a personal project of the main author whilst at university. Having encountered the barriers caused by dyslexia and the lack of educational tools that supported individuals with reading fluency difficulties, a research project slowly evolved into an actual application. More than 100 individuals made up of speech therapists, teachers, parents and children were asked what they felt was lacking in the currently available tools on the market for those with dyslexia. The most important thing that resulted from the interviews was the conclusion that there were three main aspects that were important to the users. The tool should be based on recent scientific evidence; adults wanted to be able to see the progress of the children and the tool had to be motivating and fun to play.

The research also highlighted the fact that the games or tools currently on the market had two of the three aspects, but never the entire collection. The three aspects turned into three 3 main pillars (motivation, evidence based, and tracking possibilities) when designing the tool that became Karaton. Throughout the building of the Karaton System there was a very close collaboration between the development team and teaching staff to ensure a proper balance between gamification elements and academic value.

Every mini-game that was built for the various strategies also had extensive user testing with children to ensure the goal for each game was clear, with as few instructions as possible. Other than the regular user testing with children there were also two larger scale testing phases. The first one was with 20 selected speech therapists who could test the system when it was still in development as a Beta version (March 2017). Their suggestions were integrated in the final release seven months later.

Another test phase took place in January 2019. This was focused on the use of Karaton in schools. 32 schools signed up to join this test phase. Classes usually consisted of about 30 children. The results from this test phase showed that it was a very intensive process for teachers to customize all settings in the system to each individual child's needs. This was the beginning of a decision tree structure algorithm to enhance usability for the teachers.

1.2 Current Version of Karaton

In its current version Karaton is an educational adventure game that combines a real gaming experience with personalised literacy support. The Karaton system consists of two parts. The first one is Karaton, a serious game for children (Torbeyns et al. 2015). The main goal of this game is to provide children with different types of exercises based on their specific reading level in an engaging environment that improves reading fluency and reading motivation while boosting reading confidence (De Coster 2018). At the outset, it is important to take account of the fact that many of the players may be disaffected readers or those struggling with written language. Therefore, the design of the game involves very easy to understand interactions that are graphically stimulating. Children can navigate through the game without having to read complex instructions.

The central aim of the game is gathering materials to build a customised paradise on a deserted island. That requires the player to work through a series of mini-games, each time gathering more materials. So, the gaming time is divided between practicing reading and building the paradise. Each mini-game offers a specific reading exercise. These are scientifically based on recent reviews of effective reading interventions (Galuschka et al. 2014; Scheltinga et al. 2016). The mini-games are 'chopping wood' and 'sawing wood' to exercise splitting words in syllables, 'cleaving rocks' and 'ore oven' to exercise word recognition, 'lianes' and 'binding lianes' to practice flash word reading and, lastly the 'dodo-race' and 'balancing duel' to practice spelling. Every time a task is correctly fulfilled (usually involving reading or writing a specific word) the child gains an item (wood, stones, lianes,...) that can be used to build furniture for his/her home.

The second part of the app is built around the Karaton Academy. This is a platform designed for parents and educational professionals to track and monitor the progress of their child. So, the game can be steered in two modes, an automatic mode and a manual mode. In the manual mode educational professionals can customise all the presented words in the different mini games and adapt it, based on their own insights, as to the educational needs of the child. Of course, this customisation depends on the characteristics of the mini-game (e.g. flash duration, amount of syllables, phonemes included, amount of distractors). Each time an exercise is completed the child receives feedback and his/her progress is logged. In the automatic mode a decision tree algorithm is used to decide if the child should advance to the next level. To date 50 levels are defined, based on several aspects of the word that are presented in the exercises: amount of syllables, syllable length and phonemic structure (CV[1], VC, CVC, CCVC, CVCC, ...), morphological structure of the word (composition, prefixes, suffixes),...

2 Methodology

At present, the decision tree algorithm for each type of exercise uses the predetermined steps provided in the design of the game and the professionals manually evaluate all the data gathered from children's input. For example over a four month period, 35 students and 8 teachers using Karaton provided sufficient data to allow teachers to not only see progress, but also use personalisation strategies based on the children's data to inform the next steps, such as a new mini-game or a repeat of a task where success was not obvious. This process is the basis for the predictive technology planned in the next phase.

To implement AI algorithms in the game, the aforementioned progress data and level recommendations produced by the existing decision tree algorithms will be gathered as training data. It is felt that this type of training data is suitable for an end-to-end ANN (Artificial Neural Network) based machine-learning model. The progress data, based on users' personalised information (e.g. reading level), the difficulty level of each mini-game associated with reading exercises, users' response times and game scores, will be normalised to feed into the proposed ANN model. As progress data has been evaluated by professional experts, their feedback will also be transferred into the

---

[1] C = consonant / V = vocal.

training data to help build up this end-to-end machine learning model. Based on the children's reading levels and performance in each game, the trained AI model will be used to predict the personalised difficulty level of the next game and provide a recommendation service, thereby creating an individualised learning path for each child.

3 Results and Discussion

The results from this work have yet to be completed, but currently experts involved in the A is for A project have analysed all the data from the different reading techniques and compared them with previous results. At present they have to assess the best course of action and adjust the parameters which can be a subjective judgement. Therefore this method is only as good as the assessment made by the person who is doing it and how often the assessment is carried out.

It appears that the use of AI techniques could offer a more detailed analysis of the particular words (and letters) that have been found to be incorrectly read and the creation of a personalised word list that is more specific to the needs of the child. For example when children make common errors such as reversals, with the letters b and d in some words, the use of machine learning captures these mistakes and integrates words using these letters into the next exercise level, so they can be repeated. The trials have also highlighted that there may be numerous combinations of letters that children mix up. Instead of trying to program all these separate rules, machine learning can help to detect the different combinations and provide useful information to teachers and other educational professionals. At a more advanced stage, the system could also be used as an assessment tool for individual reading strategies and their particular effectiveness for each child, as well as for the development of successive reading stages.

Moreover, the recent work undertaken has the potential to offer children with poor literacy skills improved support at a more targeted level, whilst increasing the effectiveness of the training offered. The use of AI also allows professionals to more easily detect these variations at an early stage and spend more time on particular difficulties in their own intervention or instruction. More individualised exercises or mini-games could be added where needed and the designers would receive enhanced feedback for the next stage of the app development.

Preliminary data of a recent randomized control trial (Gheeraert and Hendrix, in prep.) indicated that the Karaton game had at least the same effect on reading development as a training strategy using traditional interventions, e.g. repeated book reading. However, the affective processes that come with these activities are in favour of the game. Pupils enjoyed using the variety of mini-games and did not feel they were forced to start training with the app. Moreover, playing the game for a certain period of time increased their motivation to read and have fun while reading (De Coster 2018).

When discussing the outcomes of the research and in order to create a better understanding of the effective mechanisms of the game and further optimize the algorithms, it was felt that the separate mini-games should be offered specifically to struggling readers. This would be for a certain period of time to track their performance in detail. Thus offering the necessary extra information to train the AI system and create a better algorithm to adapt the mini-games to the 'zone of proximal development' of the child for that specific reading strategy. Aspects such as graphemes included in the word, structure of the word (e.g. CVC or CCVC), errors made, reaction time of the response etc. could be used to match the difficulty level of the exercises with the skills level of the child. Furthermore, with a study in a larger group of children, the vocabulary database could be ordered, based on word level difficulty. The internal software could also be organized in an intelligent way, so that this ordering would adapt to the way each child plays a mini-game.

4 Conclusion

Early discussions about the use of AI models in Karaton have produced some indications that the methodologies chosen have the potential to enhance the app and better support those children finding certain aspects of typical literacy skills difficult to master.

On the games side an AI intervention would enable the offering of different types of vocabulary for each mini-game tailored to those that a child likes to play. There could also be incremental changes to the kind of materials the games provide for the building activities, that might increase in complexity to challenge and encourage the child. An example of this would be that a player has to collect 10 pieces of wood to build a chair in the early stages, but has to collect 50 pieces of wood at a more advanced stage in order to build a more complex object.

At present making sure there is a balance between instruction and degree of effort required to complete a game is one of the hardest parts in the design process. If the game is too easy a child will lose interest. Make it too hard and they will feel a failure. AI could be of enormous benefit in this balancing act and the games' internal economy. There is a fine balance to be made between resources gained versus spent and support for literacy difficulties, whilst providing a confidence boost for players.

Current insights into the characteristics of these e-learning tools for reading, their actual implementation in schools and their effectiveness for children's reading development and motivation are limited. This research has highlighted the need to address this gap by systematically analyzing the characteristics and implementation of the available electronic teaching tools in the domain of reading. There is also the need to review the effectiveness of these tools for children's reading development and motivation, as well as developing a toolkit for teachers to enhance the effective implementation of strategies involving the use of electronic technologies in their classrooms.

Acknowledgements. The authors would like to thank the European Commission Erasmus + project funding for "A is for App"[2] involving a collaboration between four European countries (Belgium-Flanders, the Czech Republic, the Netherlands, the United Kingdom) and between researchers and practitioners (teachers and professionals working in Centres for Dyslexia). In the framework of this project, Karaton is being used in 10 schools in Belgium and Czech Republic through randomised trials and qualitative interviews with fourth graders in primary school.

---

[2] https://www.aisforapp.eu/.

References

De Coster, S.: KARATON. Een leesgame voor leeszwakke en dyslectische kinderen: een pilootstudie naar de bruikbaarheid en effectiviteit van KARATON. HOGent, Mens en Welzijn, Gent (2018)

Dehaene, S.: Reading in the Brain. The New Science of How We Read. Penguin Books, New York (2009)

Galuschka, K., Ise, E., Krick, K., Schulte-Körne, G.: Effectiveness of treatment approaches for children and adolescents with reading disabilities: a meta-analysis of randomized controlled trials. PLoS One **9**(2), e89900 (2014). https://doi.org/10.1371/journal.pone.0089900

Gheeraert, A., Hendrix, S.: Effect van een App voor de stimulering van leesvloeiendheid bij leeszwakke leerlingen uit het vierde leerjaar (Masterthesis under supervision of prof. dr. Pol Ghesquière & prof. dr. Joke Torbeyns). Leuven: KU Leuven (in prep.)

Ritchie, S.J., Bates, T.C.: Enduring links from childhood mathematics and reading achievement to adult socioeconomic status. Psychol. Sci. **24**, 1301–1308 (2013)

Scheltinga, F., Wang L., Voeten, R. Verhoeven. L.: Interventions for reading problems and dyslexia: what works? (rapportage NWO) (2016)

Snowling, M.: Dyslexia. 2 edn. Oxford Blackwell Publishing, Oxford (2000)

Torbeyns, J., Lehtinen, E., Elen, J. (eds.): Describing and Studying Domain-Specific Serious Games. AGL. Springer, Cham (2015). https://doi.org/10.1007/978-3-319-20276-1

Can We Unify Perception and Localization in Assisted Navigation? An Indoor Semantic Visual Positioning System for Visually Impaired People

Haoye Chen, Yingzhi Zhang, Kailun Yang$^{(\boxtimes)}$, Manuel Martinez, Karin Müller, and Rainer Stiefelhagen

Institute for Anthropomatics and Robotics, Karlsruhe Institute of Technology, Karlsruhe, Germany
kailun.yang@kit.edu

Abstract. Navigation assistance has made significant progress in the last years with the emergence of different approaches, allowing them to perceive their surroundings and localize themselves accurately, which greatly improves the mobility of visually impaired people. However, most of the existing systems address each of the tasks individually, which increases the response time that is clearly not beneficial for a safety-critical application. In this paper, we aim to cover scene perception and visual localization needed by navigation assistance in a unified way. We present a semantic visual localization system to help visually impaired people to be aware of their locations and surroundings in indoor environments. Our method relies on 3D reconstruction and semantic segmentation of RGB-D images captured from a pair of wearable smart glasses. We can inform the user of an upcoming object via audio feedback so that the user can be prepared to avoid obstacles or interact with the object, which means that visually impaired people can be more active in an unfamiliar environment.

Keywords: Visual localization · 3D reconstruction · Semantic segmentation · Navigation assistance for the visually impaired

1 Introduction

With the help of mobility aids such as a global navigation satellite system (GNSS) device, it is possible for visually impaired people to travel more independently. Although such mobility aids can navigate visually impaired people to the entrance of the right target building, the unknown indoor environment remains a labyrinth for them [3]. The situation indoors is a more demanding challenge than outdoors, as each room can have a different layout and indoor navigation systems are not on the market. For visually impaired people it is difficult to find their own way to the desired destination without the company of a personal

© Springer Nature Switzerland AG 2020
K. Miesenberger et al. (Eds.): ICCHP 2020, LNCS 12376, pp. 97–104, 2020.
https://doi.org/10.1007/978-3-030-58796-3_13

guide. In addition, the arrangement of movables can change when returning to a familiar place, which can be dangerous for people with visual impairments if they rely on their memory for navigation.

On the other hand, vision-based navigation aids have made remarkable progress in recent years [5,8,20], making it possible to perceive the environment and localize oneself effectively, which significantly improves the mobility of visually impaired people. However, most of these tools work outdoors and address each task separately, which increases the response time that is clearly not advantageous for safety-critical assisted navigation. In these scenarios, a system, which can capture and convey both positional and cognitive messages, offers significant support to visually impaired people.

In this paper, we aim to cover scene perception and localization desired by navigation assistance in a unified manner. We present a semantic visual localization system for the visually impaired under indoor circumstances, in order to help them to acquire the overall information about their surroundings and relative position of objects nearby. The system reconstructs a 3D copy of the user's surroundings in real time from a stereo camera. Meanwhile, it associates semantic concepts of nearby objects with corresponding entities in the 3D reconstruction by using pixel-wise semantic segmentation. As the system maps the real world into a digital one, we can estimate the user's location according to the camera position in the 3D map. Finally, through audio feedback, semantic concepts combined with their position can give the user intuitive awareness and understanding of their surroundings (e.g., the system can tell the user what kind of obstacles are in front of him or tell him where a door is).

2   Related Work

In recent years, the robotics community has well explored Simultaneous Localization and Mapping (SLAM) [2] problems. Visual-SLAM research still has a substantial potential thanks to astonishing achievements by computer vision and computer graphic techniques. ORBSLAM [9] exhibits a system for monocular, stereo, and RGB-D cameras, including loop closing, relocalization, and map reuse. ElasticFusion [18] is capable of estimating a dense 3D map of an indoor environment. Kimera [14] enables mesh reconstruction and semantic labeling in 3D. However, there is still a huge gap between localization and assistance, as visually impaired people always rely on the surrounding semantic information to localize themselves, which is not necessarily mapped to the corresponding positioning results from visual SLAM algorithms.

Deep neural networks have achieved excellent results in semantic segmentation. SegNet [1] was presented as an encoder-decoder architecture for pixel-wise semantic segmentation. ENet [10], Fast-SCNN [11] and ERFNet [12,13] were proposed as efficient architectures for fast inference. ACNet [4] introduced an attention complementary module to exploit cross-modal features, which is also used in RFNet [17] that facilitates real-time RGB-D segmentation. In this work, we use RFNet due to its real-time performance and fusion capability. Despite these progress, in previous wearable systems, semantic segmentation has only been used for unified scene perception [20], leaving rich opportunities open to assist localization.

In the field of assisted navigation with computer vision methods for visually impaired people, Lin et al. [5] proposed an outdoor localization system for visually impaired pedestrians. Hu et al. [3] presented an indoor positioning framework based on panoramic visual odometry, which attained robust localization performance due to the large field of view. Lin et al. [6] put forward a data-driven approach to predict safe and reliable navigable instructions by using RGB-D data and the established semantic map. Liu et al. [7] built a solution for indoor topological localization with semantic information based on object detection, which is the closest to our work. Our work differs from these works as we aim to use the dense semantic maps produced by an RGB-D segmentation network to improve localization, since the pixel-wise results, which are extremely informative during orientation and navigation, not only allow the user to recognize nearby objects, but also facilitate the detection of walkable areas.

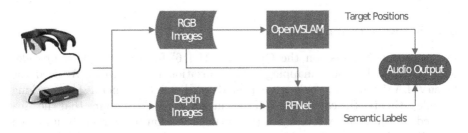

Fig. 1. An overview of the proposed system. The smart glasses provide RGB images to OpenVSLAM to establish localization and mapping. Meanwhile, the RFNet generates semantic labels from the RGB and depth images. We select the target positions with their semantic labels to produce audio prompts for the user.

3   System Description

In this section, we describe the hardware and software components as well as the interaction of the components of the entire system. Figure 1 gives an overview of the proposed system.

3.1   Hardware Components

The system consists of a RealSense camera R200, a pair of bone-conduction earphones, as well as an NVIDIA Jetson AGX Xavier processor. The camera and earphones are integrated into a pair of wearable smart glasses, as it is shown in Fig. 2. We perform the semantic segmentation and localization on the embedded processor Xavier in real time.

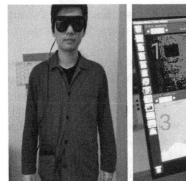

Fig. 2. Devices and the real-time results of our system. The left image shows the user wearing the devices. The blue box in left image indicates the smart glasses while the orange box indicates the Xavier processor. The windows on the screen exhibit (1) the depth image, (2) the input frame for the SLAM system, (3) the semantic segmentation result and (4) the 3D map.

3.2   Software Components

Our approach is based on the OpenVSLAM [16] framework, which provides our system with robust mapping and localization in real time. We feed the OpenVSLAM with color images captured by the RGB camera. The tracking module estimates the camera pose of the current frame. We assume that the area covered by the camera reveals an interesting direction for a visually impaired user. We utilize the 3D landmarks generated by the mapping module in the current frame to calculate the distance between the user and the objects. In this scenario, the camera center is considered as the location of the user. We choose the area within a distance of half a meter to one meter as the target area. In parallel, our system takes the color images and the depth images to the image segmentation component of our system. Subsequently, we acquire the semantic labels of the target area from the segmentation results. Normally, our target area covers several semantic labels. It is trivial to determine the final label by choosing the most frequent label of this area. The semantic segmentation approach is derived from the RFNet [17], a real-time fusion network. It provides the system with fast inference and high accuracy of semantic segmentation by fusing RGB-D information from the camera, as shown in Fig. 3.

Training of the Computer Vision Model. We trained the RFNet with the SUN RGB-D indoor scene understanding benchmark suit [15]. SUN RGB-D contains 10355 RGB-D images with dense indoor semantic labels of 37 classes. We resized all images to 480×640 and applied data augmentation during the training. The pixel classification accuracy is 15.5% on 2000 test images. Figure 3 shows some results of RFNet on the SUN RGB-D dataset. We use Intel RealSense R200 as the input device for both the SLAM part and segmentation part.

The stream resolution is 480×640 with a frame rate of 60 fps. As shown in Table 1, We achieve approximately 69.3 ms/frame inference speed of the semantic segmentation and 59.9 ms/frame tracking speed of the SLAM system, which is fast for navigation assistance on the portable embedded processor. Figure 4 shows the mapping results in small rooms. When the system detects objects near the user, the system generates a audio feedback with semantic information every 1 s.

3.3 Interaction of the Components

Figure 1 shows the general interaction of the components of our proposed system. In order to support reliable obstacle avoidance, we keep searching for the nearest landmarks to the camera center in the map. When the distance is reaching a certain interval (i.e., between 0.5 m and 1 m), the user is informed of the semantic label of the target area. We embed this information in a sentence (e.g., "A table is in front of you") and send it to a text-to-speech module to generate audio feedback for the user.

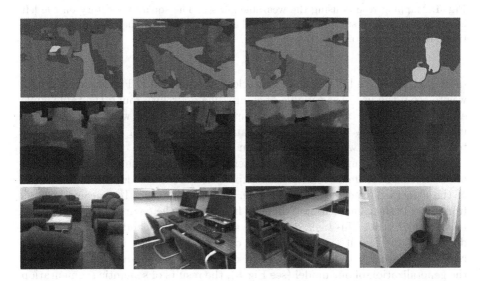

Fig. 3. Semantic segmentation results on SUN RGB-D dataset. From top to bottom: semantic maps, depth maps and RGB images.

4 Pilot Study

Our system aims to enable navigation in unstructured indoor environments. Thus, the user must be made aware of impassable areas in their path, as well as possible obstacles. Hence, we focused our evaluation on the ability to detect obstacles and objects blocking the path. However, we also evaluated our prototype through a user study where a blindfolded participant walked around a

Table 1. System specifications and speed analysis.

Camera resolution	Camera fps	Inference speed	Mean tracking time
480 × 640	60 fps	69.3 ms/frame	59.9 ms/frame

Fig. 4. Mapping results using the wearable glasses. The square trajectory on the left image indicates the result of walking around a table. The right image shows the walking trajectory along a corridor.

table with chairs and other small obstacles along the path. The goal of the task was to see if the user was capable of completing a circuit around the table while evading all possible objects. In this regard, the system test was successful. The user received timely audio feedback that warned him of all obstacles, and the test was completed without any collision with an obstacle.

On the other hand, the test was useful to identify some of the limitations of our device that impacted the user experience. On one side, the field of view of the camera did not cover all areas in front of the user. To prevent hazards from outside the camera frame, the user had to scan the environment by slightly moving their head. This task, however, was quite intuitive and posed no problem during the test, but it was noted that a device with a larger field of view would be advantageous for this application. A second limitation found was that due to the generalization of our model (see Fig. 5), the results of semantic segmentation differ under various environments. This resulted in a handful of times where obstacles that were not present on the scene were nonetheless notified to the user. While the user had no problem dealing with them, those diminish the confidence of users in the system, and thus further improvements in the semantic segmentation would benefit the user experience.

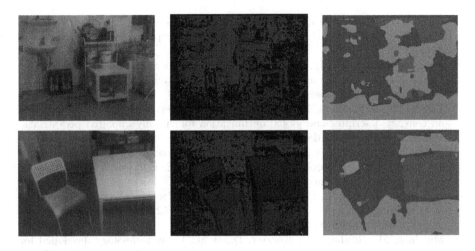

Fig. 5. Semantic segmentation results in our indoor environments.

5   Conclusions

We presented an approach for visually impaired people to gain more mobility and orientation capacity in an indoor environment. The system makes it possible to provide additional information that it is not easy to obtain with traditional mobility aids such as the white cane. Combined with semantic contents of the environment, the system can provide visually impaired people with different options of their actions (i.e., not only avoidance but also interaction).

In future work, we plan to use the semantic information to improve the localization further (i.e., to estimate what kind of room the user is currently located in). We also will test our system with persons with visual impairments to adapt the system to their special needs. Furthermore, we will robustify semantic perception in real-world domains [19] and improve the computational efficiency of the visual positioning system.

Acknowledgement. The work is partially funded by the German Federal Ministry of Labour and Social Affairs (BMAS) under the grant number 01KM151112. This work is also supported in part by Hangzhou SurImage Technology Company Ltd. and in part by Hangzhou KrVision Technology Company Ltd. (krvision.cn).

References

1. Badrinarayanan, V., Kendall, A., Cipolla, R.: SegNet: A deep convolutional encoder-decoder architecture for image segmentation. IEEE Trans. Pattern Anal. Mach. Intell. **39**(12), 2481–2495 (2017)
2. Cadena, C., Carlone, L., Carrillo, H., et al.: Past, present, and future of simultaneous localization and mapping: toward the robust-perception age. IEEE Trans. Robot. **32**(6), 1309–1332 (2016)

3. Hu, W., Wang, K., Chen, H., et al.: An indoor positioning framework based on panoramic visual odometry for visually impaired people. Measure. Sci. Technol. **31**(1), 014006 (2019)
4. Hu, X., Yang, K., Fei, L., Wang, K.: ACNet: Attention based network to exploit complementary features for RGBD semantic segmentation. In: International Conference on Image Processing (2019)
5. Lin, S., Cheng, R., Wang, K., Yang, K.: Visual localizer: outdoor localization based on convnet descriptor and global optimization for visually impaired pedestrians. Sensors. **18**(4), 2476 (2018)
6. Lin, Y., Wang, K., Yi, W., Lian, S.: Deep learning based wearable assistive system for visually impaired people. In: Proceedings of the IEEE International Conference on Computer Vision Workshops (2019)
7. Liu, Q., Li, R., Hu, H., Gu, D.: Indoor topological localization based on a novel deep learning technique. Cognitive Comput. **12**(3), 528–541 (2020). https://doi.org/10.1007/s12559-019-09693-5
8. Martinez, M., Roitberg, A., Koester, D., et al.: Using technology developed for autonomous cars to help navigate blind people. In: Proceedings of the IEEE International Conference on Computer Vision Workshops (2017)
9. Mur-Artal, R., Tardós, J.D.: ORB-SLAM2: An open-source SLAM system for monocular, stereo, and RGB-D cameras. IEEE Trans. Robot. **33**(5), 1255–1262 (2017)
10. Paszke, A., Chaurasia, A., Kim, S., Culurciello, E.: Enet: A deep neural network architecture for real-time semantic segmentation. arXiv:1606.02147 (2016)
11. Poudel, R.P., Liwicki, S., Cipolla, R.: Fast-SCNN: fast semantic segmentation network. arXiv:1902.04502 (2019)
12. Romera, E., Alvarez, J.M., Bergasa, L.M., Arroyo, R.: ERFNET: Efficient residual factorized convnet for real-time semantic segmentation. IEEE Trans. Intell. Transport. Syst. **19**(1), 263–272 (2018)
13. Romera, E., Bergasa, L.M., Yang, K., et al.: Bridging the day and night domain gap for semantic segmentation. In: Intelligent Vehicles Symposium (2019)
14. Rosinol, A., Abate, M., Chang, Y., Carlone, L.: Kimera: an open-source library for real-time metric-semantic localization and mapping. In: International Conference on Robotics and Automation (2019)
15. Song, S., Lichtenberg, S.P., Xiao, J.: SUN RGB-D: A RGB-D scene understanding benchmark suite. In: 2015 IEEE Conference on Computer Vision and Pattern Recognition (CVPR) (2015)
16. Sumikura, S., Shibuya, M., Sakurada, K.: OpenVSLAM: a versatile visual slam framework. In: Proceedings of the 27th ACM International Conference on Multimedia (2019)
17. Sun, L., Yang, K., Hu, X., et al.: Real-time fusion network for RGB-D semantic segmentation incorporating unexpected obstacle detection for road-driving images. arXiv:2002.10570 (2020)
18. Whelan, T., Salas-Moreno, R.F., Glocker, B., et al.: Elasticfusion: real-time dense slam and light source estimation. Int. J. Robot. Res. **35**(14), 1697–1716 (2016)
19. Yang, K., Bergasa, L.M., Romera, E., Wang, K.: Robustifying semantic cognition of traversability across wearable RGB-depth cameras. Appl. Opt. **58**(12), 3141–3155 (2019)
20. Yang, K., Wang, K., Bergasa, L.M., et al.: Unifying terrain awareness for the visually impaired through real-time semantic segmentation. Sensors. **18**(5), 1506 (2018)

IBeaconMap: Automated Indoor Space Representation for Beacon-Based Wayfinding

Seyed Ali Cheraghi$^{(\boxtimes)}$, Vinod Namboodiri , and Kaushik Sinha

Department of Electrical Engineering and Computer Science,
Wichita State University, Wichita, KS, USA
sxcheraghi@shockers.wichita.edu,
{vinod.namboodiri,kaushik.sinha}@wichita.edu

Abstract. Traditionally, there have been few options for navigational aids for the blind and visually impaired (BVI) in large indoor spaces. Some recent indoor navigation systems allow users equipped with smartphones to interact with low cost Bluetooth-based beacons deployed strategically within the indoor space of interest to navigate their surroundings. A major challenge in deploying such beacon-based navigation systems is the need to employ a time and labor-expensive beacon planning process to identify potential beacon placement locations and arrive at a topological structure representing the indoor space. This work presents a technique called IBeaconMap for creating such topological structures to use with beacon-based navigation that only needs the floor plans of the indoor spaces of interest.

Keywords: Indoor wayfinding · Accessibility · Machine learning · Internet of things (IoT) · Computer vision

1 Introduction and Related Works

Recent advances in global positioning systems (GPS) and mapping technologies provide accurate and simple to use means for wayfinding for outdoor environments. For indoor environments, reading and following signs remains the easiest and most reliable option because GPS and associated advances for outdoor environments do not apply. This has, however, meant that indoor wayfinding has remained a challenge for the blind and visually impaired (BVI) in our society. Indoor environments can be geographically large and intimidating such as grocery stores, airports, sports stadiums, large office buildings, and hotels. A solution to the indoor wayfinding problem for the BVI also has broad applications for the sighted population. Recent work has developed a system of wayfinding for the BVI using low-cost, stamp-size Bluetooth Low Energy (BLE) "beacon" devices embedded in the environment [1,3,6] that interact with smartphones carried by users. Such beacon-based navigation systems have achieved promising preliminary results indicating that they may be a viable solution for indoor

© Springer Nature Switzerland AG 2020
K. Miesenberger et al. (Eds.): ICCHP 2020, LNCS 12376, pp. 105–113, 2020.
https://doi.org/10.1007/978-3-030-58796-3_14

wayfinding for the BVI if some of the underlying challenges to the deployment of such systems can be solved.

Exploring an indoor space and its information for someone who is blind requires knowing the information somehow beforehand and have it presented when the person approaches the proximity of a Point of Interest (POI). This information can be entered manually by a human about the entire indoor space which is the current and traditional approach to beacon planning. Manual determination of all beacon placement locations and path computations is time-consuming and labor-expensive, especially for large indoor spaces. Such an approach requires the manual identification of walking paths on a floor plan, marking of points of interest, determining the distance between any two points of interest, determining the orientation between them for navigation, computing shortest paths between points of interests, and subsequent adjustments to optimize the resulting paths that may require further iterations of the entire process.

None of the efforts so far had designed a fast, and largely automated method for representing indoor spaces as topological structures for accurate and timely beacon-based navigation. Such a method (as proposed in this work) will benefit all current efforts in deploying indoor beacon-based navigation systems. Work related to creating representations of indoor spaces have been around for a while (e.g. [7,8]). These can mainly be differentiated based on the approach used in collecting the required information and in the techniques employed to create the desired representations. Prior work such as in [2] can help create indoor space representation through floorplans which serve as inputs to IBeaconMap. IBeaconMap differs from this class of work by taking files in simple image formats or PDFs as input and employing a combination of computer vision and machine learning techniques. In addition to marking points of interests on floor plans as beacon locations, IBeaconMap can also mark strategic points such as intersections which are important for BVI navigation. None of the previous work on indoor space representations focused on providing outputs catering to the special needs for beacon-based wayfinding that include beacon location markings, indoor paths connecting these locations, a weighted connectivity graph as topological structure representation, and directional orientations for paths. The web-based mapping tool developed as part of NavCog [1], the only other tool with a similar objective as IBeaconMap, requires a user to mark all beacon locations and walking paths first on a floor plan image. This higher-level of manual involvement is expected to not scale well thus rendering the tool not as desirable in many situations.

Additional approaches for indoor space representations beyond extraction from architectural floor plans are that of robotic mapping and crowdsourced approaches [9]. Robotic mapping approaches are likely to be more expensive to implement and time-intensive while crowdsourced approaches, although inexpensive and maybe even free, will not be as accurate or fast as IBeaconMap. Further, the recent work on using crowdsourcing to deploy beacons in [5] assumes that beacon locations are already known; thus, IBeaconMap could be a useful first tool to create location markings where beacons can then be placed in a crowdsourced fashion.

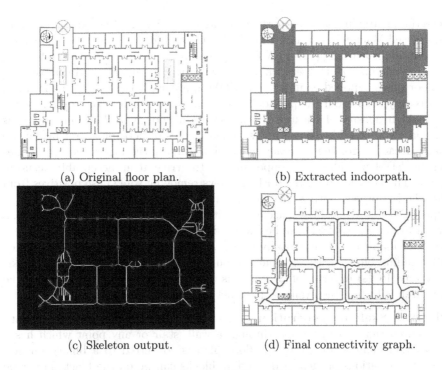

(a) Original floor plan.

(b) Extracted indoorpath.

(c) Skeleton output.

(d) Final connectivity graph.

Fig. 1. Outputs from execution of IBeaconMap on a floor plan.

2 Overall Approach

A floor plan image's analysis is performed in four phases:

Phase 1: Indoor path identification - The goal of phase 1 is to extract the indoor path and adjoining POIs from the floor plan. The walking path connects all the building blocks (doors, stairs etc.) to each other, so finding it first makes it easier to find POIs. Furthermore, having the indoor path helps find the shortest path from any office or point of interest to any other. Walking paths were found by identifying the largest contiguous block of pixels within the indoor space; this contiguous block of pixels has to be the walking path with all other areas within the floor plan having disconnections due to doors, walls, stairs etc. The largest contiguous area[1] is then labeled so that it can be marked off as the walking path. Figure 1b demonstrates the original floor plan with the gray area added manually for illustration purposes to show the indoor path in the original image.

Phase 2: Building block detection - After obtaining the foreground, the next step is to find all the required building blocks in a floor plan and get the specific coordinates of their locations. To achieve this goal, IBeaconMap provides three different approaches: feature detection and matching (FDM), feature

---

[1] Any area to be added or removed from consideration as a restricted area can be marked as such in floor plan pre-processing steps.

detection, matching, and Support Vector Machine (SVM) [4] as one approach to Supervised Machine Learning (FDM + SML), and feature detection and supervised machine learning (FD + SML). The reason to use three different techniques is to provide options to users when faced with varying quality and complexities of floor plans supplied as input. The FDM approach is the fastest of the three, and is very accurate if the provided floor plans are of high resolution and without a high density of features. If the provided floor plan does not meet this criteria, as is possible when using scanned images of floor plan drawings made many decades ago, the accuracy can suffer. Having the other two approaches besides FDM provides more opportunities to arrive at an acceptably accurate result. The addition of SML to FDM allows removing some false positives from the FDM approach output, helping improve accuracy. For cases where FDM is expected to have very high inaccuracies, it can be skipped altogether. Instead, a pre-processing step of FD can be executed to first collect all possible features in the floor plan (a computationally intensive step) followed by the SVM to classify building blocks with reasonable accuracy. After obtaining building blocks' locations (POIs) in terms of (x, y) pixels using one of the above techniques, the next step is to find the available path between them.

Phase 3: Skeleton generation - To connect one POI to another, a path is required that does not pass through a wall, stair or any point which has a color other than white (after the floor plan is converted to a binary image). Since the locations of identified building blocks can be on the black line or be blocked in some ways, we desire to map them onto specific pixels of the indoor path already found. To achieve this, the boundary pixels of the indoor path are removed without letting the indoor path break apart. Then by using euclidean distance, the closest points on the indoor path skeleton to the building blocks are located (Fig. 1c).[2]

Phase 4: Connectivity graph generation - After mapping building blocks[3] on the indoor path skeleton, we need to find the paths connecting any POIs which will lead to creating a connectivity graph on which path computations for navigation can be performed. To determine one-hop path distances between POI's, the IBeaconMap algorithm considers the indoor path skeleton to be the only non-zero pixels in the floor plan image. This by itself does not provide the one-hop paths between POIs, but the skeleton can be traversed in a breadth-first fashion beginning from a POI pixel by pixel to find various features. The connectivity graph arrived at for the example floor plan under consideration is shown in Fig. 1d.

---

[2] The function bwmorph used comes from the equivalent MATLAB function that was used to perform the skeleton generation operation.

[3] If there were errors in building block detection, post-processing steps can correct them; after such steps the connectivity graph generation phase is executed again.

3   Evaluation

Two metrics were chosen to show the effectiveness of IBeaconMap. The first metric is that of accuracy of IBeaconMap's output in terms of the number of beacon locations correctly identified versus those that were incorrect. The incorrect ones are further broken down into beacon locations that were missed and those that were redundantly added. A correct identification of a beacon location involves finding a POI and intersections. A visual comparison of beacon location marking outputs from a manual beacon planning process is also presented to provide a visual sense of accuracy of IBeaconMap. A manual approach is expected to be the most accurate as a skilled human can best determine where a beacon should be placed through an on-site survey. The question to us was "is there a way for us to significantly automate the beacon planning process while preserving as much of the accuracy of the manual process?". The second metric is the processing time for IBeaconMap to take a floor plan as input and produce its output. This metric is thus a measure of the reduction in time and labor in arriving at beacon locations and connectivity graph for indoor navigation. Any manual post-processing required to fix inaccuracies would need to be added onto this time for a fairer comparison with a completely manual process; however, the aim with IBeaconMap was to keep the manual corrections to be minimal.

3.1   Basic Results

The basic results are from the FDM scheme, which is typically the recommended scheme (due to its low processing time) unless the floor plans have low resolution or very high density of building blocks. The basic results presented here use the indoor walking path detection of building blocks only option as this option is expected to be more commonly used.

Figure 2 shows the beacon location marking results using FDM on two floor plans that were of high resolution; one from a shopping mall and the other a small research building with offices and laboratories. For each floor plan, beacon locations identified by a manual process (finding all POIs visually and marked) are shown along with those generated by IBeaconMap. It can be seen that the outputs are remarkably accurate. The major difference can be seen as the small mismatch in locations at each point of interest such as doors, stairs etc. which accounts for over half of an deviations seen and is easily correctable. This mismatch was because the manual process intentionally marks beacon locations on the side of a door or stairs while IBeaconMap marks them at the center leaving those who deploy the beacons to make the decision as to which side to place the beacon. In addition IBeaconMap marks additional locations at intersections which would be very useful during navigation. If two POIs are very close to each other, within a distance of c meters (we used $c = 2$ m in this paper), IBeaconMap just affixes one beacon location that can serve both points. Some POIs that perhaps would have been omitted as beacon locations during a manual process (due to knowledge that those POIs will not be useful), are marked by IBeaconMap in the shown image; such location can be removed manually.

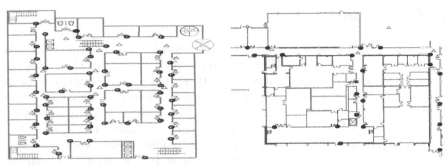

(a) Beacon location markings on the Shopping Mall floor plan.

(b) Beacon location markings on the Research Building floor plan.

Fig. 2. Beacon locations as output on two different floor plans provided as input. Blue solid circles indicate beacon locations marked by a manual process while red triangles show beacon locations from IBeaconMap. (Color figure online)

The computation time for both indoor floor plans considered in Fig. 2 were analyzed on an Intel i5-5200U CPU (2.20 GHz) with 8 GB RAM on a 64-bit Windows 10 OS. The Shopping Mall floor plan took 15.64 s in total to provide the final outcome while Research Building only took 22.07 s. The computation for the former is faster as it has fewer building blocks/features that need to be detected next to the indoor path. Thus, these typical floor plans can be analysed to not only provide beacon locations to use, but they also provide a connectivity graph for navigation in under 1 min. An entire building with multiple floors thus can be analyzed (and generation of connectivity information and beacon locations) in an automated fashion in the order of minutes to a few hours depending on its size. A manual process, that involved drawing walking paths, marking beacon locations, measuring and entering graph data structure connectivity information, weights, and directional orientations as experienced by the authors for the research building floor plan in [3], took over 1 h to arrive at similar outcomes; larger buildings with many more POIs would have taken many more hours if not days per floor. It is important to remember that there may be post-deployment alterations required for which an automated tool again can make changes easier.

3.2 Comparison of Building Block Detection Techniques

Evaluation results from four different floor plans are shown here. Many other floor plans were analyzed and tested to ensure that the results shown here are representative of a larger trend. The first two (Research Building and Shopping Mall) are those already seen in Figs. 2a and 2b. An additional two, called Large Area and Scanned Image respectively, were added. The Large Area floor plan is of a 75,000 sq. ft indoor facility with a large number of potential POIs, some of which are densely congregated as well. The fourth floor plan was the same as the first (Research Building), but a low-resolution (200 dpi) scanned image. These Large Area and Scanned Image floor plans were used to test the worst case for FDM and see how the SML based algorithms helped in such cases.

Table 1. Comparison of Building Block Detection Techniques - Indoor Path Only

		Correct	Incorrect		Processing Time (s)			Correct	Incorrect		Processing Time (s)
			Missed	Redundant					Missed	Redundant	
Research Building	FDM	30	1	3	22.07	Large Area	FDM	105	1	23	173.62
	FDM+SML	29	2	2	40.5		FDM+SML	98	8	16	282.83
	FD+SML	31	0	12	51.94		FD+SML	105	1	18	285.79
Shopping Mall	FDM	49	0	12	15.64	Low-Resolution Image	FDM	22	9	6	14.46
	FDM+SML	49	0	4	41.46		FDM+SML	21	10	3	26.1
	FD+SML	49	0	1	44.41		FD+SML	31	0	15	38.80

Table 2. Comparison of Building Block Detection Techniques - Full Floor Plan

		Correct	Incorrect		Processing Time			Correct	Incorrect		Processing Time
			Missed	Redundant					Missed	Redundant	
Research Building	FDM	63	4	16	11.30	Large Area	FDM	237	11	97	185.73
	FDM+SML	60	7	14	31.87		FDM+SML	233	15	59	351.38
	FD+SML	67	0	9	67.94		FD+SML	248	0	68	875.97
Shopping Mall	FDM	49	0	40	18.77	Low-Resolution Image	FDM	42	25	30	6.6
	FDM+SML	49	0	27	25.18		FDM+SML	42	25	20	21.3
	FD+SML	49	0	0	81.33		FD+SML	67	0	13	45.99

Indoor path detection only - The results for the detection along indoor walking path only is shown in Table 1. It can be seen that all three building block detection schemes perform with a high accuracy in terms of correctly identifying POIs with very few missed detections. The fast FDM scheme does very well for the smaller and simpler floor plans (Research Building and Small Area) and looks adequate for such cases. The FD + SML scheme helps improve detection accuracy significantly in the case of the low-resolution scanned image where FDM does not do well. The FD + SML scheme also seems to work better than FDM for floor plans with high density as in the Large Area floor plan. The FDM + SML scheme acts primarily as an "enhancer" to the FDM scheme, helping reduce some of the redundant locations identified, sometimes however at the cost of adding some more to missed detections. All schemes have some redundant identifications (false positives) which will need to be "scrubbed off" through a post-processing step as shown in Fig. 3. In terms of processing time, FDM was the fastest and FD + SML typically took the most time.

Full floor plan detection - The results for the entire floor plan building block detection is shown in Table 2. This being the worst case for building block detection due to the presence of multiple layers, it can be seen that the number of redundant beacon locations identified are larger; however, most POIs are still correctly identified. The FD + SML scheme again improves upon that of the FDM scheme when image resolution is poor or has a high density of POIs. The relative processing times of each scheme remains the same as in the indoor path only case, except that there is an overall increase due to the consideration of the entire floor area. As the floor plan area increases (as in the Larger Area floor plan), the FD + SML scheme processing time does increase faster than the other schemes due to its need to execute its three step process.

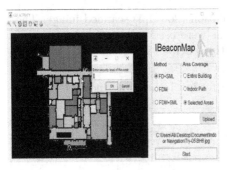
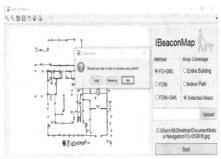

(a) Marking restricted areas and assigning restriction levels.

(b) Post-processing option to correct any errors on beacon markings on floor plan.

Fig. 3. Snapshots of IBeaconTool options.

4   Conclusion

This work presented a largely automated technique called IBeaconMap to prepare an indoor space for beacon-based wayfinding for the BVI and other sighted users. Such a technique solves the current challenge of creating indoor space representations in a time and labor-efficient manner. Evaluations show IBeacon-Map to be fast computationally and reasonably accurate (depending on input resolution and space characteristics) thus presenting itself as a scalable tool in preparing all indoor spaces for beacon-based wayfinding in the future.

Acknowledgement. This work has been supported by NSF award #1951864.

References

1. Ahmetovic, D., Gleason, C., Ruan, C., Kitani, K., Takagi, H., Asakawa, C.: Navcog: A navigational cognitive assistant for the blind. In: International Conference on Human Computer Interaction with Mobile Devices and Services. ACM (2016)
2. Alzantot, M., Youssef, M.: Crowdinside: Automatic construction of indoor floor-plans. In: Proceedings of the 20th International Conference on Advances in Geographic Information Systems, pp. 99–108 (2012)
3. Cheraghi, S.A., Namboodiri, V., Walker, L.: Guidebeacon: Beacon-based indoor wayfinding for the blind, visually impaired, and disoriented. In: IEEE Pervasive Communications (PerCom), pp. 121–130 (2017)
4. Cortes, C., Vapnik, V.: Support-vector networks. Mach. Learn. **20**(3), 273–297 (1995)
5. Gleason, C., Ahmetovic, D., Toxtli, C., Savage, S., Bigham, J.P., Asakawa, C.: Luzdeploy: A collective action system for installing navigation infrastructure for blind people. In: Web For All. ACM (2017)
6. Kim, J.E., Bessho, M., Kobayashi, S., Koshizuka, N., Sakamura, K.: Navigating visually impaired travelers in a large train station using smartphone and bluetooth low energy. In: Proceedings of the 31st Annual ACM Symposium on Applied Computing, SAC 2016. pp. 604–611. (2016)

7. Krūminaitė, M., Zlatanova, S.: Indoor space subdivision for indoor navigation. In: Proceedings of the Sixth ACM SIGSPATIAL International Workshop on Indoor Spatial Awareness. pp. 25–31. ISA '14 (2014)
8. Niua, L., Song, Y.: A schema for extraction of indoor pedestrian navigation grid network from floor plans. In: The International Archives of the Photogrammetry, Remote Sensing and Spatial Information Sciences. vol. XLI-B4. Prague, Czech Republic (July 2016)
9. Zhang, Y., Liu, J., Hoffmann, G., Quilling, M., Payne, K., Bose, P., Zimdars, A.: Real-time indoor mapping for mobile robots with limited sensing. In: The 7th IEEE International Conference on Mobile Ad-hoc and Sensor Systems (IEEE MASS 2010). pp. 636–641 (Nov 2010)

XR Accessibility – Learning from the Past, Addressing Real User Needs and the Technical Architecture for Inclusive Immersive Environments

XR Accessibility – Learning from the Past and Addressing Real User Needs for Inclusive Immersive Environments

Introduction to the Special Thematic Session

Joshue O Connor[1]([⊠]), Shadi Abou-Zahra[1],
Mario Covarrubias Rodriguez[2], and Beatrice Aruanno[2]

[1] W3C Web Accessibility Initiative (WAI), Cambridge, USA
joconnor@w3.org
[2] Department of Mechanical Engineering, Politecnico di Milano, Milan, Italy

Abstract. XR is an acronym used to refer to the spectrum of hardware, software applications, and techniques used for virtual reality or immersive environments, augmented or mixed reality and other related technologies. The special thematic session on 'XR Accessibility' explores current research and development as well as presenting diverse approaches to meeting real user needs in immersive environments. The contributed research papers range from using spatial sound for object location and interaction for blind users, to alternative symbolic representation of information, Augmented Reality (AR) used in rehabilitation for stroke patients and vocational skills training for students with intellectual disabilities. The session also explores what we can learn from previous research into immersive environments – looks at opportunities for future research and collectively explores how we can together iterate accessibility standards.

Keywords: Accessibility · Virtual reality · Augmented Reality · Immersive web · Rehabilitation · Serious games · Inclusive design · Usability

1 Introduction

The discipline of web accessibility can now be considered to some degree 'traditional'. There are established conventions that are used or considered part of best practice to support accessible design and development. Whether it is users needing to access simple structured text and information via webpages, consume rich media and its alternatives or interact with more complex dynamic web applications in a way that works with complex assistive technologies like screen readers - there is now greater understanding of what these diverse user needs are, as well as what is required to support those needs and how a designer or developer may make this content more accessible to people with disabilities.

There is certainly more work to do, via awareness raising and advocacy required from disability groups, standards bodies and so on but we can say a solid foundation

© Springer Nature Switzerland AG 2020
K. Miesenberger et al. (Eds.): ICCHP 2020, LNCS 12376, pp. 117–122, 2020.
https://doi.org/10.1007/978-3-030-58796-3_15

has been laid by the combined hard work and dedication of those actively involved and engaged in removing barriers for people with disabilities.

Simple practices like adding text alternatives, structuring page content using appropriate semantics, correctly labelling form inputs and controls have all become core skills and part of best practice for the accessibility aware designer and developer.

However, the technical landscape is forever in flux and while the needs of people with disabilities may arguably be considered a constant in relation to these changes the dynamic nature of technology demands consistent attention and is ever presenting new challenges that need to be addressed.

2   The Relevance of XR for Accessibility

XR presents many opportunities and challenges to the 'traditional' model and practices of accessible web design and development. In some cases it extends it, in that current best practices can be applied or extended in new or novel ways but in other instances may confound it.

This is largely because as distinct from traditional web content, in practice, very little is understood about the needs of people with disabilities within immersive environments.

To further compound this problem there are assumptions that can be made on the basis of previous knowledge and experience in 2D web that may not always be helpful in XR. XR presents a new advanced model, with inherent opportunities and challenges for the user and designer/developer alike. We need to both identify and distinguish areas where current practices of traditional design and development are useful, from where they need to be rethought.

It is then important to be able to iterate abstractions such as applicable principles to practical requirements in a way that meets real user needs, in order to both challenge the assumptions of a priori knowledge in this area, as well as ask new questions.

This process will help us build on the acquired collective knowledge that is reflected in world leading accessibility standards like WCAG [1].

2.1   Lessons Learned and Building on Previous Research

We have an advantage in meeting any new technical challenge in emerging technology if we take care to not ignore previous legacy research in new XR accessibility initiatives. As mentioned, it is arguable that the needs of people with disabilities do not change very much, only the technology changes.

Understanding this as a principle can lead to solid practical approaches to addressing new technical challenges. Not understanding this as a principle can lead to tokenism, or poorly implemented solutions that do not meet real user needs.

If we adopt this view, we can build on meeting these needs iteratively. There is current work going on in this space at the W3C Web Accessibility Initiative (WAI) for example on 'XR Accessibility User Requirements' that aims to inform the reader of practical user needs and potential requirements that should be addressed in XR environments. It outlines the complexity of understanding XR, introduces some accessibility challenges, accessibility multimodal support for a range of input and output devices, and the importance of customisation and personalisation.

It then outlines accessibility user needs for XR and their related requirements, followed by information about related work that may be helpful to understand the complex technical architecture and processes behind how XR environments are built and what may form the basis of a robust accessibility architecture for XR [2].

2.2   XR Research - the Benefits of Co-design and Usability Testing

XR is an exciting and challenging space to work in and many of the papers presented in this session demonstrate the benefits of co-design and including users in research and development work [5, 6].

Primarily it is important to gain a clear understanding of diverse user needs in this space. This can be done by conducing usability testing under an experienced user test facilitator or building platforms with active input from users who have diverse needs. These methods and interactions with real users will help give deeper designers and developers a rich insight that will inform better design and development decisions.

Once you have a clear understanding of diverse user needs, practical requirements can follow to meet these needs. Without that broad understanding it is hard to have a clear vision of what these requirements should be, as they may be developed with only a mere hazy idea of what they may be.

Good accessibility practices can also leverage the nexus between various cohort requirements – and expert experienced usability test facilitation can spot where there may be competing needs between the requirements of one group and another and not suggest user interface changes that benefit one cohort over another.

This will be a potentially greater challenge in XR accessibility and also illustrates the need for personalization, customization and so on that is fit for purpose to address conflicting cohort user needs. This is something that is not discussed much in the accessibility community but may become more prominent in addressing accessibility user needs in emerging technologies like XR.

Ultimately, we can learn much from these inclusive design processes, facilitate better social inclusion, build personalised abstractions of immersive environments that are interoperable and fit a person's particular ability and need, without contradicting any other set of needs.

The ability to personalise an XR user environment gives broad scope and potential to true bespoke XR that is inclusive. Abstractions like this can be built on strong semantics, interoperability with various device APIs and assistive technologies [3].

3   Uniting Multi-disciplinary Approaches

XR accessibility is being explored in these papers via multi-disciplinary approaches, which are critical for the successful amalgamating of UX, serious games, the creation of new semantic architectures, better accessibility standards, XR software development and an inclusive immersive web.

Many who are skilled in inclusive design come from diverse backgrounds and leverage these broad range of skills in unforeseen ways. Unique perspectives and the unification of collective creative thinking with inclusive design methodologies help to facilitate better technologies and imaginative solutions.

There is then potential for work on XR accessibility to promote the social model of disability - via the broader adoption of the outcomes of this research. Mainstreaming of innovation originally from the disability space may bring XR related assistive technologies to the masses via ubiquitous devices, such as what currently happens with the sort of sophisticated assistive technology already embedded in widely available iOS or Android devices or indeed any other future platforms that will be broadly commercially available.

Regarding valuable progression of the social model, the mainstreaming of this work is also a chance to reframe the technological discussion around the spectrum of different types of disabilities to better accept the user and their inherent ability as they are, and continue to explore the options around use of any given technology to better support that ability.

A further opportunity is to identify that ability and look at intelligently supporting functional need in the context of that user's ability.

4   Challenges in XR

There are challenges for assistive technology users in XR and ensuring ease of use and better interoperability within immersive environments. This can be as a result of complexity when using various input devices simultaneously, or the need for a high degree of precision coupled with timing accuracy and simultaneous action or by requiring tricky gestures to complete a task.

While some of these issues can be mitigated by the careful customisation of an assistive technology setup for the user, or remapping gestures to simpler patterns - there are other challenges around legacy support for older assistive technologies and how interactions can be mapped in XR to existing user setups.

There are other more generic issues with motion sickness and sensory conflict that are common with many users of XR but these may be even more severe for people with disabilities.

Other technical challenges include the need for an architecture that inherently supports accessibility. This may be modular and involve the combined development of advanced semantics, designed to describe specific parts of the immersive eco-system - relationships between objects, persons, places things their state and so on.

In immersive environments it is imperative that the user can understand – within the context of their mode of choice - what objects are, understand their purpose, as well as another qualities and properties. These include interaction affordance, size, form, shape, relational information and other inherent properties or attributes such as even an object's fragrance in order to create advanced multi modal systems.

4.1   Integrating XR Technologies for Young People with Cognitive Issues

There are other challenges in terms of integrating these technologies for young people with cognitive impairments to help them understand what parts of XR they can use and what can be helpful to them.

Co-design of interfaces and applications involving users with cognitive impairments could be very helpful so the affordances that are available to the user are commonly expressed and understood.

A challenge is that the perceived value of an XR system may not be immediate - the user may not understand the technology - or the features that will help them.

Getting this right reduces the potential for pressed a 'wrong fit technology' upon a user and ensuring technologies are not developed without clear understanding of user needs.

Gaining acceptance of these technologies is still an issue and we do not want to reproduce the issue of 'device abandonment' in the XR space [4].

5   Discussion and Conclusion

We have seen how accessibility features may lead to mainstream innovation for the majority population, voice commands for example are now widely used. We believe this will likely also be the case for XR; in fact, some papers here already seem to indicate the potential for such mainstream innovation.

All the papers presented and represented in this session indicate both valuable current work in an exciting emergent field, as well as laying the groundwork for future research.

They also reflect the importance of a multi-disciplinary approach that must gather all the various threads that make up emerging accessible technologies and architectures, whether in the browser or via other devices.

These papers reflect the existence of current vibrant inclusive design practices and the value inherent in clearly understanding diverse user needs and then ensuring related requirements both come from and meet those needs.

Finally, any future accessibility standards that are going to successfully address emergent technologies will need to be built upon substantial understanding of these diverse user needs. The research that we present in this special thematic session are examples of crucial contributions to this understanding.

References

1. W3C Web content accessibility guidelines 2.1. https://www.w3.org/TR/WCAG21/. Accessed 11 Jun 2020
2. W3C Web accessibility initiative (WAI) - XR accessibility user requirements. https://www.w3.org/TR/xaur/. Accessed 11 Jun 2020
3. WebXR standards and accessibility architecture https://www.w3.org/WAI/APA/wiki/WebXR_Standards_and_Accessibility_Architecture_Issues. Accessed 11 Jun 2020

4. Phillips, B., Zhao, H.: Predictors of Assistive Technology Abandonment. Assistive Technology: The Official Journal of RESNA 5(1), 36–45 (1993). https://www.researchgate.net/publication/13125783_Predictors_of_Assistive_Technology_Abandonment

5. AlMousa, M., Al-Khalifa, H., AlSobayel, H.: Move-IT: a virtual reality game for upper limb stroke rehabilitation patients. In: ICCHP 2020 17th International Conference on Computers Helping People with Special Needs Proceedings

6. Usability of virtual reality vocational skills training system for students with intellectual disabilities. In: Published in ICCHP 2020 17th International Conference on Computers Helping People with Special Needs Proceedings

7. Aruanno, B., Caruso, G., Rossini, M., Molteni, F., Carlos, M.E., Covarrubias, M.: Virtual and augmented reality platform for cognitive tele-rehabilitation based system. In: Published in ICCHP 2020 17th International Conference on Computers Helping People with Special Needs Proceedings

Usability of Virtual Reality Vocational Skills Training System for Students with Intellectual Disabilities

Ting-Fang Wu[1(✉)], Yung-ji Sher[1], Kai-Hsin Tai[2,3], and Jon-Chao Hong[2,3]

[1] Graduate Institute of Rehabilitation Counseling, National Taiwan Normal University, 162, Sec. 1 Heping East Road, Taipei, Taiwan
{tfwu, siaa}@ntnu.edu.tw
[2] Institute for Research Excellence in Learning Sciences, National Taiwan Normal University, Taipei, Taiwan
star99xin@gmail.com, tcdahong@gmail.com
[3] Department of Industrial Education, National Taiwan Normal University, Taipei, Taiwan

Abstract. Virtual reality has been applied to education widely since technology developed quickly. In order to apply the "Virtual Reality Vocational Skills Training System" to vocational high school students with intellectual disabilities, this study simplify the operation of the original system and develop an easy-to-use version to meet the learning needs of students with intellectual disabilities. Therefore, the purpose of this study is to test the usability of the easy-to-use version through the questionnaire, and to compare the operating efficiency between the easy-to-use version and the original one. Eight students with intellectual disabilities participated in the study. The results indicated that most students expressed that the easy-to-use version had good usability, and reduced the operation time and the number of wrong actions, as well as enhanced the accuracy. Overall, this designed "Virtual Reality Vocational Skills Training System" can be applied to the training of vocational skills for students with intellectual disabilities.

Keywords: Virtual reality · Students with intellectual disabilities · Vocational skill training · Usability

1 Introduction

Virtual reality (VR) is a scene generated by a computer that simulates the real environment, and has been gradually applied in education. VR can simulate the real life situation and may enhance learning and transfer skills to everyday circumstances [1]. Tam et al. used a 2-D VR system to train persons with intellectual disabilities (ID) to shop. The result indicated that the VR program appears effective in training persons with ID in learning a community living skill [1]. Tsang and Man investigated the efficacy and effectiveness of VR as a cognitive intervention for enhancing vocational outcome. The results indicated that the participants in the VR-based vocational training group performed better in cognitive function compared with the therapist-administered group and a conventional

© Springer Nature Switzerland AG 2020
K. Miesenberger et al. (Eds.): ICCHP 2020, LNCS 12376, pp. 123–129, 2020.
https://doi.org/10.1007/978-3-030-58796-3_16

group. Both the VR-based vocational training and therapist-administered groups showed the better work performance after training [2]. Smith et al. used the virtual reality system to train the interview skills of patients with post-traumatic stress syndrome and got the positive results [3]. VR provides the opportunities for learners to repeat as many times as they need, and to adjust their learning speeds based on their abilities. Therefore, VR seems to be suitable for training persons with ID [1]. In addition, persons with disabilities do not need to consider the consequences of errors even if they make mistakes in performing tasks in a VR environment. Persons with disabilities can learn in a safe and motivating environment [1]. Da Cunha, Neiva, and da Silva reviewed the literature in applying VR for training persons with cognitive impairments, and found that 61% of the studies indicating VR is effective for training persons with autism, intellectual disabilities, and other cognitive disorders [4]. Among those reviewed articles, only 2 out of 28 studies focused on the population of persons with ID. In the literature, VR has a positive effect towards learning skills for persons with disabilities. However, whether it is applicable to students with ID still needs more empirical data to support. We have already developed the Virtual Reality Vocational Skill Training (VRVST) System, which was designed for training individuals to learn new vocational skills via VR system. In order to provide training for students with ID, we developed an easy-to-use version for fulfilling this purpose. Usually a new system is developed, the first step is to perform the usability test of this system. Therefore, the purpose of this study is to test the usability of the easy-to-use version of the VRVST System.

Usability usually refers to the elegance and clarity of computer design or website human-machine interface [5]. Usability test is a necessary process in human-machine interface design. Designers can enhance usability through usability testing and improving the current interface. In this study, a questionnaire survey, where users fill out the subjective feeling after operating the easy-to-use version of VR system, was conducted as a usability test [6]. In addition, in order to understand whether students with intellectual disabilities will improve their performance using the easy-to-use version of VR system, the operational performance of the original version and the easy-to-use version were compared.

2   Method

2.1   Participants

Eight students with ID participated in this study with their parental consents. They were recruited from vocational high schools in Metropolitan Taipei area. Students with ID were diagnosed and identified by the local education authority based on the following criteria: (a) significant limitations in intellectual functions (reasoning, learning, and problem solving), (b) significant limitations in adaptive behaviors, which includes a range of everyday social and practical skills, and (c) this disability originates before the age of 18 [7]. All the participants met the above criteria. The following table (Table 1) shows the individual scores of 8 students in Wechsler Intelligence Scale for Children-IV. The average scores of the participants in the Full Scale Intellectual Quotient (IQ) is 53; the average scores of the participants in Verbal Comprehension Composite, Perceptual Reasoning Composite, Working Memory Composite, and Processing Speed Composite are 60.9, 54.8, 60.4, and 56.1 separately.

Table 1. Participants' Scores of Wechsler Intelligence Scale for Children-IV

	Full Scale IQ	Verbal comprehension	Perceptual reasoning	Working memory	Processing speed
Subject 1	43	50	45	57	50
Subject 2	46	55	45	60	50
Subject 3	68	74	72	75	62
Subject 4	47	56	50	54	50
Subject 5	53	71	48	60	68
Subject 6	60	58	79	54	50
Subject 7	54	58	45	69	62
Subject 8	53	65	54	54	57
Average	53.0	60.9	54.8	60.4	56.1

2.2   Tools

Virtual Reality Vocational Skills Training System (VRVST System)

The VRVST System was developed by the research team of Professor Jon-Chao Hong at National Taiwan Normal University, in Taipei, Taiwan. It was designed to train students to learn a new vocational skill. For the module of learning to be a kitchen assistant, the VRVST System consists of 8 common kitchen preparation tasks, such as: cutting cucumber, cutting cabbage, and peeling radish. Through the comprehensive work analysis, each kitchen preparation task is analyzed into 8 to 18 steps based on the complexity of the task, and the students can learn the task step by step by following the cues embedded in the VRVST System. There are several different kinds of cues in this system, for example, the VRVST system provides the order of cutting cucumber steps and tips on where to cut (Fig. 1a). In addition, there are blue flashes to indicate where items should be placed (Fig. 1b).

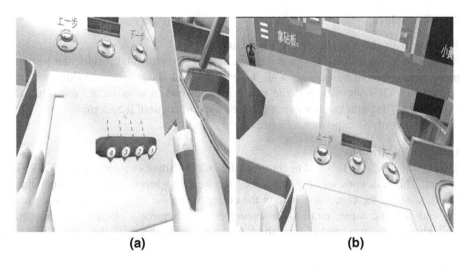

(a)   **(b)**

Fig. 1.   (a) Step by step tips for cutting cucumber were provided (b) Blue flash tips for reminding where the chopping board should be placed (Color figure online).

Easy-to-Use Version of VRVST System

The VRVST System was originally intended to design for vocational high school students to learn vocational skills. In order to make this original system applicable to students with ID, this study simplified the operation of the original VRVST system and developed an easy-to-use version to meet the learning needs of students with ID. There were two differences between the original and easy-to-use versions: (a) Added voice prompts: Since the students with ID usually have poor literacy, voice prompts may provide more direct cues for persons with ID, and (b) Simplified the control buttons: Due to the poor dexterity of the students with ID, they often fail to manipulate the selection action in the original system which require the coordination of the thumb and the index. Therefore, in the easy-to-use version, the operator only needs to put the handle to the target and press the key to select.

VR Hardware Equipment

The experimental hardware equipment used in this study included Acer Windows Mix Reality headset (AH101 model), which has a built-in gyroscope, acceleration sensor, magnetometer (compass) and proximity sensor, as well as Acer AR/VR remote controller.

System Usability Scale

The questionnaire, System Usability Scale (SUS), was used to test the usability of the easy-to-use version of VRVST System. It was developed by Brooke, and is a widely used standardized questionnaire in testing the perceived usability of computer programs, systems and website pages [8]. The SUS is a Likert's five-point scale, which the higher the score, the better the user perceive the usability of the system is. The products with SUS scores above 70 indicate the acceptable usability, and if the products' SUS scores less than 70 means should be considered candidates for increased scrutiny and continued improvement, and be marginal at best. Products with scores less than 50 should be considered for significant concern and judged to be unacceptable [5, 9].

2.3 Procedure

Familiar with the VR Hardware Equipment

In order to avoid unfamiliar operation affecting the experimental results, the participants were asked to be familiar with the experimental equipment, including how to operate the VR controller, and the entire experimental process before entering the experiment. The participants will not enter the experiment until they were familiar with the operation of the experimental equipment.

Conduct Experiment

The participants were required to complete the task of cutting cucumber in the VRVST system. This task consists of 8 steps; they are wearing gloves, picking the chopping board, washing the cucumber, putting the cucumber on the cutting board, cutting out the ends of cucumber, cutting the cucumber into 5 pieces, placing the chopped cucumbers in the tray, and placing the tray in the specified area.

In order to eliminate the effect of repeat practice on score improvement, the counterbalance order of operating two versions of the VRVST system was used. For example, if the first student operated the original version first and followed by the easy-to-use version, then the second student will operate the easy-to-use first and followed by the original version. Four of the eight students used the easy-to-use version first, and the other four used the original version first.

Fill in the SUS Questionnaire
After completing the experiment, the students were asked to fill in the SUS questionnaire to report their perceived usability about the VRVST system. If the student cannot read the text due to poor literacy, the researcher will read the question and the student answered the question orally.

2.4   Measurement Parameters and Data Analysis

The students' operational efficacy in the original version and in the easy-to-use version were compared to indicate which version has better operating efficiency. Three parameters, time spent, accuracy, and movement errors, in completing the task of cutting cucumber were used as indicators of operational efficacy. All data was calculated and recorded by the VRVST system automatically. The shorter the time spent, the higher the accuracy, and the fewer movement errors, indicate the better the operating efficiency. The followings are the definitions of those parameters.

- Time spent: Time required to complete all steps in the task
- Accuracy: Correct steps divided by total steps
- Movement errors: The number of errors in various actions, including not following the instruction line when cutting vegetables, gesture errors of assisting hand when cutting vegetables, the size of the cut vegetables is not even, and so on.

In addition, the Wilcoxon related sample test in the SPSS 23 was used to analyze the differences in the operating performance of students between the original version and the easy-to-use version.

3   Results

3.1   Students' Operational Efficiency in Original and the Easy-to-Use Versions

The results indicated that students performed better in the easy-to-use version. The total time spent in completing the task was significantly less, the accuracy was significantly higher, and the number of movement errors was significantly lower in the easy-to-use version when compared to those in the original version (Table 2).

Table 2. Students' operational efficiency in original and the easy-to-use versions.

	Original	Easy-to-use	P
Time spent (sec)	471.0(±154.9)	184.8(±77.2)	<0.001**
Accuracy (%)	75.4(±1.0)	82.8(±6.5)	.012*
Movement errors	20.0(±8.8)	8.0(±7.7)	.016*

$*p < .05, **p < .01$

3.2 Students' Perceived Usability About the VRVST System

The SUS scores filled out by the participants are presented in Table 3. The students' SUS scores ranged from 47.5 to 90, showing considerable variation. If divide those scores into groups, we found that five out of eight have their SUS scores over 70, which indicating they perceive the VRVST System having good usability. Two participants have their SUS scores between 50 and 70 indicating the marginal usability. Only one student's SUS score is less than 50, which means the system is considered unacceptable usability. However, according to the qualitative statements of students after using the VRVST System, students expressed that this system was easy to operate, and the voice prompts in easy-to-use version was helpful for them performing the tasks more intuitively, without spending time to look at the text prompts.

Table 3. The SUS Scores of the 8 students

Student #	1	2	3	4	5	6	7	8
SUS score	90	75	75	47.5	52.5	75	67.5	70

4   Discussion and Conclusion

This study explored the usability of the VRVST System for students with ID from two aspects: students' subjective feelings and objective operational performance. The results showed that most students' SUS scores were high, which indicating the acceptance of this system. Among the 8 students, 5 students had SUS scores above 70, supporting a considered acceptable system; 2 students reported scores between 50–70 showing a "marginal" system; only one student (Students number 4) scored less than 50, which means the system is considered unacceptable.

The reason why the students number 4 scored lower in the SUS may due to some items have relatively low scores. For example, his/her score of the item "I will often use this VR game" was relatively low than others. Further inquire about the reason for the low score of this question, this student answered that since the VR system is not widely available, he would not use it frequently. In addition, some students scored low in another item "I need help from others when playing this VR game". Actually, all the participants were able to operate the VR system independently, they only need some assistance in setting up the system before entering the game. Meanwhile, students with ID also provided qualitative feedback about the system. They all responded positively to this system, such as: easy to operate, the well-integrated overall function of the system, and easy to learn quickly in using this system. The clarity of the questionnaire presentation may need to be defined more clearly for further study.

From the objective view, the students performed significantly better in the easy-to-use version than in the original one. According to the qualitative statements, the participants expressed that the voice prompts in the easy-to-use version provides more intuitive cues than text prompts. That might be the reason for their better performance in the easy-to-use version. Whether objective data or subjective expression demonstrated that the easy-to-use version VR system seems to be suitable for students with ID to learn a new daily task. In the future, we will continue to use this system to collect more empirical data to understand the learning curve or leaning path of students with ID. In addition, factors affecting learning in the VR environment for students with ID will also be investigated.

Acknowledgment. The authors would like to thank the Ministry of Science and Technology of the Republic of China for financially supporting this research under Grant MOST 108-2511-H-003-045.

References

1. Tam, S.F., Man, D.W.K., Chan, Y.P., Sze, P.C., Wong, C.M.: Evaluation of a computer-assisted, 2-D virtual reality system for training people with intellectual disabilities on how to shop. Rehabil. Psychol. **50**(3), 285 (2005)
2. Tsang, M.M., Man, D.W.: A virtual reality-based vocational training system (VRVTS) for people with schizophrenia in vocational rehabilitation. Schizophr. Res. **144**(1–3), 51–62 (2013)
3. Smith, M.J., et al.: Virtual reality job interview training for veterans with posttraumatic stress disorder. J. Vocat. Rehabil. **42**(3), 271–279 (2015)
4. da Cunha, R.D., Neiva, F.W., da Silva, R.L.D.S.: Virtual reality as a support tool for the treatment of people with intellectual and multiple disabilities: a systematic literature review. Revista de Informática Teórica e Aplicada **25**(1), 67–81 (2018)
5. Bangor, A., Kortum, P., Miller, J.: Determining what individual SUS scores mean: Adding an adjective rating scale. J. Usabil. Stud. **4**(3), 114–123 (2009)
6. Ghasemifard, N., Shamsi, M., Kenar, A.R.R., Ahmadi, V.: A new view at usability test methods of interfaces for human computer interaction. Global. J. Comput. Sci. Technol. **15**(1) (2015). [Special issue]. https://computerresearch.org/index.php/computer/article/view/1126
7. Schalock, R.L., et al.: Intellectual disability: definition, classification, and system of supports. American Association on Intellectual and Developmental Disabilities, 11th edn. Washington, DC (2010)
8. Brooke, J.: SUS: a quick and dirty usability scale. In: Jordan, P.W., Thomas, B., Weerdmeester, B.A., McClelland, I.L., (Eds.) Usability Evaluation in Industry, pp. 189–194, Taylor and Francis, London (1996)
9. Bangor, A., Kortum, P., Miller, J.A.: The System Usability Scale (SUS): an empirical evaluation. Int. J. Hum-Comput. Int. **24**(6), 574–594 (2008)

Virtual and Augmented Reality Platform for Cognitive Tele-Rehabilitation Based System

Beatrice Aruanno[1], Giandomenico Caruso[1], Mauro Rossini[2], Franco Molteni[2],
Milton Carlos Elias Espinoza[3], and Mario Covarrubias[1(✉)]

[1] Dipartimento di Meccanica, Politecnico di Milano, Milan, Italy
`mario.covarrubias@polimi.it`
[2] Rehabilitation Centre, Valduce Hospital, Villa Beretta, Costa Masnaga, Italy
[3] ITESM, Santa Fe, Mexico

Abstract. Virtual and Augmented Reality systems have been increasingly studied, becoming an important complement to traditional therapy as they can provide high-intensity, repetitive and interactive treatments. Several systems have been developed in research projects and some of these have become products mainly for being used at hospitals and care centers. After the initial cognitive rehabilitation performed at rehabilitation centers, patients are obliged to go to the centers, with many consequences, as costs, loss of time, discomfort and demotivation. However, it has been demonstrated that patients recovering at home heal faster because surrounded by the love of their relatives and with the community support.

Keywords: VR/AR · Cognitive rehabilitation · Gaming ·
LeapMotion · Oculus rift

1 Introduction

The ambition of the Virtual and Augmented Reality Platform based on Tele-Rehabilitation is to combine assistance with appropriate feedback to close the loop in cognitive learning strategy for the home. The tele-rehabilitation system is based on the use of low cost sensors, connected with a gaming module for cognitive-motor rehabilitation, and integrated with an infrastructure connecting the patient at home with therapists at hospitals who monitor the rehabilitation exercises. Specifically, the ambition of the Platform is to strengthen and extend rehabilitation services, including community-based rehabilitation, and assistive technology. The platform addresses people with Cognitive Disability. Cognitive Disability (CD) is a broad concept encompassing intellectual or cognitive deficits derived from either specific neurodevelopmental disorders (e.g., Autism) or problems emerging later in life such as brain injuries or neurodegenerative diseases like dementia. Most individuals with CD often experience co-occurring difficulties

© Springer Nature Switzerland AG 2020
K. Miesenberger et al. (Eds.): ICCHP 2020, LNCS 12376, pp. 130–137, 2020.
https://doi.org/10.1007/978-3-030-58796-3_17

in different areas such as language and speech, memory, learning, social behavior and motor skills [4]. Designed in cooperation with CD specialists (psychologists and therapists) of three Rehabilitation Center in the north of Italy, the VR/AR platform aims to promote the understanding and execution of some basic tasks that are typical of domestic routines, helping people with CD to improve their autonomy in everyday life, or at least to make them less dependent on caregivers.

2 The VR/AR Platform

The VR/AR platform allows us to implement a set of exercises for cognitive rehabilitation. The interaction with virtual objects is performed through hand and body movements and gestures. The most innovative aspect of the platform is that the interaction is performed by using the Oculus rift, the LeapMotion, the Kinect sensors and the HoloLens in a unique platform.

2.1 Architecture

The VR/AR platform is used by the patients, by the neurologist in charge of the patient and by other clinical specialists (e.g., by the neuropsychologists and physiotherapists). Each of the users has proper functions: the patient can see the daily exercises therapy, the neurologist can assign, modify or evaluate the therapeutic plans, the medical staff can check how the rehabilitation is going. The interaction of the different users and the logical architecture of the platform are showed in Fig. 1.

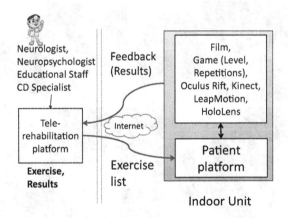

Fig. 1. VR and tele-rehabilitation architecture.

The Indoor Unity represents the patient's interaction with the platform.

The main software tools we used in the implementation of the VR/AR platform are Unity and Visual Studio. The scripts are coded in C-Sharp, which is more supported than other programming languages by both Microsoft and Unity documentation. The application source consists of Unity assets and C-Sharp scripts. Unity assets are managed by the Unity engine and include the 3D models used for the different scenes and holograms, the UI elements, and the Mixed Reality Toolkit. The Mixed Reality Toolkit is a collection of components provided by Microsoft, which accelerates the development of applications for Microsoft HoloLens and other Windows Mixed Reality headsets. For instance, the input module contains scripts that interpret inputs such as gaze, gesture, and voice, and the spatial mapping module is used to map the real world into the MR environment.

3   Gesture Interaction

We have developed a visualization and interaction system integrated with the gaming module that visually renders the virtual environment for rehabilitation and also the user's virtual hands and body in real-time. This functionality requires tracking the user's hands and body in the physical space. In order to provide a realistic immersiveness, the tracking and the representation of the user's hands and body in the virtual environment should be accurate and timely. Figure 2 shows a training session. In fact, some studies have shown that if the users are able to see the virtual rendering of their hands and legs and their movements relative to the movements of other objects there is a much better chance that they will feel that the virtual hands embodies their intentions and actions [3].

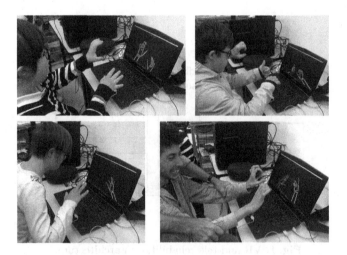

Fig. 2. Gesture interaction training.

The gesture interaction is performed through the LeapMotion and Kinect Sensors in the cognitive exercise who are supported by the Oculus Rift VR device.

While for the HoloLens the hand gestures (air-tap) enable the interaction with holograms or other digital contents. Instantaneous air-tap selects and activates the gazed interactive element. Prolonged air-tap enables drag and drop.

4 VR/AR Rehabilitation Exercises

The exercise database consists of three different categories which are connected through a film database and a picture database. A film is used in order to catch the attention of the user. One of the strengths of the platform is its customizability and modularity. Customizability is particularly important in applications for people with CD, who have enormously different cognitive and motor skills and evolving therapeutic or educational needs. In each VR/AR activity it is possible to choose the "configuration" that is most suitable for the specific user, for instance the level of difficulty, the number and the kind of objects involved in the task, the film who is connected to the cognitive exercise. A high modularity also facilitates design extensions and technical improvements, like the addition of new levels and new objects, which can be performed with a little implementation effort.

– **Category 2:** Exercise $\Longrightarrow$ Film: This category of exercises starts directly with the rehabilitation exercise and the video is seen by the patient only if the exercise has been completed. The film is used as an award.

4.1 Database Exercise

A set of 10 cognitive exercise have been developed as can be seen from Fig. 3.

The exercises have been designed in order to offer a more effective and customized training for cognitive deficiencies, allowing for an easy customization and definition of exercises; offering the possibility of performing training programs in autonomy, without the need of the continuous presence of caregiver/parents, but under their continuous monitoring, and which can be performed quietly at home; allowing CD specialist to use a complete and rich set of data recorded from the exercises executed by the users to improve knowledge on rehabilitation and therapies. There already exist, some projects that explore therapeutic approaches based on social stories [5] and storytelling [6], mostly targeting young people with Autism [2,8]. The benefits of MR in the CD arena are much less explored. To our knowledge, the only HoloLens application that addresses people with Cognitive Disability is the one reported in [1], which addresses people with Alzheimer's Disease. The application consists of a set of tasks that aims to slow down mental decline by strengthening short-term memory and spatial memory (which are usually damaged by Alzheimer's Disease).

5 Users Study

In our research, a user study has been carried out in order to test the VR/AR platform initially with healthy people. In particular, we were interested in

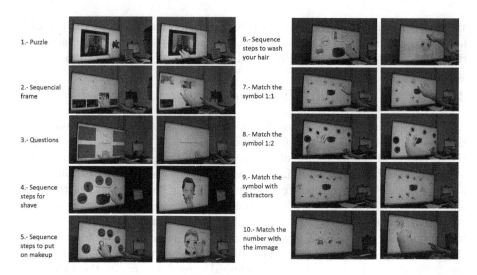

1.- Puzzle

2.- Sequencial frame

3.- Questions

4.- Sequence steps for shave

5.- Sequence steps to put on makeup

6.- Sequence steps to wash your hair

7.- Match the symbol 1:1

8.- Match the symbol 1:2

9.- Match the symbol with distractors

10.- Match the number with the immage

Fig. 3. Exercise database

checking if any issues may arise during the use of the Virtual Reality application, in particular any issues related to gesture interactions.

5.1 User Study with Healthy Subjects

10 healthy users, 6 female and 4 male, aged between 18 and 23 participated to the preliminary tests. Before the test, the participants were asked to fill in a pre-test questionnaire with their data, confidence to use games and also hand gestural technologies. In addition, we asked the participants to compile a symptoms check-list related to the sense of sight.

Participants were instructed about the task, and they were allowed to use the hand gestural approach until they felt sufficiently confident. The task consisted in using the 'Cancel and go' exercise.

The test lasted approximately 8 min. Figure 4-a shows the user while starts with the exercise with the left hand. Figure 4-b shows the instant in which the user is cancelling the image of the rehabilitation exercise.

The questionnaire was organized in a 6 points Likert-scale, from 1 (which is the most negative value) to 6 (which is the most positive value).

5.2 Analysis of the Results

The charts on Fig. 5 show the results of the questionnaires.

The VR application achieved a high evaluation rate relatively to the aspects concerning the system in general, a quite positive evaluation of the easiness in using it as a whole (chart **a** in Fig. 5).

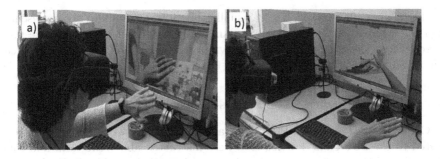

Fig. 4. 'Cancel and go exercise'

The *knowledge acquisition* section of the test intended to go more in details in understanding and evaluating the system from the user's perspective. Chart **b** in Fig. 5 shows the results. Overall, the collected data show a positive evaluation. Only one user assigned a very low rate for what concerned the easiness of using the system the first time. But the same user was convinced that the following time it would have been easier and more natural to use it.

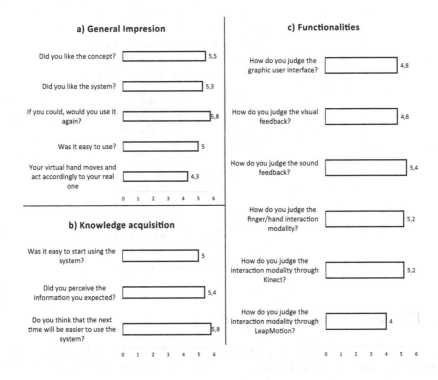

Fig. 5. Results of tests performed by the healthy subjects.

These anomalies however, were usually short-termed and did not represent a significant impact in the user's performance, and in general in the overall results. Nevertheless, these anomalies were known to happen [7] and therefore expected. This preliminary study was designed to cope with these issues.

5.3   User Study with CD Subjects

15 CD subjects from the ASPOC association [9] aged between 19 and 22 participated to the SUS tests. Participants were instructed about the task, and they were allowed to use the hand gestural approach until they felt sufficiently confident. Also in this case, the task consisted in using the '**Cancel and go**' exercise. The same exercise than in the user study with healthy subjects. The test lasted approximately 10 min. Figure 6 shows the SUS results.

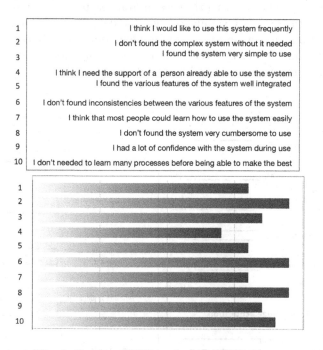

Fig. 6. Results of SUS performed by CD users.

6   Discussion and Conclusion

The paper describes a VR/AR platform based on hand and body gesture interaction. We have performed some tests in order to prove our approach. The preliminary test results reported in the paper are positive for what concerns the quality of the hand and body gesture interaction while executing the cognitive exercise. On this basis, we conclude that the gestural interaction system provides users with an effective and natural method to interact with the rehabilitation exercises. The study results, although preliminary, highlight a high degree of likeability. Still, for people with severe forms of CD. In the shorter term, we will add new cognitive exercise and more complexity levels; they will be inspired by stories, films and cartoons currently used during regular therapeutic activities, and partially designed by people with CD through a co-design process. We will also include more options for the current activities and will implement new types of tasks, already designed with the therapists in our team.

References

1. Aruanno, B., Garzotto, F., Rodriguez, M.C.: HoloLens-based mixed reality experiences for subjects with alzheimer's disease. In: Proceedings of the 12th Biannual Conference on Italian SIGCHI Chapter (CHItaly 2017), Article 15, 9 p. (2017)
2. Bozgeyikli, L., Raij, A., Katkoori, S., Alqasemi, R.: A survey on virtual reality for individuals with autism spectrum disorder: design considerations. IEEE Trans. Learn. Technol. **11**, 133–151 (2018)
3. Cameron, C., et al.: Hand tracking and visualization in a virtual reality simulation, pp. 127–132, April 2011
4. American Psychiatric Association Diagnostic: Statistical manual of mental disorders. American psychiatric pub. (2013)
5. Gelsomini, M., Garzotto, F., Matarazzo, V., Messina, N., Occhiuto, D.: Creating social stories as wearable hyper-immersive virtual reality experiences for children with neurodevelopmental disorders. In: Proceedings of the 2017 Conference on Interaction Design and Children (IDC 2017), pp. 431–437 (2017)
6. Gelsomini, M., Garzotto, F., Montesano, D., Occhiuto, D.: Wildcard: a wearable virtual reality storytelling tool for children with intellectual developmental disability. In: 38th Annual International Conference of the IEEE Engineering in Medicine and Biology Society (EMBC) Orlando, FL, pp. 5188–5191 (2016)
7. Guna, J., Jakus, G., Pogacnik, M., Tomazic, S., Sodnik, J.: An analisis of the precision and reliability of the leap motion sensor and its suitability for static and diynamic tracking. Sensors **14**, 3702–3720 (2014)
8. Josman, N., Ben-Chaim, H.M., Friedrich, S., Weiss, P.L.: Effectiveness of virtual reality for teaching street-crossing skills to children and adolescents with autism. Int. J. Disabil. Hum. Dev. 49–56 (2011)
9. Aspoc Onlus (2020). http://www.aspoc.it//. Accessed 04 Apr 2020

An Immersive Virtual Reality Exergame for People with Parkinson's Disease

Weiqin Chen$^{(\boxtimes)}$, Martin Bang, Daria Krivonos, Hanna Schimek, and Arnau Naval

Oslo Metropolitan University (OsloMet),
POB 4 St. Olavs plass, 0130 Oslo, Norway
Weiqin.Chen@oslomet.no

Abstract. Parkinson's disease is a neurodegenerative disorder that affects primarily motor system. Physical exercise is considered important for people with Parkinson's disease (PD) to slow down disease progression and maintain abilities and quality of life. However, people with PD often experience barriers to exercises that causes low-level adherence to exercise plans and programs. Virtual Reality (VR) is an innovative and promising technology for motor and cognitive rehabilitation. Immersive VR exergames have potential advantages by allowing for individualized skill practice in a motivating interactive environment without distractions from outside events. This paper presents an immersive virtual reality (VR) exergame aiming at motor training on fingers and hand-and-eye coordination. The results from the usability study indicate that immersive VR exergames have potential to provide motivating and engaging physical exercise for people with PD. Through this research, we hope to contribute to evidence-based design principles for task-specific immersive VR exergames for patients with Parkinson's Disease.

Keywords: Immersive virtual reality · Exergame · Parkinson's disease

1 Introduction

Parkinson's disease (PD) is a neurodegenerative disorder affecting one in every 100 people over the age of 60 [1]. Apart from motor symptoms such as tremor and freezing of gait, cognitive symptoms in memory and executive function also cause challenges in daily living. PD affects primarily motor systems and exercises are found beneficial for people with PD in slowing down the decline and maintaining physical and cognitive abilities and quality of life [2]. However, people with PD often experience barriers to exercises which causes low level of adherence to exercise plans and programs [3]. Motivation is a critical factor for exercise adherence, which in turn is associated with important health benefits and improved quality of life [4]. Exergames which provide enjoyable exercise experiences and further increase the intrinsic motivation to adhere to the exercise programs are therefore becoming an increasingly popular alternative rehabilitation method for people with PD [5, 6].

Virtual Reality is an innovative and promising technology for motor and cognitive rehabilitation. A recent meta-analysis and systematic literature review conducted by

© The Author(s) 2020
K. Miesenberger et al. (Eds.): ICCHP 2020, LNCS 12376, pp. 138–145, 2020.
https://doi.org/10.1007/978-3-030-58796-3_18

Triegaardt et al. [7] on VR in rehabilitation of 1031 patients with PD found that VR training improved a number of outcomes in patients with PD including motor functioning, balance and coordination, cognitive function and quality of life. VR exergames have potential advantages by allowing for individualized skill practice in a motivating and engaging interactive environment. However, current VR exergames are mostly based on commercial game consoles such as Nintendo Wii, Sony PlayStation Eye and Microsoft's Kinect. These games are often either too difficult for patients with PD or the games progress too quickly, failing to provide impairment-focused training or specifically address patients' needs [8]. More specifically, these games are non-immersive VR, where the real physical world is enhanced by computer-generated digital information and users are not fully immersed in the virtual environment, therefore their experience can be interrupted. Immersive Virtual reality exergames, on the other hand, fully immerse users in the game, often with the help of a head mounted display (HMD) which allows users to focus entirely on the game without distractions from outside events.

This research aims to explore the potentials of fully immersive Virtual Reality exergames for people with PD. We have developed a simple VR exergame focusing on motor training on fingers and hand-and-eye coordination based on HTC vive and conducted user testing with patients with PD in a rehabilitation center to study the usability of the game.

2 Related Work

Virtual Reality has been recognized as a promising tool for rehabilitation purposes by providing just-in-time feedback, allowing for repetitive practice, stimulating both cognitive and motor abilities simultaneously. Among others VR exergames have been used for rehabilitation of patients with cardiovascular disease [9] patients with spinal cord injury [10], and stroke patients [11].

For people living with PD, VR has mainly been used for gait and balance training [12, 13]. According to the recent systematic literature review [14] which examined eight trials with Virtual Reality therapy involving a total of 263 participants with PD, benefits of VR therapy include increased step and stride length and improvement in gait and balance. All the eight trials used non-immersive VR technology such Nintendo Wii.

In recent years with the increasing offers and decreasing price of immersive VR technology on the market, a few more studies have used immersive VR technology such as HTC vive and Oculus Rift for gait and balance training for people with PD [15, 16].

It is also suggested that Virtual Reality exergames hold some drawbacks for people with PD, such as cognitive overload and cyber sickness [5], and custom-made VR applications developed to offer disease-specific exercise may be able to overcome the drawbacks and prove to be more beneficial than commercial VR systems. However, there are very few custom-made VR immersive VR applications and most of the VR exergames are non-immersive and focus on training gait and balance. Even fewer VR applications are developed for training other aspects of motor systems than gait and balance for people with PD.

3 Design and Development

The prototype design is based on an earlier project which focused on developing a mobile app for people with PD to carry on physical exercises using a human-centered design approach [17] where focus group interviews were conducted in a rehabilitation center with 20 people with PD and 7 health care workers. The design and implementation have taken an iterative process.

Related VR exergames and their design were studied in order to learn from their experiences. Design principles and considerations related to exergames and VR have been taken into considerations. For example, Burke et al. [18] identified two design principles for rehabilitation games: *meaningful play* where feedback and scoring mechanism are helpful for maintaining engagement, and *challenge* where different levels of difficulty are (dynamically) offered to target to the diversity of knowledge, skills, and needs of patients. Shaw et al. [19] discussed fiver major challenges in virtual reality exergame design: to overcome possible cyber sickness; to provide accurate motion control; to select appropriate view for the player; to address health and safety risks during high intensity exercises; and to address the issue of feedback latency.

People with PD often exhibit reduced manual dexterity that leads to difficulties in daily activities such as buttoning clothing, tying shoelaces, and handwriting. According to research by Agostino et al. [20], Parkinson's disease impairs individual finger movements more than gross hand movements. Vanbellingen et al. [21] shows that an intensive, task specific home-based dexterity training program significantly improved fine motor skills in Parkinson's disease and the effect generalized to dexterity-related activities of daily living (ADL) functions. Dockx et al. [14] recommended to study VR application in different disease stages to determine whether VR technology plays a role in the prevention of physical deterioration in early-stage Parkinson's disease and in the management of disease progression in the moderate to late stages.

The VR exergame prototype we have developed focuses on patients in early stage of PD and on exercise for hand-eye coordination and finger movements, in order to slow down the deterioration of motor performance in fingers. We aim to provide an easy to learn and use, motivating and enjoyable experience for the patients.

The exergame was developed on HTC vive and Unity was used as the game engine. Users wear the Head Mounted Display and use the controllers to play the game while sitting down to avoid sickness and keep safe. Feedback to users is provided visually and through the controllers. Both visual and haptic feedback are provided immediately without noticeable delay. The game consists of a simple interface where the user can choose the game setting in Cloud or Galaxy, as shown in Fig. 1. After that, the game shows balloons in different colors and background depending on the choice made by the user in the previous step. The user can move the controllers to target on the balloons and use finger to press the trigger and shoot. With each hit, a score will be shown. After the game is over, the user can see the total score.

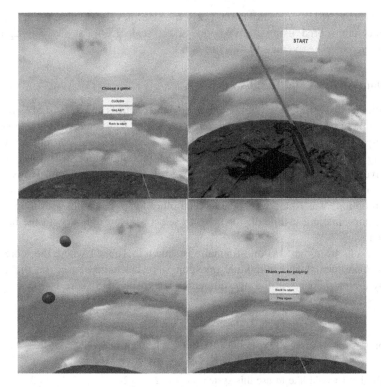

Fig. 1. Screenshots of the first prototype

4 Evaluation

The user testing of the developed prototype was conducted at a rehabilitation center for patients with PD. Five early-stage PD patients participated in the testing. The participants consisted of two female and three male patients, with an age range 65–74 years old and an average of 5.6 years with PD. Participants rated themselves as 'intermediate' when asked about their computer knowledge and skills.

4.1 Setting and Procedure

First, the purpose of the user testing and procedure was introduced and consent form was signed. After a pre-interview focusing on the demographic information, each participant was helped with putting on the Head Mounted Display and picked up the controllers. They were explained the basic of Virtual Reality and how the game should be played. They were then asked to play the game for two rounds (one in Cloud and one in Galaxy) and encouraged to think aloud and comment freely. After the two rounds, a post-interview was conducted to better understand their experience and gather feedback for improvement. Notes were taken during interviews as well as when the participants playing the game. Each participant was then asked to complete a System

Usability Scale (SUS) questionnaire [22]. In SUS, levels of agreement with ten statements are scored using a five-point Likert scale from 'strongly disagree' to 'strongly agree'. The average SUS score is 68.

4.2   Data Analysis and Results

The participants were able to quickly understand the controls and the visual elements of the game including the trigger motion and laser select. The underlying game concept (shooting objects in a virtual environment) was well liked and participants reacted positively to the trigger mechanic. They found that the game was both fun and immersive, simple to use, and that they enjoyed its competitive nature. However, we have also identified some usability challenges. For example, the placement of the selection options was found too close to each other for participants with more intense hand tremors, making it difficult for them to select a given option with the handheld controller.

The results from the SUS questionnaire is shown in Table 1 where the scores from individual participant and individual question were calculated based on the choices made by the participants in the questionnaire. The mean SUS score is 90.

Table 1. Overview of the SUS scores.

Question (1-strongly disagree, 5-strongly agree)	Participant/Score					Mean
	P1	P2	P3	P4	P5	
1. I think that I would like to use this system frequently	2	2	2	4	3	2.6
2. I found the system unnecessarily complex	4	4	4	3	4	3.8
3. I thought the system was easy to use	4	4	4	4	3	3.8
4. I think that I would need the support of a technical person to be able to use this system	3	4	4	3	4	3.6
5. I found the various functions in this system were well integrated	3	4	4	4	4	3.8
6. I thought there was too much inconsistency in this system	1	4	3	3	4	3
7. I would imagine that most people would learn to use this system very quickly	4	4	4	4	4	4
8. I found the system very cumbersome to use	4	4	4	4	4	4
9. I felt very confident using the system	2	4	4	4	4	3.6
10. I needed to learn a lot of things before I could get going with this system	3	4	4	4	4	3.8

The participants have also made some suggestions regarding the game mechanics including different gameplay options such as size, moving speed, location, and type of the objects to hit, different scores for different types of objects, and their distances to the player in the virtual world. In addition, they thought that different backgrounds, settings, music and colors could make the game more engaging and immersive.

5 Further Development

Based on the feedback from user testing of the first prototype, we have further developed the game with following improvements: level of difficulties; leader board for high scores; size, moving speed, location of balloons and their distances to the player; progress bar and number of streaks, and sound and animation.

We have also addressed some general usability issues such as spaces between options so that PD patients with hand tremor do not choose options by mistakes. Figure 2 shows some screenshots of the improved prototype including the new features and functions based on user feedback.

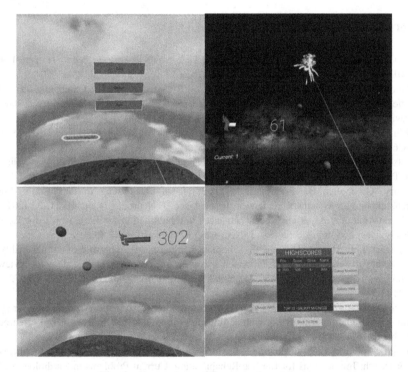

Fig. 2. Screenshots of the second prototype

6 Conclusion and Future Work

In this paper, we have presented an immersive VR exergame prototype and the evaluation. The prototype was found user-friendly and it was well received by the participants. The high System Usability Scale scores indicated high levels of acceptability, ease of use, learnability and confidence when using the prototype. The small number of participants in the evaluation does not allow us to make any conclusions. However, the results indicate that immersive VR exergames is a promising tool for patients with PD. The evaluation also provides valuable input that guided further improvement of the prototype. More user testing with larger number of participants and longitudinal study are necessary in order to improve the usability of the game and understand its effects on improving hand-eye coordination and finger movements.

Through this research, we have found that although there are considerable research on exergames for rehabilitation in general and for people with PD specifically, there is a lack of evidence-based design guidelines for immersive VR and research on exergames with fully immersive VR for rehabilitation purpose is limited. Future research should therefore focus on design principles for task-specific immersive VR exergames for patients with Parkinson's Disease taking into consideration the special needs of this user group.

References

1. Tysnes, O.B., Storstein, A.: Epidemiology of Parkinson's disease. J. Neural Transm. **124**(8), 901–905 (2017). https://doi.org/10.1007/s00702-017-1686-y
2. Goodwin, V.A., Richards, S.H., Taylor, R.S., Taylor, A.H., Campbell, J.L.: The effectiveness of exercise interventions for people with Parkinson's disease: a systematic review and meta-analysis. Mov. Disord. **23**, 631–640 (2008)
3. Ellis, T., et al.: Barriers to exercise in people with Parkinson disease. Phys. Ther. **93**, 628–636 (2013)
4. Afshari, M., Yang, A., Bega, D.: Motivators and barriers to exercise in Parkinson's disease. J. Parkinsons Dis. **7**, 703–711 (2017)
5. Barry, G., Galna, B., Rochester, L.: The role of exergaming in Parkinson's disease rehabilitation: a systematic review of the evidence. J. Neuroeng. Rehabil. **11**, 33 (2014)
6. Garcia-Agundez, A., et al.: Recent advances in rehabilitation for Parkinson's disease with exergames: a systematic review. J. Neuroeng. Rehabil. **16**, 1–17 (2019)
7. Triegaardt, J., Han, T.S., Sada, C., Sharma, S., Sharma, P.: The role of virtual reality on outcomes in rehabilitation of Parkinson's disease: meta-analysis and systematic review in 1031 participants. Neurol. Sci. **41**, 529–536 (2019). https://doi.org/10.1007/s10072-019-04144-3
8. Fernández-González, P., et al.: Leap motion controlled video game-based therapy for upper limb rehabilitation in patients with Parkinson's disease: a feasibility study. J. Neuroeng. Rehabil. 16, (2019)
9. Bond, S., Laddu, D.R., Ozemek, C., Lavie, C.J., Arena, R.: Exergaming and Virtual Reality for Health: Implications for Cardiac Rehabilitation. Current Problems in Cardiology (2019)
10. Palaniappan, S.M., Duerstock, B.S.: Developing rehabilitation practices using virtual reality exergaming. In: IEEE International Symposium on Signal Processing and Information Technology (ISSPIT), pp. 90–94, Louisville, KY, USA (2018)
11. Brien, J.O., Roberts, D., Monaghan, K.: Virtual reality to improve motor function after stroke: past, present, and future (open access). J. Neurol. Neurosur. **10**(2), 112–116 (2019)
12. Liao, Y.-Y., Yang, Y.-R., Cheng, S.-J., Wu, Y.-R., Fuh, J.-L., Wang, R.-Y.: Virtual reality–based training to improve obstacle-crossing performance and dynamic balance in patients with Parkinson's disease. Neurorehabil. Neural Repair **29**, 658–667 (2015)

13. Freitag, F., et al.: Is virtual reality beneficial for dual-task gait training in patients with Parkinson's disease? A systematic review. Dement Neuropsychologia **13**(3), 259–267 (2019)
14. Dockx, K., et al.: Virtual reality for rehabilitation in Parkinson's disease. The Cochrane database of systematic reviews 12, (2016)
15. Janeh, O., et al.: Gait training in virtual reality: short-term effects of different virtual manipulation techniques in parkinson's disease. Cells **8**, 419 (2019)
16. Kim, A., Darakjian, N., Finley, J.M.: Walking in fully immersive virtual environments: an evaluation of potential adverse effects in older adults and individuals with Parkinson's disease. J. Neuroeng. Rehabil. **14**, 16 (2017)
17. Upsahl, K., Vistven, A., Bergland, A., Chen, W.: A mobile app supporting exercise adherence for people with Parkinson's disease. In: Miesenberger, K., Kouroupetroglou, G. (eds.) ICCHP 2018. LNCS, vol. 10897, pp. 464–467. Springer, Cham (2018). https://doi.org/10.1007/978-3-319-94274-2_67
18. Burke, J.W., et al.: Optimising engagement for stroke rehabilitation using serious games. Visual Comput. **25**(12), 1085 (2009)
19. Shaw, A.L., et al.: Challenges in virtual reality exergame design. In: Proceedings of the 16th Australian User Interface Conference (AUIC), Sydney, pp. 61–68, Australian Computer Society Inc. (2015)
20. Agostino, R., Curra, A., Giovannelli, M., Modugno, N., Manfredi, M., Berardelli, A.: Impairment of individual finger movements in Parkinson's disease. Mov. Disord. **18**, 560–565 (2003)
21. Vanbellingen, T., et al.: Home based training for dexterity in Parkinson's disease: a randomized controlled trial. Parkinsonism Relat. Disord. **41**, 92–98 (2017)
22. Brooke, J.: SUS: a "quick and dirty" usability scale. In: Jordan, P.W., Thomas, B., Weerdmeester, B.A., McClelland, I.L. (eds.) Usability Evaluation in Industry, pp. 189–194. Taylor and Francis, London (1996)

Augmented Reality for People with Low Vision: Symbolic and Alphanumeric Representation of Information

Florian Lang$^{(\boxtimes)}$, Albrecht Schmidt, and Tonja Machulla

LMU Munich, Frauenlobstr. 7a, 80337 Munich, Germany
{florian.lang,albrecht.schmidt,tonja.machulla}@ifi.lmu.de

Abstract. Many individuals with visual impairments have residual vision that often remains underused by assistive technologies. Head-mounted augmented reality (AR) devices can provide assistance, by recoding difficult-to-perceive information into a visual format that is more accessible. Here, we evaluate symbolic and alphanumeric information representations for their efficiency and usability in two prototypical AR applications: namely, recognizing facial expressions of conversational partners and reading the time. We find that while AR provides a general benefit, the complexity of the visual representations has to be matched to the user's visual acuity.

Keywords: Augmented reality · Low vision · Symbolic and alphanumeric representation

1 Introduction

A large percentage of people with visual impairment (VI), including those who have been diagnosed as legally blind, have residual visual functions [6], such as intact peripheral vision with a central scotoma. These individuals often prefer using vision to other modalities – especially, when visual information better supports the current task (e.g., navigation, identification of objects), or when audition and touch are occupied by other tasks. Hence, there is a large potential for the research and development of assistive solutions that provide adapted visual feedback.

A promising approach is the use of augmented reality (AR), presented through head-mounted displays (HMD), to enhance or substitute degraded visual information. When compared to traditional assistive solutions, such as CCTV or optical magnifying glasses, HMDs have the advantage of being mobile and hands-free. Also, AR glasses will likely become an everyday device in the next decades, reducing the stigma that is often associated with the use of assistive devices [7]. A number of recent studies have demonstrated possible applications for AR, such as enhancing text for reading [10] or poorly-lit ledges [13]. There is comparably less work regarding how AR goggles could be used to substitute degraded or imperceptible visual information [14]. In the present paper, we

K. Miesenberger et al. (Eds.): ICCHP 2020, LNCS 12376, pp. 146–156, 2020.
https://doi.org/10.1007/978-3-030-58796-3_19

investigate how different representation formats of such substituting information influence the efficiency and usability of AR assistance.

Missing visual information can be substituted by recoding it into a visual format that is more readily perceived by a user with a visual impairment. Here, we distinguish between two basic types of representations: alphanumeric and symbolic. Alphanumeric representation refers to the recoding of visual information into words and numbers. Symbolic representations can be analogues to the information they are substituting for, e.g., when they are pictorial in nature. Alternatively, they can be visually simple or abstract symbols that are easy to perceive and recognize (e.g., a red square, a blue circle etc.) but have little resemblance to the information they stand for. The present research evaluates symbolic and alphanumeric representations of information in AR. For this, we identified two viable use cases from prior interviews with persons with VI: i) reading the time off of conventional watches, and ii) identifying the emotional expression on the face of a conversational partner. Accordingly, we developed two assistive AR functions: one to augment a physical watch with either an analogue/symbolic or a digital/numeric representation of time and another one that overlays the face of a conversational partner with an additional symbolic or textual representation of their current facial expression (angry, sad, happy). Our results show that AR can provide a recognition benefit in both use cases and is generally well-received by persons with VI.

2   Related Work

There is some prior work that we considered in the design of our study, in particular regarding the cognitive processes associated with symbolic and alphanumeric representations as well as the use case of augmenting emotional expressions. We are not aware of any scientific work on augmenting clocks visually, most likely due to the fact that there are alternative solutions such as using zoom or audio output on smartphones. However, especially older participants who lived most of their live without any VI and are now faced with gradual vision loss indicated to us that they would like to continue using wristwatches. Here, AR can provide a simple solution without the necessity of having to modify one's life-long routines, e.g., display a large virtual clock in AR after the user performs the typical gesture of looking at their wristwatch. In contrast, using a future AR device should not require that much of a behavioral adaptation, as many older users already wear normal glasses.

Symbolic vs Alphanumeric. Alphanumeric representation of information is very common, especially in user interfaces. Thus, for most users, information processing can be expected to be very efficient without much practice due to a high level of familiarity with the task. Nevertheless, there are two main reasons to evaluate the feasibility of providing information in a symbolic format. First, alphanumeric representation typically requires a higher visual acuity compared to symbols, especially if the latter are sufficiently simplified. Second, information in written form takes longer to comprehend than pictorial information [8] and can require more attentional resources to process, leading to cognitive capture [12].

Use Case Emotions. Persons with visual impairments often have difficulties perceiving nonverbal conversational clues, such as facial expressions [2], making social interactions challenging. To support a user during a conversation, an assistive system has to be able to first extract and process these clues and then convey the information in an adapted format to the user. For both steps, relevant prior work exists. Recognising facial expressions from images is a long standing challenge in computer vision [3]. Handcrafted algorithms run in real time and exceed 70% accuracy on mobile devices such as smartphones [11] and reach 97% accuracy on stationary setups with controlled lightning conditions [5]. A neural network can provide more robustness to image properties or fuse multiple modalities [4]. For presenting the information, several researchers have proposed solutions for people with VI using audio [1] or tactile [2] feedback. Zuniga et al. proposed a system providing visual feedback [14]. They presented colored patches in a smartphone-based virtual reality to indicate the current facial expression of a conversational partner as well as a miniature image of the face in the visual periphery, albeit without evaluation with their target group. Here, we test different symbolic and alphanumeric representations for their efficiency to communicate emotional expressions.

3   Prototypes and Real World Feasibility

We are currently implementing a prototype for emotion recognition and communication using the Microsoft HoloLens. When a user indicates the start of a conversation, computer vision is used to detect faces and determine facial expressions. In case multiple faces are detected, the largest or most centered face is selected. The information is recoded into an alternative visualization (for details see below) and displayed to the user. The user can adjust the details of this visualization such as its size, position, brightness, and type. The augmentation appears either relative to the screen or to the detected face.

Similarly, clock faces can be recognized [9] and augmented. Pilot tests with two individuals with VI showed that positioning the augmentation around a wristwatch is cumbersome, as the watch has to be placed in the comparably narrow field of view of the HoloLens. This means the user had to either tilt their head down unnaturally or lift their arm high in front of their face. Therefore, we pursued an ego-centric approach where the augmentation is always displayed inside of the field of view. We used a smartwatch to trigger the augmentation using a wake-up gesture or a tap on the display. Therefore, users used to regular wristwatches do not need to learn a new gesture. Again, the user can set the type, color, brightness, and position of the augmentation according to personal preferences. A visualization of both prototypes is shown in Fig. 1.

Fig. 1. The figure shows the functionality of the two systems in a real world setting. In the left image the facial expression of a conversational partner is augmented to indicate the smiling (Source without augmentation: WOCInTechChat.com (www.flickr.com/photos/wocintechchat/25392590663/ License: www.creativecommons.org/licenses/by/2.0/)). The right side shows a wristwatch which is augmented by the HoloLens. In both cases our system provides a large and simplified representation of information.

4   Methods

We used an iterative approach including feedback from persons with VI to design and develop several early prototypes of the two assistive functions and the different information representations. In the following, we report a formal evaluation of the current prototype.

Participants. Participants were reimbursed with 12 EURO/hour. Three individuals with VI participated in the study (P1: 20-year-old male, severe binocular vision loss, 0.04 visus; P2: 24-year-old female, binocular low vision with good color vision, 0.14 visus; P3: 81-year-old female, central vision loss, 0.17 visus). P1 and P2 tested both assistive functions. They had no prior experience with AR devices. P3 tested the clock augmentation and provided feedback on an earlier version of the emotion representations; she has had extensive experience with the HoloLens due prior testing of other research prototypes at our institution. Unfortunately, data collection was interrupted by the Covid-19 pandemic. Although, the generalizability of the current dataset may be limited, we are convinced that it provides constructive insights for future empirical studies and interface design.

Apparatus. The AR system is implemented in Unity 3D with the Mixed Reality Toolkit from Microsoft and deployed to a HoloLens. A computer—connected via a dedicated WLAN Router—using the virtual input functionality from the

Microsoft HoloLens App controls the application. We implemented the app on the wristwatch in Java (Watch OS 2/Android). We use the touch screen of the devices as input.

Study Design. Our primary aim was to test different information representations. Thus, we did not use the full systems described in the above "Prototype" section. This simplified the study setup and removed potential confound variables. In each study, we only display the augmentation, i.e., show the visualization for an emotion without a corresponding conversation and a time of day without the triggering gesture.

Both studies consist of four conditions, presented in randomized order for each participant to mitigate order and training effects. In the emotions study, one of four different representations was presented in each condition, namely: one textual (alphanumeric) representation, henceforth termed "Text", and the three symbolic representations Emoticons, Abstract, and Colors (see Fig. 2). In each condition, we displayed representations of the three emotions happy, sad, and angry (following [14]). Each condition consisted of 9–15 training and 15 test trials. Maximum font size of the text was chosen such that the longest word (in German) fit in the field of view of the HMD (approx. visual angle of 17° vertical and 34° horizontal). In the Emoticons condition, we used default emoticons from IOS, as had been suggested by P3 in a prior iteration of the design process. In the Abstract condition, we simplified the emoticons by only displaying the mouth, and for 'angry' the eyebrows. In the Colors condition, we asked each participant to select their own preferred three colors (from a set of seven), one for each emotion, for the reason that there is no wide-spread consensus on the association between colors and emotions.

In the clock study, we presented the time either directly in the HoloLens (without augmenting a physical clock or triggering gesture) or on a wristwatch, either using a symbolic (analogue clock face) or numerical (digital time) representation (see Fig. 3), resulting in four conditions each consisting of four training and six test trials. Here, the wristwatch conditions serve as baselines.

We presented the stimuli in the HoloLens on the physical accommodation plane of the device (2 m distance) and a height of 50 cm resulting in 14.2° of the visual field and locked to the center of the screen (therefore no calibration of the HoloLens was required). The wristwatch Huawei Watch 2 has a round display with a screen size of 3.05 cm, resulting in 17.3° of the visual field at 10 cm distance or 5.8° at 30 cm distance. Each stimulus was displayed until the participant gave an answer regarding the perceived time or emotion.

Procedure. We offered to meet with participants at the nearest station of public transport. When arriving in our lab they sat down on a chair and were introduced to the HoloLens. After filling out a consent form, we reminded the participants that they were allowed to abort the study at any point or take breaks in case they felt uncomfortable.

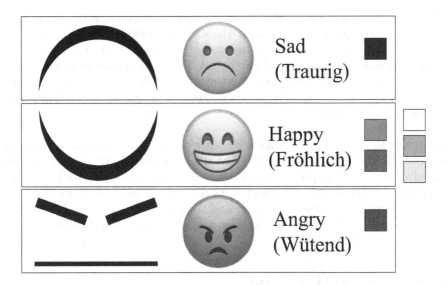

Fig. 2. The figure shows the different representations for sad, happy, and angry from top to bottom and from left to right in the conditions Abstract, Emoticons, Text (English and German), and Colors. The three colors on the far right were not mapped to any emotion by any of the participants.

Fig. 3. The figure shows the symbolic representation of clocks in the top row and the numerical representation in the bottom row. The size ratio between the visualizations in the HoloLens (left column, black and white inverted) and on the wristwatch (right column) equals the perceived size ratio in the real world when holding the watch at a distance of approximately 10 cm. This illustrates that some of the advantage found in the HoloLens conditions is likely to result from the possibility of displaying the information subtending a larger visual angle within the field of view.

Clock. We first confirmed that the participants could perceive the clock. Participants were allowed to freely chose the distance between their eyes and the wristwatch. Afterwards, we started the study by showing the first training trial. The participant was asked to read the time aloud as soon as they were able to recognize it. They were allowed to read the time in any format they wish (e.g., "half past 2", "two-thirty", etc.). We recorded the accuracy of participants' answers and their response time.

Emotional Expressions. First, we asked each participant to choose a mapping between the three emotions and three of the seven colors. Afterwards, we displayed all visualizations and confirmed that our assumed mapping for Emoticons and Abstract aligned with the expectations of the participant. Next, we displayed the stimuli analogue to the clock study and the participant had to name the perceived emotion. A button press displayed the next stimulus and response times and accuracy were recorded.

5   Results and Discussion

We first analyse the quantitative measures of response time in seconds (RT) and the error (E). Afterwards, we discuss subjective feedback given by the participants.

Emotional Expressions. None of the participants made an error when naming the displayed emotions. As all participants reported not being able to recognize facial expressions in real-life settings (P1: "When really close and with good illumination, I can sometimes recognize the teeth, when somebody laughs"), all four types of representations yield an advantage in conversation and provide a benefit to users.

Mean RT was highest for Emoticons (2.01 s), although both participants reported to regularly receive emoticons in instant messages. The remaining conditions had comparable RTs (Text 1.83 s; Abstract 1.83 s; Colors 1.89 s, see Fig. 4), albeit with differences in the standard deviation. Text (0.39 s) and Emoticons (0.34 s) have higher standard deviations than Abstract (0.08 s) and Colors (0.02 s). The subjective feedback provides an explanation for the larger spread. P1 stated, that Text is hard to read and he just focused on the shape of the word after reading it once during training and Emoticons are only distinguishable by the large white mouth or the red color. P2, with a higher visual acuity, reported Text to be easy to read and could recognize small details, e.g., the thin mouth, for Emoticons. We conclude that alphanumeric and complex symbolic representations are more strongly affected by the visual acuity of the participant, while simple symbolic representations are more robust.

Clock. All participants were able to read the time both in the HoloLens and on the wristwatch. Using the HoloLens resulted in both faster and more accurate responses when determining the current time compared to the respective

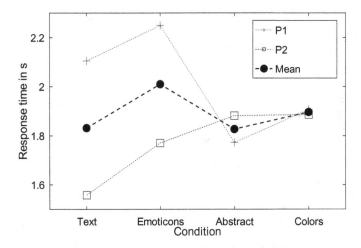

Fig. 4. The figure shows the response times for the four visual representations of emotion. While P1 (red cross) and P2 (blue square) achieved similar results for Abstract and Colors, P1 took longer for Text and Emoticons and P2 was faster in these conditions. The mean across participants (black circle) is slightly higher for Emoticons compared to the other conditions; however, as the results of the individual participants differ substantially from each other, it is unclear whether this observation is due to the small sample size. (Color figure online)

condition on the wristwatch (see Figs. 5 and 6). Further, responses to numerical representations were faster (HoloLens: 2.74 s vs. 5.92 s; Watch: 5.23 s vs. 7.46 s) and more accurate (HoloLens: 0.00 vs. 1.67; Watch: 1.00 vs. 2.33) than to symbolic representations. Here, the errors in the conditions with symbolic representation resulted from a misreading of the hour hand, e.g., 8:55 read as 9:55, or a mixup of the hands, e.g., 10:45 read as 8:55. Other types of inaccuracies (8:35 read as 8:30) were only observed once. All errors for numerical representations originate from visually similar digits, e.g., 8 instead of 3, or 6 instead of 5.

The participants reported preferring the AR-presentation in the HoloLens to the wristwatch. They also compared it to their usual means of obtaining the time and further confirmed some of the above findings. For instance, the advantage of the augmentation is likely attributable to the possibility of magnification and accompanying decrease in visual clutter. P1 said "The HoloLens requires less effort" and "The space between the clock hands is easier to perceive on the HoloLens". P2 was amazed by the numerical representation in the HoloLens, "The numbers are huge, even larger than on my mobile phone, this is great". P3 complained about the size of the numerical representation on the wristwatch "This is really small, and the numbers are very close together. This is hard for me".

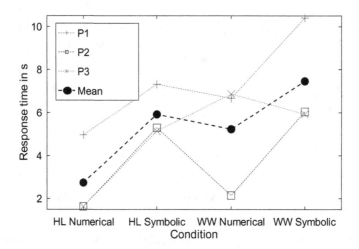

Fig. 5. The figure shows the response times for reading the time of day for displaying the information in the HoloLens (HL) or on the wristwatch (WW). The average over all participants (black circle) shows that participants were faster using the HoloLens compared to the wristwatch and numerical compared to symbolic representation.

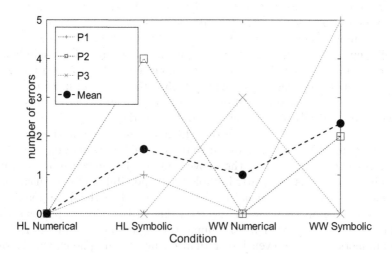

Fig. 6. The figure shows the number of errors for reading the clock. In the condition with numerical representation, results were less error prone than in the condition with symbolic representations. Additionally, participants achieved better results with the HoloLens (HL) compared to the wristwatch (WW).

6   Conclusion

Our results demonstrate that the HoloLens enables users to recognize facial expressions and further provides a benefit over a wristwatch when reading the time. Alphanumerical representations are easier to read, as long as the visual acuity of the user is sufficient to resolve the displayed text. However, if the visual acuity is too low to read even large text in the HoloLens, a symbolic representation can provide a good or even better alternative. In general, simple symbolic visualizations are more robust against differences in acuity. In conclusion, an AR system, especially if customized to the visual acuity of the user, can assist in everyday situations to individuals with low vision, either by providing access to previously non-accessible information or by helping to process available information faster.

Acknowledgements. F. Lang was supported by the German Federal Ministry of Education and Research as part of the project IDeA (grant no. 16SV8102). A. Schmidt and T. Machulla were supported by the European Union's Horizon2020 Programme under ERCEA grant no. 683008 AMPLIFY. We would also like to thank the reviewers and ACs for their work and valuable feedback.

References

1. Ashok, A., John, J.: Facial expression recognition system for visually impaired. In: Hemanth, J., Fernando, X., Lafata, P., Baig, Z. (eds.) ICICI 2018. LNDECT, vol. 26, pp. 244–250. Springer, Cham (2019). https://doi.org/10.1007/978-3-030-03146-6_26

2. Buimer, H.P., et al.: Conveying facial expressions to blind and visually impaired persons through a wearable vibrotactile device. PLoS One **13**, e0194737 (2018). https://doi.org/10.1371/journal.pone.0194737

3. Fasel, B., Luettin, J.: Automatic facial expression analysis: a survey. Pattern Recogn. **36**(1), 259–275 (2003). https://doi.org/10.1016/S0031-3203(02)00052-3. https://linkinghub.elsevier.com/retrieve/pii/S0031320302000523

4. Fragopanagos, N., Taylor, J.G.: Emotion recognition in human-computer interaction. Neural Netw. **18**, 389–405 (2005). https://doi.org/10.1016/j.neunet.2005.03.006

5. Happy, S.L., George, A., Routray, A.: A real time facial expression classification system using local binary patterns. In: 4th International Conference on Intelligent Human Computer Interaction: Advancing Technology for Humanity, IHCI 2012 (2012). https://doi.org/10.1109/IHCI.2012.6481802

6. Pararajasegaram, R.: Low vision care: the need to maximise visual potential (2004)

7. Parette, P., Scherer, M.J.: Assistive technology use and stigma. Educ. Train. Dev. Disabil. **39**(3), 217–226 (2004)

8. Potter, M.C., Faulconer, B.A.: Time to understand pictures and words. Nature **253**(5491), 437–438 (1975). https://doi.org/10.1038/253437a0

9. Scharf, P.: Clock face detection (2012). https://github.com/amulware/ip-clock-face-detection

10. Stearns, L., Findlater, L., Froehlich, J.E.: Design of an augmented reality magnification aid for low vision users. In: ASSETS 2018 - Proceedings of the 20th International ACM SIGACCESS Conference on Computers and Accessibility (2018). https://doi.org/10.1145/3234695.3236361
11. Suk, M., Prabhakaran, B.: Real-time mobile facial expression recognition system- a case study. In: IEEE Computer Society Conference on Computer Vision and Pattern Recognition Workshops (2014). https://doi.org/10.1109/CVPRW.2014.25
12. Charissis, V., Patera, M.: Symbolic vs alphanumeric representations in human machine interface design. In: Communication: Understanding/Misunderstanding - Proceedings of the 9th World Congress of the IASS/AIS - Helsinki-Imatra, 11–17 June, 2007, pp. 276–284. The International Semiotics Institute at Imatra, Helsinki (2009)
13. Zhao, Y., Kupferstein, E., Castro, B.V., Feiner, S., Azenkot, S.: Designing AR visualizations to facilitate stair navigation for people with low vision. In: UIST 2019 - Proceedings of the 32nd Annual ACM Symposium on User Interface Software and Technology (2019). https://doi.org/10.1145/3332165.3347906
14. Zuniga, R., Magee, J.: Conversation aid for people with low vision using head mounted display and computer vision emotion detection. In: Miesenberger, K., Kouroupetroglou, G. (eds.) ICCHP 2018. LNCS, vol. 10897, pp. 44–50. Springer, Cham (2018). https://doi.org/10.1007/978-3-319-94274-2_7

Enhancing Interaction and Accessibility in Museums and Exhibitions with Augmented Reality and Screen Readers

Leandro Soares Guedes[1,2]($\boxtimes$), Luiz André Marques[2], and Gabriellen Vitório[2]

[1] Università della Svizzera italiana (USI), Lugano, TI, Switzerland
leandro.soares.guedes@usi.ch
[2] Federal Institute of Mato Grosso do Sul (IFMS), Campo Grande, MS, Brazil
leandro.guedes@ifms.edu.br, lamfsantos5@gmail.com, gaby18vsilva@gmail.com
http://www.leandro.guedes.com.br

Abstract. Throughout the evolution of humanity, technologies have served as support for new evolutionary horizons. It is an unambiguous fact that technologies have positively influenced the masses, but they have also brought a remoteness with local cultures, often making them oblivious. Among the new technologies and forms of interaction, we have augmented reality and screen readers that allow the device to read the content. This paper presents AIMuseum. It aims to facilitate accessing and interacting with cultural environments for people with different abilities, combining the use of technologies with local museums, artworks, and exhibitions. The work was evaluated with 38 users, ranging from 16 to 41 years old, and five declared having one type of disability. They used the application and answered a questionnaire. The results showed a positive experience and improved the users' interest in the artworks and their additional information.

Keywords: Artworks · Museums · Interaction · Augmented reality · Screen reader · Accessibility

1 Introduction

Throughout the evolution of humanity, technologies have been used for new evolutionary horizons. From the typewriter to the most modern devices, humans search for something that meets their desires in terms of ergonomics, usability, automation, and utility.

The so-called augmented reality (AR) can be defined as an interface based on the overlap of digitally generated virtual information (dynamic images, sounds, etc.) with the user's real environment, using modern devices such as smartphones. When this virtual information is brought into real space, using the user's natural interactions, we have the presence of augmented reality.

It is important to consider people with different abilities. Inclusive applications help people with special needs to interact and use them. Accessibility is

K. Miesenberger et al. (Eds.): ICCHP 2020, LNCS 12376, pp. 157–163, 2020.
https://doi.org/10.1007/978-3-030-58796-3_20

essential for allowing people to access and interact with multiple devices, enhancing independence and freedom.

This paper presents AIMuseum. It aims to facilitate accessing and interacting with cultural environments for people with different abilities, combining the use of technologies with local museums, artworks, and exhibitions.

Fig. 1. Using AIMuseum to interact with a photograph and its QR code. The user have can read and listen to details about the picture.

2   Related Works

AR is nowadays a widely accepted technology, however not yet so widespread socially. It keeps a system with three characteristics: it combines the real with the virtual, brings interactivity in real-time, and adjusts virtual objects in the three-dimensional environment.

We can use QR codes to track printed markers, which will be captured by a camera, and subsequently mapped by software [8]. This type of application allows visitors in an exhibition to have eye contact with details not perceived in real life.

Neto et al. [7] propose a tourism guide for smartphones using AR and QR codes' technologies. Tillon et al. [10] describe the results of experiments conducted during museum visits with a mobile guide using markerless augmented reality. Heikkinen [3] used a JSARToolKit library with APIgetUserMedia WebRTC to run augmented reality applications on the Web. Some other works applied augmented reality to museums' exhibitions, such as [1, 9], and [4].

The use of immersive technology, like VR, has also been used for works in Museum Exhibitions, such as [2, 6], and [12]. Likewise, recent works present natural interaction [5] and experience model for mixed reality in the museum [11].

3 Enhancing Interaction and Accessibility

We developed AIMuseum, an application to facilitate accessing and interacting with cultural environments for people with different abilities, combining the use of technologies with local museums, artworks, and exhibitions.

We built the application on the Unity game engine using the C# programming language. We used Vuforia as API (Application Programming Interface) to create augmented reality. It was done by associating information received through the camera (from QR codes) with its predefined database, then projecting a two or three-dimensional image from this association.

QR Codes were selected as markers for the present work, because, as they use black and white, it becomes easier to identify the image even in low light conditions. We adapted their size and quality according to our preliminary tests.

To develop the Screen Reader accessibility feature, we used a UI Accessibility Plugin for Unity that makes it possible to read QR codes associated texts in different languages.

While developing the application, it was necessary to choose, catalog, and model some artworks. For the 3D modeling, we used Blender, which consists of an open-source program to make models, animations, textures. One 3D example, while being modeled, can be seen in Fig. 2.

We select the current artworks from local museums and free collections available. The works include paintings, objects, and photographs.

Objects were photographed at different angles to allow modeling. It is important to note that this is not a digital reconstruction of the works but manual modeling, seeking to reproduce faithfully. We do not intend to substitute the users' experience with the real artworks, but to make them more accessible and easy to understand.

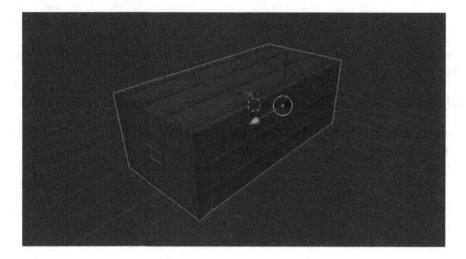

Fig. 2. Ancient chest 3D model.

The application interface is intuitive and straightforward. It uses a responsive User Interface (UI) design, adaptable to the user's device (smartphone or tablet). It also allows users to configure settings such as volume, font size, and language.

The application UI can be found in Fig. 3. In Fig. 3a the main screen. Pressing Next, the user will find the instructions page, Fig. 3b. Pressing on options, Fig. 3c, the settings will appear to personalize the app.

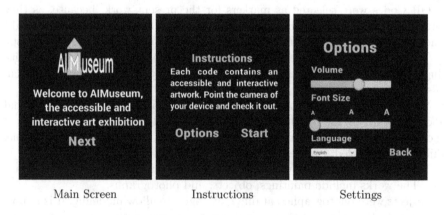

Main Screen   Instructions   Settings

Fig. 3. AIMuseum user interface.

When the users configure the application and open it, they can scan a QR code automatically. It is just necessary to point the device to the QR code. We can check an example of scanning in Fig. 1.

The user can access extra information about the artwork, such as title, year of creation, description, the context of production, and copyright.

If the screen reader is on, the user can listen to all extra information. This inclusive feature is essential for people with disabilities, such as visually impaired or intellectually disabled people.

One example of a 3D model scanned by AIMuseum is available in Fig. 4. The QR code and the white background are real-life objects, while the sword (Rapier) and its label are virtual objects generated by the application.

Fig. 4. AR showing a Rapier 3D model.

4   User Evaluation

To validate the development, we tested the application at a local exhibition. We aim to promote the interaction of the community with artworks and making them easily accessible.

We evaluated the work for two afternoons. We invited participants using banners and social network invitations.

We had 38 participants in total, ranging from 16 to 41 years old, with a mean age of 28. The participants were 54% female and 46% male. Three participants declared to have low vision, and two participants reported to have reading difficulties.

They used the application freely for about 5 min and then answered a questionnaire. There were ten artworks available, and we can check some of the AIMuseum generated artworks used in the user evaluation in Fig. 5.

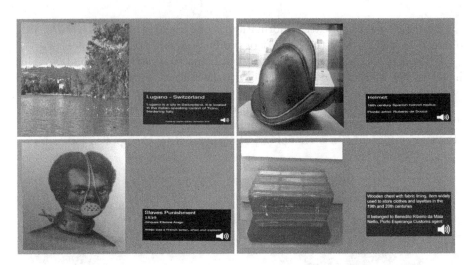

Fig. 5. Augmented Reality exhibition examples.

On a Likert scale of 1 to 5, being one very unsatisfied and five very satisfied, we obtained:

- 87% very satisfying and fast QR code scanning experience
- 92% very satisfying screen reader (text-to-speech) experience
- 89% very satisfying and intuitive interface experience
- 89% very satisfying usability experience
- 87% very satisfying overall experience

The results showed a positive experience and improved the users' interest in the artworks and their additional information. The majority of participants found the interaction easy, and the public's approach to the works was relaxed and straightforward, demonstrating that the use of new technologies became part of our current lives.

Some interesting comments: two participants that declared having low vision said they could understand the artwork in a novel way, and wanted to have this extended for other artworks. One participant that stated having reading difficulties commented that the screen reader helped to focus.

5   Conclusions and Future Work

Developing this research was a very productive experience. During the development, it was possible to be in contact with several artworks and regional artifacts. Also, the presentation of the application to the target audience exceeded expectations, making the community's interaction with works of art and their feedback very significant.

Comparing AIMuseum with other similar works interacting with available artworks, the screen reader enhanced the experience for AR. Our work made artworks accessible for the population with low vision and reading difficulties. Also, it can be fun for children and older people.

Unfortunately, we did not have the number of participants with special needs that we wanted. So we could analyze all-new challenges that they could face. We are sure some adjusts have to be made in future work to include, for example, blind users and people with difficulty moving.

Therefore, we suggest a few more activities for future work:

- Add new forms of reading and accessing markers
- Add pictures and audios to the gallery
- Share content in social networks
- Test future versions with people having other types of disabilities.

References

1. Braga, I.F., Landau, L., Cunha, G.G.: Realidade aumentada em museus: as batalhas do museu nacional de belas artes. Virtual Reality Sci. Visual. J. **4**(1), 35–55 (2011)
2. Haguenauer, C., Cunha, G.G., Cordeiro Filho, F., Araujo, M.C.M., Pastorino, L., de Freitas Lohmann, A.: Projeto museu virtual: Criação de ambientes virtuais com recursos e técnicas de realidade virtual. Virtual Reality Sci. Visual. J. **1**(2), 1–13 (2008)
3. Heikkinen, I.: Writing augmented reality applications using JSARToolKit, February 2012. https://www.html5rocks.com/en/tutorials/webgl/jsartoolkit_webrtc/
4. Keil, J., et al.: A digital look at physical museum exhibits: designing personalized stories with handheld augmented reality in museums. In: Digital Heritage International Congress (DigitalHeritage), 2013. vol. 2, pp. 685–688. IEEE (2013)
5. Kyriakou, P., Hermon, S.: Can I touch this? Using natural interaction in a museum augmented reality system. Digit. Appl. Archaeol. Cultural Heritage **12**, e00088 (2019)
6. Marques, M.A., Costa, T.K., Machado, L.S., Nettos, C.: Representação do sítio arqueológico da pedra de ingá com realidade virtual. In: Anais do Workshop de Realidade Virtual e Aumentada, Santos, Brasil (2009)
7. da Silva Neto, P.C., Nunes, C., dos Santos Nunes, E.P.: Integrando recursos de realidade aumentada e código de barras bidimensionais no desenvolvimento de um guia de turismo (2011)
8. da Silva, U.L., Braga, R.F., Scherer, D.: Uso de qr code e realidade aumentada como suporte a visitação de museu. In: Anais dos Workshops do Congresso Brasileiro de Informática na Educação, vol. 1 (2012)
9. da Silveira, A.L.M., pela UFRGS, I., Biazus, M.C.V.: A realidade aumentada aplicada a museologia (2010)
10. Tillon, A.B., Marchal, I., Houlier, P.: Mobile augmented reality in the museum: can a lace-like technology take you closer to works of art? (2011)
11. Trunfio, M., Campana, S.: A visitors' experience model for mixed reality in the museum. Curr. Issues Tourism **23**(9), 1053–1058 (2020)
12. Wojciechowski, R., Walczak, K., White, M., Cellary, W.: Building virtual and augmented reality museum exhibitions. In: Proceedings of the Ninth International Conference on 3D Web Technology, pp. 135–144. ACM (2004)

Guidelines for Inclusive Avatars and Agents: How Persons with Visual Impairments Detect and Recognize Others and Their Activities

Lauren Thevin[1,2](✉) and Tonja Machulla[1,3]

[1] LMU Munich, 80337 Munich, Germany
tonja.machulla@ifi.lmu.de
[2] UCO-Bretagne Sud, Arradon, France
lthevin@uco.fr
[3] TU Dortmund, Dortmund, Germany

Abstract. Realistic virtual worlds are used in video games, in virtual reality, and to run remote meetings. In many cases, these environments include representations of other humans, either as stand-ins for real humans (avatars) or artificial entities (agents). Presence and individual identity of such virtual characters is usually coded by visual features, such as visibility in certain locations and appearance in terms of looks. For people with visual impairments (VI), this creates a barrier to detecting and identifying co-present characters and interacting with them. To improve the inclusiveness of such social virtual environments, we investigate which cues people with VI use to detect and recognize others and their activities in real-world settings. For this, we conducted an online survey with fifteen participants (adults and children). Our findings indicate an increased reliance on multimodal information: **vision** for silhouette recognition; **audio** for the recognition through pace, white cane, jewelry, breathing, voice and keyboard typing; **sense of smell** for fragrance, food smell and airflow; **tactile information** for length of hair, size, way of guiding or holding the hand and the arm, and the **reactions of a guide-dog**. **Environmental and social cues** indicate if somebody is present: e. g. a light turned on in a room, or somebody answering a question. Many of these cues can already be implemented in virtual environments with avatars and are summarized by us in a set of guidelines.

Keywords: Virtual reality · Accessible avatars and agents · Virtual environment · Blindness · Low vision

1 Introduction

Virtual reality (VR) technology allows users to visit virtual environments and to interact with them. This increasingly includes interactions with virtual representations of other human users and artificial characters controlled by the computer,

© Springer Nature Switzerland AG 2020
K. Miesenberger et al. (Eds.): ICCHP 2020, LNCS 12376, pp. 164–175, 2020.
https://doi.org/10.1007/978-3-030-58796-3_21

Fig. 1. Avatars with cues usable by sighted and people with visual impairments: wristband and jewelry making noise with the movement of the avatar, distinctive voice or laughter and telling the identity, different size (audio and tactile cues), pace, loud or specific breathing pattern.

termed avatars and agents, respectively. Much recent research focuses on improving the appearance of such virtual humans and how different characteristics such as emotional expressiveness, personalization, or motion profiles influence the quality of the interpersonal interaction. As with many other features of VR environments, current representations of human characters rely heavily on visual aspects. As a result, they are less accessible to users with visual impairments. Difficulties include not being aware of the presence of other characters, or not being able to discern their location, identity, or activity. As a result, persons with visual impairments face a higher threshold when it comes to joining in social or collaborative VR experiences. Recently, there have been efforts to increase the accessibility of VR for people with VI [23]. So far, these efforts have focused on improving interactions with physical features of the VR environment. Our work aims to also improve inclusiveness in terms of social and collaborative aspects of VR. To this end, we investigated how people with VI determine presence, identity, and activity of other humans in real-world settings. These factors are likely to influence whether a person will approach others with the goal of engaging in a social interaction: first, a person with VI has to be aware of the presence of potential interaction partners; second, the identity of co-present persons might play a role for certain types of interactions (such as a banter between friends); and third, the activity might determine whether the other person is available for an interaction or not (e.g., a working colleague should not be interrupted). We created an online survey answered by fifteen adults and minors with VI. We present the results of this survey and propose guidelines for the creation of inclusive virtual characters, that can be implemented at present with currently available technological solutions (Fig. 1).

2   State of the Art

Representation of Avatars and Agents in Interactive Virtual Environments. Virtual environments support more and more interactive and collaborative activities [15], such as physical and cognitive therapies [3,11], training [12,14,17], gaming, telepresence for meeting [18], and communication with conversational agents [13,16]. All of these applications require the representation of oneself or others in virtual space, in the form of (self-)avatars or virtual agents. These representations rely strongly on visual cues, as these are considered essential for the realism and faithfulness of avatars [19]. Hence, many research efforts focus on photo-realistic avatars as well as visual rendering of life-like motions and non-verbal cues. For example, research on therapy to counter perceived body image distortion in anorexia has used biometrically correct virtual bodies, so the visual representation is realistic [3,11]. Crisis management training [12,17] and surgery training [14] aims to teach collaboration with virtual agents and other users to improve collective work. The representation of others and virtual agents has mostly made use of visual feedback.

Occasionally, multisensory cues are used to increase the realism and individuality of avatars, e.g., in the context of communication. Here, it is increasingly common to additionally implement auditory cues (synthetic voices, Voice Over Internet Protocol (VoIP), etc.; e.g., [17] and [14]. Voices rendering is known as a key part of collaborative skills and avatar realism, combined with visual cues [19]. Rarely, social interactions in VR include other auditory cues and tactile feedback to the user, such as a touch to the forearm or shoulder [6,7].

As of yet, it is unclear whether these developments are conducive to creating inclusive virtual environment. Improving on fine visual detail is unlikely to create strong cues for people with VI, and the current focus on voices ignores other potential auditory sources as cues to the presence and identity of others.

Accessibility of Virtual Reality for People with VI. Multiple projects have specifically investigated VR for people with VI. It is now possible to navigate auditory, sometimes audio-visual, virtual environments without vision using a force-feedback joystick and environmental cues through audio-tactile feedback [10], with a keyboard to explore an virtual audio environment [2], with smartphone applications using and gesture [4,5], and by physically walking in a virtual or augmented room [9,20]. Two works propose virtual white canes: one simulates a whitecane with a braking system [22], and another work designed a virtual white cane through vibration in the hand controller of the VR system [8]. In all of these works, the user interacts with physical aspects of the VE only, such as exploring virtual environments and interact with them. As far as we are aware, there are no virtual characters present, thus ignoring the potential for collaborative experiences.

3 Method and Participants

3.1 Design of the Survey

We created a questionnaire to gather insights into the strategies and cues used by persons with VI in real-world settings when attempting to detect and identify others with the goal of initiating an interaction. To this end, we developed 20 questions, falling into several different categories. The full set of questions is provided Table 1. A first set of categories covers four types of mutual awareness in social and collaborative settings: environmental awareness, user and interaction awareness, action awareness, and organization awareness [1]. As summarized in [21], environmental awareness refers to sharing the same space (Q1), action awareness is being aware of the concurrent actions of the other users (Q6), interaction and user awareness concerns knowing the available interactions and knowing who the other users are (Q2, Q3, Q4, Q5, Q8, Q9), and organizational awareness is about knowing and sharing the implications of context on the group (Q7). The question Q8, Q9, Q19 and Q20 aim to identify the good practices for both representing people and initiating interaction in virtual environment. Further, we asked about the use of the senses (Q10 to 15), as well as potential other information found in literature and blogging (Q16–17) and one open question (Q18).

3.2 Protocol

The survey was self-administered. It was organized as follow:

- **presentation of the goal of the study, confidentiality and consent form**. For minors, this part was read and agreed upon by the participants' legal guardian, for legal reasons (it was the only part that required another person to answer for the minor participants).
- **demographic information**. Information regarding age, gender, and the level of vision was collected.
- **survey**. The twenty questions presented Table 1.

3.3 Participants

We send our survey to three blind adults first, so they could verify the accessibility and the questions. We then distributed our survey to professionals of two schools for people with visual impairments in France. The schools send our surveys to former students and to parents of current students. Questionnaire responses were returned by fifteen participants in total, i.e., eight adults and seven minors under the age of eighteen years old. For confidentiality reasons and to respect the consent form terms, we do not provide the individual demographics. However, we will describe here individually each demographics dimension (gender, age, and level of vision). Regarding the adults' group, 6 participants were male, 2 were female, and 0 other. The average age is 38 years old, with a

Table 1. The twenty questions of the survey, and the categories. Awareness categories: Environmental, Interaction and User, Action and Organizational. Other categories: Use of senses, Other potential cues, Open question, and Good practices.

Category	Question
Environmental	**Q1.** When you enter a room, how do you notice a person is present?
Interaction and User	**Q2.** When you meet up with people you know for a social appointment in a public space, how do you recognize them?
Interaction and User	**Q3.** When you meet people you know by coincidence in a public space, how do you recognize them?
Interaction and User	**Q4.** When you meet people you do not know, how do you know you have never met them?
Interaction and User	**Q5.** In the first few second after meeting a person for the first time, which factors (such as perceptual cues) influence your first impression of this person (a nice person, an unsympathetic person, a shy person, an extrovert person)?
Action	**Q6.** How do you identify that a group of people is present in a room you enter? How do you identify the activity of the group?
Organizational	**Q7.** How do you know if it is socially appropriate to join the activity of a group of people, for instance a conversation?
Interaction and User, Good practices	**Q8.** When do you find a person easy to recognize?
Interaction and User; Good practices	**Q9.** When do you find a person difficult to recognize?
Use of the senses	**Q10.** Do you use vision for it? If you use vision to identify people, what cues do you use to recognize them?
Use of the senses	**Q11.** Do you use touch for it? If you use touch to identify people, what cues do you use to recognize them?
Use of the senses	**Q12.** Do you use temperature perception for it? If you use temperature perception to identify people, what cues do you use to recognize them?
Use of the senses	**Q13.** Do you use air flow perception for it? If you use air flow perception to identify people, what cues do you use to recognize them?
Use of the senses	**Q14.** Do you use audio perception for it? If you use audio perception to identify people, what cues do you use to recognize them?
Use of the senses	**Q15.** Do you use smell perception for it? If you use smell perception to identify people, what cues do you use to recognize them?
Other potential cues	**Q16.** Do you use location and context for it? If you use location and context to identify people, what cues do you use to recognize them?
Other potential cues	**Q17.** If you have one, do you use information from your guide dog for it? If you use information from your guide dog to identify people, what cues do you use to recognize them?
Open question	**Q18.** What other cues do you use to recognize people?
Good practices	**Q19.** When somebody approaches you and you can't identify the person because you either don't know or remember the person, what are the most helpful cues to identify who it is?
Good practices	**Q20.** What do you want people not to do to alert you from their presence or to identify themselves? For example, because the action startles or annoys you or is not helpful.

standard deviation of 18 years. The range is from 19 to 67 years old, with the following values: 19, 20, 21, 26, 48, 48, 52 and 67. 2 participants were low vision, 5 were blind with light perception, and 1 was blind without light perception. Regarding the minors' group, 5 participants were male, 1 was female, and 1 was other. The average age is 12 years old, with a standard deviation of 4 years. The range is from 6 to 16 years old, with the following values: 6, 10, 10, 10, 14, 15, 16. 1 participant was low vision, 2 were blind with light perception, and 4 were blind without light perception.

4   Results

In the following, we analyze participants' responses in terms of their own observational and behavioral strategies as well as strategies by others that are used to: detect and subsequently identify a person as known or unknown (Sects. 4.1, 4.2 and 4.3), and identify their activity (Sect. 4.4). In Sect. 4.5, we summarize strategies that others might use to initiate an interaction. Numbers in round brackets indicate the number of participants who mentioned a particular fact.

4.1   Detecting the Presence of Others

Observation strategies: Vision is used to identify silhouettes (2 participants), although audition is more commonly used, by paying attention to noises people make (9 participants) through their activities (indistinct noise, voice, breathing, typing on a computer, pace noise) or by being directly greeted by somebody in the room. Participants also use smells (4 participants), such as parfume, food, hygiene products such skin care and aftershave, touch for airflow perception and clothes, and, interestingly, a sense of a co-presence (5 participants) in form of passive echolocation or a feeling of being observed. Smell can help to estimate the distance of another person.

Behavioral Strategies: Participants mention saying hello and then waiting whether somebody answers. The direction of the answer can help to visually search for the other person. An indirect strategy is trying to detect whether the light in a room is turned on since rooms containing people are often illuminated. This is useful when visual capabilities are insufficient to recognize silhouettes but light perception is possible.

4.2   Identifying a Known Person

Observation Strategies: People can be identified visually by the individual shape of their silhouettes (2 participants), and their face if close enough (2 participants). However, eleven of the participants do not use vision at all to identify others. Visual or tactile feedback is used to recognize somebody by their hair (tactile, 2 participants; visually, 2 participants), their clothes (3 participants), the size (silhouette, tactilely when guiding by the height of the leading arm, with audio when talking). Audition is used to pay attention to the voice (14 participants; sample needs to be long enough to disambiguate identity), to person-specific sounds like laughter (2 participants), way of breathing (3 participants), moving and walking (3 participants). Other person-specific sounds mentioned were the way to playing with a pen, typing on a keyboard, and sounds from jewelry. Jewelry can also help to identify a person by touch. Two participants said they do not dare too much using active tactile exploration, as it may make others uncomfortable. Passive tactile feedback is used to recognize close relatives (e.g., by the way how another person grabs one's arm or how they guide, how their hands feel, musculature). Smell and fragrance can help (10 participants), but do not always give a clear cue to identity. Participants also mentioned using passive echo-location signature for identification (2 participants). Lastly, guide-dog reactions indicate that a person is known; however, this does usually not help to identify the person (2 participants).

Behavioral Strategies: Some participants let people approach and present themselves (5 participants). To this end, they define a precise meeting point (3 participants) and make their arrival known (4 participants; by phone, calling out loud, or hitting the white cane on the floor). The context can help to disambiguate persons (colleagues in the workplace, landlord inside a specific house). Other people can draw attention to themselves by calling out or waving at the person with VI.

Miscellaneous: One participant reports never going out without a sighted guide; two others report they are not able to identify people and have to rely on others approaching them. A person that is easy to identify has a recognizable voice (9 participants) or breath, a particular smell or fragrance (3 participants), makes distinctive noises (wrist bands, keys, heels, personal style of walking (3 participants), person in a wheelchair). A person is difficult to recognize if it is difficult to identify their voice (7 participants; person not talking, or too quiet, strong similarity to the voice of another person). Similarly, a person that does not move or is encountered out of their usual context is difficult to recognize, as well as encounters within large public spaces, with too many people (4 participants) and too much noise (3 participants). Lastly, familiarity plays a role—a person that is encountered less often is more difficult to recognize (4 participants) because there were insufficient opportunities to learn distinctive elements for identification (clothes, pace, voices, way of grabbing).

4.3   Identifying that a Person Is Unknown

Observation Strategies: In general, the cues are the same as when identifying a known person; however, without any correspondence in memory: participants use the voice (10 participants), typical words or gestures, way of grabbing the arm or guiding, silhouette and smell.

Behavioral Strategies: The fact that participants do not know a person is usually confirmed during the conversation and by asking questions. Sometimes, the course of the conversation will lead to the realization that the participant wrongly assumed to be talking to a known person.

4.4 Identifying an Activity

Observation Strategies and Joining an Activity: Ongoing activities can be identified visually from gestures and, in case of physical activities, movements of human silhouettes (2 participants). Audition is particularly helpful to pick up noises that humans or materials emit (9 participants; e.g., from a keyboard, specific sounds of a familiar activity such as board games tokens or cooking tools) as well as the density of the noise, the number of different voices and the content of the conversation are considered useful cues to the activity (6 participants), or the general atmosphere of the room (2 participants; e.g., tavern vs. meeting). Smell and touch give information about the material used (cooking, smell of a pen when drawing). Three participants indicated they would not participate in an activity or a conversation if they are not explicitly included by the others or invited to join.

4.5 Approaching a Person with VI to Start an Activity

In the following, we summarize good and bad strategies mentioned by our participants regarding how others can identify themselves and initiate an activity.

Good Practices: In many situations, it is helpful if the approaching person states their name (8 participants), their function or job (3 participants), and the context of previous encounters (5 participants). If the person is unknown, they should indicate why they are approaching and, if applicable, the name of the person who send them. When others did not present themselves properly, our participants' strategies are to ask who it is (4 participants), asking possible past memories or if there have been previous encounters (2 participants), and asking questions in general.

Bad Practices: Several participants stated that sudden and unannounced physical contact is undesirable, such as catching somebody who is moving with a white cane by the arm to stop them (2 participants), pat them on the shoulder (2 participants), or touching otherwise without prior consent (4 participants). Approaching somebody silently can generate negative effects, like surprise or making the participants uncomfortable because they failed to hear the person's approach. Addressing a person with VI verbally has its pitfalls, as well: others may not speak up long enough for them to be identified (e.g., "Hello" is too short), a call out from too far away can lead to a visual search for the caller but without a successful localization, and calling and speaking loudly at close distance may have startling effects (3 participants).

First Impression: What influences the first impression somebody makes on a person with VI? Participants stated that they rely on concrete cues: the handshaking, the tone and intonation of the voice (10 participants), if there is a warm feeling in the voice, the way of speaking and the words used (three participants), the attention the person pays, the face, and the overall behavior (2 participants). One participant stated that he or she can notice if the visual handicap will be an obstacle from the voice and the intonation.

5   Creating Inclusive Virtual Characters

The responses to our questionnaire suggest a number of extensions that can be made to virtual characters to increase their accessibility for persons with VI with current technologies that we describe in the first subsection. The answers also open future perspectives that we describe in the second subsection.

5.1   Adaptation Possible with Current Technologies

Visual Attributes. Avatars and agents should have distinctive silhouettes, clothes (shapes, color), and faces, to be easily recognized even with low vision. They could have personalized movement patterns, e.g., with idle animation or when talking. A light turned on in a virtual room can indicate that an avatar or agent is present. Some adjustments make VR potentially more accessible, for instance avoiding the necessity of eye to have to adapt to differences in brightness, e.g., when changing virtual environments (e.g., rooms, or from outside to inside).

Audio Attributes. Voice is a highly valuable cue to identify people, in particular if the avatar is talking long enough. Distinctive voices, e.g., in terms of pitch, differentiate between characters. With only three voices with referring to gender (feminine, masculine, mixed) a user can differentiate between three characters. Vocabulary, speed, and rhythm add specificity. Other person-specific sounds such as breathing, laughter, way of walking, or wearing different types of shoes (heels, sport shoes, squeaky shoes) improve the chances of identifying the virtual character. Pace can be a cue to decide whether to start an interaction or not (e.g., walking fast may imply little time). Identity and social cues could be conveyed by any sound-generating activity linked to a habit (playing with a pen, tapping finger nails on the table), to objects (keys, chains, sword), or to jewelry (wristbands, ear rings).

Multimodal Attributes. The height of a person can be represented visually as well as via spatialized audio feedback. The cloth of virtual characters' garments can be represented visually by a texture as well as by distinctive sounds like rustling and swishing. Avatars in a wheelchair can be a very recognizable by their silhouette and associated sounds.

Airflow. Airflow from a fan could simulated that someone just came closer or walked by.

Interactions. Initiating an interaction is a crucial prerequisite for collaboration. Therefore, it is important that it is transparent to the user how they can join activities. The user should be able to address the entire virtual room, equivalent to "Hello?" , using voice or through a controller. The virtual characters, either agents or avatars, should detect it (broadcast to remote users or audio recognition for agents). The user may want to send a directed call to a particular character (virtual phone call, virtual poke) or semi-directed call (like making noise with the white can). The virtual characters should be able to answer, wave at the person or get closer. They may spontaneously address the user and present themselves or even invite the user to join. The virtual space should ease recognition of characters and activities (e.g., by being a meeting point, providing distinctive activity sounds, or good separation of multiple voices). The place of meeting (noisy, full of people or not) make the recognition difficult or not.

5.2   Future Implementations for Virtual Reality

Smell. Combined with airflow, a fragrance dispenser could indicate that some-one is in the room; the distance from this person could be indicated by smell intensity. Many flavors, fragrances and spices exist, liquid or other (vanilla, chocolate, coconut, mint, banana, musk, cedar, cumin, curry, basil, cinnamon), even scent kits, and can be used to give smell feedback.

Tactile Feedback for Shapes. Tactile feedback helps to recognize jewelry by touch, the face and objects that help identifying the person.

Tactile Feedback for Materials. Tactile feedback could indicates hair (long, short, no hair) with only on actuator at the hand level for the user. Tactile feedback for cloth can be added to visual and audio-feedback.

Tactile Feedback for Human Contact. Tactile feedback can give a lot of information, to identify a person and to make a first impression. In real life, tactile feedback for recognition is used during handshakes, guiding and even to know the size and the musculature of the person.

Guide Dog. A virtual guide dog could react differently depending on the time spent with a virtual character or a real person controlling the avatar.

Passive Echo-Location. Passive echo location is the ability to feel shapes and obstacles from reverberations without emitting a sound purposefully for echoing. If it can be more efficiently modeled in VR, it could be a new means to feel spaces and people.

6   Discussion and Perspectives

We presented the results of an online survey on the strategies used by people with VI for detecting and identifying people as well as on-going activities in real environments. We use the findings to propose solutions for inclusive collaborative VE, with inclusive representations of virtual characters and activities. Many of these solutions can already be implemented, while others will become achievable with future technological developments. Further, our work is applicable to any virtual environment such as for multiplayer games, applications with non-player characters, training environments, telepresence scenarios, or video conferencing. It may require new ways of recording and broadcasting people, to add information beyond the currently predominant video stream. Our future research will focus on designing and evaluating such virtual characters with people with and without VI.

Acknowledgments. We thank the participants and the institutions that distributed our survey, especially IRSA and Ocens. This work was supported by the European Union's Horizon2020 Program under ERCEA grant no. 683008 AMPLIFY.

References

1. Ahn, H.J., Lee, H.J., Cho, K., Park, S.J.: Utilizing knowledge context in virtual collaborative work. Decis. Support Syst. **39**(4), 563–582 (2005)
2. Connors, E.C., Chrastil, E.R., Sánchez, J., Merabet, L.B.: Virtual environments for the transfer of navigation skills in the blind: a comparison of directed instruction vs. video game based learning approaches. Front. Hum. Neurosci. **8**, 223 (2014)
3. Cornelissen, K.K., McCarty, K., Cornelissen, P.L., Tovée, M.J.: Body size estimation in women with anorexia nervosa and healthy controls using 3D avatars. Sci. Rep. **7**(1), 1–15 (2017)
4. Guerreiro, J., Ahmetovic, D., Kitani, K.M., Asakawa, C.: Virtual navigation for blind people: building sequential representations of the real-world. In: ASSETS 2017. ACM, Baltimore (2017)
5. Guerrón, N.E., Cobo, A., Olmedo, J.J.S., Martín, C.: Sensitive interfaces for blind people in virtual visits inside unknown spaces. Int. J. Hum. Comput. Stud. (2019). https://doi.org/10.1016/J.IJHCS.2019.08.004
6. Haans, A., Ijsselsteijn, W.: Mediated social touch: a review of current research and future directions. Virtual Reality **9**(2–3), 149–159 (2006)
7. Hoppe, M., Rossmy, B., Neumann, D.P., Streuber, S., Schmidt, A., Machulla, T.K.: A human touch: Social touch increases the perceived human-likeness of agents in virtual reality. In: Proceedings of the 2020 CHI Conference on Human Factors in Computing Systems, pp. 1–11 (2020)
8. Kreimeier, J., Götzelmann, T.: First steps towards walk-in-place locomotion and haptic feedback in virtual reality for visually impaired. In: Extended Abstracts of the 2019 CHI Conference on Human Factors in Computing Systems, p. LBW2214. ACM (2019)
9. Kunz, A., Miesenberger, K., Zeng, L., Weber, G.: Virtual navigation environment for blind and low vision people. In: Miesenberger, K., Kouroupetroglou, G. (eds.) ICCHP 2018. LNCS, vol. 10897, pp. 114–122. Springer, Cham (2018). https://doi.org/10.1007/978-3-319-94274-2_17
10. Lahav, O., Mioduser, D.: Construction of cognitive maps of unknown spaces using a multi-sensory virtual environment for people who are blind. Comput. Huma. Behav. **24**(3), 1139–1155 (2008). https://doi.org/10.1016/j.chb.2007.04.003
11. Mölbert, S.C., et al.: Assessing body image in anorexia nervosa using biometric self-avatars in virtual reality: Attitudinal components rather than visual body size estimation are distorted. Psychol. Med. **48**(4), 642–653 (2018)

12. Nakanishi, H., Koizumi, S., Ishida, T.: Virtual cities for real-world crisis management. In: van den Besselaar, P., Koizumi, S. (eds.) Digital Cities 2003. LNCS, vol. 3081, pp. 204–216. Springer, Heidelberg (2005). https://doi.org/10.1007/11407546_10

13. Negrón, A.P.P., Vera, R.A.A., de Antonio Jimenez, A.: Collaborative interaction analysis in virtual environments based on verbal and nonverbal interaction. In: 2010 Ninth Mexican International Conference on Artificial Intelligence, pp. 129–133. IEEE (2010)

14. Paiva, P.V., Machado, L.S., Valença, A.M.G., Batista, T.V., Moraes, R.M.: Simcec: a collaborative VR-based simulator for surgical teamwork education. Comput. Entertain. (CIE) **16**(2), 1–26 (2018)

15. Pan, X., Hamilton, A.F.D.C.: Why and how to use virtual reality to study human social interaction: the challenges of exploring a new research landscape. Br. J. Psychol. **109**(3), 395–417 (2018)

16. Pejsa, T., Gleicher, M., Mutlu, B.: Who, me? How virtual agents can Shape conversational footing in virtual reality. IVA 2017. LNCS (LNAI), vol. 10498, pp. 347–359. Springer, Cham (2017). https://doi.org/10.1007/978-3-319-67401-8_45

17. Rudinsky, J., Hvannberg, E.T., Helgason, A.A., Petursson, P.B.: Designing soundscapes of virtual environments for crisis management training. In: Proceedings of the Designing Interactive Systems Conference, pp. 689–692 (2012)

18. Shachaf, P.: Cultural diversity and information and communication technology impacts on global virtual teams: an exploratory study. Inf. Manag. **45**(2), 131–142 (2008)

19. Steed, A., Schroeder, R.: Collaboration in immersive and non-immersive virtual environments. In: Lombard, M., Biocca, F., Freeman, J., IJsselsteijn, W., Schaevitz, R.J. (eds.) Immersed in Media, pp. 263–282. Springer, Cham (2015). https://doi.org/10.1007/978-3-319-10190-3_11

20. Thévin, L., Briant, C., Brock, A.M.: X-road: virtual reality glasses for orientation and mobility training of people with visual impairments. ACM Trans. Access. Comput. (TACCESS) **13**(2), 1–47 (2020)

21. Thévin, L., Brock, A.: How to move from inclusive systems to collaborative systems: the case of virtual reality for teaching O&M. In: CHI 2019 Workshop on Hacking Blind Navigation (2019)

22. Zhao, Y., et al.: Enabling people with visual impairments to navigate virtual reality with a haptic and auditory cane simulation. In: Proceedings of the 2018 CHI Conference on Human Factors in Computing Systems, p. 116. ACM (2018)

23. Zhao, Y., Cutrell, E., Holz, C., Morris, M.R., Ofek, E., Wilson, A.D.: Seeingvr: a set of tools to make virtual reality more accessible to people with low vision. In: Proceedings of the 2019 CHI Conference on Human Factors in Computing Systems, pp. 1–14 (2019)

Motiv'Handed, a New Gamified Approach for Home-Based Hand Rehabilitation for Post-stroke Hemiparetic Patients

Sarah Duval-Dachary[1], Jean-Philippe Chevalier-Lancioni[1],
Mauro Rossini[2], Paolo Perego[1], and Mario Covarrubias[3(✉)]

[1] Dipartimento di Design, Politecnico di Milano, Milan, Italy
[2] Valduce Hospital, Villa Beretta, Rehabilitation Centre, Costa Masnaga, Italy
[3] Dipartimento di Meccanica, Politecnico di Milano, Milan, Italy
mario.covarrubias@polimi.it

Abstract. This document summarizes a master thesis project trying to bring a new solution to hemiplegia rehabilitation, one of the numerous consequences of strokes. A hemiplegic patients observe paralysis on one side of their body, and as so, loses autonomy and their quality of life decreases. In this study, we decided to only focus on the hand rehabilitation aspect. However, there is a clear tendency in stroke patients to stop training regularly when returning home from the hospital and the first part of their rehabilitation is over. They often experience demotivation, having the feeling that they will never get back to a fully autonomous person ever again and tend to put their training aside, especially when they do not see clear and visible results anymore. This is also due to the supervised training becoming sparser. All of this results in patients stagnating or even worse, regressing. Thus, we decided to offer a motivating solution for hand rehabilitation at home through gamification.

Keywords: Stroke · Hand · VR rehabilitation · Gamification

1 Introduction

According to the World Health Organization, 15 million people suffer strokes worldwide each year which can sometimes cause death. Survivors are left with neurological and cognitive issues. Ninety percent of the surviving victims experience some degree of paralysis [1]. As to regain mobility and voluntary movement, they need a continued rehabilitation and therapy following the stroke where repetition is key [2].

This paper aims at explaining our work in providing a home-based hand rehabilitation device for hemiparetic patients. We will first go through the research phase that led us to our concept decision, from studying the stroke condition and the rehabilitation process, to what has already been done in the post-stroke hand rehabilitation field. Then we will explain what our concept consists in, finishing with the complete description of the physical and virtual prototype, looking at all the challenges we encountered and all the solutions we found.

© Springer Nature Switzerland AG 2020
K. Miesenberger et al. (Eds.): ICCHP 2020, LNCS 12376, pp. 176–183, 2020.
https://doi.org/10.1007/978-3-030-58796-3_22

2   State of the Art

We looked for all types of rehabilitation devices for the upper limb implementing technological assets, as exoskeletons, clinical devices, and innovative products. We did not include the devices like the elastic bands, balls, cubes, games, etc., that can be used in any type of rehabilitations. Some of the considered products are on the market, others are just research projects, or concepts. We will here present only the devices that inspired us. For a more comprehensive state of the art, we invite you to read the two following master thesis [3, 4].

After going over the different kinds of products that we found, the ones that seemed the most relevant were:

- Saebo Rejoyce: A workstation with an 3-axis arm and 6 different types of grips working with a graphic interface for 2D games. Allows movements in every direction while grip training. It aims at working on everyday life movements.
- Saebo VR devices: A hand tracking device allowing the patients to control a game with their hands. No intermediary device is necessary.
- WIM [5] and Fit Mi from Flint Rehab devices: Both are small, simple and innovative devices that take a different approach regarding rehabilitation, using a gamified approach.
- Bimeo Pro from Kinestica: A device is a physical interface between the patient and a 2D game, using the valid side to help the disabled one.
- Project of F. Carneiro, R. Tavares, J. Rodrigues and P. Abreu [6]: A device that interacts with VR. In their case, they are showing the deformation and the motion of the object in the VR environment.

From all the products that we have reviewed, it appears that there recently is a clear trend for training's gamification. Most products come with a graphical interface or 2D games trying to enhance the patients' rehabilitation experience. However, a lot of them look outdated which is not really appealing. Given the result of our study, we decided to follow this direction and develop a product that allows gamified training.

3   User Analysis

3.1   Users

Our users are patients that were victims of a stroke and suffer from hemiplegia or hemiparesis and the medical team that is following them. In our case, we focus on patients, who experienced hand paralysis and already regained some hand mobility and are relieved from spasticity. It corresponds to the patient that were just sent home after the end of their rehabilitation in hospital and/or clinic. Patients tend then to stop training as frequently as they were, because the frequency of their supervised session is decreasing. It sometimes implies stagnation in their rehabilitation, but it can also cause the regression of their mobility gains.

Thus, the aim of our product is to motivate the patients to regularly train at home thanks to a device they can use by themselves.

Moreover, since this product will be used in a medical context, the training and the device will have to be adapted to each patient individually. Our secondary user, the medical team, will have to take care of it.

3.2 Users Study

To know a little bit more about our users we decided to create some questionnaires in different languages (italian, french, english) that we distributed on Facebook pages and to therapists and stroke survivors among our entourage. Unfortunately, the outcome of those questionnaires is quite irrelevant since we did not get as much engagement as we wish we would have. However, by going to the Villa Beretta clinic, witnessing exercise sessions, and interviewing patients and therapists, we learned that they are willing to do any exercises as long as they can see tangible results.

In addition, we learned that some patients that had the possibility to go home, had to come twice or three times a week for training sessions of two hours to a half day. It requires time and imposes a rigid organization. Moreover, it obliges the patient to train also at home to continue to keep progressing quickly.

Furthermore, we noticed that the exercises were really repetitive, and the machines were big and expensive. We look for alternative solutions focused on home training on the internet. Various tutorials were stressing out the importance of making progress as obvious as possible thanks to simple tricks. The offered exercises were still really repetitive.

Finally, from our personal experience and the experience of our relatives, we found out that, doing rehabilitation exercises everyday was almost the same as doing physical preparation (sport). In both cases the most difficult part is to stay motivated.

3.3 The Rehabilitation Process and Repetitive Exercises

The rehabilitation process consists in going through numerous repetitions of the same exercise in order to trigger the brain functional reorganization process. Repeating the same exercises can get boring very quickly, which explains the current trend of gamified training. As we saw in the state of the art, gamification consists in the use of 2D or 3D games on a flat screen.

We thought about going further by using a Virtual Reality (VR) game for hand rehabilitation, since it would completely immerse the users into the task they are performing. Virtual reality being a fairly new technology, it is not yet so widespread but it sure will become a standard in the near future. A review of different VR systems for stroke rehabilitation [7] indeed revealed that these systems were useful and recommended for rehabilitation. Then it comforts us in using a VR solution for our product. By VR we mean a 3D game in which the user is immersed in thanks to a VR headset.

4 The Product: Motiv'Handed

4.1 Concept

Our concept is to create a modular, compact and adaptive device which would focus on ADL-based exercises while being unobtrusive in order to motivate the user to train in any circumstances. It then requires having a discrete appearance, not looking like a medical object to avoid shame or any idea of this nature. The idea is to break down as many barriers as we can that can go in the way of sticking to a regular training schedule. It is a hybrid product, which can be used with or without a Virtual Reality Headset. Finally, it is a 3D-printed device, which allows it to be printed with different dimensions, thus it is possible to adapt it to best fit any patient's hand size.

We chose to reproduce with our device Activities of Daily Living, thus any progress with the product would be directly applicable to real life circumstances. This seemed like the most motivating solution for patients.

The object as standalone will consist in different grips assembled on a single object. You can visualize them on Fig. 1 that shows the various motions that can be done with the object. With this arrangement we are trying to cover as many grips as a user can encounter and must deal with daily.

Fig. 1. Product characteristics and grips.

4.2 Design

Shape. In order to fill in the requirement for it to be unobtrusive, we decided to go for a bottle-shaped object that would fit in any environment. It is important for us that the users would not be ashamed of bringing it with them outside. As each single patient have a different hand size, we made the device adaptative. A parametric 3D model based on a single sketch allows the therapist to change its dimensions thanks to two inputs: the patient's hand length and width.

Technical Solutions. In order to be able to track the patients' training and be able to interact with our video game we had to use different components:

- Potentiometers and rotary encoders to monitor which rotational grip is being actuated,
- An electronic montage using a Velostat material sheet to monitor pressure applied on the power grip,

- An Arduino board, a microcontroller, with an integrated Bluetooth low energy module and IMU sensor,
- A battery, for a portable and autonomous device.

Manufacturing Process and Material. To be able to make each product with a customized size, we needed to use a process that allowed it. We decided to go for 3D printing. Indeed, nowadays 3D printers are becoming more and more accessible, lowering the production cost, especially for objects that must be produced in small series as in our case. Regarding the material, among the two most common materials used in 3D printing we decided to use PLA, which is cheap, comes in a lot of colors, is less toxic than ABS, and offers sufficient mechanical properties.

4.3 Device

After making sure our 3D model was feasible and shock resistant, we decided to print it ourselves using a Fused Deposition Modeling printer. It contains 19 parts to print which takes up to 60 h. To this, needs to be added the post-processing and assembly time. By summing all up, building a complete device can take one week and a half of work for a single person with just one printer at disposal.

4.4 Use

As said before the product comes with a VR game but is however usable with or without VR. Indeed, we did not want to force people to have to put a 3D headset to use the device. In addition, it really brings meaning to the idea of a portable device that the patients can bring with them during their trips. In this way they can maintain a high training frequency wherever they might go.

To use the device with VR, the patients need a VR headset and a free desk in front of a chair. Thus, it will be used mostly at home or in a clinic. On the contrary, the device as a stand-alone product can be used everywhere, just by connecting it to the corresponding app and doing the exercises given by the therapists (Fig. 2).

Fig. 2. Use cases and real prototype/rendering comparison.

5 The App

5.1 Companion App

The app (not entirely implemented, only graphics and logic of the app were realized) will connect the therapists to their patients and allow them to monitor from their application their patient's progress. They will be able to change their patient's program remotely based on their performance, communicate with them or recommend a new appointment in case, for example, adjustments need to be done with the device.

5.2 Unity App

Our unity application aims at motivating the patients to exercise regularly by providing a pseudo realistic environment while gamifying the tasks to execute. Its second goal is to help the patient in getting a difficulty level that suits them and monitors their progress in order to provide adequate exercises. Moreover, it aims at providing for the lack of contextual setting that the patients may feel when using the regular app program.

Interaction Modes. The interactions within our game has been thought to always revolve around hand training. There are then two modes of interaction:

- Direct interaction: without the use of our device, hand tracking and interaction with the virtual environment is ensured by the Leap Motion. It is a very natural and seamless interaction. There, we decided to use movements that were not actually among the movement list that the device allowed to perform, but are still often practiced during rehabilitation, like pinching and pointing.
- Interaction through our device: For actions representing an ADL task, the interaction will be performed using a specific part of the device. The part that the user will have to use will be indicated in real time with specific icons.

User Interface. In Virtual Reality, the environment evolves with where the user is looking at. Which means that the UI cannot be static in the environment. Therefore, we decided to use a Leap Motion feature that sticks a menu with interactive buttons to the user's palm. One of them allows the user to switch between motion mode and free interaction mode, the second brings the player back to the main menu, to save or quit the game. The other UI element of the game is an interactive white crosshair displayed at exact center of the user's view. It becomes green when the player can interact with an object of the game.

Player Movement. For our user we decided to allow two kinds of motion: translation of the player forward and backward, and rotation of the camera around the player. Both are performed thanks to given gestures tracked and recognized by the Leap Motion. To translate the users should point forward with their index or backward with their thumb. To rotate the camera the players should perform a pinch with each hand, positioned one next to another. Then, if they want to rotate right, they just draw their right hand towards the right, and vice versa (Fig. 3).

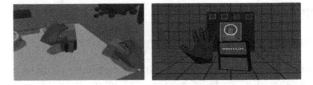

Fig. 3. Direct interaction on the left and example of interface on the right.

Presentation of the Game. Our game is a mix between a simulation game and a casual game. It is based on the popular principle of the Escape Game. The user is locked inside a series of rooms and must reach the final one to earn specific objects/points.

In order to access the next room, the users must solve puzzles in a specific sequence that will allow them to unlock the door to the next room. Those puzzles will require the user to use their devices to interact with the game and then solve them.

An Example of a Puzzle: The First One in the Game. At the beginning of the game you need to power some knobs in order to change the color of four cubes to match the ones above the door (Fig. 4).

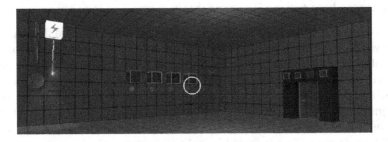

Fig. 4. 1st room of the game.

The repetitive aspect of the training is achieved in two ways: by increasing the number of puzzles to solve or by increasing the number of motions per puzzle.

6   Experience on People with no Disability

We had the opportunity to test our device on some people with no disability, including ourselves. We feared we would lose the device's position between two interactions, as the eyes are covered by the headset and the device is not visible in the game. Instead we notice that we quickly find it and it is not an issue.

The physical device was working but required fine tuning to insure a more stable and durable connection to the microprocessor. Regarding the game prototype, it was necessary to dimension it better. The player would feel small inside our environment. Furthermore, the translation triggers needed better tunings. In this state, it was not conceivable to test it with a stroke patient. Due to a lack of time we did not continue the project.

7   Conclusion

Developing a home-based rehabilitation device brings a lot of advantages to the patients, who can thus train in a familiar environment when it is the most convenient for them. Gamifying it gives the users an additional motivation to train. But Motiv'-Handed is more than just a product offering a home-based gamified rehabilitation training. Indeed, it differentiates itself from the other products on the market, thanks to the following characteristics:

- its portability: the stroke survivors do not need any more to stay at home for training but can also go outside to enjoy fresh air or bring Motiv'Handed with them on weekend or vacation, never breaking their training routine
- its variety of trained grips: six different grips used in activities of daily living can be trained
- its adventure video game: the patients go through a real game that is involving them, and where they can practice ADL gestures
- its accessibility: it is available to a large public at low production costs
- its adaptability: each hand is different and thus the main dimensions of the product can be change to the various hand sizes

We achieved to develop a functional prototype with the main sensors of the device and paired it with a game prototype. Thus, we proved the feasibility of our concept. After correcting the flaws of the prototype, a test with stroke patient will be conceivable.

References

1. Stroke Paralysis. Portea. https://www.portea.com/physiotherapy/stroke-paralysis#section_1. Accessed 15 June 2020
2. Recovering from Hand Weakness after Stroke. Saebo. https://www.saebo.com/stroke-hand-weakness-recovery/. Accessed 15 June 2020
3. UHMA, a new solution for post-stroke home-based hand rehabilitation for patient with hemiparese, Duval–Dachary Sarah, Master thesis (2019)
4. Motiv'Handed, a new home-based hand rehabilitation device for post-stroke hemiparetic patients, Chevalier–Lancioni Jean-Philippe, Master Thesis (2020)
5. WIM, Jenny Holmsten website. https://www.jennyholmsten.com/wim. Accessed 15 June 2020
6. Carneiro, F., Tavares, R., Rodrigues, J., Abreu, P., Restivo, M.: A gamified approach for hand rehabilitation device. Int. J. Online
7. Engineering (iJOE), January 2018. Virtual reality for therapeutic purposes in stroke: A systematic review. S. Viñas-Diza, M. Sobrido-Prieto. s.l. : Elsevier España, S.L.U (2015)

Move-IT: A Virtual Reality Game for Upper Limb Stroke Rehabilitation Patients

Maram AlMousa[1], Hend S. Al-Khalifa[1($\boxtimes$)] (iD), and Hana AlSobayel[2]

[1] Information Technology Department, College of Computer and Information Sciences, King Saud University, Riyadh, Saudi Arabia
hendk@ksu.edu.sa
[2] Department of Rehabilitation Sciences, College of Applied Medical Sciences, King Saud University, Riyadh, Saudi Arabia

Abstract. Stroke rehabilitation plays an important role in recovering the life-style of stroke survivors. Although existing research proved the effectiveness and engagement of Non-immersive Virtual Reality (VR) based rehabilitation systems, however, limited research is available on the applicability of fully immersive VR-based rehabilitation systems. In this paper, we present the development and evaluation of "Move-IT" game designed for domestic upper limb stroke patients. The game incorporates the use of Oculus Rift Head Mounted Display (HMD) and the Leap Motion hand tracker. A user study of five upper limb stroke patients was performed to evaluate the application. The results showed that the participants were pleased with the system, enjoyed the game and found it was exciting and easy to play. Moreover, all the participants agreed that the game was very motivating to perform rehabilitation exercises.

Keywords: Virtual Reality · Serious game · Rehabilitation · Stroke · Upper limp · Fully immersive · Head Mounted Display

1 Introduction

Stroke or brain attack is a disease that occurs when a blood stream or part of the brain is ruptured or blocked by a blood clot [1]. At the point when this happens, brain cells are left without oxygen and will start to die within minutes. Once the cells cannot work, the part of the body they control cannot work either, which can make daily activities difficult to stroke survivors [2]. Technically speaking, the affected side of the brain determines the affected area of the body, for example, when the stroke occurs in the right part of the brain, the left part of the body will be affected and vice versa. Moreover, when the stroke occurs in the lower part of the brain, the damage of the body will be greater [3]. Furthermore, stroke disease is classified as the third cause of death in the world after heart and cancer diseases [4].

According to the World Health Organization, there are 15 million people who suffer from stroke worldwide each year [5]. About 5 million of these people die, while 5 million become permanently disabled. Nation wise, statistics indicate that more than 100 strokes occur daily in the Kingdom of Saudi Arabia [6]. Many experts expect that the

© Springer Nature Switzerland AG 2020
K. Miesenberger et al. (Eds.): ICCHP 2020, LNCS 12376, pp. 184–195, 2020.
https://doi.org/10.1007/978-3-030-58796-3_23

rate of stroke will rapidly grow as a result of the increasing population ages, occurrence of high blood pressure, number of smokers, incidence of diabetes and obesity [7].

There are four types of stroke treatment: prevention therapy, medical treatments, surgical treatment, and physical therapy (Rehabilitation) [4]. Stroke rehabilitation is a post stroke treatment that helps stroke survivors to become as independent as possible and have a better control of their life. According to Gunasekera and Bendall [8] Rehabilitation is defined as "a dynamic process of planned adaptive change in lifestyle in response to unplanned change imposed on the individual by disease or traumatic incident".

Rehabilitation helps patients to relearn basic skills such as eating, dressing, and walking, which were lost due to the damage of stroke. Rehabilitation is generally performed in hospitals in the early stages after stroke [9]. As the treatment advances, patients often need to go to specialized units for a supervised outpatient therapy. Finally, the last stage consists of home-based programs that may involve the professionals' visits in order to permit the patient to develop his/her skills in home environment.

The tests of rehabilitation programs proven that the patient's function recovers by performing a series of repeated exercises identified with a certain goal [10]. There are several typical movements practiced in upper limp rehabilitation following stroke, which are usually relevant to daily life [2] such as: reach towards object, grasp object, manipulate object, release object, and single handed and bimanual tasks. Nonetheless, this treatment approach suffers from the absence of patient motivation for performing several repetitive tasks at regular intervals. Moreover, health care providers need to ensure that this treatment program is completed by outpatients. Therefore, the focus of recent research has been on Virtual Reality (VR) based rehabilitation systems, as they were proven to be much effective and engaging than conventional rehabilitation therapy. However, most of these systems are non-immersive.

A recent Cochrane review [11], looking at using VR in stroke rehabilitation, showed growing evidence on the benefits of VR and interactive video gaming on improving upper limb function and activities of daily living function when used as an adjunct to the usual rehabilitation program. However, the clinical trials that are so far available did not have sufficient power to reach a conclusion on the effectiveness of VR on upper limb performance among people with stroke [9]. The lack of sufficient evidence warrants more research on this area. Therefore, our contribution in this paper contains two parts as an extension of our published work in [12]:

1- Present the development of Move-IT game, which is fully immersive VR game designed for stroke upper limb rehabilitation exercises.
2- Evaluate the game feasibility and usability via interviews and observation during test sessions.

The rest of the paper is organized as follows: Sect. 2 illustrates Move-IT game design and implementation. Section 3 reports the evaluation of Move-IT game, and finally. Section 4 concludes the paper with the game limitations and future work.

2 Move-IT Game Design and Implementation

Move-IT game is a fully immersive VR game, which is especially designed for stroke upper limb rehabilitation exercises. The patient needs to perform several arm rehabilitation movements in order to complete the game. The game incorporates the use of Oculus Rift Head Mounted Display (HMD) and the Leap Motion hand tracker. It was developed using the following tools: Unity game engine, Oculus SDK, and Leap Motion SDK.

The story of the game is very simple. It is about a regular person who needs to move some colored cubes arranged in a certain order on a shelf and place them into their boxes next to him. There will be two different colors of cubes and a box for each color. These boxes are located in the right and left side of the user. The user is required to move the cube to the box of the same color (as shown in Fig. 1). Moreover, the game can be played either seated or standing to allow stroke patients who need support or who are unable to stand to use the game. In addition, Move-IT game includes one option, which allows the user to restrict using one hand to achieve the game tasks or using both. The default option is using both hands.

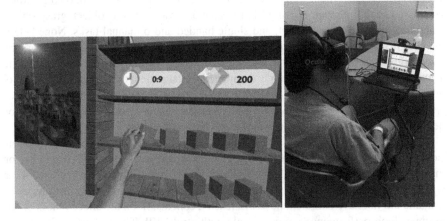

Fig. 1. (left): A Player hand grasping a cube; (right) The environment set-up with a patient

The main user interface of our game module is comprised of four main options:

1. Warm up exercise option that enables the patient to warm up before starting the game.
2. Rehabilitation game option that allows the patient to perform the rehabilitation exercise in an engaging form.
3. Training option that enables the user to try and play the game without any constraints such as time or score.
4. Non-immersive game option that enables the patient to play game without the HMD.

To set an appropriate level of challenge, the game provides users with a variety of difficulty levels that are increased gradually as the user proceed in the game. There are several factors that determine the difficulty of the level. These factors are the number of cubes on the shelf, the arrangement of cubes, and the number and height of the shelves.

There are four different levels of difficulty offered in the game to maintain the user's engagement and to suit a verity of upper limb stroke patients with different severities. The game mainly focuses on the user's upper extremity movements, and requires the patient to perform numerous arm rehabilitation movements. These movements are shoulder flexion to 90° and 120° to reach the cubes on the shelves, shoulder extension, abduction and adduction to move the cubes into the boxes on the right and left sides, hand extension, grasp and release. Moreover, these shoulder movements include implicitly the elbow flexion and extension. These movements are described by images in Table 1.

Table 1. Movements description as suggested by [13]

Movement	Image
Shoulder flexion and extension	
Shoulder abduction and adduction	
Elbow flexion and extension	

The movements included in the game were provided by the occupational therapists (OTs) and physical therapists (PTs) of Sultan Bin Abdulaziz Humanitarian City (SBAHC) and King Fahad Medical Center (KFMC).

There were multiple visits to both centers. The first visit included conducting a focus group with a number of specialists from both centers where several questions were raised and answered. These questions were about the stroke patient's characteristics, the processes and approaches of the rehabilitation therapy, the rehabilitation sessions for inpatients and outpatients, the upper limb rehabilitation exercises, the assessment and evaluation outcome measures, and the VR-base rehabilitation game requirements. The focus group lasted for about one hour in each center.

The second visit involved on-site observation of patients, OTs and PTs during the rehabilitation session, which included interviewing the OTs and PTs, as well. This observation lasted for four hours in SBAHC. It was important to gather reliable information, take notes and get a clearer view of what is the actual rehabilitation therapy activities and environment.

Additionally, Move-IT game has a target time duration identified for each level, to assess the suitability of this level to the user. For example, when the user finishes the current game level before the target time, this means that the level is very easy to the user and s/he needs to pass to the next level. While, spending much time to achieve the game's goal, the game will determine either that this level is suitable to the user and s/he needs to replay it again, or that this level is very hard to the user and s/he needs to be moved to the previous level; depending on the amount of extra time spent. All these decisions are done transparently without the user's knowledge or disturbance to permit him/her to enjoy the game without frustrations.

The user will earn 50 points for each cube he grasps and placing it in the right box. If the user puts the cube in the wrong box, s/he will not earn any point. These points will be displayed during the game and a total of the points won will be displayed at the end of the game. The user statistics option contains records of the user's movement data that are presented in a simple way with graphs; hence the patient could easily read and understand.

3   Evaluation

A pilot evaluation was conducted at Sultan Bin Abdulaziz Humanitarian City (SBAHC) in Saudi Arabia; a total of five patients participated in this pilot evaluation. Prior to conducting the evaluation with real stroke patients, several occupational therapists from SBAHC were invited to actually use the game, propose their suggestions and confirm whether the game is ready to be used on real patients. Their main suggestions are summarized in the following points:

- Modifications on the warm-up exercise so that it focuses on the shoulder and elbow exercises only, excluding hand exercises, which are very difficult to stroke patients.
- Adding a training mode to train the patients before trying the game.
- Adding a non-immersive level (using Leap Motion hand tracker only) that is equivalent to the first level of the original game to enable patients to try between immersive and non-immersive game and choose their preference.

Therefore, all these recommendations were implemented and added to the game before conducting our evaluation with the patients.

3.1 Environment Set-Up

The evaluation was conducted in a quiet and closed room at SBAHC. The laptop that contains our game is placed at a regular computer desk. The Oculus Rift positional tracker is attached to the top of the laptop's monitor. The patient sits on a chair facing the laptop while wearing the Oculus Rift HMD with the leap motion attached to it, at a distance of about 80 cm from the positional tracker. Figure 1 (right) shows the environment set-up with a patient. A therapist assistant was present in the room during the evaluation for prompt assistance.

3.2 Participants

A sample of five stroke patients was recruited in the study as shown in Table 2. SBAHC Institutional Review Board (IRB) has granted ethical approval and the participants were selected according to the following inclusion criteria, which was determined with the help of SBAHC therapists:

- First episode stroke,
- Need for upper limb rehabilitation,
- Minimum ability to grasp and raise arm to 90° within functional rate,
- Ability to speak and understand,
- Not involved in other study during our study period.

All the five patients were male, 56–61 aged. They were from SBAHC as the evaluation was conducted there. Their muscle power differs from each other; most of them have 3+/5 muscle power, while the other two have 3/5 and 4/5 muscle power. Moreover, none of them has experienced playing video games before except for two patients (P2, P4) who used to be expert gamers in Sony PlayStation. In addition, none of them has tried an HMD, except (P1) who has used it once very shortly, just for watching.

Table 2. Collected information of participating demographics

P#	Gender	Age	Start of stroke	Muscle power	Affected hand	Dominant hand	Gamer	Have used HMD
P1	Male	60	2 months	3+/5	Left	Right	No	Once, very shortly
P2	Male	58	5 years	3/5	Left	Right	Yes, daily before stroke (PlayStation)	No
P3	Male	56	2 months	3+/5	Left	Right	No	No
P4	Male	60	1 year	4/5	Left	Right	Yes, weekly (PlayStation)	No
P5	Male	61	3 months	3+/5	Right	Right	No	No

3.3   Method, Results and Discussion

In order to measure the usability of our game, we used quantitative measures to collect performance data such as the time spent on each game level, the number of errors and the number of assistance required to complete the game tasks. In addition, we used qualitative measures to collect preference data such as the participant's opinion, expectation and experience of the game [14]. On the other hand, the feasibility of the game was measured by the number of patients who was able to complete all the given game sessions without inconvenience or harms.

Once the participant accepts and signs the consent form, a pre-interview was conducted. The goal of this interview is to gather patient's demographic information such as gender and age, clinical characteristics such as post stroke period and affected side, and his experience with video games and HMDs.

Next, during the test session, we have adopted the observation usability evaluation method to watch the participants while they interact with the game and take notes. The computer screen actions and time spent on each task was recorded.

Participants were asked to complete several tasks in the game. These tasks include:

- Task 1: performing the warm-up exercises,
- Task 2: trying the game in training mode, once the patient is able to grasp one cube and move it to its box successfully he will be moved directly to the real game (task 3).
- Task 3: playing three rounds of the game starting with the first level.
- Task 4: playing one round of our game, which is equivalent to the first level.

All the participants completed the given tasks successfully, except one participant (P1) who could not complete Task 2, which was about trying the game in training mode. From our observation, we found that this patient was not able to achieve any progress in the game because he was not able to control his virtual hands movement correctly. He was only considering his real hands movement and distance from the virtual game objects, which prevented him from reaching and grasping the cubes successfully. Therefore, he was moved directly to Task 4 where it does not require cubes movements. However, this patient declared later that the game is very useful especially for younger ones.

Interestingly, all the patients have earned the maximum score in the completion game levels. However, they varied in the time spent to finish these various levels. Figure 2 shows the time spent on each level for each patient in seconds. It reveals that the best result was achieved by patient (P4) who spent the shortest time in all game levels compared to the other patients. His impressive performance was due to the fact that he was higher functioning and has a video game experience. In addition, we can notice that all patients spent less time on level two than level one. Perhaps, because they learned the game rules from level one and became more skilled in the game. Besides, level two has the same number of cubes and only differs in their placement on the shelf. Moreover, we can notice that all the patients spent more time on the non-immersive level than the other levels, although this level was equivalent to the first and second levels in terms of difficulty. This indicated that the patients struggled in this level more than the other original game levels (the fully-immersive levels).

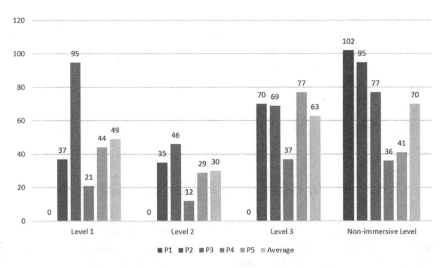

Fig. 2. Time spent on each level in seconds

Figure 3 shows the number of errors and assistance required to complete the game for each patient, which were considerably small. In fact, some patients have not made any error and did not need any assistance. Perhaps, because that the game concept and rules were explained during the tutorial session. Besides, patients were able to try the game first in the training level (Task 2). However, most of the errors were related to grasping the cube correctly. As some patients attempt to grasp the cube while their hand is already closed; they need to open their hand and then grasp it near to the cube, similar to the way objects are grasped in real world.

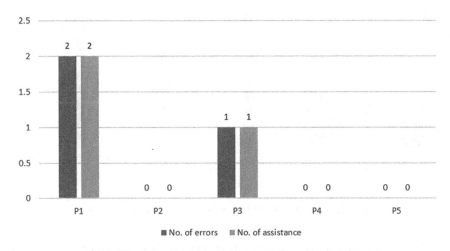

Fig. 3. Number of errors and assistance for each participant

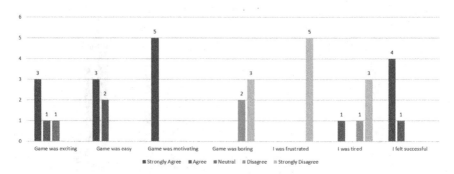

Fig. 4. Questions related to usability of the game

After the patients completed the evaluation tasks, we conducted a post-interview to measure the overall impression of Move-IT game. The questions were ranked according to Likert scale, which is based on five scale (5 means strongly agree and 1 indicates strongly disagree) to assess the user experience of Move-IT game, and if they had encountered any difficulties while playing. In The entire evaluation sessions took about 30–45 min for each participant.

Figure 4 illustrates that most patients have enjoyed the game and found it exciting and easy to play. Moreover, all the patients agreed that the game was very motivating to perform the rehabilitation exercises. None felt bored, frustrated or tired except one patient (P1) who felt tired but with joy; because he thinks the more effort the more arm function recovery. In Addition, all the patients felt successful after playing the game.

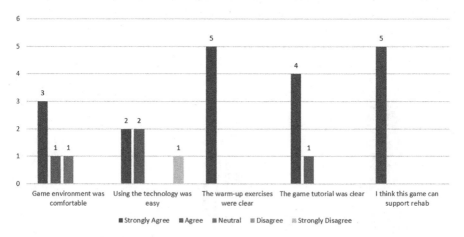

Fig. 5. Questions related to usability of the overall system

Figure 5 reveals that most patients indicated that the game environment (the living room, game colors, and sound) was comfortable. In fact, some stated that it was encouraging to continue playing and perform the rehabilitation exercises. Additionally, most of the patients considered using VR technology easy, except one patient (P1) who could not complete the fully immersive levels. All the patients agreed that the warm-up exercises and the game tutorial were clear and well described. Finally, they all indicated that the game could support rehabilitation. Actually, one patient has pointed that it can support any arm exercise in general not only rehabilitation exercises.

Moreover, we asked the patients what did they enjoy and prefer more: the fully immersive or the non-immersive version of the game. Remarkably, 80% of them stated that the fully immersive version was more exciting, the game objects are bigger and the virtual hand movements were more reasonable and easier to control. Surprisingly, one of them played the fully immersive levels without wearing his medical glasses and still preferred it over playing the non-immersive level with his glasses on. This could be possibly because the games' objects were big enough and have colors which standout from the rest of the game environment.

Furthermore, we have also asked them whether they prefer our game or the other conventional rehabilitation games. 60% of them chose the conventional games because they prefer dealing with solid objects that can be touched physically. Besides, these games were easier to set-up. Additionally, 80% of them would like to use the VR game again and recommend it to others. None of the patients have faced any issues during the game sessions expect one patient (P1), who had a slight headache at the beginning of the training level for a short period of time.

Also, patients were asked to give their suggestions and recommendations to improve the game. Most of them gave the same suggestion, which is adding more set of games to increase diversity and prevent getting bored. Finally, our game was found to be feasible for most of stroke patients. As 80% of the patients were able to complete all the given game levels easily and shortly without taking breaks between them.

From the previous results, we can confirm that a well-designed fully immersive VR-based rehabilitation system can provide a higher sense of amusement and inspiration to stroke patients than non-immersive VR-based rehabilitation systems. Moreover, it was proven to be usable and feasible to stroke patients with medium and high arm functional abilities. Nevertheless, most of the stroke patients still prefer the traditional rehabilitation games for the reason that dealing with real physical game objects is more convenient for them. This can be somewhat resolved by incorporating the use of real objects such as game controllers or using haptic gloves.

Furthermore, the system needs to include several set of games in order to maintain the user motivation and enjoyment, cover more rehabilitation exercises, and suit many stroke patients with different severities.

4   Conclusion and Future Work

The lack of patient's motivation is a serious challenge that faces stroke rehabilitation programs. This project aimed to propose a solution to overcome this issue by introducing a fully immersive VR-based rehabilitation system and assessing its usability and feasibility to determine its applicability to stroke patients and to the stroke rehabilitation process. Our proposed game "Move-IT", proved to be usable, feasible and safe rehabilitation tool to enhance arm motor function among patients in various stages of recovery after stroke. It also encouraged and motivated further rehabilitation.

There were some challenges that were related to the VR field such as health side effects of using fully-immersive VR technology, which include dizziness, nausea, headache and eye strain [15]. In our game, we tried to reduce these side effects by implementing the following:

- Reducing the head movements required to achieve the game goals.
- Removing the Head-Up Display (HUD) that was distracting and annoying while using the HMD and placing its elements (game score, timer, and exit button) inside the game world (i.e. on one of the room walls).
- Building a virtual game environment that has correct dimensions and distances that are similar to real world.

Future work will involve adding other set of games to increase diversity and cover all the rehabilitation movements. In addition to recording the patients' movement data and allowing their therapists to monitor them remotely through developing a portal for the therapists where they can view their patients' movements data, monitor their progress and receive notifications whenever their patients perform the rehabilitation exercises. Furthermore, clinical pilot study will be conducted to assess the effectiveness of our game.

References

1. "What is stroke?" Stroke.org, 16 July 2014. http://www.stroke.org/understand-stroke/what-stroke. Accessed 20 May 2020
2. Burke, J.: Games For Upper-limb Stroke Rehabilitation (Seminar). University of Ulster, Northern Ireland, 29 March 2010
3. A stroke occurs when the brain is damaged due to lack of blood supply. http://www.brainandnerves.com/uk/blood-vessels-of-the-brain/stroke/. Accessed 20 May 2020
4. Khujah, A.: Stroke Rehabilitation, 17 February 2012. http://archive.aawsat.com/details.asp?section=15&article=664001&issueno=12134#.WHQSn1N97X5. Accessed 20 May 2020
5. WHO|The world health report 2002 - Reducing Risks, Promoting Healthy Life, WHO. http://www.who.int/whr/2002/en/. Accessed 20 May 2020
6. Alhazani, 100 stroke cases accure in SA daily, 13 September 2013. http://www.alarabiya.net/ar/saudi-today/2013/09/17/اليومية-الدماغية-السكتة-بالسكتة-اصابة-100-تسجل-السعودية.html. Accessed 20 May 2020
7. Alsinani, F.: 6000 of stroke cases accure in Kingdom of Saudi Arabia yearly, Riyad newspaper, 14 Apr 2005. http://www.alriyadh.com/56594. Accessed 23 May 2020
8. Gunasekera, W., Bendall, J.: Rehabilitation of neurologically injured patients. In: Moore, A.J., Newell, D.W. (eds.) Neurosurgery. Springer Specialist Surgery Series, pp. 407–421. Springer, London (2005). https://doi.org/10.1007/1-84628-051-6_23
9. Burke, J.W., McNeill, M., Charles, D., Morrow, P., Crosbie, J., McDonough, S.: Serious games for upper limb rehabilitation following stroke. In: Proceedings of the 2009 Conference in Games and Virtual Worlds for Serious Applications, Washington, DC, USA, 2009, pp. 103–110 (2009)

10. Rego, P.A., Moreira, P., Reis, L.: Serious games for rehabilitation: a survey and a classification towards a taxonomy. In: 5th Iberian Conference on Information Systems and Technologies (CISTI), pp. 1–6 (2010)
11. Laver, K.E., George, S., Thomas, S., Deutsch, J.E., Crotty, M.: Virtual reality for stroke rehabilitation. Cochrane Database Syst. Rev. no. 9, p. CD008349, September 2011
12. AlMousa, M., Al-Khalifa, H.S., AlSobayel, H.: Requirements elicitation and prototyping of a fully immersive virtual reality gaming system for upper limb stroke rehabilitation in Saudi Arabia. Mobile Information Systems (2017). https://www.hindawi.com/journals/misy/2017/7507940/. Accessed 23 May 2020
13. Grimm, F., Gharabaghi, A.: Closed-loop neuroprosthesis for reach-to-grasp assistance: combining adaptive multi-channel neuromuscular stimulation with a multi-joint arm exoskeleton. Front. Neurosci. **10**, 284 (2016)
14. Dörner, R., Göbel, S., Effelsberg, W., Wiemeyer, J. (eds.): Serious Games, Foundations, Concepts and Practice. Springer, Cham (2016). https://doi.org/10.1007/978-3-319-40612-1
15. Yagv, B.: Overview of virtual reality technologies. In: Presented at the Interactive Multimedia Conference, University of Southampton, United Kingdom (2013)

Serious and Fun Games

Serious and Fun Games

Introduction to the Special Thematic Session

Cecilia Sik-Lanyi(✉)

University of Pannonia, Egyetem Str. 10, Veszprem 8200, Hungary
lanyi@almos.uni-pannon.hu

Abstract. Serious and Fun Games Special Thematic Session aims to bring together academic scientists, researchers, Ph.D. students and research scholars to exchange and share their experiences and research results on all aspects of Game-Based Learning and Serious Games helping people with disabilities and people who need special education. The target groups of these Serious Games are blind people or people with low vision, hearing impairment, motion challenges, learning problems or children with special diets for example type 1 diabetes, or food allergy. It also provides an interdisciplinary platform for researchers, practitioners, and educators to present and discuss the most recent innovations and trends. Moreover, to share and concern practical challenges encountered, and solutions adopted in the fields of Game-Based Learning and Serious Games. High-quality research contributions describing original and unpublished results of conceptual, constructive, empirical, experimental, or theoretical work in all areas of Game-Based Learning and Serious Games were cordially invited for presentation at the STS.

Keywords: Serious Game · Universal design · Special thematic session

1 A Few Words About Serious Games

Comenius advised teachers to organize lessons into easily assimilated steps to make learning gradual, cumulative, and pleasant [1, 2]. He emphasized the function of playing as a pedagogically effective activity. Today, we could say that Comenius' ancient motto, Schola Ludus, has found new meaning in the modern use of interactive educational programs that use play and games as pedagogical tools [3].

Playing games, including intelligent serious games, shows all of the attributes needed for 'flow' according to Sellingmann and Csikszentmihaly [4]: playing computer games is a challenging activity which requires skills, it contains action and demands awareness, it has clear goals and provides the player with immediate feedback. During the process of playing, absolute concentration on the task is required. A well-designed game transports its players to their personal flow zones, delivering genuine feelings of pleasure and happiness [5].

The term "serious games" denotes digital games serving serious purposes like education, training, advertising, research and health. Compared to traditional interventions, these games may help elderly people to improve their health by enhancing

© Springer Nature Switzerland AG 2020
K. Miesenberger et al. (Eds.): ICCHP 2020, LNCS 12376, pp. 199–204, 2020.
https://doi.org/10.1007/978-3-030-58796-3_24

physical fitness and coordinative abilities by combining increased motivation, game experience like fun and game flow and training. Serious games, particularly adventure and shooter games, already play an important role in prevention and rehabilitation, e.g. to enhance health-related physical activity, improve sensory-motor coordination [6, 7].

Serious games are electronic games whose main purpose is "serious" and not to simply entertain. The primary "serious" purposes can be to teach or train in areas such as education, semiformal educational settings, health care, advertising, politics, etc. [8]. Digital games, simulations, virtual environments and mixed reality/media that provide opportunities to educate or train through responsive narrative/story, gameplay or encounters [9]. Serious games is built with pedagogical principles and education and training purposes, supported by gaming techniques and entertainment [10]. A classification referring to games that are specifically designed for a particular purpose. These games are often for education, training, and advertising, and are more often used in particular industries like health care and the military [11].

Initially, serious games where considered to be games with a purpose. The basic idea behind serious games is to hide important and time-consuming tasks behind a gaming veil. They are games that have scope beyond recreation [12].

The idea of using games or game technologies for "serious", e.g., educational purposes is as old as the idea of "learning games", but is not limited to those forms. As opposed to games designed for entertainment, serious games can be defined as computer games aiming towards an underlying second "off-game" goal that differs from in-game goals such as finishing a level or gaining high scores. Beyond the surface of gaming actions—or embedded into those—, serious games try to evoke learning processes or even complex experiences (e.g., through taking the perspective of political refugees, trying to bring them out of a danger zone). Computer game art can be seen as a related form of serious games, aiming, for example, towards open aesthetical experiences rather than following didactic concepts and defined learning goals [13].

Do not think that only young people play. In 2018, people aged 65+ outnumbered children under five years old globally for the first time in history [14]. By 2050, over 16% of the world's population will be 65 years or older [15]. According to Nielsen and even as far back as 2012, reports showed us that over 70% of US disposable income is controlled by individuals aged 65 and above [16]. This consumer age-group is not a stranger to games. "Peak NES (Nintendo Entertainment System) sales" happened when they were in their 30 s and 40 s, with many of their children engrossed in the first generation of Mario and Zleda games. Furthermore, this age group is currently one of the most engaged mobile game player segments in the world. The largest group of mobile gamers is 55+ (albeit this is also the largest age bracket within the data). As such, taking any learnings to heart on how to serve this growing group of diehard mobile gamers with a high income [17]. The work of Carvelho et al. [18] has confirmed positive results on a population with visual disabilities, while Baker [19] has arrived to similar positive and encouraging results working with people with autism, and also Schneider et al. [20], who worked with persons with dyslexia. Brown et al. [21] proved in their project the effectiveness of combining serious games with mobile apps, which can be used anywhere, to reach a higher level of independence of persons with Down's syndrome.

Intelligent serious games are raising many hopes for developments in the educational field and in the rehabilitation in the upcoming decades. Numerous studies have demonstrated the effectiveness and usefulness of serious games not only in education [22–24] but also in rehabilitation in e.g. stroke patients [7].

2 The Session of Serious and Fun Games

This year we have 4 papers, from various European countries. The STS presentation "Serious and Fun Games" tries to achieve progress here to the Future Perspectives in AT, eAccessibility and eInclusion. The target groups could be very wide: pre-school children, young and elderly people. Everybody likes to play. Moreover, if the game is not only for entertainment but it helps people with special needs. If their designs based on the universal design, these games are excellent.

One of this year's papers deals with a newly developed serious game for preschool-age children who have been newly diagnosed with type 1 diabetes. The software consists of two parts, an editor and a game part. The editor part is for the parents, so they can adjust the game according to their child's daily allowable carbohydrate meals. Parents can upload pictures and data of meal/food into the game database. The game main menu contains four games for the children: "True/False quiz", "Which food has more/fewer carbs", "Take it to your plate" and the reward game: "Feed the figure" game. This paper shows the design, development and evaluation process of the game. The evaluation process has been based on the System Usability Scale. It is an innovative game because it is useful for children who have multiple diseases e.g. diabetes and gluten or lactose sensitivity.

The accessibility development on the mobile game is more difficult than in regular computer applications. Most computer games are not developed to be played by people with special needs [25], because they cannot access input sensors and graphical user interface in a sufficient way. Mobile card games are a quite popular and large group of games available in the Google Play store. Dobosz and Adamczyk have selected 15 most popular of them for their analysis. The accessibility features in their study were e.g. custom control, configurable colours, voice messages, audio messages, vibrations, etc. It was found that most games do not meet even half of the verified attributes of availability. Furthermore, the same set of games was analyzed in terms of actions performed: get a card, discard a card, returning a card to the opponent, etc. After analysis, it was found that most card games have only a few actions. The authors have also investigated the Question-Answer mode. However, some games that are placed in the card game genre involve a board or cards that are arranged on the table in a special way (as solitaires). In consequence, a list of question in the Question-Answer will be uselessly long. In their investigation, a group of 11 voluntaries participated in the study. They play the game several times (30 min).

Game interactions require physical manipulation of game controls by hands and body motions (such as keyboard, mouse, gamepad and joystick), which may exclude people with motor disabilities. Although gaze control transforms game controls and liberates the hands, challenges remain on how to design gaze control for different game mechanics and various motor disabled people. The problem is that people with motor disability may have difficulties playing games with conventional game controls requiring physical manipulation, such as keyboard, mouse, gamepad and joystick. The research question is: What is the acceptance of gaze control among novice players and people with upper-limb motor disability for game accessibility? What would need to be improved upon regarding usability and game experience to enhance acceptance? Answering these questions, the authors of the next paper presented a game accessibility study of gaze control modality for novice players and disabled people and addressed two research questions. First, gaze control modality demonstrated possible game accessibility to people with motor disabilities. The acceptance of gaze control among novice players and upper-limb motor disabled people for game accessibility is high. Second, it indicates that the challenge of game mechanics and the accuracy of the gaze-control system are two significant impact factors. The game mechanics need to be designed thoughtfully for the conditions of people with disabilities, including gaze-control-friendly user interfaces, appropriate challenge, simple game scenes, and appropriate game duration for each round to avoid being overwhelmed by visual feedback and eye fatigue. Furthermore, the accuracy of gaze control system should be improved to enhance the acceptance of gaze-control modality.

Nishchyk et al. present a prototype of an augmented reality exergame for elderly people to perform physical exercise at home. A user-centered design approach was adopted to guide the design and development process. The research aimed to create a safe exercising environment with a game narrative to motivate elderly users to exercise. The first prototype has been developed with a few basic exercises as a proof of concept but has a possibility of extension during the next development iterations. The results of the first prototype testing have shown that the game has potential to achieve the goal of the research. The participants have shown a positive attitude towards the prototype. They also have provided a useful feedback, which would help with further development.

3 Conclusion

The presentations in this Special Thematic Session are the first steps in the ICCHP conference series to introduce the newest serious games for special needs users. Hopefully, there will be similar sessions in future conferences. Moreover, we also hope that the youngest scientist generations will be motivated by this Special Thematic Sessions.

Acknowledgements. This introduction to the "Serious and Fun Games" could not have come into being without the financial support of Széchenyi 2020 programme under the project No EFOP-3.6.1-16-2016-00015.

References

1. Comenius, J.A.: Great didactica of John Amus Comenius. Russell & Russell, New York (1896)
2. Smolik, F.: Comenius: a man of hope in a time of turmoil. Christian History **6**, 15–18 (1987)
3. Kapp, K.M.: The Gamification of Learning and Instruction: Game-based Methods and Strategies for Training and Education. Wiley, San Francisco (2012)
4. Seligman, M.E.P., Csikszentmihalyi, M.: Positive psychology: an introduction. Am. Psychol. **55**(1), 5–14 (2000)
5. Chen, J.: Flow in games (and everything else). Commun. ACM **50**(4), 31–34 (2007)
6. Weimeyer, J., Kleim, A.: Serious games in prevention and rehabilitation-a new panacea for elderly people? Eur. Rev. Aging Phys. Act. **9**(1), 41–50 (2012)
7. Sik Lanyi, C., Szucs, V.: Motivating rehabilitation through competitive gaming. In: Vogiatzaki, E., Krukowski, A. (eds.) Modern Stroke Rehabilitation through e-Health-based Entertainment, pp. 137–167. Springer, Cham (2016). https://doi.org/10.1007/978-3-319-21293-7_5
8. Arriaga, P., Esteves, F., Fernandes, S.: Playing for better or for worse? health and social outcomes with electroninc gaming. In: Handbook of Research on ICTs for Human-Centered Healthcare and Social Care Services, pp. 48–69. IGI Global Publisher (2013). https://doi.org/10.4018/978-1-4666-3986-7.ch003
9. Gallegos, B., Kepple, M.T., Bukaty, C.A.: Using video gameplay to measure achievement for students with disabilities: a new perspective to grading and achievement reporting. In: Handbook of Research on Gaming Trends in P-12 Education, pp. 326–352. IGI Global Publisher (2016). https://doi.org/10.4018/978-1-4666-9629-7.ch016
10. Neto, J., Mendes, P.: Game4Manager: more than virtual managers. In: Handbook of Research on Serious Games as Educational, Business and Research Tools, pp. 108–134. IGI Global Publisher (2012). https://doi.org/10.4018/978-1-4666-0149-9.ch006
11. Taylor, L.N.: Gaming ethics, rules, etiquette, and learning. In: Handbook of Research on Effective Electronic Gaming in Education, pp. 1057–1067. IGI Global Publisher (2009). https://doi.org/10.4018/978-1-59904-808-6.ch061
12. Pavlidis, G.P., Markantonatou, S.: Playful education and innovative gamified learning approaches. In: Handbook of Research on Educational Design and Cloud Computing in Modern Classroom Settings, pp. 321–341. IGI Global Publisher (2008). https://doi.org/10.4018/978-1-5225-3053-4.ch015
13. Fromme, J., Jörissen, B., Unger, A.: (Self-) educational effects of computer gaming cultures. In: Handbook of Research on Effective Electronic Gaming Education, pp. 757–775 (2009). IGI Global Publisher. https://doi.org/10.4018/978-1-59904-808-6.ch043
14. Deutsche Welle News, 17 June 2019
15. https://www.dw.com/en/world-population-to-reach-97-billion-by-2050-un/a-49241728
16. United Nations: WorlD Population Ageing (2019)
17. https://www.un.org/en/development/desa/population/publications/pdf/ageing/WorldPopulationAgeing2019-Highlights.pdf
18. Nielsen, J.: Introducing Boomers: Marketing's Most Valuable Generation (2012)
19. https://www.nielsen.com/us/en/insights/report/2012/introducing-boomers–marketing-s-most-valuable-generation/
20. Tath, W.: How to successfully cater to older players (2020)
21. https://www.gamesindustry.biz/articles/2020-07-06-how-to-successfully-cater-to-older-players

22. Carvelho, T., Allison, R.S., Irving, E.L., Harriot, C.: Computer Gaming for Vision Therapy. IEEE, Washington, D. C. (2008)
23. Baker, M.J.: Incorporating the thematic ritualistic behaviors of children with autism into games. J. Positive Behav. Interv. (2000). http://journals.sagepub.com/doi/abs/10.1177/109830070000200201
24. Schneider, W., Roth, E., Ennemoser, M.: Training phonological skills and letter knowledge in children at risk for dyslexia: a comparison of three kindergarden intervention programs. J. Educ. Psychol. **92**, 284–295 (2000)
25. Brown, D.J., McHugh, D., Standen, P.J., Evett, L., Shopland, N., Battersby, S.J.: Designing location based learning experiences for people with intellectual disabilities and additional senzory impairments. Comput. Educ. **56**(1), 11–20 (2011)
26. Sik Lanyi, C., Brown, D.J., Standen, P., Lewis, J., Butkute, V.: User interface evaluation of serious games for students with intellectual disability. In: Miesenberger, K., Klaus, J., Zagler, W., Karshmer, A. (eds.) ICCHP 2010. LNCS, vol. 6179, pp. 227–234. Springer, Heidelberg (2010). https://doi.org/10.1007/978-3-642-14097-6_37
27. Sik Lanyi, C., Brown, D., Standen, P., Lewis, J., Butkute, V.: Results of user interface evaluation of serious games for students with intellectual disability. Acta Polytechnica Hungarica 9(1), 225–245 (2012). http://www.uni-obuda.hu/journal/Issue33.htm
28. Sik-Lanyi, C., Szucs, V.: Play for children with disabilities: some reflections on the results on the users' needs and on the role of technologies. In: Allodi Westling, M., Zappaterra, T. (eds.) Users' Needs Report on Play for Children with Disabilities - Parents' and children's views. pp. 117–123. De Gruyter Poland Ltd, Warsaw/Berlin (2017)
29. Sik-Lanyi, C.: Colour-Fidelity and Barrier-Free Design of Virtual Worlds and Games. The Theses Submitted for the Habilitation Procedure at the University of Pannonia, Veszprem, Hungary (2017)

A Study on Gaze Control - Game Accessibility Among Novice Players and Motor Disabled People

Lida Huang$^{(\boxtimes)}$ ⓘ and Thomas Westin ⓘ

Department of Computer and Systems Sciences, Stockholm University,
Stockholm, Sweden
{lida.huang, thomasw}@dsv.su.se

Abstract. Gaze control is a substitution for disabled people to play computer games. However, many disabled people may be inexperienced in games and/or novices using gaze-control. This study presents a game accessibility approach using gaze control modality for novice players and disabled people. A workshop was conducted involving a playtest on three games with gaze-control. The game experiences were observed, recorded, and evaluated with mixed methods. The study estimated the gaze control game accessibility by System Usability Scale (SUS), Game Experience Questionnaire (GEQ), and an open-ended questionnaire. The gaze control modality demonstrated possible game accessibility to people with motor disabilities. The results also indicate that the challenge of game mechanics and the accuracy of the gaze-control system are two significant impact factors. Further research will be conducted on gaze-control games including more disabled people, and also develop the data analysis methods for evaluating gaze-control modality for game accessibility.

Keywords: Gaze control · Game accessibility · Motor disabled · Novice

1 Introduction

Computer games are a global cultural phenomenon that calls for inclusion of all, regardless of disabilities or other limitations. Game interactions require physical manipulation of game controls by hands and body motions (such as keyboard, mouse, gamepad and joystick), which may exclude motor disabled people [1]. Gaze control is a substitution for motor disabled people to play some computer games, but many may be novices of using this relatively new modality. Although gaze control transforms game controls and liberates the hands, challenges remain on how to design gaze control for different game mechanics and various motor disabled people. The problem is that motor disabled people may have difficulties playing games with conventional game controls requiring physical manipulation, such as keyboard, mouse, gamepad and joystick. The research questions are: What is the acceptance of gaze control among novice players and upper-limb motor disabled people for game accessibility? What would need to be improved upon regarding usability and game experience to enhance acceptance?

© Springer Nature Switzerland AG 2020
K. Miesenberger et al. (Eds.): ICCHP 2020, LNCS 12376, pp. 205–216, 2020.
https://doi.org/10.1007/978-3-030-58796-3_25

2 Related Research

2.1 Gaze-Control Interaction

Gaze-control interaction has emerged in computer games in recent years. Early applications of eye gaze as game control modality can be retrieved in a research article from 2004 when Layba J et al. [2] implemented an eye-tracking game control experiment, with the Tobii ET-1750 eye tracker. Following this gaze control experiment, more researchers have tried to design and optimize more gaze-control game mechanics over the past decade [3–5]. There are various game mechanics for gaze control, summarized in five categories as *Selection & Commands, Aiming & Shooting, Navigation, Implicit Interaction,* and *Visual Effects* [6]. Ramirez et al. further classified *Selection & Commands, Aiming & Shooting,* and *Navigation* as the primary game mechanics for gaze control [7]. Both *gaze selection* and *gaze aiming & shooting* are operated by eye fixation [8, 9], which is the principal function of human eyes. *Gaze selection* is when people gaze at an object on the screen, the cursor (which is the gaze plot) can click or select the object [10]. In some games, the fixation has to last for a dwell time to trigger the selection [11, 12]. *Gaze aiming & shooting* indicates aiming at a target and shoot it, for example, firing [13] and pinpoint bombing [14]. And *gaze navigation* means the game camera (field of vision) follows where the eyes look [13]. Some games used saccade for *gaze navigation* [15] (rapid movement of the eye between fixation points), and some other games use head orientation as direction control [16].

2.2 Game Accessibility and Game Experience

Game accessibility can be defined as the usability of computer games under restricted circumstances (e.g., motor impairment, visual impairment, and auditory impairment) [17]. Game accessibility in gaze-control modal is affected by deliberately designed challenges of different games, i.e., normative game rules and performative game mechanics [18]. S. Almeida et al. [19] summarize the effects of eye-tracking technologies on different game genres, showing that racing games are less accessible with eye tracking. As racing games require a long duration of gazing and visual attention, unexpected eye distractions or non-intentional absence of gaze are likely to cause in-game crashes. Antunes. J et al. [20] noted that multimodal, for example, keyboard integrated with gaze control is more accessible than unimodal gaze control, proven in a shooting game playtest.

Furthermore, gaming skills of players also affect game experiences. Cain M. S et al. shows that novices spend significantly more response time in unfamiliar game tasks and are less flexible in switching tasks [21]. When novice players encounter game failure, they may be frustrated to utilize a novel game control modal in the future. This is especially relevant for accessibility where novel game controls are common. However, the views of novice players and motor disabled people for gaze control have been less explicated in previous research.

3 Methodology

This study presented a game accessibility approach using gaze-control modality for novice players and disabled people. A workshop was conducted involving a sample of eight mid-age to elderly people with multiple sclerosis, stochastically selected by an organization for multiple sclerosis. Two of the participants had severe motor disabilities in hands and arms, and two were middle level disabled in hands and arms, four were minor disabled in hands.

Three typical gaze control modals were tested utilizing an infrared eye tracker (*Tobii 4C*) in three games: (1) *Beatshot* (BS)[1], a shooting game, game mechanics used gaze fixation to hit the moving target while avoiding the interfering penalties. (2) *Patin Grappin* (PG)[2], a navigating game, the game mechanics used gaze control to control a skier going downhill, turning and jumping by a grappling hook with a rope to make long jumps. Turning was implemented by head orientation (head yawing for left and right, pitching for up and down) and grappling by dwell clicks, looking at clouds for perhaps a second. (3) *Fast Sight* (FS)[3], a cooperative racing game with a multimodal of keyboard and eye gaze, to control the avatar rolling across a valley. Aiming at the falling rocks from aside and press Space key simultaneously to shoot the rocks, while pressing Left and Right keys to control direction and avoid obstacles on the way.

3.1 Pre-game Session

An introduction about the eye tracker and the three tested gaze-control games were given. Each participant signed an informed consent form for participating in the study. Then, the participants watched the presentation of how to use eye tracker and short tutorials on how to play the tested games. Next, each of them played the tested games to get familiar with the graphical user interfaces for the tested games in five minutes.

3.2 Playtest Session

A playtest was conducted per participant with one-to-two minutes for *Beatshot*, a variation of time with *Patin Grappin* that depended on how long the player was able to get before s/he failed, and two minutes with *Fast Sight*. *Fast Sight* was tested with two participants at a time, pairing one severe disabled participant to gaze control and one with better motor ability to command the keyboard. The total time per playtest session was ten minutes including time to shift between games. Observation were noted based on a systematic user experience scheme of the observations (see Table 1 in the Results section). The gameplay was recorded by the screen recorder *Bandicam v4.2.0.1439* and the user interaction was recorded by a video camera installed behind the participants. The performances of the eight participants were observed and recorded. The in-game observation with participants' behaviors was thematically coded based on five game

---

[1] https://gaming.tobii.com/games/beatshot/.

[2] https://www.youtube.com/watch?v=sHNrzG2zR_o.

[3] https://gaming.tobii.com/games/fast-sight/.

experience dimensions: *Enjoyment* [22], *Flow* [23], *Immersion* [24], *Challenge* [25], and *Sensory experience* [26] with gaze control.

3.3   Post-game Session

The participants were asked to complete the System Usability Scale (SUS) [27] and Game Experience Questionnaire (GEQ) [28]. Then, retrospective think-aloud of observation results and video recordings were included, in which the participants were asked to explain why they answered the questionnaires the way they did. Furthermore, the participants were asked to answer an open-ended questionnaire. The SUS results were estimated with maximum likelihood estimation (MLE) and t-distribution. This work hypothesizes that the user experience rating of novice players and disabled people is in Gaussian distribution (Normal distribution). Therefore, it implemented the MLE estimation to indicate the result of the target group. The GEQ results for the three gaze-control modals were estimated by eight game experience dimensions: *Competence, Sensory experiences, Flow, Challenge, Tension/ Annoyance, Negative affect, Positive affect, and Tiredness.* The *Tiredness* here is also designed as a specific dimension for eye fatigue caused by gaze control. The results from eight participants were computed with arithmetic mean and standard deviation. The open-ended questions about gaze control were developed based on playtesting questions in Fullerton et al. [29]. The answers of eight participants were summarized by merging similar answers and listing the representative answers.

4   Results and Analysis

The gaze control modality demonstrated possible game accessibility to people with motor disabilities. The results also manifest that the challenge of game mechanics and the accuracy of the gaze-control system are two significant impact factors for game accessibility. Note that the observation form is a presentation of findings that were corroborated from the significant behaviors and refined from the repeated answers (Table 1).

4.1   Playtest Session

The observation provides a triangulation of the oral answers given by participants. It also reveals some unintentional in-game motions of the participants and explains the reason why they have such game experiences.

Enjoyment. Most of the participants enjoyed the games. Negative emotions only occurred when they faced in-game crashes or gaze control inaccuracy.

Flow. Although the participants were novices with gaze control, they desired to learn how to score more and they became better during the gameplay session.

Table 1. Observation form.

Observed Dimensions		Players' Behaviors
Enjoyment	Positive	–The player showed interest in the game –The player expressed his/her desire to play the game again –The player felt enjoyment when they were playing the games
	Negative	–The player did not want to replay the game –The player wanted to quit the game in the middle of the game
Flow	Positive	–The player tried to learn new skills and desire to score more –The player performed better by playing more time
	Negative	–The player was not skillful when playing the game as a novice.
Immersion	Positive	–The player was very concentrated playing the game, with some unintentional gasps, cheering, exclamations and body language –The player revealed emotions in-game. When the player failed the game, he/she expressed a depressed/emulative spirit. When the player won a high score, he/she expressed delight
	Negative	–The player could not make swift with the game task –The player could not devote himself/herself to the gameplay
Challenge	Positive	–The player believed he/she can do (gaze control) better next time –The player asked about the other players' scores and wanted to compete with them
	Negative	–The player failed the game even he/she tries hard –The player expressed pressure on the gameplay by gaze control –The player wanted to quit the game after several failures
Sensory experience	Positive	–The player did/did not notice the eye tracker and showed a comfortable/uncomfortable reaction with the eye tracker –The player commanded the unimodal of gaze control very well/just well
	Negative	–The player's gaze plot was dislocated on the screen –The player's gaze was lost by eye tracker and the software –The player commanded the unimodal of gaze control badly

Immersion. The participants showed the most significant immersion in *Beatshot*. For the other two games, some participants were focused on the game. However, some participants had some problems that affected the immersion: **a)** The buttons of the two games' menus were too small for most people to click on correctly, considering the gaze control has limited precision. Particularly, two participants also had difficulties on gazing at falling rocks in the racing game due to inaccuracy of the gaze control; **b)** The participants reacted slower than the speed of the game. In *Patin Grappin*, the participants spent more time on searching the game scene than racing on the racetrack.

Challenge. The unimodal gaze control required much effort, especially when the game mechanics were complicated, the participants felt eye strain after playing for a while. For gaze control, the participants had to look at numerous information in the scene and try to control the game by eye-gaze simultaneously. *Patin Grappin* and *Fast Sight* have more sophisticated controls and are thus harder to start playing.

Sensory Experience with Gaze Control. In terms of the gaze control, three participants encountered different degree of difficulties on gaze tracking, thus caused the games to crash, especially in *Patin Grappin*. In terms of the hardware sensor, the participants showed no sign of distraction from the infrared lights of the eye tracker. Firstly, the participants noticed the lights, but when they played games, they focused on the game.

The factors that caused the gaze control's inaccuracy observed were: **A)** Three participants had unintentional head movements while playing. This situation recognized as unintentional movements and inevitable when the players are immersive in-game. **B)** One participant was significantly shorter than the others. When she sat in front of the computer, her position was remarkably lower than the other participants as her wheelchair was at a fixed height compared to the regular, adjustable chair. The eye tracker in front of the laptop screen could hardly capture her eyes (intermittently).

4.2   Post-game Session

Gaze Control Usability. To indicate the usability for the group of novice players and disabled people, the playtest session was estimated by SUS and the data was evaluated by MLE and t-distribution (see Fig. 1). The estimated Gaussian model (mean = 80.625, std = 13.332) and the t-distribution model of the eight users (mean = 79.362, std = 13.332, df = 7) are in the B level of SUS standard [29]. The height of each bar illustrates the likelihood of the user's SUS score. As shown by the SUS distribution curve, the gaze control usability has the highest likelihood at 80.625 and is downward by aside.

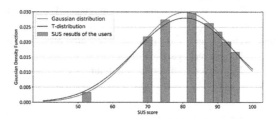

Fig. 1. Histogram of the SUS distribution model estimated by MLE and t-distribution. The histogram illustrates the score of the eight participants. The height of the histogram is the Gaussian Kernel Density (KDE) value indicating the likelihood of the SUS scores.

Gaze-Control Game Experiences. The results of GEQ (see Fig. 2) show no statistical significance (p > 0.05, t-test) between the three game modals. The highest game experience dimension was the *Positive affect*, which decreased remarkably from 2.925 to 2.563 following the game sequences *Beatshot* (BS), *Patin Grappin* (PG) to *Fast Sight* (FS). Similarly, the *Competence* decreased from 2.45 to 2.0 in the three games.

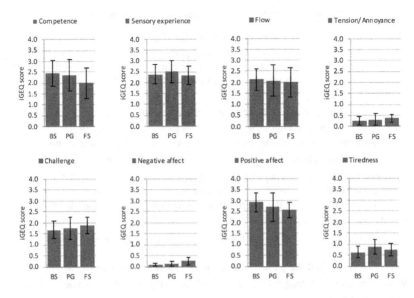

Fig. 2. Game experience dimensions estimated based on GEQ scores of the three games: *Beatshot* (BS), *Patin Grappin* (PG), and *Fast Sight* (FS). The value of each dimension is the score mean ± standard deviation of the eight participants. T-test on the three games indicates no statistical significance between the GEQ values of the three games (p > 0.05).

The *Sensory experiences* fluctuated slightly between 2.3 and 2.5, while the *Flow* was almost static in approximately 2.0 in the three games. The *Challenge* is between 1.6 and 1.9. The lowest dimensions were *Tension/Annoyance and Negative affect* between 0 and 0.4. The *Tiredness* for gaze control is between 0.6 and 0.9.

The open-ended interview showed that most participants had positive perspectives on the gaze control modality. Notably, there were two remarkable gaze control designs reported by the participants. First, the eye tracker can transform the tracking modes as tracing left/right eye or both eyes, which enabled the accessibility of divergent squint people. Second, the cooperative multimodal design with gaze control and keyboard enabled severe hand disabled participants play more complex game mechanics together with another player. The remaining open-ended questions confirmed what was found in the observations. The result of the open-ended interview was showed in Table 2.

Table 2. Answers from the open-ended questionnaire.

Q	What was your first impression of gaze-control games?
A	–It is my first time to hear about eye-tracking games, and it is exciting and fresh to me –I read the news that there were devices people can connect and control the computer with eye gaze, is it (Tobii) the device on the news? –I want to try it!
Q	Has the impression changed after you play the gaze control games?
A	–It is more complicated than I thought to play eye-tracking games –I felt disappointed that I could not play the game because it cannot track my eyes. (PG)
Q	Is there something challenging in using the gaze control modals?
A	–The eye-tracking device could not track my eyes, so I could not enjoy the game –Play games with gaze control is very difficult for me, especially to play the skiing game –I tried to fix my gaze on the target, but it was not on the right location where I gazed.
Q	Did the gaze control modals drag or bug at any point?
A	–Yes. The game (PG) could not capture my eye gaze, so the game crashed once it launched –Yes. When I played the game (BS), my gaze plot was always in the wrong place
Q	Were there particular features that you found satisfying in terms of game mechanics of gaze control models?
A	–The unimodal of gaze control is convenient for playing games –It is thoughtful of the system that can track a single eye (divergent squint) –The cooperate modal is helpful for me. (The participants with severe hand disabilities.) –When I played BS, the prized targets had the same color as the punished targets. The colors are disguising, and it is a challenge to shoot the right target. (Positive commend)
Q	How well do you think you performed the gaze control in-game?
A	–Very well, I worked better than the other people. (Feeling proud) –Just OK –Not very well
Q	Were the procedures and rules of gaze-control games easy to understand?
A	–Yes. The unimodal is easy to understand
Q	What do you think the cons and pros with gaze control of the games?
A	–The eye-tracking system worked not very well to capture my eyes –The game speed (FS) is too fast to control the avatar –The buttons in the game (FS) were in a small size, and the gaze plot was unsteady (PG and FS), I could not gaze at the button correctly –At the beginning of the games (PG and FS), I had to learn information of the game scenes (by my eyes), too many figures came from me, and I felt too rush to control the avatar (by eye gaze) appropriately –Watching the scene and controlling the target at the same time was intensive and stressful –There was a little eye strain after playing the games. I could not keep playing for a long time. I hope the game can designed as pause after playing for a while

5   Discussion

This study tested three typical gaze-control modals, covering primary gaze-control game mechanics: *Selection & Commands*, *Aiming & Shooting*, and *Navigation* [7]. While the study used existing games developed by others, the acceptance of the games may have been affected by the situation and presentation by the authors. The gaze control game accessibility is discussed in three perspectives: usability, gaze-control game experiences and the designs in gaze-control modal.

5.1   Gaze Control Usability

The average SUS results demonstrated that the gaze-control modality manages to provide accessibility for most novice players and disabled people. This work hypothesizes that the user experience rating of novice players and disabled people is in Gaussian distribution (Normal distribution), while the rating of the small probability sample is in t-distribution. The likelihood model of Gaussian distribution predicted with MLE differs from the model of t-distribution. It implies that the exact gaze-control acceptance may be higher than the expectation of the sample. This study introduces MLE to address the problem that severely upper-limb motor disabled people are a relatively small group of society who are not readily available for game accessibility research recruitment. Thus, it concludes a reliable estimation of the gaze-control acceptance among the novice players and the disabled people.

5.2   Gaze-Control Game Experiences

The results of GEQ and the open-ended questionnaire indicate that the gaze-control game accessibility is affected by the eye-tracking accuracy and the game mechanic design. In the GEQ results, the values of *Competence*, *Sensory experiences*, *Flow*, *Challenge*, *Positive affect* are considerably high, while the values of *Tension/ Annoyance*, *Negative affect* are low, suggesting high game accessibility of gaze control among the majority. The GEQ results in the three gaze-control modals are examined by t-test and show no statistical significance between each other. The cause can derive from the GEQ scales (0-4). Only five-integer-scales caused the SD values between participants in each game remarkably significant than the difference between games.

Although the p-value with t-test shows no statistical significance between the three games, combined with the observation, the minor trends can show the differences between the three game experiences. The *Competence* and *Positive affect* slightly decrease from BS to FS, while the *Challenge*, *Tension/Annoyance*, and *Negative affect* slightly increase. It shows an inversed correlation between game difficulties and the command of gaze control. The participants present strong learning abilities of gaze control in BS, which has the most straightforward game mechanic. However, they report the difficulties of PG and FS. In PG, the participants have difficulties in controlling the avatar on the racetrack. When the avatar falls out, they find it hard to find a new racetrack by saccade and head yawing control simultaneously. In FS, the participants think the game pace is too fast for them to control the direction. Although keyboards were controlling the direction, the game performance of the keyboard player was affecting the gaze-control player.

The *Tiredness* increased gradually in PG and FS. Corresponding to the observation, the participants proposed that eye fatigue arose when the game mechanics are more challenging in the post-game interview section. When the game scenes are complex (PG and FS), the participants reported tension and visual overload due to the massive information. It is more likely to cause eye strain and cognition overload in a started period of the games.

5.3   Designs in the Gaze Control Modals

Minimum Button Size. This study finds that significant number of gaze-control players have difficulties on aiming at the rocks in FS as they are in smaller size compared to the targets in BS. This situation also occurs during the game menu selection in FS. It indicated that the gaze plot has minor jitters, so the size of a selected or aiming target should be designed big enough to be accessible. Earlier findings proved that target sizes below 1.5–2° caused increased selection error [30, 31], while recent studies noted gaze calibrating difficulties on a minimum target size about 3° [32, 33]. Also, eye gaze selection time (period between target initialization and gaze entry into the target circle) increased remarkable when the target size bellowed 2° [34]. In light of these studies, the button size above 2° ensure game accessibility of gaze control.

Special Needs of Motor Disabilities. The observation manifests that gaze control should consider people with various severe motor disabilities and individual conditions (e.g., eye divergent squint and body height). It reveals the accessibility demand for synchronizing eye trackers individually and gaze-adaptive methods for special needs.

6   Conclusion

The current work presented a game accessibility study of gaze control modality for novice players and disabled people and addressed two research questions. First, gaze control modality demonstrated possible game accessibility to people with motor disabilities. The acceptance of gaze control among novice players and upper-limb motor disabled people for game accessibility is high. Second, it indicates that the challenge of game mechanics and the accuracy of the gaze-control system are two significant impact factors. The game mechanics need to be designed thoughtfully for the conditions of disabled peoples, including gaze-control-friendly user interfaces, appropriate challenge, simple game scenes, and appropriate game duration for each round to avoid being overwhelmed by visual feedback and eye fatigue. Furthermore, the accuracy of gaze control system should be improved to enhance the acceptance of gaze-control modality.

Future research will focus on a broader range of gaze-control games, a larger scale of disabled people, and also develop more data analysis methods for evaluating gaze-control game accessibility. This study suggests that game duration is an impact factor on gaze control game accessibility. However, it cannot inform about the optimal game duration for gaze control. Thus, it raises a further question of how long game duration should be in gaze-control games. Appropriate game duration (ensures game enjoyment whilst avoiding eye fatigue) will be examined in future research.

Acknowledgments. Thanks to AISM, Genoa, Italy for their kind invitation to conduct the study. The study was funded via the EU project RISEWISE < EU project reference number No 690874 > Thanks to Tobii company providing the eye tracker for the study.

References

1. Poole, A., Ball, L. J.: Eye tracking in HCI and usability research. In: Encyclopedia of human computer interaction pp. 211–219. IGI Global (2006)
2. Leyba, J., Malcolm, J.: Eye tracking as an aiming device in a computer game. Course work (CPSC 412/612 Eye Tracking Methodology and Applications by A. Duchowski), Clemson University, 14 (2004)
3. Isokoski, P., Joos, M., Spakov, O., Martin, B.: Gaze controlled games. Universal Access Inf. **8**(4), 323 (2009)
4. Antunes, J.,Santana, P.: Gaze-Oriented gameplay in first-person shooter games. In: Proceedings of the 24th Portuguese Meeting on Computer Graphics and Interaction (EPCGI), pp. 231–232 Guimarães, Portugal, 12–13 October 2017
5. Isokoski, P., Joos, M., Spakov, O., Martin, B.: Gaze controlled games. Universal Access Inf. **8**(4), 323–337 (2009)
6. Eduardo, V., Marcus, C.: The emergence of eyeplay: a survey of eye interaction in games. In: Proceedings of the 2016 Annual Symposium on Computer-Human Interaction in Play (CHI PLAY 2016). ACM, New York, NY, USA, 171–185 (2016)http://dx.doi.org/ https:// doi.org/10.1145/2967934.2968084
7. Ramirez Gomez, A., Gellersen, H.: Looking outside the box: reflecting on gaze interaction in gameplay. In: Proceedings of the Annual Symposium on Computer-Human Interaction in Play. pp. 625–637 (2019, October)
8. Duchowski, A.T.: Eye Tracking Methodology: Theory & Practice. Springer Verlag, London, UK (2003)
9. Morimoto, C.H., Koon, D., Amir, A., Flickner, M.: Pupil detection and tracking using multiple light sources. Image Vision Comput. **18**, 331334 (2000)
10. Vidal, M., Bulling, A., Gellersen, H.: Pursuits: spontaneous interaction with displays based on smooth pursuit eye movement and moving targets. In: Proceedings of the 2013 ACM international joint conference on Pervasive and ubiquitous computing. pp. 439–448 (2013, September)
11. Wilcox, T., Evans, M., Pearce, C., et al.: Gaze and voice based game interaction: the revenge of the killer penguins[J]. SIGGRAPH Posters 81(10.1145): 1400885.1400972 (2008)
12. Castellina, E., Corno, F.: Multimodal gaze interaction in 3D virtual environments. COGAIN **8**(2008), 33–37 (2008)
13. Schaefer, C., Menges, R., Schmidt, K., Kuich, M., Walber, T.: Schau genau! an eye tracking game with a purpose. Applications for Gaze in Games (2014)
14. Lennart, E.N., Michael, K., Calvin, L., Regan, L. M.: Biofeedback game design: using direct and indirect physiological control to enhance game interaction. In: Proceedings of the SIGCHI conference on human factors in computing systems. ACM, 103–112 (2011)
15. Anders, M.N., Anders, L.P., John, P.H.: Gaming with gaze and losing with a smile. In: Proceedings of the Symposium on Eye Tracking Research and Applications. ACM, 365–368 (2012)
16. Smith, J. D., Graham, T. N.: Use of eye movements for video game control. In: Proceedings of the 2006 ACM SIGCHI international conference on Advances in computer entertainment technology. pp. 20–es (2006, June)

17. Whitaker, R.: Accessibility. Developing Inclusive Mobile Apps, pp. 1–16. Apress, Berkeley, CA (2020). https://doi.org/10.1007/978-1-4842-5814-9_1
18. Sicart, M.: Defining Game mechanics. Game Studies, 8(2) (2008)
19. Almeida, S., Veloso, A., Roque, L., Mealha, Ó.: The eyes and games: a survey of visual attention and eye tracking input in video games. (2011)
20. Antunes, J., Santana, P.: A study on the use of eye tracking to adapt gameplay and procedural content generation in first-person shooter games. Multi. Technol. Int. 2(2), 23 (2018)
21. Cain, M.S., Landau, A.N., Shimamura, A.P.: Action video game experience reduces the cost of switching tasks. Atten. Percept. Psycho. 74(4), 641–647 (2012)
22. Mekler, E.D., Bopp, J.A., Tuch, A.N., Opwis, K.: A systematic review of quantitative studies on the enjoyment of digital entertainment games. In: Proceedings of the SIGCHI Conference on Human Factors in Computing Systems, CHI 2014, pp. 927–936. Toronto, Canada, (2014)
23. Brockmyer, J.H., Fox, C.M., Curtiss, K.A., McBroom, E., Burkhart, K.M., Pidruzny, J.N.: The development of the Game Engagement Questionnaire: a measure of engagement in video game-playing. J. Exp. Soc. Psychol. 45(4), 624–634 (2009)
24. Jennett, C., Cox, A.L., Cairns, P., Dhoparee, S., Epps, A., Tijs, T., Walton, A.: Measuring and defining the experience of immersion in games. Int. J. Hum-comput. St. 66(9), 641–661 (2008)
25. Vorderer, P., Klimmt, C., Ritterfeld, U.: Enjoyment: at the heart of media entertainment. Commun. Theor. 14(4), 388–408 (2004)
26. Calvillo-Gámez, E.H., Cairns, P., Cox, A.L.: Assessing the core elements of the gaming experience[M]//Game user experience evaluation, pp. 37–62. Springer, Cham (2015)
27. Brooke, J.: SUS: a "quick and dirty" usability scale. In: Jordan, P.W., Thomas, B., Weerdmeester, B.A., McClelland, A.L. (eds.) Usability Evaluation in Industry. Taylor and Francis, London (1986)
28. Ijsseltein, W. A., Poels, K., De Kort, Y.: The game experience questionnaire: Development of a self-report measure to assess player experiences of digital games. FUGA technical report, Deliverable 3.3, Technical University Eindhoven, (2008)
29. Fullerton, T.: Game design workshop: a playcentric approach to creating innovative games. CRC press, (2014)
30. Sven-Thomas, G., Michael, H., Sebastian, P., Boris, M.V.: Evaluating requirements for gaze-based interaction in a see-through head mounted display. In: Proceedings of the 2008 Symposium on Eye Tracking Research Applications. ACM, 91–94 (2008)
31. Colin, Ware., Harutune, H.M.: An evaluation of an eye tracker as a device for computer input. In: Acm sigchi bulletin, Vol. 17. ACM, 183–188 (1987)
32. John, P.H., Vijay Rajanna, I., Scott, M., Per, B.: A Fitts' law study of click and dwell interaction by gaze, head and mouse with a head-mounted display. In: Proceedings of the Workshop on Communication by Gaze Interaction. ACM, p. 7 (2018)
33. Yuan, Y.Q., Robert, J.T.: The eyes don't have it: an empirical comparison of head-based and eye-based selection in virtual reality. In: Proceedings of the 5th Symposium on Spatial User Interaction (SUI 2017). ACM, New York, NY, USA, 91–98 (2017).https://doi.org/10.1145/3131277.3132182
34. Schuetz, I., Murdison, T.S., MacKenzie, K.J., Zannoli, M.: An explanation of fitts' law-like performance in gaze-based selection tasks using a psychophysics approach. In: Proceedings of the 2019 CHI Conference on Human Factors in Computing Systems (CHI 2019). Association for Computing Machinery, New York, NY, USA, Paper 535, 1–13 (2019) https://doi.org/10.1145/3290605.3300765

Accessibility of Mobile Card Games

Krzysztof Dobosz[✉][iD] and Artur Adamczyk

Department of Algorithmics and Software, Silesian University of Technology,
Akademicka 16, Gliwice, Poland
krzysztof.dobosz@polsl.pl, artuada442@student.polsl.pl

Abstract. The article describes a study aimed at developing an interaction template for mobile card games for visually impaired gamers. First, accessibility features of existing mobile card games were analyzed. Then various types of actions in common card games were studied and classified to proper categories. Next a simplified layout was proposed in a simplified form of single card view. The interaction mode also was limited to six simple gestures. This approach was used in the sample game. Finally, the new approach was evaluated obtaining satisfactory results.

Keywords: Game accessibility · Mobile games · Card games ·
Visually impaired

1 Introduction

The mobile games markets currently include many items, and their number is still growing. One type of them is mobile games, which become popular because of their ease of being able to be played anywhere and anytime [10]. However, there are still not many mobile games developed for players with special needs, such as people with visual impairment. The accessibility that focuses on the ease access to all game contents should be one of the mandatory elements in every mobile game. Awareness of game developers about the need of game accessibility is still growing, and appropriate guides are being created. However, they are often too general and difficult to fit into the appropriate category of games.

This study focused on a gesture template suitable for interaction in mobile card games. As a result, when the visually impaired gamer launches any mobile card game first time, most gestures should be intuitive for him.

2 Background

Accessibility in games is defined as the ability to play a game despite limiting conditions, which can be temporary functional limitations or permanent disabilities – such as blindness, deafness or reduced mobility [15]. The accessibility

This work was co-financed by SUT grant for maintaining and developing research potential.

development of mobile game is more difficult than in the case of regular computer applications [2]. Most computer games are not developed to be played by people with special needs [13], because they cannot access input sensors and graphical user interface in sufficient way [5].

A very important issue is the integration of assistive technology in the guidelines [14]. In the area of game accessibility very important role plays the Independent Game Developers Association (IGDA). IGDA includes the Special Interest Group on Game Accessibility with a passion for game accessibility. IGDA-GASIG recommends several guidelines that can be used as a reference for developing the accessibility of computer games [3]. Although, the recommendation is proposed for applications used by gamers with different kinds of impairment, in some cases, the guidelines cannot be applied properly [17]. Players who are blind often meet an incompatibility of screen readers and games when want to get access to information about elements of interaction. Even players with low vision need options for increasing the size or contrast of game elements [12,16].

Anticipating that awareness of the existence of players with special needs will be growing among mobile game developers, the set of design rules should be increased so that emerging applications meet specific accessibility expectations. Some guides present recommendations and accessibility guidelines focused specifically on the assessment and support for the development of accessible digital games. Other guidelines are dedicated to audio game developers, where attention is especially paid to the audio feedback interface [4,9]. Another research focuses on structuralization and organization of the main guidelines of accessibility for audio games in mobile platforms [1]. The development of alternative design can be conducted by using participatory design approach [11]. This approach is considered to be able to create interaction design which is appropriate with the participants wish [11]. However, this is not the best way to create general, universal accessibility templates. Some solutions show that it is enough to develop a good interaction engine and the game data can be taken from external files, as in the case of mobile gamebooks [8]. At present we can develop multimodal interfaces. The research [7] compared the effectiveness of using various control interfaces. This study presented that the best result obtained by gestures means that the implementation of other not so commonly used methods of interaction for mobile games may not be useful.

3   Methodology

The methodology followed in this study consisted of four phases: review of existed mobile card games, comparison of actions in card games, proposal of game layout and gesture-action pairing, and evaluation of the prototype accessible card game. The starting point of the work was the search and studying of papers concerning mobile game accessibility. This study also includes the investigation of the main accessibility guidelines for mobile games. Looking for fully accessible mobile card games in the most popular gaming stores, nothing was found. Therefore, it was decided to analyze the existing games for any elements of accessibility.

The research next stage consisted of card games analysis for types of actions. Then after the consultation of the individual who was visually impaired, the template of gesture-action pairing and gesture-action mode were proposed. In the last part of the study, we verified accessible card game implemented using proposed template of the interaction.

4   Review of Mobile Card Games

Mobile card games are quite a popular and large group of games available in the Google Play store. It would be impossible to test all of them. Therefore, the 15 most popular were selected for analysis: *Kuku* (G1), *Macau* (G2), *Pig* (G3), *Oczko* (G4), *Bishop's buttocks* (G5), *Pan* (G6), *Kemps* (G7), *Bluff* (G8), *War* (G9), *Thousand Schnapsen* (G10), *Durak* (G11), *Rummy* (G12), *Poker* (G13), *Blackjack* (G14), *Sixty-Six* (G15). Next among them, two implementations of each type with the highest rating and number of downloads. Various aspects of accessibility were assessed for them. Solitaires were excluded for the analysis, because each of them requires placing a card on the table in a strictly defined place and quite complex operations related to changing their location during the game.

Table 1 summarizes all analyzed games and accessibility features. An 'X' has been placed next to each feature fulfilled. Analyzing the data contained in the table, it was found that most games do not meet even half of the verified attributes of availability. Some of them (G1, G3, G6, G15) do not have any features that facilitate playing for the disabled. The biggest surprise may be caused by the fact that the TalkBack - a screen reader dedicated by Google for the disabled, was not supported by any of the games. The most common facilities found in the tested games are: hints, audio messages and access to the rules of the game or tutorial.

Table 1. Accessibility features in mobile card games

	G1	G2	G3	G4	G5	G6	G7	G8	G9	G10	G11	G12	G13	G14	G15
A. Custom. control	–	–	–	–	–	–	–	–	–	x	–	–	–	x	–
B. Hints	–	–	–	x	–	–	–	x	x	–	–	–	x	x	–
C. No small cards	–	–	–	–	–	–	–	–	–	–	–	–	–	–	–
D. No small fonts	–	–	–	–	–	–	–	–	–	–	–	–	–	–	–
E. Configurable colors	–	–	–	–	–	–	–	–	x	–	–	–	x	–	–
F. Help/tutorial	–	x	–	x	–	–	x	–	–	–	x	x	x	x	–
G. Voice messages	–	–	–	–	–	–	–	–	–	–	–	–	x	–	–
H. Audio messages	–	x	–	–	–	–	–	–	–	–	–	–	x	x	–
I. Vibrations	–	x	–	–	–	–	–	–	–	–	–	–	–	–	–
J. Conf. diffic. level	–	–	–	–	–	–	–	–	–	–	–	x	x	–	–

Development of the accessibility features is not a hard task. Features B, C, D, G, I, J are easy to implement and require only adequate awareness of the developers about accessibility to be considered. Voice messages can be handled by Text-To-Speech mechanism if the application architecture does not support the TalkBack screen reader. Features E and F are related to the way of displaying cards on the hand and require a change of approach to the user's interface and presenting the cards in a different form. Configurable game control (A) can be accomplished by using an intuitive control template that will be universal for all mobile card games.

5 Towards the Universal Layout and the Interaction Template

5.1 Game Layout

When developing the graphical interface, the game designer also determines how the control will take place. Usually, control in mobile games is done by precisely indicating the appropriate elements of the graphic interface, e.g. cards, on a touch screen of the device.

To eliminate this problem, the principle of displaying only one face card at the same time can be applied on the screen. *Single Card View* (SCV) is a great convenience for the visually impaired, especially - low vision people. Thus, all the actions that a player could make at a given moment would relate either to that particular card or to the entire game in general. This solution does not impose on the user a specific way to use the smartphone (horizontally or vertically). The consequence of this method of displaying is the need to reserve proper gestures for viewing cards on a hand. Left and right swipes can be selected, or alternatively, swipe only in one direction.

5.2 Card Game Analysis

The same set of games was analyzed in terms of actions performed: get a card, discard a card, returning a card to the opponent, etc. Each of them was played five times recording the type of performed actions. The summary is presented in the Table 2. All of identified actions can be simplified to *Take* and *Discard* type, or use both. The *Other* row covers information about additional actions related to special game rules.

Table 2. Comparison of actions in card games

	G1	G2	G3	G4	G5	G6	G7	G8	G9	G10	G11	G12	G13	G14	G15
Take	–	36%	55%	90%	–	22%	–	–	33%	–	38%	41%	–	63%	44%
Discard	–	60%	45%	–	50%	78%	–	90%	67%	75%	55%	20%	–	–	55%
Transfer	75%	–	–	–	–	–	96%	–	–	4%	–	–	–	–	–
Return	–	–	–	–	–	–	–	–	–	–	–	39%	–	–	–
Exchange	–	–	–	–	–	–	–	–	–	–	–	–	27%	–	–
Other	25%	4%	–	10%	50%	–	4%	10%	–	21%	7%	–	63%	37%	1%

The frequency of actions is important when designing the accessible game interface. It determines which moves should be assigned to easy-to-use keys, gestures, etc. After analysis, it was found that most card games have only a few actions. It is good information in the context of design the accessible mobile card games. In this case, the limited number of simple gestures available on the touchscreen will not be a barrier to the implementation of a new way of interaction.

5.3   Gesture-Action Pairing

Many mobile games use screen buttons. Unfortunately, blind gamers often cannot properly hold the device to be able to play the game by using that kind of interaction [6]. Thus, when designing a new interaction template, the following principles of associating gestures with actions were adopted: the set of gestures should be limited, most frequently actions should be associated with the simplest gestures performed anywhere on the screen. Other actions should be accessed in a special Question-Answer mode (QA mode). Hence, proposed interaction template uses only six gestures as follows:

- *swipe left* and *swipe right* navigate between cards on a hand,
- *swipe up* discards the current card,
- *swipe down* gets the card from the deck/dealer,
- *single tap* emits a message about current card,
- *double tap* turns on the QA mode.

The QA mode is a sequence of questions about additional actions. The following gestures are available in this mode:

- *swipe left* and *swipe right* navigate between questions,
- *single tap* equals the "YES" answer, then exits the QA mode immediately,
- *double tap* turns off the QA mode.

6   Evaluation

The proposed interaction template and layout have been implemented in a prototype game: *BlackJack* (Fig. 1). The game was created in a multiplayer mode including three predefined computer players. All gestures have been implemented using proposed approach. Only *swipe up* gesture was inactive due to the lack of appropriate action in the rules of the game. Maximum four (depending on the current situation in the game) questions were available in the QA mode for *BlackJack* game: *Don't you want more cards?*, *Do you double down?*, *Do you want to split cards?*, and *Do you want to insure?* In order to speed up the game, gestures in the QA mode have stopped speaking current question and move control to the next one.

The introduced elements of the mobile application implement accessibility features. Configurable game control (A feature in the Table 1) has been replaced

Fig. 1. Accessible mobile *BlackJack*.

by a developed interaction template. The set of questions in the QA mode plays a role of hints (B), because the availability of the question depends on the current state of the game, cards on a hand, discarded table, etc. The SCV layout (C, D features) although is not customizable, it shows cards in natural contrast colors (E): black and red symbols on a white background. Moreover, next accessibility features have been implemented: the tutorial is immediately read at the star instead of splash screen (F), voice messages informs about current game state (G), confirmation of gesture detection is done by audio beep (H) and vibration (I). The configurable difficulty level (J) has been replaced by a bidding algorithm dynamically adaptable to the player level.

A group of 11 voluntaries participated in the study: 3 women and 8 men - in the age range 21–50. They play the game several times (30 min). Then they completed a short questionnaire with a 5-point Likert scale answers. The most interesting two of them gave satisfying results: *The method of interaction is intuitive* (M = 4.42, MSE = 0.67) and *Feedback is sufficient* (M = 4.58, MSE = 0.52).

7   Conclusions

The proposed approach of the game control, limits the number of available gestures to six types: swipes in four directions, taps and double taps. In a standard mode, swipes are associated with the basic card actions on the hand, while in QA mode they are used to view optional actions in the game. A single tap works for information (as for screen readers) about the current card in the normal mode. Double tap is used to switch between modes. This approach and SCV layout should allow for the efficient implementation of many mobile card games.

However, some games that are placed in the card game genre involve a board, or cards are arranged on the table in a special way (as solitaires). In consequence a list of questions in the QA will be uselessly long. Therefore, another special interaction mode could be included to the template to enable navigation among the cards placed on the table. This issue is a topic of the future work.

References

1. Araújo, M.C.C., Façanha, A.R., Darin, T.G.R., Sánchez, J., Andrade, R.M.C., Viana, W.: Mobile audio games accessibility evaluation for users who are blind. In: Antona, M., Stephanidis, C. (eds.) UAHCI 2017. LNCS, vol. 10278, pp. 242–259. Springer, Cham (2017). https://doi.org/10.1007/978-3-319-58703-5_18
2. Archambault, D., Ossmann, R., Gaudy, T., Miesenberger, K.: Computer games and visually impaired people. Upgrade **8**(2), 43–53 (2007)
3. Bierre, K., et al.: Accessibility in games: motivations and approaches. White paper, International Game Developers Association (IGDA) (2004)
4. Teixeira Borges, O., de Borba Campos, M.: "I'm blind, can i play?" Recommendations for the development of audiogames. In: Antona, M., Stephanidis, C. (eds.) UAHCI 2017. LNCS, vol. 10278, pp. 351–365. Springer, Cham (2017). https://doi.org/10.1007/978-3-319-58703-5_26
5. Buaud, A., Svensson, H., Archambault, D., Burger, D.: Multimedia games for visually impaired children. In: Miesenberger, K., Klaus, J., Zagler, W. (eds.) ICCHP 2002. LNCS, vol. 2398, pp. 173–180. Springer, Heidelberg (2002). https://doi.org/10.1007/3-540-45491-8_38
6. Csapó, Á., Wersényi, G., Nagy, H., Stockman, T.: A survey of assistive technologies and applications for blind users on mobile platforms: a review and foundation for research. J. Multimodal User Interfaces **9**(4), 275–286 (2015). https://doi.org/10.1007/s12193-015-0182-7
7. Dobosz, K., Ptak, J.: How to control a mobile game. In: Miesenberger, K., Bühler, C., Penaz, P. (eds.) ICCHP 2016. LNCS, vol. 9758, pp. 523–529. Springer, Cham (2016). https://doi.org/10.1007/978-3-319-41264-1_71
8. Dobosz, K., Ptak, J., Wojaczek, M., Depta, T., Fiolka, T.: Mobile gamebook for visually impaired people. In: Miesenberger, K., Fels, D., Archambault, D., Peňáz, P., Zagler, W. (eds.) ICCHP 2014. LNCS, vol. 8547, pp. 309–312. Springer, Cham (2014). https://doi.org/10.1007/978-3-319-08596-8_49
9. Garcia, F.E., de Almeida Neris, V.P.: Design guidelines for audio games. In: Kurosu, M. (ed.) HCI 2013. LNCS, vol. 8005, pp. 229–238. Springer, Heidelberg (2013). https://doi.org/10.1007/978-3-642-39262-7_26
10. Jeong, E.J., Kim, D.J.: Definitions, key characteristics, and generations of mobile games. In: Mobile Computing: Concepts, Methodologies, Tools, and Applications, pp. 289–295. IGI Global (2009)
11. Mahardhika, G.P., Kurniawardhani, A., Yolhanda, D.: Mobile games interaction design for people with visual impairment using participatory design approach. In: IOP Conference Series: Materials Science and Engineering, vol. 482, p. 012039. IOP Publishing (2019)

12. Mark, C., Spohn, S.: A pratical guide to game acessibility. The AbleGames Foundation (2012)
13. Miller, D., Parecki, A., Douglas, S.A.: Finger dance: a sound game for blind people. In: Proceedings of the 9th International ACM SIGACCESS Conference on Computers and Accessibility, pp. 253–254 (2007)
14. Ossmann, R., Miesenberger, K.: Guidelines for the development of accessible computer games. In: Miesenberger, K., Klaus, J., Zagler, W.L., Karshmer, A.I. (eds.) ICCHP 2006. LNCS, vol. 4061, pp. 403–406. Springer, Heidelberg (2006). https:// doi.org/10.1007/11788713_60
15. SIG, I.G.A.: Accessibility in games: motivations and approaches (2004). Accessed 15 June 2015
16. Yuan, B.: Towards generalized accessibility of video games for the visually impaired. Ph.D. thesis (2009)
17. Yuan, B., Folmer, E., Harris, F.C.: Game accessibility: a survey. Univ. Access Inf. Soc. **10**(1), 81–100 (2011)

Developing a Serious Game for Children with Diabetes

Cecilia Sik-Lanyi[1(✉)], György Erdős[1], and Andras Sik[2]

[1] University of Pannonia, Egyetem Str. 10, Veszprem 8200, Hungary
lanyi@almos.uni-pannon.hu
[2] Prolan Innolab Kft., Szentendrei út 1-3, Budakalasz 2011, Hungary

Abstract. A Serious Game has been developed for preschool-age children who have been newly diagnosed with type 1 diabetes. The name of this game is "for kids with diabetes" the shorter version is "4KidsDiab". The 4KidsDiab program consists of two parts, an editor and a game part. The editor part is for the parents and they can adjust the game according to their child's daily allowable carbohydrate meals. Parents can upload pictures and data of meal/food into the game database. The main menu of the game contains four games for children: "True/False quiz", "Which food has more/fewer carbs", "Take it to your plate" and the reward game: "Feed the figure" game. This paper shows the design, development and evaluation process of the game. The evaluation process has been based on the System Usability Scale. It is an innovative game because it is useful for children who have multiple diseases e.g. diabetes and gluten or lactose sensitivity.

Keywords: Serious Games · Preschool-age children · Life management · Lactose/gluten sensitivity

1 Introduction

1.1 Background

In the United States, diabetes is increasing in prevalence, and it is now the seventh leading cause of death; if today's trends continue, by the year 2050, an estimated 48.3 million people in the United States will have type 1 or type 2 diabetes—almost double the current number [1].

The type 1 diabetes disease develops in childhood and the number of patients has tripled in the last thirty years. Currently, the estimated number of children with type 1 diabetes in the world is close to 601,000 [2], and under the age of 15, approximately 80,000 new cases are registered yearly [3]. In Hungary, all six-hundredths of children under the age of 15 are affected, and it is a particularly worrying phenomenon that the incidence of the disease in the youngest (under 6 years) age group increases disproportionately even compared to older children. Type 1 diabetes has become one of the most common chronic childhood diseases these days.

Lifestyle factors do not play a role in the development of type 1 diabetes unlike it is common in type 2 diabetes due to poor eating habits. Type 1 diabetes is an autoimmune

© Springer Nature Switzerland AG 2020
K. Miesenberger et al. (Eds.): ICCHP 2020, LNCS 12376, pp. 225–232, 2020.
https://doi.org/10.1007/978-3-030-58796-3_27

disease caused by a disorder of the immune system. The cause of type 1 diabetes has not been revealed in medicine in recent decades, only predisposing factors are known, such as familial accumulation, cow's milk consumption under one year of age, and some viral infections. Diagnosis at the earliest possible stage would be extremely important.

Therapeutic options have evolved at a tremendous pace over the past 30 years, there are insulin pumps and sensors, which not only significantly improved patients' quality of life, but minimized the risk of complications. By 2027 it is predicted that the market for insulin pens alone will be worth some 8.3 billion U.S. dollars.

1.2 Aim of the Development

Despite modern tools, in the case of type 1 diabetes, the lives of children need to be organized on an extremely strict agenda. There is no special diet, the recommendations are in line with the principles of healthy eating, only certain fast-absorbing carbohydrates are on the ban list, but the time, number and amount of meals are predetermined.

The treatment of diabetes is real teamwork, in collaboration between the pediatrician, the educator nurse, the dietitian, the pediatric diabetologist and the psychologist, but civil society also has a prominent role to play [3].

Patients who have type 1 or type 2 diabetes have daily self-management responsibilities that are essential for keeping their blood glucose level under control - such as measuring blood glucose, taking medications or insulin as needed, eating appropriate foods, being aware of symptoms, responding quickly when blood glucose rises too high or falls too low, and adhering in other ways to their individual treatment plan - and poor self-management that fails to control blood glucose adequately, which is a serious problem for many diabetes patients, can lead to severe complications or early death [4].

The lifestyle of diabetic children and their families changes drastically at a glance after the diagnosis. Not only parents but also children need to learn a lot.

To sum it up, a big number of children live with managing type 1 diabetes. Those children need guidance and knowledge near to diagnosis and during ongoing management in order to cope with their condition. It was our motivation to develop a Serious Game to help kids with type 1 diabetes learn the new knowledge they need.

2 Method

Firstly, we have reviewed the literature to find what similar serious games are available.

We have found some video games e.g.:

Lieberman [4] 14 video games, there were released in the period of 1992-2011 but none of them was for preschool-age children.

The game in the Pouw's thesis at the University of Twente was developed for primary school children [5].

In [6] authors reviewed 18 articles that described the design and evaluation of games for diabetes from technical, methodological, and theoretical perspectives. They undertook searches covering the period 2010 to May 2015. Few of them were developed for children (not for little children) and some of them were not available in English.

Carb Counting with Lenny [7] game is downloadable from the AppStore. In spite of the fact that the developers recommend it for age rating 4+ the screens contain several text pieces of information and it is available only in English, moreover the overall rating is 2.9 out of 5.

MyDiabetic game [8] is a very complex game, however, this complexity can be a disadvantage for our target audience. The game tries to cover as many aspects of diabetes as possible. The game is a result of three years of research. Unfortunately, this game is not available in Hungarian either.

Then we have realized the lack of age-appropriate education for younger children with type 1 diabetes. We have followed a user-centered design approach. Therefore, we have consulted pediatric dietitian on how to educate newly diagnosed children with type 1 diabetes. The consultations have helped in formulating the scope and we have defined the functional requirements which can be summarised as follows:

- The program can be run on as many platforms as possible, but the two most important are Android and Windows.
- The game should be designed so that it can be easily upgraded to other platforms.
- The controls of the game should be clear and simple so that anyone who uses it can handle it without any difficulty.
- Age group would be preschool children who do not have literacy skills and thus cannot access written information.
- The game would be based inside the clinical setting, in order for the clinicians and parents to be involved as well in the process.
- The game will focus on four mini-games for children and an editor program for parents and pediatric dietitians, which can be used to expand the game's database.

Since young children of this age are not able to set their own learning goals, feedback from those who are educating them is very important. Hence, care professionals, teachers, parents, and staff healthcare had been interviewed. The knowledge and experiences of the participants uncover the health, education and lifestyle needs of the children with diabetes. Those needs have been thereafter translated into the requirements for the game. Those requirements consist of all the non-functional goals which are related to education about the disease.

3 Discussion

The 4KidsDiab program consists of two parts, an editor and a game part. The two parts have different constraints and functional functions, so we have chosen development tools that better specialize in the tasks. The editor is QT Creator, the game has been created in a development environment called Game Maker Studio.

QT Creator is a C++ based development environment. We have chosen it because it's easy to create a user interface, and the editor itself is well documented, making it easier to fix bugs.

Game Maker Studio is a popular game development engine that uses its own language, GML. Game Maker Studio specializes specifically in the development of two-dimensional games, which is a big advantage in this case. It has a built-in graphics creator/editor, which is also a great help during development. Using Game Maker Studio we are able to develop new games on many platforms. It can develop for Windows, Android, IOS, and Ubuntu, among others.

3.1 4KidsDiabGame

The game part contains four games: "True/False quiz", "Which food has more/fewer carbs", "Take it to your plate" and the reward game: "Feed the figure" game.

The task in the "True/False quiz" (Fig. 1) is to choose the right answer for the question. It means that the statement of the question is true or false. E.g.:

- It is important that I exercise a lot, drink enough water. (True)
- My blood sugar levels can go up from a lot of movement. (False)
- A lot of movement can drop my blood sugar level. (True)
- I always have to have some carbs with me. (True)
- I have to drink at least 2 dl of milk every morning. (False)
- Milk should not just be drunk; it should be calculated. (True)
- Honey should not be eaten. (True)

These sentences and instructions are read by children's voices in the game.

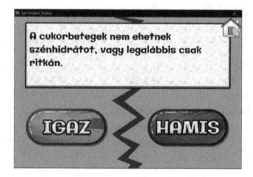

Fig. 1. A screenshot of the "True/False quiz".

The photos of two foods are on the screen in the "Which food has more/fewer carbs" game (Fig. 2). Children have to choose the picture based on the right answer to the question.

Fig. 2. A screenshot of the "Which food has more/fewer carbs" game.

Children have to choose food for a meal in the "Take it to your plate" game (Fig. 3). They can choose foods for breakfast, lunch dinner, etc. from the database. The carbohydrate is calculated based on their allowable value which had been uploaded by their parents in the editor mode. It is a very hard game for little kids.

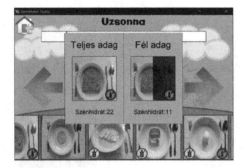

Fig. 3. A screenshot of the "Take it to your plate" game.

The fourth, reward game is the "Feed the figure" game (Fig. 4). It is a traditional snake game. If the child gives a portion of good food for the snake the snake will be longer. If the child gives bad food for the snake, it will be shorter and sick.

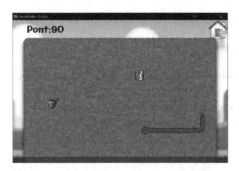

Fig. 4. A screenshot of the "Feed the figure" game.

3.2   Editor for Parents

Parents can upload pictures and data of meal/food into the game database. These data are (Fig. 5):

- Name of the food
- Category of the food (fruit, meat, vegetables, baked goods, etc.),
- The carbohydrate content of the food
- The food is usually serviced for (breakfast, lunch, snack, dinner, supplementary dinner),
- It contains fast or slow absorbing carbohydrate,
- It is allowed to eat anytime, it is forbidden to eat, children can eat but parents have to calculate its carbohydrate content
- Does it contain gluten or lactose?

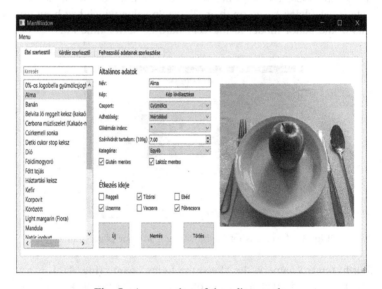

Fig. 5. A screenshot of the editor mode.

Parents can upload questions for "True/False quiz" game e.g.:

- I can drink milk at any time. (False)
- I can never drink milk. (False)
- I can drink milk when there is a meal and mom/dad calculate the carbohydrate content. (True)
- I can drink tea made with sweetener at any time. (True)
- I can get a teaspoon of honey at any time. (False)
- If my blood sugar is low, I can safely eat chocolate. (False)

Parents can upload pictures and food date for the "Which food has more/fewer carbs" and "Take it to your plate" games. The necessary and eatable carbohydrate is adjustable based on the children needs by the parents in the editor mode.

3.3 Evaluation

The "4KidsDiab" serious game is under evaluation. We have asked little preschool-age children and their parents and pediatric dietitians to test our game.

For testing, System Usability Scale (SUS) [9], more precisely a modified version was used in the Google Form. The questionnaire asks questions that are alternately positive and then negative statements. Users have had to answer the questions on a Likert scale of 1 (strongly disagree) to 5 (strongly agree). In our modified SUS questionnaire, there are 15 instead of 10 questions. Moreover, it is further divided, the first 10 questions of the test are for parents and the remaining 5 questions (questions 11–15) are for children. The first 5 questions are interested in the editing program, while all the others are opinions on the game:

1. The operation of the editing program is simple and straightforward.
2. The editing program is unnecessarily overcomplicated.
3. Managing the editing program is easy to learn.
4. I need the help of an expert to be able to manage the editing program.
5. Using the editor is fast and problem-free.
6. The user interface of the game does not correspond to a child's play.
7. The game is useful for young children.
8. The sub-games are too complicated.
9. Game management is easy to learn.
10. The game is difficult to use.
11. I will play the game often.
12. The game is too simple.
13. I can learn a lot from the game.
14. I don't like the game.
15. I can play the game alone.

The modified SUS questionnaire was filled by 10 users (7 adults and 3 children). The results' evaluation based on the SUS Interpreting Scores. The maximum scores are 100. In our case, the parents' score was 81.25 and the children's score was 80.5. So we can state that both the parents' and children's scores are "Excellent" based on the SUS [9] evaluation. (SUS score above 80.3, the letter grade is "A", the adjective rating is "Excellent").

4 Conclusion

A Serious Game has been developed for preschool-age children who have been newly diagnosed with type 1 diabetes. The game has been designed on the children's needs and conceptions and implemented based on the knowledge of pediatric dietitians. It contains a database with photos and data of several foods and meals. Finally, it has been evaluated for its learning effectiveness and usability. Our game is an innovative game not only because it is for preschool-age children, but it contains allergic information for children who have gluten or lactose intolerance.

Acknowledgements. The authors would like to thank Dóra Henn, Anna Mesterházi-Kövecses and Márta Molnár-Nemes, dietitians of the Ferenc Csolnoky Hospital in Veszprém for their professional advice.

References

1. Hayes, B.M., Aspray, W. (eds.) Health Informatics: A Patient-Centered Approach. MIT press, Cambridge (2010): https://books.google.hu/books?hl=hu&lr=&id=GCd5qpAVxLMC&oi=fnd&pg=PR5&ots=VwHnBqS18O&sig=I2GOfPWP0gUD4GE3ZFbA8wFj2ts&redir_esc=y#v=onepage&q&f=false
2. Elflein, J.: Children and type 1 diabetes worldwide – key facts (2019). https://www.statista.com/statistics/241818/key-facts-on-children-and-type-1-diabetes-worldwide/#statisticContainer
3. Semmelweis's news: The number of children with type 1 diabetes is increasing year by year (in Hungarian). http://semmelweis.hu/hirek/2019/01/09/evrol-evre-tobb-az-ovodaskoru-1-es-tipusu-diabeteszes/
4. Liebarman, D.A.: Video games for diabetes self-management: examples and design strategies. J. Diabetes Sci. Technol. **6**(4), 802–806 (2012). https://doi.org/10.1177/193229681200600410
5. Pouw, I.H.: You are what you eat: serious gaming for type 1 diabetic persons. Student thesis at the University of Twente (2015). https://essay.utwente.nl/68139/
6. Lazem, S., Webster, M., Holmes, W., Wolf, M.: Games and diabetes: a review investigating theoretical frameworks, evaluation methodologies, and opportunities for design grounded in learning theories. J. Diabetes Sci. Technol. **10**(2), 447–452 (2016). https://doi.org/10.1177/1932296815604634
7. Carb Counting with Lenny . https://apps.apple.com/us/app/carb-counting-with-lenny/id516080517
8. MyDiabetic game. http://my-diabetic.cz/en/index.html
9. System Usability Scale. https://www.usability.gov/how-to-and-tools/methods/system-usability-scale.html

An Augmented Reality Game for Helping Elderly to Perform Physical Exercises at Home

Anna Nishchyk[(✉)], Wim Geentjens, Alejandro Medina, Marie Klein, and Weiqin Chen

Oslo Metropolitan University, St. Olavs Plass, 0130 Oslo, Norway
annani@oslomet.no

Abstract. People are living longer nowadays. Unfortunately, this positive tendency is marred by various age-related health issues, which people experience. Falling is one of the most serious and common of them. Falls negatively influences elderly' everyday living and significantly decreases quality of their life. Physical exercises is a proven method for preventing falls. However, it is only effective when training is regular and exercise techniques are correct. This paper presents a prototype of an augmented reality exergame for elderly people to perform physical exercise at home. The research is focusing on developing a solution for both above-mentioned issues: augmentation with Microsoft Kinect and various sensors assists in creating a safe game environment, which can helps to perform exercises with right technique; gamification elements contribute to users' motivation to train regularly. A user-centered design approach was adopted to guide the design and development iterative process. User testing of the first prototype was performed and demonstrated positive attitudes from participants. Feedback from user testing will be used for the next development iterations.

Keywords: Augmented reality · Exergame · Fall prevention · Elderly · Physical exercises

1 Background

Population around the world is rapidly ageing and the numbers are only increasing each year [12]. Unfortunately, with age the majority of elderly people are losing muscle mass and strength, which could lead to limited mobility, decrease in postural control and increase of risk of falling and related injuries [5, 6]. Falling is one of the most common and serious age-related issues, which negatively affects the health of elderly and their well-being. About 1/3 of community dwelling older people over 65 experience a fall annually [4, 6].

Many research have been focusing on different fall prevention methods [4, 6, 9, 10]. A number of articles demonstrated that regular physical exercises can help to reduce the amount of falls and improve health conditions [3, 4, 10]. Training is recognized as an effective and cost-efficient fall prevention method [3–5]. However, exercises also have risks, related to wrong technique and wrong speed of the training [7]. It could also be challenging to perform exercises regularly, especially for elderly people, who have

© The Author(s) 2020
K. Miesenberger et al. (Eds.): ICCHP 2020, LNCS 12376, pp. 233–241, 2020.
https://doi.org/10.1007/978-3-030-58796-3_28

experienced a fall before and developed a fear of falling. According to the literature, up to 24-55% of seniors have a fear of falling [8].

The use of different interventions, such as video exercising games, virtual and augmented reality games as a method of physical exercise "delivering" has shown its effectiveness based on a number of research studies [10, 11]. Literature have shown that variety of "exergames" can increase motivation to exercise as well as level of enjoyment for different users, including elderly people [10, 11]. Modern technologies such as sensors and other various input devices have made it possible to determinate a user's exercise performance and show it to the user through a usable interaction interface [11].

However, most of the tested interventions have limitations for the aged generation related to different factors, including a lack of accessibility and usability for people with low technology tolerance, low safety level, etc. [11]. Most of the mentioned interventions are commercial and were not designed to the specific purpose of helping elderly people to perform physical exercises [11].

There is a lack of exergames intervention, which are specifically designed and developed for elderly users. The goal of this research is to create a system with two major focuses: first, to create a safe game environment, which can help to perform exercises with right techniques and reduce risk of traumatic mistakes; second, the elements of the gamification and the game's narrative can motivate users to do the training regularly. Additionally, the interface of the game should be accessible and usable for elderly people.

One of the interventions, which has been investigated before and demonstrated its effectiveness for fall prevention, is augmented reality [1]. Augmented Reality is a technology, which presents a combination of artificial and real elements (aligned with each other) in a real environment; it is three-dimensional, interactive and working in a real time [13]. Augmented reality is highly useful for training purposes, especially due to its ability to create contextual situational experience [15].

The end goal of the research is to demonstrate how augmented reality game, specifically developed for our target group, could help elderly to perform physical exercises, improve their health conditions and, as a result, prevent from falls, which could significantly enhance their quality of life. In terms of this research, our target users will be elderly people (any person over 60), anyone with limited mobility or a person who is prone to lose muscle mass easier.

2 Methods

Since the focus of the research is to create a system specifically designed and developed for a certain user group, User-centered design approach has been chosen. This approach helps to focus on the needs of potential users, gain deeper understanding of the issues which they have and clarify how to create the product which they could get maximum benefit of [2].

The design and development process will consist of several iterations with user testing at the end of each iteration. For now, the first iteration is finished, the results of it will be presented in this paper.

3 Design and Development

In order to start the design of the first prototype, various recommendations on how to design for elderly users were investigated. To represent the research's target group and to better understand the need of our target users, two personas were created in the beginning of the design process.

Based on previous research, similar systems and created personas, the following requirements have been defined: creating an indoor solution, which could be used at home to provide safeness and confidence (performing exercises in the familiar environment increases the level of safety); a user should be able to play the game alone, without additional supervision or/and a partner (elderly people often live alone).

Three important components were considered for the design and development. First, physical exercises, which will be chosen as the exercises "packed" in the game shell, should be suitable for the research and its target group. Second, hardware, including sensors, main purpose of which is to make sure the participants' safety (that the exercises are performed with the right technique). Third, the narrative of the game, its levels and achievements, which will motivate a user to play the game and perform the exercises regularly.

The solution consists of a user-friendly adventure game, created for elderly people using Augmented Reality concept. The augmentation was created by the use of Kinect camera, additional sensors and Arduino. The game has a plug and play solution and well-explained interface (see Fig. 1).

Fig. 1. Set-up of the game.

3.1 Exercises

The chosen exercises program is a low-intensity resistance training program with slow movement (LST method) developed by Prof. Ishii [14]. It helps to increase muscle mass and strength, and it is effective and safe for elderly people, which can help to avoid some possible injuries [14]. These exercises are recommended by The National

Health Service (the publicly funded healthcare system of the United Kingdom), as suitable for elderly people.

The game is about a pirate and his parrot walking on an island trying to look for a treasure chest. During their trip, they have to pass different challenges before finding the treasure chest. To pass different level of difficulty, a user needs to perform different physical exercises, which fits in the narrative of the game (for examples, "hand swings" exercises allows the parrot to fly, etc.).

3.2 Game Narrative

The game idea aims to engage a user and create a possibility to add new scenarios with new types of exercises easily. It also allows using different methods of motivation like score, rewards, unlockable levels, etc.

The game consists of set of missions (tasks). Completing each task allows the player to move forward from point A to point B in the game narrative scenario. To complete each task the player needs to perform a particular physical exercise. The game scenario was designed in a way which helps logically fit each physical exercise into game narrative. During the first game development iteration, presented in this paper, two tasks were developed. Figure 2 shows a mock-up of one of the tasks.

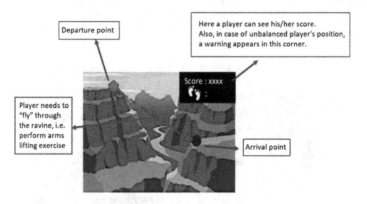

Fig. 2. Mock-up of second task.

The first task is to climb a staircase in order to start the journey and leave hometown. The exercise the player needs to perform is to walk with high knees on a spot to imitate staircase climbing (see Fig. 3).

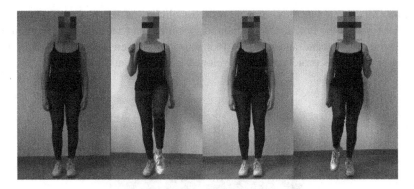

Fig. 3. A demonstration of the first exercise.

The next game stop is located on top of a mountain in front of a ravine, so the player needs to "fly" through it as a parrot. To "fly" the player needs to repetitively lift arms to shoulder height (parallel to the ground) and keep elbows straight and then lower arms slowly to starting position (see Fig. 4).

Two more exercises were selected and scripted into game tasks' scenario, but have not been developed yet.

3.3   Hardware

Kinect. Different technologies have been investigated in order to find the best solution for the research. The final choice was Microsoft Kinect. It is a device with a digital camera, which helps with the posture recognition. The technology was used to recognize player's body, map it as a simple skeleton and distinguish the positions of the body during exercising. Kinect is an open source technology and Microsoft offers a well-documented Software Development Kit for it. A large developers' community has been using the technology. Much useful information is available.

Fig. 4. A demonstration of second exercise.

Arduino. Making a safe environment was established as the main priority for the research. A part of the functions is to monitor balance, heart rate and fall detection. For this purpose, a wristband and pressure foot sensors has been designed. Based on the foot sensor design its prototype was developed (see Fig. 5 and Fig. 6).

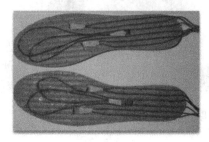

Fig. 5. Front of the foot sensor insole with the connected sensors.

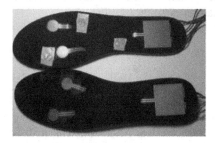

Fig. 6. Back of the foot sensor insole with the connected sensors.

Open-source electronic microcontroller board and prototyping platform Arduino was used to prototype foot sensors. Several round and square pressure sensors were placed on different parts of insoles. Through simple serial Bluetooth modules the system gets data from foot pressure sensors. Then in real time the program calculates each foot "sum" and "average" pressure and compares right and left foot numbers. If the difference in average is more than 15%, a real time warning appears on the screen and notifies the player that his/her position is unbalanced.

4   User Testing and Results

The prototype was tested with three participants. The age of participants ranged from 43 to 62 years old. Two of them were men and one was a woman. One of the participants had shoulder mobility problem, another had issues with his lower back. Although the main research target group is elderly, it was decided to include 43-years old participant into user testing due to his mobility issue and lack of physical exercises on a daily basis.

In order to collect demographic information about the participant, an interview was conducted before user testing procedure. The participants were then asked to turn on the system and play the game following the instructions on the screen. The users' interaction with the game was observed by researchers in order to identify issues experienced during the process. After the user testing, post-testing interview was conducted to collect participants' feedback and understand their attitude towards the game.

All the participants managed to finish playing the whole game. The overall feedback was positive. All of them stated that the game was comfortable to play, and the speed and the length of the explanatory videos were correct to understand the exercises. The participants also reported that the additional information collected through the sensors was very useful.

The participants have also provided some feedback, which will be used for the next iteration of the development. For instance, all the participants stated that the narrative of the game is interesting and engaging, however more themes could be added in order to add a variety to the exercising experience. One of the participant claimed that the length and speed of the videos are suitable, but the possibility to skip the video should be available, especially considering that the game could be repeated by a user many times. The participants commented that the game could be more motivating, so it would be important to add more motivation methods (score, rewards, unlockable levels, etc.). One of the participants also emphasized that a few times during the game when he made a mistake, he did not receive feedback. So more feedback from the game to a user should be added in order to increase the usability of the system.

5   Conclusion and Future Work

The research aimed to create a safe exercising environment with a game narrative to motivate elderly users to exercise regularly and correctly. The first prototype has been developed with a few basic exercises as a proof of concept, but has a possibility of extension during the next development iterations.

The results of the first prototype testing have shown that the game has potential to achieve the goal of the research. The participants have shown a positive attitude towards the prototype. They have also provided some useful feedback, which would help with further development. Although the game is designed for home use, it may also be used in health institutions, for instance, in nursing homes.

In the next development iterations, the prototype will be developed further taking into consideration the user testing results. It is planned to involve more users in next user testing iterations. After the last iteration, a longitudinal study will be conducted to investigate the effect of the exergame on elderly health conditions and its effectiveness as a fall prevention intervention.

References

1. Bruun-Pedersen, J.R., Pedersen, K.S., Serafin, S., Kofoed, L.B.: Augmented exercise biking with virtual environments for elderly users: a preliminary study for retirement home physical therapy. In: 2nd Workshop on Virtual and Augmented Assistive Technology (VAAT) IEEE, pp. 23–27 (2014)
2. Ceccacci, S., Germani, M., Mengoni, M.: User centred approach for home environment designing. In: Proceedings of the 5th International Conference on PErvasive Technologies Related to Assistive Environments, pp. 1–8 (2012)
3. El-Khoury, F., Cassou, B., Charles, M.A., Dargent-Molina, P.: The effect of fall prevention exercise programmes on fall induced injuries in community dwelling older adults: systematic review and meta-analysis of randomised controlled trials. BMJ **347**, f6234 (2013)
4. Gillespie, L.D., et al.: Interventions for preventing falls in older people living in the community. In: Cochrane Database of Systematic Reviews, vol. 9 (2012)
5. Goodwin, V.A., et al.: Multiple component interventions for preventing falls and fall-related injuries among older people: systematic review and meta-analysis. BMC Geriatr. **14**(1), 15 (2014)
6. Hauer, K., Lamb, S.E., Jorstad, E.C., Todd, C., Becker, C.: Systematic review of definitions and methods of measuring falls in randomised controlled fall prevention trials. Age Ageing **35**(1), 5–10 (2006)
7. Kojima, T., et al.: EXILE: experience based interactive learning environment. In: Proceedings of the 7th Augmented Human International Conference, pp. 1–2 (2016)
8. Levy, F., Leboucher, P., Rautureau, G., Komano, O., Millet, B., Jouvent, R.: Fear of falling: efficacy of virtual reality associated with serious games in elderly people. Neuropsychiatr. Dis. Treat. **12**, 877 (2016)
9. Lo Bianco, M., Pedell, S., Renda, G.: A health industry perspective on augmented reality as a communication tool in elderly fall prevention. In: Proceedings of the International Symposium on Interactive Technology and Ageing Populations (2016)
10. Mirelman, A., et al.: V-TIME: a treadmill training program augmented by virtual reality to decrease fall risk in older adults: study design of a randomized controlled trial. BMC Neurol. **13**(1), 15 (2013)
11. Pisan, Y., Marin, J.G., Navarro, K.F.: Improving lives: using Microsoft Kinect to predict the loss of balance for elderly users under cognitive load. In: Proceedings of the 9th Australasian Conference on Interactive Entertainment: Matters of Life and Death, pp. 1–4 (2013)
12. United Nations, Department of Economic and Social Affairs, Population Division: World Population Ageing 2017. ST/ESA/SER.A/408 (2017)
13. Van Krevelen, D.W.F., Poelman, R.: A survey of augmented reality technologies, applications and limitations. Int. J. Virtual Reality **9**(2), 1–20 (2010)
14. Watanabe, Y., Tanimoto, M., Ohgane, A., Sanada, K., Miyachi, M., Ishii, N.: Increased muscle size and strength from slow-movement, low-intensity resistance exercise and tonic force generation. J. Aging Phys. Act. **21**(1), 71–84 (2013)
15. Yuen, S.C.Y., Yaoyuneyong, G., Johnson, E.: Augmented reality: An overview and five directions for AR in education. J. Educ. Technol. Dev. Exchange (JETDE) **4**(1), 11 (2011)

Large-Scale Web Accessibility Observatories

Large Scale Web Accessibility Observatories

Introduction to the Special Thematic Session

Yehya Mohamad[✉] and Carlos A. Velasco[✉]

Fraunhofer Institute for Applied Information Technology FIT, Schloss
Birlinghoven, 53757 Sankt Augustin, Germany
{yehya.mohamad,carlos.velasco}@fit.fraunhofer.de

Abstract. This paper is an introductory to the special thematic session "Web Accessibility Observatories". The presented papers in this session tackle different dimensions of accessibility evaluation from different perspectives e.g. user requirements elicitation for large scale evaluation of websites, using meta data of digital artefacts such as chatbots to assess their accessibility, physical versus digital accessibility and tools to evaluate easy language on websites. Holistic web accessibility evaluation is a complex task that requires powerful cloud infrastructure to cope with the huge amount of data produced during the evaluation process according to legal frameworks.

Keywords: Accessibility · Large scale · Monitoring bodies · Easy language · Chat bot · Web accessibility · Mobile applications · Digital accessibility · Physical accessibility

1 Introduction

Accessibility refers to the design of products, devices, services, or environments for people with disabilities e.g. accessibility of computer software systems such as web and mobile applications. The concept of accessible design ensures both "direct access" (i.e., unassisted) and "indirect access" meaning compatibility with a person's assistive technology (for example, computer screen readers). Accessibility and usability of physical devices including wearables, sensors and actuators requires special attention to ensure access and ease of use for users with disabilities and elderly persons throughout the entire development life cycle. This can be achieved in case of web and mobile applications through consideration of accessibility guidelines already from the user requirements phase to design, development and finally evaluation phase at running time. Usable and accessible design features of physical gadgets include aspects related to workflow (suitability for typical user tasks, etc.), interaction design (conformance to user expectations, e.g., dialogue design), information presentation (clear and consistent page layout, wording) [3]. Evaluating the virtual prototypes of physical devices can be achieved by using simulated users.

Accessibility is strongly related to universal design which is the process of creating products that are usable by people with the widest possible range of abilities, operating within the widest possible range of situations. This is about making things accessible to all people (whether they have a disability or not) and to enhance user experience.

© Springer Nature Switzerland AG 2020
K. Miesenberger et al. (Eds.): ICCHP 2020, LNCS 12376, pp. 245–249, 2020.
https://doi.org/10.1007/978-3-030-58796-3_29

As mentioned above accessibility should be considered in all dimensions of product life cycles from the user requirement phase, design, specification and development. There are main while a lot of approaches and tools to support the consideration of accessibility at all phases of product life cycle. Evaluation and monitoring of the accessibility status at every phase is probably the most important category.

Web and mobile apps' accessibility has seen a lot of attention especially form W3C/WAI[1]-Web Accessibility Initiative, where many accessibility guidelines have been created such as Web Content Accessibility Guidelines WCAG[2] and Authoring Tools Accessibility Guidelines ATAG[3] etc.

One of the accessibility questions, which was discussed in the last years was about automatic versus expert evaluation of websites and mobile applications. There is a consensus that a holistic approach combining both of them should be followed in order to achieve good and cost effective state of accessibility.

Furthermore accessibility was in the last decades internationally subject for regulatory efforts based on the work of W3C/WAI e.g. in the USA in form of section 508, in Europe in the form of Web Accessibility Directive WAD and respectively the implementation of WAD in national laws in the EU member states.

The Web Accessibility Directive (WAD)[4] establishes accessibility requirements for websites and mobile applications of public sector bodies, which public sector bodies needed to start applying since 23 September 2019.

WAD defines accessibility as *"principles and techniques to be observed when designing, constructing, maintaining, and updating websites and mobile applications in order to make them more accessible to users, in particular persons with disabilities"*. The content of websites and mobile applications includes textual as well as non-textual information, downloadable documents and forms, and two-way interaction such as the processing of digital forms and the completion of authentication, identification and payment processes.

WAD's accessibility requirements describe what must be achieved for the user to be able to perceive, operate, interpret and understand a website, a mobile application and related content. But it does not specify what technology should be selected for each website, online information or mobile application. WAD defines mobile applications as *"application software designed and developed, by or on behalf of public sector bodies, for use by the general public on mobile devices such as smartphones and tablets. It does not include the software that controls those devices (mobile operating systems) or hardware"*.

WAD aims to ensure that the websites and mobile applications of public sector bodies are made more accessible based on common accessibility requirements. It defines the four principles of accessibility as:

- **perceivability**, meaning that information and user interface components must be presentable to users in ways they can perceive.

---

[1] https://www.w3.org/WAI/.

[2] https://www.w3.org/WAI/standards-guidelines/wcag/.

[3] https://www.w3.org/WAI/standards-guidelines/atag/.

[4] Directive (EU) 2016/2102 of the European Parliament and of the Council of 26 October 2016 on the accessibility of the websites and mobile applications of public sector bodies (OJ L 327, 2.12.2016, p. 1).

- **operability**, meaning that user interface components and navigation must be operable.
- **understandability**, meaning that information and the operation of the user interface must be understandable; and
- **robustness**, meaning that content must be robust enough to be interpreted reliably by a wide variety of user agents, including assistive technologies.

This regime of such requirements needs the implementation of large-scale accessibility observatories at micro (single website) and macro (organization up to member state) level. Observatories as a regime software must provide easy access for monitoring bodies, web commissioner, web accessibility experts and web developer. The monitoring body selects the required websites in a sample that fulfills the WAD requirements; the web commissioner can conduct the automatic evaluation of the websites of the sample, the web commissioner can provides then access to the web accessibility expert to conduct the manual part of the evaluation based on the automatic evaluation results. A combined report out of the automatic and manual results should be created automatically and the results should be made available to the monitoring body and other stakeholder. On the other side, the web commissioner can provide access to the web developer to correct any detected issues during the evaluation. These observatories require holistic technologies and sophisticated powerful cloud infrastructure that requires a lot of development and experimentation to reach efficient and cost effective results as described in th WADcher[5] project [1, 2]. The WADcher project is building a large-scale infrastructure by integrating extended and enhanced existing web accessibility solutions, and by making them customizable to the needs of different stakeholders in EU member states. This will result in the minimisation of costs and development-time along with increased scalability, accessibility and usability for all types of end-users including older users and users with special needs.

WADcher will be a large-scale infrastructure by integrating extended and enhanced existing web accessibility solutions, and by also making them customizable to the needs of different stakeholders in EU Member States, to meet the requirements of the WAD in all European public sector websites and mobile applications, while minimising costs and development-time along with increased scalability, accessibility and usability for all types of end-users, to enable "Web Access by Default".

WADcher users should be able to readily and reliably achieve WAD Compliance of their web sites and mobile applications through

- WAD Compliance Evaluation - using a choice of appropriate Accessibility Assessment Tools.
- WAD Accessibility Statements
- Periodic Simplified Monitoring
- Periodic In-Depth Testing.
- Evaluation Reports for WAD Monitoring Bodies
- Periodic National WAD Compliance Reports.

---

[5] https://wadcher.eu/.

The WADcher Observatory aims at facilitating web commissioners to govern accessibility policy of the sites for which they are responsible. It is comprised of three different components, namely:

1. **Dashboard** which is responsible for the visualization of the evaluation results,
2. **Aggregation Manager** which connects the automatic evaluation results with the feedback of the experts, described in the following section, and
3. **Machine learning** results and the big data analytics component, which assists the dashboard in summarizing the evaluation results.

In the following, we will present four research papers that tackle crucial questions of accessibility evaluation aspects from different angels.

2 Areas Covered by This STS

The papers presented in this STS elaborate on questions including the following:

1. Maria Laura de Filippis et al. present a common framework and guidelines on how to assess the perceived quality of interaction of chatbots. They investigate these aspects from a system's perspective; the subjective experience of quality derives from the interaction between the user and the application under specific conditions and contexts. They investigate then how factors of perceived quality of interaction are measured in studies of AI-based agents that support people with disabilities or special needs through a systematic literature review performed in accordance with the PRISMA[6] reporting checklist. The results of the present study suggest that informal and untested measures of quality are often employed when it comes to evaluating user interactions with AI agents. This is particularly relevant in the health and well-being domain, where researchers set out to measure the clinical validity of tools intended to support people with disabilities or special needs.
2. Ana Iglesias et al. introduces the Comp4Text online readability evaluation tool, which is able to calculate the readability level of a web page based on classical linguistic measures (sentence to sentence), and detects unusual words and abbreviations. The authors introduce Comp4Text checker, a new web readability evaluation tool for Spanish web pages, based on classical linguistic measures and making recommendations to improve the readability of the web pages in a very visual way.
3. Christophe Ponsard et al. present a paper about the accessibility evaluations of digital and physical worlds. Digital services reduce the need to physically move hence to have to face physical accessibility barriers, but it becomes then more critical to make sure they are not replaced by digital accessibility barriers. In order to assess the interplay of both worlds from the accessibility perspective, the authors collected available data and used automated tools from three different perspectives: one starting from physically accessible places and looking at the digital accessibility of their online services, the second going the other way and finally a representative

---

[6] http://prisma-statement.org/.

sample of services from the same smart city. They found a good combined level of accessibility in about one third of the places. Mutual strengthening could also be observed, usually greater on the digital accessibility side and revealing that awareness actions in one field also contribute to improve the other.

4. Fabio Paternò et al. present a paper about user requirements elicitation for large-scale accessibility evaluations of websites. They argue that the recent European legislation emphasizes the importance of enabling people with disabilities to have access to online information and services of public sector bodies. To this regard, automatic evaluation and monitoring of Web accessibility can play a key role for various stakeholders involved in creating and maintaining over time accessible products. They then present the results of elicitation activities that they carried out in the WADcher project to collect experience and feedback from Web commissioners, developers and content authors of websites and web applications. The purpose was to understand their current practices in addressing accessibility issues, identify the barriers they encounter when exploiting automatic support in ensuring the accessibility of Web resources, and receive indications about what functionalities they would like to exploit in order to better manage large-scale accessibility evaluation and monitoring. Each of these stakeholders represents a user role with specific requirements that emerged during their research and which have been considered in the design phase.

3 Future Research Areas

The presented papers in tis STS cover a wide range of topics related to accessibility evaluation methods, techniques and practices. As mentioned above accessibility evaluation is a complex multidimensional task involving full stack technical layers and various stakeholder such as developer, tester, policy maker etc. Accessibility evaluation research should cover in future beside the feasibility of semi-automatic large-scale monitoring pilots additional state of the art topics like Artificial Intelligence, Machine Learning, Mixed and Augmented Reality etc.

References

1. Spyrou, A., et al.: WADcher: A Unified Web Accessibility Assessment Framework (2019). https://www.thinkmind.org/articles/smart_accessibility_2019_2_20_80032.pdfs
2. Mohamad, Y., Velasco, C.A., Kaklanis, N., Tzovaras, D., Paternò, F.: A holistic decision support environment for web accessibility. In: Miesenberger, K., Kouroupetroglou, G. (eds.) ICCHP 2018. LNCS, vol. 10896, pp. 3–7. Springer, Cham (2018). https://doi.org/10.1007/978-3-319-94277-3_1
3. Mohamad, Y., Nordbrock, G., Gappa, H., Velasco, A.C.: Study on elicitation and detection of emotional states with disabled users. In: Miesenberger, K., Bühler, C., Penaz, P. (eds.) ICCHP 2016. LNCS, vol. 9758, pp. 563–570. Springer, Cham (2016). https://doi.org/10.1007/978-3-319-41264-1_76

Preliminary Results of a Systematic Review: Quality Assessment of Conversational Agents (Chatbots) for People with Disabilities or Special Needs

Maria Laura de Filippis[1]([⊠]) [iD], Stefano Federici[1] [iD],
Maria Laura Mele[1] [iD], Simone Borsci[2,3,4] [iD], Marco Bracalenti[1],
Giancarlo Gaudino[5], Antonello Cocco[5], Massimo Amendola[5],
and Emilio Simonetti[6]

[1] Department of Philosophy, Social and Human Sciences and Education,
University of Perugia, Perugia, Italy
marialauradefilippis@gmail.com
[2] Department of Cognitive Psychology and Ergonomics, Faculty of BMS,
University of Twente, Enschede, The Netherlands
[3] Department of Surgery and Cancer, Faculty of Medicine, NIHR London IVD,
Imperial College, London, UK
[4] Design Research Group, School of Creative Arts, Hertfordshire University,
Hatfield, UK
[5] DGTCSI-ISCTI, Directorate General for Management and Information
and Communications Technology, Superior Institute of Communication
and Information Technologies, Ministry of Economic Development, Rome, Italy
[6] Department of Public Service, Prime Minister's Office, Rome, Italy

Abstract. People with disabilities or special needs can benefit from AI-based conversational agents, which are used in competence training and well-being management. Assessment of the quality of interactions with these chatbots is key to being able to reduce dissatisfaction with them and to understand their potential long-term benefits. This will in turn help to increase adherence to their use, thereby improving the quality of life of the large population of end-users that they are able to serve. We systematically reviewed the literature on methods of assessing the perceived quality of interactions with chatbots, and identified only 15 of 192 papers on this topic that included people with disabilities or special needs in their assessments. The results also highlighted the lack of a shared theoretical framework for assessing the perceived quality of interactions with chatbots. Systematic procedures based on reliable and valid methodologies continue to be needed in this field. The current lack of reliable tools and systematic methods for assessing chatbots for people with disabilities and special needs is concerning, and may lead to unreliable systems entering the market with disruptive consequences for users. Three major conclusions can be drawn from this systematic analysis: (i) researchers should adopt consolidated and comparable methodologies to rule out risks in use; (ii) the constructs of satisfaction and acceptability are different, and should be measured separately;

© Springer Nature Switzerland AG 2020
K. Miesenberger et al. (Eds.): ICCHP 2020, LNCS 12376, pp. 250–257, 2020.
https://doi.org/10.1007/978-3-030-58796-3_30

(iii) dedicated tools and methods for assessing the quality of interaction with chatbots should be developed and used to enable the generation of comparable evidence.

Keywords: Chatbots · Conversational agents · People with disability · People with special needs · Usability · Quality of interaction

1 Introduction

Chatbots are intelligent conversational software agents which can interact with people using natural language text-based dialogue [1]. They are extensively used to support interpersonal services, decision making, and training in various domains [2–5]. There is a broad consensus on the effectiveness of these AI agents, particularly in the field of health, where they can promote recovery, adherence to treatment, and training [6, 7] for the preparation of different competencies and the maintenance of well-being [3, 8, 9]. In view of this, an evaluation of the perceived quality of engagement with chatbots is key to being able to reduce dissatisfaction, facilitate their possible long-term benefits, increase loyalty and thus improve the quality of life of the large population of end-users that they are able to serve. Chatbots are interaction systems, and irrespective of their domain of application, their output in terms of the quality of interaction should be planned and measured in conjunction with their users, rather than by applying a system-centric approach [1]. A recent review by Abd-Alrazaq and colleagues [6] found that in the field of mental health, researchers typically only test chatbots in a randomized controlled trial. The efficiency of interaction is seldom assessed, and is generally done by looking at non-standardized aspects of interaction and qualitative measurements that do not require comparisons to be made. This unreliable method of testing the quality of interaction of these devices or applications through a wide and varied range of variables is endemic in all fields that use chatbots, and makes it difficult to compare the results of these studies [1, 10, 11]. While some qualitative guidelines and tools have emerged [1, 12], it is still hard to find agreement on which factors should be tested. As argued by Park and Humphry [13], the implementation of these innovative systems should be based on a common framework for assessing the perceived interaction quality, in order to prevent chatbots from being regarded by their end-users as merely another source of social alienation, and being discarded in the same way as any other unreliable assistive technology [14, 15]. A common framework and guidelines on how to determine the perceived quality of chatbot interaction are therefore required. From a systems perspective, a subjective experience of consistency arises from the interaction between the user and the program in specific conditions and contexts. Subjective experience cannot be measured merely by believing that the optimal performance of the system as perceived by the user is the same as a good user experience [16]. The need to quantify the objective and subjective dimensions of experience in a reliable and comparable manner is a lesson that has been learned by those in the field of human-computer interaction, but has yet to be learned in the field of chatbots, as outlined by Lewis [17] and Bendig and colleagues [18]. Chatbot developers are forced to rely on the umbrella framework provided by the International

Organization for Standards (ISO) 9241-11 [19] for assessing usability, and ISO 9241-210 [20] for assessing user experience (UX), due to the absence of a common assessment framework that specifies comparable evaluation criteria. These two ISO standards define the key factors of interaction quality: (i) effectiveness, efficiency and satisfaction in a specific context of use (ISO 9241-11); and (ii) control (where possible) of expectations over time concerning use, satisfaction, perceived level of acceptability, trust, usefulness and all those factors that ultimately push users to adopt and keep using a tool (ISO 9241-210). Although these standards have not yet been updated to meet the specific needs of chatbots and conversational agents, the two aspects of usability and UX are essential to the perceived quality of interaction [21]. Until a framework has been developed and broad consensus reached on assessment criteria, practitioners may benefit from the assessment of chatbots against these ISO standards, as they allow for an evaluation of the interactive output of these applications. This paper examines how aspects of perceived interaction quality are assessed in studies of AI-based agents that support people with disabilities or special needs. Our systematic literature review was conducted in accordance with the PRISMA reporting checklist.

2 Methods

A systematic review was carried out of journal articles investigating the relationship between chatbots and people with disabilities or special needs over the last 10 years. To determine whether and how the quality of interaction with chatbots was evaluated in line with ISO standards of usability (ISO 9241-11) and UX (ISO 9241-210), this review sought to answer the following research questions:

R1. How are the key factors of usability (efficiency, effectiveness, and satisfaction) measured and reported in evaluations of chatbots for people with disabilities or special needs?
R2. How are factors relating to UX measured and reported in assessments of chatbots?

We included in our review studies that: (i) referred to chatbots or conversational interfaces/agents for people with disabilities or special needs in the title, abstract, keywords or main text; (ii) included empirical findings and discussions of theories (or frameworks) of factors that could contribute to the perceived quality of interaction with chatbots, with a focus on people with various types of disability.

We excluded records that did not include at least one group of end-users with a disability in either the testing or the design of the interaction, and studies that focused on: (i) testing emotion recognition during the interaction exchange, or assessing applications for detecting the development of disability conditions or disease; (ii) chatbots supporting people with alcoholism, anxiety, depression or traumatic disorders; (iii) the assessment of end-user compliance with clinical treatment, or assessment of the clinical effectiveness of using AI agents as an alternative to standard (or other) forms of care without considering the interaction exchange with the chatbot; and (iv) the ethical and legal implications of interacting with AI-based digital tools. Records were retrieved from Scopus and the Web of Science using the Boolean operators (AND/OR) to combine the following keywords: chatbot*, conversational agent*, special needs, disability*. We searched only for English language articles.

3 Results

A total of 147 items were retrieved from Scopus and Web of Science. A further 53 records were added based on a previous review of chatbots in mental health in [6]. After removing eight duplicates, a scan of the remaining 192 records by title and abstract was performed by two authors (MLDF, SB). Articles that defined their scope as including the assessment of interactions between chatbots and conversational agents and people with various types of intellectual disabilities or special needs were retained. The full text of 68 records was then scanned to look for articles mentioning methods and factors for assessing the interactions of people with disabilities or special needs with chatbots. The final list consisted of 15 documents [3, 8, 9, 22–33], 80% of which had already been discussed in previous work by Abd-Alrazaq et al. [6] for different purposes.

Of the 15 records that matched our criteria, 80% examined AI agents in terms of supporting people with autism and (mild to severe) mental disabilities, while the other 20% focused on the testing of applications to support the general health or training of people with a wide range of disabilities. The main goal of 66.6% of the applications was to support health and rehabilitation, while the remaining studies focused on solutions to support learning and training for people with disabilities. In terms of their approach to assessment, 46.7% of the studies used surveys or questionnaires, 26.7% applied a quasi-experimental procedure, and the remaining 26.7% tested chatbots using randomized controlled trials (i.e., testing the use of the agent versus standard practice with a between design) that assessed several aspects relating to the quality of the interaction. Factors relating to usability (i.e., effectiveness, efficiency, and satisfaction) were partly assessed, with 80% of the studies reporting measures of effectiveness, 26.7% measures of efficiency and 20% measures of satisfaction. In terms of UX, acceptability was the most frequently reported measure (26.7% of the cases) while a few other factors (e.g., engagement, safety, helpfulness, etc.) were measured using various approaches.

4 Discussion

The results suggest that the main focus of studies of chatbots for people with disabilities or special needs is the effectiveness of such apps compared with standard practice, in terms of supporting adherence to treatment. The results can be summarized in accordance with our research questions as follows:

R1. A total of 80% of the studies [3, 8, 9, 23, 25, 27, 30–33] tested the effectiveness of chatbots according to the ISO standard [19], i.e., the ability of the app to perform correctly, allowing the users to achieve their goals. Only 26.7% of the studies [9, 25, 26, 32] also investigated efficiency, by measuring performance in terms of time or factors relating to the resources invested by participants to achieve their goals. Only 20% [9, 22, 23] referred to an intention to gather data on user satisfaction in a structured way, and only one study [23] used a validated scale (e.g., the System Usability Scale, or user metrics of UX [34]). In another, practitioners adapted a standardized questionnaire without clarifying the changes to the items [22], and a qualitative scale was used in a further study [9].

R2. Acceptability was identified as an assessment factor in 26.7% of the studies [9, 22, 24, 25]. Despite the popularity of the technology acceptance model [35, 36], acceptability was measured in a variety of ways (e.g., lack of complaints [25]) or treated as a measure of satisfaction [24]. A total of 53% of the studies used various factors to assess the quality of interaction, such as the overall experience, safety, acceptability, engagement, intention to use, ease of use, helpfulness, enjoyment, and appearance. Most used non-standardized questionnaires to assess the quality of interaction. Even when a factor such as safety was identified as a reasonable form of quality control, in compliance with ISO standards for medical devices [37] and risk analysis [38], the method of its measurement in these studies was questionable, i.e., assessing a product to be safe based on a lack of adverse events [9].

5 Conclusion

The results of the present study suggest that informal and untested measures of quality are often employed when it comes to evaluating user interactions with AI agents. This is particularly relevant in the domain of health and well-being, where researchers set out to measure the clinical validity of tools intended to support people with disabilities or special needs. The risk is that shortcomings in these methods could significantly compromise the quality of chatbot usage, ultimately leading to the abandonment of applications that could otherwise have a positive impact on their end-users. Three major findings can be identified from this systematic analysis. (i) Researchers tend to consider a lack of complaints as an indirect measure of the safety and acceptability of tools. However, safety and acceptability should be assessed with consolidated and comparable methodologies to rule out risks in use [37–39]. (ii) Satisfaction, intended as a usability metric, is a different construct from acceptability, and these two constructs should be measured separately with available standardized questionnaires [39, 40]. (iii) Although dedicated tools and methods for assessing the quality of interaction with chatbots are lacking, reliable methods and measures to assess interaction are available [17, 19, 21, 37], and these should be adopted and used to enable the generation of comparable evidence regarding the quality of conversational agents.

References

1. Radziwill, N.M., Benton, M.C.: Evaluating quality of chatbots and intelligent conversational agents. arXiv preprint arXiv:1704.04579 (2017)
2. Ammari, T., Kaye, J., Tsai, J.Y., Bentley, F.: Music, search, and IoT: how people (really) use voice assistants. ACM Trans. Comput.-Hum. Interact. **26** (2019). https://doi.org/10.1145/3311956
3. Beaudry, J., Consigli, A., Clark, C., Robinson, K.J.: Getting ready for adult healthcare: designing a chatbot to coach adolescents with special health needs through the transitions of care. J. Pediatr. Nurs. **49**, 85–91 (2019). https://doi.org/10.1016/j.pedn.2019.09.004
4. Costa, S., Brunete, A., Bae, B.C., Mavridis, N.: Emotional storytelling using virtual and robotic agents. Int. J. Hum. Robot. **15** (2018). https://doi.org/10.1142/S0219843618500068
5. Dmello, S., Graesser, A.: AutoTutor and affective AutoTutor: learning by talking with cognitively and emotionally intelligent computers that talk back. ACM Trans. Interact. Intell. Syst. **2** (2012). https://doi.org/10.1145/2395123.2395128
6. Abd-Alrazaq, A.A., Alajlani, M., Alalwan, A.A., Bewick, B.M., Gardner, P., Househ, M.: An overview of the features of chatbots in mental health: a scoping review. Int. J. Med. Inf. **132** (2019). https://doi.org/10.1016/j.ijmedinf.2019.103978
7. Fadhil, A., Wang, Y., Reiterer, H.: Assistive conversational agent for health coaching: a validation study. Methods Inf. Med. **58**, 009–023 (2019)
8. Burke, S.L., et al.: Using virtual interactive training agents (ViTA) with adults with autism and other developmental disabilities. J. Autism Dev. Disord. **48**(3), 905–912 (2017). https://doi.org/10.1007/s10803-017-3374-z
9. Ellis, T., Latham, N.K., DeAngelis, T.R., Thomas, C.A., Saint-Hilaire, M., Bickmore, T.W.: Feasibility of a virtual exercise coach to promote walking in community-dwelling persons with Parkinson disease. Am. J. Phys. Med. Rehabil. **92**, 472–485 (2013). https://doi.org/10.1097/PHM.0b013e31828cd466
10. Balaji, D., Borsci, S.: Assessing user satisfaction with information chatbots: a preliminary investigation. University of Twente, University of Twente repository (2019)
11. Tariverdiyeva, G., Borsci, S.: Chatbots' perceived usability in information retrieval tasks: an exploratory analysis. University of Twente, University of Twente repository (2019)
12. IBM http://conversational-ux.mybluemix.net/design/conversational-ux/practices/
13. Park, S., Humphry, J.: Exclusion by design: intersections of social, digital and data exclusion. Inf. Commun. Soc. **22**, 934–953 (2019)
14. Federici, S., Borsci, S.: Providing assistive technology in Italy: the perceived delivery process quality as affecting abandonment. Disabil. Rehabil. Assist. Technol. **11**, 22–31 (2016). https://doi.org/10.3109/17483107.2014.930191
15. Scherer, M.J., Federici, S.: Why people use and don't use technologies: introduction to the special issue on assistive technologies for cognition/cognitive support technologies. NeuroRehabilitation **37**, 315–319 (2015). https://doi.org/10.3233/NRE-151264
16. Bevan, N.: Measuring usability as quality of use. Softw. Qual. J. **4**, 115–130 (1995). https://doi.org/10.1007/BF00402715
17. Lewis, J.R.: Usability: lessons learned… and yet to be learned. Int. J. Hum.-Comput. Interact. **30**, 663–684 (2014). https://doi.org/10.1080/10447318.2014.930311
18. Bendig, E., Erb, B., Schulze-Thuesing, L., Baumeister, H.: The next generation: chatbots in clinical psychology and psychotherapy to foster mental health – a scoping review. Verhaltenstherapie (2019). https://doi.org/10.1159/000501812
19. ISO: ISO 9241-11:2018 Ergonomic Requirements for Office Work with Visual Display Terminals – Part 11: Guidance on Usability. CEN, Brussels (2018)

20. ISO: ISO 9241-210:2010 Ergonomics of Human-System Interaction – Part 210: Human-Centred Design for Interactive Systems. CEN, Brussels (2010)
21. Borsci, S., Federici, S., Malizia, A., De Filippis, M.L.: Shaking the usability tree: why usability is not a dead end, and a constructive way forward. Behav. Inform. Technol. **38**, 519–532 (2019). https://doi.org/10.1080/0144929x.2018.1541255
22. Ali, M.R., et al.: A virtual conversational agent for teens with autism: experimental results and design lessons. arXiv preprint arXiv:1811.03046 (2018)
23. Cameron, G., et al.: Assessing the usability of a chatbot for mental health care. In: Bodrunova, S.S., et al. (eds.) INSCI 2018. LNCS, vol. 11551, pp. 121–132. Springer, Cham (2019). https://doi.org/10.1007/978-3-030-17705-8_11
24. Konstantinidis, E.I., Hitoglou-Antoniadou, M., Luneski, A., Bamidis, P.D., Nikolaidou, M.M.: Using affective avatars and rich multimedia content for education of children with autism. In: 2nd International Conference on PErvasive Technologies Related to Assistive Environments (PETRA 2009), pp. 1–6 (2009). https://doi.org/10.1145/1579114.1579172
25. Lahiri, U., Bekele, E., Dohrmann, E., Warren, Z., Sarkar, N.: Design of a virtual reality based adaptive response technology for children with autism. IEEE Trans. Neural Syst. Rehabil. Eng. **21**, 55–64 (2013). https://doi.org/10.1109/TNSRE.2012.2218618
26. Ly, K.H., Ly, A.-M., Andersson, G.: A fully automated conversational agent for promoting mental well-being: a pilot RCT using mixed methods. Internet Interv. **10**, 39–46 (2017). https://doi.org/10.1016/j.invent.2017.10.002
27. Milne, M., Luerssen, M.H., Lewis, T.W., Leibbrandt, R.E., Powers, D.M.W.: Development of a virtual agent based social tutor for children with autism spectrum disorders. In: International Joint Conference on Neural Networks (IJCNN 2010), pp. 1–9 (2010). https://doi.org/10.1109/IJCNN.2010.5596584
28. Razavi, S.Z., Ali, M.R., Smith, T.H., Schubert, L.K., Hoque, M.: The LISSA virtual human and ASD teens: an overview of initial experiments. In: Traum, D., Swartout, W., Khooshabeh, P., Kopp, S., Scherer, S., Leuski, A. (eds.) IVA 2016. LNCS (LNAI), vol. 10011, pp. 460–463. Springer, Cham (2016). https://doi.org/10.1007/978-3-319-47665-0_55
29. Smith, M.J., et al.: Job offers to individuals with severe mental illness after participation in virtual reality job interview training. Psychiatr. Serv. **66**, 1173–1179 (2015). https://doi.org/10.1176/appi.ps.201400504
30. Smith, M.J., et al.: Virtual reality job interview training for individuals with psychiatric disabilities. J. Nerv. Mental Dis. **202**, 659–667 (2014). https://doi.org/10.1097/NMD.0000000000000187
31. Tanaka, H., Negoro, H., Iwasaka, H., Nakamura, S.: Embodied conversational agents for multimodal automated social skills training in people with autism spectrum disorders. PLoS ONE **12**, e0182151 (2017). https://doi.org/10.1371/journal.pone.0182151
32. Wargnier, P., Benveniste, S., Jouvelot, P., Rigaud, A.-S.: Usability assessment of interaction management support in Louise, an ECA-based user interface for elders with cognitive impairment. Technol. Disabil. **30**, 105–126 (2018). https://doi.org/10.3233/TAD-180189
33. Smith, M.J., et al.: Virtual reality job interview training in adults with autism spectrum disorder. J. Autism Dev. Disord. **44**(10), 2450–2463 (2014). https://doi.org/10.1007/s10803-014-2113-y
34. Borsci, S., Federici, S., Bacci, S., Gnaldi, M., Bartolucci, F.: Assessing user satisfaction in the era of user experience: comparison of the SUS, UMUX and UMUX-LITE as a function of product experience. Int. J. Hum.-Comput. Interact. **31**, 484–495 (2015). https://doi.org/10.1080/10447318.2015.1064648
35. Venkatesh, V., Morris, M.G., Davis, G.B., Davis, F.D.: User acceptance of information technology: toward a unified view. MIS Q.: Manag. Inf. Syst. **27**, 425–478 (2003)

36. Federici, S., Tiberio, L., Scherer, M.J.: Ambient assistive technology for people with dementia: an answer to the epidemiologic transition. In: Combs, D. (ed.) New Research on Assistive Technologies: Uses and Limitations, pp. 1–30. Nova Publishers, New York (2014). https://doi.org/10.13140/2.1.3461.4405
37. IEC: IEC 62366-1:2015 Medical Devices – Part 1: Application of Usability Engineering to Medical Devices. CEN, Brussels (2015)
38. ISO: ISO 14971:2007 Medical Devices – Application of Risk Management to Medical Devices. CEN, Brussels (2007)
39. Borsci, S., Federici, S., Mele, M.L., Conti, M.: Short scales of satisfaction assessment: a proxy to involve disabled users in the usability testing of websites. In: Kurosu, M. (ed.) HCI 2015. LNCS, vol. 9171, pp. 35–42. Springer, Cham (2015). https://doi.org/10.1007/978-3-319-21006-3_4
40. Borsci, S., Buckle, P., Walne, S.: Is the lite version of the usability metric for user experience (UMUX-LITE) a reliable tool to support rapid assessment of new healthcare technology? Appl. Ergon. **84**, 103007 (2020)

Comp4Text Checker: An Automatic and Visual Evaluation Tool to Check the Readability of Spanish Web Pages

Ana Iglesias[1]([⊠]) [iD], Ignacio Cobián[1] [iD], Adrián Campillo[1] [iD],
Jorge Morato[1] [iD], and Sonia Sánchez-Cuadrado[2] [iD]

[1] Computer Science and Engineering Department,
Universidad Carlos III de Madrid, Madrid, Spain
aiglesia@inf.uc3m.es
[2] Library and Information Science Department,
Universidad Complutense de Madrid, Madrid, Spain

Abstract. One important requirement for a web page to be accessible for all, according to the current international recommendations from the W3C Accessibility Initiative is that the text should be readable and understandable to the broadest audience possible. Nowadays, unfortunately, the information included in the web pages are not easy to read and understand to everybody. This paper introduces the Comp4Text online readability evaluation tool, which is able to calculate the readability level of a web page based on classical linguistic measures (sentence to sentence) and detect unusual words and abbreviations. Moreover, it provides recommendations to solve the readability problems and show everything in a very visual way. Thanks to this tool, the web page designers and writers could improve their sites, being easier to be read and understand for all. Currently, Comp4Text is based on the Spanish language, but it can be easily extended to other languages if the readability metrics and easy-to-read rules are well-known.

Keywords: Web pages readability · Automatic tool · Accessibility

1 Introduction

Currently, and increasingly, we are immersed in a digital society that pretends to make our lives easier. However, unfortunately, not everybody is able to access to the digital information and services provided yet because of accessibility barriers. This proposal is focused on one of the bases of accessibility: the readability of the web pages' text, according to the current international recommendations from the W3C Accessibility Initiative (WAI)[1].

---

[1] WAI accessibility principles: https://www.w3.org/WAI/fundamentals/accessibility-principles/ (accessed on June '20).

© Springer Nature Switzerland AG 2020
K. Miesenberger et al. (Eds.): ICCHP 2020, LNCS 12376, pp. 258–265, 2020.
https://doi.org/10.1007/978-3-030-58796-3_31

The accessibility barriers on the Internet become especially important and worrying when they are related to the individual's rights, like public information from the Government, or services as education, health, employment or social activities, among others. That is why digital inclusion is a world-wide strategy nowadays, to ensure that everybody, regardless of their functional abilities/disabilities (physical or cognitive), can contribute-to and benefit-from the digital economy and society.

This paper presents Comp4Text, an online readability evaluation tool which can help web pages' designers and writers to improve their documents and make them readable for all.

2 Literature Review

2.1 Readability Tools

There exist different types of tools which try to test or adapt the documents to make the text more readable according to the reader's needs.

Some of the tools are focused on making the text more perceivable and readable by customizing the visual presentation of the contents. Typically, this type of tools are called *legibility tools*. This kind of text adaptation is very useful for people with visual impairments who usually experience eyestrain, fatigue or headaches among others when reading. Examples of these tools are the ATBar[2] (by the University of Southampton), and the Accessibility Enabler[3] (by Hike Orders). Both tools are toolbars to help users to customize the way they view and interact with web pages by changing the background, font style, font size, line spacing, etc. of the web pages.

Some other efforts have been focused on providing a better understanding by customizing the text to the user's needs by modelling and graphically representing more than one version of text through Variant Graphs, like the TadER project [1] or Stemmaweb project [2]. Web applications were developed following this proposal, as the CollateX[4] web tool or Stemmaweb[5] tool, showing directed acyclic graphs, horizontally aligned, with the different versions of the text fragments.

Other research projects are focused on computing and showing the text readability based on typical linguistic measures to check whether the content is easy-to-read. More information about linguistic readability measures are provided in the next section. The linguistic measures are highly language dependent, and most of them are developed for English language, as Readability Text Tool[6] (by webFX), the Document Readability Text Tool[7] (by Online-utility.org), the Readability Grader[8] (by Jellymetrics) or the

---

[2] ATBar: https://www.atbar.org/ (accessed on June '20).

[3] Accessibility Enabler: https://hikeorders.com/accessibility/home/ (accessed on June '20).

[4] CollateX: https://collatex.net/ (accessed on June '20).

[5] Stemmaweb: https://stemmaweb.net/ (accessed on June '20).

[6] Readability Text Tool: https://www.webfx.com/tools/read-able/ (accessed on June '20).

[7] Document Readability Text Tool: http://www.online-utility.org/english/readability_test_and_improve.jsp (accessed on June '20).

[8] Readability Grader: https://jellymetrics.com/readability-grader/ (accessed on June '20).

Reading Effectiveness Tool[9] (by Clear Language and Design - CLAD). A tool for Italian language can also be found in the literature, the Vàmola[10] (by Regione Emilia-Romagna).

However, specific readability tools have not yet been developed for the Spanish language. This paper presents a new visual proposal for a readability testing tool for Spanish language: Comp4Text. The next subsection introduces a state of the art related to typical and new linguistic measures in readability. Many of these measures have been considered and some of them implemented in the CompText tool, as we detail in the next sections, where the tool is introduced.

2.2   Readability Measures

Metrics to estimate readability of texts in English emerged in the 1950s in the educational field applied to level the text at the corresponding school age. These metrics were based on characteristics such as the number of characters, number of syllables, number of words, sentences, and paragraphs. Different metrics were created based on the size of different parts of the text, or by selecting two or three combinations of indicators (Flesh-Kinkaid, Gunning-Fog, Coleman-Liau Index, SMOG Index or ARI). In fact, more than 70 indexes have been developed [3, 4], including some for Romance languages such as Spanish, French or Italian. Main metrics proposed for Spanish language were Inflesz, Legibilidad μu (Lμ), Gutiérrez Polini's readability metric, Flesh-Fernández Huerta, and Szgriszt-Pazos among others [5]. In general, these formulas penalize writing with polysyllabic words and long and complex sentences. Texts score improve when simpler and shorter words and sentences are used.

Researchers Dale and Chall [6] proposed a derived approach, based on the frequency of use of a word. Their hypothesis assumes that the frequency of use of a word shows that there is a community of users that understands its meaning, and therefore reflects the familiarity that readers have regarding the term. They proposed a list of simple words that included a value on the familiarity of the word with which they could presumably estimate the educational level that would correspond to the text.

The result of applying the comprehensibility metrics provides a value that establishes the text difficulty on a scale of five or seven levels depending on each formula. Flesh index proposed five values: 1) very easy, 2) easy, 3) standard, 4) difficult, and 5) very difficult. Flesh Fernández-Huerta index created seven levels: 1) very easy, 2) easy, 3) fairly easy, 4) standard, 5) fairly difficult, 6) difficult, 7) very difficult. These metrics have successfully served their purpose for decades.

2.3   Discussion

After an in-depth analysis of the current readability checker tools in this section, we have realized that none of them is specific for the Spanish language. Therefore, due to the high language dependency of the readability linguistic measures, Comp4Text

---

[9] Reading Effectiveness Tool: http://clad.tccld.org/measuring-readability/ (accessed on June '20).

[10] Vàmola: http://www.validatore.it (accessed on June '20).

checker covers this issue, based on the linguistic indexes described in the previous subsection.

Moreover, the new tool introduced on this paper will try to maintain the accessibility and improve the usability of the readability checker tools for English and Italian language mainly in four different points: showing graphically and directly in the web page the main readability errors or warnings found, reducing the location problems that other tools have (indicating, for instance, a line code); making recommendations for improving the readability of specific sentences and unusual words; allowing to show and download summary reports in standard formats (.pdf and .json); and facilitate user interaction by allowing users to navigate the website dynamically (following the links) and checking the readability of other web pages online.

Inclusive methodologies, as the Accessibility Conformance Evaluation Methodology [7] and Universal Design Principles [8] have been taken into account from the very beginning of the Comp4Text' design in order to obtain an accessible and usable product.

As a first step, a study of the current readability tools for Spanish language and other languages was conducted, finding that most readability tools were developed for English language. In this step, an automatic readability checker tool was selected to be the focus of the study, taking into account and trying to solve the differences with the previous ones.

Moreover, an in-depth study of the best linguistic measures to take into account for the Spanish language and the adaptation of classical measures to the new type of text, as well as study of recommendations to improve the text based on linguistic research works was performed.

The first prototype of the Comp4Text tool, introduced in this paper, was designed and implemented in a laboratory environment (at the University). Then, two accessibility experts made a heuristic accessibility evaluation of the application according to the w3c methodology [7], defining the evaluation scope, exploring the target website, selecting and auditing a representative sample and reporting the findings. Automatic accessibility checker tools were also used during the developing process, as WAVE[11] and aChecker[12] web accessibility evaluation tools. Then, all these findings were fixed to ensure an appropriate accessibility level. As future work, an in-depth user evaluation is going to be performed for the Comp4Text tool, before its public web upload, to ensure its accessibility for all.

3 Comp4Text Application

The Comp4Text application is an online readability evaluation tool which provides a visual representation of readability issues within the document. The aspect is similar to WAVE accessibility tool (see Fig. 1). At present, it calculates the readability for Spanish language of web pages (providing the URL). In the near future, it will be able

---

[11] WAVE web accessibility evaluation tool: https://wave.webaim.org/ (accessed on June '20).

[12] aChecker web accessibility evaluation tool: https://achecker.ca/ (accessed on June '20).

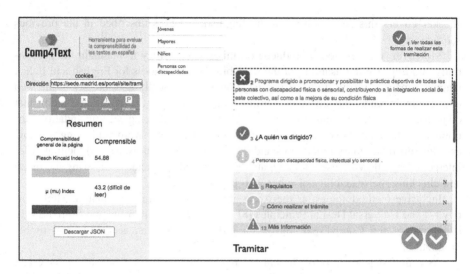

Fig. 1. Screenshot 1 of Comp4Text. Summary of classical readability measures. (Color figure online)

to calculate the readability of documents (including the most common documents formats: .txt, .doc, .pdf, etc.) or plain text.

Classical readability measures for the Spanish language have been used to calculate the sentences readability: Flesch-Kincaid index (Fernández-Huerta Index) [9] in 1958 and mu index [5] in 2006. Both indexes are based on the number of years of education that a person needs to be able to understand the text easily on the first reading and they are very similar according to attributes used in their construction. However, the two of them are used to check the accurateness of traditional measures within the time (there is a difference of more than 50 years between them).

On the other hand, to estimate the readability of the words in the document (detecting unusual words and abbreviations), word frequency and familiarity measures have been used. Each word in the text is associated with a frequency value from Current Spanish Reference Corpus (CREA for its Spanish acronym) [10]. According to that frequency value, the words in the text are classified into three different levels (very frequent, frequent and not frequent words) using the Zipf's law and Goffman's transition point approach [11]. Moreover, the application is able to provide a list of synonyms from the Spanish version of Wordnet lexical database[13] to suggest other options to improve readability.

Figure 1 shows the interface of the readability tool. On the right frame, the web page evaluated is shown visually. On the left frame, a summary of the web page readability is shown, using the Flesch Kincaid Index -that measures the understability-, and the Mu Index-that measures how difficult is the web page to read. Moreover, scrolling down in the left frame of the web page, the tool details the number of complex

---

[13] Wordnet lexical database por Spanish language: https://wordnet.princeton.edu/ (accessed on June '20).

sentences (marked with a square icon in red within an x letter), the number of easy sentences (marked with a round icon in green within a tick symbol), the number of sentences which medium readability (marked with a round icon in yellow within an exclamation symbol) and the number of sentences that weren't evaluated (marked with a light blue icon within an exclamation). Figure 2 shows this information.

By clicking any tag, on the left frame, the sentences on that category are marked on the web page right-side. For instance, in Fig. 1 we can see how the first sentence has been framed with a red and dashed line (complex sentence) and the corresponding squared and red icon. Moreover, the other sentences and non-common words are also marked with their corresponding readability icon (red-green-yellow-blue icons), where a number is used to identify each one of the icons on the text, needed to identify the readability problems in the final report.

A more detailed information of the readability evaluation is popped-up by clicking on any error or warning icon on the right frame. Figure 2 shows a screenshot of the application when un icon has been clicked, popping-up detailed information about the problem and how to solve it. For instance, if a complicated word or sentence is detected, suggestions for what to do to improve its readability are shown. Moreover, the user can feedback this information, rating it, including a new recommendation and how sure is of this recommendation.

One of the most important differences to other readability evaluation tools is that, similar to WAVE application, the application introduced in this paper annotates errors and warnings in-line and visually on the document, taking into account accessibility, but focused on readability evaluations. It underlies instantly and visually the elements (sentences or words) on the document that are causing the possible reading problems after sliding the mouse over it or its paper tag.

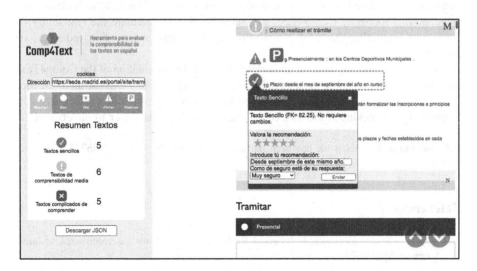

Fig. 2. Screenshot 2 of Comp4Text. Details of readability evaluation for a sentence. (Color figure online)

The application has been designed according to the W3C recommendations, accomplishing the WCAG 2.0[14] accessibility guidelines and, at the same time, using colourful error and warning icons in order to be easily identified in the document, even if the document is a colourful web page.

The application also allows building a final readability evaluation report of the web page, allowing to download a .json report. This report includes a summary of the readability problems found, within a list of sentences that are suggested to be rewritten and a list of unusual words to be changed to improve readability and how to fix the readability issues are provided in the report.

4 Conclusions and Planned Activities

This paper introduces Comp4Text checker, a new web readability evaluation tool for Spanish web pages, based on classical linguistic measures and making recommendations to improve the readability of the web pages in a very visual way.

This new tool take into account accessibility and usability issues: it shows graphically and located in the original webpage, the main readability errors or warnings found, reducing the location problems that other tools present; it makes recommendations for improving the readability of specific sentences and unusual words; it shows and allows to download summary reports in standard formats (.pdf and .json); and it makes easier the interaction of the users, allowing them to navigate dynamically on the website (following the links).

In the near future, API services and extensions for the most Chrome and Firefox browsers are going to be developed. Currently, it calculates the readability for Spanish language of web pages (providing the URL), but it could be easily adapted to other languages, considering their specific linguistic measures and tools to provide recommendations. Moreover, Comp4Text will soon be able to calculate the readability of documents (including the most common documents formats: .txt, .doc, .pdf, etc.) or plain text.

We are also working now on an in-depth accessibility evaluation of the Comp4Text checker, being necessary to involve final users in the accessibility evaluation of the tool before publishing it. Moreover, an in-depth user evaluation of the tool effectively will be performed, checking if the tool contributes to render texts easier to understand.

Acknowledgment. This work has been partially funded by the CSO2017-86747-R Spanish project.

References

1. TAdER – Text Adaptability is Essential for Reading. http://www.tader.info/scrolling.html. Accessed April 2020

---

[14] WCAG 2.0 guidelines (W3C): https://www.w3.org/TR/WCAG20/ (last access on June, 2020)

2. Jänicke, S., et al.: TRAViz: a visualization for variant graphs. Digit. Scholarsh. Humanit. **30** (suppl_1), i83–i99 (2015)
3. Social Science Consulting, "TextQuest". http://textquest.de/shop/product_info.php?products_id=3. Accessed April 2020
4. Morato, J., Sánchez-Cuadrado, S., Gimmelli, P.: Estimación de la comprensibilidad en paneles de museos. EPI **27**(3), 570 (2018)
5. Baquedano, M.M.: Legibilidad y variabilidad de los textos. Boletín De Investigación Educacional [Artículo De Revista] **21**, 13–25 (2006)
6. Dale, E., Chall, J.S.: A formula for predicting readability. Educ. Res. Bull. **27**, 11–28 (1948)
7. Web Accessibility Conformance Evaluation Methodology (WCAG-EM) v1.0. https://www.w3.org/TR/WCAG-EM/. Accessed April 2020
8. Story, M.F.: Maximizing usability: the principles of universal design. Assist. Technol. **10**(1), 4–12 (1998)
9. Fernández-Huerta, J.: Medidas sencillas de lecturabilidad. Consigna **214**, 29–32 (1959)
10. Real Academia Española: Banco de datos (CORDE). Corpus diacrónico del español. http://www.rae.es. Accessed April 2020
11. Urbizagástegui Alvarado, R., Restrepo Arango, C.: La ley de Zipf y el punto de transición de Goffman en la indización automática. Investigación Bibliotecológica **25**(54), 71–92 (2011)

Towards Cross Assessment of Physical and Digital Accessibility

Christophe Ponsard[1]([✉]), Jean Vanderdonckt[2], and Vincent Snoeck[3]

[1] CETIC Research Center, Charleroi, Belgium
cp@cetic.be
[2] Louvain School of Management, LLN, Louvain-la-Neuve, Belgium
jean.vanderdonckt@uclouvain.be
[3] Atingo, Namur, Belgium
vincent.snoeck@atingo.be

Abstract. Our digital and physical worlds are becoming increasingly interconnected. Digital services reduce the need to physically move hence to have to face physical accessibility barriers, but it becomes then more critical to make sure they are not replaced by digital accessibility barriers. In order to assess the interplay of both worlds from the accessibility perspective, we collected available data and used automated tools from three different perspectives: one starting from physically accessible places and looking at the digital accessibility of their online services, the second going the other way and finally a representative sample of services inside a smart city. Globally, we found a good combined level of accessibility in about one third of the places. Mutual strengthening could also be observed, usually greater on the digital accessibility side and revealing that awareness actions in one field also contribute to improve the other.

Keywords: Physical accessibility · Digital accessibility · Assessment · Automated tools

1 Introduction

Physical world accessibility is about ensuring that the capabilities of physical places (e.g. administrations, shops, cultural places) matches the (dis)ability of people visiting them in order to ensure optimal access for all, including for the estimated 15% of the population living with some kind of impairment [21]. Currently our world is undergoing a strong digitalisation process: online maps are becoming precise to the point they capture the inner structure of buildings, the accessibility of several places is being ranked using crowdsourcing, Artificial Intelligence can provide help to guess the content of images, etc. This results in a wide range of new opportunities to break accessibility barriers and also better combine physical and digital aspects of accessibility, from removing the need to move using fully digital services to the in-depth preparation of a visit to a specific place and the constant guidance during the travel to cope with the unforeseen.

© Springer Nature Switzerland AG 2020
K. Miesenberger et al. (Eds.): ICCHP 2020, LNCS 12376, pp. 266–274, 2020.
https://doi.org/10.1007/978-3-030-58796-3_32

Physical Accessibility (PA) requirements are now well defined and documented, such as in the ISO21542 standard [8]. However, assessing physical accessibility is not straightforward because it requires identifying physical obstacles depending on the impairments, e.g. a doorstep for a wheelchair, no braille on lift buttons for blind people, audio only announcements for deaf people. Experts can reliably evaluate this accessibility by applying a well-defined measurement procedure and Web-oriented reporting [13]. However, the limited number of trained experts strongly restricts the ability to assess at large scale and keep the information up to date. On the other hand, dedicated social media apps like jaccede.com [9] or wheelmap.org [20] enable a crowdsourcing approach through the consolidation of partial information reported by different users, each with her own point of view, which may lead to inconsistency. Both approaches are naturally complementary and can efficiently be combined together, through the use of open linked data techniques [14].

Although information and communication technologies are a clear enabler for physical accessibility, it is also raising new obstacles as the end-users need to use a computer or mobile interface to make sure some place is physically accessible. Hence Digital Accessibiltiy (DA) needs to be considered. The Web Accessibility Initiative (WAI) [18] provides specific guidelines like Web Content Accessibility Guidelines (WCAG) to help Web developers making Web sites accessible [19] while dynamic content is addressed through (Accessible Rich Internet Applications (ARIA). Many useful evaluation and repair tools are also proposed, including for tailored and optimised usability and accessibility evaluation [17].

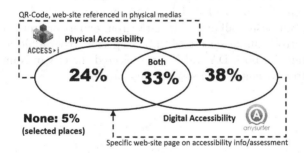

Fig. 1. The interplay between physical and digital accessibilities

Looking at both physical and digital accessibility together raises interesting questions about the current level of maturity and awareness about each kind of accessibility, the possible correlation between them, and what kind of synergies can further enhance the user experience. Through a preliminary unpublished study, we manually gathered and processed a first limited data set in Belgium from Access-I (for physical accessibility) [4] and AnySurfer (for digital accessibility) [2]. Both kinds of accessibility are summarised in Fig. 1 which already shows a satisfactory level of physical accessibility in 60% of cases, of digital accessibility in 70% of cases and both in 33% of cases.

In order to push our investigation further, we decided to set up a wider and more automated assessment. This required a better methodology relying on the available data sources but also avoiding some related bias, e.g. organisations specifically reviewed or labelled for accessibility are more mature that those randomly evaluated by occasional visitors through crowdsourcing. Our priority is to ensure a data collection methodology that supports automation and yield comparable data even if some identified aspects of accessibility (requiring manual work) are not completely evaluated. In addition, we also decided to collect specific indicators reporting about accessibility scenarios ranging across both worlds, the simplest one being the presence of "how to get there" information in a website, or conversely, reporting about the website of a place (maybe using a QR code).

This paper is structured as follows. First, Sect. 2 present our methodology as well as the data and tools used to carry out our assessments. Section 3 presents the results collected so far. Section 4 performs some analysis and discussion on them. Finally, Sect. 5 draws some conclusions and presents our future work.

2   Methodology and Tools

To answer the question "How does PA and DA relate ?", we used a triple approach:

- starting from an available PA data set (from access-i) and assessing the related DA through dedicated automated web assessment tool.
- starting from an available DA data set (from anysurfer) and assessing its PA (when relevant) using all available data (from expert or crowdsourced) data.
- using a control sample selected inside a specific geographic location which good coverage for both DA and PA: we selected the city of Namur (Belgium) which is strongly engaged in a smart city process.

Accessibility

These checks highlight opportunities to improve the accessibility of your web app. Only a subset of accessibility issues can be automatically detected so manual testing is also encouraged.

Names and labels — These are opportunities to improve the semantics of the controls in your application. This may enhance the experience for users of assistive technology, like a screen reader.

▲ <frame> or <iframe> elements do not have a title

▲ Image elements do not have [alt] attributes

Fig. 2. Example of typical physical assessment summary [7]

About the DA assessment, several tools are available to assess the WCAG at a specified level. Some can be directly run online. However, considering the additional requirements to be Open Source or freely usable with export capabilities reduces the number to a handful, usually based on the same underlying libraries like a11y project or pa11y [11]. After considering platforms able to scan a whole website such as BOSA accessibility check server [12] and Tanguru [10], we decided to use a separated crawler (crawl4j) to better control the visit (e.g. search depth, ignore irrelevant pages). As DA checker, we selected Google Lighthouse [7] which is a more general tool also assessing performance and search engine optimisation. It is mature and has an easy to use and well specified scoring mechanism (see Fig. 2). It relies on 35 key accessibility criteria, mainly for visually and auditory impaired, covering much of what WCAG tools automatically check for level AA. Of course, a whole set of manual checks are discarded making the assessment inaccurate. **Our DA score index is computed on the average Lighthouse score of the website, on a scale from 0 (worse) to 10 (best).**

Fig. 3. Example of typical physical assessment summary [4]

About PA accessibility, we relied on available local expert databases coming from access-i (collective of experts) and sometimes from access-city (focused on wheelchairs and providing more open data) [1,4]. The crowdsourced information was extracted from jaccede [9] and wheelmap [20] through available APIs. **Our PA score is computed as the average of the scores on 4 main categories related to physical (wheelchair), visual, auditory and cognitive impairments. Like for DA, the scores are ranked on a scale from 0 (worse) to 10 (best).** For example, the simplified red-orange-green codes are respectively translated to 0, 5 and 10, resulting in a score of 7.5 for the case depicted on Fig. 3. When available more detailed scores can also be used using different mappings. A cross validation/alignment of those mappings is performed when different sources are available.

In order to assess more specific **awareness indicators linking both DA and PA**, we used a qualitative approach by looking for the following elements inside the website, from the most basic to the most advanced:

- presence of basic information about address, maps, opening hours
- mention of PA in "contact/how to get/access" page(s)
- mention of e-services or special on-site service (e.g. sign language tour)
- mention of an accessibility policy

- mention of specific DA or PA labels
- specialised controls (e.g. font size, contrast, video remote interpretation).

Table 1. Characteristics and scores of our data sets

#	Name	Type	Website URL	DA score	PA score	Mixed indicator
DA1	Kust Pass	Multiple	kustpas.be	9.7	–	none
DA2	Piet Devos	Home	pietdevos.be	9.7	–	none
DA3	Pink House	Meeting rooms	hetrozehuis.be	8.4	7	map, label
DA4	CPAS Charleroi	Administr	cpascharleroi.be	9.3	8	map, charter
DA5	Stavelot Abbey	Religous	abbayedestavelot.be	9.3	5	map, label, virtual visit
PA1	Media cité	Shopping mall	mediacite.be	7.7	6.8	map, hours, label
PA2	Loncin Fortress	Fortress	fortdeloncin.be	8.1	6.8	audio, map, hours
PA3	Gileppe Lake	Touristic dam	gileppe.com	9.8	7	raw address
PA4	Jalhay Tourism	Tourist office	tourismejalhaysart.be	8.8	3	broken map
PA5	Mariemont Museum	Museum	musee-mariemont.be	7	8.5	address, label, info
SC1	Decathlon	Sport shop	decathlon.be	5.5	9	map, hours
SC2	Citizen house	Administr	namur.be/	8.4	8.3	map, hours, e-services, charter
SC3	CGT	Tourist office	tourismewallonie.be	8.4	6	raw address
SC4	Namur Expo	Meeting hall	namurexpo.be	8.8	8.5	map, (faq)
SC5	Rops Museum	Museum	museerops.be	3.0	7.5	address, dog
SC6	County Palace	Administr	gouverneurnamur.be	8.7	3.0	nothing
SC7	NAM-IP	Museum	nam-ip.be	5.5	4.0	map, hours, info
SC8	Terra Nova	Fortress	citadelle.namur.be	6.6	6.5	map, page, special visits
SC9	IBIS	Hotel	all.accor.com/hotel/3151/	8.9	6	map, hours
SC10	Namur Cathedral	Religious	cana.be	6.8	6	address, hours
SC11	St Loup Church	Religious	eglise-saint-loup.be	8.3	6.5	map, label
SC12	INNO Galleria	General store	inno.be/fr/stores/store_namur	8.4	8	map (inc. internal), hours
SC13	1PasseTemps	Restaurant	1passetemps.be	7.7	6.8	hours, info
SC14	Royal Snail	Hotel	theroyalsnail.com	7.1	3.0	address
SC15	Namur Station	Railway station	belgianrail.be/.../namur.aspx	7.3	8	info

3   Assessment Results

Table 1 reports about 25 representative samples coming from our three different sources: DAx initiated from the DA side, PAx from the PA side and SCx located in the smart city of Namur. The first columns characterise each place by their name, type, URL. The next columns give the assessment from the DA, PA and mixed perspectives. Note that the first two places could not be fully assessed because one had multiple locations and the second was private.

4   Analysis and Discussion

DA Analysis. The DA score are quite high across all categories (mean: 7.7, std dev: 1.5). This is likely related to be our tool not capturing the whole set of accessibility requirements, but this means most websites achieve good compliance with essential requirements. About the tooling itself, it proved quite reliable although some adaptation were sometimes required depending on the specific configuration, e.g. to correctly isolate specific pages part of a bigger website. More flexible tools are also emerging to cope with the fact that different viewpoints and different requirements need to be considered when checking a website [3]. On the long run they also shape how the accessibility standards evolve.

PA Analysis. The PA score is a bit lower with a wider spread (mean: 6, 5, std: 1.8). Although lower, those numbers may appear quite good as physical accessibility is more difficult to achieve in terms of adaptation cost, especially to very old infrastructures. This bias may be related to the fact the selection of places was done on important places for which accessibility was already pointed out. However, it means for such places the actions lead to measurable results.

Mixed Indicators. Most places stick to a minimal link using address and opening hours (many closed in the present version due to COVID19 lockdown). The map is present in about 60% of the websites. An interesting interrelation is the announcement of remote service in administrations, again here the COVID19 crisis may have encourage such updates but some were present before this event. Conversely, for very inaccessible places like fortress or underground, special adapted services may be proposed upon request. From this point of view, the digital can compensate the lack of accessibility (or the interdiction of accessibility in the case of the COVID19 crisis). E.g. a mobile phone application (hopefully accessible) maybe available as museum guide but also to give a remote experience. Virtual tours are also quite easy to create nowadays. A more complex immersive scenarios may be envisioned such as the used of virtual reality but is more complex and costly to implement and also needs to be accessible [16]. However they pave the way to new kinds of experience across both worlds. Going beyond the PA or DA, another important dimension is the social goal, e.g. to have a common experience which can also be achieved through digital means. Gamification is another area worth investigating from that point of view [15].

No Strong Direct Link Between DA and PA. Looking at relationship between DA and PA does not reveal any direct correlation between them. Considering a threshold score of 7.0 between less satisfactory and more satisfactory level, we can compute that about 74% of places have good DA, 34% have good PA and 22% have both which is lower as in our initial survey. Digital accessibility is quite better. The explanation can lie in the increased importance of digital presence and the lower effort required to achieve it compared to PA. Indeed, a Web site is easier and less expensive to repurpose than a building. However, the fraction of the considered places currently achieving both dimensions is still small which means that those issues are still largely being considered separately. A good point is that 60% of the places with good PA accessibility have also good digital accessibility which can indicate that awareness leads to change in that way. The other way, the ratio is much lower (only 30%). Again, the cost of change is probably a barrier to go beyond the awareness level.

About the Intertwining of PA and DA. PA and DA should also not be considered in isolation but in a mixed global scenario where each play its role on a part of the experience. Considering the whole experience from the preparation to the travel, arrival to finally reach the purpose of a visit may require a variable mixture of digital and physical activities. A typical scenario can include using a computer in preparation phase, a smartphone on the move and a specific device at the destination (e.g. lift). End-to-end scenarios are commonly used, e.g. for sports events [6] or tourism [5,14] but do not focus explicitly on each kind of experience and possible alternatives.

The Use of Labels is not Very Convincing Both for PA and DA: currently many labelled sites do not advertise about it or report a broken link. Finding the accessibility information is globally difficult and is comparable to locating the contact page with the additional uncertainty that the information might simply not be reported. Considering accessibility portal as a potential answer leads to other issues such as finding them and being sure of their quality. Probably an interesting move is that accessibility information should be gathered by search engines like what is done for location and opening hours.

Threat to Validity: our current dataset is still quite small which threatens the statistical validity of our analysis. We carefully selected the places for diversity and selected different strategies: from PA to DA, from DA to PA and in a smart city. However, our conclusions would benefit from a bigger dataset. At this stage our approach is quite well automated for DA but has a bigger bottleneck on the PA side because we are dependent on data sources that are partial, of different quality and not easy to aggregate. Starting from existing mature assessments, a total data set of 200 fully automated evaluations is beyond our reach. Another threat is to check the accessibility scores. DA scores are more homogeneous in nature but their automation only covers a restricted subset of web accessibility standards. The scores also needs to be evaluated from the complementary point of view of various kind of impairments. Actually both kind of scores can be broken down in different subscores with sometimes overlapping checks but which allows us to carry out validation sessions with the concerned people.

5   Conclusion and Future Work

In this paper, we have proposed a method for the joint assessment of digital and physical accessibility and proposed supporting tools, essentially for the digital side while the physical side relies more on a diversity of data source mixing expert and crowdsourcing. We thoroughly analysed a subset of 25 locations, with a stronger focus on a nearby smart city.

We are currently busy extending our validation by considering an enlarged data set and by involving impaired people to check our PA and DA scores from their point of view. We also plan to release our tooling in Open Source and to publish the resulting data using available open data platforms. Our further research steps will be to refine our global indicators at impairment level, to quantify our mixed indicators and to develop a specific crawling agent that can help detecting such highly valuable information inside websites.

Acknowledgement. This work was partly funded by the Walloon Region and ERDF through the IDEES CO-INNOVATION project (nr. ETR121200001379). Thanks to CAWAB partners and AnySurfer for the data they provided. Special thanks to Lyse Saint Jean for her contribution to our first assessment campaign.

References

1. Acces City: Website. http://www.anlh.be/accescity
2. AnySurfer: Accessible Internet for All. https://www.anysurfer.be/en
3. Broccia, G., Manca, M., Paternò, F., Pulina, F.: Flexible automatic support for web accessibility validation. Proc. ACM Hum.-Comput. Interact. **4**, 1–24 (2020)
4. CAWAB: Accessibility Information Portal (in French). http://www.access-i.be
5. DWP: The Inclusive and Accessible Stadia Report. Department for Work and Pensions (2015). www.gov.uk/dwp
6. Ellcessor, E.: Blurred lines: accessibility, disability, and definitional limitations. First Mon. **20**(9) (2015)
7. Google: Lighthouse (2016). https://developers.google.com/web/tools/lighthouse
8. ISO: ISO21542:2011 - Building construction - accessibility and usability of the built environment (2011)
9. Jaccede.com: Pour une cité accessible. http://www.jaccede.com
10. Kebri, M., et al.: Tanaguru (2015). https://github.com/Tanaguru/Tanaguru
11. Manning, R., et al.: Pa11y is your automated accessibility testing pal (2013). https://github.com/pa11y/pa11y
12. OpenFed: BOSA Accessibility Check (2012). https://openfed.github.io/AccessibilityCheck
13. Ponsard, C., Snoeck, V.: Objective accessibility assessment of public infrastructures. In: Miesenberger, K., Klaus, J., Zagler, W.L., Karshmer, A.I. (eds.) ICCHP 2006. LNCS, vol. 4061, pp. 314–321. Springer, Heidelberg (2006). https://doi.org/10.1007/11788713_47

14. Ponsard, C., et al.: A mobile travel companion based on open accessibility data. In: Miesenberger, K., Bühler, C., Penaz, P. (eds.) ICCHP 2016. LNCS, vol. 9759, pp. 245–252. Springer, Cham (2016). https://doi.org/10.1007/978-3-319-41267-2_33
15. Smith, K., Abrams, S.: Gamification and accessibility. Int. J. Inf. Learn. Technol. **36**, 104–123 (2019)
16. Teófilo, M., et al.: Evaluating accessibility features designed for virtual reality context. In: IEEE International Conference on Consumer Electronics (ICCE), pp. 1–6 (2018)
17. Vanderdonckt, J., Beirekdar, A.: Automated web evaluation by guideline review. J. Web Eng. 4(2), 102–117 (2005)
18. W3C: Web Accessibility Initiative. https://www.w3.org/WAI
19. W3C: Web Content Accessibility Guidelines. http://www.w3.org/TR/WCAG
20. Wheelmap Community: Collaborative website about wheelchair accessibility. http://wheelmap.org/en
21. WHO: Disability and Health - Key Facts (2018). https://www.who.int/news-room/fact-sheets/detail/disability-and-health

Requirements for Large Scale Web Accessibility Evaluation

Fabio Paternò[1]([✉]), Francesca Pulina[1], Carmen Santoro[1],
Henrike Gappa[2], and Yehya Mohamad[2]

[1] CNR-ISTI, Human Interfaces in Information Systems Laboratory,
Via Moruzzi 1, Pisa, Italy
{fabio.paterno, francesca.pulina,
carmen.santoro}@isti.cnr.it
[2] Fraunhofer-Institute for Applied Information Technology,
Sankt Augustin, Germany
{henrike.gappa, yehya.mohamad}@fit.fraunhofer.de

Abstract. The recent European legislation emphasizes the importance of enabling people with disabilities to have access to online information and services of public sector bodies. To this regard, automatic evaluation and monitoring of Web accessibility can play a key role for various stakeholders involved in creating and maintaining over time accessible products. In this paper we present the results of elicitation activities that we carried out in a European project to collect experience and feedback from Web commissioners, developers and content authors of websites and web applications. The purpose was to understand their current practices in addressing accessibility issues, identify the barriers they encounter when exploiting automatic support in ensuring the accessibility of Web resources, and receive indications about what functionalities they would like to exploit in order to better manage accessibility evaluation and monitoring.

Keywords: Accessibility guidelines · Automatic evaluation · Monitoring

1 Introduction

Web accessibility is evolving because it has to respond to the demands posed by the digital transformation of our society while considering the changes in the interactive technologies used for implementing and accessing Web sites. Such changes have stimulated also new developments in terms of the associated accessibility guidelines standards, and new obligations imposed on public sector bodies as regards the compliance of public Web services. The recent WAD directive aims to obtain large scale monitoring of the adoption of accessibility guidelines. For this reason, all people involved in the commissioning and development of Websites and mobile applications of public sector bodies need to act towards providing Web services accessible for all citizens. To this end, they also need to be supported in the process of evaluating and monitoring the accessibility of their services. Thus, in the course of the EU-funded

© The Author(s) 2020
K. Miesenberger et al. (Eds.): ICCHP 2020, LNCS 12376, pp. 275–283, 2020.
https://doi.org/10.1007/978-3-030-58796-3_33

research project WADcher[1] (Web Accessibility Directive Decision Support Environment) we have investigated to what extent the current automatic support provides useful help in accessibility validation activities, and what requirements a novel monitoring platform should provide to be a valid support in managing accessibility over time with respect to the accessibility standards and the WAD directive. For this purpose, we have carried out various activities aiming at better understanding the problems experienced by relevant user groups (developers, designers, experts and policy makers), and their accessibility knowledge and current work processes in order to identify user requirements for developing and providing a sustainable framework for the periodic monitoring and assessment of the Web accessibility state. This paper summarizes and discusses such activities useful for identifying requirements for large scale Web Accessibility evaluation.

2   State of the Art in Guidelines and Automatic Tools for Web Accessibility Evaluation

The recent European legislation has stressed the importance of the right of people with disabilities to have access to online information and services of the public sector bodies. In fact, the European Accessibility Directive (WAD) 2016/2102 requires websites and Web applications to be compliant to the Web accessibility guidelines and standards, namely the European standard EN 301 549, which refers currently to the Web Content Accessibility Guidelines (WCAG) 2.1. In addition to this, it requires that public sector bodies periodically monitor the accessibility level of the Web services and compile a Web Accessibility Statement regarding their monitored Web services.

In this perspective automatic evaluation of Web accessibility [1] can play a useful role. Thus, we carried out a first analysis of the currently available solutions in terms of tools, which can support stakeholders in assessing accessibility compliance, detecting barriers, supporting Web developers in knowing how to solve them and commissioners and public bodies in monitoring the accessibility over time.

Such analysis indicated that support for the latest version (2.1) of the WCAG, which is the W3C recommendation since June 2018, is still limited because of the difficulties for several accessibility tool developers to easily update the functionalities of their validators. One possible tool architecture that supports the update of the guidelines to validate with limited effort is described in [9]. Moreover, among the tools that consider the recent guidelines, there are some that consider just a few features of Web pages (such as the colour contrast between foreground and background items), others that are not freely available, or that do not offer the checking against the AAA level of conformance. Often the analysis is limited to single pages and not to group of pages or even entire Web sites. As regards detecting barriers and showing them in the evaluation results, we noticed that the provided reports in some cases code-oriented, which means that issues of non-compliance are showed in the code line where they occur, thus it could be difficult for commissioners and experts who do not have Web

---

[1] https://wadcher.eu/.

programming knowledge to fully understand accessibility barriers in order to better act upon them.

Overall, a solution to Web accessibility assessment, comprehensive of all the possible useful features is still lacking. Investigations of accessibility evaluation tools conducted in the past have actually pointed out various issues [2, 4, 6–8]. They already revealed that such tools should provide more support for developers in conducting accessibility audits as well as in understanding and fixing errors. It would be desirable for interested users that a validation environment provides customized presentations of its results based on their role. The majority of the tools do not provide the visualization of the errors/warnings on the rendered Web page. WAVE was an exception since it provides this kind of report, while also providing the pinpointing of problems in the source code. Regarding commercial solutions, the Deque's aXe browser extension and Siteimprove extension allow the developer to highlight issues on the running Web page. In general, there are accessibility-related features in which Web developers are more interested, and others that are more relevant to non-accessibility experts and public officials. In the end, only a few of the analyzed tools provide, in the full report, a dashboard that keeps track of the accessibility improvements, allowing the monitoring of the accessibility status over time. Such advanced feature is mainly provided by commercial services and solutions, whereas freely available tools and plugins provide users with an evaluation of the current version of the Website or Web page, without keeping track of previous accessibility evaluation results and improvements over time. Beyond this, assessment results are in the majority of cases reported and persisted using proprietary formats, i.e. several tools do not follow the Evaluation and Report Language (EARL) recommended by W3C[2]. The imergo® Web Compliance Suite has used EARL as assessment result format from the beginning in its developments. This decision was as well followed in the design of the WADcher data model, so all assessment results are conforming to EARL and are serialized as JSON-LD objects. One further issue is that the validation tools need to be able to provide their results in different formats that consider the different stakeholders that can use them, as it happens in MAUVE++ [3].

3 Investigating Knowledge Level About Accessibility Evaluations and Resulting User Needs

In the following, we present the results of elicitation activities that we carried out in WADcher in order to collect experiences and feedback from Web commissioners, developers and content authors of Websites and Web applications. A similar research work regarding the extent to which the importance of Web accessibility is perceived by potential users, and how accessibility is actually implemented was done [5] some years ago; but accessibility standards have evolved as well as the Web technologies, thus the results of our work can provide an updated overview on such topic.

---

[2] https://www.w3.org/WAI/standards-guidelines/earl/.

3.1 Methodology

The project's objective is to develop a supportive environment that helps the afore-mentioned WADcher target groups to create and maintain over time accessible products, thus we need to understand if they already use tools to exploit automatic support in ensuring the accessibility of the Web resources, and what are the functionalities they would like to exploit in order to better manage the accessibility evaluation and monitoring.

We carried out three main requirements elicitation activities: online questionnaires, interviews and a workshop. The objectives of our user research were to understand:

- to what extent people working in Web content development and commissioning are considering accessibility validation in their working routine;
- what is the perceived importance of Web accessibility compliance in the organizations they work; what their level of knowledge regarding Web accessibility standards is;
- what kind of accessibility evaluation activities they perform (manual, automatic, evaluation with experts);
- if they take advantage of using automatic evaluation tools and plugins.

In addition to these objectives, we wanted to investigate what information stakeholders look for in the reports generated by automatic accessibility evaluation tools; what kind of information and support they need from such tools, and what the features that they do not find but they would like to have available in them are.

We designed two multi-language online questionnaires to be filled remotely, one addressed to Web commissioners and people in charge of maintaining Websites and their accessibility, and one addressed to more technical stakeholders, namely Web developers and content authors. Questionnaires were divided into multiple sections, each one aimed to gather the following information: personal information and professional background; how they consider accessibility during work (for the commissioning or development part); their knowledge about Web accessibility guidelines, standards, and best practices; their knowledge regarding automatic accessibility assessment tools; suggestions based on what they like or dislike of such tools, and on what feature(s) they would like them to have to be a helpful support. The questionnaires were disseminated across the European countries from which partners of the WADcher project come from (Ireland, Italy, Greece, Austria, and Germany), through mailing lists of people employed in the public sector and personal contacts. Then, we interviewed some stakeholders. One interview was done in Germany and it involved a Web content author/accessibility expert; other two interviews were conducted in Italy and involved a Web content editor and a Web editorial staff member.

Moreover, a workshop was organized in Italy at AgID[3] (AgID is the Italian organization in charge of monitoring the accessibility of public Web sites). The workshop was attended by about 40 people who work in accessibility in different organizations and with different roles. We involved them in a moderated discussion

---

[3] https://www.agid.gov.it/.

regarding accessibility standards and the WAD directive, their current workflow in considering accessibility, obstacles in considering and evaluating accessibility of the Web resources they are responsible of.

3.2 Results

Online Survey. We gathered feedback from 387 Web commissioners and from 148 Web developers and content authors through online questionnaires; people came from five European countries (Ireland, Italy, Greece, Austria, and Germany). As regards Web commissioners, 223 respondents are males and 164 females; they have an age ranging from 21 to 75 years old (mean 49; σ: 8, 7). They are mainly employees of organizations of medium size operating in the public sector (mainly at a local level: municipalities and schools). Most of them (131) have a management role (e.g. ICT/IT managers, school officials); 52 are responsible for websites; 44 have a technical role. As regards Web developers and content authors, 99 respondents are males and 49 females; their age is ranging from 25 to 72 years old (mean 44,4; σ: 10, 4). They are mainly employees of large companies and organizations, with a medium or high level of expertise in Web accessibility.

A first general consideration is that people involved in our elicitation activities have limited knowledge of accessibility assessment tools, and they usually encounter difficulties in both considering accessibility and evaluating it in their projects.

Web commissioners who answered the online questionnaire for the great majority have an intermediate level of accessibility knowledge, even if the same people answered that they have an elementary level in knowing the problems faced by people with disabilities in accessing the Web. The accessibility topic is perceived moderately important in their organizations: this can be due to the fact that they do not have a proper education in this topic, or that the accessibility compliance is not a requirement for their websites. But for commissioners who consider accessibility as a requirement there are difficulties in managing it in their workflow, and the reasons of such difficulties are the limited knowledge regarding standards (the 28,4% of them does not know any accessibility guideline and standard) and how to make Web resources compliant, and lack of time and resources. In terms of accessibility evaluation methods used they indicated: automatic evaluation with tools (148), manual guidelines review (142), HTML/CSS validation (127), expert testing (73), test with users (71), inspection with assistive technologies (64).

The answers from Web developers and accessibility experts, instead, indicate largely good knowledge regarding accessibility; only the 16,2% does not know any accessibility guideline and standard. In their workflow, they usually consider accessibility compliance in the final development phase. In fact, in most experiences, automatic evaluation tools are used in the pre-release step, when the product is almost ready. We noted that a lot of respondents from Italy are working in the educational sector. Web developers and content authors who work in this field, but in general those who work for public administrations, have to do with Web applications addressed to citizens of all ages who have the right to be informed and benefit from the public services provided via Web: it is of crucial importance that the contents be accessible to everyone, included people who need to access Web services using assistive technologies. In general, when they cannot work towards ensuring that Web applications meet the accessibility standards is because of commissioner's imposition, lack of time and knowledge, and budget limitations.

Workshop. The workshop had a broad audience: 19 Web developers, 11 content providers, 9 accessibility experts and evaluators, 1 blind person who participates to evaluation tests. They are employed in the fields of health care, government, education, banking, PAs (mainly large organizations). In the workshop some organizations reported that the accessibility checks of their websites are performed with tests with impaired users, HTML and CSS validation, and manual evaluation by accessibility experts. There is still a lack of culture about accessibility in the organizations where they work, but it emerged that organizations are more aware about accessibility if disabled people work within them. During the discussion, developers mentioned as one of the problems they face in considering accessibility is to maintain it over time and not just at the first release of the application. Examples of expected features in tools for accessibility evaluation that emerged are: the possibility to have customization options, such as filter relevant information by disability type, and/or by interface element type; a hierarchical analysis of the pages that compose the Website (in particular, the analysis of pages that are more subject to uploads and editing); the possibility to store the log of the identified errors, in order to be able to do the comparison the before and after situation, in a monitoring perspective; contextual help: help contextual to errors/alerts with links to checkpoints and additional examples, extraction of results with type of error (perhaps a code), URL, and location of the problematic element, in order to use results in next scripts; analysis of pages based on the device (to avoid that hidden elements, such as menus in mobile version, are analyzed), the analysis of PDF documents' accessibility.

Interviews. From the interviews carried out we gathered suggestions that emerged also from the questionnaires' answers, such as: integrating accessibility guidelines into Content Management Systems used to update the websites, allowing the sorting of results by elements/topics (for example, tables, images, operability by keyboard), providing links and tips for possible solutions of the identified issues of non-compliance.

Discussion. Unfortunately, not all commissioners and developers from whom we gathered feedback had used accessibility evaluation tools; in particular, 55% of the commissioners and 31% of the developers had not used them at all.

We asked people who used them at least once if there are obstacles in using them that they want to point out. As regards the support given by automatic evaluation tools, sometimes developers find difficulties in including dynamic content in the evaluation process, in the restrictions imposed by Content Management Systems, but also in other limitations of such tools, such as the detection of several false positives; the limited guidance on how to fix the detected issues; the effort they make in understanding the explanation of the violated success criterion and in general of the detected issue, thus, for example, they would like to have also suggestions on how to solve them.

Based on their knowledge of available accessibility assessment tools, they recommended the features they would expect from them. Among those, in general, they indicated a report tailored to the technical level of the user, by providing one more technical report addressed to developers, and one addressed to commissioners and content authors; the support in checking also dynamic content; giving measures representing the overall accessibility level reached.

Web commissioners, in particular, stressed the importance of having access to a non-technical report, where issues and trends are showed in a more graphical manner, without the details of the code, or in general the adaptation of the results report to the user role. They would appreciate that issues are grouped by gravity, that is by the impact level on the overall accessibility, and by the element(s) that are affected by the reported violations, so to organize the interventions in the code by groups of elements. They are also interested in knowing which categories of disabled users are more affected by the issues, and, in relation to this, they mentioned that it could be useful to filter the results by type of disability.

Web developers expressed the need to have more supporting information in relation to the identified issues: more and clearer examples of the identified violations, tips for the solution of the error, examples of interventions in the code in order to solve the barrier, customized solutions, showed in tooltips or modal sections. Then, they would like the possibility to aggregate recurring errors and to filter the potential false positives. In the end, they need that tools are able to efficiently evaluate also the dynamic code (analysis of scripts, analysis in the various states of the application). Another feature they would appreciate to better manage the fixing of the detected issue is the note-taking functionality, or being able to compile a to-do list of the interventions. The possibility to store the log of the identified errors, in order to be able to compare the before and after situation, in a monitoring perspective is also expected from automatic tools. They are also interested in metrics, such as the frequency of each error type (based, for example, on the different success criteria), a percentage representing how much the evaluated resource is still not accessible, the compliance level.

4   Conclusions

The recent European directive requires structured monitoring of existing public Web applications, which can be achieved only with automatic support. The results gathered in the presented study provide useful insights on how stakeholders address issues concerning accessibility evaluation, know and use methods and tools for accessibility evaluation, and what they need for efficient evaluation and monitoring of the Web resources of their interest. In addition, they also provide indications of how accessibility is perceived in organizations and the level of importance it has. Overall, this study has made it possible to better understand to what extent accessibility assessment tools are used and provide useful support, and how they can be improved. More detail on the elicitation activities carried out is available in the project deliverables.

The insights gathered from both the analysis of the available solutions and the elicitation of users' needs can be useful for all those who design and develop automatic support for accessibility evaluation, and have been used as a basis for the initial design of the WADcher tools. In fact, WADcher is intended as a set of tools composing a platform where accessibility evaluation results are accessed by Web commissioners, accessibility experts, Web developers and the monitoring bodies of the European countries. Each of these stakeholders represents a user role with specific requirements that emerged during our research and which have been considered in the design phase. In particular, the WADcher platform includes two main environments: a) the Observatory, which provides overview information on audits and trends over time of the evaluated sites, a dedicated area for compiling the Web Accessibility Statement as well as services targeted at national monitoring bodies and b) the Decision Support Environment, which for each audit supports the use of the results provided by external automatic evaluation tools to fix reported errors, and resolve audit results where expert decision is needed. The first one is addressed to the needs of Web commissioners and the monitoring bodies; the second one, instead, is addressed to developers and accessibility experts.

Acknowledgments. This work was partially funded by the European Commission H2020 programme; Contract number 780206; WADcher. The authors would like to acknowledge the support of the WADcher consortium.

References

1. Abascal, J., Arrue, M., Valencia, X.: Tools for web accessibility evaluation. In: Yesilada, Y., Harper, S. (eds.) Web Accessibility. HIS, pp. 479–503. Springer, London (2019). https://doi.org/10.1007/978-1-4471-7440-0_26
2. Abduganiev, S.G.: Towards automated Web accessibility evaluation: a comparative study. Int. J. Inform. Technol. Comput. Sci 9(9), 18–44 (2017)
3. Broccia, G., Manca, M., Paternò, F., Pulina, F., Flexible automatic support for web accessibility validation. In: Proceedings of the ACM on Human-Computer Interaction, vol. 4, EICS, Article 83, June 2020. https://doi.org/10.1145/3397871. 24 pages
4. Fernandes, N., Kaklanis, N., Votis, K., Tzovaras, D., Carriço, L.: An analysis of personalized Web accessibility. In: Proceedings of the 11th Web for All Conference, p. 19. ACM (2014)
5. Yesilada, Y., Brajnik, G., Vigo, M., Harper, S.: Exploring perceptions of Web accessibility: a survey approach. Behav. Inf. Technol. 34(2), 119–134 (2015)
6. Petrie, H., King, N., Velasco, C., Gappa, H., Nordbrock, G.: The usability of accessibility evaluation tools. In: Stephanidis, C. (ed.) UAHCI 2007. LNCS, vol. 4556, pp. 124–132. Springer, Heidelberg (2007). https://doi.org/10.1007/978-3-540-73283-9_15
7. Tanaka, E.H., Vieira da Rocha, H.: Evaluation of Web accessibility tools. In: IHC + CLIHC 2011: Proceedings of the 10th Brazilian Symposium on Human Factors in Computing Systems and the 5th Latin American Conference on Human-Computer Interaction, October 2011, pp. 272–279 (2011)
8. Paternò, F., Schiavone, A.: The role of tool support in public policies and accessibility. ACM Interact. 22(3), 60–63 (2015)

9. Schiavone, A.G., Paternò, F.: An extensible environment for guideline-based accessibility evaluation of dynamic Web applications. Univ. Access Inf. Soc. **14**(1), 111–132 (2015). https://doi.org/10.1007/s10209-014-0399-3

Accessible and Inclusive Digital Publishing

STS on Accessible and Inclusive Digital Publishing

Introduction to the Special Thematic Session

Reinhard Ruemer[1(✉)] and Valentin Salinas López[2]

[1] Verein BookAccess, 4040 Linz, Austria
reinhard.ruemer@bookaccess.at
[2] Johannes Kepler University Linz, Altenbergerstraße 69, 4040 Linz, Austria
valentin.salinas_lopez@jku.at

Abstract. The special thematic session on Accessible and inclusive Digital Publishing consists of a wide range of publications in this area. It will show efforts undertaken to understand the role of accessibility within a company, practical methods for accessing and structuring digital content and ways of improving the evaluation of digitally created content.

Keywords: Digital publishing · Accessibility · World Wide Web · EPUB · PDF

1 Introduction

In a perfect world, we would see the considerations regarding the accessibility of the published content considered in every step of the publishing process. From the authoring and design phase to the technical implementation and all stages of production and marketing.

In the real world, we are far away from such a situation. Digital publishing still has a way to go to become an inclusive process. Although, there are several well-documented resources available regarding the accessibility e.g. the WCAG-Guidelines [1] and there is also commitment from governments regarding the accessibility of digital published content [2, 3] in the day to day production process accessibility is still not as much implemented as it could be. There are many reasons why this is happening. At the top is the lack of knowledge on the practical side of accessible publishing by the responsible actors. As a result, a large share of the digitally available documents is not - or only on a very shallow level - accessible. Just to illustrate the magnitude of the problem, in 2017 the European Blind Union estimates that the share of accessible books for visually impaired persons (VIP) ranged between 7% and 20% in the EU. In recent times, a number of initiatives with different approaches have emerged to address this issue. One of them is the co-funded by the Erasmus + Programme of the EU: Supporting Inclusive Digital Publishing through Training (SIDPT). The aim of this project is supporting the publishing industry in the creation and delivery of accessible digital publications, in order to help it to comply with new legislative context of accessibility in digital publications. To this end, it focuses on the provision of practical

© Springer Nature Switzerland AG 2020
K. Miesenberger et al. (Eds.): ICCHP 2020, LNCS 12376, pp. 287–293, 2020.
https://doi.org/10.1007/978-3-030-58796-3_34

accessibility training material for professionals working in the publishing sector. It covers most of the publication process from content creation and design to production and marketing of digital works. Due to the complexity of the publishing process and the wide variety of actors involved, the SIDPT's partners conducted a survey through publishers in Austria, France and the Netherlands to get a better understanding of the current situation and actual needs. Below, there are some interesting findings regarding to the actual digital publishing, accessibility awareness in the sector and topics in which they are interested the most.

Digital publishing is widespread through the publishing industry due to more than three-quarters of respondents said the organizations they work for already publish digital works. Another noticeable fact is the popularity of digital formats, which raise some accessibility concerns, like PDF or EPUB2 (Fig. 1).

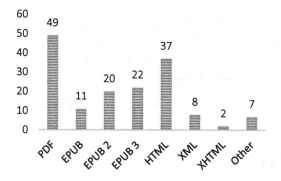

Fig. 1. Popularity of digital publishing format among respondents.

Over 50% of participants said their organization had not implemented yet digital accessibility in their workflow, but they were working on it. The most hopeful point is that many of them already implemented actions that affect positively on the accessibility of their outcomes (Fig. 2).

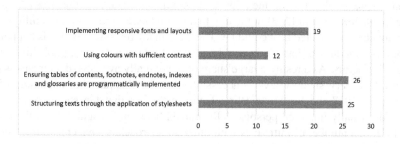

Fig. 2. Tasks that respondents already complete and affect positively to accessibility.

Regarding to accessibility awareness, over 50% consider accessibility to be a social and moral responsibility. However, 30% answered that they did not start to integrate accessibility in the publishing workflow yet (Fig. 3).

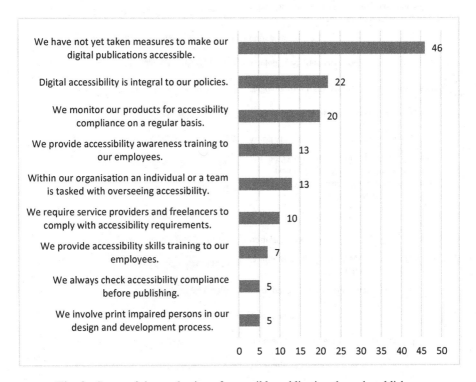

Fig. 3. Status of the production of accessible publication through publishers.

Only a few publishers have received some form of accessibility training, and these are mostly respondents intervening towards the end of the book production phase. This fact is depicted in Fig. 4, where is possible to notice the few people who answered they got some sort of training and most of them work in production (Fig. 5).

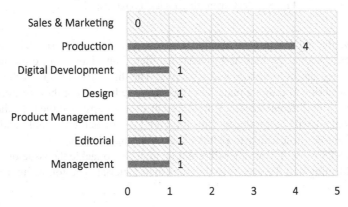

Fig. 4. Accessibility trainings taken by respondents and professional profiles.

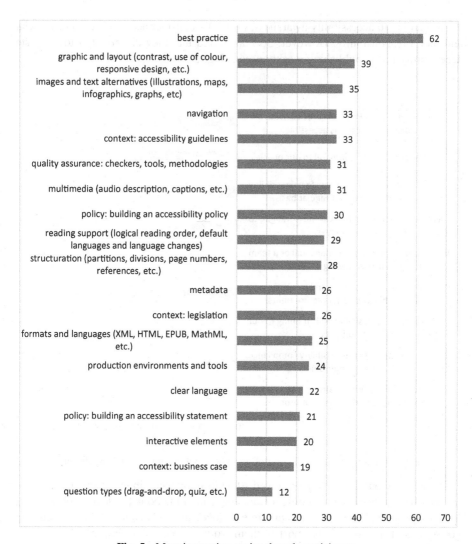

Fig. 5. Most interesting topics though participants.

Finally, the SIDPT project decided to produce training material tailored for the different professional profiles and present it ordered and labeled in order to provide quick and easy access to lessons and resources. The distinctive feature of the project is that the production of training material is based on the findings of the described survey. It will target the different needs of the different user groups identified. In the coming months, content will be produced with the core goal of being a simple and comprehensive resource for learning to publish accessible digital works.

In this STS we will hear other different approaches to tackle the issue of accessible digital publishing and the access to the published material. The following section will give a short overview on how the authors tackle different issues in the process of making content available to people with special needs.

2   Content

2.1   Practitioner's Perception of Web Accessibility: Roles, Process and Scope

Providing usable web information and services to as many people as possible confronts web practitioners with a demanding task. The present study provides insights on how Web Accessibility is perceived in practice. A total of 163 web practitioners in various professional roles reported their perspective on roles primarily responsible for Web Accessibility, on key phases in the development process and on types of disabilities mainly considered. Results show that non-technical roles are perceived to be less involved, that Web Accessibility is mainly considered in the conceptual design and development phase only, and that efforts focus on people with visual impairments. Based on these findings, recommendations for research and practice are discussed.

A Multi-site collaborative sampling for Web Accessibility Evaluation

Many sampling methods have been used for web accessibility evaluation. However, due to the difficulty of web page feature extraction and the lack of unsupervised clustering algorithm, the result is not very well. How to optimize the manual workload of different websites under the premise of ensuring that the overall manual workload remains the same during multi-site collaborative sampling is an important issue at present. To solve the above problems, we propose a Multi-site collaborative sampling method to obtain the final sampling result of each website. The effectiveness of the two sampling methods proposed in this paper is proved by experiments on real website datasets [4].

2.2   A Multi-site Collaborative Sampling for Web Accessibility Evaluation

Many sampling methods have been used for web accessibility evaluation. However, due to the difficulty of web page feature extraction and the lack of unsupervised clustering algorithm, the result is not very well. How to optimize the manual workload of different websites under the premise of ensuring that the overall manual workload remains the same during multi-site collaborative sampling is an important issue at present. To solve the above problems, we propose a Multi-site collaborative sampling method to obtain the final sampling result of each website. The effectiveness of the two sampling methods proposed in this paper is proved by experiments on real website datasets [5].

2.3 Towards More Efficient Screen Reader Web Access with Automatic Summary Generation and Text Tagging

Readers with 20/20 vision can easily read text and quickly perceive information to get an overview of the information within a text. This is more challenging for readers who rely on screen readers. This study investigated factors affecting successful screen reading in order to shed light on what contributes towards the improvement of screen reading access. Text extraction, summarization, and representation techniques were explored. The goal of this work leads to the development of a new summarization technique, referred to as On Demand Summary Generation and Text Tagging (ODSG&TT). This technique makes use of a summarization algorithm and a text tagging algorithm developed by Algorithmia, which enables on the fly and on-demand summarization of text and keyword generation. The focus of the screen reader is transferred to the keywords using a button control. The intention is to provide summaries with minimum user navigation effort to simplify the screen reading process [6].

2.4 A Series of Simple Processing Tools for PDF Files for People with Print Disabilities

This paper presents a simple tool to process PDF files for people with print disabilities. They consist of the following three titles: "PDFcontentEraser", "PDFfontChanger" and "PDFcontentExtracter." PDFcontentEraser is a tool to remove a certain type of elements in a PDF file. PDFfontChanger is a tool to replace the selection of fonts in a document. By default, all fonts are replaced by "Universal Design Font for Digital Textbooks" (UD font) developed by Morisawa Inc. PDFcontentExtracter is a tool to retrieve the components of a PDF file. It can output in the following three forms: (1) character information, image location and path location in XML, (2) image files, and (3) the shapes of paths, the shapes of characters and the locations of images in SVG [7].

2.5 Layout Analysis of PDF Documents by Two-Dimensional Grammars for the Production of Accessible

This paper proposes the use of two-dimensional context-free grammars (2DCFGs) for layout analysis of PDF documents. In Japan, textbooks are considered to be the primary teaching instruments that are necessary to guarantee the quality of education, and audio textbooks have been available for students with print disabilities in compulsory education. In order to create any type of audio textbooks, it is necessary to obtain the information of structure and the reading order of documents of regular textbooks in PDF. It is not simple task because most PDF files only have the information how to print them out, and page-layouts of most textbooks are complex [8].

3   Conclusion

As we could see, there are many different approaches to make published content accessible. Still many of the presentations and the underlying work done is connected to the adaptation and processing of already published material. We would like to see more research and efforts put into the actual information creation process. The potential benefit of the principles of multi-channel publishing put into practice is much greater and can save a lot of work and time spent for making content afterwards accessible.

References

1. Web Content Accessibility Guidelines (WCAG) 2.0 Homepage. https://www.w3.org/WAI/GL/WCAG20/. Accessed 18 June 2020
2. Section 508 Homepage. https://www.section508.gov. Accessed 18 June 2020
3. Marrakesh Treaty to Facilitate Access to Published Works for Persons Who Are Blind, Visually Impaired or Otherwise Print Disabled. Homepage https://wipolex.wipo.int/en/text/301019. Accessed 18 June 2020
4. Vollenwyder, B., Opwis, K., Brühlmann, F.: Practitioner's perception of web accessibility: roles, process and scope. In: Miesenberger, K., Covarrubias Rodriguez, M., Penaz, P. (eds.) ICCHP 2020, LNCS, vol. 10896. Springer, Heidelberg (2020)
5. Yu, Z., Bu, J., Shen, C., Wang, W., et al.: A multi-site collaborative sampling for web accessibility evaluation. In: Miesenberger, K., Covarrubias Rodriguez, M., Penaz, P. (eds.) ICCHP 2020, LNCS, vol. 10896. Springer, Heidelberg (2020)
6. Sarwar, U., Eika, E.: Towards more efficient screen reader web access with automatic summary generation and text tagging. In: Miesenberger, K., Covarrubias Rodriguez, M., Penaz, P. (eds.) ICCHP 2020, LNCS, vol. 10896. Springer, Heidelberg (2020)
7. Nakamura, S., Kohase, K., Fujiyoshi, A.: A series of simple processing tools for PDF files for people with print disabilities. In: Miesenberger, K., Covarrubias Rodriguez, M., Penaz, P. (eds.) ICCHP 2020, LNCS, vol. 10896. Springer, Heidelberg (2020)
8. Kohase, K., Nakamura, S., Fujiyoshi, A.: Layout analysis of PDF documents by two-dimensional grammars for the production of accessible textbooks. In: Miesenberger, K., Covarrubias Rodriguez, M., Penaz, P. (eds.) ICCHP 2020, LNCS, vol. 10896. Springer, Heidelberg (2020)

How Web Professionals Perceive Web Accessibility in Practice: Active Roles, Process Phases and Key Disabilities

Beat Vollenwyder(✉) ⓘ, Klaus Opwis, and Florian Brühlmann ⓘ

Center for Cognitive Psychology and Methodology, Department of Psychology,
University of Basel, Basel, Switzerland
{beat.vollenwyder,klaus.opwis,florian.bruehlmann}@unibas.ch

Abstract. Providing usable web information and services to as many people as possible confronts web professionals with a challenging task. The present study delivers insights about how Web accessibility is perceived in practice. Using a survey, a total of 163 web professionals in various roles reported their evaluation of Web accessibility implementation in their projects with regard to three aspects: the professional roles primarily responsible for Web accessibility, key phases in the development process, and the types of disabilities primarily considered. Results show that non-technical professional roles are perceived to be less involved in the development process, that Web accessibility considerations are mainly restricted to the design and implementation phases of projects, and that efforts focus predominantly on the needs of people with visual impairments.

Keywords: Web accessibility · Web professionals · Awareness · Survey

1 Introduction

Web accessibility aims to provide usable web information and services to as many people as possible. It thereby contributes substantially to the web's role in enabling and promoting equal participation in society [6]. However, web professionals face a challenging task when considering Web accessibility in their work. The first hurdle to overcome relates to its basic adoption in industrial practices. Here, it is essential that all organisational levels acquire a fundamental awareness and understanding of Web accessibility [12]. Insufficient knowledge gives rise to potentially harmful misconceptions about Web accessibility, such as beliefs that too few people benefit from it, that Web accessibility compromises aesthetics and technologically advanced solutions, or that the responsibility for addressing accessibility concerns lies solely in the hands of the developers [3,6]. Consequently, Web accessibility issues are often deprioritised relative to other requirements [13]. In contrast, findings show that Web accessibility contributes to improved performance and perceived usability for all user groups [9].

K. Miesenberger et al. (Eds.): ICCHP 2020, LNCS 12376, pp. 294–302, 2020.
https://doi.org/10.1007/978-3-030-58796-3_35

The actual implementation of Web accessibility poses further challenges. To address the needs of users with disabilities, web professionals are required to gain a thorough understanding of how to design and implement accessible solutions for individual forms of sensory, motor and cognitive impairments. They need to consider not only how the various set-ups that are available for assistive technologies, such as screen readers, screen magnifiers and alternative input mechanisms [2,11] can be employed, but also how they will be handled by people with different skill levels [14]. Further, web professionals are confronted with a large heterogeneity of constantly evolving web technologies. While this constitutes a major strength in terms of flexibility and adaptability, it can present an obstacle to the consideration and implementation of Web accessibility [5].

Several Web accessibility guidelines are available that provide information and advice on how to overcome these challenges. The Web Content Accessibility Guidelines (WCAG) are one of the most widely applied resources: They serve as the de facto standard for Web accessibility and are referenced in the policies of several countries [17]. However, despite the availability of the second edition of the WCAG since 2008 and their incorporation in legislation, adoption rates of Web accessibility standards still remain low. In February 2020, over 98% of the top million home pages on the web have detectable WCAG failures [18].

In a recent study, we aimed to identify the contributing factors underlying this neglect [15]. We identified three key determinants motivating web professionals to consider Web accessibility. First, users should actively communicate their specific needs. This can be facilitated by involving users with special needs in the development process. Second, web professionals should consider Web accessibility as an integral part of their professional role. They should become conscious of their responsibility to promote Web accessibility and ensure that expertise in implementing Web accessibility effectively is developed and supported. Third, Web accessibility should be perceived as beneficial for the overall quality of a product. This can be supported by promoting Web accessibility as a quality feature for all user groups.

As part of the aforementioned study [15], a subset of the participating web professionals were asked to comment on their evaluation of Web accessibility implementation practises in their own projects. These insights contribute to a deeper understanding of the professional roles that are primarily responsible for Web accessibility, the phases in the development process that are key to adoption and implementation, and the types of disabilities that are most often considered. The present paper reports these findings and discusses implications for Web accessibility research and practice.

2 Method

2.1 Participants and Design

An online survey was advertised via various computer science and human-computer interaction newsletters and mailing lists across Switzerland. The study description addressed, "all specialists who participate in the creation of websites and web applications (developers, designers, project managers, etc.)". As an incentive, participants could take part in a lottery for two gift vouchers worth CHF 50.- (approximately EUR 46.-). A total of 166 participants completed the online survey, of which 163 participants (age $M = 37.1$, $SD = 8.5$, range 20–65; 53 women, 110 men) were included in the analysis. Three participants were removed from the sample, because their response time exceeded one hour. On average, the study took 16 min ($SD = 8.5$ min, range 2.5–56) to complete.

The majority of participants completed the questionnaire in German ($N = 146$), followed by French (9) and English (8). When describing their main role as web professional, most participants reported being employed in functional testing (32), management (29), user research and usability testing (14), product owner (13) visual design (13) and development (12). Compared to other employees at their organisation, the participants reported moderate business ($M = 5.42$, $SD = 1.26$; all items measured on a 7-point Likert-type rating scale, where $1 = $ *very low*, and $7 = $ *very high*) and technical expertise ($M = 4.31$, $SD = 1.66$) in web development. Similar ratings were reported regarding personal factors: Web accessibility interest ($M = 5.48$, $SD = 1.27$), knowledge ($M = 4.85$, $SD = 1.51$) and familiarity with WCAG ($M = 4.59$, SD $= 1.59$). Sixteen participants reported a disability, including visual ($N = 9$), hearing (2), motor (1) and cognitive (1), as well as unspecified (3) impairments.

Most participants reported working in large organisations with more than 250 employees ($N = 81$), followed by middle-sized organisations with 10 to 250 employees (52), and small organisations with under 10 employees (30). Organisations were active in the private sector (106), the public sector (57), science and education (35), trusts, societies or non-governmental organisations (26), and other domains (23). The main geographical regions of the organisations' operations were Switzerland (134), Europe (14), global (13), and other individual or not further specified countries (2). Regarding legal obligations on Web accessibility, participants stated that a majority of their organisations were not obliged to consider Web accessibility (79), followed by organisations that were fully (38) and partially (10) obliged. A sizeable number of participants were not aware of the exact legal requirements of their organisation (36).

2.2 Procedure

Participants were first asked to describe their professional role and to rate their business and technical expertise in web development. Further, participants were asked whether they were familiar with the term 'Web accessibility', which was a requirement for taking part in the present study. Participants who were neither aware nor informed about this issue were screened out and could not complete the questionnaire. Participants then rated their level of personal interest in Web accessibility, their knowledge about it, and their familiarity with WCAG. This was followed by questions regarding the size, domain, location and legal obligations of the participants' organisation. Participants were also asked to report which professional roles (e.g., product owner, visual designer) were responsible for matters of Web accessibility in their organisation, the phases (e.g., analysis, design; see also [1]) involved in the development process and to report which types of disabilities (e.g., hearing impairments, motor impairments) were considered in their implementation efforts.

3 Results

With regard to specifying the professional roles of the individuals in their organisation who hold primary responsibility for Web accessibility, participants listed professionals in interaction design ($N = 80$, 49.1%; multiple answers were possible), development (75, 46.0%), and user research and usability testing (68, 41.7%), followed by visual design (59, 36.2%) and dedicated accessibility experts (54, 33.1%). Professional roles in management (26, 16.0%) and functional testing (21, 12.9%) were mentioned the least. Full results are presented in Table 1.

Table 1. Professional roles primarily responsible for Web accessibility. Multiple answers were possible.

Key web professionals	N	%
Interaction design	80	49.1
Development	75	46.0
User research & usability testing	68	41.7
Visual design	59	36.2
Accessibility expert	54	33.1
Project management	46	28.2
Content specialist	42	25.8
Product owner	35	21.5
Business analysis	33	20.2
Management	26	16.0
Software architecture	26	16.0
Other	25	15.3
Functional testing	21	12.9

With regard to identifying the phases in which Web accessibility is considered during the development process, participants mentioned the implementation ($N = 111$, 68.1%; multiple answers were possible) and design (104, 63.8%) phases most frequently, followed by analysis (55, 33.7%), operation (54, 33.1%), as well as the deployment phase (43, 26.4%). A substantial number of participants reported that Web accessibility is not considered at all in their organisation's development process (36, 22.1%). A schematic representation of the results is presented in Fig. 1.

Participants reported that most of their organisation's Web accessibility efforts focus on people with visual impairments ($M = 5.23$, $SD = 1.89$; all items

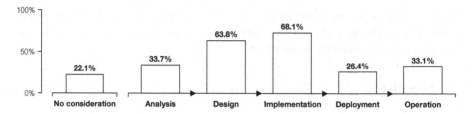

Fig. 1. Bar diagram presenting the percentage values per phase, in which Web accessibility is considered during the development process. Multiple answers were possible.

measured on a 7-point Likert-type rating scale, where $1 = very\ low\ importance$, and $7 = very\ high\ importance$), blindness ($M = 4.87$, $SD = 2.21$), and motor impairments ($M = 3.77$, $SD = 2.03$), whereas deafness ($M = 3.30$, $SD = 2.04$), hearing impairments ($M = 3.27$, $SD = 2.07$), as well as learning and attention disorders ($M = 3.09$, $SD = 1.91$) receive less attention. All results are presented in Table 2.

Table 2. Participant responses rating the types of disabilities that are most often considered in Web accessibility efforts on a 7-point scale of ascending importance.

	M	SD
Visual impairments	5.23	1.89
Blindness	4.87	2.21
Motor impairments	3.77	2.03
Deafness	3.30	2.04
Hearing impairments	3.27	2.07
Learning and attention disorders	3.09	1.91

4 Discussion

4.1 Professional Roles Primarily Responsible for Web Accessibility

The role of the developer is identified as being one of the professional roles that is primarily responsible for considering Web accessibility. While this result was expected from previous insights [6], it is a more recent development to observe interaction design, user research and usability testing professionals emerge in this category. This may reflect discussions about the need for accessible solutions to go beyond the provision of basic access, and include aspects related to usability (e.g., effectiveness, efficiency and satisfaction) and user experience (e.g., affect, trust or aesthetics) [8]. Encouragingly, these results are in line with the strong agreement among accessibility experts that Web accessibility must be grounded in user-centred methodologies [19] and show that this understanding is in the process of being established in practice. Dedicated accessibility experts, however, were not reported among the top ranks. Even though most participants reported being part of a large organisation, accessibility experts may still be less common or less well known, and therefore receive less recognition than other roles. It may also indicate that accessibility experts are occupied with promoting a general awareness and understanding of Web accessibility, rather than being directly involved in development projects [12]. Finally, less technical professional roles, such as product owner, business analysis and management were rarely mentioned. This research corroborates previous studies in finding non-technical roles to be less aware of accessibility issues [4,19]. The absence of concern for Web accessibility in non-technical roles may compromise the adoption strategies of their organisation, as these professionals are often in charge of prioritising or funding requirements.

4.2 Key Phases in the Development Process

Web accessibility seems to be mostly considered in the design and implementation phases of the development process. While this may be appropriate for the development of a new product, few participants reported that Web accessibility was considered while adding new functionalities once the product was operational. Given that many products are often continuously improved after their initial launch, this poses a potential pitfall in ensuring the quality of web information and services as products continue to evolve [1]. For instance, if the login mechanism of a web service is updated and not tested for Web accessibility, it may block users from obtaining otherwise perfectly usable content. However, the present study did not include any questions concerning whether a product is developed iteratively, for instance, in applying an agile methodology. This may have influenced how participants rated the implementation and the subsequent development during operational phases. The issue of Web accessibility is also less prominent in the analysis phase, including during definition of the business case and risk analysis assessment. This may reflect the widespread belief that few people benefit from Web accessibility, and that it therefore provides only a limited competitive edge for a business [3]. It might also be closely tied to the aforementioned finding that non-technical and managerial professionals tend to be less involved in the provision of accessible web information and services. At worst, this lack of involvement and the resulting omission in the analysis phase may ultimately have a detrimental impact on people's lives by excluding them from various spheres of private, social, economic or political life. Also, the neglect of such issues may have legal consequences for an organisation in the future [17].

4.3 Types of Disabilities Primarily Considered

Most reported Web accessibility efforts are focused on visual impairments. Previous studies found that accessibility experts rated users with visual impairments as being an important target group, but not the only beneficiaries [19].

In contrast, the present findings reveal that there is a bias against users with non-visual impairments in practice. This bias may be due to the perception of the web as being a mainly visual medium and confirms widespread misconceptions that Web accessibility only benefits users with visual impairments [3]. In contrast, learning and attention disorders are only rarely considered. This is in line with ongoing discussions regarding the persisting need to reduce barriers for people with cognitive disabilities in current Web accessibility practice and policy [7]. Hence, it is important to highlight the beneficial effects of Web accessibility for all user groups, while potentially problematic aspects, such as contradictory findings regarding language complexity in the web, should be further explored to provide guidance for practice [10, 16].

5   Conclusion

The present study provides insights into how web professionals evaluate the implementation of Web accessibility in practice. While there is evidence that user-centred practices in combination with Web accessibility are in the process of being established, non-technical web professionals tend to be less involved in supporting accessibility issues. Web accessibility is mainly considered in the design and implementation phases of the development process. The lack of attention to Web accessibility during the analysis phase and ongoing developments may result in missed opportunities and less accessible solutions after the product's initial release. Future research should therefore explore how Web accessibility can be promoted among all professional roles and during the complete development process of a product. Further, results indicate that most Web accessibility efforts predominantly focus on people with visual impairments. It is therefore recommended to actively promote awareness and understanding of Web accessibility and to broaden the perspective at all organisational levels. We hope that these findings will guide further research activities and support web professionals in their quest to make the web more inclusive.

Acknowledgements. We are grateful to Elisa Mekler for her helpful feedback and Hermione Miller-Moser for her editorial assistance in revising this manuscript. The study was registered with the Institutional Review Board of the University of Basel under the number D-005-16.

References

1. Abou-Zahra, S.: Web accessibility evaluation. In: Harper, S., Yesilada, Y. (eds.) Web Accessibility. HCIS, pp. 79–106. Springer, London (2008). https://doi.org/10. 1007/978-1-84800-050-6_7
2. Barreto, A.: Visual impairments. In: Harper, S., Yesilada, Y. (eds.) Web Accessibility. HCIS, pp. 3–13. Springer, London (2008). https://doi.org/10.1007/978-1-84800-050-6_1

3. Ellcessor, E.: <ALT = "Textbooks">: Web accessibility myths as negotiated industrial lore. Crit. Stud. Media Commun. **31**(5), 448–463 (2014).https://doi.org/10.1080/15295036.2014.919660

4. Freire, A.P., Russo, C.M., Fortes, R.P.M.: The perception of accessibility in Web development by academy, industry and government: a survey of the Brazilian scenario. New Rev. Hypermedia Multimed. **14**(2), 149–175 (2008). https://doi.org/10.1080/13614560802624241

5. Harper, S., Chen, A.Q.: Web accessibility guidelines. World Wide Web **15**(1), 61–88 (2011). https://doi.org/10.1007/s11280-011-0130-8

6. Henry, S.L.: Understanding web accessibility. In: Thatcher, J., et al. (eds.) Web Accessibility: Web Standards and Regulatory Compliance, pp. 1–51. Apress, Berkeley (2006). https://doi.org/10.1007/978-1-4302-0188-5_1

7. Lewis, C.: Cognitive and learning impairments. In: Harper, S., Yesilada, Y. (eds.) Web Accessibility. HCIS, pp. 15–23. Springer, London (2008). https://doi.org/10.1007/978-1-84800-050-6_2

8. Power, C., Cairns, P., Barlet, M.: Inclusion in the third wave: access to experience. In: Filimowicz, M., Tzankova, V. (eds.) New Directions in Third Wave Human-Computer Interaction: Volume 1 - Technologies. HIS, pp. 163–181. Springer, Cham (2018). https://doi.org/10.1007/978-3-319-73356-2_10

9. Schmutz, S., Sonderegger, A., Sauer, J.: Implementing recommendations from web accessibility guidelines: a comparative study of nondisabled users and users with visual impairments. Hum. Factors: J. Hum. Factors Ergon. Soc. **59**(6), 956–972 (2017). https://doi.org/10.1177/0018720817708397

10. Schmutz, S., Sonderegger, A., Sauer, J.: Easy-to-read language in disability-friendly web sites: effects on nondisabled users. Appl. Ergon. **74**, 97–106 (2019). https://doi.org/10.1016/j.apergo.2018.08.013

11. Trewin, S.: Physical impairment. In: Harper, S., Yesilada, Y. (eds.) Web Accessibility. HCIS, pp. 37–46. Springer, London (2008). https://doi.org/10.1007/978-1-84800-050-6_4

12. Urban, M., Burks, M.R.: Implementing accessibility in the enterprise. In: Thatcher, J., et al. (eds.) Web Accessibility: Web Standards and Regulatory Compliance, pp. 69–83. Apress, Berkeley (2006). https://doi.org/10.1007/978-1-4302-0188-5_3

13. Velleman, E.M., Nahuis, I., van der Geest, T.: Factors explaining adoption and implementation processes for web accessibility standards within eGovernment systems and organizations. Univ. Access Inf. Soc. **16**(1), 173–190 (2015). https://doi.org/10.1007/s10209-015-0449-5

14. Vigo, M., Harper, S.: A snapshot of the first encounters of visually disabled users with the web. Comput. Hum. Behav. **34**, 203–212 (2014). https://doi.org/10.1016/j.chb.2014.01.045

15. Vollenwyder, B., Iten, G.H., Brühlmann, F., Opwis, K., Mekler, E.D.: Salient beliefs influencing the intention to consider web accessibility. Comput. Hum. Behav. **92**, 352–360 (2019). https://doi.org/10.1016/j.chb.2018.11.016

16. Vollenwyder, B., Schneider, A., Krueger, E., Brühlmann, F., Opwis, K., Mekler, E.D.: How to use plain and easy-to-read language for a positive user experience on websites. In: Miesenberger, K., Kouroupetroglou, G. (eds.) ICCHP 2018. LNCS, vol. 10896, pp. 514–522. Springer, Cham (2018). https://doi.org/10.1007/978-3-319-94277-3_80

17. Waddell, C.D.: Worldwide accessibility laws and policies. In: Thatcher, J., et al. (eds.) Web Accessibility: Web Standards and Regulatory Compliance, pp. 547–579. Apress, Berkeley (2006). https://doi.org/10.1007/978-1-4302-0188-5_17

18. WebAIM: The WebAIM Million, February 2019. https://webaim.org/projects/million. Accessed 12 Jun 2020
19. Yesilada, Y., Brajnik, G., Vigo, M., Harper, S.: Exploring perceptions of web accessibility: a survey approach. Behav. Inf. Technol. **34**(2), 119–134 (2014). https://doi.org/10.1080/0144929X.2013.848238

Towards More Efficient Screen Reader Web Access with Automatic Summary Generation and Text Tagging

Usama Sarwar and Evelyn Eika[(✉)]

Oslo Metropolitan University, 0130 Oslo, Norway
{s310272,Evelyn.eika}@oslomet.no

Abstract. Readers with 20/20 vision can easily read text and quickly perceive information to get an overview of the information within a text. This is more challenging for readers who rely on screen readers. This study investigated factors affecting successful screen reading in order to shed light on what contributes towards the improvement of screen reading access. Text extraction, summarization, and representation techniques were explored. The goal of this work leads to the development of a new summarization technique, referred to as On Demand Summary Generation and Text Tagging (ODSG&TT). This technique makes use of a summarization algorithm and a text tagging algorithm developed by Algorithmia, which enables on the fly and on-demand summarization of text and keyword generation. The focus of the screen reader is transferred to the keywords using a button control. The intention is to provide summaries with minimum user navigation effort to simplify the screen reading process.

Keywords: Automatic summarization · Screen reader · Visually impaired · Reading · Skimming · Accessibility

1 Introduction

Digital information is increasingly being used in communications. This trend requires that citizens obtain information electronically. Hence digital information must be made easily available for all readers, including the visually impaired who rely on screen readers to gain access to information. Most screen readers that assist the visually impaired read the text in an iterative manner. Since these tools present text sequentially, it is difficult for users to scan for items of interest or importance compared to people who read text with their eyes. Browsing through the digital documents thus becomes a slow and often pains-taking process for the screen reader user. A more intelligent screen reader that leads to more efficient navigation through the electronic document would hold potential for greatly assisting users in accessing information. This study investigates challenges that screen reader users commonly encounter and explores text extraction techniques as a potential remedy for achieving more effective screen reading.

Screen readers are software tools developed to enable the visually impaired to use computers. These tools read aloud with a synthetic voice and they are commonly used

© Springer Nature Switzerland AG 2020
K. Miesenberger et al. (Eds.): ICCHP 2020, LNCS 12376, pp. 303–313, 2020.
https://doi.org/10.1007/978-3-030-58796-3_36

by the visually impaired to access the web. Readers who rely on their eyes form an overview of the contents by simply visually scanning the webpage; the screen reader users are not using their eyes but have to construct what is there bit by bit [1]. What visually oriented readers regard as a simple task such as getting advice online for a web product/service may not be trivial for a screen reader user [1]. As expressed by a user who had limited experience with screen readers, intensive navigating through the library' websites took much longer time (twice or three times as much) to search for information compared to visually oriented readers [2]. Though screen readers assist users greatly, limitations exist and need to be resolved to provide more accessible use. Some weaknesses include reading irrelevant visual presentation elements, employing a simple top-to-bottom and left-to-right reading strategy leading to lengthy waiting for relevant information, unable to deliver structural information of the page, intertwining content reading with links reading that causes confusions and inconveniences for listeners who have to wait for links' meanings to be clarified or select long wrong moves in websites due to ineffective ordering of links' list, impractical links selection scheme because of audio synchronization difficulties, along with the synthetic voice reading all pieces of information on the page (content, links, landmarks, etc.) with the same intonation throughout [3].

Automatic text summarization techniques are proposed as a means to help screen reader users reduce cognitive workload by generating meaningful summaries of long texts. Many artificial Intelligence algorithms are developed based on natural language processing. However, the process of using such software is not simple. It often involves navigation challenges for screen reader users as they have to shift their focus from different applications. Summarization may include multiple steps: (1) Select the text to summarize. (2) Copy the selected text. (3) Open the text summarizer through webpage, plugin link, or desktop software. (4) Paste the copied text into the software. (5) Generate the summary. (6) Read it through the screen reader. (7) Come back to the original text (webpage or other electronic text). (8) Users must start reading again from the initial point as the context is lost. These steps may seem simple but require effort; the overall purpose of saving effort is thus lost. Moreover, some web-based summary generators return the summaries in dialog boxes or alerts, and such popups reduce accessibility.

Given the challenges that users encounter when navigating using the screen reader, this work aims to minimize the efforts involved through an integrated approach where the summary is available as part of the regular screen reader reading flow. The following questions are asked: Can effective screen reading be achieved with minimized navigation? Can lengthy text reading of website screen reading be simplified?

This paper is organized as follows. Related work is presented, followed by sections of method and results. Discussion is then offered based on findings gathered, closed by a conclusion.

2   Related Work

According to Borodin et al. [4], browsing the Web with screen readers can be challenging because of accessibility and usability problems. Accessibility issues associated with screen reader users have also been identified in websites of higher education [5]. The basic readability of the text affects all readers [6–9], and it has been demonstrated that readability features such as sentence length affect screen reading performance [10]. It is nearly impossible to access some content through screen readers. One common example is an image without an alternative text. Screen readers will ignore such images which then become "invisible" to the readers. Though the screen reading technology is advancing with new features, new web technologies emerge at an even faster pace and the discrepancies lead to inaccessibility. Implementing an accessible website without any rich media is by some viewed as laborious [11] as W3C recommendations are implemented differently in different browsers. Ensuring accessibility with rich media is even more challenging. For instance, the Flash multimedia content was inaccessible to screen reader users for years [4]. With HTML 5 introducing canvas, content inaccessibility may arise again that will affect the working of web technologies with screen readers.

Screen readers are usually slow to use because they read out the content sequentially at a fixed rate. It is known that interactions of screen reader users are slower than those of users who make use of the visual interface [11, 12]. Repeated navigation links and complex search functions were among main accessibility issues for screen reader users [13]. As also proposed, users' needs such as adapting the speed of the screen reader should be considered in web accessibility evaluations [14]. Still, navigational constrains remained in current screen readers, and multimodal technologies enhancing non-visual interface were proposed to provide navigational cues to assist users [15].

Skimming is an effective way of quickly reviewing large amount of information, where the readers' eyes rapidly explore the visual contents. However, this is not easy for screen reader users. Screen readers typically rely on text-to-speech techniques or tactile braille displays to convey the digital content non-visually allowing users to navigate through the content marked up by HTML tags for headings, paragraphs, links, and buttons [16]. A screen reader scans the whole page from start till the end that makes the process sequential and potentially time-consuming. Screen-readers have features to accelerate access where users can jump more rapidly through the content a sentence at a time, jump across lines, paragraphs, sections, pages, and traverse lists of links and headings. Although these functions provide great improvements, they do not provide the same flexibility, speed, and freedom as visual skimming of information would [17].

Although as a comprehension strategy the screen reader user could filter through the document by choosing a faster screen reading speed, it has drawbacks of increasing users' cognitive load since more concentration is required. The increased attention thus demanded could reduce word comprehension as some participants experienced and result in overall reduced comprehension [18]. Further, linear presentation gives users little room for maneuvering information selection hence fatiguing their working memory, which in turn is found to reduce efficiency of information processing [19].

There exists, also, a trade-off between speed reading and comprehension accuracy, and fast reading pace that hinders reread could cause misinterpretation because of word ambiguity and sentence complexity [20]. As recommended, screen reader users should be given flexibility to change reading speed as current tools already offered, or to relocate information space for individual users' preferences [18].

Because of the low bandwidth of a serial audio interface and braille displays, screen reader users spend considerably more time identifying the information they need compared to users who skim visually [4]. The cognitive load increases when a user has to process a large amount of information [21]; for screen reader users, the cognitive load is even higher as they have to listen, remember, and process the content that is presented sequentially. As experienced by some users, they resort to listen to the whole document since it is nearly impossible to identify specific parts of the document [18]. The assumption of this work is that by reducing the amount of information through summarizing techniques consequently reduces the cognitive load of screen reader users.

Automatic summarization approaches are used to summarize the textual content while preserving its essence [22]. Two main classes of text summarization techniques exist, namely summarization by extraction and summarization by abstraction [22]. According to [23], summarization by extraction deals with selecting the most prominent and meaningful phrases from the content. Summarization by abstraction is constricting sentences [22, 24], which involves rephrasing the content by automatically filling out a template [25].

Various algorithms have been proposed to foster faster screen reading. For example, skim reading is available in JAWS (Job Access With Speech) 6.0 and later. Skim reading refers to gaining the gist of a text without using all the details [20]. This feature has a simple implementation where users can swiftly review long documents by reading the first line or sentence of each paragraph. JAWS also provides users with looking up for specific phrase and words and with generating summaries of the text for users' overview of the whole content and for detailed reading if it is relevant. Users could also make rules to read in certain patterns, but they cannot be applied to all contents. Users' experience was that JAWS skimming was not useful for content skimming and it was similar to navigating paragraphs with a different purpose, hence not efficient [16, 18]. Specifically, users indicated that they used regular navigation shortcuts for skimming since no tools provided adequate content skimming support [16].

Accessible skimming is a concept introduced by Ahmed et al. [16]; it is also a form of non-visual skimming. The summarization algorithm uses a text extraction technique with the following steps: (1) Generate variable sized summaries of the text. (2) Each sentence is summarized to cover the complete text. (3) Phrases are extracted such that the meaningful connections between the words hold. This technique has been successful in facilitating screen reading as opposed to using regular shortcuts [16]. An additional shortcut was enabled to let users switch between the summary and the original text while preserving the reading position within the text so that the users could return to the same spot after listening to the generated summary without having to reread from the beginning of the article [16].

Tag Thunder [26] is a cloud content representation system. It works based on principles of content summarization and concurrent speech synthesis [27]. Tag Thunder implements content presentation as follows: The Web Page is segmented into several zones, then key words are extracted through text extraction techniques, and extracted key terms are concurrently vocalized on an audio track to echo the positions and visual properties of respective zones. It enables users to filter out the content of interest and determine the desired zone for further navigations.

Fig. 1. ODSG&TT enabled webpage.

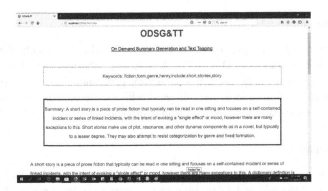

Fig. 2. The webpage appears with ODSG&TT executed.

3   Method

To answer the research questions, an experiment with a prototype involving screen reader users and questionnaire feedback was conducted. The goal was to contribute towards improved screen reading.

3.1   Equipment

Nonvisual Desktop Access (NVDA) screen reader was used for the experiment. NVDA ensures nonvisual access to and interaction with Windows OS and other applications [28].

3.2 Prototype Framework

A prototype named On Demand Summary Generation and Text Tagging (ODSG&TT) was implemented using PHP version 5.6.35 and the jQuery library version 3.3.1. Because this was a controlled experiment, we only used localhost with a WAMP server. WampServer is a Windows web development environment [29]. We used the Summarizer summarizing algorithm [30] developed on Algorithmia [31] platform. It is a developed algorithm and can be used with an API Key. AutoTag [32] is another library developed at Algorithmia [31] that was used to extract keywords of texts. The prototype setup was run on a computer running Windows 10 Enterprise version with Mozilla Firefox version 63.0.3 (64-bit) and Google Chrome Version 70.0.3538.102 (Official Build, 64-bit).

Figure 1 shows a website with the ODSG&TT functionality enabled. Users can generate the keywords and summary of the text within the webpage; they can also decide if they want to skip the keywords and summary and continue.

Figure 2 shows that there are two additional sections generated within the same webpage shown in Fig. 1, namely the sections keywords and summary. The original text is still there, and it will be read after the screen reader reads out these two sections. This gives users a rapid clue about whether the text is relevant and interesting or not. If yes, the screen reader will continue reading the detailed text as well; otherwise, the user can simply move to another webpage.

3.3 Questionnaire

An interview using five questions was conducted to elicit feedback. The questions addressed the efficiency of ODSG&TT: Does it serve the purpose of summary generation? Is it faster than the other two summary generation techniques (see the procedure section)? Is it simple to use? Does it address the navigation issues? Does it simplify the screen reading when generating summaries?

3.4 Participants

Twenty participants ($N = 20$) were recruited for the study. They all had information technology backgrounds and knew how to use screen readers or were familiar with concepts of using screen readers.

3.5 Procedure

The participants were first given instructions about the task. Participants were blindfolded as it was challenging to recruit actual screen reader users. One-to-one sessions were conducted. A summary was generated from a website and read with the NVDA screen reader; the time taken was measured using Resoomer. A second summary was generated using a browser plugin and read using the NVDA screen reader; the time taken was measured via Chrome Plugin Text-Summarizer. A third summary was generated using ODSG&TT (also read with the NVDA screen reader), and the time taken was measured. A questionnaire-based interview was then conducted.

3.6 Analysis

A one-way repeated ANOVA was used, with summarization technique as the independent variable and summarization time as the dependent variable. SPSS was used for the statistical computations.

4 Results

4.1 Processing Time of Summarization Techniques

The results indicated that compared to the Plugin and Website processes, the ODSG&TT summarization technique required less time. These repeated measures were conducted at a significance level .05 with a 95% confidence interval. The following figure indicates the mean time taken in seconds to generate the summary of the text (Fig. 3).

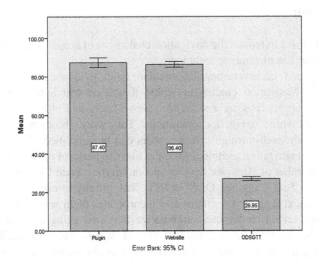

Fig. 3. Bar chart for calculated means with 95% confidence interval.

The observations did not violate the assumption of sphericity ($\chi^2(2) = 3.718$, $p = .156$). The ANOVA showed that there was a significant difference in summarization time for the three summarization techniques ($F(2, 38) = 1439.5$, $p < .001$, $\eta p^2 = .987$). Bonferroni post-hoc analysis revealed that the plugin summarization technique ($M = 87.4$, $SD = 5.315$) and the website summarization technique ($M = 86.4$, $SD = 3.22$) exhibited almost the same summary generation time. Hence, the two techniques were not significantly different. However, the ODSG&TT summarization technique ($M = 26.9$, $SD = 2.23$) took significantly less time. These results support the claim that ODSG&TT is a faster summarization technique compared to the two other alternatives.

4.2 Questionnaire Feedback

Most participants (80%) expressed that ODSG&TT addressed the purpose satisfactorily and succeeded in performing the intended functionality. However, one-fifth of the participants (20%) thought it did not entirely address the purpose. In response to the second question, as high as 95% of the participants perceived that the prototype was faster than the two other summary generation techniques while only 5% of the participants did not perceive that it was any faster. As for simplicity, most of the participants found the prototype simple and straight forward to use as no complex calculations or processes were involved. More than half of the participants (70%) responded that this system was simple while 30% thought it was moderately simple.

Concerning navigation challenges, most (75%) were of the opinion that ODSG&TT addressed the navigation challenges while one-fourth of the participants (25%) disagreed. As for simplifying the screen reading experience, the majority of the participants (85%) responded that it did simplify the screen reading while 15% disagreed.

5 Discussion

This research aimed to reduce the navigation challenges of screen reader technology by exploring a new summarization technique.

Perceiving and understanding information quickly is not straightforward with screen readers. Navigation challenges within digital content indicate that improved techniques and approaches are needed to achieve faster and effective screen reading with less cumbersome navigation operations. This work shows how the access to lengthy text on the web through screen readers can be simplified.

Existing summarization techniques require users to perform many steps. In order to minimize the number of steps, we developed a prototype named On Demand Summary Generation and Text Tagging (ODSG&TT). This prototype uses the existing summarization and text tagging algorithms and incorporates them within the website. The prototype helps screen reader users summarize long text using a button control. By pressing the button the summarized text and keywords are dynamically displayed within the webpage, and the focus of screen reader is also transferred to the keywords section.

With the current implementation, the regular text reading starts automatically after reading the summary. Some participants also suggested that there should be a pause with instruction that lets users know that summary is finished and if they want to continue or change the search. Future work may enhance the prototype by combining with smart devices to provide users with flexibility. Users may be able to give a voice command to devices such as Alexa and Siri to generate the summary of an article or text, and the prototype can run in the backend. A summary will then be generated and read aloud by the device.

Overall, the results show that the proposed technique does simplify the screen reading process because the focus of the screen remains within the webpage and the navigation procedures are reduced. The screen reader users do not have to swap the focus between different applications to access content.

6 Conclusion

Visual reading is not the same as screen reading. Screen reader users face several navigation challenges. The work shows that a lengthy text can be summarized within the same webpage, eliminating the need to shift focus between a given webpage and a summarizing tool. After reading the summary users can decide whether or not they want to continue. Participants' feedback also shows that ODSG&TT does not involve complex navigation and control transfers, making it faster and easier to use. Future work involves enhancing the prototype by letting users know when a summary is finished and explicitly asking them if they want to continue reading.

References

1. Gerber, E.: The benefits of and barriers to computer use for individuals who are visually impaired. J. Vis. Impairment Blindness **97**(9), 536–550 (2003)
2. Mulliken, A.: There is nothing inherently mysterious about assistive technology: a qualitative study about blind user experiences in US academic libraries. Reference and User Services Quarterly **57**(2), 115–126 (2017)
3. Di Blas, N., Paolini, P., Speroni M., Capodieci, A.: Enhancing accessibility for visually impaired users: the Munch's exhibition. In: Bearman, D., Trant, J., (eds.) Museums and the Web 2004. Selected Papers from an International Conference, Archives & Museum Informatics, Arlington, Washington, U.S.A (2004)
4. Borodin, Y., Bigham, J.P., Dausch, G., Ramakrishnan, I.V.: More than meets the eye: a survey of screen-reader browsing strategies. In: Proceedings of the 2010 International Cross Disciplinary Conference on Web Accessibility (2010)
5. Parajuli, P., Eika, E.: A comparative study of accessibility and usability of norwegian university websites for screen reader users based on user experience and automated assessment. In: Antona, M., Stephanidis, C. (eds.) HCII 2020. LNCS, vol. 12188, pp. 300–310. Springer, Cham (2020). https://doi.org/10.1007/978-3-030-49282-3_21
6. Eika, E., Sandnes, F.E.: Assessing the reading level of web texts for WCAG2.0 compliance —can it be done automatically? In: Di Bucchianico, G., Kercher, P. (eds.) Advances in Design for Inclusion. Advances in Intelligent Systems and Computing, vol 500. Springer, Cham (2016). https://doi.org/10.1007/978-3-319-41962-6_32
7. Eika, E., Sandnes, F.E.: Authoring WCAG2.0-compliant texts for the web through text readability visualization. In: Antona, M., Stephanidis, C. (eds.) UAHCI 2016. LNCS, vol. 9737, pp. 49–58. Springer, Cham (2016). https://doi.org/10.1007/978-3-319-40250-5_5
8. Eika, E.: Universally designed text on the web: towards readability criteria based on anti-patterns. Stud. Health Technol. Inform **229**, 461–470 (2016)
9. Kaushik, H.M., Eika, E., Sandnes, F.E.: Towards universal accessibility on the web: do grammar checking tools improve text readability? In: Antona, M., Stephanidis, C. (eds.) HCII 2020. LNCS, vol. 12188, pp. 272–288. Springer, Cham (2020). https://doi.org/10.1007/978-3-030-49282-3_19
10. Kadayat, B.B., Eika, E.: Impact of sentence length on the readability of web for screen reader users. In: Antona, M., Stephanidis, C. (eds.) HCII 2020. LNCS, vol. 12188, pp. 261–271. Springer, Cham (2020). https://doi.org/10.1007/978-3-030-49282-3_18

11. Chapdelaine, C., Gagnon, L.: Accessible video description on-demand. In: Proceedings of the 11th International ACM SIGACCESS Conference on Computers and Accessibility, pp. 221–222 (2009). https://doi.org/10.1145/1639642.1639685

12. Sun, S.-Y., Shieh, C.-J., Huang, K.-P.: A research on comprehension differences between print and screen reading. S. Afr. J. Econ. Manage. Sci. **16**(5), 87–101 (2013)

13. Gerber, E.: Technology and persons with disabilities. In: Proceedings of the 17th Annual International Conference of California State University Northridge (CSUN) (2002)

14. Vigo, M., Kobsa, A., Arrue, M., Abascal, J.: User-tailored web accessibility evaluations. In: Proceedings of the eighteenth conference on Hypertext and hypermedia, pp. 95–104 (2007)

15. Murphy, E., Kuber, R., McAllister, G., Strain, P., Yu, W.: An empirical investigation into the difficulties experienced by visually impaired Internet users. Univ. Access Inf. Soc. **7**(1–2), 79–91 (2008). https://doi.org/10.1007/s10209-007-0098-4

16. Ahmed, F., Borodin, Y., Soviak, A., Islam, M., Ramakrishnan, I.V., Hedgpeth, T.: Accessible skimming: faster screen reading of web pages. In: Proceedings of the 25th Annual ACM Symposium on User Interface Software and Technology, pp. 367–378. ACM (2012). https://doi.org/10.1145/2380116.2380164

17. Bigham, J.P., Cavender, A.C.: Evaluating existing audio CAPTCHAs and an interface optimized for non-visual use. In: Proceedings of the SIGCHI Conference on Human Factors in Computing Systems, pp. 1829–1838. ACM (2009). https://doi.org/10.1145/1518701.1518983

18. Machulla, T., Avila, M., Wozniak, P., Montag, D., Schmidt, A.: Skim-reading strategies in sighted and visually-impaired individuals: a comparative study. In: Proceedings of the 11th Pervasive Technologies Related to Assistive Environments Conference, pp. 170–177 (2018)

19. Wickens, C.D., Gordon, S.E., Liu, Y.: An introduction to human factors engineering. Course material (1998)

20. Rayner, K., Schotter, E.R., Masson, M.E., Potter, M.C., Treiman, R.: So much to read, so little time: How do we read, and can speed reading help? Psychol. Sci. Public Interest **17**(1), 4–34 (2016)

21. Sweller, J.: Cognitive load during problem solving: effects on learning. Cogn. Sci. **12**(2), 257–285 (1988). https://doi.org/10.1016/0364-0213(88)90023-7

22. Ahmed, F., Borodin, Y., Puzis, Y., Ramakrishnan, I.V.: Why read if you can skim: towards enabling faster screen reading. In: Proceedings of the International Cross-Disciplinary Conference on Web Accessibility, pp. 1–10 (2012)

23. Goldstein, J., Kantrowitz, M., Mittal, V., Carbonell, J.: Summarizing text documents: sentence selection and evaluation metrics. In: Proceedings of the 22nd Annual International ACM SIGIR Conference on Research and Development in Information Retrieval, pp. 121–128. ACM (1999). https://doi.org/10.1145/312624.312665

24. Berger, A.L., Mittal, V.O.: OCELOT: A System for Summarizing Web Pages. In: Proceedings of the 23rd Annual International ACM SIGIR Conference on Research and Development in Information Retrieval, pp. 144–151, (2000). https://doi.org/10.1145/345508.345565

25. Jacobs, P.S.: To parse or not to parse: relation-driven text skimming. In: Proceedings of the 13th Conference on Computational Linguistics - Volume 2, pp. 194–198 (1990). https://doi.org/10.3115/997939.997973

26. Manishina, E., Lecarpentier, J.-M., Maurel, F., Ferrari, S., Busson, M.: Tag thunder: towards non-visual web page skimming. In: Proceedings of the 18th International ACM SIGACCESS Conference on Computers and Accessibility, pp. 281–282. ACM (2016). https://doi.org/10.1145/2982142.2982152

27. Guerreiro, J., Gonçalves, D.: Scanning for digital content: how blind and sighted people perceive concurrent speech. ACM Trans. Access. Comput. **8**(1), (2016). https://doi.org/10.1145/2822910
28. NVDA: About NVDA. November 18, 2018, from NV Access website (2017). https://www.nvaccess.org/about-nvda/
29. WampServer: Retrieved November 19, 2018, from WampServer website (n.d.). http://www.wampserver.com/en/
30. Algorithmia: Summarizer - Algorithm by nlp. Retrieved November 19, 2018, from Algorithmia website (n.d.). https://algorithmia.com/algorithms/nlp/Summarizer
31. Algorithmia: Algorithmia - Deploy AI at Scale. Retrieved November 19, 2018, from Algorithmia website (n.d.). https://algorithmia.com
32. Algorithmia: AutoTag - Algorithm by nlp. Retrieved November 19, 2018, from Algorithmia website (n.d.). https://algorithmia.com/algorithms/nlp/AutoTag

A Series of Simple Processing Tools for PDF Files for People with Print Disabilities

Shunsuke Nakamura, Kento Kohase, and Akio Fujiyoshi(✉)

Graduate School of Science and Engineering, Ibaraki University, Hitachi, Japan
{20nm726r,20nm711h,akio.fujiyoshi.cs}@vc.ibaraki.ac.jp

Abstract. This paper presents simple processing tools for PDF files for people with print disabilities. They consist of the following three tools: "PDFcontentEraser", "PDFfontChanger" and "PDFcontentExtracter." PDFcontentEraser is a tool to remove a certain type of elements in a PDF file. PDFfontChanger is a tool to change a selection of fonts in a document. PDFcontentExtracter is a tool to retrieve the components of a PDF file.

Keywords: Print disability · Accessibility · PDF documents · Universal design font

1 Introduction

In our daily life, we often read digital documents on the web. Official documents from governments, event guides, floor maps of station, and operating manuals of electronic appliances are usually available in the Portable Document Format (PDF). Therefore, the existence of hard-to-read PDF documents is a big issue for all people, especially for people with print disabilities. A print disability is a difficulty or inability of reading printed material because of a visual, physical, perceptual, developmental, cognitive, or learning disability. Figure 1(a) is a typical example of hard-to-read PDF document. The characters stay on the background image, the gradations of color are too steep, and the selection of fonts can be improved. Fortunately, if we process the document, a readable document can be obtained as shown in Fig. 1(b). This study presents simple tools to process PDF files for people with print disabilities.

Editing software for PDF files has not been widely used. There are commercial tools for editing PDF files, such as "Adobe Acrobat Pro" and "Adobe Illustrator." These tools are capable of editing PDF files freely at a high quality. However, they are not developed for general people, but for DTP engineers. Their prices are very high, and a lot of training is necessary to master them. There are some free tools for handling PDF files such as PDFBox application [1] and PDFtk server [2]. However, they are not user-friendly and does not have enough function for editing to produce readable PDF files.

© Springer Nature Switzerland AG 2020
K. Miesenberger et al. (Eds.): ICCHP 2020, LNCS 12376, pp. 314–320, 2020.
https://doi.org/10.1007/978-3-030-58796-3_37

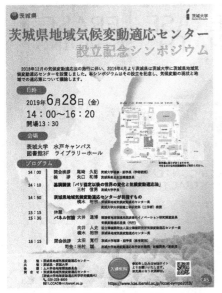

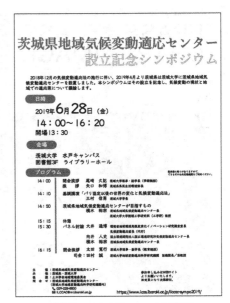

(a) An Example Hard-to-Read Document   (b) Converted Document in PDF

Fig. 1. An Example of Conversion of PDF Files (a poster for an announcement of the start-up symposium of Ibaraki Local Climate Change Adaptation Center, Ibaraki University).

The authors have experience of handling PDF files because the authors' laboratory has been producing Multimodal Textbooks [3,4] for students with print disabilities. Multimodal Textbooks are paper-based textbooks with audio support utilizing invisible 2-dimensional codes and digital audio players with a 2-dimensional code scanner. They were used by 1,110 students in 2018 in Japan. The simple processing tools for PDF files presented in this paper are a reformulation of software developed for the production of Multimodal Textbooks.

The simple processing tools for PDF files are designed for general users including people with print disabilities. They consist of the following three tools: "PDFcontentEraser", "PDFfontChanger" and "PDFcontentExtracter." They are developed in Java using Apache PDFBox library and run on Windows. The usage is very simple. When they are installed on a PC, icons are placed on the desktop as shown in Fig. 2. A PDF file is processed by a drag-and-drop operation to these icons.

PDFcontentEraser is a tool to remove a certain type of elements in a PDF file. A PDF file mainly consists of characters, images, paths, and shadings. This tool can selectively erase all elements of a certain type. PDFfontChanger is a tool to change a selection of fonts in a document. As a default setting, all fonts are replaced by "Universal Design Font for Digital Textbooks" (UD font) [5] developed by Morisawa Inc. The converted document (Fig. 1(b)) is obtained by erasing all images and all shadings using PDFcontentEraser and by changing

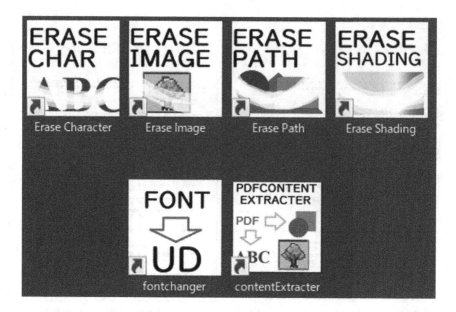

Fig. 2. The icons of the simple tools

all fonts to the UD font from the original document (Fig. 1(a)). PDFcontentExtracter is a tool to retrieve the components of a PDF file. It can output a retrieved
information in XML format.

To evaluate the usability of the simple tools, we measure the working times
for conversions of a PDF file using the simple tools and Adobe Acrobat Pro.
With the simple tools, the conversions were finished much faster without any
mistakes.

2   Simple Processing Tools

The simple processing tools for PDF files are developed on Java with the Apache
PDFBox library and run on Windows.

2.1   PDFcontentEraser

This tool is to remove a certain type of elements in a PDF file. As shown in Fig. 3,
main elements of a PDF file are characters, images, paths, and shadings. When
this tool is installed on a PC, 4 icons are placed on the desktop (the upper
row of Fig. 2). The way to use this tool is just a drag-and-drop operation of a
PDF file to one of the icons. An output file is created in the same folder with a
new file name (the original file name + "_wo_" + the initial letter of the erased
elements). If we want to delete more than one type of elements, we can continue
the drag-and-drop operations.

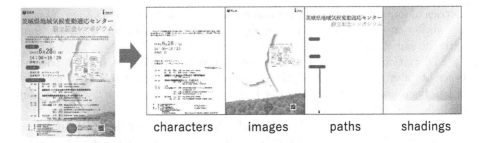

characters   images   paths   shadings

Fig. 3. Main elements of a PDF file

When a person wants to remove annoying background under characters in a document, the tool can remove the images and shadings on the background. In addition, the tool helps for productions of large-printed teaching materials. When characters stay on images overlappingly, the tool can erase all characters over images, and we can obtain clean images from a PDF file.

PDFcontentEraser is a convenient tool for all people to make a readable PDF files. It has been used to create large-printed textbooks for low vision students in Japan.

2.2   PDFfontChanger

This tool is to change a selection of fonts in a document. The usage of the tool is also a drag-and-drop operation to the icon. As a default setting, all fonts are replaced by "Universal Design Font for Digital Textbooks" (UD font) [5] developed by Morisawa Inc. (Fig. 4). From the "Windows 10 Fall Creators Update" in 2017, UD font becomes one of standard fonts in Windows 10 with Japanese language pack. If UD font is not installed on a PC, the tool uses Arial font instead.

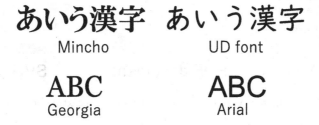

あいう漢字   あいう漢字

Mincho   UD font

ABC   ABC

Georgia   Arial

Fig. 4. Sample of Glyph of UD font, Arial, and Georgia

Though we can change a selection of fonts using Adobe Acrobat Pro, page-layouts of the document might be broken sometimes due to differences of glyph metrics of fonts. PDFfontChanger can replace fonts without any change of page-layouts because each character is replaced by the same character of another font with the same size at the same position.

PDFfontChanger should be used by someone incapable of reading specific types of fonts. In Japan, there are some children who cannot read Mincho font. It has been used to change fonts of large-printed textbooks for low vision and dyslexic students in Japan.

Unlike a conversion to PDF/UA (PDF/Universal Accessibility), the tool does not change the reading order of an original PDF file because this tool is mainly designed for a person who wants to read a document on a screen or a sheet of printed paper. Elementary and junior high school teachers may also want to use this tool. After creating printed materials to be distributed, all the fonts can be replaced for some students who have difficulty of reading particular fonts.

2.3 PDFcontentExtracter

This tool is to retrieve the components of a PDF file. It is a command line tool. It can extract images, character information (position, bounding box, font name, Unicode, and color) and the shapes of paths. This tool can output in the following three forms: (1) character information, image location and path location in XML, (2) image files in PNG, and (3) the shapes of paths, the shapes of characters and the locations of images in SVG (Fig. 5).

PDFcontentExtracter can be used for the development of new PDF processing tools by others.

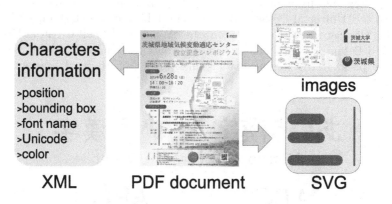

Fig. 5. Types of outputs of PDFcontentExtracter

3   Evaluation

In order to evaluate the usability of the simple processing tools, we compare the time needed to convert a PDF file by using the simple tools and Adobe Acrobat Pro.

3.1   Method

For experimental subjects, 3 university students were employed. They are familiar with using Acrobat Pro.

They were asked to convert the PDF file shown in Fig. 1(a) to the new one shown in Fig. 1(b) by deleting all images and shadings and replacing all font to UD font.

As shown in Fig. 6, the task can be done using PDFcontentEraser and PDF-fontChanger as follows. First, drag-and-drop the file to the "Erase Image" icon and the "Erase Shading" icon. Next, drag-and-drop the output file to the "Font to UD" icon. Then, the requested PDF file is obtained.

Using Acrobat Pro, on the other hand, there are two ways to delete elements in a PDF file: (1) clicking items directly on the document view and pushing the delete key, and (2) showing the content panel, and selecting items there. Changing a selection of fonts can be done by selecting text objects on the document view and choosing a new font from a drop-down list in the side panel. When a selection of fonts is changed, the layout of some text objects becomes broken and needs to be fixed.

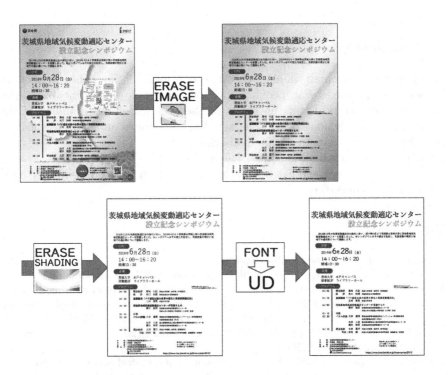

Fig. 6. Operations using processing tools

3.2 Result

The result is shown in Table 1. All subject can convert the document faster with the simple tools than Acrobat Pro. When they used Acrobat Pro, all subjects choose the document view to select items. They made some mistakes using Acrobat Pro; Subject A erased a text object and left a shading object, Subject B selected a wrong font and forgot to fix the layout of a text object, and Subject C deleted a necessary path object.

Table 1. Result of Experiment

	Working time		Number of mistakes	
	Acrobat Pro	Simple tools	Acrobat Pro	Simple tools
Subject A	1 min 31 sec	12 sec	2	0
Subject B	44 sec	10 sec	2	0
Subject C	1 min 10 sec	12 sec	1	0

4   Conclusion

This paper has presented simple processing tools for PDF files. These tools were developed to be used by all people, especially for people with print disabilities and their supporters. From the result of the evaluation, the usability of the simple tools was demonstrated. The simple processing tools for PDF files are available on the website of authors' laboratory:

http://apricot.cis.ibaraki.ac.jp/PDFtools/

In the future, we would like to explore collaboration between the simple tools and PDF/UA converters.

References

1. Apache PDFBox. https://pdfbox.apache.org/
2. PDF Labs PDFtk. https://www.pdflabs.com/tools/pdftk-the-pdf-toolkit/
3. Fujiyoshi, A., Fujiyoshi, M., Ohsawa, A., Ota, Y.: Development of multimodal textbooks with invisible 2-dimensional codes for students with print disabilities. In: Miesenberger, K., Fels, D., Archambault, D., Peňáz, P., Zagler, W. (eds.) ICCHP 2014. LNCS, vol. 8548, pp. 331–337. Springer, Cham (2014). https://doi.org/10.1007/978-3-319-08599-9_50
4. Takaira, T., Tani, Y., Fujiyoshi, A.: Development of a unified production system for various types of accessible textbooks. In: Miesenberger, K., Bühler, C., Penaz, P. (eds.) ICCHP 2016. LNCS, vol. 9758, pp. 381–388. Springer, Cham (2016). https://doi.org/10.1007/978-3-319-41264-1_52
5. Morisawa Inc., Universal Design Fonts (in Japanese). https://www.morisawa.co.jp/fonts/udfont/

Layout Analysis of PDF Documents by Two-Dimensional Grammars for the Production of Accessible Textbooks

Kento Kohase, Shunsuke Nakamura, and Akio Fujiyoshi[✉]

Graduate School of Science and Engineering, Ibaraki University, Hitachi, Japan
{20nm711h,20nm726r,akio.fujiyoshi.cs}@vc.ibaraki.ac.jp

Abstract. This paper proposes the use of two-dimensional context-free grammars (2DCFGs) for layout analysis of PDF documents. In Japan, audio textbooks have been available for students with print disabilities in compulsory education. In order to create accessible textbooks including audio textbooks, it is necessary to obtain the information of structure and the reading order of documents of regular textbooks in PDF. It is not simple task because most PDF files only have the information how to print them out, and page-layouts of most textbooks are complex. By using 2DCFGs, we could obtain useful information of regular textbooks in PDF for the production of accessible textbooks.

Keywords: Accessible textbooks · Layout analysis · PDF documents · Two-dimensional grammars

1 Introduction

In Japan, textbooks are considered to be the primary teaching instruments that are necessary to guarantee the quality of education, and audio textbooks have been available for students with print disabilities in compulsory education. They are mainly Multimedia DAISY Textbooks [1] (Fig. 1(a)), Multimodal Textbook [2] (Fig. 1(b)), and AccessReading [3] (Fig. 1(c)). DAISY is a world standard for digital audio books, and textbooks in the format are provided by Japan Society for Rehabilitation of Persons with Disabilities (used by 10,039 students in 2018). Multimodal Textbooks are paper-based textbooks with audio support utilizing invisible 2-dimensional codes and digital audio players with a 2-dimensional code scanner, provided by the authors' laboratory in Ibaraki University (used by 1,110 students in 2018). AccessReading is digital textbooks in DOCX or EPUB format used with a screenreader on a PC or tablet, provided by Research Center for Advanced Science and Technology, the University of Tokyo (used by 520 students in 2018). Audio textbooks as well as other types of accessible textbooks, such as braille textbooks and large-print textbooks, are made by the efforts of volunteer groups on low budgets in Japan. Since Barrier-Free School Textbooks Act was enforced in Japan in 2008, volunteer groups can obtain PDF files of textbooks from textbook publishing companies.

© Springer Nature Switzerland AG 2020
K. Miesenberger et al. (Eds.): ICCHP 2020, LNCS 12376, pp. 321–328, 2020.
https://doi.org/10.1007/978-3-030-58796-3_38

(a)Multimedia DAISY Textbook   (b)Multimodal Textbook   (c)AccessReading

Fig. 1. Major types of audio textbooks in Japan

(a)   (b)

Fig. 2. Page layout of an English textbook published by Sanseido Co., Ltd.

In order to create any type of audio textbooks, it is necessary to obtain the information of structure and the reading order of documents of regular textbooks in PDF. It is not simple task because most PDF files only have the information how to print them out, and page-layouts of most textbooks are complex. Figure 2 is an example of page-layouts of textbooks. A page-layout is composed of a variety of entities such as texts, lines, words, figures, tables and images (Fig. 2(a)). Region of these entities should be assigned functional or logical labels such as header, footer, main content, sub content, page number, image, etc. (Fig. 2(b)). Hence, we want to have an automatic way to analyze the layout of PDF documents. Though machine learning has attracted attention recently, there are not enough training dataset of the page-layouts of textbooks. This paper proposes the use of two-dimensional context-free grammars (2DCFGs) [4] for layout analysis of PDF documents.

In the formal language theory, 2DCFGs are thought as a powerful tool for layout analysis of two-dimensional objects [5]. For parsing documents with a 2DCFG, we can adopt classical bottom-up or top-down algorithm like CKY or Earley parser. However, there is a problem of using 2DCFGs because their computational complexity for parsing is exponential or a high degree of polynomial in size of inputs. To deal with this, some studies proposed to parse liner projections of the input by 1D grammars. This approach results in a good performance, but has drawbacks such as a weaker expressive power caused by the simplified parsing. Průša and Fujiyoshi introduced a subclass of 2DCFGs where productions have a nonterminal rank reducing property. Parsing documents with a rank-reducing 2DCFG is much faster because they can generate regular languages in the case of 1D productions and be applied a simple top-down parsing algorithm using 1D grammars to reduce the number of backtracks. We think their expressive power is sufficient to model page-layouts of textbooks.

The parsing algorithm is implemented as a function of Multimodal Publication Producer [6], which is an unified production system for various type of accessible textbooks, developed by the authors' laboratory. It is used to create Multimodal Textbooks, and its latest version is available on the website [7]. Because of the new parsing algorithm, the cost of production of Multimodal Textbooks was much reduced.

For an evaluation of the proposed method, we compare its result to those of two titles of commercial OCR software and two titles of commercial PDF authoring software, namely, FineReader (ABBYY), Yomitorikakumei (Panasonic), Shunkan PDF (Antenna House), and Acrobat Pro (Adobe). Three types of PDF documents are prepared: (1) a section of a tale (1 page, 204 characters), (2) tables of Chinese characters (Kanji) from a textbook in Japanese (1 page, 869 characters), and (3) a section of conversations from a textbook in English (1 page, 479 characters). Text files are created from the PDF documents using the five programs (the proposed method and the four titles of commercial software). The outputs are normalized by eliminating unnecessary spaces and symbols. The correct answers of reading order were manually created. We calculate Levenshtein distances between the each output and the correct answer. The score of the proposed method is the best for the three types of documents among the five programs.

This paper is organized as follows. Layout analysis by two-dimensional grammars is described in Sect. 2. Evaluation of the proposed method is described in Sect. 3. Finally, a conclusion of the proposed method is described.

2 Layout Analysis by Two-Dimensional Grammars

2.1 Definition of Two-Dimensional Context-Free Grammars

A two-dimensional context-free grammar (2DCFG) is a tuple $\mathcal{G} = (\mathcal{N}, \mathcal{T}, \mathcal{P}, S)$, where $\mathcal{N}$ is a set of nonterminals, $\mathcal{T}$ is a set of terminals, $S \in \mathcal{N}$ is the initial nonterminal and $\mathcal{P}$ is a set of productions in one of the following forms:

$$(1)\ N \to A, \quad (2)\ N \to A\,|\,B, \quad (3)\ N \to A\,/\,B,$$

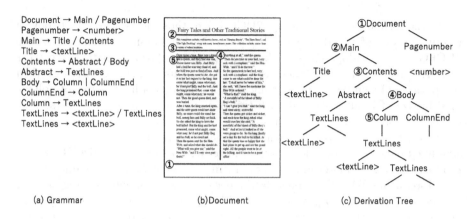

(a) Grammar   (b)Document   (c) Derivation Tree

Fig. 3. Example of layout analysis by a 2DCFG

where $N \in \mathcal{N}$ and $A, B \in \mathcal{T} \cup \mathcal{N}$. The productions follow the Chomsky normal form. A production of type (2) generates a horizontal connection composed of A and B. Analogously, a production of type (3) generates a vertical connection composed of A and B.

Figure 3(a) is an example of a 2DCFG, which is used to parse documents composed of regions of a title, an abstract, a page number, and two columns consisting of text lines. When we parse a document (Fig. 3(b)) using the grammar, a derivation tree can be obtained (Fig. 3(c)). Elemental regions are assigned terminals such as "⟨textLine⟩" and "⟨number⟩". "⟨textLine⟩" means a group of adjoining characters of the same font and size, while "⟨number⟩" means a group of adjoining digits. A production of type (2) or type (3) divides a set of elemental regions into two parts by assigning a nonterminal to each of them.

2.2 Rank-Reducing Property

We say that a 2DCFG $\mathcal{G} = (\mathcal{N}, \mathcal{T}, \mathcal{P}, S)$ is rank-reducing iff, for each $N \in \mathcal{N}$, N is assigned a positive integer which is called a rank of N, and, for each production $N \to B$, $N \to A \,|\, B$ or $N \to A \,/\, B$, the values of rank are $N \geq B > A$, i.e., a nonterminal generates nonterminals whose rank is not greater than its. Let $\mathcal{G}_{\mathrm{T}}$ and $\mathcal{G}_{\mathrm{L}}$ are 1D grammars generated from a rank-reducing 2DCFG as described in [4]. Then, both $\mathcal{G}_{\mathrm{T}}$ and $\mathcal{G}_{\mathrm{L}}$ generate a regular language . This fact can be used to reduce a number of backtracks in a parsing process.

2.3 Top-Down Parsing Algorithm

Algorithm 1 shows an execution of the top-down parsing. The first call of PARSE passes to it a grammar $\mathcal{G} = (\mathcal{N}, \mathcal{T}, \mathcal{P}, S)$, the initial nonterminal S and the set of terminal regions "terms". Procedure MATCHES (terms, V) returns true iff "terms" contains the only terminal region assigned by $V \in \mathcal{N} \cup \mathcal{T}$. Procedure FINDSPLITPOINTS (terms, P) detects all vertical/horizontal cuts by production

P. Given a vertical/horizontal cut (determined by a point s), SPLIT (terms, s, P) divides terminal regions of "terms" into two parts.

Algorithm 1. Top-down parsing

Input: $\mathcal{G} = (\mathcal{N}, \mathcal{T}, \mathcal{P}, S)$, $V \in \mathcal{N} \cup \mathcal{T}$, terms
1: **procedure** PARSE($\mathcal{G}$, V, terms)
2:    **if** $V \in \mathcal{T}$ **and** MATCHES(terms, V) **then**
3:        **return** true
4:    **for each** $P \in \mathcal{P}$ **do**
5:        **if** $P = V \rightarrow A$ **and** PARSE($\mathcal{G}$, A, terms) **then**
6:            **return** true
7:        **else if** $P = V \rightarrow A \,|\, B$ **or** $P = V \rightarrow A \,/\, B$ **then**
8:            SplitPoints = FINDSPLITPOINTS(terms, P)
9:            **for each** $s \in$ SplitPoints **do**
10:                [termsA, termsB] = SPLIT(terms, s, P)
11:                **if** PARSE($\mathcal{G}$, A, termsA) **and** PARSE($\mathcal{G}$, B, termsB) **then**
12:                    **return** true
13:    **return** false

2.4 Implementation

The parsing algorithm is implemented as a function of Multimodal Publication Producer [6], which is an unified production system for various types of accessible textbooks. The system is an application software developed on Java with standard widget toolkit (SWT) and Apache PDFBox library [8]. It runs on multi-platforms: Windows and OS X. Neighboring characters are grouped based on the gap between their bounding boxes. Each group of characters is defined as an elemental region consisting of a bounding box and a word content. We input a list of productions of a 2DCFG as a text file, and the grammar can be changed by editing the text file. Thus, the layout analysis can be used for various types of page-layouts.

2.5 Grammars for Describing of Page-Layouts of Textbooks

There are many types of layouts of a textbook. A textbook in Japanese language has pages such as tales, table of contents, guides, and some types of tables of Chinese characters (Kanji). In order to analyze these pages with different layouts, it is necessary to describe a grammar for each layout of pages. We described 10 different grammars for a textbook in Japanese language, and they are selected automatically or manually in the system. For example, a grammar describing a page of a tale from a textbook in Japanese language composed of 17 nonterminals and 25 productions, and a grammar describing a page of a table of Chinese characters composed of 29 nonterminals and 43 productions.

Figure 4 is a result of layout analysis of a page of a tale. When the page is parsed by the grammar, a derivation tree whose internal nodes are labeled by a nonterminal of the grammar can be obtained (Fig. 4(**b**)). The reading order and the classification of elements are determined by the derivation tree. Figure 4(**a**) shows the classification obtained from the derivation tree. A classification consists of a variety of entities such as BODY, HEAD, NOTE and AUXILIARY for a page of a tale.

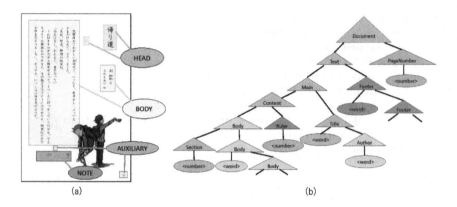

(a)   (b)

Fig. 4. A Result of layout analysis of a textbook

3   Evaluation

For an evaluation of the proposed method, we compare five programs: Multimodal Publication Producer, FineReader (ABBYY), Yomitorikakumei (Panasonic), Shunkan PDF (Antenna House), and Acrobat Pro (Adobe).

3.1   Methods

Three types of PDF documents are prepared: (1) a section of a tale (1 page, 204 characters), (2) tables of Chinese characters (Kanji) from a textbook in Japanese (1 page, 869 characters), and (3) a section of conversations from a textbook in English (1 page, 479 characters). The orders of elements stored in PDF documents are unchanged as they were made in textbook publishing companies. The elements of the document (2) starts from the bottom line though its appropriate reading order should start from the top line.

Text files are created from the PDF documents using the five programs, and then, they are normalized by eliminating unnecessary spaces and symbols. The correct answers of reading order were manually created. Levenshtein distances between each output and the correct answer are calculated.

3.2   Results

The Levenshtein distances between outputs and the correct answer are shown in Table 1. Acrobat Pro just outputs a text file in the order of elements stored in a PDF file. The results of the document (1) shows that the other programs do a kind of layout analysis because their outputs are better than Acrobat Pro. The results of the document (2) shows that layout analysis does not always work properly. The layout of the document (2) requires groupings of elements as shown in Fig. 5(a). However, Shunkan PDF put the elements in a simple order without groupings as shown in Fig. 5(b). The results of FineReader and Yomitorikakumei tend to be poor because they first convert PDF documents into raster images and then use their OCR engines to recognize characters. Misrecognitions occur for some characters.

Table 1. Levenshtein distances to the correct answer

Document	(1)	(2)	(3)
Multimodal Publication Producer	10	0	46
FineReader	53	430	142
Yomitorikakumei	40	630	231
Shunkan PDF	16	780	512
Acrobat Pro	62	280	423

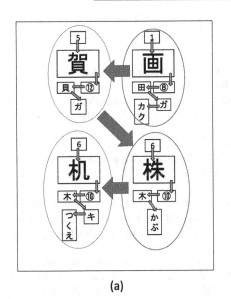 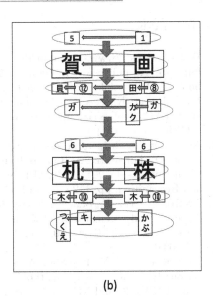

(a)   (b)

Fig. 5. Groupings of elements of the document (2)

3.3   Discussion

If the order of elements in a PDF document is maintained correctly, Acrobat Pro outputs without problems. Shunkan PDF can analyze accurately if layout is simple. FineReader and Yomitorikakumei are equipped with OCR engines, so they can recognize characters in images and vector graphics.

By describing a grammar to model page-layouts, the proposed method can analyze page-layouts with high accuracy. We think the expressive power of rank-reducing 2DCFGs is sufficient to model page-layouts of textbooks used in compulsory education in Japan.

4   Conclusion

This paper proposed the use of two-dimensional context-free grammars (2DCFGs) [4] for layout analysis of PDF documents. Implementing the parsing algorithm as a function of Multimodal Publication Producer [6], a detailed layout analysis ot the textbooks becomes possible.

At present, we have only grammars for page-layouts of textbook for compulsory education in Japan. In the future, we want to design a grammar which is suitable to analyze all page-layouts of the documents.

The latest version of Multimodal Publication Producer with the parsing algorithm for 2DCFGs is available on the website [7].

References

1. DAISY. https://www.dinf.ne.jp/doc/daisy/book/
2. Fujiyoshi, A., Fujiyoshi, M., Ohsawa, A., Ota, Y.: Development of multimodal textbooks with invisible 2-dimensional codes for students with print disabilities. In: Miesenberger, K., Fels, D., Archambault, D., Peňáz, P., Zagler, W. (eds.) ICCHP 2014. LNCS, vol. 8548, pp. 331–337. Springer, Cham (2014). https://doi.org/10.1007/978-3-319-08599-9_50
3. AccessReading. https://accessreading.org/
4. Průša, D., Fujiyoshi, A.: Rank-reducing two-dimensional grammars for document layout analysis. In: 2017 14th IAPR International Conference on Document Analysis and Recognition, pp. 1120–1125 (2017)
5. Álvaro, F., Cruz, F., Sánchez, J.-A., Ramos Terrades, O., Benedi, J.-M.: Structure detection and segmentation of documents using 2D stochastic context-free grammars. Neurocomputing **150**, 147–154 (2015). https://doi.org/10.1016/j.neucom.2014.08.076
6. Takaira, T., Tani, Y., Fujiyoshi, A.: Development of a unified production system for various types of accessible textbooks. In: Miesenberger, K., Bühler, C., Penaz, P. (eds.) ICCHP 2016. LNCS, vol. 9758, pp. 381–388. Springer, Cham (2016). https://doi.org/10.1007/978-3-319-41264-1_52
7. Multimodal Publication Producer. http://apricot.cis.ibaraki.ac.jp/MultimodalPublicationProducer/
8. PDFBox. https://pdfbox.apache.org/

A Multi-site Collaborative Sampling for Web Accessibility Evaluation

Zhi Yu[1,2,3]($\boxtimes$), Jiajun Bu[1,2,3], Chao Shen[1,2,3], Wei Wang[1,2,3],
Lianjun Dai[4], Qin Zhou[4], and Chuanwu Zhao[5]

[1] Zhejiang Provincial Key Laboratory of Service Robot, College of Computer
Science, Zhejiang University, Hangzhou, China
{yuzhirenzhe,bjj,shenchao,wangwei_eagle}@zju.edu.cn
[2] Alibaba-Zhejiang University Joint Institute of Frontier Technologies,
Hangzhou, China
[3] Ningbo Research Institute, Zhejiang University, Ningbo, China
[4] China Disabled Persons' Federation Information Center, Beijing, China
{dailianjun,zhouqin}@cdpf.org.cn
[5] Zhejiang Toman Intelligent Manufacturing Technology Co., Ltd,
Xinchang, China
zhaocw@zjtoman.com

Abstract. Many sampling methods have been used for web accessibility
evaluation. However, due to the difficulty of web page feature extraction and the
lack of unsupervised clustering algorithm, the result is not very good. How to
optimize the manual workload of different websites under the premise of
ensuring that the overall manual workload remains the same during multi-site
collaborative sampling is an important issue at present. To resolve the above
problems, we propose a multi-site collaborative sampling method to obtain the
final sampling result of each website. The effectiveness of the two sampling
methods proposed in this paper is proved by experiments on real website
datasets.

Keywords: Information accessibility · Accessibility evaluation · Sampling
method · Active learning · Semi-supervised clustering

1 Introduction

The rise of various e-commerce websites has connected our online and offline lives.
However, most of these websites were not designed with information access methods
for people with disabilities in mind. For example, the visually impaired can only read
the content of a web page by reading screen software and traversing the focus. If the
website is designed without considering the compatibility of the reading screen software, it will block the people with visual impairment from accessing the information.
Instead, according to the survey in 2010, there were 85.02 million disabled people in
China, and the number of disabled people in the world exceeded 1 billion. In order to
meet the requirements of information accessibility, anyone can obtain information

K. Miesenberger et al. (Eds.): ICCHP 2020, LNCS 12376, pp. 329–335, 2020.
https://doi.org/10.1007/978-3-030-58796-3_39

equally and effectively under any circumstances. The information gap of disabled people in the current Internet information age deserves attention.

In order to enable people with disabilities to enjoy the benefit of Internet information on an equal basis with able-bodied people, the World Wide Web Consortium (W3C) published the first website content accessibility guide [1] (WCAG 1.0) in 1995. Website provides effective guidance. With the wide application of this guide in countries around the world, and considering some existing limitations, the W3C released WCAG2.0 in November 2008 [2]. WCAG2.0 has made a lot of supplements to WCAG1.0. It is designed with practicality in mind. It is no longer limited to specific technologies, and has made many compatibility considerations for future technologies.

Based on this, we have developed a web accessibility evaluation system for the Chinese government. Through accessibility assessment of the website, we obtain website detection results and suggestions to guide website accessibility reconstruct. However, affected by the lack of automatic detection tools, the detection process still requires the participation of accessible experts. For the thousands of web pages, manual inspection of each webpage becomes impractical, so web page sampling came into being. Because the quality of the sampling effect will directly affect the website's ultimate barrier-free overlap, which sampling algorithm is currently a major problem.

Existing web accessibility evaluation sampling methods give more consideration to how to extract which pages within a web site as a sample collection for accessibility assessment. In actual testing tasks, a batch of websites are usually evaluated at the same time. However, due to the limitation of accessibility testing expert resources, how to reasonably allocate the number of expert resources to each website (that is, how to determine when the total number of samples is fixed, the sample and quantity of each website) is often overlooked. The current number of samples for each website is usually determined by the number of pages on the website. If the number of pages on the website is larger, the sample set obtained by sampling will be larger, so more accessibility testing experts will be assigned for testing, and vice versa, The less. However, this method of allocating expert resources according to the number of website pages does not take into account the impact of website complexity, resulting in a higher overall sampling error.

In the process of multi-site collaborative sampling, it is unreasonable to only consider the number of website pages to determine the sample and quantity of each website. We should also fully consider the impact of differences in website structure. To solve the above problem, this paper proposes Multi-site collaborative sampling. The effectiveness of this method proposed in this paper is proved by experiments on real website datasets.

2 Related Work

In this part, we briefly review the related works in web page sampling methods for Web accessibility evaluation.

Random sampling guarantees that every page in the website will be sampled with equal probability. However, the distribution of checkpoints is not evenly distributed. For example, a verification code is a checkpoint that appears on only a few pages. For a website with a large number of pages, when random sampling is used, there will be a high probability that web pages containing verification code will not be extracted, causing sampling errors.

The Ad-hoc sampling method proposed by W3C/WAI and UWEM [3] first sets sampling rules in advance by domain experts. However, the shortcomings of this method are also obvious. Due to the complex website structure and the huge number of websites, it is difficult to accurately find different types of web pages. In addition, due to human intervention, this method requires high cost and has certain subjectivity.

The random walk sampling method [4] consists of two phases: 1) the walk phase: starting from the homepage of the website, selecting a webpage from the URL out of the webpage with probability p to visit; returning to the previous visit pages with probability 1−p; 2) Sampling phase: Take a specified number of web pages from the pages visited during the wandering phase as the final sample. Because the random walk sampling method does not need to obtain a complete set of web pages, compared with random sampling, the calculation and storage overhead are relatively small. In addition, compared with Ad-hoc sampling, because no manual intervention is required, this method is more objective. However, this method tends to select lower-level web pages as samples, ignoring deep-level web pages, so that the most representative web pages in the entire website cannot usually be obtained.

In order to make the sampling samples reflect the characteristics of checkpoints, King et al. Proposed a sampling method based on the distribution of checkpoints [5]. This method first uses automatic detection tools to count the automatic detection results of each web page, and then based on the automatic detection of these web pages. The detection results are clustered. Finally, according to the cluster size, random sampling is performed from each cluster to form the final sample set. This method is based on the inaccurate assumption that the distribution of automatic checkpoints is the same as the distribution of manual checkpoints, which leads to errors in the detection of manual detection items.

Zhang [6] proposed a semi-supervised method based on active prediction to try to solve the problem of web page sampling and evaluation based on web structure checkpoints. This method again actively learns appointments to the picked webpages, and actively selects the best alternative webpages for manual detection, so that it can get smaller errors while reducing its detection cost. The limitation of this method is that it divides the accessibility results into only two categories: pass and fail, this simple pass and fail cannot judge the performance of the two websites on the checkpoint more accurately.

3   Sampling Method

How to optimize the manual workload of different websites under the premise of ensuring that the overall manual workload remains the same during multi-site collaborative sampling is an important issue at present.

Inspired by the idea of turning accessibility sampling problems into active prediction problems proposed by [6], we use an active learning method based on a sample selection strategy that combines uncertainty and representativeness. Compared with an active learning method based on a statistical model, this method has a lower computational complexity, but the difficulty of this method lies in how to select each iteration. Measure the uncertainty and representativeness of each sample.

We use Hinted SVM [7] to ensure that the training query hyperplane can better distinguish untrained sample web pages. By integrating the Active Learning Webpage Sampling Model with Hinted SVM, we can obtain the active learning webpage sampling algorithm AL-HSVM (Active Learning Hinted SVM) based on the hinted support vector machine.

Initially, we randomly select a small number of web pages Pl for manual detection, and then in each iterative process of active learning, first select a subset Ph from the undetected web page set Pu as the hint pool, and then use Hinted SVM training from Pl and Ph. The training obtained the hyperplane h. Finding the closest webpages to h from the undetected webpage set Pu can be regarded as the webpage with the highest uncertainty and the best representation, that is to say, it needs manual detection in the next cycle. And all the similar pages will be removed from the hint pool.

In the process of collaborative sampling of multiple websites, because the numbers of pages corresponding to each website are different, we find the most uncertain pages according to Hinted SVM in each website, and then delete them in the hint pool The number of similar pages is also different. For a website with a simple structure, it only contains a small number of page templates, but the number of pages generated by these page templates is large. When we delete similar pages, we can usually delete a large number of similar pages. Therefore, the size of the current hint pool can reflect the complexity of the website structure to a certain extent. If in the current iteration step, the hint pool still contains a lot of web pages, it means that there are still many different templates in this site that have not been detected by the query hyperplane, so more detection resources need to be allocated for it to make hint pool size reduction. In order to avoid the impact of the difference in the number of pages on different websites, we use the ratio of the number of pages in the hint pool to the total number of pages on the website to horizontally compare the size of the hint pool for different websites.

Therefore, our sampling strategy is: First, each website randomly selects a small number of web pages for detection, obtains a set of detected web pages, and initializes the hint pool for all undetected web pages. In each subsequent iteration, we calculate the hint pool size of each site, select the site with the largest size and perform an AL-HSVM iteration on it. While selecting web pages for expert detection, all pages with a similar structure to this page are removed from the hint pool. Repeat the above steps until the number of samples reaches the specified total number of samples.

4 Experiment

We do an experiment to verify the validity of our method in real Web accessibility evaluation data. We will start with dataset description.

This experimental data set was collected by the accessibility detection system on October 24, 2018, and these sites were also tested for accessibility based on the detection entries and accessibility scores for each web page were obtained. There are five websites in this experimental data set, the first two of which are provincial disability federations, the third one is a website of a unit directly under the China Disabled Persons' Federation, and the last two are social websites with a high daily frequency.

4.1   Experiment for Single Website Sampling

First we do the experiment to verify the prediction model based on the web pages selected by active learning can obtain better prediction results with less detection cost than the prediction model established by randomly selected web pages.

As can be seen from the Fig. 1, which shows the accuracy of different sampling methods, AL-HSVM not only considered the uncertainty of the detection result of the webpage when selecting the webpage, but also considered the representativeness of the webpage in the entire website. Therefore, compared to AL-Uncertainty, a sampling method that only considers the uncertainty of webpage detection results, and AL-Representative sampling method, which only considers the representativeness of webpages, AL-HSVM is significantly higher than them in prediction accuracy. It can be found that the AL-HSVM method can obtain higher prediction accuracy under fewer web pages.

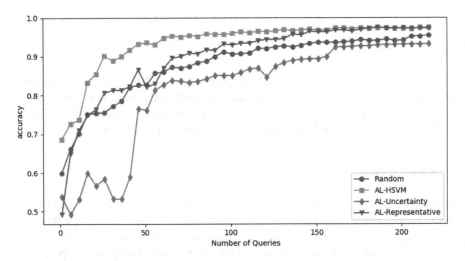

Fig. 1. The accuracy of different sampling method.

4.2   Experiment for Multi-site Collaborative Sampling

Another experiment is mainly used to verify the effectiveness of multi-site collaborative sampling algorithm based on active learning. It is verified that the method can more reasonably allocate the sample number of each website and determine which pages are extracted from each website under a certain total sample number, so that the total sampling error is minimized.

In addition to the collaborative learning algorithm based on active learning proposed in this article, the comparison algorithms in this experiment include:

In this experiment, we use the sum of the sampling errors of all websites as the evaluation criteria. The result is shown in Fig. 2.

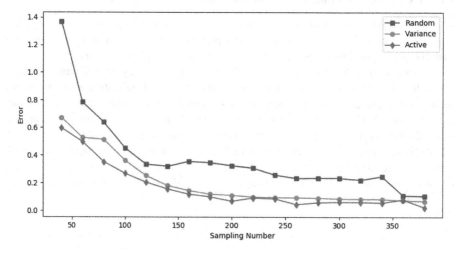

Fig. 2. The accuracy of different sampling method.

We can clearly see that the total sampling error of the multi-site collaborative sampling algorithm based on active learning is significantly lower than the other two methods. Furthermore, let us observe that when the total number of samples is 75, the number of samples and the sampling error representation of each website.

5 Conclusion

We propose a multi-site collaborative sampling method based on active learning. This method aims to more reasonably determine the number of samples for each website and which pages to use as samples, under the condition of manual detection costs, so as to minimize the overall sampling errors. This method uses a hinting-based support vector machine's active learning sampling algorithm. When selecting the next webpage to be detected, in addition to combining the uncertainty of the webpage detection results, it also treats the undetected webpages as hint, check the distribution of web pages as one of the basis for selection. After that, through the improved hint pool reduction strategy and the multi-site collaborative sample selection strategy, each time a sample is taken from the website with the smallest hint pool to obtain the final sampling results of each website. At the same time, many different types of experiments are designed. The sampling method proposed in this paper is compared with the current commonly used accessibility evaluation sampling methods. The performance of each sampling method on multiple different types of website data sets is verified.

Although the sampling method proposed in this paper effectively reduces the sampling error, there are still some shortcomings. In the multi-site collaborative sampling method, we divide the detection results of each web page into two types: Pass and Fail. However, the result is too high. It is rough and cannot effectively reflect the accessibility differences between different web pages. In the future, we can try to refine the accessibility detection results.

Acknowledgments. This work is supported by Alibaba-Zhejiang University Joint Institute of Frontier Technologies, The National Key R&D Program of China (No. 2018YFC2002603, 2018-YFB1403202), Zhejiang Provincial Natural Science Foundation of China (No. LZ13F020001), the National Natural Science Foundation of China (No. 61972349, 61173185, 61173186) and the National Key Technology R&D Program of China (No. 2012BAI34B01, 2014BAK15B02).

References

1. Chisholm, W., Vanderheiden, G., Jacobs, I.: Web content accessibility guidelines 1.0. Interactions 8(4), 35–54 (2001)
2. World Wide Web Consortium: Web content accessibility guidelines (WCAG) 2.0 (2008)
3. Velleman, E., Velasco, C.A., Snaprud, M., et al.: D-WAB4 unified web evaluation methodology (UWEM 1.0). Technical report, WAB Cluster (2006)
4. Ulltveit-Moe, N., Snaprud, M., Nietzio, A., et al.: Early results from automatic accessibility benchmarking of public European web sites from the european internet accessibility observatory (EIAO) (2006)
5. King, M., Thatcher, J.W., Bronstad, P.M., et al.: Managing usability for people with disabilities in a large web presence. IBM Syst. J. 44(3), 519–535 (2005)
6. Zhang, M., Wang, C., Yu, Z., et al.: Active learning for Web accessibility evaluation. In: Proceedings of the 14th Web for All Conference on the Future of Accessible Work, p. 16. ACM (2017)
7. Li, C.L., Ferng, C.S., Lin, H.T.: Active learning using hint information. Neural Comput. 27(8), 1738–1765 (2015)

AT and Accessibility for Blind and Low Vision Users

An Overview of the New 8-Dots Arabic Braille Coding System

Oussama El Ghoul[1]([envelope]) [ID], Ikrami Ahmed[2]([envelope]), Achraf Othman[1]([envelope]) [ID],
Dena A. Al-Thani[1]([envelope]) [ID], and Amani Al-Tamimi[1]([envelope])

[1] Mada Center, Al Nasr Tower B, 8th Floor, Doha, Qatar
{oelghoul, aothman, aaltamimi}@mada.org.qa,
dalthani@hbku.edu.qa
[2] Qatar Social and Cultural Center for Blind, Doha, Qatar
ikrami.ahmad@gmail.com

Abstract. Considering the rapid technological development and especially for assistive technology, the six-point Braille system has become insufficient to meet the needs of the blind and enable them to read, write content, and, to publish accessible documents. This system is not sufficient to write and produce scientific contents that contain several symbols. Despite this need, the Arabic language still lacks an eight-point coding system. In this context, this paper aims to present a unified eight-point Braille system and present it to Arab communities to get benefit from it in developing digital content for blind people. The Arabic language differs from the Latin and other languages in the number of letters and diacritics, which makes the coding system different from the one used in these languages. In this work, we studied the symbols used in the Arabic language and the current Braille system and looked for methods and recommendations regarding the design of the eight-point Braille system. A methodology and a set of principles have been identified that have been adopted in preparing the system, and rules for coding have been established.

Keywords: Braille · 8 dots Braille · Assistive technology · Accessibility

1 Introduction

Braille is the only and unique method that enables blind or deaf-blind people who have difficulties to access to printed materials to read and write. In fact, the ability to write and read in braille opens the door to knowledge, intellectual freedom, equal opportunity and personal security. Nowadays The cost of Braille electronic devices has begun to decrease significantly, which means that a larger segment of the blind - especially in developing countries - can access Braille electronic devices, but there is not enough content to support the Arab Braille.

Although Braille has become important for teaching literature and science for blind people, Braille's coding of the Arabic language is still not developed to accommodate scientific symbols such as those used in mathematics, physics, or even chemistry. This is because the eight-point Braille coding system is not yet adopted.

K. Miesenberger et al. (Eds.): ICCHP 2020, LNCS 12376, pp. 339–345, 2020.
https://doi.org/10.1007/978-3-030-58796-3_40

In this context, this paper aims to present an eight-point braille coding system for the Arabic language. A scientific methodology for identifying symbols has been designed upon by relying on five rules that are subject to six principles that have been adjusted by following previous studies.

2 Related Work

The six-dots Braille systems allow encoding of a maximum of 63 characters, which is sufficient to encode letters, numbers, punctuation marks, and some signs of the approved Braille system. However, these systems do not provide enough coding capacity for coding symbols used in science such as mathematics, physics, chemistry or even music. Hence the importance of the eight-dots coding system, which enables coding up to 255 symbols. This gives sufficient scope for the inclusion of all the important symbols. Using this system allows people with visual disabilities to read and write scientific, literary and artistic contents. Adopting a Unified Arabic Braille coding system is become important to allow Arabic blinds to create and read Arabic content.

Worldwide there are two primarily unified braille systems that are mostly used: The Unified English Braille UEB and The Nemeth Uniform Braille System NUBS [2, 6]. Both are used to transcribe and represent all letters and formats used on English documents into braille. The UEB is more suitable for text representation, in fact, it's derived from the classic six-dot Braille that encodes 26 small letters and 14 punctuation symbols with one cell. However, NUBS is mainly used for representing mathematical and scientific contents. Unfortunately, there are many mismatches between the two systems.

3 Motivation

According to many blind people, the current Braille coding system suffers from several limitations. In this context, the Mada Center for Assistive Technology conducted a questionnaire on the problems and limitations that users of the current Arab Braille see and want to fix. The questionnaire covered all Arab countries, and we got 80 answers from 17 countries. The questionnaire was directed to all persons who use this system from teachers, students and other users. We received 80 answers, as 67% of people who completed the questionnaire are using Braille to learn and/or read, which indicates the importance of this system in their daily lives (Fig. 1). The answers also confirmed that 96% participant are fluent in Arabic braille and 77% of them are fluent in a coding system other than Arabic, which means that their answers will be based on a comparison between the Arab Braille system and other systems. This makes their answers more realistic and accurate. In fact, 72% of the participants confirmed that they are daily users of Braille.

After analysing the results we concluded that 70% of the participants think that the current Arabic Braille contains many limitations. Furthermore, 83% of the participants believe that work should be done to develop the current Arab Braille system.

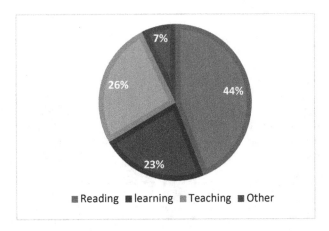

Fig. 1. For which purposes you use Braille?

Concerning the limitations of the Arabic Braille we prepared a set of 8 options to be chosen by the participants. Each participant can choose one or many options and he can propose additional limitation.

List of limitations :

- **L1** : Some symbols and signs are not defined in Arabic Braille, such as new symbols that appeared in modern software and applications, non-Arabic characters that entered the Arabic language to encode local dialects, and so on.
- **L2** : There are ambiguities and inconsistencies between many letters and symbols, with more than one symbol sharing the same bullet representation in Braille.
- **L3** : Relying on the reader's ability to distinguish the symbol through the context, which makes the Arab braille inappropriate for all literary and artistic contexts and makes it difficult to learn.
- **L4** : Problems in writing Arabic texts via devices.
- **L5** : There are low-usage letters or symbols that can be replaced by used ones that are not present in the current system.
- **L6** : Inconsistent Braille usage rules for typing numbers and spaces before and after symbols.
- **L7** : Others.
- **L8** : No-Limitations.

As shown on the following Chart, 50% of participants confirms that the current Arabic Braille does not encode some importants signs and symbols that appeared in moder software and applications or the new non-Arabic characters that entered the Arabic language to encode local dialects. Furthermor, many participants complain of confusion and inconsistencies between many letters and symbols, with more than one symbol sharing the same dot representation in Braille.

We asked participant about the use of 8-dot Braille to overcome the limitations of the current 6-dot Arabic Braille. 67% of them think that by adding 2 additional dots we

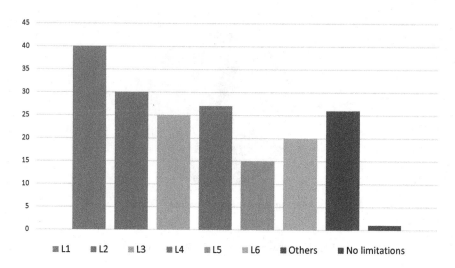

Fig. 2. Limitations of the current Arabic Braille system.

can encode more symbols and decrise the confusion and the inconsistencies rate between many letters and symbols.

The results of the survey confirms that the development of an 8-dot for Arabic language is important an become a request from the Braille users communities (Fig. 2).

4 Specificities of the Arabic Language

The Arabic alphabet is the alphabet that uses the Arabic letters for writing, and it is described as the most complete writing system, it included most of the sounds that a person can speak; derived from it many of the alphabets and the alphabet remained the most used for many centuries and is currently the most used writing system after the alphabet Latin. Many languages rely on the Arabic alphabet for writing, such as Urdu, Ottoman, Kurdish, and Malay [3, 4].

Arabic letters are written from right to left, in a style that depends on joining the letters of one word to each other, and these alphabets include 28 basic letters, and some consider them 29 letters as Hamza is a separate letter.

Contextual adjustments can be made to some letters [6]. The following characters are not individual letters, but are contextual adjustments of some Arabic characters ى : آ ة

The Arabic language is distinguished from the rest of the other languages by the 8 diacritics that are drawn on its letters, and diacritics are signs and movements to set the letters to be pronounced correctly [5].

Some languages that use the Arabic alphabet to write in their language add some additional letters, in order to translate some foreign letters phonetically, here are some of those letters:

- ڤ - which is used to denote the letter "V" in Latin characters when phonetic translation. This letter is also used in writing dialects that pronounce this sound. The letter "ڤ" is usually used in the phonetic translation of the Latin "V". This letter is used to express the sound "Pa".
- پ - used to indicate the letter "P" when transliterating. Therefore, the word "7up" can be copied in this way: "سفن أب ", or in this way: "سفن أپ ". The letter is also used in Persian and Urdu.
- چ - Cha: The letter is used to clarify the sound [tʃ], in Persian, Urdu, and Kurdish. Sometimes the letter is used in phonetic translation, although the Arabic word "Cha" is used using the compound "تشا".
- گ - it refers to the non-thirsty "gym" in some languages.
- ژ - Zhi, (by breaking Zain). This letter is used to express a spoken frictional voice that comes out from behind the "palate", in the Persian, Kurdish, Urdu and Uyghur languages. This letter is used to translate sounds that are of foreign origin. It is rare for the sound "[ʒ]" to appear in the Arabic language, and the shin "ش" is usually used in the phonetic translation of this sound "[ʒ]". This letter is used in Persian and Urdu.

According to our study on the Arabic language, at least 45 symbols should be reserved for encoding the Arabic letters.

5   Methodology

An eight-dot Braille Unicode is defined by the Unicode Consortium. It offers an encoding capacity of 256 symbols using a single cell [1]. Based on the Unicode Braille we proposed a new mapping for the Arabic 8-dots Braille.

The proposed Arabic eight-dot Braille maps most-used one-cell symbols – it contains:

- 29 small letters
- 3 contextual adjustment letters
- 8 diacritics {ó̈ ó̇ ó̂ ǒ̈ o̦ ȯ̦ ó̇ ó̇}
- 10 digits
- 35 punctuations and computer symbols
- 26 Greek symbols {α β θ δ ε φ γ η ι χ κ λ μ ν ο π ∑ ρ σ τ υ Ω ξ ψ ζ}
- 14 basic math symbols
- 10 trigonometrical, logarithmic, and calculus symbols
- 9 set theory & logic symbols
- 5 geometry symbols
- 8 formatting symbols
- 21 patterns towards new indictors/prefixes {superscript, subscript, start-radical, endradical, start-radical-index, ovelay-above, overlay-below, overlay-across, cancel-previous, endsubscript/superscript/radical-index/overlay, tally-markindicator, bullet-prefix, set-tactile-graphics-mode, set-braillegraphics-mode, set-math-mode, end-math/graphics-mode, setlanguage, set-currency, set-braille-code-system}
- Thus Braille-8 becomes an extension of classic six-dots braille.

Table 1. Principles used for creating the Unified Arabic Braille Encoding System

Principle	Description
Compression	Map as many symbols as possible to a single braille cell. This principle aims to reduce the number of cells used to encode texts and facilitate reading.
Intra-Similarity	Considering the existence of a 6-dot code. It is important to maintain a link with the 6-dot encoding system.
Inter-Similarity	Maintain a minimum of similarity with transition rules adopted by other languages.
Unambiguity	Ensure the coherence of the code when a combination of more that one cell is used to encode a character.
Consistency	Use the same transition rules to encode characters of the same category.
User friendly	Use a tactile based assignment/mapping for characters encoding to suit visually challenged users.
Coverage	Unified Arabic Braille should cater to the needs of math, science, and computer science, as well as the transcribing codes.
Foresight	Consider possible expansions in other areas (e.g. scientific braille, computer braille) by providing unbounded cells or sharing characters.

In order to control the coding process through scientific rules, we have defined a set of principles that we will rely on when deciding which symbols to adopt. We adopted a set of principles proposed by [2] and we added one principle that we considered important (User friendly).

The adopted process was carried out in the following stages: 1- Defining the list of symbols used in the six-point system, including indicators and structuring symbols. 2- Defining the list of new symbols and indicators. 3- Classifying symbols into groups. 4- Applying the following rules [2] to encode the set of symbols of each group.

Rule 1: Retain the 6-dot representation. According to the principle of Intra-Similarity, the priority was given to the symbols mapped to one 6-dot cell.

Rule 2: Maintain as much as possible the system adopted in UEB and NUBS. It aims to maximize Inter-Similarity.

Rule 3: Use the dots 7 and 8 to encode the group's identifier. In order to have a structured representation. It aims to have a user-friendly representation.

Rule 4: Use the dots 3 and 6 to encode the sub-groups identifier if needed.

After finishing the development of the new 8-Dots Braille system we implemented it on the opensource Liblouis library. The proposed tables are published on the last version of Liblouis (3.14). The tables can be now downloaded and used for free. We planified to conduct a new survey in order to evaluate the new library after weeks of uses.

6   Conclusion

In this paper, we presented a new Unified Arabic eight-dot braille system. The system is created according to a set of rules that we defined in order to follow the international requirements. The methodology of implementation and identification of rules was done by researchers and persons with visual impairments and blinds in all milestones through focus groups and one-to-one discussion. This approach helps us to get into consideration all challenges that face Braille-users and to understand the need to have a new 8-dots braille system.

References

1. ISO/TR 11548–2:2001, 1st ed., Part 2: Communication aids for blind persons identifiers, names and assignation to coded character sets for 8-dot Braille characters Latin alphabet based character sets. International Standards Organization. Zurich, Switzerland (2001)
2. Kacorri, H., Kouroupetroglou, G.: Design and Developing Methodology for 8-dot Braille Code Systems. In: Stephanidis, C., Antona, M. (eds.) UAHCI 2013. LNCS, vol. 8011, pp. 331–340. Springer, Heidelberg (2013). https://doi.org/10.1007/978-3-642-39194-1_39
3. Martos, A., Kouroupetroglou, G., Argyropoulos, V., Deligiorgi, D.: Towards the 8-dot Nemeth braille code. Lect. Notes Comput. Sci. **8547**, 533–536 (2014)
4. Abdallah, M.A., Khairuddin, O.: "Quranic Baille System", World Academy of Science, Engineering and Technology,4–6,2008
5. Abualkishik, A., Omar, K.: Framework for translating the Holy Quran and its reciting rules to Braille code. In: International Conference on Research and Innovation in Information Systems (ICRIIS), 2013. IEEE (2013)
6. Vistrit, G.: Braille-8 – the Unified Braille Unicode System. In: IEEE International Conference on Advanced Networks and Telecommunications Systems (ANTS), ISBN: 978–1-5090-2193-2, (2016)

Image-Based Recognition of Braille Using Neural Networks on Mobile Devices

Christopher Baumgärtner, Thorsten Schwarz(✉), and Rainer Stiefelhagen

Study Centre for the Visually Impaired, Karlsruhe Institute of Technology,
Engesserstr. 4, 76131 Karlsruhe, Germany
thorsten.schwarz@kit.edu
https://www.szs.kit.edu

Abstract. Braille documents are part of the collaboration with blind people. To overcome the problem of learning Braille as a sighted person, a technical solution for reading Braille would be beneficial. Thus, a mobile and easy-to-use system is needed for every day situations. Since it should be a mobile system, the environment cannot be controlled, which requires modern computer vision algorithms. Therefore, we present a mobile Optical Braille Recognition system using state-of-the-art deep learning implemented as an app and server application.

Keywords: Optical Braille Recognition · Deep learning · Mobile devices

1 Introduction

The Convention on the Rights of Persons with Disabilities aims to ensure that all people with disabilities are fully included in all areas of society. This also implies that people with blindness can communicate with people without blindness without obstacles. Since Braille is the printed script of people who are blind, knowledge of Braille would improve cooperation, e.g. for teachers at regular schools or lecturers at universities who teach blind students. However, learning Braille is very difficult due to different Braille systems such as Braille with six or eight dots, contractions, shorthand, Braille for various languages, Braille for music, math and other fields, which makes it even harder to learn. Mobile approaches on a modern smartphone or a tablet that allow scanning with an on-board camera and translating Braille into text could solve this problem, without using a special hardware. A system like that needs to overcome different challenges. First, it must detect and recognize embossed Braille using a camera. When a mobile system is used, the environment in which the data is collected cannot be controlled, which in turn is a challenge for the computer vision algorithms used. A second challenge arises from the documents themselves. Braille documents can be created using various techniques and therefore the output looks very different, which makes it difficult to recognize Braille. Another problem is the conversion

© Springer Nature Switzerland AG 2020
K. Miesenberger et al. (Eds.): ICCHP 2020, LNCS 12376, pp. 346–353, 2020.
https://doi.org/10.1007/978-3-030-58796-3_41

of recognized Braille into text. The transliteration is not trivial. Braille characters are ambiguous and depend on the system used. The identification of the system and contractions must also be addressed.

In this paper, we present the development of a mobile Optical Braille Recognition (OBR) system using state-of-the-art deep learning techniques.

2 Related Work

There are many approaches dealing with Optical Braille Recognition. An overview of seven different optical Braille recognition algorithms are given by Isayed and Tahboub (2015) [7]. They derive a common pipeline used in most publications. First, data is captured, mostly using flatbed scanners. Then the images are converted to gray-scale. A rotation correction is done using projections of the image onto the x- and y-axis. This method is also used for extracting the different lines and columns Braille is arranged in. The Braille dots are usually detected using static or dynamic threshold algorithms on a global or local level. To improve the results and to remove unwanted noise, morphological operations are utilized. After the dots are segmented, a grouping is performed. Therefore the lines and columns are used to divide the text in single character cells. The characters are recognized by splitting every cell in its 6- or 8-dot structure. Every possible dot position is checked for existence of a dot. The translation is usually done via translation tables.

Besides the papers discussed in [7], there are some other interesting approaches not using flatbed scanners. Hentzschel et al. (1995) introduce the twin-shadow-approach [5]. Their system uses a fixed camera, directly over the document, and two light sources. The lights are placed on the right and left side of the document at an angle. The system takes two pictures, using one light individually. The two images show the same scene but different lighting and shadows. The two pictures are used to calculate the difference picture. By doing this, nearly everything but the different shadows can be removed.

Schwarz et al. [13] presented a system based on [5]. They mounted a camera in a black box, and for lighting, several LED-stripes are placed on each side. By taking the brightness gradient into account, this system can remove the print from objects. The result only displays the Braille embossing. They also utilize the dedicated library, Liblouis* [9], for reverse translation from Braille to text. It uses translation tables for numerous different Braille languages and variants to convert text to Braille. Based on these tables a reverse translation is implemented. The drawback of the system is that it is far from being mobile.

Considering current approaches of optical character recognition (OCR), the state of the art is based on neural networks. These models haven't been used in OBR yet, but show great results in general OCR. One of these approach was published by Shi et al. [14] in 2016. They use a combination of Convolutional Neural Networks (CNN) and Long Short-Term Memories (LSTM) for OCR. Image features are extracted using the CNN creating multiple feature maps. The columns of these maps are used as input for a bidirectional LSTM successively.

The LSTM creates a per-frame prediction distribution over all possible characters. A transcription layer generates the final text output based on the predictions. Building upon the architecture of Shi et al., Deng et al. [2] introduce another model using CNNs and LSTMs. In addition to the former architecture, Deng et al. used an attention mechanism to take spatial information into account. Their system is used to recognize mathematical equations from images. The attention mechanism yields better performance for this problem. This leads back to the spatial arrangement of symbols being critical for mathematical equations.

3   The Mobile Braille Scanner

In our approach, we use different smartphones, like a Huawei P20 Lite and a P20 Pro as a mobile Braille scanner combined with a server for computationally intensive processes. For this purpose, we develop a mobile application for the smartphone with the aim of capturing images of Braille documents and translating Braille into standard text using modern image processing. By outsourcing the majority of the image processing to an external server, the requirements for the smartphone are low, which means that the App requires Android 8 (API level 26 [4]) or higher.

3.1   Design Challenges

A great challenge for a mobile system is that images may vary widely in background, lighting and overall quality of the image. Former approaches [5,13] use controlled lighting to make the dots more visible. Inspired by that, we use a flashlight to create shadows for each Braille dot. We observed that the flashlight increases the visibility of the Braille by creating bright spots and shadows. But in contrast to a scanned document, the page is very uneven lit. Moreover, depending on the ambient lighting, the effect of the flashlight may vary. Those images can not be easily processed using simple threshold algorithms and morphological operations. Thus, we use modern deep learning architectures to detect and recognize Braille.

3.2   Processing Pipeline

The processing pipeline is shown in Fig. 1. First, the images are cropped. After converting to gray-scale, a line detection is performed. Therefore a Faster R-CNN [12] is used. Faster R-CNNs are neural networks based on a CNN and Region-Proposal Network, which are used for object detection. The model is pre-trained on the COCO data set [10] and fine-tuned with our own data set.

After line detection, the cropped lines are used as an input for character recognition. A histogram equalization is applied to increase the contrast. We use a model based on the architecture of Deng et al. [2] with a standard attention mechanism. To train the model from scratch, we use a second data set which is discussed in more detail in the subsequent Sect. 3.3.

3.3   Generation of the Training and Evaluation Corpus

We used three different types of corpora to cover different scanning conditions in our training and evaluation corpora: (i) images of pages of a book printed with three different embossers[1] to obtain a variation of different embossing techniques, (ii) generated images on the basis of the first corpus and sentences from the dataset "German Vocabulary" of Leipzig University [11], where the lighting conditions and background are varied to simulate shots from different angles with different background (iii) images of documents that contain both, normal print and Braille.

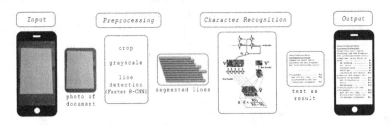

Fig. 1. Processing pipeline including preprocessing with line detection and character recognition

Neural networks are usually trained on annotated data. Therefore, we needed segmented data for our training regime, containing bounding boxes of lines for line detection and line images for OBR in Braille and normal print, as well as a mapping for Braille to normal print. We captured images of our first corpus without additional light source because it was pure Braille without normal print. The corpus was semi-automatically annotated and manually corrected. Annotating, however, is time-consuming and laborious and large amounts of data are required to develop robust models for neural networks. Therefore, we automatically generated the second corpus together with the annotations for lines, characters and mappings in order to significantly enlarge the training corpus. The third corpus contained images of documents either embossed with Emfuse

Table 1. Data set for Optical Braille Recognition. Number of lines for training, validation and test

Images of	Pure Braille		Braille+ print	Overall
	Embossed	Generated		
Training	9.000	50.000	13.795	72.795
Validation	1.250	11.100	1.050	13.500
Test	1.000	10.000	1.737	12.737

---

[1] Emfuse, EmBraille from Viewplus and Everest from Index Braille.

or came from pharmaceutical packages. With this corpus our models had to learn to distinguish between normal print and Braille. Table 1 gives an overview of the data sets used for OBR. The data set for line detection was created from the segmented lines of the previous data set. It contains 1305 images of Braille documents and 31.005 objects. The data set is split into 24.989 training samples, 2.978 validation samples and 3.038 test samples.

3.4   Implementation

We implemented an **Android App** for image capturing, pre-processing and result output (Fig. 2). The two deep learning models for line detection and for OBR are running on a **server using tensorflow-serving** [3] and docker. The app sends the cropped image to the server for line detection. The resulting Braille lines are sent to the server one by one for Braille recognition. The process of scanning a document using our system is shown in Fig. 2.

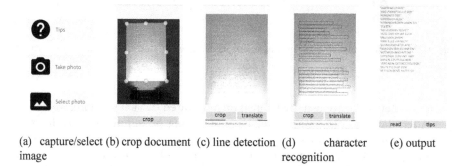

(a) capture/select (b) crop document (c) line detection (d)   character   (e) output
image   recognition

Fig. 2. Screenshots taken from the Android App.

4   Evaluation

We evaluated our approach twofold: (i) The deep learning models are validated using the test data from our data sets, and (ii) The usability of the application is evaluated by carrying out a user study.

4.1   Line Detection Model

The model for line detection is evaluated using the COCO object detection metric [10]. This metric is based on the intersection over union (IoU), which measures the overlap between two bounding boxes. For different IoU-thresholds the average precision (AP) is calculated. The higher the IoU-threshold is chosen, the better the bounding boxes have to align to be considered a successful detection.

Our model reaches a AP@IoU(0.5) of 0.91 and a AP@IoU(0.5;0.95;0.05) of 0.59. The scores for each IoU-threshold are shown in Fig. 3. In general the results are satisfying but it can be seen, that the results for higher IoU-thresholds get worse. Considering the detection being the foundation for character recognition, better results for higher thresholds would be desirable. Therefore mainly a larger data set needs to be created.

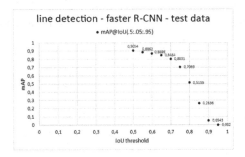

Fig. 3. Evaluation of line detection using the COCO metric.

4.2   Optical Braille Recognition Model

Optical Braille Recognition is evaluated using the test data split into documents with and without additional print without any generated images. We use the Levenshtein distance/edit distance (ed) [8] to compare the ground truth to the prediction of our model. It counts the insertions, deletions or substitutions needed to change string $s1$ to $s2$. Based on this distance we calculate the "Character-Error-Rate (cer)" which is defined as $cer(s1, s2) = \frac{ed(s1,s2)}{max(|s1|,|s2|)}$. We calculate the ed and cer for every line length independently. The evaluation with documents of Braille with additional print is shown in Fig. 4a. The model works well for short and long lines. On average, the models achieve a cer of 0.02 and an ed of 0.362 operations. Figure 4b shows the model's performance on non printed documents without synthetic data. The results deviate greatly from the printed documents. The model reaches a cer of 0.11. The biggest difference between these two types of data is the use of a flashlight. It was only used with printed documents because the print has much more contrast than embossing at ambient light. To check, if it is part of the worse results, a few images of the same documents were taken using the additional light. The results with these images are shown in Fig. 4c. The model reaches much better scores on this data. This observation confirms that the correct illumination is crucial.

4.3   User Study

To evaluate the usability of the app, we performed a user study with participants which don't have regular contact to blind persons. This study involved 7

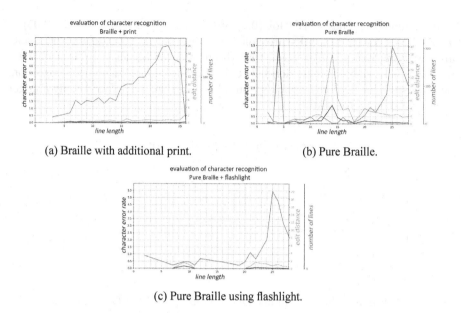

(a) Braille with additional print.

(b) Pure Braille.

(c) Pure Braille using flashlight.

Fig. 4. Evaluation of Optical Braille Recognition

persons with an average age of 40 (29–61, 4 female and 3 male). The task of each participant was to scan a document and get results from our system. There were three types of documents available: without print, printed with matching text and a pharmaceutical packaging. An additional light source was available. First, the participant were introduced to the task. Then the smartphone was handed over with the app already running.

Every participant was able to complete the task without help. To evaluate usability, the participants were asked to fill out a questionnaire consisting of general questions, User-Experience-Questionnaire (UEQ) [6] and System Usability Scale (SUS) [1]. We received a SUS score of 90% and overall very good UEQ ratings. The results show that the system is well usable for an average person. The questionnaire provided some valuable feedback to further improve the application. The participants suggested that it should be possible to adjust the results from the line detection, to include automatic orientation recognition, or a functionality to save and load results.

5 Conclusions

We present a new approach to Optical Braille Recognition using a mobile device and state-of-the-art computer vision algorithms. Our system is based on a Faster R-CNN architecture for Braille line detection. For character recognition, a combination of a CNN and LSTM is used. To capture the important spatial information of Braille, an attention mechanism is included. The models are trained with custom data sets. An Android application is developed which is used to capture the images and show the results. Both deep learning models are hosted using TensorFlow-serving and docker. This architecture allows for easy updates of both neural networks without updating the app itself.

In the future, some improvements to the application like automatic orientation detection of Braille writing are considered. To further improve the performance of both deep learning models, more annotated data has to be collected. Therefore, a special data collection application can be created to get interested contributors to participate. To make the system accessible for blind or visually impaired users, a fixture could be used to hold the smartphone and document in a fixed position. This would also allow for some controlled lighting to further improve performance.

References

1. Brooke, J., et al.: SUS: a quick and dirty usability scale. In: Usability Evaluation in Industry, pp. 189–194 (1996)
2. Deng, Y., Kanervisto, A., Ling, J., Rush, A.M.: Image-to-markup generation with coarse-to-fine attention. In: Proceedings of the 34th International Conference on Machine Learning, vol. 70, pp. 980–989. JMLR. org (2017)
3. Google: Tensorflow (2019). https://www.tensorflow.org/. Accessed 5 Jan 2020
4. Google: Android sdk (2020). https://developer.android.com/studio/releases. Accessed 14 Apr 2020
5. Hentzschel, T., Blenkhorn, P.: An optical reading system for embossed Braille characters using a twin shadows approach. J. Microcomput. Appl. 18(4), 341–354 (1995)
6. Hinderks, A., Schrepp, M., Thomaschewski, J.: User experience questionaire (2020). https://www.ueq-online.org/. Accessed 18 Mar 2020
7. Isayed, S., Tahboub, R.: A review of optical braille recognition. In: 2015 2nd World Symposium on Web Applications and Networking (WSWAN), pp. 1–6. IEEE (2015)
8. Levenshtein, V.I.: Binary codes capable of correcting deletions, insertions, and reversals. Soviet physics doklady 10, 707–710 (1966)
9. Liblouis* (2019). http://liblouis.org/. Accessed 4 Dec 2019
10. Lin, T.-Y.: Microsoft COCO: common objects in context. In: Fleet, D., Pajdla, T., Schiele, B., Tuytelaars, T. (eds.) ECCV 2014. LNCS, vol. 8693, pp. 740–755. Springer, Cham (2014). https://doi.org/10.1007/978-3-319-10602-1_48
11. Quasthoff, U., Richter, M.: Projekt Der Deutsche Wortschatz (1998)
12. Ren, S., He, K., Girshick, R.B., Sun, J.: Faster R-CNN: towards real-time object detection with region proposal networks. CoRR abs/1506.01497 (2015). http://arxiv.org/abs/1506.01497
13. Schwarz, T., Dolp, R., Stiefelhagen, R.: Optical braille recognition. In: Miesenberger, K., Kouroupetroglou, G. (eds.) ICCHP 2018. LNCS, vol. 10896, pp. 122–130. Springer, Cham (2018). https://doi.org/10.1007/978-3-319-94277-3_22
14. Shi, B., Bai, X., Yao, C.: An end-to-end trainable neural network for image-based sequence recognition and its application to scene text recognition. IEEE Trans. Pattern Anal. Mach. Intell. 39(11), 2298–2304 (2016)

Developing a Magnification Prototype Based on Head and Eye-Tracking for Persons with Low Vision

Thorsten Schwarz[✉], Arsalan Akbarioroumieh, Giuseppe Melfi,
and Rainer Stiefelhagen

Study Centre for the Visually Impaired, Karlsruhe Institute of Technology,
Engesserstr. 4, 76131 Karlsruhe, Germany
thorsten.schwarz@kit.edu
https://www.szs.kit.edu

Abstract. Severe visual impairments make it difficult for users to work on a computer. For this reason, there is great demand for new technical aids on the computer to compensate for these limitations. Current magnification software makes it possible to adjust the screen content, but due to the lack of overview and the time-consuming use of the mouse it is sometimes difficult to find the right content. If another physical disability is involved, working on a computer often becomes even more difficult. In this paper, we present the development of an affordable magnification system based on a low-cost eye-tracking device, which can be adjusted to the visual impairment without the need for a mouse or keyboard by using the line of vision derived from eye or head movements. Two studies with experts and potential users showed the usefulness of the system.

Keywords: Eye-tracking · Head-tracking · Magnifier · Magnification software · Low vision aid

1 Introduction

Nowadays computers are all around us and life without them is unimaginable. For most people, computers are the most convenient way to get things done, whether it's everyday life or work. However, not everyone can take full advantage of digital information because of a visual impairment such as albinism, glaucoma, retinopathy, macular degeneration, often accompanied by nystagmus, strabismus, limited field of vision and false color vision. Thus, people low vision have problems when working with computers because they often try to use the same working techniques as people with full sight. They usually use various tools

© Springer Nature Switzerland AG 2020
K. Miesenberger et al. (Eds.): ICCHP 2020, LNCS 12376, pp. 354–363, 2020.
https://doi.org/10.1007/978-3-030-58796-3_42

on the computer to be able to work, such as magnifying software (e.g. Zoom-Text,[1] SuperNova Magnifier[2] or screen reader software (e.g. JAWS,[3] NVDA[4]) to compensate their reduced vision. Current magnification software allows the screen content to be adapted to the visual impairment in terms of magnification factor and color settings. Since the enlarged screen content does not adapt to the width of the screen, they must constantly scroll to capture the content. Skimming over a text is no longer possible and reading becomes more difficult. In addition, people with low vision can easily lose track of what is happening on the screen due to the magnification. If another physical disability is involved, working on a computer becomes even more difficult and inefficient. Moreover, commercial assistive technologies are expensive and many people with disabilities cannot afford a suitable efficient system.

It is therefore necessary to develop intuitive solutions that enable efficient work with low vision. Thus, the aim of this work was to develop an affordable magnification system based on a low-cost eye-tracking device, which can be adjusted to the visual impairment without the need of a mouse or keyboard by using the direction of vision derived from eye or head movements.

The paper is structured as follows: First, we present related work, then we describe the development of our prototype and its functions as well as the design challenges. In Sect. 4, we present a pilot study with sighted experts and a second study with users with low vision. Finally, we draw our conclusions.

2 Related Work

Various approaches have already investigated eye-tracking approaches as a possible method of controlling the computer instead of using the keyboard and mouse.

Xuebai et al. [13] developed an application with low-cost eye trackers. Their application recognizes the user's gaze and places the cursor at the corresponding position of the gaze. Missimer et al. [8] created a camera-based system that monitors the eyes of users and uses the position of the head to control the cursor. Eriksson-Backa et al. [2] designed a magnification system that uses the gaze point. This system is also suitable for users with physical disabilities and for users with low vision. However, the user must wear special glasses to control the system. Chin et al. [1] designed a system for computer users with disabilities who cannot use their hands due to spinal disabilities. The system uses electromyogram (EMG) signals from muscles in the face and gaze point coordinates as inputs. Lupu et al. [4] developed a system for communication with people with neuro-locomotor disabilities using eye tracking. The eye-tracking system is

---

[1] Zoomtext. https://www.zoomtext.com/ (Retrieved 04/13/2020).

[2] SuperNova Magnifier. https://yourdolphin.com/products/individuals/supernova-magnifier-screen-reader (Retrieved 04/13/2020).

[3] JAWS. https://www.freedomscientific.com/products/software/jaws/ (Retrieved 04/13/2020).

[4] NVDA. https://www.nvaccess.org/ (Retrieved 04/13/2020).

based on a webcam mounted on glasses for image processing. The eye movement is recorded by a special device and the voluntary blinking of the eye is correlated with a pictogram or keyword selection reflecting the patient's needs. In 2013, Lupu et al. proposed another communication system [5] using head-mounted video glasses based on eye tracking. The system tracks the eye movements of the user and consequently the mouse pointer is moved on the screen. Salunkhe et al. [11] proposed an eye tracking system to control the movement of the computer mouse pointer and simulated a mouse click by influencing the blinking. Similarly, Meghna et al. [7] developed a tool based on a virtual mouse with head-tracking that uses the method of classification to recognize features. Shengwen Zhu (2017) [12] developed a magnification system using the inexpensive Tobii eyeX eye-tracker. The goal of the work was to design and implement a magnification system for people with impaired vision. Almost all requirements of the work of Shengwen Zhu [12] were taken as a basis for this study. WenChung Kao et al. [3] developed a magnification software that recognizes the user's gaze point on the screen based on a digital camera and changes the size of the local image. The main problem with this approach is that the magnification window jumps around and does not move smoothly. Stephan Pölzer et al. (2018) [9] proposed a modular magnification tool based on the inexpensive Tobii EyeX eye tracker for users with visual impairments such as nystagmus and users without visual impairments. The tool has no graphical interface and starts from the command line. They include the technique described by [10] to solve the problem of the moving window for users with nystagmus.

Since the goal of this work was to develop a magnification system and not an eye tracker, the focus was on finding the best algorithm for a stable magnification window. Thus, when the magnification system uses the eye's gaze points that it receives directly from the eye tracker, the magnification window is unstable and wobbles a lot. WenChung Kao's idea to limit the magnification window was very helpful. The limit within the magnification window helps the system to react more stable. The magnification window only moves when it receives the eye's gaze outside the limit.

3   Development of the Eye-Tracking Magnifier Prototype

The magnification tool has been developed in an iterative and incremental development process. We pursued the idea of co-design development by involving both potential users with visual impairments and experts working with people with visual impairments in order to get feedback as early as possible for the design of an intuitive interface.

3.1   Description of the System

We chose the Tobii 4 C eye-tracker[5] as the core part of the prototype. It has a sampling rate/frequency between 80–90 Hz and is connected to a computer via

---

[5] https://gaming.tobii.com/tobii-eye-tracker-4c/ (Retrieved 04/13/2020).

USB and mounted in the middle of the bottom edge of the screen. In addition, the system also offers head tracking, which could be an alternative if eye tracking is not feasible. The software was developed entirely in C# to create the most efficient, accessible tool possible.

3.2   Design Challenges

During our development process, we faced three challenges: (i) a stable magnification window, (ii) a magnification window with smooth movements, and (iii) maintaining an overview of the screen.

Stabilizing the Magnification Window. The biggest challenge in developing a magnification software with an eye tracker for people with low vision is the question of when to move the magnification window. We have tried to stabilize our magnification window by using the collected gaze points of the eye tracker. It turned out that for users without visual impairment, the viewpoint remains in a small area around the fixation target, i.e. in most cases the distance is less than 50 pixels. For users with low vision, however, the distance can be up to 1000 pixels, which would lead to rapid jumps of the magnification window. Thus, we defined a limit for eye movements within which the magnification window remains stable (see Fig. 1). Within this area, eye movements can jump back and forth without affecting the position of the magnification window, and only when the eye moves outside the area does the magnification window move. The size of the boundary is also very important. If the area of the inner box is too small, the eye movement may jump out slightly and the window will start to wobble slightly. If the area is too large, the magnification window may be difficult to move. The size of the inner box depends on the size of the magnification window, and it is a small area in the middle of the magnification window. The default width and height of the inner box is set to half the width and height of the magnification window. When the user's eye movements are inside the inner box, the magnification window remains stationary, and only when the eye movements are outside this box does the window move.

Fig. 1. Inner box inside the magn. window

Smoothing the Movement of the Magnification Window. The second challenge was to determine how the magnification window moves. If only the viewpoint function outside the inner box is considered for the movement of the window, the window does not move smoothly but jumps to the point. And this is not optimal when the user wants to read a text horizontally or vertically. Therefore the speed of the movement must be determined. The speed of the movement must be set so that it is inversely proportional to the zoom factor. This means that the window moves slower with a zoom factor of 8 and faster with a zoom factor of 2.

Keeping the Overview of the Screen. Another challenge was to determine the correct ratio between the magnification window and the overall screen. A higher magnification factor requires a larger screen to display the visual information that covers most of the main screen. This made it easy for users to lose track of the main screen. An approach to solve this problem was developed by Ashmore et al. [6]. They used a fisheye lens with the highest zoom factor in the center and a lower zoom factor at the edges of the fisheye lens. This approach was not accepted by the users in our pilot study and was therefore replaced by a "Where am I" function.

3.3   Functions

In our prototype, we implemented an eye (head) controlled and a mouse controlled magnification mode. The final tool includes the following five functions: (i) Magnification, (ii) Settings, (iii) Automatic determination of the best control mode, (iv) Tool-internal eyetracker calibration process, and (v) Instructions. The goal of our approach was to develop software that is easy to use, covers all expected functions and provides the functionality of normal magnification software for the majority of users (Fig. 2).

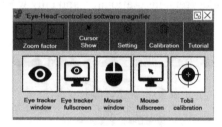

Fig. 2. User interface of the eye-head-controlled magnifier

4   Pilot Study

We have qualitatively evaluated the magnification system in two ways: in a first step with experts without visual impairment and in a second step with users with various eye diseases. The tasks for the test procedure were the same for all users:

1. Use Tobii's own calibration procedure to calibrate the eye tracker.
2. Use the internal calibration process to find out the best tracking mode.
3. Set the most convenient configurations.
4. Start using the magnification for reading.

4.1   Pilot Test with Experts Without Visual Impairment

In the first pilot study, six sighted experts working with people with visual impairments were invited to test the software. In all tests, the calibration process of the Tobii Eye Tracker was successfully completed. The magnification tool was tested with both the head tracking mode and a combination of head and eye tracking. There was no clear preference regarding the tracking mode. Some users preferred the combination of head and eye tracking because the magnification window moved or reacted faster than in eye tracking mode alone. For other users, however, eye tracking was the best solution. The goal of the first user study was to evaluate our internal calibration tool and the general functions of the magnification software to optimize the system.

Results. The following two features have been added according to user feedback: (1) Freezing, i.e. stopping the movement of the magnification window to allow reading even when the eyes are moving outside the bounding box, and (2) integration of a shortcut key for finding the main menu.

4.2   Pilot Test with Users with Low Vision

In our second pilot study, three students with low vision (two male and one female) were invited to test the tool.

Participants. Table 1 shows an overview of the three participants (P) regarding their eye disease, the magnification factor they used, how the calibration was performed, which tracking method was preferred (eye, head) or whether they preferred to work with the mouse.
Participant 1 had problems using Tobii Eye Tracker's own calibration process due to the used colors, contrasts and size of the calibration points. Therefore, the calibration was done manually. Another problem was his habit of moving his head too close to the monitor, which meant that the eye tracker could not determine the eye positions. As a result, the tool could not respond optimally. Therefore the participant was asked to test the software in mouse-controlled

Table 1. Overview of the participants and their preferred interaction method

Participants	Gender	Eye disease	Mag. factor	Tobii's own calibration	Eye/Head tracking	Mouse
P1	Male	Tunnel vision	10x	Manually	Not working	Preferred
P2	Male	Nystagmus	5x	Manually	Eye preferred	Not preferred
P3	Female	Strabismus	9x	Manually	Head preferred	Not preferred

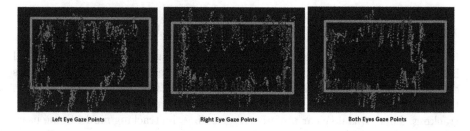

Left Eye Gaze Points   Right Eye Gaze Points   Both Eyes Gaze Points

Fig. 3. Gaze points from left, right and both eyes of participant 2 with nystagmus during the internal calibration process

mode. This made it possible to interact with the software easily and smoothly. The participant also mentioned that the color representation is much better than with other magnification tools.

Participant 2 could also not successfully complete the calibration process of the eye tracker. However, our internal calibration process could be used to select the best eye tracking mode. The results are shown in Fig. 3. Based on the results of the calibration, the internal tool suggested the tracking mode "right eye". The test result was surprisingly good and the magnification software was stable during the test. The user found the software easy to use and very promising. Since the user has nystagmus, he mentioned that the freezing functions were very useful for him. In the second part of the test, the combined head-eye tracking was tested for comparison. This option causes a faster movement of the magnification window. Due to this speed increase combined with the high zoom factor, it was difficult to follow a sentence or find the beginning or end of a sentence. In the third and last part of the evaluation, only head-tracking was used. The magnification window was surprisingly stable in the middle of the screen. In the case that the participant turned his head too far to the left or right, the magnification window became unstable. However, the user mentioned that he needed time to train with this mode. The user also said that it was better to move the magnification window only along the X axis and not up and down when trying to read something. Locking the direction would be a desirable feature here.

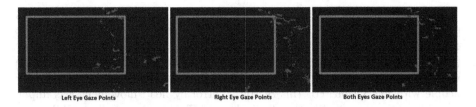

Fig. 4. Gaze points from left, right and both eyes of the third participant user during the internal calibration process

The eyes of the **3rd participant** were directed in different directions (strabismus), which tempts the participant to balance the steering with the "stable" eye. The Tobii calibration process was again not completed successfully (not even by pointing manually at the calibration points on the screen). The internal calibration process was tested to find the best control mode again (see Fig. 4). The result was that the eye tracker could not detect the gaze points in the current case and suggested using the head tracking mode. For this participant, the head-tracking mode worked very well and she was able to interact with the software in this mode better than other users. She mentioned that she already noticed that she could use the software better when she was using it for a longer time and became more familiar with the controls. Finally, she was asked to test the software with the mouse-driven mode. Although she had been using other magnification tools for years, in her opinion the color definition of color filters in the presented magnification tool (e.g. inverted color filters) was better than the other tools.

Results. The following three features were added based on feedback from participants with low vision: (1) "Where am I" function. This function is triggered by pressing a key combination that shows the user the position of the current magnification area by a large red circle on the entire screen. (2) Shortcut key to adjust the color inversion filter to the magnification window. (3) The magnification window should follow the keyboard focus.

5   Conclusions

In this paper, we presented a user-centered approach to the development of a novel software magnification system. It is based on a low cost eye-head tracking system, where the magnification window is displayed on the screen at the same position as the fixation target. In this way, the user maintains an overview of the screen and can work with the mouse in the original sense instead of using it for scrolling. For optimization, the software is not limited to the eye positions, but also offers the possibility to evaluate head movements and uses them to control the magnification window.

Our pilot studies indicate that the combined eye-head magnification tool presented in this paper is helpful for almost all users with low vision. We also expect that it can provide great added value for people with limited mobility (paraplegia). The evaluation of the prototype has also shown that interaction via a purely eye-based control is very difficult or even impossible for some of the people with low vision. For this reason, control by head movement was implemented as mouse control in the classical sense. This opens up all possibilities of individual control for the user. The user studies also pointed out that in many cases it makes sense to use only one eye instead of both for control, since most people have a so-called guiding eye.

Finally, we plan to continue user testing with a larger number of people with low vision. The tool can be found on our website (https://www.szs.kit.edu) and can be used after registration and the willingness to participate in a survey. We would appreciate any feedback in order to gather further experiences and suggestions for improvement.

References

1. Chin, C.A., Barreto, A., Cremades, J.G., Adjouadi, M.: Integrated electromyogram and eye-gaze tracking cursor control system for computer users with motor disabilities. J. Rehabil. Res. Dev. **45**(1), 161–174 (2008)
2. Raudonis, V., Paulauskaite-Taraseviciene, A., Maskeliunas, R.: Vision enhancement technique based on eye tracking system. In: Eriksson-Backa, K., Luoma, A., Krook, E. (eds.) WIS 2012. CCIS, vol. 313, pp. 150–160. Springer, Heidelberg (2012). https://doi.org/10.1007/978-3-642-32850-3_14
3. Kao, W.C., Huang, K.J., Chiu, Y.C., Hung, M.Y., Shen, C.W.: Real-time image magnifier with visible-spectrum gaze tracker. In: 2018 International Symposium on Consumer Technologies (ISCT), pp. 22–23. IEEE, Piscataway, NJ (2018). https://doi.org/10.1109/ISCE.2018.8408907
4. Lupu, R.G., Ungureanu, F., Bozomitu, R.G.: Mobile embedded system for human computer communication in assistive technology. In: Letia, I.A. (ed.) 2012 IEEE International Conference on Intelligent Computer Communication and Processing (ICCP), pp. 209–212. IEEE, Piscataway, NJ (2012). https://doi.org/10.1109/ICCP.2012.6356187
5. Lupu, R.G., Ungureanu, F., Siriteanu, V.: Eye tracking mouse for human computer interaction. In: E-Health and Bioengineering Conference, EHB 2013, pp. 1–4. IEEE, Piscataway, NJ (2013). https://doi.org/10.1109/EHB.2013.6707244
6. Ashmore, M., Duchowski, A.T., Shoemaker, G.: Efficient eye pointing with a fisheye lens. http://andrewd.ces.clemson.edu/research/vislab/docs/gi05.pdf
7. Meghna, S.M., Ashlesha, T., Kachan, K.L., Baviskar, A.: Head tracking virtual mouse system based on ad boost face detection algorithm (2016). http://www.ijritcc.org/download/conferences/ICMTEST_2016/ICMTEST_2016_Track/1467100132_28-06-2016.pdf
8. Missimer, E., Betke, M.: Blink and wink detection for mouse pointer control. In: Makedon, F. (ed.) Proceedings of the 3rd International Conference on PErvasive Technologies Related to Assistive Environments, p. 1. ACM, New York, NY (2010). https://doi.org/10.1145/1839294.1839322

9. Pölzer, S., Gander, E., Miesenberger, K.: Gaze based magnification to assist visually impaired persons. In: Miesenberger, K., Kouroupetroglou, G. (eds.) ICCHP 2018. LNCS, vol. 10897, pp. 333–337. Springer, Cham (2018). https://doi.org/10.1007/978-3-319-94274-2_46

10. Pölzer, S., Miesenberger, K.: Assisting people with nystagmus through image stabilization: Using an arx model to overcome processing delays. In: 2017 Annual International Conference of the IEEE Engineering in Medicine and Biology Society. IEEE Engineering in Medicine and Biology Society, pp. 1222–1225 (2017). https://doi.org/10.1109/EMBC.2017.8037051

11. Salunkhe, P., Patil, A.R.: A device controlled using eye movement. In: 2016 International Conference on Electrical, Electronics and Optimization Techniques (ICEEOT), pp. 732–735. IEEE, Piscataway, NJ (2016). https://doi.org/10.1109/ICEEOT.2016.7754779

12. Zhu, S.: Software magnifier with eye-tracking for visually impaired (February 2017). https://www.szs.kit.edu/english/287_1037.php

13. Zhang, X., Liu, X., Yuan, S.M., Lin, S.F.: Eye tracking based control system for natural human-computer interaction. Comput. Intell. Neurosci. **2017**, 5739301 (2017). https://doi.org/10.1155/2017/5739301

Numeric Key Programming: Programmable Robot Kit for both Visually Impaired and Sighted Elementary School Students

Yoshihiko Kimuro[1(✉)], Takafumi Ienaga[1], and Seiji Okimoto[2]

[1] Fukuoka Institute of Technology, 3-30-1, Wajiro-Higashi, Higashi-ku,
Fukuoka-shi, Fukuoka-ken 811-0295, Japan
kimuro@fit.ac.jp
[2] Fukuoka Special Needs Education School for the Visually Impaired,
114, Ushijima, Chikushino-shi, Fukuoka-ken 818-0014, Japan

Abstract. In the informational society, it seems that elementary school students should learn programming and a robot kit such as LEGO is used as one of adequate programming materials. However, almost all programming tools for beginners employ graphical user interface, so visually impaired students cannot use such programming tools. To reduce the problem, we have proposed a new programming material only using a numeric keypad and a mobile toy robot. In this paper, we show the architecture of our programming environment. And we had experimental classes, which were focused on the ease of use it for both visually impaired and sighted students. As a result, visually impaired students were able to obtain the programming skill within 15 min at maximum from their first touch of the robot. On the other hands, sighted students spent only 5 min to use the robot.

Keywords: Visually impaired · Programming · Robot kit · Elementary school

1 Introduction

In the informational society, it seems that elementary school students should learn programming so that they come to know what they can do with a computer and what they cannot. However, almost all programming tools for beginners employ graphical user interface [1], so visually impaired students cannot use such programming tools easily. To reduce or resolve the problem, many researchers have studied on programming languages, programming environments and programming materials for the visually impaired [2].

A. Hadwen-Bennett et.al reported their work, which was based on the result of surveys on published scientific international journals in the view point of accessibility of programming environment for the visually impaired [3]. They classified

© Springer Nature Switzerland AG 2020
K. Miesenberger et al. (Eds.): ICCHP 2020, LNCS 12376, pp. 364–370, 2020.
https://doi.org/10.1007/978-3-030-58796-3_43

these papers into four categories; i.e. Text-Based Language (TBL) accessible, Block-Based Language (BBL) accessible, Physical artefacts, and Auditory and haptic feedback. However, most studies were only for visually impaired. Namely, there is no aspect that both visually impaired and sighted students can learn programming together.

J.D.Oliveria et.al. focused on using robots in programming education and surveyed relating many papers [4]. As a result of the survey, they pointed out the effectiveness of robots and 34 recommendations on robot programming for visually impaired. Unfortunately, it was more difficult to use the robot such as "LEGO" for visually impaired than sighted. Otherwise, authors introduced an original robot system "P-CUBE" proposed by Motoyoshi, which used physical blocks with RFID tags for programming. However, the special robot for visually impaired could not be used by sighted because there was no additional merit to use it instead of LEGO. Therefore, the accessibility of a robot for visually impaired should be as simple as for sighted.

2   Our Idea

First, we have to say our aim. The aim is not only to teach programming but also to teach the principle of the computer. Namely, the computer consists of a processor and a memory, as a minimal component, and a program stored in the memory is loaded into the processor and the program is executed. As a result, the computer can work according to the program. If the program includes some mistakes, the computer wrongly works according to the mistakes. If human cannot make a program, the computer cannot work. To learn these facts, students make a computer program by themselves, we think.

As an easy programming tool for beginners, visual programming languages such as "Scratch" have been employed. Such language can reduce a syntax error and a typing mistakes. However, our methodology is just the opposite of a conventional programming language for beginners.

Our aim is as follows.

1. Both visually impaired and sighted students can use a programmable robot with the same accessibility.
2. In order to teach a concept of a robot (a computer), our programmable robot is able to accept wrong program codes produced by typing mistake or syntax errors.

Figure 1 shows the overview of our mobile robot, which has a small keypad. Our robot programming system belongs to Text-Based Language (TBL). Needed keys for programming are only ten numeric keys, which are from 0 to 9. And two keys are used for "RUN" and "Reset" commands. Using these twelve keys, our mobile robot can be programmed.

3   Specification of Our Programmable Robot

3.1   Command Set

A command set of our robot has five basic commands, which are motion- and sound-related, and three flow control commands, which are "For", "If" and "While" statements (Table 1).

Fig. 1. Overview of programmable robot "KOROBO SP"

The basic commands consist of "opcode" and "operand", that is a two words command. Using a one digit number, namely from "0" to "9", working time of transition and rotation of the robot can be programmed. In the sound command, a number means a musical scale. Moreover, if "0" is set at a certain basic command as an operand, the command works as not stop command but random motion.

As flow control commands of our mobile robot, there are three statements, i.e., loop (for), conditional branch (if), and conditional loop (while). The loop procedure executes sequential statements sandwiched with "FOR n" and "NEXT" by n times. In the case of "FOR 0", this FOR block behaves as an infinite loop. The conditional branch is described by a block structure with "IF condition" and "ENDIF". A conditional expression consists of identifier of sensors and the state ON/OFF.

Figure 2 shows some sample programs. It is easy for everyone to understand the codes. In these figures, programs are written in English, but learners need not to remember these command names. The details will be explained in the following subsection.

Table 1. Robot programming commands

Category	Command	Parameter	Description
Basic	FW	d	Move forward (0:random)
	BK	d	Move backward (0:random)
	LR	d	CCW rotation (0:random)
	RR	d	CW rotation (0:random)
	BEEP	d	Musical scale (0:random)
Control	FOR	d	Loop block (d:times, 0:inf)
	NEXT	-	End of loop
	IF	Sensor ID & State	Conditional branch block
	ENDIF	-	End of IF block
	ENDWHILE	-	End of WHILE block (with IF)
Operation	RUN/STOP	-	Execution/temporal stop
	RESET	-	Clear program memory

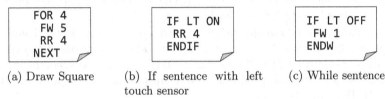

(a) Draw Square   (b) If sentence with left touch sensor   (c) While sentence

Fig. 2. Sample programs

3.2 Programming Method

Our employed keypad is the most significant part of our programmable robot material. The keypad is just the same as buttons layout of a phone which is common in the world and visually impaired students can understand easily and quickly. This is because the visually impaired often use the phone than sighted students. Accessibility of the keypad for visually impaired is only a convex part on the "5" key.

The robot commands "forward", "backward", "turn left", and "turn right" are located at in front, in back, at left and at right of a center key "5" respectively (Fig. 3). Namely, key layout directly means motion commands. The key "5" is used for sound command in our system.

The flow control commands are located at the rest of the above keys. For example, "FOR" and "NEXT" are set at "1" and "3" keys respectively. "IF" and "ENDIF" are set at "7" and "9" respectively. The position of keys for choosing sensors corresponds to the actual sensor position of the mobile robot. "RUN/STOP" button and "Reset" button are set at the right and left of "0".

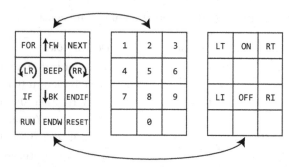

Fig. 3. Commands layout and its state transition

3.3 Implementation

The base of our mobile robot (Fig. 1) is a toy robot (MR-9172) released by EK-JAPAN co. This robot kit has two motors, two IR (Infra-Red) sensors, two touch sensors, and a buzzer. We added Arduino UNO microcontroller board and a numeric keypad to the base robot kit.

A firmware for a command interpreter explained at the Sect. 3.1 and 3.2 is installed on the Arduino board. The program codes input from the keypad are automatically stored on EEPROM (Fig. 4). So there is no SAVE command. Now, our firmware can store 250 program steps at maximum. The depth of nesting of each FOR, IF, WHILE is 10.

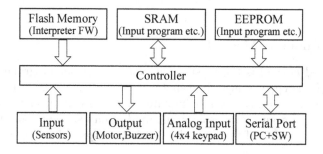

Fig. 4. Block diagram

4 Experiment

Using our mobile programmable robots, we had an experimental class at Fukuoka Blind Elementary School. Participants were two pupils aged 8 and four pupils aged 10. The number of totally blind was 2 and low vision was 4. The time length of the programming class was about 45 min. Each participant used one robot by themselves. As an additional material, we prepared the reflate explaining the layout of commands in braille and huge fonts.

First, participants knew a structure of the robot with their hands. Next, they learned "Reset" and "RUN" buttons. They could understand beeping when they push keys. After that, they pushed "2" and "5" key successively, then pushed "RUN". As a result, all visually impaired were able to know the behavior of the robot caused by their own program. After participants knew the "Move forward" command, they could find the other commands "backward", "turn left", "turn right" experimentally.

We set a video camera to grasp how long the visually impaired students needed to obtain the programming skill (Fig. 6(a)). From the video, all students can make a sequential code and execute it on the robot within 15 min at maximum from their first touch of the robot(Fig. 5). On the other hand, sighted people also tried this programmable robot at the other place. The 127 participants were from kindergarten students to adults. As a result, almost all participants can make a sequential program within 5 min from they touched the robot for the first time. Moreover, we confirmed that visually impaired junior high school students could learn until conditional branch within two hours. Figure 6(b) shows that they made a guide dog robot which can avoid obstacles.

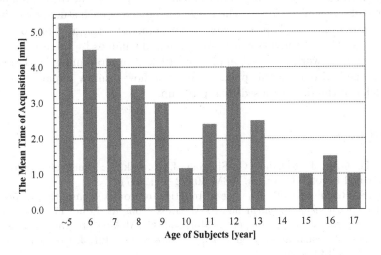

Fig. 5. The mean time of acquisition in age of subjects. Note: There is no participant aged 14.

As the results of these facts, we consider that inclusive computer education, which is for students who have or don't have visually impaired could be achieved by using our programmable robot kit.

(a) The experimental class   (b) Guide dog robot with blind student

Fig. 6. Snapshots

5 Conclusion

We proposed a new programmable robot and its programming system. Our new programmable robot can be used for both visually impaired and sighted. Further, we explained the robot command in English in this paper, but the command does not depend on English. Always the mother language of each student can be used to learn programming. This is because each command is assigned into one button from "0" to "9" so students can make command's names by themselves.

As a future work, we will apply our 10 key programming system onto a programmable drone. In this plan, we focus on how visually impaired can know a behavior of the drone caused by a program.

References

1. Bau, D., Gray, J., Kelleher, C., Sheldon, J., Turbak, F.: Learnable programming: blocks and beyond. Commun. ACM **60**, 72–80 (2017)
2. Ludi, S., Reichlmayr, T.: The use of robotics to promote computing to precollege students with visual impairments. ACM Trans. Comput. Educ. **11**, 20 (2011)
3. Hadwen-Bennett, A., Sentance, S., Morrison, C.: Making programming accessible learners with visual impairments: a litereature review. Int. J. Comput. Sci. Educ. Sch. **2**(2), 3–13 (2018)
4. Damasio Oliveira, J., de Borba Campos, M., de Morais Amory, A., Manssour, I.H.: Teaching robot programming activities for visually impaired students: a systematic review. In: Antona, M., Stephanidis, C. (eds.) UAHCI 2017. LNCS, vol. 10279, pp. 155–167. Springer, Cham (2017). https://doi.org/10.1007/978-3-319-58700-4_14

Art Karshmer Lectures in Access to Mathematics, Science and Engineering

AUDiaL: A Natural Language Interface to Make Statistical Charts Accessible to Blind Persons

Tomas Murillo-Morales[✉] and Klaus Miesenberger

Institute Integriert Studieren, Johannes Kepler University,
Altenbergerstraße 69, 4040 Linz, Austria
Tomas.Murillo_Morales@jku.at

Abstract. This paper discusses the design and evaluation of AUDiaL (Accessible Universal Diagrams through Language). AUDiaL is a web-based, accessible natural language interface (NLI) prototype that allows blind persons to access statistical charts, such as bar and line charts, by means of free-formed analytical and navigational queries expressed in natural language. Initial evaluation shows that NLIs are an innovative, promising approach to accessibility of knowledge representation graphics, since, as opposed to traditional approaches, they do not require of additional software/hardware nor user training while allowing users to carry out most tasks commonly supported by data visualization techniques in an efficient, natural manner.

Keywords: Natural language interface · Statistical charts · Accessibility · Annotation

1 Introduction

In order to foster the inclusion of blind and visually impaired persons in the information society it is paramount that they have full access to information in all its forms, a sizeable amount of which is based on or supported by visual means. Graphically displayed information in the form of statistical charts, networks, and maps (which, as a whole, we will refer to as *diagrams*), is commonly employed in newspapers, didactic materials, finance, and many other aspects of daily life. Diagrams exploit the natural perceptual, cognitive, and memorial capacities of human beings so that the represented information can be more easily processed and understood by sighted readers. However, blind persons are generally excluded from accessing diagrammatic representations of data. Diagrams and other graphics have been labelled as "the last frontier in accessibility" [7], since current alternative accessible versions thereof are either not functionally equivalent [8] (e.g. tabular descriptions, sonified diagrams), they have to be greatly simplified and must be authored by a sighted expert using specialized devices (tactile graphics), or some substantial training must be undertaken by

© The Author(s) 2020
K. Miesenberger et al. (Eds.): ICCHP 2020, LNCS 12376, pp. 373–384, 2020.
https://doi.org/10.1007/978-3-030-58796-3_44

the end user (interactive software) before becoming accustomed to their peculiarities so that they can be used efficiently.

In this paper, we expand on our previous concept of a non-visual accessible web interface to diagrams [12] by introducing AUDiaL (Accessible Universal Diagrams through Language), a prototype of a Web-based NLI to semantically-enhanced statistical charts adapted to the specific needs of blind users. NLIs are an innovative means for non-visually accessing diagrams that possess many benefits in comparison with traditional accessible diagrams, namely:

- NLIs leverage a skill that is mastered early in life, natural language, which makes them a useful and efficient way for people to interact with computers. In addition, given that "verbal communication must be employed as the primary means to present [...] visual information to people who are blind" [10], NLIs emerge as a reasonable interactive approach that enables blind persons to access and navigate diagrams.
- Web-based NLIs do not require users to install new hardware or software, since they can be accessed, like any other well-designed website, through the combination of standard Web browsers and assistive technologies such as screen readers. This allows users to forego most of the training time which would be otherwise required to operate a more complex traditional user interface, thus fostering their take-up by the visually impaired population.
- Natural language can express information at different conceptual levels. The knowledge embedded in a diagram can be communicated from low-level facts e.g. the specific value of an individual data point, to high-level, abstract concepts e.g. the general trend described by a time series, thereby preserving, to a certain extent, the functional equivalence of the original diagram regardless of its complexity. This functional equivalence is however limited by the fact that natural language, unlike tactile approaches, is unable to provide direct perceptual access to spatial information [16]. On the other hand, a one-to-one correspondence between the original diagram and its tactile counterpart leads to perceptually cluttered and unusable displays except for very simple diagrams [16]. As a result, most blind persons do not even attempt to read a tactile diagram [7].
- A number of annotation techniques, some of which are discussed in [14], may be employed to compensate for the lack of sight when employing a NLI. These techniques include the ability for users to annotate and bookmark individual graphic objects, high-level summary generation, sequential and hierarchical navigation of graphic objects, clustering of related graphic objects, navigational breadcrumbs, and quick-jumps to salient nodes of the diagram.

However, despite their increasing popularity, research on NLIs is rarely motivated by the goal of accessibility [5]. Existing approaches to accessibility of diagrams supported by natural language are either constrained to providing static, high-level descriptions of the diagram's contents (see e.g. [4]), or are limited to providing output in natural language, whereas input is given by means of keyboard combinations that need to be learned (see e.g. [6]). Therefore, we have designed

AUDiaL as a pure NLI in which both user input and system output are characterized in natural language. In the following, we briefly outline the architecture of AUDiaL and some preliminary evaluation results with blind users.

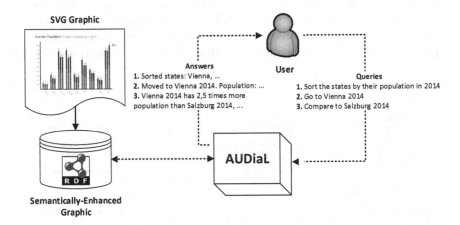

Fig. 1. High-level overview of AUDiaL in its problem context. AUDiaL enables (blind) users access information that is visually displayed in statistical charts by means of queries performed in natural language. Example diagram, user queries, and system answers are shown.

2 AUDiaL: Accessible Universal Diagrams Through Language

AUDiaL is a Web-based prototype of a natural language interface (NLI) to semantically-enhanced statistical charts in RDF[1]. It was designed with the goal of evaluating whether blind persons find NLIs a usable, effective means of accessing information displayed visually. Figure 1 displays AUDiaL in its problem context. Namely, the developed framework consists of two core independent components:

- **Semantically-enhanced graphic**: The semantics embedded in a diagram can be characterized at different levels of abstraction by means of formal underpinnings i.e. a knowledge base (KB) on visualization [13]. We have developed a hierarchical set of ontologies for visualization, whose resources may be associated to graphical primitives of a vectorized diagram in SVG format in order to formalize its semantics. This combination of raw SVG graphical data and its associated formal semantics is known as a semantically-enhanced graphic.

---

[1] We are currently working on guidelines for the authoring of semantically-enhanced diagrams in RDF. For a general introduction to RDF, the reader is referred to the RDF primer, available at https://www.w3.org/TR/rdf11-primer/.

– **AUDiaL prototype**: A Web-based NLI allows blind persons to execute analytical and navigational low-level tasks on a semantically-enhanced graphic.
As introduced in [12], we first carried out an analysis on which tasks are
commonly undertaken by sighted persons with the support of visualization
techniques, and characterized them as formal resources in our hierarchy of
ontologies for visualization. AUDiaL allows these tasks to be performed in a
non-visual manner by means of queries in natural language. The rest of this
paper describes AUDiaL in greater detail and reports some initial evaluation
results.

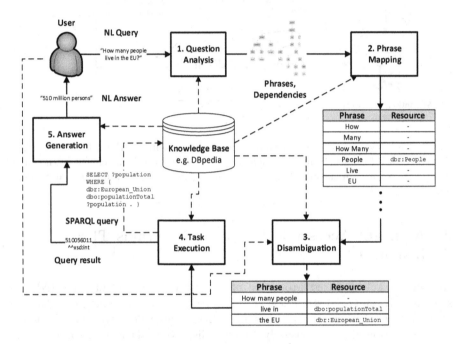

Fig. 2. Prototypical process flow of question answering over knowledge bases.

3   Natural Language Processing Pipeline

The workflow of a prototypical natural language (NL) to knowledge bases (KB)
pipeline is shown in Fig. 2. AUDiaL implements all phases of such a pipeline,
where the KB consists of a semantically-enhanced graphic and, optionally, one
or more domain ontologies that augment the knowledge of the diagram with
external domain knowledge, as follows.

1. **Question Analysis**: This phase analyses the syntactic features of the input
natural language query. The input query is first normalized. Next, a Parse
Tree (PT) of the query is generated via an external Stanford CoreNLP Server

[11] instance. The PT is then analyzed following several heuristics resulting in a number of Potential Ontology Concepts (POCs). POCs are phrases of the input query that have the potential of being mapped to resources in the KB (e.g. "People" and "EU" in Fig. 2). We generate POCs by extending the approach of FREyA [2]. In addition, we introduce the concept of Cardinal Query Filters (CQFs), which are also generated during this phase and correspond to phrases of the query that modify the selection of triples retrieved from the KB before executing a task or the triples that are output as a result of executing a task (e.g. "more than 1000" or "approximately 20").

2. *Phrase Mapping*: This phase aims to map each of the query's phrases found during the previous phase to zero or more resources of the KB. For example, the phrase "People" could be mapped to a literal resource, for example `"People^^xsd:string"` underpinning a label's text in a semantically-enhanced diagram through a datatype property occurrence. This phase not only searches for query phrases as-is in the KB, but also lemmatized versions and synonymic phrases thereof.

3. *Disambiguation*: The disambiguation phase resolves any remaining POCs, QCFs, and disambiguates between KB resources that have been mapped to the same query phrase during the previous phase of the pipeline. An automatic consolidation phase takes place first, which aims to automatically resolve any unresolved and ambiguous phrases. All remaining unresolved elements are settled by explicitly asking the user in mapping and disambiguation dialogues following the approach described in [3] which we have extended to include QCF resolution. An example mapping dialogue is shown in Fig. 6 along with further information about this phase.

4. *Task Execution*: This phase is in charge of executing the corresponding task stemming from a consolidated user query. First, the resources corresponding to the task(s) to be executed are identified. If no task is found, it defaults to a filtering task in which all elements in the graphic that match the user's query are simply listed. Next, a number of KB triples that match the resources and CQFs of the consolidated user query are retrieved. Lastly, the chosen analytical task is executed on the matching triples. For example, some of the tasks currently recognized include retrieving an average of values, determining the trend of values with respect to a metric axis, clustering graphic objects according to some of their attributes, or jumping between graphic objects. The complete list of implemented low-level tasks can be consulted in [12].

5. *Answer Generation*: Lastly, the task result is expressed in a suitable manner, depending on the task, in natural language and dynamically embedded into AUDiaL's accessible Web interface. The user may now input a new query, and the processing pipeline will be executed again from the beginning.

Besides retrieving knowledge from the graphic and domain ontologies, AUDiaL additionally supports user-specific annotation of graphic elements in order to aid users with navigating complex graphics more efficiently by bookmarking elements, selecting home nodes during navigation, or simply adding customized information to that already contained in the diagram. Moreover, a high-level summary of the graphic as a whole may be requested at any time [14]. These techniques aim to compensate for the lack of sight of AUDiaL's user base. For example, bookmarking methods were implemented with the goal of preventing the overloading of the users' working memory when navigating complex diagrams.

4   Evaluation

An initial evaluation of AUDiaL was carried out with 9 visually impaired participants (5 females, 4 males; 7 fully blind, 2 near blind; average age $\mu = 24.11$, standard deviation $\sigma = 12.17$), all of whom had more than 5 years Web browsing experience and who were familiar with the concepts of bar and line charts. Most of them (89%) reported that their preferred means for accessing diagrams was a textual or tabular version thereof, with a single person reporting a preference for tactile graphics.

A statistical difference-making experiment [18] was designed, as follows. Two diagrams (a stacked bar chart and a simultaneous combination of a bar chart and a line chart sharing the same metric space) of similar complexity (depicting the equivalent of around 80 tabular values each) were semantically enhanced with Semantic Annotator for Inkscape (SAI) [15] and uploaded to a running instance of AUDiaL. Participants were provided user accounts and asked to solve eight tasks of varying difficulty on both diagrams. Around half of the participants were asked to answer the first batch of tasks using AUDiaL, and the second batch of questions using a tabular or tactile version of the diagram according to their individual preference. The other half of the participants were asked to employ the traditional alternative first, followed by AUDiaL. This process, known as a complete counterbalanced, repeated measures, task-based evaluation design, enables us to halve the number of participants needed while minimizing potentially harmful sequence effects (e.g. participant fatigue) in the evaluation [2].

Tasks included initial simple questions that could be answered by consulting the high-level summary of the diagram e.g. "How many bars are there in the chart?", meant to get participants accustomed to using the prototype; tasks of intermediate difficulty that could not be solved by asking a single question and introduced mapping and disambiguation dialogues e.g. "Write the two Austrian regions having the maximum and minimum population in 2004, respectively", to complex questions that required participants to acquire a mental model of the diagram as a whole e.g. "Which regions increased in population between 2004 and 2014?". Participants were not trained in using the prototype, being simply instructed to input free-formed questions in the only text field of the user interface. Each evaluation session lasted for approximately 150 min, with two intermediate breaks. System logs were collected in order to determine the time it took participants to solve (or withdraw) each task. Moreover, the efficiency in solving each task in a scale from 0 (solved it with ease) to 2 (task failed) was gathered. Participants were also asked to answer two complementary user satisfaction surveys.

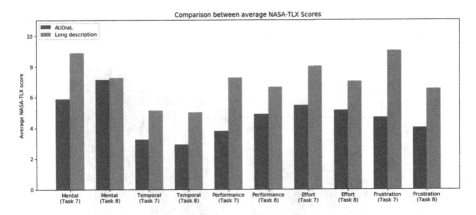

Fig. 3. Comparison of average NASA-TLX scores.

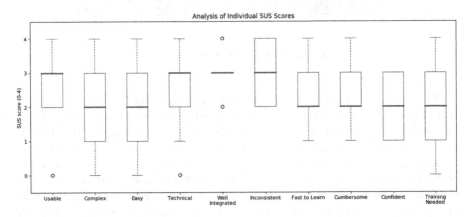

Fig. 4. Analysis of individual SUS scores obtained by AUDiaL.Analysis of individual SUS scores obtained by AUDiaL.

Given that the number of participants is insufficient to derive a statistically significant measure of the differences in task efficiency and efficacy between using AUDiaL as opposed to other methods, in the following we lay our focus on reporting the user satisfaction metrics we have collected. After having completed the two hardest tasks (task 7 and 8) with either AUDiaL or by consulting the diagram's alternative long description, users were asked 5 feedback questions in order to compute the NASA Task Load Index (NASA-TLX, [9]) scores for each task. This index is a widely used assessment tool that rates user perceived workload to assess a system's effectiveness. Results, as depicted in Fig. 3, show that, on average, users rate tasks performed on AUDiaL as less mentally demanding, faster to solve, and less frustrating than the same tasks being solved with support of a long description of the diagram.

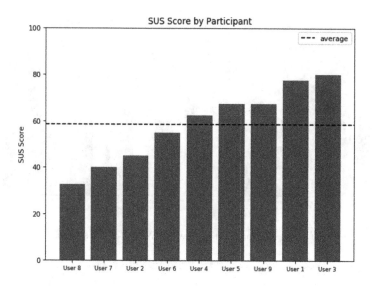

Fig. 5. SUS scores by participant.

The last part of the evaluation had participants answer the System Usability Scale (SUS) questionnaire (the *de facto* standard satisfaction measure of system usability evaluation in industry [1]) about their experiences with AUDiaL. SUS has been shown to produce the most reliable results among all sample sizes when compared to four other website usability questionnaires. Moreover, it can be used on small sample sizes with reliable results, with a reported accuracy of 75% with a sample size of 8 [17]. The results, shown in Fig. 4 and Fig. 5, exhibit that participants had somewhat mixed subjective impressions of AUDiaL. On the one hand, users found it, for the most part, usable and consistent. However, the presence of many dialogues (Fig. 6) that had to be resolved before an answer to some queries could be computed resulted on some users finding the prototype complex to use. This resulted in most participants resorting to a strategy of asking simple, short questions that they felt were less likely to provoke system prompts. The obtained average SUS score of 58.61 is an acceptable result. However, as seen in Fig. 5, scores greatly varied between individual participants. When inquired individually, users that gave the lowers scores reported a very low interest in statistics and mathematics in general. For example, the participant who gave the lowest score mentioned that she "hated maths" and initially thought the session was about tactile geographical maps. Another participant who gave AUDiaL a low usability score reported that he felt he was "just crunching numbers". However, he conceded that AUDiaL was "easier and much faster" than using a table or a tactile graphic. Another participant reported that even she though the system was "interesting and useful for blind people" she "would rather read a table" because she was already used to her screen reader's shortcuts when navigating HTML tables. This was a common motif among participants,

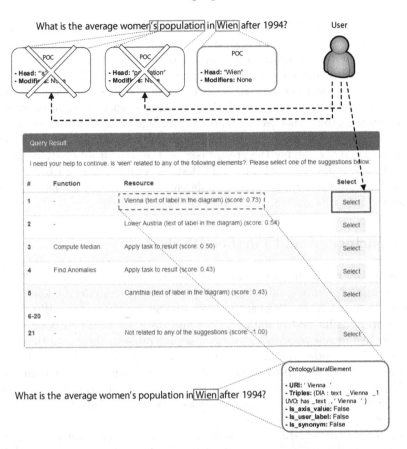

Fig. 6. Example of an (adapted) mapping dialogue. The user should select the resource on the 1st row (the literal *Vienna*) as the resource that the POC corresponding to the phrase "Wien" should be mapped to, resulting in the resolution of the unknown phrase ("Wien") to a specific resource of the underlying semantically-enhanced graphic (*Vienna*). The remaining two POCs were previously discarded by mapping them to *None* elements (last row of the mapping dialog). This process results in a consolidated user query that may now be resolved in the task execution phase of the processing pipeline. The bottom of the figure shows a consolidated query consisting of three ontology concepts ("average", mapped to an analytical task; and "women" and "Wien", mapped to literals corresponding to labels in the diagram), and a CQF ("after 1994") which will filter out the output triples having objects less than or equal to 1994 before generating the final answer.

who often requested for a list of available commands or queries understood by the system. Another common complaint was that the suggestions given by the mapping and disambiguation dialogues were not clear, especially when inputting long, complex queries.

On the other hand, participants who gave the highest score had previously attended courses on statistics and were generally more engaged and interested in the tasks performed during the evaluation, declaring that the prototype was "really fun" and that they would likely use such a system in their day-to-day lives. A participant reported that AUDiaL made the diagram "easier to understand" compared to the long description alternative, since she would always "get stuck" on the table. Another one said that AUDiaL was "very interesting" and that she enjoyed the interactivity it provided as opposed to the static nature of the table. While solving the given tasks on the tabular alternative, she commented "this is not so much fun" and that she would rather go back to using the dialogue prototype if possible. A different user said "I wish I had more time to get to know this system, I am sure I could do better".

5   Conclusions and Further Work

In conclusion, the evaluation results outlined in this paper show that NLIs display promising results in allowing blind persons to access information displayed visually in statistical charts in an autonomous and natural manner. Blind persons with a previous interest in data analysis and statistics found NLIs an engaging and effective means of accessing diagrams preferable to their traditional counterparts. On the other hand, our NLI prototype failed to provoke an interest in such matters in the case of participants already apathetic about them. These results suggest that such an approach may be of special interest in educational settings, where blind and sighted students could engage together in the same problems supported by diagrams.

The implemented NLI still presents much room for improvement, especially regarding the disambiguation phase of the NLP pipeline (Fig. 2). In addition, time constrains during evaluation sessions prevented us from evaluating whether the techniques that aim to compensate for the lack of sight when navigating complex diagrams (e.g. node annotation) enable blind persons to use the NLI more efficiently. In the future we intend to evaluate these aspects as well as an improved version of AUDiaL.

References

1. Brooke, J.: SUS: a retrospective. J. Usability Stud. **8**(2), 29–40 (2013)
2. Damljanović, D.: Natural language interfaces to conceptual models. Ph.d. thesis, University of Sheffield (2011)
3. Damljanović, D., Agatonović, M., Cunningham, H., Bontcheva, K.: Improving habitability of natural language interfaces for querying ontologies with feedback and clarification dialogues. Web Semant. Sci. Serv. Agents World Wide Web **19**, 1–21 (2013)
4. Demir, S., Oliver, D., Schwartz, E., Elzer, S., Carberry, S., McCoy, K.F.: Interactive sight into information graphics. In: Proceedings of the 2010 International Cross Disciplinary Conference on Web Accessibility (W4A). ACM, New York (2010)

5. Feng, J., Sears, A.: Speech input to support universal access. In: Stephanidis, C., (ed.) The Universal Access Handbook. Human Factors and Ergonomics. CRC Press, Boca Raton (2009)
6. Ferres, L., Lindgaard, G., Sumegi, L., Tsuji, B.: Evaluating a tool for improving accessibility to charts and graphs. ACM Trans. Comput. Hum. Interact. (TOCHI) 20(5), 28 (2013)
7. Gardner, J.: Can mainstream graphics be accessible? Inf. Technol. Disabil. E J. 14(1) (2014). http://itd.athenpro.org/volume14/number1/gardner.html
8. Goncu, C., Marriott, K.: GraVVITAS: generic multi-touch presentation of accessible graphics. In: Campos, P., Graham, N., Jorge, J., Nunes, N., Palanque, P., Winckler, M. (eds.) INTERACT 2011. LNCS, vol. 6946, pp. 30–48. Springer, Heidelberg (2011). https://doi.org/10.1007/978-3-642-23774-4_5
9. Hart, S.G.: NASA-task load index (NASA-TLX); 20 years later. In: Proceedings of the Human Factors and Ergonomics Society Annual Meeting, vol. 50, no. 9, pp. 904–908 (2006). https://doi.org/10.1177/154193120605000909
10. Keane, K.: Interactive scientific graphics: recommended practices for verbal description (2014)
11. Manning, C.D., Surdeanu, M., Bauer, J., Finkel, J., Bethard, S.J., McClosky, D.: The Stanford coreNLP natural language processing toolkit. In: Proceedings of 52nd Annual Meeting of the Association for Computational Linguistics: System Demonstrations, pp. 55–60 (2014)
12. Murillo-Morales, T., Miesenberger, K.: Non-visually performing analytical tasks on statistical charts. In: Cudd, P., de Witte, L. (eds.) Studies in health technology and informatics, vol. 242, pp. 339–346. IOS Press (2017)
13. Murillo-Morales, T., Miesenberger, K.: Ontology-based semantic support to improve accessibility of graphics. In: Sik-Lányi, C., Hoogerwerf, E.J., Miesenberger, K. (eds.) Studies in Health Technology and Informatics, vol. 217, pp. 255–260. IOS Press (2015)
14. Murillo-Morales, T., Miesenberger, K.: Techniques for improved speech-based access to diagrammatic representations. In: Miesenberger, K., Kouroupetroglou, G. (eds.) ICCHP 2018. LNCS, vol. 10896, pp. 636–643. Springer, Cham (2018). https://doi.org/10.1007/978-3-319-94277-3_98
15. Murillo-Morales, T., Plhák, J., Miesenberger, K.: Authoring semantic annotations for non-visual access to graphics. J. Technol. Pers. Disabil. 6, 398–413 (2018)
16. O'Modhrain, S., Giudice, N.A., Gardner, J.A., Legge, G.E.: Designing media for visually-impaired users of refreshable touch displays: possibilities and pitfalls. IEEE Trans. Haptics 8(3), 248–257 (2015). https://doi.org/10.1109/TOH.2015.2466231
17. Tullis, T.S., Stetson, J.N.: A comparison of questionnaires for assessing website usability. In: Usability Professional Association Conference (2004)
18. Wieringa, R.J.: Design Science Methodology for Information Systems and Software Engineering. Springer, Berlin, Heidelberg (2014). https://doi.org/10.1007/978-3-662-43839-8

EuroMath: A Web-Based Platform for Teaching of Accessible Mathematics

Donal Fitzpatrick[1]([⊠]) [ID], Azadeh Nazemi[1],
and Grzegorz Terlikowski[2]

[1] School of Computing, Dublin City University,
Glasnevin Dublin 9, Dublin, Ireland
donal.fitzpatrick@dcu.ie
[2] Faculty of Exact and Natural Sciences, Siedlce University of Natural Sciences
and Humanities, Siedlce, Poland

Abstract. One of the main goals of students' education is the acquisition of skills that will determine their functioning in the so-called community of knowledge and their success in the labour market. In 2006, the European Parliament (EP) described, defined, and issued recommendations concerning the acquisition of key competences in individual subjects and general knowledge by young people completing their compulsory education. Among the four subject-defined competences are those pertaining to mathematics and basic scientific and technical skills, as well as IT competences. The need to acquire mathematical abilities concerns amassing the aptitude to develop and use mathematical thinking in solving problems arising from everyday situations, with an emphasis on process, action, and knowledge. However, for many persons who are either blind or vision-impaired, there remains considerable barriers to equal participation in disciplines which rely on mathematical content. This paper describes the EuroMath project which has, over the past three years, developed a web-based solution to enable mathematical communication between teachers and students. Note that we do not stipulate whether the student or teacher is the individual with the visual disability. Rather, we assume that said individual can fulfil either role. To this end, the EuroMath platform has been designed to enable the person who is blind or vision-impaired to create mathematical content or acquire it from others.

Keywords: Accessible mathematics · Braille · STEM accessibility

1 Introduction

One of the main goals of students' education is the acquisition of skills that will determine their functioning in the so-called community of knowledge and their success in the labour market. In 2006, the European Parliament (EP) described, defined, and issued recommendations concerning the acquisition of key competences in individual subjects and general knowledge by young people completing their compulsory education. Among the four subject-defined competences are those pertaining to mathematics and basic scientific and technical skills, as well as IT competences. The need to acquire mathematical abilities concerns amassing the aptitude to develop and use

K. Miesenberger et al. (Eds.): ICCHP 2020, LNCS 12376, pp. 385–392, 2020.
https://doi.org/10.1007/978-3-030-58796-3_45

mathematical thinking in solving problems arising from everyday situations, with an emphasis on process, action, and knowledge.

One of the primary barriers to successful engagement by many blind students in STEM (Science, Technology, engineering and Mathematics) subjects is the lack of available and accessible solutions and resources to assist in working with this type of content. To rectify this situation partners at Dublin city University (Ireland), royal Dutch visio (the Netherlands) and NASK (Project coordinator, Poland) have been working in collaboration to develop a technological platform known as EuroMath. This web-based solution facilitates creation of math-based exercises, worksheets and other resources by a teacher who uses the traditional printed notation, and the presentation of this material in various accessible formats such as speech, large print, Unified English Braille and the Braille notation used in Poland (BNM). The tool also enables the blind student to peruse mathematical material, complete exercises, and answer quizzes etc. using their preferred input modality, and to have them translated back to standard printed notation.

The goals of this project are:

- To enable blind and vision-impaired students and their teachers to communicate mathematical concepts in a manner and using modalities which are most appropriate to their needs.
- To ensure that the blind and vision-impaired student can access the platform using technology with which they are already familiar such as their screen reader, note-taker, and/or Braille display of choice.
- To ensure that all project artefacts are built on open standards.

This work builds on previous efforts, entitled Platmat [1] which focused on the development of a suite of windows-based tools to provide access to mathematics for blind and vision-impaired students and their teachers in Poland. This award-winning project demonstrated that the techniques underpinning the EuroMath project were effective in providing communication mechanisms for mathematical content. The EuroMath platform seeks to provide a freeform editor which incorporates textual, mathematical and graphical elements. During the initial phases of design and explo-ration, it became apparent that many students did not, in fact, use traditional Windows-based computers to engage with their educational resources. Thus, a primary concern became how best to facilitate access to the content using a variety of devices and Operating Systems; not to mention input and output modalities. Thus, the EuroMath platform was developed using open web standards to cater for the diverse usage pat-terns of the demographic.

As well as providing a platform for the preparation and manipulation of mathe-matical material the EuroMath platform also seeks to provide a portal for the sharing of content. This portal has several functions which are:

- To enable a teacher to save learning content which can then be accessed by their students;
- To provide a mechanism for students to upload their solutions to problems and exercises provided by their teacher;

- To enable teachers to share examples of best practice which others may use in turn to teach their students.

The remainder of this paper will focus on the platform itself. It provides a brief overview of the state-of-the-art on which this project is based. It will also describe the design and implementation of the platform as well as the steps taken to evaluate its efficacy. We conclude with a discussion of the impact this work may have in the context of both teachers and students and outline some plans for future development.

2 State of the Art

One of the key decisions which must be made when considering the design of a suite of tools to provide access for blind and visually impaired people is the means of presenting the information to the target user. In order to implement this ideal, the notion of what information to present needs to be decided on first, followed by how to present this material. It is therefore important to understand the reading process, in order to fulfil the dual purpose of determining both what and how to present the relevant information to the user.

A key feature which is present in the visual reading process is the role of the printed page. This medium affords the reader not only the facility to act as an external memory, but also facilitates a highly refined control over the flow of information. In his Ph.D. thesis Stevens [2] states that Raynor [3] describes reading as: "...the ability to extract visual information from the page and comprehend the meaning of the text". Stevens also tells us that reading can be divided into three main domains:

- The process of understanding what has been read.
- The input of information from a physical, external source, into the reader's memory via the visual system;
- The recognition of words and their integration into higher level structures such as sentences [2].

These design decisions have enormous implications for the presentation of mathematical material in an educational context. It is imperative that students be afforded the opportunities to learn and/or manipulate formulas, rather than diverting large amounts of additional cognitive effort to memorising content. In [4], it has been shown that reading equations to blind students does involve a significantly increased cognitive load. Thus, the goal of any system should be to ensure that, to the greatest extent possible, this is reduced.

3 Platform Design and Implementation

3.1 Initial Research

Prior to embarking on the implementation phase, research was conducted into the state of educational activity in respect of mathematics in the partner countries; namely Ireland, the Netherlands and Poland. It is beyond the scope of this paper to describe the findings of this work in detail; however, the reader is directed to [5] for further information. What was discovered was that for many blind students both the design of the curriculum and a lack of access to relevant technologies were amongst the major barriers to completion of studies. It also emerged that devices such as Braille notetakers (such as those manufactured by Humanware and Hims Inc.) were very much utilised by the students in question. This report greatly informed and guided the design process for the EuroMath platform.

3.2   Design and Implementation

As was stated in the introductory section, a key principle of this research was that all components and related artefacts should be based on open standards and web technologies. To this end, the editor was designed using components built in accordance with the w3C web standards. The user interface components are all built using HTML, CSS and JavaScript whilst underlying internal representations of mathematics have been built on MathML. This ensures interoperability with other web-based technologies and ensures compatibility with screen readers and other Assistive Technology commonly utilised by blind and vision-impaired people.

Like other such tools, the EuroMath editor has a very standard look-and-feel. It contains menus, toolbars, and an area wherein one may input the desired content. There are several different types of material one may add to a document in this platform. They include text, mathematical equations and graphics. Each of these are presented in a manner which is accessible to users both with and without vision.

The EuroMath editor has been designed to satisfy several key criteria. Firstly, Students should be able to interact with mathematical content using a variety of input and/or output modalities. To that end, it is possible to explore using Braille (UEB as well as the BNM notation used in Poland), synthetic speech (using screen readers such as NVDA or JAWS) and large print; or indeed combinations of the above. It is not the intention of the developers to be in any way prescriptive by dictating which method a student should use to access the material. To facilitate this, the following have been implemented:

- An editor based on Tiny MCE [6] which has been significantly extended to enable the input and the display of mathematics. The extensions have been achieved through the use of provided APIs and customisation of underlying CSS code.
- A lightweight JavaScript converter developed as part of the EuroMath project to translate from MathML to Unified English Braille (and vice Versa).
- A converter which enables translation of Mathematical content to and from BNM.
- Incorporation of the MathJax [7] library which enables perusal of the information using synthetic speech.
- components which enable mathematics to be input using AsciiMath [8], Unicode, or Braille.
- The ability to input using Unified English Braille notation (either via a Qwerty-based keyboard or an external Braille display) and to have it translated into Printed representations.

- The ability to insert graphics in SVG format, and to explore them using touchscreen enabled devices. Note that it is also possible for blind users to prepare rudimentary graphics through a simple command-language, and the specification of coordinates and dimensions.
- Interoperability with external tools such as Desmos [8].
- The ability to emboss textual, mathematical and graphical material onto paper.

4 Example Use Case

Whilst recognising other stellar efforts in this space such as [10, 11] The EuroMath platform seeks to provide a freeform editor which incorporates textual, mathematical and graphical elements in a single document. The following is a simple scenario of use.

During the Covid-19 pandemic, a teacher in a mainstream school wishes to create exercises for her student who is blind. Because of the social distancing requirements imposed, it is not possible for the teacher to provide the exercise in a face-to-face manner. She decides to use the EuroMath platform. To this end, she opens the website and is greeted with the EuroMath interface.

The teacher writes some explanatory text in which she describes the assignment for the day. She then adds some mathematical content using the Unicode editor. The EuroMath platform renders the textual and mathematical content into Braille; the student's preferred modality. This exercise is then saved onto the Euromath Portal.

The student logs onto the EuroMath Portal and downloads his exercise. He accesses the content using Braille, and answers the questions using the same modality. The EuroMath platform translates the textual and mathematical material back into the standard printed notation with which his teacher is familiar. This is then saved to the portal by the student. She can now look at the student's work and provide appropriate feedback.

5 Evaluation

The evaluation methodology has been based on a multi-phased approach. Firstly, internal review took place to determine whether each of the components worked as expected. This necessitated testing with a variety of screen reader and browser combinations, as well as utilising devices such as notetakers which are commonly used by blind and vision-impaired people. It should be noted that two of the developers on this project were themselves blind and have extensive experience of the screen reader and browser technologies used to verify the functional completeness of the components of the EuroMath platform. Once all issues had been resolved, then the second phase, comprising expert review from stakeholders, took place.

In this series of evaluations, a functional description of the project was provided to teachers of mathematics. Whilst some had experience in teaching this material to blind and vision-impaired students, it was not deemed to be a prerequisite for participation. It was felt that, as this platform would be used in a mainstream educational setting, input from individuals who had no prior knowledge of teaching mathematics to those with visual disabilities was deemed to also be desirable. Teachers were simply asked to explore the functionality of the platform, and to use it to prepare lessons, or any other types of document containing mathematical content they thought appropriate. They were asked to envisage scenarios in which they might use this system in a classroom situation, or to provide homework and/or quizzes to their students for completion in an independent-learning situation. they were asked to engage with the platform over a period of weeks, and to note their responses on a survey which was then returned to the project partners. They were permitted to contact partners to seek guidance on any aspect of the platform which was not clear. During this phase students were also given access to the platform and were also asked to complete and return the same survey. In this discussion, results will be described in the context of Irish participants comprising 3 mainstream teachers of mathematics, one blind student, and one teacher with expertise in teaching students who are blind or vision impaired.

Whilst acknowledging the lack of a laboratory-based controlled set-up, it was felt that a more long-term study of this nature would yield better results. Firstly, this approach gave the participants time and leisure to explore the platform using their own equipment and circumstances of use. Secondly, it provided a broader more nuanced set of opinions on the overall usability and suitability of the system. At this juncture, it is only appropriate to acknowledge a glaring limitation in the evaluation described here. We are aware that no inferences can or should be drawn from results gained from only one blind student. Consequently, no statistical data is provided here as we feel that it would be unsound, and unreproducible should others attempt to duplicate our efforts. Thus, we present the findings as anecdotal only. In justification for this lack, we wish to point out that, owing to the restrictions imposed by the Irish government, it was not permissible for evaluators to enter schools and consequently the original face-to-face data-gathering exercises had to be abandoned. It is our intention to undertake the originally scheduled evaluations with younger blind and vision impaired students once restrictions have been lifted and they, and their teachers, return to school.

The context of use for the three mainstream teachers was as follows: A student was undertaking a first-year mathematics course as part of a degree programme in an Irish university. The EuroMath project was proposed as a solution to provide access to learning resources, exercises and assessments for this semester-long module. The evaluation had several key objectives:

- Could teachers and other relevant support staff/content creators provide the same, or analogous resources to the blind student?
- Could the blind student receive and access the resources?
- Could the blind student use the EuroMath platform to complete the exercises and/or assignments provided?

Results gleaned from all participants were extremely positive. In the Irish context teachers with experience of supporting blind and vision-impaired students recognise the potential that the EuroMath platform offers. The ability to remotely deliver material to the student was considered a significant bonus. What was noteworthy in the feedback, however, was the comments on the newly developed converter for Unified English Braille. Again, comments from teachers suggest that given the newness of this Braille code, accurate translation of mathematical material is not widely available. For teachers in the mainstream educational context, the most noted feature was that the EuroMath platform negated the need for the teacher to learn Braille in order to communicate with their students who were blind. This, it was felt, represented the removal of a significant stumbling block in the educational process. Teachers provided materials to their blind students who were able to interact with the content thus prepared. Indeed, it is noteworthy that the blind student who took part in the evaluation process successfully used the EuroMath platform in order to access their learning content. Both student and teachers did uncover functional bugs which have been addressed in the post-evaluation phase.

6 Conclusion

The overarching goal of the EuroMath project has always been to design an innovative multi-tool ICT platform to support teachers and learners with visual impairments in math instruction. Access to EuroMath solutions will be freeware. The project attempts to meet ICT needs that will level the playing field for learners with visual impairments in gaining math competencies aligned with the elementary and secondary education curricula in the partner countries (Ireland, Poland and the Netherlands). Both learners educated in the inclusive and mainstream settings, along with their teachers, will also benefit from the outcomes of the project.

The outcomes of the evaluation undertaken in the three partner countries, and described here in the context of Irish responses, certainly demonstrate an appetite for the EuroMath concept. That a cohort of mainstream teachers and a blind student were able to prepare and access materials using the platform, and consequently guarantee that said student could complete a first year university module in mathematics speaks to the efficacy of the platform, however more work needs to be carried out with younger students to ensure that it is suitable for those with less technical experience.

Given the modular design of the platform, we see no reason why, with the addition of minor modifications, it cannot be extended to cater for the curricula in other countries. Of most relevance, however, is that as the EuroMath platform, being web-based, is ideally suited to online/remote delivery of learning material. As has been seen from the dramatic shift to this type of educational provision caused by the Covid-19 epidemic, the need for tools which can ensure equal participation of blind and vision-impaired students in an online educational setting are vital. EuroMath is perfectly positioned to cater for the needs of face-to-face or remote learning, and thus can offer students and teachers alike the opportunity to overcome the educational challenges which have, thus far, formed a significant barrier for many blind and vision-impaired students.

References

1. Platmat portal. http://www.platmat.pl:8181/Platmat/index.xhtml. Accessed
2. Stevens, R.D.: Principles for the design of auditory interfaces to present complex information to blind computer users (1996)
3. Rayner, K., Pollatsek, A.: The Psychology of Reading. Prentice Hall, Upper Saddle River (1989). 15 June 2020
4. Gillan, D.J., Barraza, P., Karshmer, A.I., Pazuchanics, S.: Cognitive analysis of equation reading: application to the development of the math genie. In: Miesenberger, K., Klaus, J., Zagler, W.L., Burger, D. (eds.) ICCHP 2004. LNCS, vol. 3118, pp. 630–637. Springer, Heidelberg (2004). https://doi.org/10.1007/978-3-540-27817-7_94
5. Fitzpatrick, D., Murray, S., van Leendert, A., Brzostek-Pawłowska, J., Rubin, M.: A comparative analysis of ICT tools and the mathematical education of blind and visually impaired people in Ireland, Poland, the Netherlands, and neighbouring countries. Accessed 15 Jun 2020
6. TinyMCE. https://www.tiny.cloud/. Accessed 15 Jun 2020
7. MathJax: Beautiful math in all browsers. https://mathjax.org. Accessed 15 Jun 2020
8. AsciiMath. http://asciimath.org/. Accessed 15 Jun 2020
9. Desmos|Free Math. https://www.desmos.com/. Accessed 15 Jun 2020
10. Soiffer, N.: The benetech math editor: an inclusive multistep math editor for solving problems. In: Miesenberger, K., Kouroupetroglou, G. (eds.) ICCHP 2018. LNCS, vol. 10896, pp. 565–572. Springer, Cham (2018). https://doi.org/10.1007/978-3-319-94277-3_88
11. Sorge, V., Krautzberger, P., Dooley, S.: Generating and using accessible mathematics on the web, in accessing higher ground (2016)

Multidisciplinary Experience Feedback on the Use of the HandiMathKey Keyboard in a Middle School

Frédéric Vella[1], Nathalie Dubus[2], Cécile Malet[2], Christine Gallard[2], Véronique Ades[2], William Preel[2], and Nadine Vigouroux[1(✉)]

[1] IRIT, UMR CNRS 5505, Paul Sabatier University, 118 Route de Narbonne Cedex 9, 31062 Toulouse, France
{frederic.vella,nadine.vigouroux}@irit.fr
[2] ASEI, Jean Lagarde Center, 1 Avenue Tolosane, 31520 Ramonville-Saint-Agne, France

Abstract. There is a poorly addressed input area in the accessibility field that deals with the input of scientific elements including mathematical formulas. Few studies have addressed this issue although Word and Open Office editors offer input interfaces consisting of button bars associated with mathematical symbols and an "input sheet". The analysis of input activity with these tools with disabled children has revealed that the use of these bars is complex and tiring. HandyMathKey is virtual keyboard co-designed by specialized teacher and human-interaction researchers to address the difficulties of numerical mathematical input tools. The purpose of this paper is to describe the observation method implemented in a 4th grade class at the Centre Jean Lagarde in Toulouse and to report few results on usability of HMK.

Keywords: Input of mathematical formulas · Disabled children · Virtual keyboard · Evaluation

1 Introduction

Assistive technologies are often inappropriate or even abandoned due to the lack of inclusion of end-users or their ecosystem [1], especially in the field of inclusive education [2]. A numerical keyboard for mathematical input, HandiMathKey (HMK), was designed by implementing a co-design method in which teachers and occupational therapists expressed the demands for such an innovation based on their expertise, starting from the observation of the difficulties of young adolescents in school for the production of mathematical writings [3]. The purpose of this paper is to describe the observation method implemented in a 4th grade class at the Centre Jean Lagarde in Toulouse and to report few results on usability of HMK.

© Springer Nature Switzerland AG 2020
K. Miesenberger et al. (Eds.): ICCHP 2020, LNCS 12376, pp. 393–400, 2020.
https://doi.org/10.1007/978-3-030-58796-3_46

2 State of the Art

Information and communication technologies on computers, or tablets, can become an assistive technology that makes the learning process more accessible. Indeed, handwriting is a difficult and tiring task for students with grapho-motor deficits. Benoit & Sagot [4] have analyzed and identified the difficulties encountered by a student with neurodevelopmental disorders in order to determine special educational needs. This is why keystroking on the computer keyboard, combined with word processing software, is recommended for text entry. Rogers & Case-Smith [5] studied the relationships between handwriting and keyboarding performance of sixth-grade students and reported "some children with difficulty in handwriting may nonetheless become proficient in using a keyboard to wordprocess". While text input has been the subject of numerous studies [6, 7] for disabled people, there has been little research for mathematical formulas input. At the elementary and middle school levels, it is difficult to be autonomous in mathematics for students who cannot write by hand. Indeed, learning in this subject requires inserting symbols not available on a conventional keyboard and writing in a non-linear way.

There is a poorly addressed input area in the accessibility field that deals with the input of scientific elements including mathematical formulas. Few studies have addressed this issue although Word and Open Office editors offer input interfaces consisting of button bars associated with mathematical symbols and an "input sheet". The analysis of input activity with these tools with disabled children has revealed that the use of these bars is complex and tiring. Dmaths[1], MathType[2], MathMagic Lite[3], MathCast[4], ...are some interactive applications that lets you create mathematical notation. Windsteiger [10] has designed a graphical user interface based on the possibility to have dynamic objects (sliders, menus, checkboxes, radio buttons, and more) but within the specific framework of the Mathematica programming environment. Their goal was to facilitate the use of the Mathematica programming environment. Elliott and Bilmes [11] proposed the CamMath application that allows the creation and manipulation of mathematical formulas using a speech recognition system. They reported that this input modality is useful for students or professionals with motor disabilities. In addition, the use of this modality results in fewer errors and faster input of mathematical formulas than when using a keyboard and pointing device [12]. Indeed, these authors have explored a multimodal input method combining handwriting and speech. Their hypothesis is that the multimodal input may enhance computer recognition and aid user cognition. They reported that novice users were indeed faster, more efficient and enjoyed the handwriting modality more than a standard keyboard and mouse mathematics interface, especially as equation length and complexity increased. However, although speech recognition is a useful modality for people with motor disabilities, it could be on the one hand intrusive in crowded environments (schools, etc.) and on the other hand, it would have degraded performance in noisy environments.

---

[1] https://www.dmaths.org.

[2] http://www.dessci.com/en/products/mathtype.

[3] http://www.mathmagic.com.

[4] http://mathcast.sourceforge.net/home.html.

3   HandiMathKey Virtual Keyboard

The ASEI Jean Lagarde Centre in Toulouse and the IRIT laboratory have implemented the User Centred Design Method [8] and the ISO 9241-210 [9] standard for the co-design of the HandiMathKey (HMK) mathematical input keyboard.

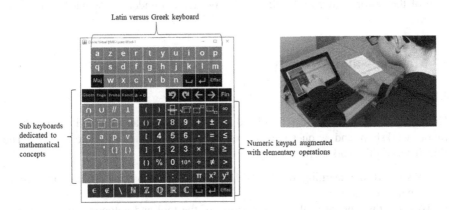

Fig. 1. Handimathkey used at the centre Jean Lagarde by a child with disabilities.

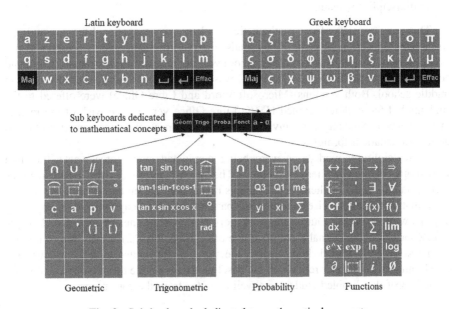

Fig. 2. Sub keyboards dedicated to mathematical concepts.

This HMK keyboard aims to address the limitations of use that users with disabilities encountered with dedicated mathematical editors or integrated in text editors (see [3]). The HMK keyboard is a multi-block integrated keyboard composed of sub keyboards (See Fig. 1) to meet the mathematical needs of middle and high school students. The background color of the sub keyboards (See Fig. 2) and the font size can be adjusted to meet accessibility needs. The HMK keyboard is currently available for each of the editors (Microsoft Office and Libre Office) under the Windows operating system.

4   Materials and Methods

4.1   Study Design

The participatory action research utilized a mixed method: an interdisciplinary observation workshop and a questionnaire on the utility and usability of HMK. The objectives of this workshop are:

- To support the learning of the HMK keyboard by putting it into practice in mathematics class.
- To assist the student in the appropriation of the tool and autonomy in the face of writing mathematics on digital media, to encourage his or her practice during personal work in secretarial work and to bring up needs and difficulties to the multidisciplinary team.

This team consists of one mathematics teacher, one occupational therapy and one specialized education assistant. They leads observe how the students accept and use HMK. This field study has lasted one school year at the Jean Lagarde rehabilitation and education Center in Toulouse. The HMK was proposed to 9 students in fourth year in middle school. Both versions (Microsoft Word and Libre Office) were offered to the students but the children learned HMK, Libre Office version, the wish of the mathematics teacher. Students were invited to use HMK in all their mathematics class to write mathematical formulas.

Interdisciplinary workshops were being conducted every three weeks (i.e. five workshops, outside mathematics class). The teacher introduces the HMK features corresponding to the mathematical concepts being taught; then the students are invited to do mathematical exercises and the occupational therapist may assist them in getting to grips with the HMK. During the workshop, two types of data are recorded: 1) notes of teacher and occupational therapist in the case report form; 2) activity log of the use of HMK. After five workshop sessions the students are invited to reply to answer a questionnaire. This paper reports on the baseline data from the questionnaire and some verbatims of the disabled students as well as notes from the case report.

4.2   Participants

The study population consists of 9 students (see Table 1), with motor disability: two of whom have associated tremors, one has a visual impairment, one an emotional disability and another a learning impairment. The modes of writing mathematical formulas were distributed as follows: 5 of them performed handwritten input (HW); 7 used personal computers (PC); 5 used personal assistant (PA). 2 of them (P2 and P9) had never used a computer before the study. On the contrary, the children (P6 and P7), who have the most difficulty with handwritten input (level 4 much difficulty), were already using the PC for input (Microsoft editor). 4 have levels of difficulty (level 3 with difficulty), one has little difficulty (level 2) and 2 have no difficulty (level 1).

Table 1. Participants profile

Children	Impairment	Mode of writing mathematics	Computer use	Difficulty level
P1	Motor	HW + PC	Yes	3
P2	Motor + learning disorders	HW	No	1
P3	Motor, right-hand predominant	HW + PC	Yes	1
P4	Motor	PC + PA	Yes	3
P5	Motor	HW + PC + PA	Yes	2
P6	Motor + emotional disorders	PC	Yes	4
P7	Motor with tremor + visual impairment	PC + PA	Yes	4
P8	Motor with tremor nts (+dysgraphia)	HW + PC + PA	Yes	3
P9	Motor	PA	No	3

5 Results

5.1 Data Analysis of Questionnaire

We have chosen to report the preliminary results of the following two questions: Q1: Is HMK easier to use than Libre Office mathematical functions? Q2: Do I feel less tired using HMK than Libre Office functions? These two questions have been evaluated on a Likert scale (1: disagree at all, 2: disagree rather than agree; 3: agree rather than disagree; 4: agree completely). Figure 3 shows a mean score of 3.25 ($\pm$1.03) for ease of use and 3.5 ($\pm$0.75) for a less tiring use situation with HMK. The ease of use score could be improved due to residual bugs in the version used during this experiment.

We also wanted to find out their ability and level of satisfaction in using the HMK keyboard by means of the following two questions: Q1: Do I feel able to use HMK on my own? Q2: Overall, I am happy using HMK. These two questions are evaluated with a score ranging from 1 to 10 (Q1: 1: I am not at all capable, 10: I am fully capable; Q2: 1: I am not at all happy, 10: I am very happy). Figure 4 shows that the mean ability to use is 7.25 $\pm$ 1.16 and the mean degree of satisfaction is 6.37 $\pm$ 2.13. These results show that HMK is an easy input tool thanks to its attractive button representation and layout. The degree of satisfaction is acceptable although we observe a large variation between subjects. As observed by the multi-disciplinary workshop team, the students have increasingly taken ownership of the tool over the course of the school year and we hope that the degree of satisfaction will increase.

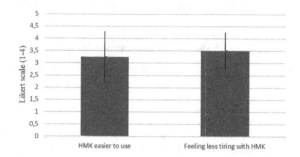

Fig. 3. Likert scale (1–4) for easiness and fatigue.

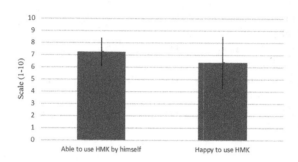

Fig. 4. Easy and satisfaction scale from 1 to 10.

5.2 Feedback from Multidisciplinary Team

The teacher and the occupational therapist have reported dialog and observations. First the behaviour and the enjoyment were different according the children. They expressed different assessments depending on their typing habits and acceptability of HMK. P1 said she did not like the HMK too much. She was generally reluctant to use the computer tool. However, when she was asked to use HMK, she did quite well. P2 told us she was not interested in the HMK because she preferred to write mathematics by hand. During the HMK sessions, she has been able to demonstrate some skills but she was not yet really taking the initiative to use this tool. P3 had a very good mastery of the HMK. He recognized the interest of the HMK in terms of time saving. P4 had a good mastery of the HMK. She used it in class without being requested and rarely asked for help from the teacher or the occupational therapist. P5 was able to invest himself to input mathematical formulas with HMK thanks to the support of an adult.

In autonomy, he does not wish to use it. P6 reported that he found that the HMK allowed him to write mathematics formulas faster, but he was accustomed to the physical keyboard. P7 found that the HMK allowed her to be faster but no less tired. Indeed, she was a fairly good mastery of HMK. P8 told us he was faster with HMK. Since the HMK experiment, he uses the computer much more easily and makes homework perfectly readable. P9 found that it was faster with HMK and that writing was less tiring. Motivation on the subject was real for him because of his difficulties in producing fine gestures.

In the inclusive school, the mathematics teacher reports that students are dependent on the AESH (Persons accompanying students with disabilities) for math class. The AESH writes in the student's place and the teacher finds this to be an obstacle to the student's progress. Indeed, the learning of mathematics is more efficient by practicing the written word as regularly as possible, even if mental arithmetic is important. The HMK perfectly meets this need. Thanks to HMK, this teacher is now able to offer a fully digital teaching for writing mathematics.

5.3   Discussion

This study confirms the interest of having a multidisciplinary team for observation and assistance in the appropriation phase of HMK. The students were all volunteers but during these workshops they did not seen the immediate interest of HMK. This interdisciplinary workshop showed that the use of HMK in mathematics class undeniably favors the acceptance of the tool and its appropriation. HMK becomes an assistive technology used by everyone in the classroom and does not point out a difficulty related to disability. It thus brings to each student the help corresponding to his needs, and according to the children it differs according to their difficulties and the levels of competence in mathematics. The students appropriated quickly HMK due to the interface affordance (the symbols are quickly understood by the students) even if they took time to perceive its interest (see Fig. 4). However, they necessarily need to be accompanied in the learning of HMK but also in the learning how to use the Libre Office text editor. The typing with HMK and Libre Office is similar to reading the mathematical formula, which makes it more affordable for students with planning and visual-spatial difficulties. Students reported that HMK is much less tiring (see Fig. 3). It would be interesting to highlight the benefits of this decrease of fatigue for young people in terms of the learning of the subject being taught (speed of grasping, duration of concentration, etc.).

6   Conclusion

The paper presents a first field study of HandiMathKey (a software keyboard for typing mathematical formulas) used by 9 motor disabled students. Questionnaire and observations were performed by a mathematics teacher and an occupational therapist during multidisciplinary workshop. The first results show that the classroom facilitates acceptability of HandiMathKey by disabled students. In general, young people adapt quickly to HMK, thanks to its intuitive layout. However, they necessarily need to be accompanied in the learning of the mathematical editor. As the sessions progressed there is a greater participation of students. This first observation over one school year made it possible to assess the relevance of the establishment of HMK as an assistive technology. These data (observations & questionnaire) must be completed by quantitative data (speed & error rate) and with more students to confirm the benefit for college.

Acknowledgments. We are thankful to the Jean Largarde Center and national education, for giving us access to students. The authors also thanks the students in the experiment.

References

1. Guffroy, M., Nadine, V., Kolski, C., Vella, F., Teutsch, P.: From human-centered design to disabled user & ecosystem centered design in case of assistive interactive systems. Int. J. Sociotechnology Knowl. Dev. **9**(4), 28–42 (2017)
2. Federici, S., Borsci, S.: Providing assistive technology in Italy: the perceived delivery process quality as affecting abandonment. Disabil. Rehabil. Assist. Technol. **11**(1), 22–31 (2016)
3. Bertrand, E., Sauzin, D., Vella, F., Dubus, N., Vigouroux, N.: HandiMathKey: mathematical keyboard for disabled person. In: Miesenberger, K., Bühler, C., Penaz, P. (eds.) ICCHP 2016. LNCS, vol. 9759, pp. 487–494. Springer, Cham (2016). https://doi.org/10.1007/978-3-319-41267-2_68
4. Benoit, H., Sagot, J.: L'apport des aides techniques à la scolarisation des élèves handicapés. La nouvelle revue de l'adaptation et de la scolarisation **43**, 19–26 (2008)
5. Rogers, J., Case-Smith, J.: Relationships between handwriting and keyboarding performance of sixth-grade students. Am. J. Occupational Therapy **56**(1), 34–39 (2002)
6. Pouplin, S., et al.: Effect of a dynamic keyboard and word prediction systems on text input speed in patients with functional tetraplegia. J. Rehabil. Res. Dev. **51**(3), 467–480 (2014)
7. Polacek, O., Sporka, A.J., Slavik, P.: Text input for motor-impaired people. Univ. Access Inf. Soc. **16**(1), 51–72 (2015). https://doi.org/10.1007/s10209-015-0433-0
8. Norman, D.A.: The design of everyday things: Revised and expanded edition. Basic Books, New York (2013)
9. ISO, I.: 9241: Ergonomic requirements for office work with visual display terminals-Part 11: Guidance on usability. ISO, Geneva (1998)
10. Windsteiger, W.: Theorema 2.0: A graphical user interface for a mathematical assistant system (2013). arXiv preprint arXiv:1307.1945
11. Elliott, C., Bilmes, J.: Computer based mathematics using continuous speech recognition. Striking a C[h]ord: Vocal Interaction in Assistive Technologies, Games and More (2007)
12. Anthony, L., Yang, J., Koedinger, K.R.: Evaluation of multimodal input for entering mathematical equations on the computer. In: CHI 2005 Extended Abstracts on Human Factors in Computing Systems, pp. 1184–1187 (2005)

Rainbow Math

A Case Study of Using Colors in Math for Students with Moderate to Severe Dyslexia

Neil Soiffer[1]([⊠]) [iD] and Jennifer L. Larson[2]([⊠]) [iD]

[1] Talking Cat Software, Portland, OR 97229, USA
soiffer@alum.mit.edu
[2] My City School, 855 27th Ave., San Francisco, CA 94121, USA
jennifer@mycityschool.com

Abstract. The goal of Rainbow Math is to investigate what font-related changes can be made to aid students with dyslexia and other learning disabilities. As part of the initial step, we developed software that allows students do customize coloring of text, modify the text's spacing and style on a per-character basis. Additionally, students can use color to visually distinguish what is between parentheses, brackets, etc. Testing with 13 middle school students showed that most students liked larger fonts, extra spacing between operators, bold fonts, and highlighting of parenthesized expressions. Their self-chosen preferences resulted in decreased reading times and decreased errors.

Keywords: Math accessibility · Dyslexia · Fonts for dyslexia · Learning disabilities · Reading impairments · Visual processing

1 Background

Dyslexia is a developmental learning disability that interferes with the ability to read/recognize and spell words. Dyslexia affects an estimated 5%–10% of the U.S. population and varies significantly in its severity. Its symptoms also vary depending on age [11].

Many studies on dyslexia have been performed for readability and comprehension of *text*, both on paper and on a computer. Based on results of past studies, [10] focused on those things found most useful to change. Their study group was larger than previous studies and used eye tracking to help make sense of the results. They found that (in order of importance) font size (18–24pt), character spacing (0–14% increase), text and background color, and text grey scale were the most important factors related to reducing fixation time; the longer the eye is "stuck", the more the reader is working to read the text. Their results with color did not completely match those of previous studies. In particular high contrast is often not recommended for people with dyslexia [1], but in their study, subjects preferred black on yellow, although eye tracking showed it had the highest fixation times. Factors not found to be important were line spacing, paragraph spacing, and column width. This group was composed of Spanish

© Springer Nature Switzerland AG 2020
K. Miesenberger et al. (Eds.): ICCHP 2020, LNCS 12376, pp. 401–409, 2020.
https://doi.org/10.1007/978-3-030-58796-3_47

readers, so results may not carry forward to English *text* readers, but do seem relevant for reading *math* because language differences are small in mathematics.

On computers, special fonts for dyslexic readers have been devised. However, several recent studies have cast doubt on their usefulness [9, 14]. Both of these studies show that italic fonts tend to increase reading time; italic fonts are typically used for variables in math. There do not appear to be any studies related to math, fonts, and dyslexia.

Many interventions to help with reading involve coloring. Colored lenses and overlays have long been used to aid reading because it is believed to reduce visual stress, although some studies have challenged their usefulness, at least for adults with dyslexia [17]. [8] showed that using a warm color such as peach for a background on a computer increased reading speeds among dyslexics and the general population by 50% over a cold color. [7] studied various coloring techniques such as coloring words different colors, coloring the start and end of words differently, and coloring each syllable differently. They found that "color wins against all of the known typesetting similarities such as underline, italic and bold fonts playing together" (p. 5).

The work above is about static text. On a computer, dynamic effects are possible. The most common technique is to read the text aloud. This can be done alone or with reinforcement by highlighting the words as they are spoken. Several meta-analyses have come to mixed conclusions on the effectiveness of read aloud as summarized in [15]. The authors performed their own meta-analysis. They concluded that read aloud may assist students with reading comprehension, but there are many variables that might moderate the effect. As they note, earlier computer voices were very mechanical and lacked prosody that makes human speech more interesting to listen to; many of the studies reviewed involved human readers. The ability to highlight words as are they are spoken is less well studied. [4] studied dyslexic children reading Japanese, so the results are not necessarily applicable to reading English. They found that sentence highlighting with blue background most strongly reduced eye fixation time. A second study they performed found that in side by side comparisons, students preferred blue sentence backgrounds along with blue or yellow word highlights, but no actually reading was done in the second study. [16] compared computer text to speech (TTS) with and without highlighting to silent reading, read aloud, and listen only. TTS (with and without highlighting) improves comprehension scores for students with dyslexia. Only children with reading & language impairments benefited from highlighting.

All of the above studies involved text, not computer reading of math. To the authors' knowledge, Project SMART [5] and its follow-on MeTRC study [6] are the only studies that involved math with synchronized highlighting. The first study involved 48 middle school students with learning disabilities. This study modified textbooks to use MathML to encode the math. The study used TextHELP's Read & Write Gold to read and highlight the text together with MathPlayer [12] to read and highlight the math. One textbook had systemic errors in the conversion and another had very few mathematical expressions; no benefit was seen in those texts. However, the textbook with the most math "exhibited the most consistent improvement in pre/post test scores for intervention students using the digital version in comparison to control students using the print version." The MeTRC study expanded upon the

Project SMART to include workbooks, handouts, and quizzes in the materials that were made accessible. An initial assessment consisted of 17 students who had an Individualized Education Program that included an oral accommodation in math reading aloud both word problems and math symbols. The assessment found that these students had an average error rate of 6.7% in reading the plain text word problems, but their error rate for reading symbolic math content soared to 36%. At the end of the school year, students using MathML-encoded eText were compared to a control group that used standard read aloud accommodations. Those using enhanced math had gains of 16.7 points on a standardized test versus gains of 8 points for the control group. Remarkably, the gains for the math enhanced special ed group outpaced those of the average (non-special ed) 7th graders.

2 Study Software and Plan

This paper details a preliminary investigation into whether the pencil and paper coloring ideas currently in use in some classrooms for dyslexic children will work when transferred to a computer.

Because no one has developed software to color math, the goal of this initial study is to get qualitative feedback from students and teachers as to what features are subjectively useful, not useful, and what would be useful to add in the future. In particular, does the coloring used on paper by the teachers at the school to help students "see" the math also work on computer screens.

The end goal is to incorporate the useful features of Rainbow Math into Mathshare [13], an accessible math editor. Mathshare already supports synchronized highlighting of spoken math so this study focuses only on coloring math. To ease implementation and allow freer experimentation, the software designed for this study is text-based and allows only linear math (no superscripts, square roots, or 2D fractions). Most of the students who participated in the study are still learning basic arithmetic, so this restriction is not a major hindrance. The study software consists of two web pages: one to design a set of coloring and spacing rules (teacher and student working together) and another (simpler) page for students to try out the coloring rules to solve problems.

Based on classroom experience, students with dyslexia can confuse one character for another character – e.g., '3' and '8'. They also have trouble reading thin/small characters such as "-" and ".". Classroom experience has shown that some students are resistant to using coloring because it requires them to switch pens frequently. Poor handwriting and/or dysgraphia is often associated with people with dyslexia [2]. Using a computer, software can color the math automatically so less physical and mental effort is required to write math. By moving to a computer keyboard, issues surrounding handwriting are minimized. Color coding characters and being to make individual characters bold are two known requirements for the software. Being able to easily see bracketed expressions is another design goal.

The design page is shown in Fig. 1. Any character can be changed in the following ways:

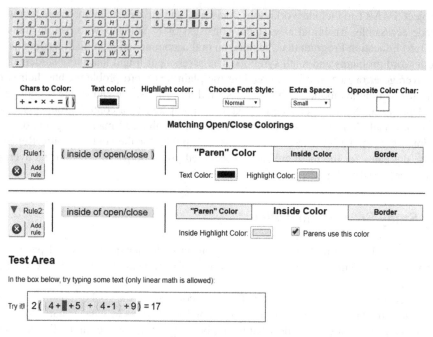

Fig. 1. Design page

- The text color and background color can be changed
- The character can be made italic, bold, or normal.
- Extra space can be added around the character.

When a character is given some coloring, the system automatically calculates the opposite background color on the color wheel, and then picks a contrasting foreground color so the user can create easily distinguished characters pairs (useful for characters that are often confused with each other). The teacher and students never made use of this feature.

The software also supports highlighting the area between matching chars. These areas can be colored or have a line drawn above, below, or around the interior of the bracketed expression. The line can be colored and its thickness changed so that it is subtle or obvious. The bracketing characters can be included or excluded from the coloring. The first version of the software supported a more complicated scheme for individual coloring of matching areas based on the open/close characters. This was found to be confusing for the teacher. Support was tried for coloring each matching area differently, but that was non-intuitive in practice. The current version will color each nesting level differently up to the number of rules that are defined. In Fig. 1, two rules are defined; nesting in the "try it" example shows the two levels of coloring. This approach seems intuitive because it makes it clearer which part of the problem to solve first.

The coloring rules can be saved and distributed to students. A page for students to use to solve problems was created but never used in testing due to time constraints.

The test page consists of lines where students can type/solve their math problems along with a palette of special symbols. There is also an area where students can control the amount of coloring used (e.g., they can lessen or remove foreground and/or background coloring). This was added because based on the teacher's experience, as students progress, they tend to need less color support. Because of space limitations and because the page was not used, it is not shown here.

After an initial round of designing colorings with 7 students and one teacher, the software was revised and a second more thorough round of testing was performed with 13 students (5 boys, 8 girls), many of them the same as in the first round. Most of the students have many other diagnoses besides dyslexia. These include dyscalculia, dysgraphia, and ADHD. The students are from a small middle school focused on children with severe reading disorders; one student is in 12th grade and attended the school when she was in middle school. The second round of testing occurred during COVID-19 shutdowns and was done via Zoom. Because of this, we were not able to control the screens and viewing environments used during the tests.

The initial round of design/testing helped refine the features the software supports and also refined the user interface so that it was easier for the teacher to create the coloring and styling the students requested. The second round incorporated six test expressions that were presented to the students in a randomized sequence. Half the expressions were shown using 14pt Arial and half using 21pt Arial[1]. The students were asked to read the expression (not solve it). The time taken and number of errors were recorded for each reading. A 14pt font was used because that is typical of what students read without accommodations, and a 21pt font was chosen because studies show many students prefer a larger font. Testing proceeded as follows:

1. Students were asked to read the first expression at 14pt, then asked to read the second at 21pt. Errors and timings were recorded for both readings and all subsequent readings.
2. The size was reduced to 14pt and the students were asked the open-ended question: "what would make this easier to read?" If they didn't suggest something, they were asked "would spacing changes to specific symbols make this easier to read?" Based on the earlier study, this was a common part of a student's eventual preference. If they said yes, they were asked which characters should have more space and were given a range of choices for the amount of space.
3. They then read the third expression and were again asked if they wanted to change anything. If they hadn't already mentioned it, they were asked "would bolding or highlighting changes to specific symbols make this easier to read?" Any requested changes were made, sometimes repeatedly until the student was satisfied with the bolding/coloring.
4. They then read the fourth expression and were again asked if they wanted to change anything. After asking if they wanted more changes, they were asked "would coloring the insides of parentheses and brackets make this easier to read?" Any

---

[1] Two students struggled to see 14pt well and 16pt was used instead; one of those students also used 26t instead of 21pt to read one question.

requested changes were made, with demonstrations of options of including/excluding the parentheses in the coloring/box.

5. They then read the fifth expressions. They were asked if they wanted to change anything.
6. The sixth and final expression was read[2].

Two examples of chosen coloring of expressions are shown in Fig. 2.

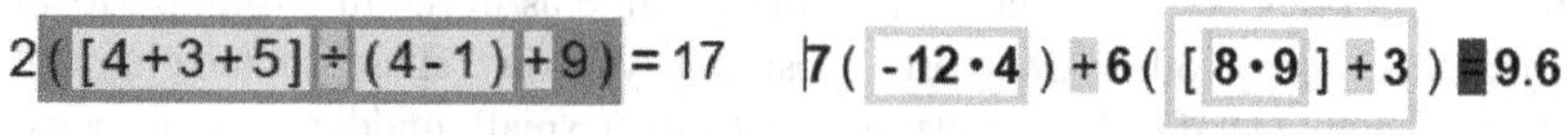

$$2([4+3+5] \div (4-1) + 9) = 17 \qquad 7(-12 \cdot 4) + 6([8 \cdot 9] + 3) = 9.6$$

Fig. 2. Two example equations with student preferences

Based on the research cited above and an initial round of testing, we hypothesized that font size, font spacing, and font colors would be features the students requested and that the error rates and time it takes to read the questions would decrease as they narrowed in on their preferred renderings.

3 Results

The primary goal of this study was to get qualitative feedback on whether students with dyslexia and other learning challenges find font-related changes helpful. Based on the students' choices/verbal feedback:

- 12 out of 13 said increasing the *font size* made the problem easier to read
- 11 out of 13 said that *spacing* things out made it easier to read
- 9 out of the 13 said *highlighting the parentheses/brackets and their contents* made the math problems easier to read and know what to do first.
- 9 out of the 13 said *bolding* the operators and/or symbols made it easier to read
- 6 out of the 13 said having the *operators and symbols* in a different *color* made it easier to see the symbols

There did not appear to be any strong similarities among the students with regard to color preference – sometimes a "+" had yellow background, sometimes purple, and sometimes it was not colored at all. During the tests, students would often say something like "purple is my favorite color, so highlight it in purple". Often, the student would modify the color to increase the contrast between foreground and background.

Students with more severe visual impairments found a greater number of changes helpful. This is shown in Table 1.

---

[2] One student stopped after reading five questions.

Table 1. Number of changes by amount of impairment

Degree of impairment	# of changes					
	0	1	2	3	4	5
Mild (B1, C1, C2, E1, E2,V1)	1	0	2	2	1	0
Moderate (T1, I1, J1)	0	0	0	1	2	0
Severe (L1, S1, A1, G1)	0	0	0	0	1	3

The expressions were of similar length, but we did not account for the different length of time it takes to read different characters/numbers in the test design. For example, "1" takes less time to read than "7". To compensate, the authors read the expressions, averaged their times, and scaled the data to reflect the relative differences in reading times. The adjusted times are reported in Table 2. The slope of a linear regression (Slope$_{e+}$) gives the trend; a negative value indicates decreasing times as testing progressed and modifications were made. Because some of the errors students made were omissions of characters, the omissions lower the time taken and skew the regression. The cells with a yellow highlight in Table 2 indicate times that include those omission errors. The regression line slope with those cells omitted is "Slope$_{e-}$".

Table 2. Adjusted Reading Times (secs) for questions (in reading order)

	B1	C1	C2	E1	T1	L1	S1	A1	I1	E2	J1	G1	V1
1	14	14	20	18	23	12	16	11	33	16	23	19	19
2	18	13	17	19	21	26	18	11	18	11	18	24	20
3	19	12	29	17	36	29	16	15	24	11	22	19	19
4	18	14	14	14	24	31	17	17	12	14	27	16	18
5	16	16	18	18	16	31	12	12	21	12	17	21	18
6	15	16	12		27	14	19	19	15	14	20	19	19
Slope$_{e+}$	0.0	0.7	−1.5	−0.6	−0.3	0.7	−0.2	1.2	−2.7	−0.1	−0.3	−0.3	−0.2
Slope$_{e-}$	−0.9	1.4		−0.6	−0.9	−3.4		1.2		0.7	−0.5	0.1	−0.2

Based on these times, the Slope$_{e+}$ and Slope$_{e-}$ values show that reading times for most students decreased as the students added their preferred modifications.

Table 3. Errors in reading questions

B1	C1	C2	E1	T1	L1	S1	A1	I1	E2	J1	G1	V1
4	6	3	0	2	8	1	0	5	6	2	0	3
0	4	2	1	0	0	4	0	4	4	1	2	0
0	6	0	0	1	0	6	0	3	3	0	3	1
0	6	3	0	0	12	3	0	4	2	4	2	0
0	0	3	0	0	15	3	0	3	0	0	2	0
0	0	2		0	0	1	0	0	0	2	1	0

Table 3 shows the errors the students made in reading the expressions. Although there appears to be a trend towards fewer errors at the end of testing, the low number of errors by most students prevents drawing any conclusions about errors decreasing significantly. The yellow highlight coloring indicates the students with the most severe visual impairments. Except for A1, they made the most errors. L1's and J1's errors initially jumped when bracketed quantities were colored; they started reading those parts first, as if they were going to solve the problems.

4 Conclusions and Future Work

With the exception of the one student who did not make changes, the students felt that the coloring and font changes would help them read, understand, and do math problems with fewer errors. This study provides evidence that they do read more quickly and that the error rate may drop with the individual modifications they made. The next step is add this functionality to Mathshare as mentioned earlier and then see if these results hold for 2D mathematical notations.

In our study, many of the students with dyslexia were also diagnosed with Attention Deficit Hyperactivity Disorder (ADHD). One estimate is that 30% of those with dyslexia also have ADHD [3]. The original coloring ideas were based on issues related to dyslexia, but research on ADHD has also indicated that coloring of background, numbers, and operators can help because it acts as visual stimulation to keep students on task [18]. As with dyslexia, [18] reports that students with ADHD and other LDs have greater deficits in math than in reading as compared to students with just ADHD. Because maintaining attention is critical in this group, additional work looking at randomizing colors or using other means to present novel stimulus on each problem is an option that should be pursued.

Acknowledgements. We would like to thank the students of My City School for participating in the study along with their parents for allowing them to participate in the study. The testing took place as COVID-19 spread in their area. They were helpful, thoughtful, and focused despite the news around them.

References

1. Beacham, N.: Dyslexia-friendly computer based learning materials. Access All Areas: Disability, Technology and Learning, 73–77 (2002)
2. "Frequently Asked Questions." *International Dyslexia Association*, dyslexiaida.org/frequently-asked-questions-2/. Retrieved March, 2020
3. International Dyslexia Association (Feb, 2020). Attention-Deficit/Hyperactivity Disorder (AD/HD) and Dyslexia. Retrieved from https://dyslexiaida.org/attention-deficithyperactivity-disorder-adhd-and-dyslexia/
4. Ikeshita, H., Yamaguchi, S., Morioka, T., Yamazoe, T.: Effects of highlighting text on the reading ability of children with developmental dyslexia: a pilot study. Int. J. Emerg. Technol. Learn. **13**(09), 239–251 (2018), https://www.learntechlib.org/p/184882/

5. Lewis, P., Noble, S., Soiffer, N.: Using accessible math textbooks with students who have learning disabilities. In: *Proceedings of the 12th International ACM SIGACCESS Conference on Computers and Accessibility - ASSETS 10*. (2010). https://doi.org/10.1145/1878803.1878829

6. Lewis, P., Lee, L., Noble, S., Garrett, B.: KY math etext project- a case study: math curriculum digital conversion and implementation.Inf. Technol. Disabil. *E-J. 13*(1), (2013)

7. Pinna, B., Deiana, K.: On the role of color in reading and comprehension tasks in dyslexic children and adults. I-Perception **9**(3), 204166951877909 (2018). https://doi.org/10.1177/2041669518779098

8. Rello, L., et al.: One half or 50%? An eye-tracking study of number representation readability. In Proc. INTERACT 2013, Cape Town, South Africa, 2013 http://nil.fdi.ucm.es/sites/default/files/interact2013-NENE.pdf

9. Rello, L., Baeza-Yates, R.: Good fonts for dyslexia. In: Proceedings of the 15th International ACM SIGACCESS Conference on Computers and Accessibility - ASSETS 2013, (2013).https://doi.org/10.1145/2513383.2513447

10. Rello, L., Baeza-Yates, R.: How to present more readable text for people with dyslexia. Universal Access Inf.Soc. **16**(1), 29–49 (2015). https://doi.org/10.1007/s10209-015-0438-8

11. Roitsch, J., Watson, S.: An overview of dyslexia: definition, characteristics, assessment, identification, and intervention. Science J. Educ. **7**(4), 81 (2019). https://doi.org/10.11648/j.sjedu.20190704.11

12. Soiffer, N.: MathPlayer v2.1. In: Proceedings of the 9th International ACM SIGACCESS Conference on Computers and Accessibility - Assets 2007, (2007). https://doi.org/10.1145/1296843.1296900

13. Soiffer, N.: The benetech math editor: an inclusive multistep math editor for solving problems. In: Miesenberger, K., Kouroupetroglou, G. (eds.) ICCHP 2018. LNCS, vol. 10896, pp. 565–572. Springer, Cham (2018). https://doi.org/10.1007/978-3-319-94277-3_88

14. Wery, Jessica J., Diliberto, Jennifer A.: The effect of a specialized dyslexia font, OpenDyslexic, on reading rate and accuracy. Ann. Dyslexia **67**(2), 114–127 (2016). https://doi.org/10.1007/s11881-016-0127-1

15. Wood, S.G., Moxley, J.H., Tighe, E.L., Wagner, R.K.: Does use of text-to-speech and related read-aloud tools improve reading comprehension for students with reading disabilities? A meta-analysis. J. Learn. Disabil. **51**(1), 73–84 (2018). https://doi.org/10.1177/0022219416688170

16. Wood, S., Shepardson, N., Keelor, J.: Empowering the Reader Through the Dynamics of Text-to-Speech. Retrieved Feb 2020 from (ATIA 2020). https://s3.goeshow.com/atia/orlando/2020/profile.cfm?profile_name=download&xtemplate&handout_key=1121C056-F04D-A206-2B64-853338BBC755

17. Uccula, A., Enna, M., Mulatti, C.: Colors, colored overlays, and reading skills. Front. Psychol. **5**, 833 (2014). https://doi.org/10.3389/fpsyg.2014.00833

18. Zentall, S.S., Tom-Wright, K., Lee, J.: Psychostimulant and sensory stimulation interventions that target the reading and math deficits of students with adhd. J. Atten. Disord. **17**(4), 308–329 (2012). https://doi.org/10.1177/1087054711430332

On Automatic Conversion from E-born PDF into Accessible EPUB3 and Audio-Embedded HTML5

Masakazu Suzuki[1](✉) and Katsuhito Yamaguchi[2]

[1] Institute of Mathematics for Industry, Kyushu University, Fukuoka, Japan
msuzuki@sciaccess.net
[2] Junior College Funabashi Campus, Nihon University, Tokyo, Japan
eugene@sciaccess.net
http://www.sciaccess.net/en/

Abstract. As a promising method to make digital STEM books in PDF accessible, a new assistive technology to convert inaccessible PDF into accessible digital books in some different-type formats are shown. E-born PDF is initially converted into text-based EPUB3, and then, it is converted into audio-embedded HTML5 with JavaScript (ChattyBook). In the conversion, various local languages can be chosen for reading out STEM contents.

Keywords: E-born PDF · Conversion · Accessible e-books

1 Introduction

"Adobe Portable Document Format (PDF)" is commonly used for the exchange of STEM (science, technology, engineering and math) contents among researchers or in various educational fields. Although the PDF/UA standard is suggested as so-called "accessible PDF" [1], it is not necessarily easy to produce a document so as to conforms to the standard of PDF/UA. Unfortunately, most of PDF documents in the world are not accessible, and it is difficult to convert a given (inaccessible) PDF into PDF/UA automatically with a concise procedure. Furthermore, it should be emphasized that there are no well-established standards for an accessible STEM document including mathematical expressions in PDF.

In most cases, when considering PDF accessibility, target disabled people are usually assumed as the blind, and the conversion of PDF into Braille or text files with LaTeX notation has been mainly treated. However, there are many dyslexic people in the print-disabled, who can read neither a Braille document nor texts in the LaTeX notation. A large number of the low vision or people who have lost their sight in not-younger days cannot, either.

As a promising method to make digital STEM books in PDF accessible, here, we show a new assistive technology to convert inaccessible PDF into accessible digital books in some different-type formats. In the next section, we classify PDF into two categories, "E-born PDF" and "image PDF." In this paper,

K. Miesenberger et al. (Eds.): ICCHP 2020, LNCS 12376, pp. 410–416, 2020.
https://doi.org/10.1007/978-3-030-58796-3_48

we give a new tool to convert E-born PDF into text-based EPUB3 (the latest release of an open-ebook-standard EPUB), and then, into audio-embedded HTML5 with JavaScript ("ChattyBook"), so that the document content including math expressions is read out without a screen reader. In the conversion, various local languages can be chosen for reading out STEM contents.

2   PDF Classification

To make our task much clearer, we begin with discussing different types of PDF. Nowadays, a PDF file is commonly produced from a digital format such as a document in Microsoft Word, LaTeX, Adobe InDesign, etc. In those PDF, the information on each character/symbol such as its character code, font type, coordinates on a page is usually embedded. You can cut and paste text information from them. As far as a math expression is concerned, its structure cannot be maintained through cut-and-pasting, but actually, its accurate character information can be detected even in the math expression by making use of a PDF parser. Based on the information, we can analyze its structure without an OCR (optical character recognition) process. We refer to such PDF as "E-born PDF" or simply, "ePDF".

On the other hand, recently, image files are usually provided in PDF, which are made by scanning or copying. In principle, such PDF has no character information. Actually, many of them include not only images but also text information (a recognition result by OCR) in the background. However, it often includes a lot of recognition errors. Concerning a math part, you cannot use such background information to analyze the math structure since it usually consists of meaningless characters/symbols. We call them "image PDF".

In some E-born PDF, to keep original layout in various display environment, characters/symbols are replaced with their scalable-vector (outline) images. In zooming-up, characters should be kept being fine, no matter how large they are magnified; however, the character information is not embedded in it. We call them "outline PDF". Although they are actually E-born PDF, from the viewpoint of recognition processing, we classify them as a kind of image PDF.

3   Accessible EPUB3

In this section, we discuss the conversion from E-born PDF into accessible EPUB3 [2]. There are several versions in EPUB3, and some of them are not compatible with each other. In this paper, we treat just EPUB3.1 which is expected to be popularized from now on. Here, we refer to it as EPUB3 or simply, EPUB.

There are two types of accessible EPUB. One of them includes audio files of aloud-reading as media-overlay, and the other does not. We call them "audio-embedded EPUB" and "text-based EPUB," respectively.

In Japan, "the Japanese Society for Rehabilitation of Persons with Disabilities" has been providing print-disabled students with e-textbooks in multimedia DAISY (Digital Accessible Information System) format [3,4]. They are now preparing to change the format of accessible e-textbooks to audio-embedded EPUB in the near future. In Japanese, four different character sets are used simultaneously in print: Chinese characters, Hiragana, Katakana and alphanumeric letters. While Hiragana and Katakana are essentially kinds of phonetic symbols, a single Chinese character or a compound of the characters usually has several ways of pronouncing, according to its context. In STEM, they are often read in a different manner from the usual. As the result, text-to-speech (TTS) engine tends to make mistakes quite frequently in reading out Japanese texts, and we do need to embed audio files of aloud-reading corrected manually in advance.

On the other hand, a TTS engine seldom makes such mistakes in English-speaking countries, and text-based EPUB is mainstream. It is possible to adopt a workflow to produce text-based EPUB initially and then, to convert it into audio-embedded EPUB. Thus, as the first step, we have developed a tool to convert E-born PDF into text-based EPUB.

4   Conversion from E-born PDF into Text-Based EPUB

As was pointed out, in E-born PDF, the structure of math formulas cannot be maintained through cut-and-pasting. However, even in their inside, the accurate information on each character/symbol such as its character code, font type, coordinates on a page is embedded.

In the latest version of our OCR software for STEM, "InftyReader" [5], by making use of "vector-image information" for printing characters/symbols, which is provided by a powerful PDF parser, we can get not only character information but the true graphical area of the original character image even in the inside of mathematical formulas. Thus, it does not need any commercial OCR engines for recognizing/analyzing STEM contents in E-born PDF. Since character codes are precisely obtained, accurate conversion into text and mathematical-structure analysis can be done [6]. Furthermore, document structures such as chapters, sections, headings can be also obtained by classifying fonts used in the PDF. Thus, we have recently implemented a new function in InftyReader so that it can convert the recognition result of E-born PDF directly into text-based EPUB, in which math expressions are represented in MathML.

5   Remaining Tasks

One of our remaining important tasks in STEM-document recognition is the segmentation of pages into figures/charts/diagrams/tables and main text areas (including math formulas). It is still difficult to realize the correct segmentation for a complicated-layout document. Analyzing the structure of tables including connected or multiple-line cells is also another remaining task. While simple tables are usually all right, InftyReader often fails at analyzing complicated-layout tables. Analyzing reading order of text areas is also difficult. As is well known, an order, in which text blocks are stored in the inside of PDF, is often different from the actual reading order. While analyzing the text order is not so difficult for a simple-layout PDF, recent school textbooks tend to have very complicated layout, and automatic text-order analysis is also a remaining important task.

In the ICCHP conference, we will show a tentative method to treat those tasks effectively, for the present. We developed an interface for InftyReader to allow users to correct manually area segmentation and their attributes including the reading order before the EPUB conversion.

6   Audio-Embedded HTML5: ChattyBook

Recently, multimedia DAISY is widely accepted as a standard of accessible e-books for various print-disabled people such as the blind, the dyslexic, etc. Accessible EPUB is essentially DAISY, Ver.4 that does not exist as a DAISY version. However, we must confess that there also remain some problems to deserve greater attention even now; that is, ordinary DAISY contents and players are not necessarily useful enough for the students with dyslexia. For instance, unlike visually disabled people, they usually do not use a screen reader, and a good TTS engine is not installed in their computers, either. Furthermore, their environment such as devices, OS, players, etc. is different from each other. You have to customize the DAISY contents frequently to meet each user's demands/environment.

To make DAISY/accessible EPUB be more useful for all, we developed a Windows application named "ChattyBooks" which converts DAISY/accessible-EPUB STEM content into audio-embedded HTML5 with JavaScript (Chatty-Book) [7]. It consists of two component modules: a converter and a file manager. If a DAISY/accessible EPUB content is dropped on the ChattyBooks icon or in the ChattyBooks main window, it is converted automatically into HTML5 with JavaScript (a ChattyBook), and it is listed on the main window (bookcase) of ChattyBooks. When double-clicking a title on the bookcase, a browser such as Google Chrome displays the content which has the almost-same functionality and operability of high-quality as the original DAISY/accessible EPUB. An advantage of this scheme is that the converted book, ChattyBook, is an HTML5 document and can be played with any standard browsers, such as Google Chrome, Firefox, Edge, Safari, etc.

ChattyBooks uses Microsoft Speech API, Ver.5 (SAPI5) as a TTS engine. If multiple SAPI5 voices are available, a user can choose any of them in the conversion. Even if the original accessible-EPUB is text-based, in ChattyBook, aloud-reading of the entire content including technical notations such as math expressions is embedded as mp3 audio files, and users can listen to it in a high-quality voice with text/math highlighting to aid their comprehension even if they do not have a good TTS engine for themselves. In addition, since it is just HTML5 with JavaScript, it can be played by any popular browsers. User need not to use any DAISY/EPUB player. Disabled users can access easily the contents with their own environment: Windows, Mac, iPad, iPhone, Android, Chrome book, etc.

7 Localization

In the latest version of our accessible STEM-document editor, "ChattyInfty3," a new localization scheme has been compiled [8]. It allows end-users to incorporate the necessary definition files for aloud reading of mathematical notations in each local language efficiently/systematically into ChattyInfty3. The users can customize the software simply by putting the definition files in a specified folder and changing some software settings; then, ChattyInfty contents including math expressions are read out in that local language.

Actually, several local-language groups/individuals have been working on developing their own language versions: Czech, French, German, Greek, Italian, Kannada, Spanish, Turkish and Vietnamese versions of ChattyInfty3, most of which have been done without our help. It shows that ChattyInfty3 is actually customizable for various local languages by making use of the localization scheme. We have recently improved InftyReader so that the localization scheme is also available in converting text-based EPUB into ChattyBook. Thus, if the necessary definition files were prepared, a user could produce an accessible STEM book in their own local language easily from E-born PDF.

8 Manner of Aloud Reading for Math Expressions

"What way of aloud reading is appropriate to access math expressions" depends on the user's characteristic; each one has their own needs. While there is no problem in reading out a simple math formula, concerning a complicated/long math expression, one should figure out what way is appropriate to make it easy to understand.

In the conversion of text-based EPUB into ChattyBook, you can choose three types of aloud-reading for math formulas. "Plain Reading" is based on one which may be most widely used in English-speaking countries (the English version). It is natural, but a spoken mathematical expression is often ambiguous just only with speech. It is assumed that people with low vision and dyslexia use it. In "Smooth Reading," minimum-necessary speech guides for blind users to grasp correctly the structure of a mathematical formula are added. "Detailed Reading" is assumed to be used when a blind user wants to know the mathematical-formula structure in the most detail.

In addition, we have also implemented a function in the application to control a time interval between math symbols or poses before/after them to make math expressions become easier to understand. Using ChattyBook, we are now planning evaluation by various print-disabled people to see which way is better for them.

9 Further Tasks in the Future

The accessibility of school textbooks is probably most important in education. As was mentioned, in Japan, the Japanese Society for Rehabilitation of Persons with Disabilities has been providing print-disabled students with accessible e-textbooks in multimedia DAISY since 2008 [3]. They produced the greater part of requested textbooks for elementary and junior-high school (291 titles in 2018), and those textbooks were provided to more-than-10,000 print-disabled students (mostly ones with developmental reading disorder).

However, concerning senior-high school or higher education, the number of textbook titles is too large, and the same service is almost impossible (more-than-1,000 titles of senior-high school textbooks are published in Japan). Instead, we can expect that senior-high-school/university students could accept automatically produced textbooks in text-based EPUB. Even if a TTS engine would fail at reading out the content, they should be able to amend those errors mentally for themselves according to the context. If so, it might be possible for us to give a quick service of making a book accessible by automatically converting E-born PDF into text-based EPUB. (In Japan, it is regulated by law that the school textbooks in E-born PDF are provided by their publishers to organizations making them accessible for students with print disabilities.)

To realize that, however, layout-analysis technologies should progress remarkably to treat complicated-layout textbooks. In Japan, the layout tends to become more and more complicated; a lot of icons, illustrations, balloons and others appear quite frequently even in high-school textbooks. The most promising approach to analyze such complicated-layout document is machine learning. To use the machine-learning technology effectively, we do need a large quantity of annotated data for the learning.

References

1. PDF/UA. https://www.iso.org/standard/64599.html. Accessed 1 June 2020
2. Schwarz, T., Rajgopal, S., Stiefelhagen, R.: Accessible EPUB: making EPUB 3 documents universal accessible. In: Miesenberger, K., Kouroupetroglou, G. (eds.) ICCHP 2018. LNCS, vol. 10896, pp. 85–92. Springer, Cham (2018). https://doi.org/10.1007/978-3-319-94277-3_16
3. Japanese society for rehabilitation of persons with disabilities. http://www.dinf.ne.jp/doc/daisy/book/daisytext.html (Japanese only). Accessed 1 June 2020
4. The DAISY consortium. http://www.daisy.org/. Accessed 1 June 2020
5. Science Accessibility Net (sAccessNet). http://www.sciaccess.net/en/. Accessed 1 June 2020
6. Suzuki, M., Yamaguchi, K.: Recognition of E-born PDF including mathematical formulas. In: Miesenberger, K., Bühler, C., Penaz, P. (eds.) ICCHP 2016. LNCS, vol. 9758, pp. 35–42. Springer, Cham (2016). https://doi.org/10.1007/978-3-319-41264-1_5
7. ChattyBooks. https://www.sciaccess.net/en/ChattyBooks/. Accessed 1 June 2020
8. Yamaguchi, K., Suzuki, M.: An accessible STEM editor customizable for various local languages. J. Enabling Technol. **13**(4), 240–250 (2019)

Tactile Graphics and Models for Blind People and Recognition of Shapes by Touch

Development of Tactile Globe by Additive Manufacturing

Yoshinori Teshima[1]([⊠])[iD], Yohsuke Hosoya[1], Kazuma Sakai[1],
Tsukasa Nakano[2], Akiko Tanaka[2], Toshiaki Aomatsu[3],
Kenji Yamazawa[4], Yuji Ikegami[4], and Yasunari Watanabe[4]

[1] Department of Mechanical Science and Engineering, Chiba Institute
of Technology, 2-17-1 Tsudanuma, Narashino, Chiba 275-0016, Japan
yoshinori.teshima@it-chiba.ac.jp
[2] National Institute of Advanced Industrial Science and Technology (AIST),
1-1-1 Higashi, Tsukuba, Ibaraki 305-8566, Japan
{tsukasa.nakano,akiko-tanaka}@aist.go.jp
[3] Special Needs Education School for the Visually Impaired,
University of Tsukuba, 3-27-6 Mejirodai, Bunkyo, Tokyo 112-0015, Japan
aomatsu@nsfb.tsukuba.ac.jp
[4] Advanced Manufacturing Team, RIKEN Advanced Science Institute,
2-1 Hirosawa, Wako, Saitama 351-0198, Japan
{kyama,yikegami}@riken.jp

Abstract. To understand geographical positions, globes adapted for tactile learning is needed for people with visual impairments. Therefore, we created three-dimensional (3D) tactile models of the earth for the visually impaired, utilizing the exact topography data obtained by planetary explorations. Additively manufactured 3D models of the earth can impart an exact shape of relief on their spherical surfaces. In this study, we made improvements to existing models to satisfy the requirements of tactile learning. These improvements were the addition of the equator, prime meridian, and two poles to a basis model. Hence, eight types of model were proposed. The equator and the prime meridian were expressed by the belt on four models (i.e., B1, B2, B3, and B4). The height of their belt was pro-vided in four stages. The equator and the prime meridian were expressed by the gutter on four models (i.e., C1, C2, C3, and C4). The width of their gutter was provided in four stages. The north pole was expressed by a cone, while the south pole was expressed by a cylinder. The two poles have a common shape in all of the eight models. Evaluation experiments revealed that the Earth models developed in this study were useful for tactile learning of the visually impaired.

Keywords: Additive manufacturing · Topography data · Globe with exact relief · Tactile 3D model · Tactile teaching material · Tactile learning

K. Miesenberger et al. (Eds.): ICCHP 2020, LNCS 12376, pp. 419–426, 2020.
https://doi.org/10.1007/978-3-030-58796-3_49

1 Introduction

Blind people can recognize various shapes through tactile sensations. For example, a tactile map creation service was offered according to the demands of the visually impaired and their helpers to disseminate the use of tactile maps [1–3]. Moreover, research on the utilization of 3D printers to help the visually impaired were conducted [4–6]. Development of the effective models for tactile learning has been reported [7–10].

The standard globes for the sighted persons have no undulations on their spherical surfaces, and countries and oceans are color-coded on the surface of such globes. Even globes for the visually impaired have been made, with possibly the oldest three-dimensional relief globe made in the United States, which is kept in the lobby of the Perkins School for the Blind. The diameter of the globe is about 135 cm (Fig. 1a). The American Printing House for the Blind has produced two types of tactile globes: one is a relief globe (Fig. 1b) with a diameter of approximately 76 cm, and the other one is the tactile and visual globe (Fig. 1c), which is a standard globe covered with a tactile overlay. The Royal National Institute of Blind People produced a tactile globe (Fig. 2a) whose diameter is about 38 cm. Nippon Charity Kyokai Foundation made a relief globe (Fig. 2b) with a diameter of about 50 cm, while Sun Kougei Inc. produced a barrier-free globe (Fig. 2c) with a diameter of about 32.

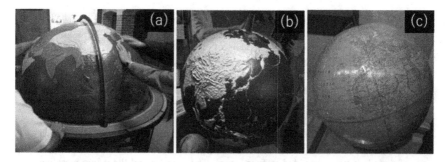

Fig. 1. (a) Relief globe (the Perkins School for the Blind), diameter: 135 cm. (b) Relief globe (American Printing House for the Blind), diameter: 76 cm. (c) Tactile and visual Globe (American Printing House for the Blind).

These globes have their own features, which are not covered in the scope of this study. Three relief globes are mentioned previously. It is noteworthy that the globes were manufactured without utilizing the exact topography data.

Recently, various additive manufacturing techniques have been developed for globe making. We can 3D print a relief globe that reconstructs the exact topography data by using additive manufacturing. To illustrate such an application, Nakano and Tanaka [11] made a relief globe (Fig. 3, S) and the models of the planets in the solar system. Their models included Venus, Earth, Mars, and Moon. The gradation of colors on the globe corresponds to the elevation of topography.

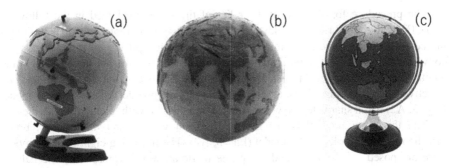

Fig. 2. (a) Tactile globe (Royal National Institute of Blind People), diameter: 38 cm. (b) Relief globe (Nippon Charity Kyokai Foundation), diameter: 50 cm. (c) Barrier-free globe (Sun Kougei Inc.), diameter: 32 cm.

Teshima et al. [12] developed relief globes that were modified from the model used by Nakano and Tanaka [11] to meet the requirement of tactile learning by the visually impaired. This paper describes in detail both the development of the tactile globe and the evaluation of the level of understanding of the visually impaired.

2 Development of Tactile Globes

The diameter of the globe used by Nakano and Tanaka [11] was 8 cm. The first phase of the modification was to change the size of globe. We formed two models with diameters of 20 cm (Fig. 3, L) and 12 cm (Fig. 3, A1). We discussed the suitable size for tactile observation among three models of diameters 20 cm (Fig. 3, L), 12 cm (Fig. 3, A1), and 8 cm (Fig. 3, S) with a blind person. Consequently, the model with a diameter of 12 cm was selected, which is suitable for tactile observation by using both hands. All diameters of the modified models are 12 cm, hereafter.

The second phase of the modification was to delete the relief of the bottom of the sea, on the globe surface, as it is very difficult for the blind to distinguish the land from the sea when such models are used. The abovementioned three models (shown in Fig. 3, S, L, A1) have the relief of the bottom of the sea. In this study, the experimental evaluation of the level of understanding was considered based on the position of the continents. Therefore, we removed the relief of the bottom of the sea (Table 1).

Table 1. Model of the earth

Topography data	ETOPO30 from National Snow and Ice Data Center
Real size (radius)	6,378 km
Relief emphasis ratio	50:1
Material	Plaster powder (Fig. 3, S, L), Nylon powder (Fig. 3, A1, A2; Fig. 4)
Diameter of models	8 cm (Fig. 3, S), 20 cm (Fig. 3, L), 12 cm (Fig. 3, A1; Fig. 4)

The procedure for deletion of the relief of the sea is explained in the following steps. First, all the values of the elevation of topography were replaced with −3000 m if the corresponding value was smaller than 0. Next, the updated elevation data were converted into the STL (Stereolithography) format, which is the file format used in the additive manufacturing technique. Finally, the model was constructed (3D printed) by selective laser sintering (the material used was nylon powder). The obtained model (Fig. 3, A2) had a sharp step between the land and the sea, without any relief in the sea.

The third and final phase of the modification was to add the equator, prime meridian, and two poles to the model (Fig. 3, A2). The following eight types of model were pro-posed. The equator and the prime meridian were expressed by the belt on models B1, B2, B3, and B4 (Fig. 4). The height of their belt was provided in four

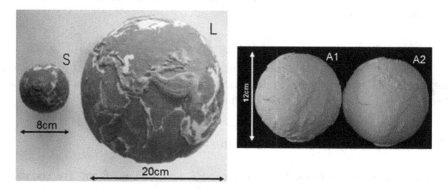

Fig. 3. (S, L) Non-modified models. Material: plaster powder (3D printing). (A1) Non-modified model. (A2) Modified model (no relief in the sea). Material: nylon powder (selective laser sinter-ing).

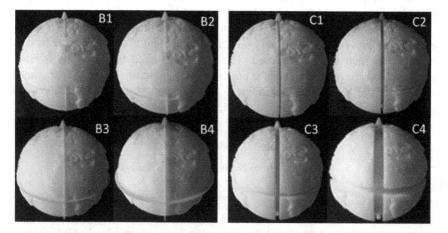

Fig. 4. Modified models. Exact topography data were utilized. Height of belt: B1 (1.2 mm), B2 (1.7 mm), B3 (3.3 mm), B4 (6.3 mm). Width of gutter: C1 (1.7 mm), C2 (3.0 mm), C3 (5.3 mm), C4 (10.2 mm). Material: nylon powder (selective laser sintering).

stages. The equator and the prime meridian were expressed by the gutter on models C1, C2, C3, and C4 (Fig. 4). The width of their gutter was provided in four stages. The north pole was expressed by a cone, while the south pole was expressed by a cylinder. The two poles have a common shape in all the of eight models.

3 Evaluation of the Level of Understanding

Eight subjects who are totally blind took part in our experiments, i.e., the investigation of level of understanding. At the beginning of the experiment, the experimenter explained the positions of both the six continents of the world and Japan to each subject. This advance explanation is shown on model B3.

Next, the subjects were requested to determine the position of each continent or Japan using their index finger, by touching one of the models using both their hands. This examination was performed with four models: B3, C3, A2, and A1.

The experimenter asked each of the subject:

(Q1) the position of the African continent
(Q2) to trace the outline of the African continent
(Q3) the position of the Antarctic continent
(Q4) the position of the Australian continent, and
(Q5) the position of Japan.

The experimenter recorded the answering time per questions.
Next, the experimenter asked the subjects:

(Q6) to decide the ranking of the four models (B3, C3, A2, A1) on the basis of their appropriateness for tactile learning
(Q7) to decide the ranking of the four models (B1, B2, B3, B4) on the basis of their appropriateness for the height of their belts
(Q8) to decide the ranking of four models (C1, C2, C3, C4) on the basis of their appropriateness for the width of their gutter, and
(Q9) the most appropriate model in questions (7) and (8).
The duration of the experiment was about 30 min per subject.

4 Results and Discussion

Tables 2, 3, 4, 5 and 6 show the main results of the experiment.

Table 2. Answering time on five questions [Q1-Q5] (Average time of eight subjects [s]).

Model	Q1	Q2	Q3	Q4	Q5	Avg.
B3	12.6	12.6	3.0	6.1	10.1	8.9
C3	18.4	18.4	3.4	9.3	4.0	10.7
A2	39.0	39.0	3.5	6.9	4.6	18.6
A1	46.0	46.0	4.6	9.4	25.5	26.3

Table 3. Q6: ranking of models (number of subjects).

Model	No. 1	No. 2	No. 3	No. 4
B3	8	0	0	0
C3	0	7	1	0
A2	0	1	7	0
A1	0	0	0	8

Order of usage of the models:

B3, C3, A2, and A1 for four subjects
C3, B3, A2, and A1 for four subjects

The last column of Table 2 shows that the best among these four models is model B3 (belt). The second best is model C3 (gutter), followed by model A2 (no relief in the sea), and, finally, model A1 (non-modified model). This order was observed to alter in the observations of Q4 and Q5. This may be attributed to the subjects' habituation, as the subjects were asked the same questions for every model.

Table 3 shows the ranking of the four models (B3, C3, A2, A1) on the basis of the suitability of tactile learning. All subjects replied that the best model was B3 and the least suitable was A1.

Table 4. Q7: ranking of belt models (number of subjects).

Model	No. 1	No. 2	No. 3	No. 4
B1	2	1	1	4
B2	1	5	2	0
B3	4	1	3	0
B4	1	1	1	4

Table 5. Q8: ranking of gutter models (number of subjects).

Model	No. 1	No. 2	No. 3	No. 4
C1	0	1	4	3
C2	4	2	2	0
C3	4	3	1	0
C4	0	2	1	5

Table 6. Q9: belt model vs. gutter model (number of subjects).

Belt model	Gutter model
8	0

Table 4 shows that model B3 had the most desirable height of 3.3 mm, among all the models. Table 5 shows that models C2 and C3 had the most desirable width of the gutter (3.0 mm and 5.3 mm, respectively).

Table 6 shows that all the subjects answered that the belt models were better than the gutter models. In the case of the gutter model, the width of the gutter leads to the removal of the exact topography. A small width is desirable; however, a gutter with a small width is difficult to recognize. In the case of the belt model, the width of the belt is constant (0.9 mm), while the height of the belt changes.

5 Conclusion

The experimental results suggest that the modified globes developed in this study (by additive manufacturing) were found to be useful for tactile learning, as confirmed by the visually impaired.

Now the question is what is the advantage of our method. In our method, the shape of the developed globe can be deformed freely, which can be used to study other geographical features. For example, it will be quite easy to create a relief globe to study the seabed. This globe possesses the relief in the sea but no relief on land, which is the reverse of model A2.

Acknowledgments. This study was partially supported by a Grant-in-Aid for Scientific Research (A) (18200049) from the Japan Society for the Promotion of Science (JSPS). We would like to thank Editage (www.editage.com) for English language editing.

References

1. Minatani, K., et al.: Tactile map automated creation system to enhance the mobility of blind persons—its design concept and evaluation through experiment. In: Miesenberger, K., Klaus, J., Zagler, W., Karshmer, A. (eds.) ICCHP 2010. LNCS, vol. 6180, pp. 534–540. Springer, Heidelberg (2010). https://doi.org/10.1007/978-3-642-14100-3_80
2. Watanabe, T., Yamaguchi, T., Koda, S., Minatani, K.: Tactile map automated creation system using openstreetmap. In: Miesenberger, K., Fels, D., Archambault, D., Peňáz, P., Zagler, W. (eds.) ICCHP 2014. LNCS, vol. 8548, pp. 42–49. Springer, Cham (2014). https://doi.org/10.1007/978-3-319-08599-9_7
3. Watanabe, T., Yamaguchi, T.: Six-and-a-half-year practice of tactile map creation service. Stud. Health Technol. Inform. **242**, 687–694 (2017)
4. Minatani, K.: An analysis and proposal of 3D printing applications for the visually impaired. Stud. Health Technol. Inform. **242**, 918–921 (2017)
5. Minatani, K.: A proposed method for producing embossed dots graphics with a 3D printer. In: Miesenberger, K., Kouroupetroglou, G. (eds.) ICCHP 2018. LNCS, vol. 10897, pp. 143–148. Springer, Cham (2018). https://doi.org/10.1007/978-3-319-94274-2_20
6. Minatani, K.: Examining visually impaired people's embossed dots graphics with a 3D printer: physical measurements and tactile observation assessments. In: Ahram, T.Z., Falcão, C. (eds.) AHFE 2018. AISC, vol. 794, pp. 960–969. Springer, Cham (2019). https://doi.org/10.1007/978-3-319-94947-5_95

7. Teshima, Y.: Three-dimensional tactile models for blind people and recognition of 3D objects by touch: introduction to the special thematic session. In: Miesenberger, K., Klaus, J., Zagler, W., Karshmer, A. (eds.) ICCHP 2010. LNCS, vol. 6180, pp. 513–514. Springer, Heidelberg (2010). https://doi.org/10.1007/978-3-642-14100-3_76

8. Teshima, Y., et al.: Models of Mathematically Defined Curved Surfaces for Tactile Learning. In: Miesenberger, K., Klaus, J., Zagler, W., Karshmer, A. (eds.) ICCHP 2010. LNCS, vol. 6180, pp. 515–522. Springer, Heidelberg (2010). https://doi.org/10.1007/978-3-642-14100-3_77

9. Teshima, Y., et al.: Enlarged skeleton models of plankton for tactile teaching. In: Miesenberger, K., Klaus, J., Zagler, W., Karshmer, A. (eds.) ICCHP 2010. LNCS, vol. 6180, pp. 523–526. Springer, Heidelberg (2010). https://doi.org/10.1007/978-3-642-14100-3_78

10. Yamazawa, K., et al.: Three-dimensional model fabricated by layered manufacturing for visually handicapped persons to trace heart shape. In: Miesenberger, K., Karshmer, A., Penaz, P., Zagler, W. (eds.) ICCHP 2012. LNCS, vol. 7383, pp. 505–508. Springer, Heidelberg (2012). https://doi.org/10.1007/978-3-642-31534-3_74

11. Nakano, T., Tanaka, A.: Making globes of the planets, 3rd Science Frontier Tsukuba, November 2004

12. Teshima, Y., et al.: Three-dimensional models of earth for tactile learning. In: Miesenberger, K., Bühler, C., Penaz, P. (eds.) ICCHP 2016. LNCS, vol. 9759, pp. 116–119. Springer, Cham (2016). https://doi.org/10.1007/978-3-319-41267-2_16

Touch Explorer: Exploring Digital Maps for Visually Impaired People

Alireza Darvishy$^{(\boxtimes)}$, Hans-Peter Hutter, Markus Grossenbacher, and Dario Merz

InIT Institute of Applied Information Technology, ZHAW Zurich University of Applied Sciences, Technikumstr. 9, P.O. Box, 8401 Winterthur, Switzerland
{alireza.darvishy,hans-peter.hutter}@zhaw.ch

Abstract. This paper describes an interaction concept for persons with visual impairments to explore digital maps. Mobile map applications like Google Maps have become an important instrument for navigation and exploration. However, existing map applications are highly visually oriented, making them inaccessible to users with visual impairments. This ongoing research project aims to develop an accessible digital map application in which information is presented in a non-visual way. Analysis of existing market solutions shows that information retention is highest when a combination of different output modalities is used. As a result, a prototype app has been created using three major non-visual modalities: Voice output (speech synthesis), everyday sounds (e.g. car traffic), and vibration feedback. User tests were performed, and based on the test results, the Touch Explorer app was developed. Initial usability tests are described in this paper.

Keywords: Visual impairment · Accessible maps · Accessibility · Output modalities

1 Introduction

According to the World Health Organisation, roughly 285,000,000 people in the world have a visual impairment [1]. Persons with visual impairments encounter many major obstacles, one of which is the difficulty in navigating and exploring unknown areas independently. In order to explore an unknown area, they cannot easily resort to maps, since the target group of commercially available maps are people with normal vision.

One solution is tactile maps, which are maps on which the information can be felt with the fingers. These are made using a special paper printing process which causes printed areas to swell upwards. However, these maps have significant disadvantages: They are expensive to produce, take up a lot of space, and generally present very little information on one page, since small details would be too difficult to distinguish by touch.

In recent decades, the presentation of geographical information has moved away from printed formats towards more convenient digital formats. Mobile map applications have become a ubiquitous and important tool for navigation and exploration. They have the advantage of being size-adjustable, meaning that the user can decide on the scope and level of detail they wish to be shown.

© Springer Nature Switzerland AG 2020
K. Miesenberger et al. (Eds.): ICCHP 2020, LNCS 12376, pp. 427–434, 2020.
https://doi.org/10.1007/978-3-030-58796-3_50

However, existing map applications are still heavily based on visual information, and, like most printed maps, are targeted towards persons with normal vision. Users with visual impairments face significant barriers when using these apps – currently, no major map app offers an accessible, intuitive or understandable presentation of map data in a non-visual format. This makes it essentially impossible for persons with visual impairments to quickly get a sense of a given environment, something which is particularly important before travelling to a new or unknown destination.

The goal of this research project is to explore how digital maps can be presented on a mobile device in an accessible and understandable way for visually impaired persons in such a manner that it offers a quick and intuitive overview of a location and its surroundings. Additionally, mechanisms should be provided to virtually navigate different layers of a digital map.

1.1 Existing Research

A handful of studies have looked into accessible map alternatives for visually impaired persons, such as 3D printed maps [2] and augmented reality maps [3]. However, these solutions are often expensive and require specialized devices or materials, making them impractical for everyday use.

In 2011, Zeng et al. [4] examined existing digital mapping systems for visually impaired persons. They concluded that, at the time the paper was published, there were still virtually no mobile applications suitable for persons with visual impairments. They noted that many different solutions were expected for the future, and suggested that audio output would offer great potential.

In a study by Poppinga et al. in 2011 [5], it was examined whether a digital map using speech and vibration provides better accessibility than standard digital maps. Test subjects were instructed to use their finger to investigate a network of streets and then attempt to draw a sketch of them on paper. The result showed that it is generally possible to provide a visually impaired person with an overview of a map using this output modalities. These findings are very promising and serve as a basis for this work. Given that smartphone technology has improved continuously since 2011, it is expected that even better results can be achieved today.

2 Initial Prototype

Two smartphone-based prototype apps were implemented in order to explore possibilities for non-visual digital map interaction. The first prototype app offered the user simplified maps of fictional places. To explore the area, the user moved their finger across the screen. The map elements were presented as rectangles for maximum clarity and simplicity. This first prototype presented a sample scenario: the user was invited to a (fictional) birthday party in a forest cabin (Fig. 1). The user's task was to use the app to get an overview of the location and its surroundings. In the app, the cabin appeared in the center of the screen; near it and around it were a forest, a lake, and one road. Using their finger to explore the map, the user encountered different vibration patterns, everyday sounds, and/or speech synthesis for each of these different elements.

Four different output methods were used for the first prototype (Table 1). These were chosen to enable all important information to be displayed as clearly as possible. In the case of forests and waters, names and exact boundaries were not of primary significance – it was more important that the user knows where a forest or body of water is located relative to other elements. Therefore, only pre-recorded audio clips were used as output, without additional vibration or voice output. This allowed users to explore the area without being distracted by less relevant information. For streets, the name and direction are of highest importance. As such, when touching the street, the device started to vibrate, and the name of the street was output once by voice. Vibrations emitted through continuous finger contact with the screen offered users a sense of the street's path. The street name was reannounced every time the street was touched again, allowing different streets to be more easily distinguished.

The forest cabin was in the center of the map. When touched, the cabin name was uttered in an endless loop.

Table 1. Overview of the map elements in the initial prototype.

Colour	Element type	Output
Green	Forest	Plays audio recording of birdsong
Blue	Body of water	Plays audio recording of water splashing
Grey	Street	$1\times$ speech output of street name, plus continuous vibration
Yellow	Building	Continuous speech output of building name

Table 1 serves as a legend to Fig. 1. It also describes which output modalities were used for the corresponding elements when the user touched them with their finger.

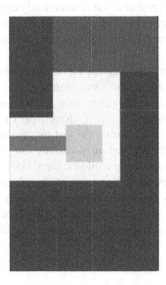

Fig. 1. Visual representation of the map for the sample scenario, as implemented in the initial prototype interface.

This first prototype was initially tested with a group of people who have normal vision. In order to be able to test the prototype with sighted persons, the map elements were hidden behind a white screen overlay. This ensured that the subjects could not see the map elements. Since this was a first attempt, only a qualitative user survey was conducted. It was based on the question of what the subjects were able to perceive and how they rated the experience.

Test subjects were able to find their way around, and in a follow-up conversation they were able to remember which elements could be found on the map. There was initially some difficulty in deciding whether the water was a lake or a river; however, most of the subjects were able to determine that it was a lake upon further exploration of the map, based on the shape of the water. They also expressed the desire to be able to learn the name of the lake through a user action. The repetitive speech output for the cabin turned out to be less than optimal: Although it was possible to identify where the cabin was located, it was difficult to determine its outline or boundaries. In addition, difficulties arose in finding the way leading to and from the cabin. For the subjects, it quickly became clear that the vibrating line was supposed to be a road. This perception was supported by the spoken street name every time the line touched. Because the finger repeatedly left and returned to the defined area of the road during touch exploration, this repeatedly led to the app speaking out the street name. Subsequent discussions with the test subjects showed that the persistent vibration for the road was perceived as too strong and disturbing.

3 Touch Explorer

Based on the feedback of the initial prototype, a second prototype, called Touch Explorer, was developed for real maps from OpenStreetMap (OSM) [6]. To that end, a process was defined and implemented that automatically converts ordinary OSM digital maps into simplified and augmented maps suitable for touch exploration (cf. Fig. 2) For the multimodal interaction, Touch Explorer uses the same concepts for haptic and audio feedback.

In order to be able to verify the concept and its implementation, the application was tested with potential users. Originally, it was planned to be tested with several visually impaired users in Switzerland. However, due to the Covid-19 pandemic, only 1 visually impaired person was able to test it, along with 10 people with normal vision, who were told to close their eyes during the test to simulate blindness.

The core of the test was three real map sections from the city of Zurich. The test subjects were observed as they freely explored the Chinese Garden, the Dolder Hotel and Bürkli Square. The tests were conducted on an iPhone 11, iPhone 8, iPhone SE 2020 and iPhone 10 S, with all devices having the current iOS version 13.4 installed. No previous information about the application and its handling was communicated to the users, so that authentic reactions to the functionality and usability could be observed.

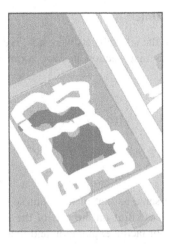

Fig. 2. Map section of the Chinese Garden in Zurich as implemented in the Touch Explorer prototype. The map shows the walled-in garden including its pond (blue), gazebo (beige), footpaths & nearby roads (white), and surrounding park (green) (Color figure online).

When the application is started, the user is informed how the instructions can be played. All test subjects were able to use the appropriate gesture without any problems so that they could then listen to the instructions. The speed of speech synthesis was generally perceived as pleasant.

3.1   First Test: Chinese Garden

First, the test subjects were given the task of exploring the Chinese Garden (Fig. 2) in an 18× zoom, without telling them where the map section was. The following objects were identified by all test subjects within a few minutes:

- grass/lawn
- footpaths
- streets
- intersections
- building
- pond
- playground

Only a few were able to identify the following objects straight away:

- bridge over the pond
- gazebo on the bridge

During the initial exploration, it was often emphasized how pleasant the haptic feedback was when crossing borders or following lines. It was easy for all test subjects to follow the course of normal roads. Footpaths could also be followed well, only the paths around and over the pond were a little more demanding. These paths branch out very often and in a very small space, which makes it difficult to form an image in your mind. When switching to 20× zoom, that was no longer a problem.

3.2 Second Test: Dolder Hotel

As with the first exploration, the test subjects were not given any previous information about the location. With this map section in 18× zoom (Fig. 3a), all objects were identified very quickly:

- forest
- train tracks
- tennis court
- footpath
- building

The zoom level was the same as that of the Chinese Garden, but the exploration was a lot quicker and with less effort on the part of the test person. This shows that there is no ideal zoom level for tactile exploration and that this must be adapted to the information density of the map section.

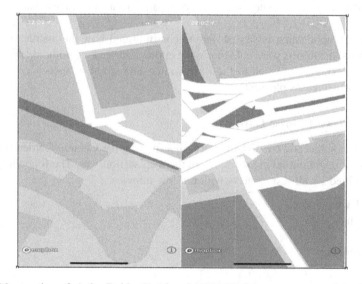

Fig. 3. Map section of a) the Dolder Hotel and b) Bürkli Square as presented in the Touch Explorer prototype.

In order to show the test subjects the limits of tactile exploration, the last task was to explore the intersection at Bürkli Square (Fig. 3b). All of the test subjects quickly became aware that the intersection consisted of footpaths, streets and tram tracks, but it was not possible for them to orient themselves because the object boundaries are so close to each other. Switching to a lower zoom level simplifies the overview somewhat, but the complexity of the intersection is no longer visible because the footpaths are hidden.

3.3   Fourth Test: Navigation Features

After the initial exploration, navigation features were tested. Zooming worked very well and was performed quickly and intuitively by the test subjects. Navigating in the four directions was also easy to learn, but it took most of the test persons a moment to get used to the section change: the map is not moved gradually as in normal map applications, but is navigated section by section. Thus, when following a line that ends at the left edge of the screen, the map jumps to the next section towards the west, and the line must be searched for at the same height on the right edge of the screen. With a little practice, this way of navigation worked well for the test persons. The "centering" function was also well received: A desired object can be moved into the center of the screen using a gesture, making it became easier to maintain an overview.

4   Outcome and Discussion

The initial prototype showed that it is possible to explore a simple map just by using vibration, everyday sounds and speech [7]. Usability tests carried out on the first prototype showed that users were able to recognize and distinguish all elements while operating the app.

The second prototype, the Touch Explorer application, met with great enthusiasm among test subjects. The integration of the OpenStreetMap metadata was also a complete success, since the user can be given a very precise understanding of a site. On the whole, the feasibility and good user experience of the interaction concept could be confirmed, but it also became apparent that the user experience of the application can be increased with additional features. During the tests many valuable ideas and suggestions were raised by the test subjects, which should be considered for further developments:

- Sample catalog: A register with all implemented objects including their noise and vibration patterns to get to know
- Scale: A feature for measuring distances with two fingers
- Status query: Output of the current situation, such as zoom level, address, stops of public transport, water, etc.
- GPS localization: Change the map section to the current location of the user
- Address search: Classic address search with the option to change location

Some of these may still be implemented in the current version of Touch Explorer, while others are left for follow-up projects.

References

1. Global data on visual impairment 2010. WHO (2012). http://www.who.int/blindness/Globaldatafinalforweb.pdf. Accessed 10 Oct 2012
2. Holloway, L., Marriott, K., Butler, M.: Accessible maps for the blind: comparing 3D printed models with tactile graphics. In: Cox, A., Perry, M. (eds.) CHI 2018 - Proceedings of the 2018 CHI Conference on Human Factors in Computing Systems, Montréal, QC, Canada, 21–26 April 2018. Association for Computing Machinery (ACM), New York (2018). https://doi.org/10.1145/3173574.3173772
3. Ducasse, J., Brock, A.M., Jouffrais, C.: Accessible interactive maps for visually impaired users. In: Pissaloux, E., Velázquez, R. (eds.) Mobility of Visually Impaired People, pp. 537–584. Springer, Cham (2018). https://doi.org/10.1007/978-3-319-54446-5_17
4. Zeng, L., Weber, G.: Accessible maps for the visually impaired. In: Proceedings of IFIP INTERACT 2011, Workshop on ADDW, pp. 54–60 (2011)
5. Poppinga, B., Pielot, M., Magnusson, C., Rassmus-Gröhn, K.: TouchOver map: audio-tactile exploration of interactive maps. In: MobileHCI 2011, pp. 545–550 (2011)
6. OpenStreetMaps. https://www.openstreetmap.org/
7. Darvishy, A., Hutter, H.-P., Frei, J.: Making mobile map applications accessible for visually impaired people. In: Ahram, T., Taiar, R., Colson, S., Choplin, A. (eds.) IHIET 2019. AISC, vol. 1018, pp. 396–400. Springer, Cham (2020). https://doi.org/10.1007/978-3-030-25629-6_61

Development of TARS Mobile App with Deep Fingertip Detector for the Visually Impaired

Yoichi Hosokawa, Tetsushi Miwa$^{(\boxtimes)}$, and Yoshihiro Hashimoto$^{(\boxtimes)}$

Nagoya Institute of Technology, Nagoya, Japan
{y.hosokawa.456,t.miwa.528}@nitech.jp,
hashimoto@nitech.ac.jp

Abstract. We propose TARS mobile applications that uses a smartphone with a camera and deep learning fingertip detector for easier implementation than using a PC or a touch panel. The app was designed to recognize the user's hand touching the images with the rear camera and provide voice guidance with the information on the images that the index finger is touching as a trigger. When performing gestures with either the index finger or thumb, the app was able to detect and output the fingertip point without delay, and it was effective as a trigger for reading. Thumb gestures are assumed to have reduced detection variances of 68% in the lateral direction because they rarely move the other four fingers compared to index finger gestures. By performing multiple detections in the application and outputting the median, the variances of detection can be reduced to 73% in the lateral direction and 70% in the longitudinal direction, which shows the effectiveness of multiple detections. These techniques are effective in reducing the variance of fingertip detection. We also confirmed that if the tilt of the device is between −3.4 mm and 4 mm, the current app could identify a 12 mm difference with an accuracy of 85.5% as an average in both of the lateral and longitudinal directions. Finally, we developed a basic model of TARS mobile app that allows easier installation and more portability by using a smart phone camera rather than a PC or a touch panel.

Keywords: Tactile graphics with an audio response system · TARS · Voice guidance gesture · Fingertip detector · Visual impairment

1 Introduction

As one way for visually impaired people to understand figures and maps, they use tactile graphics with raised shapes on the paper. While this has the advantage of allowing understanding of the shape and position of objects by touching it. it also has the disadvantage of being difficult to distinguish objects among points, lines, and description Braille on the tactile graphics. Sometimes it requires others to explain the images and the users cannot learn on their own.

Kwok et al. [1] showed that the format of the drawn the images, such as surface and contour lines, size, and height, improves the readability of the tactile graphics.

Yamamoto et al. [2], on the other hand, embedded audio descriptions in the tactile graphics so that users can focus on the image search, instead of relying on the

© Springer Nature Switzerland AG 2020
K. Miesenberger et al. (Eds.): ICCHP 2020, LNCS 12376, pp. 435–445, 2020.
https://doi.org/10.1007/978-3-030-58796-3_51

description Braille. Talking Tactile Tablet [3] is a similar device that makes it easy to read tactile graphics.

We [4] developed tactile graphics with an audio response system (TARS) which enables visually impaired people to hear an audio description of the image on the tactile graphics by using a touch panel to set the tactile graphics and a computer with a screen reader and tapping the image on the tactile graphics set on the touch panel. The device was made at a cost less than those of previous research with the advantage of portability. TARS allows visually impaired people to focus on the tactile graphics, gain a lot of information from them, and learn independently.

Simon et al. [5] revealed that deep learning from the camera images of a computer can provide fingertip detection. Miwa [6], a co-researcher, showed that the fingertip detection is 98% accurate, regardless of the type of tactile graphics, under conditions of sufficient brightness by using a smartphone camera.

We propose TARS mobile applications that uses a smartphone with a camera and deep learning fingertip detector for easier implementation than using a PC or a touch panel. The app was designed to recognize the user's hand touching the images with the rear camera and provide voice guidance with the information on the images that the index finger is touching as a trigger. Figure 1 shows the installation of the device and the tactile graphics. Initially, it was triggered by a user talking to the device, but in this research, we decided to use gestures as triggers based on the assumption that a malfunction would occur when multiple users simultaneously talk to the device. In the preliminary tests, the user's fingertip points detected by the app deviated from the actual fingertip point and voice guidance could not be made.

We assume that the following factors caused the problem:

- The fingertip detection outputs varied because the users moved their hands extensively to perform gestures.
- Since the fingertip detection logic includes inference, its output could vary every time even if the user touches the same point and sometimes could vary widely.
- The device could be set tilted and cause the fingertip detection to be misaligned with the images.

In this study, we will identify solutions to these factors and examine the development of the TARS mobile app, which can be used by visually impaired people on their own.

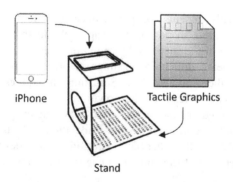

Fig. 1. Device installation

2   Methods

2.1   Application Development

According to a study by Watanabe et al. [7], 53.1% of Japanese visually impaired people own a smartphone, and 91.9% of all blind people own an iPhone. Therefore, development of the application targeted the iPhone.

Development conditions: iPhone SE (April 2020 model), 128 GB, iOS 13.4.1, Xcode 11.3. We developed a hand tracking system using Google's MediaPipe v0.5 [8]. Visually impaired people use both hands to search for images and finally obtain the information of the target with the fingertips of one hand. Therefore, we decided to use one hand for the fingertip detection. We designed an app that provides voice guidance for the user's index fingertip coordinates by activating AVSpeechSynthesizer when the user performs voice guide gestures (hereinafter "gestures"). We developed a total of four methods to activate the app, two based on the difference in fingertip detection times and two based on the difference in the types of gestures.

Methods Based on the Fingertip Detection Times. *Single detection:* Every time fingertip detection is performed, it outputs the coordinates. *Multiple detections:* After fingertip detections are performed seven times, it outputs the median value.

Methods Based on the Gesture Types. *Gesture 1:* A motion to fold the fingers other than the index finger from the condition of an open hand while touching the target image with the index finger. Figure 2 (left) shows the motion. *Gesture 2:* A motion to bend the thumb from inside to outside or outside to inside while touching the image with the index finger with an open hand. Figure 2 (right) shows the motion.

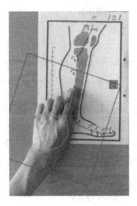

Fig. 2. Left: gesture 1 (index finger); right: gesture 2 (thumb)

2.2   Assessing the Accuracy of Fingertip Detection

We observed that when the user's fingertip touched a point, released, and touched it again, the fingertip detection did not output the same coordinates but sometimes output largely deviated coordinates. The reason was assumed to be because the fingertip detection logic includes inference. For this problem, we conducted tests with the participants to assess the degree of variance in detection.

Test participants: Seven visually impaired persons who have used Braille for more than 3 years. The test participants' data are shown in Table 1. The participants were informed of the test, understood the details, and agreed to participate.

Table 1. Test participants' data

Age	Mean: 39.7 S.D.: 11.5
Sex	Male: 5 Female: 2
Hand to touch images	Left hand: 3 Right hand: 4
Width of palm (mm)	Mean: 83.0 S.D.: 7.0
Length from fingertip to wrist (mm)	Mean: 172.1 S.D.: 13.4

After the participants practiced the gestures with voice guidance sufficiently, they conducted the test by touching one point in the image and performing the gestures to activate voice guidance. The test was conducted five times, the coordinates were recorded every time, and the variance in detection was analyzed. Also, we used js-STAR9.8.4 for the statistical analysis.

2.3   Evaluation of Deviation Between the Tactile Graphics and the Fingertip Detection Coordinates

2.3.1   Deviation Calculation

To calculate the deviations between the tactile graphics and the fingertip detection coordinates, we set two calibration points (CPs) on the image and calculated the distance ratios between the CPs and target points.

The top left of an A4 size tactile graphics in the longitudinal direction is set as the origin (0, 0). For example, CP1 (25, 25), CP2 (190, 230), and P (105, 130) are on the tactile graphics. Assume that the app detects the fingertip coordinates and output CP1 (195, 389), CP2 (810, 1156), and P (486, 798) coordinates.

- Detection coordinates: $(486 - 195)/(810 - 195) = 0.47$
- Tactile graphics coordinates: $(105 - 25)/(190 - 25) = 0.48$
- Coordinate deviation: $(0.47 - 0.48) * (190 - 25) = -1.93$

From this calculation, P was detected with a deviation of -1.93 mm from the tactile graphics in the lateral direction. In the same way, P was detected with a deviation of 4.32 mm in the longitudinal direction.

Adjustments for the Deviations. When using the app, it is expected that the above-mentioned deviations in fingertip detection and the deviations caused by device misalignment will occur. We evaluated the matching rate between tactile graphics coordinates and detection coordinates by conducting tests with participants. We selected three participants who achieved smaller detection coordinate deviations than the others in the previous test, the multiple detections and gesture test. The participants were informed of the test, understood the details, and agreed to participate. After the participants practiced the gestures sufficiently, they searched for the points of CP1 and CP2, and P1 to P9 in the image shown on the Fig. 3 and performed gestures to activate voice guidance. Based on the mean coordinates of P1 to P9 gained by the three participants, the matching rates between the tactile graphics coordinates and the fingertip detection coordinates were calculated. The matching rate was evaluated using two different adjustment methods:

- Adjustment 1: Method to calculate the detection points based on the angle difference between the line connecting CP1 and CP2 and the line connecting fingertip detection CP1 and CP2.
- Adjustment 2: Method to calculate the detection point using a constant coefficient to adjust the keystone distortion on the screen.

Fig. 3. Sample figure

3 Results

3.1 Functions of the Application

When the entire hand image was on the screen, 21 key points were detected from one hand. The key points are shown in Fig. 4 (left). The device was set with a distance to allow the rear camera to show both the image and the user's hand even when the user searches for the edge of the A4 size images in the longitudinal direction, Fig. 4 (middle and right) show the fingertip detection conditions when the device is installed at a height of 35 cm and 40 cm respectively. As a result, we decided to use the app with the device on a 40 cm height stand. The responses to voice guidance by multiple detections showed no delay compared to single detection.

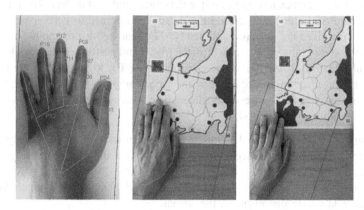

Fig. 4. Left: 21 key points; middle: image recognized from the 35 cm-stand; right: image recognized from the 40 cm-stand.

3.2 Voice Guidance Gesture Responses

Gesture responses were assessed by identifying the detected key points. The criteria for the assessment are as follows:

- Gesture1: P12(y) < P11(y) & P16(y) < P15(y)
- Gesture2: (P17(x) - P05(x))/3 > P05(x) - P03(x)

Both gestures were successfully recognized. When the gestures were recognized, the voice guidance of the index fingertip coordinates was made.

3.3 Fingertip Detection Accuracy

A variance analysis for the two factors; gesture types and multiple detections was performed based on the results of the fingertip detection test by the 7 participants. Fingertip detection variances in the lateral direction are shown in Table 2. In the lateral direction, the main effect of the gesture type was significant ($F(1, 6) = 9.79, p < 0.05$, $\eta_p^2 = 0.62$), and gesture 2 (average 5.85 pixels) had less variance than gesture 1 (average 8.61 pixels).

The main effect of multiple detections was also significant ($F(1, 6) = 26.12, p < 0.01$, $\eta_p^2 = 0.81$). Multiple detections (average 6.10 pixels) were less varied than single detection (average 8.36 pixels). The interaction effect between gesture types and multiple detections was not significant ($F(1, 6) = 1.36, p = 0.29, \eta_p^2 = 0.18$).

Fingertip detection variances in the longitudinal direction are shown in Table 3. In the longitudinal direction, the main effect of gesture type was not significant ($F(1, 6) = 0.12$, $p = 0.74$, $\eta_p^2 = 0.02$).

The main effect of the multiple detections shows a significant trend ($F(1, 6) = 4.96$, $p < 0.07$, $\eta_p^2 = 0.45$). The multiple detections (average value 6.39 pixels) show a trend that has less variances than single detection (average value 9.00 pixels.) The interaction effect between gesture types and multiple detections was not significant ($F(1, 6) = 0.17$, $p = 0.69$, $\eta_p^2 = 0.03$).

Table 2. Two-factor variance analysis in the lateral direction (pixel)

		Single detection	Multiple detection
Gesture 1	N	7	7
	Mean	10.25	6.98
	S.D.	2.24	1.96
Gesture 2	N	7	7
	Mean	6.47	5.22
	S.D.	1.86	1.69

Table 3. Two-factor variance analysis in the longitudinal direction (pixel)

		Single detection	Multiple detections
Gesture 1	N	7	7
	Mean	8.61	6.35
	S.D.	2.58	2.24
Gesture 2	N	7	7
	Mean	9.39	6.44
	S.D.	3.01	1.70

3.4 Evaluation of the Deviations Between the Tactile Graphics and the Fingertip Detection Coordinates

The tilt of the device was calculated based on the difference in angle between the line connecting CP1 and CP2 of the tactile graphics and the line connecting CP1 and CP2 of the fingertip detection. Since the tilt angle of the device is a small amount, it was converted to the length based on the device length of 138.4 mm. For example, −3.4 mm indicates that the device is tilted 3.4 mm to the right. We set the device at 5 different angles and calculated the length differences for tilt angles and calculated the deviation between the tactile graphics coordinates and the fingertip detection coordinates for each test point at every tilt angle. Then we obtained the matching rates by classifying the test point deviations into 5 ranges from 4 mm to 12 mm and dividing the number of test points in each range by the total number of test points. Tables 4 and 5 show the matching rate in the lateral direction and the match rate in the longitudinal direction under no adjustment. The matching rates increased as the tilt of the device decreased. If the device tilted by 0.2 mm, the matching rate within 6 mm in both the lateral and longitudinal directions was about 90%. The matching rate within 10 mm is as high as 100%. Also, the matching rate within 12 mm was 91% on an average in the lateral direction and 90% on an average in the longitudinal direction at any tilt angle from −3.4 to 4 mm. The matching rates by adjustment method are shown in Table 6. In the lateral direction, within 12 mm, the matching rate with no adjustment was higher than those with adjustments. In the longitudinal direction, within 8 mm, the matching rate with adjustment1 was higher than that with no adjustment by 2 points on average. In the longitudinal direction, within 6 mm, the matching rate with adjustment2 was higher than that with no adjustment by 4 points on average. Other than these cases, the matching rates with no adjustment were higher than those with adjustments.

Table 4. Matching rate in the lateral direction with no adjustment (%)

Device tilt angle (mm)		−3.4	−0.3	0.2	1.2	4.0
Range	4 mm	22	56	56	11	44
	6 mm	33	56	89	11	67
	8 mm	44	89	89	44	67
	10 mm	56	100	100	89	89
	12 mm	67	100	100	100	89

Table 5. Matching rate in the longitudinal direction with no adjustment (%)

Device tilt angle (mm)		−3.4	−0.3	0.2	1.2	4.0
Range	4 mm	22	67	78	44	0
	6 mm	33	89	89	67	11
	8 mm	56	100	100	67	11
	10 mm	89	100	100	78	11
	12 mm	89	100	100	100	11

Table 6. Matching rate by adjustment method (%)

Direction		Lateral			Longitudinal		
Method		No adj.	Adj. 1	Adj. 2	No adj.	Adj. 1	Adj. 2
Range	4 mm	38	31	33	42	42	49
	6 mm	51	49	49	58	58	60
	8 mm	67	64	62	67	71	64
	10 mm	87	80	67	76	76	71
	12 mm	91	89	71	80	80	73

4 Discussion

4.1 Variations in Fingertip Detection

When performing gestures with either the index finger or thumb, the app was able to detect and output the fingertip point without delay, and it was effective as a trigger for reading. Fingertip detection recognizes the skeletal structure of the wrist and arm, infers the position of the palm, and then calculates 21 key point coordinates based on the information. As a result, if the user moves their hands or fingers extensively, it is expected to recalculate for fingertip detection, resulting in greater coordinate variances. Thumb gestures are assumed to have reduced detection variances of 68% in the lateral direction because they rarely move the other four fingers compared to index finger gestures.

Also, the fingertip detection coordinates vary every time the same point is touched, and sometimes a very deviating value is detected. By performing multiple detections in the application and outputting the median, the variances of detection can be reduced to 73% in the lateral direction and 70% in the longitudinal direction, which shows the effectiveness of multiple detections. These techniques are effective in reducing the variance of fingertip detection.

4.2 Evaluation of the Deviations Between the Tactile Graphics and the Fingertip Detection Coordinates

By setting the calibration points in the image, we could easily identify the deviation between the tactile graphics and the fingertip detection coordinates. When printing an image, the printer driver may adjust the size of the image automatically. Deviation amounts in size vary among printers depending on the specifications or performance. Since the calculation of the deviations is relative to the calibration points, it is an effective means of determining the deviations even if the image is scaled up, reduced, or shifted in any direction. Also, because it is difficult for a visually impaired person to put the image in a fixed position, it should be effective to use the calibration points and adjust the position of the image. In order to resolve the deviation between the tactile graphics coordinates and the fingertip detection coordinates, two methods were used to calculate the coordinates using angle adjustment and keystone adjustment in this test. We found that it was the most effective to reduce the tilt of the device itself. We also confirmed that if the tilt of the device is between −3.4 mm and 4 mm, the current app could identify a 12 mm difference with an accuracy of 85.5% as an average in both of the lateral and longitudinal directions. Figure 5 shows the location of Japanese cities in circles with a diameter of about 12 mm. This application becomes a learning tool that allows users to know a city name by holding their fingers at the city's location.

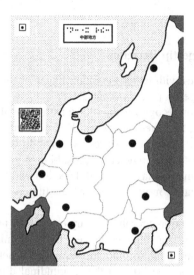

Fig. 5. The map shows cities in Chubu region of Japan

The test was conducted with the help of people who use Braille on a daily basis, and it was confirmed that the device could be installed on their own. In the future, the challenge is to develop voice guidance and user interfaces to help the users reduce the tilt of the device by themselves in setting.

Finally, we developed a basic model of TARS mobile app that allows easier installation and more portability by using a smart phone camera rather than a PC or a touch panel.

Acknowledgements. This work was supported by JSPS KAKENHI Grant Number 17H00146.

References

1. Kwok, M.G., Fukuda, T.: The new method for making tactile maps based on the human sense characteristics. IEICE technical report. Well-being Information Technology **103**(590), 55–62 (2004)
2. Yamamoto, K., Izumi, K., Inaba, J., Takayoshi, D., Yoshie, K., Higuchi, N.: Authoring tool of tactile graphics with voice explanation for teachers of schools for the blind. IEICE technical report. Well-being Information Technology **111**(424), 39–44 (2012)
3. Talking Tactile Tablet 2 (TTT). http://touchgraphics.com/portfolio/ttt. Accessed 10 June 2020
4. Hosokawa, Y.: Effect of tactile graphics with an audio response system on reading speed and accuracy of diagram. In: The 55th Conference of the Japanese Association of Special Education, Aichi, Japan, p. 83 (2017)
5. Simon, T., Joo, H., Matthews, I., Sheikh, Y.: Hand keypoint detection in single images using multiview bootstrapping. In: 2017 Proceedings of the IEEE Conference on Computer Vision and Pattern Recognition, pp. 1145–1153. (2017)

6. Miwa, T., Hosokawa, Y., Hashimoto, Y., Lisi, G.: TARS mobile app with deep fingertip detector for the visually impaired. In: Ahram, T., Karwowski, W., Vergnano, A., Leali, F., Taiar, R. (eds.) IHSI 2020. AISC, vol. 1131, pp. 301–306. Springer, Cham (2020). https://doi.org/10.1007/978-3-030-39512-4_48

7. Watanabe, T., Kobayashi, M., Minatani, K.: A survey of ICT device usage by blind people 2017 (2020). http://altmetrics.ceek.jp/article/hdl.handle.net/10191/00051465. Accessed 11 June 2020

8. Mediapipe. https://google.github.io/mediapipe. Accessed 10 June 2020

TouchPen: Rich Interaction Technique for Audio-Tactile Charts by Means of Digital Pens

Christin Engel[✉], Nadja Konrad, and Gerhard Weber

Institute for Applied Computer Science, Human-Computer-Interaction,
Technische Universität Dresden, Dresden, Germany
{christin.engel,gerhard.weber}@tu-dresden.de, nadja.konrad@posteo.de

Abstract. Audio-tactile charts have the potential to improve data analysis with tactile charts for blind people. Enhancing tactile charts with audio feedback can replace Braille labels and provide more structured information than pure tactile graphics. Current approaches lack especially in support of gestural interaction to develop useful interaction concepts for audio-tactile charts. Many approaches make use of non-standard hardware or are less mobile. That is why we investigated digital pens and their capability to increase data analysis with tactile charts. We compared two digital pens, in particular, the TipToi® pen and the Neo SmartPen M1. First, we evaluated the implementation and feasibility of five basic gestures. While the TipToi® is not suitable to support rich touch gestures, the Neo SmartPen showed in a pilot study good support of single-tap, double-tap as well as hold and line gestures. On that basis, we implemented the first prototype to demonstrate the potential of digital pens to support data analysis tasks with audio-tactile scatterplots. Afterwards, we evaluated the prototype in a pilot study with one participant. The study shows high indications for the usefulness of the presented system. The usage of the digital pen can improve the readability of a tactile chart. Our system provides audio-feedback for given tactile scatterplots in an accessible and automatic way. As a result, blind users were able to produce and use audio-tactile charts on their own by using an Android application and the Neo SmartPen.

Keywords: Audio-tactile charts · Tactile scatterplot · Digital pen · Interactive touch graphics · Blind people · Pen interaction

1 Introduction

Analysing data is a main requirement in many professions. This task can be achieved by means of information visualisations that enable fast perception of relations within the data such as correlations, cluster, or min/max values. For blind and visually impaired people, tactile charts are suitable to get access to data and their insights independently. They consist of raised lines, symbols, and

© Springer Nature Switzerland AG 2020
K. Miesenberger et al. (Eds.): ICCHP 2020, LNCS 12376, pp. 446–455, 2020.
https://doi.org/10.1007/978-3-030-58796-3_52

textures which can be perceived via touch. Embossed graphics are static representations with limited resolution (typically 20 dpi). As a consequence, they can represent a limited amount of data. Additionally, braille reading skills are needed to understand tactile charts which many blind and visually impaired people do not have [6,15]. Several approaches aim to overcome these disadvantages by enriching tactile charts with audio feedback and supporting interactivity.

Audio-tactile charts are being widely used to enable dynamic audio feedback and interacting with tactile graphics. Audio feedback is able to support reading out precise values or comparing data, detecting relationships, or exploring tactile graphic elements. Additionally, it can be used instead of Braille labels which require much space [6]. Existing approaches for audio-tactile charts mostly support simple interaction techniques and lack rich interaction concepts. While many researchers focus on interactive information visualisations which are made for the visual sense, less research address analysis tasks for interactive, audio-tactile charts. Furthermore, hardware for audio-tactile graphics is very expensive, does not support rich interaction concepts, or is not suitable for mobile use. To address these lacks, we examined the potential of digital pens with respect to their suitability to develop low cost, mobile and usable interaction concepts for audio-tactile charts. In addition, we analysed interaction tasks that audio-tactile charts could cover and developed the first prototype to evaluate the usefulness of the proposed concept.

2   Technologies for Audio-Tactile Graphics

Besides audio-tactile charts, there is a wide range of approaches providing audio-haptic charts by simulating tactile feedback by use of vibration [6] or force feedback devices such as PHANToM [13]. However, the focus in this work lies on approaches that enrich pure tactile graphics with audio-feedback. These approaches differ in terms of mobility, costs, handling, provided information and interaction modes. Furthermore, the accessibility of the generation process of audio-tactile graphics needs to be focused. On the one side, several approaches focus on technologies that can be used for audio-tactile graphics, while other approaches focus more on rich interaction concepts to realise an effective data analysis with audio-tactile charts.

Touch sensitive devices such as IVEO [5] or Tactile Talking Tablet (TTT) [10,12] were commonly used. These approaches allow the tactile graphic to be placed on a specific tablet PC. Audio feedback is provided by a tap or a double-tap gesture directly on the graphic. Therefore, the tablet has to be connected with a computer. This kind of technologies allow static audio-feedback that has to be determined in advance. The mobility is limited and the technology does not provide rich interaction techniques.

Other tablet-based approaches make use of standard tablets which were overlaid by tactile representations. *Touchplates* [8] uses acrylic plastic overlays on a tabletop or a tablet with infrared-based diffused illumination that recognizes visual markers to get the orientation and position of the overlay. This technology allows multi-touch interaction whereby touches on non-transparent overlays cannot be recognized. Other approaches do not need specific technologies such as infrared sensors to recognise overlays. For instance, the recognition and calibration of overlays can also be done by the means of capacitive codes which are embedded within the overlays by use of conductive filament [7]. *TPad* allows overlaying standard tablets with embossed, tactile graphics [11] by easily loading SVG-files into a specific app. These approaches lack in supporting rich interaction gestures because it must be possible to distinguish between intended user input and tactile graphic exploration. Authors of *TPad* reported that common multi-touch gestures were disabled for this reason. In most cases, double-tap was implemented as a selection gesture instead of a single tap to prevent unintended touches. Just one approach provides gestural interaction such as hold or lasso-gesture [2] which was applied for tactile maps and not for charts. Besides static tactile representations, dynamic, touch-sensitive pin-matrix devices also support audio feedback that was applied by Zeng et al. in several projects mostly in the context of tactile maps [16, 17]. Pin-matrix devices, for instance, made by Metec[1] support 10 point multi-touch interaction as well as additional hardware buttons for Braille input and further features. Additionally, speech output is supported. Users can interact with refreshable, tactile graphics in real-time whereby just 10 dpi resolution, and just one dot height is provided. These devices cost several thousand euros per piece and are limited in mobility and resolution.

More hardware-independent approaches which aim to augment pure tactile graphics with audio feedback, make use of computer vision or image processing techniques to recognize the intended interaction on the sheet. Baker et al. [1] placed QR-Codes directly on the graphic that can be read by a developed app to replace Braille labels in graphics. As a disadvantage, the blind user has to scan QR-Codes with the camera of the smartphone which is not practicable for fluid interaction concepts and challenging especially for blind users. Another approach comes from Fusco et al. [4] who developed a machine-vision based system that tracks the finger of blind users to enable point-and-click interaction.

Digital pens were rarely examined for practical usage together with tactile charts in the past. Just Landau et al. [9] use a digital pen that reads out printed Anoto patterns with an infrared sensor. The authors used the pen in the context of tactile maps and did not make any user studies to evaluate the usefulness of the application. Additionally, the producer does not provide an open SDK for this product anymore. In contrast, Wall et al. [14] combined a graphic tablet with simple, physical, circular overlays that can be explored by means of a digital pen. In this application, the user has to press a button on the pen to get audio feedback about the current position on the circular overlay, which makes it difficult to hold the pen steady. Beyond that, we are not aware of any approaches that use digital pens for tactile graphics in the same way we want to implement.

All in all, we identified the following disadvantages of current approaches: (1) Lack of support of rich gestures (2) Lack of ability for mobile use (3) No use of pure tactile graphic (4) Creation of audio-tactile graphic is not accessible for

---

[1] https://www.metec-ag.de/en/produkte-graphik-display.php, Retrieved on 04 April, 2020.

blind users (5) Lack of distinguishing between intended input and output (6) Requirement of specialized and expensive hardware (7) No support of simultaneous exploration and interaction with the graphic (8) No flexible usage (e.g. limitations of size or position of the tactile graphic) (9) No support of direct user input on the tactile graphic. For sure, some of these lacks were supported partly by several approaches that were discussed above. Requirements for audio-tactile graphics strongly depend on specific graphic types and goals of the analysis. Because tactile charts are useful for effective data analysis for blind and visually impaired people [3], interacting with data to address specific analysis tasks should be provided. This is the first step for the development of interaction concepts as they have already been examined for visual information visualizations. To achieve this goal, we investigated how digital pens can support exploring and analysing tactile charts and which gestural interaction can be supported. Afterwards, we propose a first interaction concept for tactile scatterplots.

3 Digital Pens for Audio-Tactile Charts

Digital pens are inexpensive, mobile, and allow fluid, direct interaction. They can be used one-handed. A main requirement for the envisaged usage is the possibility to get audio feedback dependent on user input. It should be possible to manage and identify several sheets as well as the position on the sheet. Furthermore, the creation of customised applications should be supported. Based on these requirements, we compare two digital pens that are able to interpret dot patterns.

3.1 Comparison of Digital Pens

The TipToi® is a standalone product from Ravensburger which was developed for children's books. Second, the Neo Smartpen M1 was developed to digitalise handwritten content. The TipToi® is cheaper (about 20€) than the Neo Smartpen (about 150€) and can be used without additional hardware (apart from a computer to transfer the required files to the pen) because a micro-controller, as well as a speaker, are integrated. Furthermore, they differ in their operating principle: The TipToi® works with an Anoto pattern and does not come with an official SDK to generate an object identifier (OID) or script files for the pen. Instead, an unofficial tool was developed by the community[2]. Neo SmartPen provides an SKD for different operating systems as well as documentation. While the TipToi® assigns a single identifier to interaction objects (OID) that can be encoded with Anoto pattern, Neo SmartPen uses the NCode pattern which is organised in a coordinate system so that the position on the paper can be determined by the pen. Neo SmartPen is not able to provide feedback without additional hardware. The possibility to connect the pen with other devices such as smartphones leads to the advantage that all feedback modalities and features of these devices could be used (e.g. vibration, TTS). Blind users can utilize their own devices which are familiar to them. Neo SmartPen is equipped with additional sensors to measure e.g. pressure, tilt, and rotation.

---

[2] https://github.com/entropia/tip-toi-reveng/wiki. Retrieved on 04 April, 2020.

3.2   Combining Individual Audio-Tactile Printouts with Dot Patterns

We first investigate the production of embossed graphics combined with dot patterns. Our goal is to develop an application that enables blind users to produce audio-tactile charts on their own. That is why we initially tried out printing patterns with a standard laser printer (Brother HL-5250DN). Both dot patterns were printed with a resolution of 1200 dpi and were readable by the pens. We noticed that the printed pattern was partially damaged when the pattern was touched repeatedly which decreases the recognition rate. Before embossing the graphic, the pattern must be printed on the sheet. On the reverse, the printing ink cannot reach the areas around tactile elements. Moreover, tactile printout and dot patterns have to be calibrated. When producing combined printouts for TipToi®, this has to be done manually by placing the graphic directly on the dot pattern which could be very hard especially for blind users. The Neo SmartPen requires an additional calibration step to find out where the coordinate system is placed on the sheet. Moreover, this step ensures hardware-independent printouts. To achieve this, we developed an accessible calibration process where the user just needs to identify a tactile initialisation point on the upper sheet's corner.

To test the recognition of dot patterns in combination with tactile elements, we evaluated several textures and object sizes manually. Tactile elements decrease the recognition of both dot patterns. This applies especially to raised, filled areas. The lower the embossing height, the better the detection rate. Thin lines, small elements, and rough textures do not significantly influence the recognition rate. Overlapping elements are challenging especially for the Anoto pattern because here a single code is generated per object, which - in order to be recognized - is not allowed to overlap. We believe that the recognition rate can be increased through further printing tests and improved printing. Additionally, pre-printed sheets with NCode patterns can be provided.

3.3   A Pilot Study to Evaluate Touch Gestures with Digital Pens

In a second step, we evaluated the possibility to perform and recognize gestures. We focused on common gestures that are implemented for many touch devices: Single-tap, Double-tap, Hold-Down, and Line-drawing gestures. The Neo Smart-Pen offers the possibility to realise force-touch gestures by measuring the force with which the pen is pressed onto the sheet. It has been shown that the TipToi® is not suitable for the implementation of gestures, because of limitations in programming. The tap gesture was certainly recognizable with this pen. A circle gesture could also be recognized, whereby no distinction can be made between multiple circularly arranged taps and the continuous circular gesture.

To evaluate gestures with Neo SmartPen, we developed an Android App that receives sensor data from the pen in real-time. Together with a blind student, who is a good Braille reader and has experiences with tactile charts as well as the handling of pens, we evaluated the usability and comprehensibility of the proposed gestures with the Neo SmartPen. We logged all captured sensor data and provided feedback about performed gestures for the experimenter during the whole study. The participant got audio feedback about the performed gesture. Furthermore, the participant had to use gestures to perform several tasks, e.g. tracing tactile lines, drawing lines with a specific length, lasso gestures to select elements, pointing in the middle of a circle.

Overall, the handling of the pen was not challenging for the participant. The force touch could not be recognised because the participant pressed the pen too strongly onto the sheet during the entire test. It is still unclear whether the sensor does not cover a broad enough range or whether blind people press the pen harder onto the sheet than sighted people. The hold-gesture was not only preferred, it was also often recognised instead of the force-touch, that is why we refrain from using both gestures in one application. The single-tap gesture was recognized most reliably. Apart from force-touch, the participant was able to perform all gestures easily and intuitively. Based on the study, the implementation of the gestures was adjusted again, as, for example, the threshold for the hold and double-tap was somewhat too short. Furthermore, by use of audio feedback, the participant was able to draw lines with a specific length along a tactile line and also without tactile support. The participant could frame several elements with a lasso gesture by making several small movements instead of one continous movement. This requires further testing and implementation to reliably detect lasso gestures. The user study confirmed that the dot pattern could not be detected in purely embossed areas. This can be overcome by leaving small areas with unembossed surfaces for contact points with the pen. In our study it was unchallenging for the participant to point in the unembossed middle of a tactile circle.

The pilot study indicates that the Neo SmartPen is suitable to support inter-action tasks with tactile elements. Furthermore, simple discrete and continuous gestures are applicable. Based on those findings, we developed a prototype to show the practical use of gestures in tactile scatterplots.

4   Audio-Tactile Scatterplots by Means of Digital Pens

Scatterplots are suitable for data analysis [3] and can be used to present a high amount of data. Distinguishing different symbols and the determination of precise values are challenging tasks when analysing data by means of tactile scatterplots. Especially overlying symbols are hard to distinguish. These lacks can be addressed by audio feedback. Therefore, we implemented a workflow that automates the generation of audio-tactile scatterplots which can be used with Neo SmartPen in combination with a smartphone (see Fig. 1). The structure of the SVG-file must follow a predefined structure in order to be interpreted automatically. This can be achieved by using a tool to automate the generation of tactile charts such as SVGPlott [3]. The SVG-file can be used to emboss the tactile chart. The implemented smartphone app reads the SVG-file and extracts areas, values and objects, implements gesture recognition, and automatically

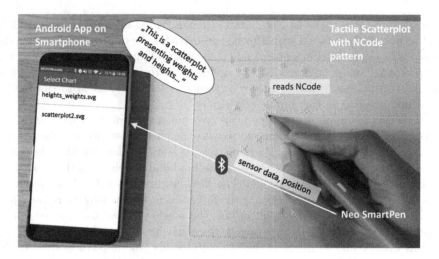

Fig. 1. Components of the application: The Neo SmartPen reads the NCode pattern from tactile scatterplot and sends it together with several sensor data to the Android application. Depending on the detected gesture and position on the page, the app provides an audio feedback to the user.

generates feedback depending on the user's input. Before the initialization, the SVG-file with the chart must be loaded into the app. Afterwards, the tactile initialization point in the diagram must be touched with the pen, so it can calculate an offset due to the printing inaccuracies.

We support the following tasks for information seeking inspired by the *Audio Information Seeking Principles* [18]: Gist, Navigate, Filter, and Detail-on-Demand. Every tactile element on the graphic provides audio feedback. Furthermore, we implemented two analysis modes: Speech and Sonification mode which can be switched by a tactile button. Sonification is suitable to provide an overview of the data while speech mode provides better support for detail-on-demand-tasks. In speech mode, single-taps provide properties of selected elements. In this way, the user is supported when exploring and understanding tactile graphic elements, such as axes, general content, or tactile symbols. A description of the chart will be provided by selecting the chart's title. When tapping on a tactile symbol, audio feedback informs about values, corresponding data sets as well as the shape of the symbol. Double-tapping at any place stops current audio output. If another element is activated while speech output is still running, the latter is automatically stopped, whereas the hold- gesture selects elements for further analysis. We implemented a distance measurement for two selected points. In addition, a line-gesture on the axes specifies the start and end of a value range for filtering. The audio feedback for filtering provides category, the number of values which lie within the specified range, and its average and its outliers. Filtering in sonification mode along the axes is realised by mapping the amount of data within the specified range to pitches. The higher the pitch the more data are located in the value range. When a single symbol is selected, the amount of data in the symbol's immediate neighbourhood is sonified (we used a threshold of 2 cm). Performing a hold-gesture on a single data point extends this radius. This feature allows a better estimation of distributions and clusters.

5 Pilot Study on Audio-Tactile Scatterplots

The results can be strongly influenced by the partly poor recognition rate, which is why we first conducted a qualitative survey with one blind participant who took already part in the first pilot study. We asked seven questions addressing the detection of outliers, counting values within a specific range, reading out precise values, and distinguish point symbols for a pure tactile and an audio-tactile scatterplot. Both scatterplots represent three different point symbols and overlaying data points.

Neither the handling of the pen nor carrying out gestures was challenging. The pen did not interrupt the exploration of the scatterplots. It was noticed that the holding of the pen has an influence on the detection rate, as the sensor must not be covered. The participant was able to connect the pen with the smartphone app and to load the scatterplot data. The participant reported that solving tasks was easier with the audio-tactile scatterplot than with the pure tactile one. Furthermore, it was stated that reading out values and symbol shapes especially for overlying symbols was improved by the use of audio feedback. However, users must first be familiar with the functions and handling in order to develop good analysis strategies. The participant suggested the following improvements. (1) Filtering data should be possible on all existing axes including doubled axes (2) Nevertheless, tactile markers should be available on the axes (3) Specifying ranges of values by drawing a line in the chart area can be helpful for the data analysis. Overall, we found some indications that the usage of Neo SmartPen for tactile scatterplots can improve data analysis.

6 Conclusion

By means of an analysis and a first pilot study, we showed that digital pens can be used to produce interactive, mobile, low-cost, audio-tactile applications. Further practical tests are necessary to improve the recognition rate of the pen on raised surfaces. The TipToi® is just useful for simple interaction tasks where the exploration of graphic elements should be supported (e.g. in form of guided tours through the graphic) or specifying precise values are demanded. In contrast, the Neo SmartPen has a high potential to support rich data analysis with tactile charts. Calculations on the data can be carried out in real-time and other output modalities of the smartphone can be used. Moreover, we showed a system that automates the generation of rich audio feedback on the basis of well-defined SVG-files. As a result, blind users were able to produce and use audio-tactile charts on their own by means of an Android application and the Neo SmartPen. More research and user studies are needed to examine further limitations and interaction concepts for audio-tactile graphics.

References

1. Baker, C.M., Milne, L.R., Scofield, J., Bennett, C.L., Ladner, R.E.: Tactile graphics with a voice: using QR codes to access text in tactile graphics. In: Proceedings of the 16th International ACM SIGACCESS Conference on Computers & Accessibility, pp. 75–82 (2014)
2. Brock, A., Jouffrais, C.: Interactive audio-tactile maps for visually impaired people. ACM SIGACCESS Access. Comput. **113**, 3–12 (2015)
3. Engel, C., Weber, G.: User study: a detailed view on the effectiveness and design of tactile charts. In: Lamas, D., Loizides, F., Nacke, L., Petrie, H., Winckler, M., Zaphiris, P. (eds.) INTERACT 2019. LNCS, vol. 11746, pp. 63–82. Springer, Cham (2019). https://doi.org/10.1007/978-3-030-29381-9_5
4. Fusco, G., Morash, V.S.: The tactile graphics helper: providing audio clarification for tactile graphics using machine vision. In: Proceedings of the 17th International ACM SIGACCESS Conference on Computers & Accessibility, pp. 97–106 (2015)
5. Gardner, J.A., Bulatov, V.: Scientific diagrams made easy with IVEO^{TM}. In: Miesenberger, K., Klaus, J., Zagler, W.L., Karshmer, A.I. (eds.) ICCHP 2006. LNCS, vol. 4061, pp. 1243–1250. Springer, Heidelberg (2006). https://doi.org/10.1007/11788713_179
6. Goncu, C., Marriott, K.: GraVVITAS: generic multi-touch presentation of accessible graphics. In: Campos, P., Graham, N., Jorge, J., Nunes, N., Palanque, P., Winckler, M. (eds.) INTERACT 2011. LNCS, vol. 6946, pp. 30–48. Springer, Heidelberg (2011). https://doi.org/10.1007/978-3-642-23774-4_5
7. Götzelmann, T.: LucentMaps: 3D printed audiovisual tactile maps for blind and visually impaired people. In: Proceedings of the 18th International ACM SIGACCESS Conference on Computers and Accessibility, pp. 81–90 (2016)
8. Kane, S.K., Morris, M.R., Wobbrock, J.O.: Touchplates: low-cost tactile overlays for visually impaired touch screen users. In: Proceedings of the 15th International ACM SIGACCESS Conference on Computers and Accessibility, pp. 1–8 (2013)
9. Landau, S., Bourquin, G., Miele, J., Van Schaack, A.: Demonstration of a universally accessible audio-haptic transit map built on a digital pen-based platform. In: Proceedings of the 3rd International Workshop on Haptic and Audio Interaction Design, pp. 23–24. Citeseer (2008)
10. Landau, S., Wells, L.: Merging tactile sensory input and audio data by means of the talking tactile tablet. Proc. EuroHaptics **3**, 414–418 (2003)
11. Melfi, G., Müller, K., Schwarz, T., Jaworek, G., Stiefelhagen, R.: Understanding what you feel: A mobile audio-tactile system for graphics used at schools with students with visual impairment. In: Proceedings of the CHI Conference 2020 (to be published) (2020)
12. Miele, J.A., Landau, S., Gilden, D.: Talking TMAP: automated generation of audio-tactile maps using smith-kettlewell's TMAP software. Br. J. Vis. Impairment **24**(2), 93–100 (2006)
13. Ramloll, R., Yu, W., Brewster, S., Riedel, B., Burton, M., Dimigen, G.: Constructing sonified haptic line graphs for the blind student: first steps. In: Proceedings of the Fourth International ACM Conference on Assistive Technologies, pp. 17–25 (2000)
14. Wall, S.A., Brewster, S.A.: Tac-tiles: multimodal pie charts for visually impaired users. In: Proceedings of the 4th Nordic Conference on Human-Computer Interaction: Changing Roles, pp. 9–18 (2006)

15. Yu, W., Ramloll, R., Brewster, S.: Haptic graphs for blind computer users. In: Brewster, S., Murray-Smith, R. (eds.) Haptic HCI 2000. LNCS, vol. 2058, pp. 41–51. Springer, Heidelberg (2001). https://doi.org/10.1007/3-540-44589-7_5
16. Zeng, L., Weber, G.: Audio-haptic browser for a geographical information system. In: Miesenberger, K., Klaus, J., Zagler, W., Karshmer, A. (eds.) ICCHP 2010. LNCS, vol. 6180, pp. 466–473. Springer, Heidelberg (2010). https://doi.org/10.1007/978-3-642-14100-3_70
17. Zeng, L., Weber, G.: Exploration of location-aware you-are-here maps on a pin-matrix display. IEEE Trans. Hum. Mach. Syst. **46**(1), 88–100 (2015)
18. Zhao, H., Plaisant, C., Shneiderman, B., Duraiswami, R.: Sonification of geo-referenced data for auditory information seeking: design principle and pilot study. In: ICAD (2004)

Environmental Sensing Technologies
for Visual Impairment

A Multi-scale Embossed Map Authoring Tool for Indoor Environments

Viet Trinh[(⊠)] and Roberto Manduchi

Department of Computer Science and Engineering, University of California,
Santa Cruz, CA, USA
{vqtrinh,manduchi}@ucsc.edu

Abstract. We introduce a multi-scale embossed map authoring tool
(M-EMAT) that produces tactile maps of indoor environments from the
building's structural layout and its 3D-scanned interiors on demand. Our
tool renders indoor tactile maps at different spatial scales, representing
a building's structure, a zoomed-in of a specific area, or an interior of a
room. M-EMAT is very easy to use and produces accurate results even
in the case of complex building layouts.

Keywords: Indoor tactile map · Map design · Map production

1 Introduction

Multiple studies have shown that, when visually impaired individuals are given
the opportunity to preview a route displayed in a tactile format, prior to an
actual travel, they are able to follow it more accurately and with fewer errors
[2,9,10]. Tactile maps give readers the layout of a venue and the spatial relationship between its landmarks, facilitating a confident self-orientation and a
safer travel. Regardless of different techniques in producing tactile graphics (i.e.,
embossing [4,27], audio-tactile pairing [3,6], or 3D printing [8,28]), it is impractical to design a one-size-fits-all tactile map because different users have different
needs of tactile feedbacks. Thus, automation of tactile map making tailored to
user needs is crucial in helping people with visual impairments.

One of the most practical challenges of automating tactile map production
is *generalization*, a process in which the map maker needs to decide which level
of detail should be rendered at a given scale, due to limited tactile resolution
[14,17]. This problem is particularly relevant for the generation of indoor tactile
maps. This is compounded by the fact that detailed maps of indoor environments
in digital format are not always publicly available. And even when they are,
they usually contain only large-scale architectural information (e.g., entrances,
staircases, offices), but not detailed layouts of interior spaces.

Findings from the focus group discussed in [26] indicate that embossing the
map of a building at different levels of detail could be provide useful spatial
information for pre-journey learning. In this paper, we introduce a multi-scale
embossed map authoring tool, or M-EMAT, that produces tactile maps of indoor

© Springer Nature Switzerland AG 2020
K. Miesenberger et al. (Eds.): ICCHP 2020, LNCS 12376, pp. 459–466, 2020.
https://doi.org/10.1007/978-3-030-58796-3_53

environments at different spatial scales on demand, including the building's architectural structure, zoomed-in of specific areas (*sections*, and a small-scale layout of a room, highlighting the spatial relationship among objects in the room. This tool is an extension of our online application, named Semantic Interior Mapology or SIM[1] [25], that allows users to trace the contour of a building and to construct the spatial layout of its interior structure, starting from the picture of a floor plan.

2   Related Work

The problems of cartographic generalization and automatic tactile map production have been investigated independently over the past few decades. However, the use of standard generalization techniques for the production of indoor tactile map that could be used by visually impaired travelers has received relatively little attention. Early works in automatic generation of tactile maps relied on data from geographical information systems (GIS) to render tactile elements of outdoor environments. For instance, TMAP [16], TMACS [27], Mapy [4], and On Demand Tactile Map [23] use OpenStreetMap as their underlying data source to generate a tactile map file of a location around a physical address that could later be printed offline using Braille embossers. These tactile elements cover important outdoor landmarks (e.g., buildings, parks, stations, road networks, rivers, etc) but not interior layouts of buildings.

Recently, there is a growing interest in technologies for automating indoor tactile map making. For example, the Audio-Tactile navigation system by Papadopoulos et al. generates audio-tactile maps from digital map files containing specific spatial information of a building [18]. Hybrid methods for the automatic generation of 3D indoor maps from AutoCAD architectural floor plans were proposed in [1,22]. This prior work only focused on the structural elements of a building, such as walls, doors, or staircases. Small-scale description of furniture items or floor covering, which can be useful for navigation without sight, were not considered.

Advances in machine learning techniques have prompted researchers to revisit the problem of cartographic generalization. Several neural-network models have been developed for the tasks of recognizing, grouping, and typifying buildings [7,20,24]. However, these models are only able to learn and predict a building's contour and the geographical distribution if groups of buildings, and may not generalize well for the representation of the layout of an indoor space.

3   The M-EMAT Development

Our embossed map authoring tool produces a digital tactile map file at a desired scale, based on the building's structure represented in *sim* [25] and the semantic layout of an interior space encoded in a *JSON* map that are collectively

---

[1] https://sim.soe.ucsc.edu.

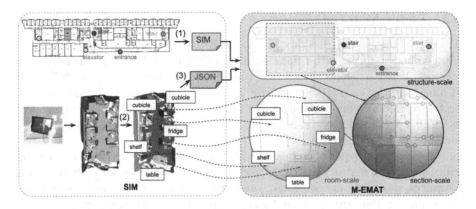

Fig. 1. M-EMAT is an extension of the SIM toolbox [25]. It allows one to (1) trace a floor plan to generate a *sim* representation, (2) import a 3D mesh of a space, and (3) segment and embed elements of interest into a *JSON* map. M-EMAT produces tactile maps at three different scales, based on the spatial information captured in SIM.

acquired from our SIM toolbox described in [25]. More specifically, M-EMAT is an extension of the SIM web application (Fig. 1) that allows one to convert an architectural floor plan and its 3D-scanned contents into a standard format (JSON). Using SIM, one can quickly trace a floor plan from an image of it, and produce a vectorized map, stored in the *sim* format [25]. Small-scale elements (such as furniture items) that are normally not available in a map can be acquired using a 3D (RGBD) camera such as Occipital's Structure Sensor,[2] which registers and stitches multiple point clouds into one 3D mesh. SIM allows one to parse the 3D scan of a room, to segment out objects of interest, and to geo-register these objects within the building's spatial layout. The object segmentation component used in SIM, which is a web-based toolkit developed in [5], lets users to manually select a connected set of mesh facets having a similar orientation, indicating the 3D scan's objects of interest. A JSON file containing all spatial information for the building is automatically generated.

3.1 Tactile Graphics Resolution

Following the study described in [21], our map authoring tool renders segments with length of at least 0.5 in (12 mm), with a minimum distance of 0.2 in (5 mm) between two segments. For easy discrimination, symbols representing different features have a minimum diameter of 0.25 in (6 mm), with minimum distance between two symbols of 0.5 in (12 mm). Braille characters for annotation of objects and spaces have size of 0.16 in × 0.26 in (4 mm × 6 mm) [11].

---

[2] Structure Sensor. https://structure.io/.

3.2   Tactile Map Design

The digital tactile map files produced by M-EMAT can be printed on a 11.5 in ×
11 in embosser sheet, with resolution of 20 DPI and a 0.5 in (12 mm) margin on
all sides. It is partitioned in two sections: the *header* (10.5 in × 3 in; 267 mm ×
76 mm); and the *body* (10.5 in × 7 in; 267 mm × 178 mm). The header contains
on the top-left the building name, the floor number, and the map scale, as well
as an arrow pointing to the North on the top-right. The body has the tactile
map at the desired scale.

There are two types of embossed features in the map: ***structural*** and ***interior***. Structural features are those traced from a building's floor plan, including
entrances, staircases, elevators, escalators, walls, and doors. Interior features represent objects that are segmented and annotated from 3D scans, such as tables,
cubicles, shelves, and other pieces of furniture. M-EMAT allows one to choose
between three different scales:

1. ***Structure-scale***: General building layout, consisting of rooms, corridors, and
   structural features. Wall are embossed as solid segments, while rooms are
   represented by untextured areas, enclosed by at least 4 walls. Corridors are
   rendered as textured areas. In this scale, the room number or door is usually
   not rendered due to space constrains.
2. ***Section-scale***: Expanded view of a specific area inside a building. In addition to the features already considered in the structure scale, a section-scale
   map also displays room numbers, room doors, and any available *interior* features. Room numbers are embossed at the center of each room, and doors are
   represented as circles along walls [13].
3. ***Room-scale***: The layout of a small area (typically a room), including walls,
   doors, and all annotated *interior* features.

Structure	entrance, staircase, elevator, escalator, wall, door
Section	wall, door, bench, couch, desk, table, shelf, chair, directory, board
Room	wall, door, cubicle, desk, couch, bench, shelf, table, cabinet, nightstand, fridge, bathtub, toilet, sink, chair, board, printer, trash can

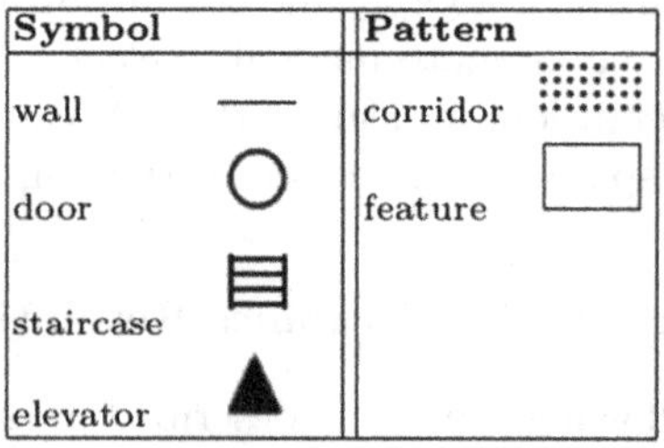 Symbol		Pattern	
wall	—	corridor	▨
door	◯	feature	▭
staircase	☰		
elevator	▲		

(a)   (b)

Fig. 2. (a) Embossed features at different map scales, and (b) tactile graphic symbols
representing these features.

The features to be embossed at different map scales when space permits
are shown in the Fig. 2-a. Tactile symbols and patterns used to represent such
features are also listed in the Fig. 2-b. Note that the staircase symbol embossed
in our maps was suggested in [12], while the other symbols were drawn from
[13]. The texture patterns were proposed in [19].

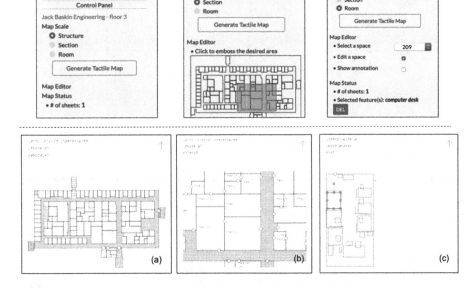

Fig. 3. The top row shows the M-EMAT control panels. The bottom row shows the generated tactile maps at 3 different scales: (a) structure, (b) section, and (c) room.

Our tactile map authoring tool limits rendering of a room or a section of a building to a single embosser sheet. The building's general layout (structure-scale) can span multiple pages; this allows for rendition of very elongated buildings. M-EMAT automatically selects the features to be rendered based on the selected scale, while adhering to tactile resolution constraints of Sect. 3.1. Figure 3 shows an example of M-EMAT's user interface at different map scales, along with the produced tactile maps.

3.3 Room-Scale Editor

Interior features at room-scale are represented by their bounding boxes, which are shaped as vertical-oriented cuboids. These cuboids are shown as rectangles in the tactile map. M-EMAT includes a simple editor (only available at the room-scale) that allows users to translate, rotate, and scale features within a boundary. This can be useful when the segmentation tools produces overcrowded, unaligned, or overlapping embossed features. The editor also allows users to merge multiple rectangles into a single polygonal feature [15], which can be helpful for objects with complex shapes. As shown in the Fig. 4, the feature #1 (a couch) was translated and then merged with another couch (#2); the coffee table (#3) was rotated to its correct orientation; and a desk (#4) and a whiteboard (#5) were both scaled down to their correct dimension. Note that if two objects (e.g., a table and a printer) are physically on top of each other, they will be represented as two stacked cuboids, which will be mapped as two nested rectangles. In this case, the innermost rectangle can be removed using the editor.

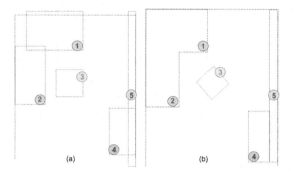

Fig. 4. A generated tactile map at the room-scale (a) before and (b) after being edited.

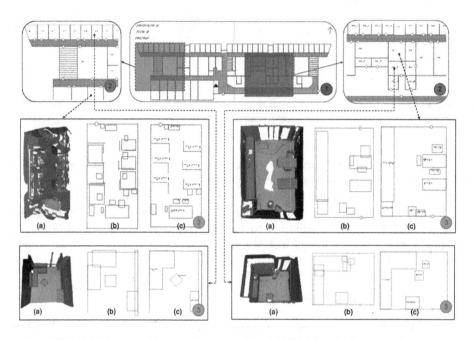

Fig. 5. Indoor tactile maps generated by M-EMAT at different scales.

M-EMAT's user-friendly interface allows one to select any region, room, or type of indoor features to be embossed. For example, one might choose to render only features that are close to walls (countertops, benches, or shelves) vs. furnitures positioned randomly in the middle of a room (tables, chairs, etc). Sample multi-scale indoor tactile maps generated by M-EMAT are shown in Fig. 5. The figure also show 3D room scans (a), their segmentation (b), and the results after manual editing (c), along with Braille annotations. These Braille annotations at the section-scale denote room numbers; whereas, in the room-scale tactile map, they annotate the interior features segmented from a 3D scan.

4   Conclusion

We introduced M-EMAT, an add-on to our existing SIM application, that enables generation of multi-scale tactile maps of a building. Using SIM, one can easily trace an existing map to generate a digital representation of the building's structure (walls, rooms, doors, stairs, elevators). M-EMAT converts this information into a format that is amenable for embossing, at the scale specified by the user, with specific constraints on the density and distances of tactile features. In addition, M-EMAT facilitates the generation of room-scale layouts by from a 3D scan of a room. This feature is particularly useful because maps at the room level are usually not available. SIM with the M-EMAT add-on is available for anyone to use at https://sim.soe.ucsc.edu.

Acknowledgments. Research reported in this publication was supported by the National Eye Institute of the National Institutes of Health under award number R01EY029033. The content is solely the responsibility of the authors and does not necessarily represent the official views of the National Institutes of Health.

References

1. Auricchio, F., Greco, A., Alaimo, G., Giacometti, V., Marconi, S., Mauri, V.: 3D printing technology for buildings accessibility: the tactile map for mte museum in pavia. J. Civ. Eng. Archit. **11**, 736–747 (2017)
2. Blades, M., Ungar, S., Spencer, C.: Map use by adults with visual impairments. Prof. Geogr. **51**(4), 539–553 (1999)
3. Brock, A., Truillet, P., Oriola, B., Jouffrais, C.: Usage of multimodal maps for blind people: why and how. In: ACM International Conference on Interactive Tabletops and Surfaces, pp. 247–248 (2010)
4. Červenka, P., Břinda, K., Hanousková, M., Hofman, P., Seifert, R.: Blind friendly maps: tactile maps for the blind as a part of the public map portal (mapy. cz). arXiv preprint arXiv:1603.09520 (2016)
5. Dai, A., Chang, A.X., Savva, M., Halber, M., Funkhouser, T., Nießner, M.: Scannet: richly-annotated 3D reconstructions of indoor scenes. In: Proceedings of the IEEE Conference on Computer Vision and Pattern Recognition, pp. 5828–5839 (2017)
6. Edwards, A.D.N., Hamid, N.N.A., Petrie, H.: Exploring map orientation with interactive audio-tactile maps. In: Abascal, J., Barbosa, S., Fetter, M., Gross, T., Palanque, P., Winckler, M. (eds.) INTERACT 2015. LNCS, vol. 9296, pp. 72–79. Springer, Cham (2015). https://doi.org/10.1007/978-3-319-22701-6_6
7. Feng, Y., Thiemann, F., Sester, M.: Learning cartographic building generalization with deep convolutional neural networks. ISPRS Int. J. Geo-Inform. **8**(6), 258 (2019)
8. He, L., Wan, Z., Findlater, L., Froehlich, J.E.: Tactile: a preliminary toolchain for creating accessible graphics with 3D-printed overlays and auditory annotations. In: Proceedings of the 19th International ACM SIGACCESS Conference on Computers and Accessibility, pp. 397–398 (2017)
9. Holmes, E., Jansson, G., Jansson, A.: Exploring auditorily enhanced tactile maps for travel in new environments. COLLOQUES-INSTITUT NATIONAL DE LA SANTE ET DE LA RECHERCHE MEDICALE COLLOQUES ET SEMINAIRES, pp. 191–196 (1996)

10. Ivanchev, M., Zinke, F., Lucke, U.: Pre-journey visualization of travel routes for the blind on refreshable interactive tactile displays. In: Miesenberger, K., Fels, D., Archambault, D., Peňáz, P., Zagler, W. (eds.) ICCHP 2014. LNCS, vol. 8548, pp. 81–88. Springer, Cham (2014). https://doi.org/10.1007/978-3-319-08599-9_13

11. U.D.O. JUSTICE: Guidance onADA standards for accessible design (2010). http://www.ada.gov/regs2010/2010ADAStandards

12. Lee, C.L.: An evaluation of tactile symbols in public environment for the visually impaired. Appl. Ergon. **75**, 193–200 (2019)

13. Lobben, A., Lawrence, M.: The use of environmental features on tactile maps by navigators who are blind. Prof. Geogr. **64**(1), 95–108 (2012)

14. MacEachren, A.M.: How Maps Work: Representation, Visualization, and Design. Guilford Press, New York (2004)

15. Martínez, F., Rueda, A.J., Feito, F.R.: A new algorithm for computing boolean operations on polygons. Comput. Geosci. **35**(6), 1177–1185 (2009)

16. Miele, J.A., Landau, S., Gilden, D.: Talking tmap: automated generation of audio-tactile maps using Smith-Kettlewell's tmap software. Br. J. Vis. Impairment **24**(2), 93–100 (2006)

17. Monmonier, M.: How to Lie with Maps. University of Chicago Press (2018)

18. Papadopoulos, K., Barouti, M., Charitakis, K.: A university indoors audio-tactile mobility aid for individuals with blindness. In: Miesenberger, K., Fels, D., Archambault, D., Peňáz, P., Zagler, W. (eds.) ICCHP 2014. LNCS, vol. 8548, pp. 108–115. Springer, Cham (2014). https://doi.org/10.1007/978-3-319-08599-9_17

19. Prescher, D., Bornschein, J., Weber, G.: Consistency of a tactile pattern set. ACM Trans. Access. Comput. (TACCESS) **10**(2), 7 (2017)

20. Sester, M., Feng, Y., Thiemann, F.: Building generalization using deep learning. ISPRS - Int. Arch. Photogramm. Remote Sens. Spat. Inf. Sci. XLII-4 (2018) **42**, 565–572 (2018)

21. Štampach, R., Mulíčková, E.: Automated generation of tactile maps. J. Maps **12**(Suppl. 1), 532–540 (2016)

22. Tang, H., Tsering, N., Hu, F., Zhu, Z.: Automatic pre-journey indoor map generation using autoCAD floor plan (2016)

23. Touya, G., Christophe, S., Favreau, J.M., Ben Rhaiem, A.: Automatic derivation of on-demand tactile maps for visually impaired people: first experiments and research agenda. Int. J. Cartogr. **5**(1), 67–91 (2019)

24. Touya, G., Zhang, X., Lokhat, I.: Is deep learning the new agent for map generalization? Int. J. Cartogr. **5**(2–3), 142–157 (2019)

25. Trinh, V., Manduchi, R.: Semantic interior mapology: a toolbox for indoor scene description from architectural floor plans. arXiv preprint arXiv:1911.11356 (2019)

26. Trinh, V., Manduchi, R.: Feeling your way around: Assessing the perceived utility of multi-scale indoor tactile maps. In: Extended Abstracts of the 2020 CHI Conference on Human Factors in Computing Systems, pp. 1–8 (2020)

27. Watanabe, T., Yamaguchi, T., Koda, S., Minatani, K.: Tactile map automated creation system using OpenStreetMap. In: Miesenberger, K., Fels, D., Archambault, D., Peňáz, P., Zagler, W. (eds.) ICCHP 2014. LNCS, vol. 8548, pp. 42–49. Springer, Cham (2014). https://doi.org/10.1007/978-3-319-08599-9_7

28. Zhang, X., et al.: Interactiles: 3D printed tactile interfaces to enhance mobile touch-screen accessibility. In: Proceedings of the 20th International ACM SIGACCESS Conference on Computers and Accessibility, pp. 131–142 (2018)

A Real-Time Indoor Localization Method with Low-Cost Microwave Doppler Radar Sensors and Particle Filter

Sylvain Ferrand$^{(\boxtimes)}$, François Alouges, and Matthieu Aussal

CMAP - Ecole Polytechnique, CNRS, IP-Paris, Route de Saclay,
91128 Palaiseau Cedex, France
sylvain.ferrand@polytechnique.edu

Abstract. We propose a novel method of localization based on low-cost continuous-wave unmodulated doppler microwave radar sensors. We use both velocity measures and distance estimations with RSS from radar sensors. We also implement a particle filter for real time localization. Experiments show that, with a reasonable initial estimate, it is possible to track the movements of a person in a room with enough accuracy for considering using this type of devices for monitoring a person or indoor guiding applications.

Keywords: Indoor localization · Doppler radar · Particle filter · Electronic travel aid

Indoor monitoring elderly people or guiding visually impaired persons (see e.g. [1]) need accurate and fast real-time localization systems. Indoor positioning is a very active research topic, and many technologies have been developed in this field (see e.g. the survey [2]). Nevertheless, unmodulated continuous wave doppler radar has been little explored for pure positioning applications, although they could be inexpensive and simple to deploy. Doppler radars are widely used in presence detectors (door opening) as well as for vehicle speed control. Unlike frequency-modulated continuous-wave (FMCW) or pulse radar, they do not measure distances. Instead, they may determine the radial velocity components of moving objects in the field of the radar.

We propose in this paper to use meager cost and rudimentary radar modules (see Fig. 1) originally designed for presence detection. This opens the door to very low cost monitoring or blind guidance applications. Unlike metrology grade sensors (e.g. Doppler radar for road control), miniature microwave radars offer minimal accuracy in the counterpart of their low cost (about 10 euros).

Those devices are used in research projects for many applications. Some researchers use them for gait monitoring and movement classification [3,4], while others try to estimate the walking speed [5] or investigate guidance and obstacle avoidance applications [6]. At first sight, it seems unreasonable to use these sensors alone to locate a person because they do not provide absolute distance measurements. This is why some researchers have used Kalman filters to combine

© Springer Nature Switzerland AG 2020
K. Miesenberger et al. (Eds.): ICCHP 2020, LNCS 12376, pp. 467–474, 2020.
https://doi.org/10.1007/978-3-030-58796-3_54

Fig. 1. A doppler radar module (CDM324).

these radar measurements with more reliable technologies that measure distances (e.g. UWB, see [7]).

We here propose a different approach in which we use the Received Signal Strength (RSS) of the radar in order to obtain a distance evaluation.

1   Measurements Model

According to the Doppler effect equation, the speed v measured by the radar can be written as :

$$v = \frac{c\,f_d}{2f_{tx}\cos(\alpha)} \tag{1}$$

with c the speed of light, f_d the Doppler frequency, f_{tx} the frequency of the radar signal (typically 24 GHz) and α the angle formed between the direction of motion and the radar beam. Notice that, for our practical application, the Doppler signal contains several frequency components related to the limb movements of the subject.

As already explained, these sensors are not designed to measure distances. However, the Received Signal Strength Indication (RSSI) provides some distance information that can nevertheless be used, although with a priori very limited accuracy. The RSSI is generally considered to be unreliable for distance evaluation, difficult to model and very sensitive to the environment (due to shading effect, reflections, lack of polarization of antennas), even if, in radio waves based triangulation methods, analytical and empirical methods have been proposed to take into account the delicate problem of reflections in indoor environment [8]). For radars, considering waves that make a round trip between the radar and the objet, the received power P_r is usually written in terms of the transmission power P_t as:

$$P_r = P_t \frac{G^2\lambda^2\sigma}{(4\pi)^3 R^4}, \tag{2}$$

where G is the antenna gain, σ the radar cross section (reflection) of the target, and λ the wavelength.

For a transmitted signal $s_t(t) = \cos(2\pi f_c t)$, neglecting the phase term, the received signal can be written as $s_r(t) = \alpha \cos(2\pi(f_c + f_d)t)$ where α is a distance dependent attenuation factor deduced from Eq. (2).

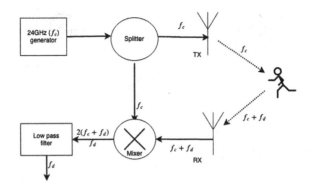

Fig. 2. The principle of a continuous wave radar.

In the sensor, the received signal is mixed with the emitted signal (c.f. Fig. 2) giving :

$$s_{mixed}(t) = \cos(2\pi f_c t)\, \alpha \cos(2\pi(f_c + f_d)t)$$
$$= \frac{\alpha}{2} \cos(2\pi(2f_c + f_d)t) + \frac{\alpha}{2} \cos(2\pi f_d t) \qquad (3)$$

Filtering the result through a low-pass filter provides a signal

$$s(t)_{IF} \propto \frac{\alpha}{2}(\cos(2\pi f_d)t) \qquad (4)$$

which permits to estimates the frequency f_d, and whose amplitude is directly proportional to the received power and can therefore be used to estimate a distance.

Rather than using the level of total energy received, we propose to use the *magnitude of the predominant frequency in the signal*, which likely corresponds to the direct path.

Eventually, the distance R is recovered from this magnitude, assuming that the target cross section is constant during movement and magnitude follows a free field k/R^4 model (cf. (2)). Since no emitter or receiver is carried, this method is naturally immune to shadowing or antenna polarization alignment problems from which RSS techniques usually suffer.

2   Real Time Localization Method

The experimental setup consists of a set of static sensors (at least two orthogonal sensors) as shown in Fig. 3. These sensors use *patch-plane antennas* and are not very directional, they have an attenuation of less than 3dB at ±60° on the horizontal plane. It is therefore advisable to move them a few metres away from the working surface to cover it completely without introducing too much attenuation linked to directivity.

The Doppler output of each sensor is connected to a suitable amplification circuit (about 60 dB) including a 5 Hz-900 Hz pass-band filter (corresponding to

Fig. 3. The experimental setup with three sensors

a maximum speed of 20 km/h). The output signals of the sensors are sampled and an autocorrelation is performed to determine the doppler frequency in the noisy signal. The magnitude is computed using a FFT.

In order to increase the precision of the system, the user can be furthermore equipped with an Inertial Motion Unit (IMU) that combines data from an accelerometer, a gyroscope and a magnetometer to estimate his/her orientation. We use an IMU composed of the low-cost MEMS (Microelectromechanical systems) sensor TDK-Inversense MPU9250 connected to a microcontroller running the Magdwick data fusion algorithm [9]. Such a device can provide orientation information with an accuracy of about 3–5°. It is a small wireless device (the size of a matchbox), that can be worn on the belt.

In the method described below, it is assumed that the user is moving in the direction of the sagittal plane (i.e. orienting himself in his direction of travel). The IMU also helps in suppressing the forward-backward ambiguity which exists when using the doppler radars alone, at least in their most simple use.

We aim at developing an algorithm for estimating the position of the subject. In that respect several difficulties need to be solved:

- Radars sensors provide highly noisy and often unusable (no sharp peaks in the spectrum) or missing measurements.
- It is impossible to distinguish motionless situations from those with no measurement (out-of-range).
- The measurement noise is not gaussian and hard to model.

To address these issues, we have developed a localization algorithm based on the particle filter (PF) method. PFs are algorithms for estimating the state of a dynamic system using Monte-Carlo methods. The PF are suitable for (strongly) non-linear models, non-Gaussian measurement noise and incomplete measurements. The particle filter algorithm is given in Algorithm 1 below.

Algorithm 1: Doppler Radar particle filter algorithm.

Result: Particle filter

(Initialisation) Random creation of a set of particles representing the possible states including speed and position

for $k = 0$ **to** Max **do**

    – For all particles: prediction of next particle state assuming a constant velocity

    – Measure sensors radial velocity, distance deduce from RSS and IMU orientation.

        • Identify static target situation (sub-threshold velocity and RSSI for all sensors)

        • Discard inconsistent measurements;

    – For all particles: Updating the particle weight taking into account the measurement;

    – Removal of Small Particles and resampling;

    – Calculation of the estimate (using a weighted average);

end

---

3 Results

3.1 Distance Estimation Accuracy

We evaluate the ranging accuracy using the magnitude of the Doppler signal alone in the case of a displacement in the direction of the axis of the sensor as well as in the case of a displacement in the orthogonal direction. First, a subject is walking back and forth towards the sensor at roughly constant walking speed. Figure 4-left compares the actual distance to the measured one. We observe that the dispersion of data increases with the distance, but we can see that the k/R^4 model provides nevertheless a realistic estimation.

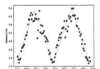

Fig. 4. Left : Measures of distance during a series of movements in the sensor axis. The blue doted line represent the real distance - Three right figures : Dispersion of distance measurement during a series of movements orthogonal to a sensor, left at 2 m, center at 3.5 m, right at 4.5 m.

We report in Fig. 4-right the distance measurements when moving in a direction orthogonal to the sensor. In this case, the model is suitable as well, but the dispersion increases sharply as the distance increases (Table 1).

Table 1. Typical ranging error while moving at different distances

	2 m	4 m	6 m
RMS Error (m)	0.62	0.7	0.77

3.2   Localization with a Particle Filter

We have implemented the device described in Fig. 3 in a surface area of 8 × 8 m.
Tests are conducted with a single person walking (speed from 0.5 to 1.5 m/s) in
this area.

Tracking on Different Courses. In order to show the tracking capabilities of
the system, we have performed different types of displacements. Some are visible
in Fig. 5.

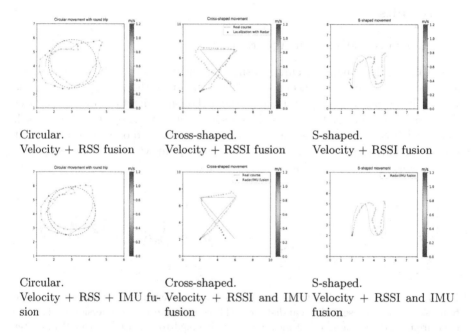

Circular.
Velocity + RSS fusion

Cross-shaped.
Velocity + RSSI fusion

S-shaped.
Velocity + RSSI fusion

Circular.
Velocity + RSS + IMU fusion

Cross-shaped.
Velocity + RSSI and IMU fusion

S-shaped.
Velocity + RSSI and IMU fusion

Fig. 5. Example of tracking with various movements. Dashed lines represent the actual
route taken by the person.

These different movements include smooth and continuous movements as well
as abrupt changes of direction, round and long trips. Theses tests were carried
out using radar RSS and velocity data but also incorporating the orientation of
the person given by the IMU.

During our tests, after initial convergence, the maximum error remains less than 1.5 m while the average error is around 0.5m. In most cases, the IMU allows to improve the quality of positioning by significantly smoothing trajectories, which is useful for the audio guidance applications we develop.

Sensor Fusion Efficiency. Figure 6 illustrate localization on a circular course using RSSI only, velocity only and data fusion. Localization using velocity can be quickly affected by drift while RSSI alone presents a rather erratic trace due to the imprecision of the measurements.

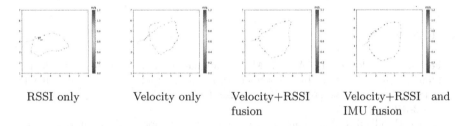

| RSSI only | Velocity only | Velocity+RSSI fusion | Velocity+RSSI and IMU fusion |

Fig. 6. Typical fusion result for an circular course

On a circular type course of about ten revolutions, including U-turns at not constant speed, the average error was about 0.4 m and 0.9 m maximum using the velocity/distance/IMU fusion. Without the IMU, the average error is about 0.7 m and 1.3 m maximum (Fig. 7).

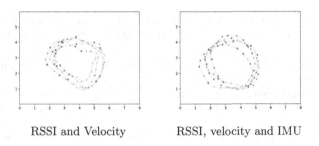

RSSI and Velocity   RSSI, velocity and IMU

Fig. 7. Tracking during a long circular course

In all experiments, the accuracy is limited by the error in the estimation of the distances and the velocities. Nevertheless, it is noticeable that no significant drift is observed even in experiments with many turns in circular courses.

4   Conclusion

Our experiments have shown that the fusion of RSSI and velocity data allows for the use of very low cost Doppler radar sensors for localization applications that do not require high accuracy. Indeed, RSSI measurements permit to limit the position drift that would be observed with velocity measurements alone.

The limited range (about 10 m) of the system is the main issue of this technology. Although limited, the accuracy could be sufficient for guidance applications. We plan to investigate further with more sensitive sensors in particular to use them for applications in guiding visually impaired people for indoor sport activities as we already did with Ultra-Wideband or RTK-DGNSS outdoor [1].

References

1. Ferrand, S., Alouges, F., Aussal, M.: An augmented reality audio device helping blind people navigation. In: Miesenberger, K., Kouroupetroglou, G. (eds.) ICCHP 2018. LNCS, vol. 10897, pp. 28–35. Springer, Cham (2018). https://doi.org/10.1007/978-3-319-94274-2_5
2. Zafari, F., Gkelias, A., Leung, K.K.: A survey of indoor localization systems and technologies. IEEE Commun. Surv. Tutorials **21**(3), 2568–2599 (2019)
3. Geisheimer, J.L., Iii, E.F.G., Marshall, W.S.: High-resolution Doppler model of the human gait. In: Radar Sensor Technology and Data Visualization, vol. 4744, pp. 8–18. International Society for Optics and Photonics, July 2002
4. Phillips, C.E., et al.: Radar walk detection in the apartments of elderly. In: 2012 Annual International Conference of the IEEE Engineering in Medicine and Biology Society, pp. 5863–5866, August 2012. ISSN: 1557-170X
5. Rui, L., Chen, S., Ho, K., Rantz, M., Skubic, M.: Estimation of human walking speed by Doppler radar for elderly care. J. Ambient Intell. Smart Environ. **9**, 181–191 (2017)
6. Tang, Y., Li, C.: Wearable indoor position tracking using onboard K-band Doppler radar and digital gyroscope. In: 2015 IEEE MTT-S 2015 International Microwave Workshop Series on RF and Wireless Technologies for Biomedical and Healthcare Applications (IMWS-BIO), Taipei, Taiwan, pp. 76–77. IEEE, September 2015
7. Wang, J., Tang, Y., Muñoz-Ferreras, J.-M., Gómez-García, R., Li, C.: An improved indoor localization solution using a hybrid UWB-Doppler system with Kalman filter. In: 2018 IEEE Radio and Wireless Symposium (RWS), pp. 181–183, January 2018. ISSN: 2164-2974
8. Benkic, K., Malajner, M., Planinsic, P., Cucej, Z.: Using RSSI value for distance estimation in wireless sensor networks based on ZigBee. In: 2008 15th International Conference on Systems, Signals and Image Processing, pp. 303–306, June 2008
9. Madgwick, S.O., Harrison, A.J., Vaidyanathan, R.: Estimation of IMU and MARG orientation using a gradient descent algorithm. In: 2011 IEEE International Conference on Rehabilitation Robotics, pp. 1–7, IEEE (2011)

An Audio-Based 3D Spatial Guidance AR System for Blind Users

James M. Coughlan[1]([⊠])[iD], Brandon Biggs[1][iD], Marc-Aurèle Rivière[2][iD],
and Huiying Shen[1][iD]

[1] The Smith-Kettlewell Eye Research Institute, San Francisco, CA, USA
{coughlan,brandon.biggs,hshen}@ski.org
[2] LITIS, University of Rouen, Normandy, France
marc-aurele.riviere@univ-rouen.fr

Abstract. Augmented reality (AR) has great potential for blind users because it enables a range of applications that provide audio information about specific locations or directions in the user's environment. For instance, the CamIO ("Camera Input-Output") AR app makes physical objects (such as documents, maps, devices and 3D models) accessible to blind and visually impaired persons by providing real-time audio feedback in response to the location on an object that the user is touching (using an inexpensive stylus). An important feature needed by blind users of AR apps such as CamIO is a 3D spatial guidance feature that provides real-time audio feedback to help the user find a desired location on an object. We have devised a simple audio interface to provide verbal guidance towards a target of interest in 3D. The experiment we report with blind participants using this guidance interface demonstrates the feasibility of the approach and its benefit for helping users find locations of interest.

Keywords: Assistive devices · Accessibility · Augmented reality · Auditory substitution · Visual impairment · Blindness · Low vision

1 State of the Art and Related Technology

Many people who are blind or visually impaired have difficulties accessing a range of everyday objects, including printed documents, maps, infographics, appliances and 3D models used in STEM education, needed for daily activities in schools, the home and the workplace. This limits their participation in many cultural, professional and educational activities. While braille labeling is often a useful means of providing access to such objects, there is only limited space for braille, and this method is only accessible to those who can read braille.

Audio labels are a powerful supplement or alternative to braille labels. Standard methods of implementing audio labels require the use of special hardware and materials, which is costly and limits their adoption. For instance, tactile graphics may be overlaid on a touch-sensitive tablet [1]. Documents or other

K. Miesenberger et al. (Eds.): ICCHP 2020, LNCS 12376, pp. 475–484, 2020.
https://doi.org/10.1007/978-3-030-58796-3_55

surfaces can be covered with a special form of paper readable by a "smart pen" [10]. The PenFriend [8] stylus uses small barcodes affixed to an object to define audio labels.

There is growing interest in using computer vision-based approaches for audio labeling. In these approaches a camera tracks the user's fingers or handheld pointer as they explore an object, enabling audio labeling for existing objects with minimal or no customization. Past computer vision approaches to audio labeling include [12], which focuses on 3D printed objects, [13], which uses a depth camera to access flat documents, and [6], which provides access to tactile graphics to students in educational settings.

We build on our past work on CamIO [3,4,11], which is short for "Camera Input-Output." We have implemented CamIO as a stand-alone iPhone app that tracks an inexpensive wooden stylus held by the user to point at locations of interest on an object (called *hotspots*). When the user points at a hotspot with the stylus tip, relevant audio information, such as text-to-speech or other sounds, is announced.

Experiments with blind participants have demonstrated the feasibility of using CamIO to access existing audio labels. Moreover, our approach allows a visually impaired user to create audio labels independently [3]. However, an ability that CamIO still lacks is the ability to provide real-time guidance to a hotspot. Without such guidance, the user must search the entire surface of an object with the stylus tip until they hear the hotspot they are seeking. This need is particularly acute in cases where the surface is lacking in tactile cues, such as the touch screen buttons on a microwave oven [3].

Guidance not only saves the user time in exploring large or intricate objects, or objects lacking in tactile features, but can enable entirely new ways of interacting with objects. For instance, a geography learning app could ask a student to point to a specific city on a world globe, and if the student has trouble finding it, the app could guide them to it in an intuitive way. Other examples could include guiding a user to a specific button on an appliance (such as a microwave oven) to perform a desired function, guiding a student to a specific element on the periodic table, or even guiding a repair-person to find a part of a machine with limited visibility. Our guidance system is inspired by recent work on auditory and haptic displays for 3D spatial guidance [5,7,9], which provide real-time audio/haptic feedback to guide a user towards a target in a virtual environment. We initially developed an interface similar to [9] for CamIO, but after preliminary testing we devised a simpler and more effective interface for our application, which we evaluated experimentally with four blind participants.

2 Overview of the CamIO System

CamIO is an augmented reality (AR) iPhone app that uses computer vision to provide audio labels for rigid 3D objects. The rigid object of interest is mounted on a *board*, which is a flat printed barcode pattern (Fig. 1) that allows CamIO to estimate the object's pose (3D translation and 3D orientation) relative to the camera. The iPhone is typically mounted on a tripod or a gooseneck cellphone holder (Fig. 1(left)) to obtain a clear view of the board and object, but in some cases [3] users may hold the iPhone by hand. The user points the tip of a passive wooden *stylus* (Fig. 1), covered with another barcode pattern, to different locations on an object. CamIO estimates the stylus tip's 3D location relative to the camera and uses the pose estimate of the board to determine the stylus tip's 3D location relative to the object. (In other words, hotspot locations are defined relative to the board, which is mounted rigidly to the object.) Whenever the tip is close enough to a pre-defined hotspot, it triggers audio information about the hotspot.

A second stylus (not shown, identical in form but distinct from the one shown in Fig. 1) is used to create new hotspots, and allows the user to make an audio recording to associate with each new hotspot. Our recent work [3] demonstrates the accessibility of this authoring process, which allows blind users to create their own annotations (hotspots and associated audio labels) independently. However, in the study presented in this paper, the experimenter was the only one who created hotspots, since the emphasis here is on providing guidance to pre-existing hotspots.

3   3D Spatial Guidance Interface

We build on the auditory display described in [9], which is intended for audio-based 3D targeting of locations in a large virtual workspace (such as a kitchen). Accordingly, the first incarnation of our guidance approach used a repeating monaural sound, whose tempo indicated how far the stylus tip is from the target, and with a pitch (low, medium or high) that indicated whether the tip needed to move up or down (or else was aligned properly in the vertical direction).

Informal tests with two blind participants (one female of age 42, who is also participant P1 in the experiment described in the next section, and one male of age 73) showed that this guidance worked satisfactorily in some cases. However, we found that the feedback was too indirect: the participants didn't always know *how* to move the stylus to increase the tempo. As a result, the resulting guidance process was unacceptably slow. Thus we devised a second, more direct guidance approach: verbal directions telling the user to move the stylus along the cardinal directions (up, down, left, right, forward or back). While the optimal direction to move the stylus tip towards the hotspot might entail a combination of these directions (e.g., simultaneously move left and up), for simplicity we issue directions along only *one* cardinal direction at a time – the direction that will most improve the alignment to the target.

We define the guidance interface as follows. The board (barcode pattern beneath the truck, see Fig. 1) defines an xyz coordinate frame, with $+x$ = right, $-x$ = left, $+y$ = forward (away from the user), $-y$ = back (towards the user), $+z$ = up and $-z$ = down. Let the desired target hotspot location be denoted (x^*, y^*, z^*), and the current location of the stylus tip be (x, y, z). Define the error vector $e = (x - x^*, y - y^*, z - z^*)$, and let index $a = argmax_i |e_i|$, i.e., a is the index (1, 2 or 3, corresponding to x, y or z, respectively) of the entry in e with the highest absolute value. In other words, a indicates which coordinate (x, y or z) is most discrepant from the target coordinate location (x^*, y^*, z^*). Then the appropriate direction is issued, e.g., "left" if $a = 1$ and $x > x^*$, "right" if $a = 1$ and $x < x^*$, "up" if $a = 3$ and $z < z^*$, etc. Directions are announced roughly twice per second whenever the stylus is visible. The target hotspot is announced when the stylus gets to within approximately 1 cm from the hotspot. No audio feedback is issued when the stylus is not visible.

4 Methods

We conducted an experiment to assess the feasibility of the spatial guidance feedback and to determine whether the feedback speeds up the target search. The experiment (see setup in Fig. 1 (left)) compared how much time a blind participant needed to find hotspots (points of interest) on a 3D object with spatial guidance vs. without it. The object was a large toy fire truck (27 cm × 12 cm × 14 cm), with K = 10 distinct hotspot locations defined in advance. The hotspots were tactilely salient features such as lights, hooks or other features that protruded from the truck. Some hotspots were in recessed locations on the truck, such as the shift stick and steering wheel (Fig. 1 (right)) in the front cabin, or on the side of the truck facing away from the participant; these hotspots were difficult to find and access, whether by fingertip or by stylus. In fact, the difficulty of accessing such locations highlights an advantage of the CamIO stylus, whose tip need not be visible to the camera. This allows the user to explore recessed areas or areas that are otherwise invisible to the camera.

Each of the 10 hotspots was searched for under both feedback conditions: G (guidance provided) and NG (no guidance). In order to minimize the influence of any possible learning effects, which could make it easier to find a hotspot the second time it was searched for, we randomized the sequence of hotspots, and alternated between NG and G trials. With 10 trials in both guidance conditions (G and NG), this resulted in a within-subject factorial design with an identical sequence of $2K = 20$ trials per participant. The participant was given up to 120 s to find each hotspot, after which a time-out was declared.

We had a total of N = 4 blind participants in our experiment (2 males/2 females, ages from 26–42). Participants P1, P3 and P4 were already familiar with the CamIO system (P4 is a co-author of this paper) while P2 was unfamiliar with it. None of the participants was told the study design before their trials, and we didn't tell them whether or not any locations would be repeated in the 20 trials.

After obtaining IRB consent, we reviewed how CamIO works if necessary and demonstrated the audio guidance feature. The experimenter launched CamIO on an iPhone 8 and positioned it on a gooseneck cellphone holder so that the camera captured the entire truck and board. Each participant spent a short time practicing with the guidance feature (on different hotspots than the one used for the evaluation), with help provided by the experimenter as needed.

Fig. 1. (left) Blind participant uses CamIO to explore a toy fire truck. The participant holds the CamIO *stylus* (a barcode pattern printed on a square wooden dowel with a pointy tip) to point to possible hotspots on the truck. The truck is glued to the *board* (a piece of paper with a separate barcode pattern), which is taped to the table. An iPhone 8 running CamIO is held by a gooseneck cellphone holder to capture a view of the truck, board and stylus. (right) Stylus points to steering wheel in the truck cabin. Though the steering wheel is in a recessed location that is not visible to CamIO, the stylus tip location can still be estimated.

In the practice phase, the experimenter explained that barriers sometimes block the user from moving in the suggested guidance direction. For instance, if in Fig. 1(right) the system directs the participant to move "forward" towards the left side mirror, the stylus will soon hit the cabin roof/wall as it moves towards the mirror; the participant must find ways around such obstacles to find the target hotspot.

Next each participant performed the formal experimental trials, which consisted of the 20-trial sequence described above. We placed a visual barrier between the participant and the object while the experimenter defined the hotspot in each trial to prevent participants from using any residual vision to see the location of the hotspot. After completing the 20 search trials, we administered a System Usability Scale (SUS) [2] to estimate the usability of the guidance system. Finally, we conducted a semi-structured interview asking what participants liked and disliked about the system, what needed to be improved, and how they might envision an ideal guidance system. Since P4 is a co-author on this paper, we did not administer the SUS or semi-structured interview to him.

5   Results and Discussion

Figures 2, 3 and 4 plot the times needed to find the hotspot in both guidance conditions, and Fig. 4 shows the raw times of each participant for each condition and hotspot. All times are in seconds; times reported as 120 s correspond to participants failing to find the target in the allotted time.

These plots show how the time to find the hotspot depends on factors such as the guidance condition (G vs. NG), the participant and which hotspot is the

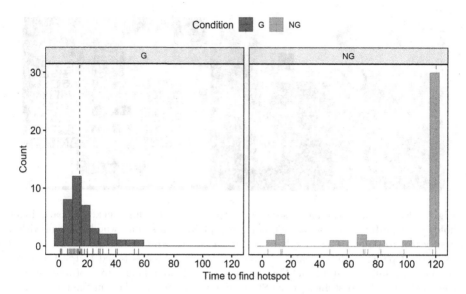

Fig. 2. Histogram of the times to find the hotspots for each guidance condition, aggregated over participants and hotspots. The vertical dashed lines represent the median scores.

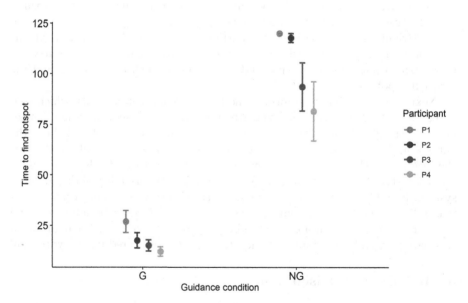

Fig. 3. Line plot showing the average time to find the hotspot ($\pm SE$) per subject and per guidance condition.

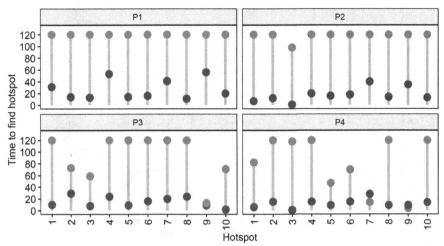

Fig. 4. Time to find target hotspot location for each participant, colored by guidance condition. This plot displays all the raw experimental data.

target. Note that G resulted in a successful target search in all cases, and in all but two cases (both for P4), target search took less time with G than with NG (visible in Fig. 4).

We used a Wilcoxon signed-rank test to compare the differences between G and NG times (see Fig. 5), paired by hotspot for each participant. The result indicated that participants performed significantly better under condition G (median $= 14.5\,\mathrm{s}$) than in condition NG (median $= 120\,\mathrm{s}$), with $V = 5$, $Z = 5.45$, $p = 5.18 \times 10^{-8}$, and an effect size of $r = 0.86$.

It should be noted that, despite our low number of participants, we had 10 pairs of measurements per participant, and a large effect-size (according to Cohen's guidelines), which should theoretically compensate for the increased type-I error rate risk inherent to running inferential statistics on a small sample.

The following System Usability Scale (SUS) scores were calculated: P1 = 65, P2 = 75, P3 = 77.5, for an average of 72.5. An SUS score of 68 is considered "average" while scores in the mid- to high 70s are considered "good"[1]. Overall, the SUS scores suggest that the guidance system is usable but needs improvement.

Next we summarize the qualitative feedback we obtained in the semi-structured interviews. All participants who provided qualitative feedback (P1, P2 and P3) acknowledged the benefit of the audio guidance that was provided, which they found intuitive and clearly superior to finding hotspots without guidance, or to more indirect ways of providing guidance (such as the early version we implemented that used tempo to signal the distance from the target and pitch to direct the stylus up or down). P3 specifically favored the "specific" instructions

---

[1] https://measuringu.com/interpret-sus-score/.

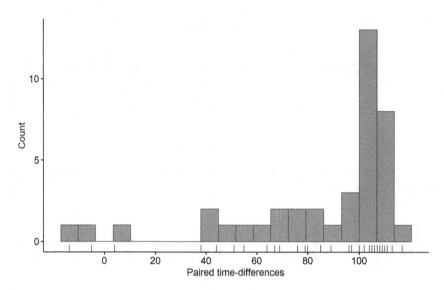

Fig. 5. Histogram of the differences (paired by hotspot & condition) in the time to find hotspots, aggregated over participants. Positive time differences indicate that the time under NG was longer than the time under G.

that the verbal feedback provided to direct the user to a hotspot, which was especially useful when the hotspot was hard to find using tactile cues alone.

However, P1 and P2 felt that the limited spatial accuracy of the CamIO system was the biggest problem that needed to be addressed; for instance, in some cases the system announced the target had been reached even though the stylus tip was hovering about 1 cm above the truck surface. (This spatial inaccuracy results from noise in the board pose and stylus tip location estimates.) P3 expressed frustration with time lag, i.e., the voice feedback tended to lag behind the current location of the stylus, even when she was moving the stylus slowly; she also felt that the speed of the repetitive speech feedback made her feel rushed.

When asked what improvements the participants wanted, P1 suggested equipping the stylus with a button that turns on the guidance feedback, and the addition of multiple vibrators on the stylus that could provide haptic feedback indicating which way the stylus should be moved. P2 suggested adding audio information similar to the earlier guidance system that the authors experimented with (Sect. 3), which would use a combination of tempo, pitch and volume changes to signal when the stylus gets closer to the target location. P3 expressed the desire that CamIO work with any ordinary pen or pencil, rather than requiring the special stylus we used.

6   Conclusion

We have devised a 3D spatial guidance system that helps a blind user find a specific location of interest on an object using CamIO, an audio-based AR system. The guidance system uses simple verbal commands ("left", "right", "up", etc.) to tell the user which direction to move the stylus tip. Experiments with four blind participants show that the guidance system significantly speeds up the search for target hotspots compared with an exhaustive search. A secondary contribution of this study is to demonstrate the ability of the CamIO stylus to access recessed or otherwise obscured locations on an object that are not themselves visible to the camera.

While we applied this guidance approach specifically to CamIO, it could be useful in any AR system, whether the system tracks the user's hands, handheld stylus or other pointing tool. Such audio-based guidance is not only helpful for blind users but is also useful in applications where visibility is limited (either by environmental conditions or because of a visual impairment), or for sighted users who prefer a cross-sensory display (e.g., audio and visual combined).

Future work will focus on refining and improving the audio interface. One possible way to speed up the guidance process is to add more specific directional feedback, e.g., "far left" would tell the user to move the stylus farther to the left than the "left" instruction. The verbal directions could be augmented with 3D spatialized sound as in [9], which could make the guidance more intuitive. Finally, we will continue to test and improve the CamIO system, with an emphasis on refining the spatial accuracy of the tip location estimates using improved computer vision algorithms.

Acknowledgments. JMC, BB and HS were supported by NIH grant 5R01EY025332 and NIDILRR grant 90RE5024-01-00. We thank Dr. Roberto Manduchi, Dr. Natela Shanidze, Dr. Santani Teng and Dr. Ali Cheraghi for helpful suggestions about the experiments.

References

1. Talking Tactile Tablet 2 (TTT) — Touch Graphics Inc
2. Brooke, J., et al.: SUS-a quick and dirty usability scale. Usabil. Eval. Ind. **189**(194), 4–7 (1996)
3. Coughlan, J., Shen, H., Biggs, B.: Towards accessible audio labeling of 3D objects. J. Technol. Persons Disabil. **8**, 210–222 (2020)
4. Coughlan, J.M., Miele, J.: Evaluating author and user experience for an audio-haptic system for annotation of physical models. In: Proceedings of the 19th International ACM SIGACCESS Conference on Computers and Accessibility, pp. 369–370. ACM, Baltimore, October 2017. https://doi.org/10.1145/3132525.3134811
5. Ferrand, S., Alouges, F., Aussal, M.: An augmented reality audio device helping blind people navigation. In: Miesenberger, K., Kouroupetroglou, G. (eds.) ICCHP 2018. LNCS, vol. 10897, pp. 28–35. Springer, Cham (2018). https://doi.org/10.1007/978-3-319-94274-2_5

6. Fusco, G., Morash, V.S.: The tactile graphics helper: providing audio clarification for tactile graphics using machine vision. In: Proceedings of the 17th International ACM SIGACCESS Conference on Computers & Accessibility - ASSETS 2015, pp. 97–106. ACM Press, Lisbon (2015). https://doi.org/10.1145/2700648.2809868

7. Guezou-Philippe, A., Huet, S., Pellerin, D., Graff, C.: Prototyping and evaluating sensory substitution devices by spatial immersion in virtual environments. In: Proceedings of the 13th International Joint Conference on Computer Vision, Imaging and Computer Graphics Theory and Applications, pp. 596–602. SCITEPRESS - Science and Technology Publications, Funchal (2018). https://doi.org/10.5220/0006637705960602

8. Kendrick, D.: PenFriend and Touch Memo: A Comparison of Labeling Tools — AccessWorld — American Foundation for the Blind (2011). https://www.afb.org/aw/12/9/15900

9. May, K.R., Sobel, B., Wilson, J., Walker, B.N.: Auditory displays to facilitate object targeting in 3D space. In: Proceedings of the 25th International Conference on Auditory Display (ICAD 2019), pp. 155–162. Department of Computer and Information Sciences, Northumbria University, Newcastle upon Tyne, June 2019. https://doi.org/10.21785/icad2019.008

10. Miele, J.: Talking tactile apps for the pulse pen: STEM binder. In: 25th Annual International Technology & Persons with Disabilities Conference (CSUN) (2010)

11. Shen, H., Edwards, O., Miele, J., Coughlan, J.M.: CamIO: a 3D computer vision system enabling audio/haptic interaction with physical objects by blind users. In: Proceedings of the 15th International ACM SIGACCESS Conference on Computers and Accessibility - ASSETS 2013, pp. 1–2. ACM Press, Bellevue (2013). https://doi.org/10.1145/2513383.2513423

12. Shi, L., Zhao, Y., Azenkot, S.: Markit and Talkit: a low-barrier toolkit to augment 3D printed models with audio annotations. In: Proceedings of the 30th Annual ACM Symposium on User Interface Software and Technology, pp. 493–506. ACM, Quebec City, October 2017. https://doi.org/10.1145/3126594.3126650

13. Thevin, L., Brock, A.M.: Augmented reality for people with visual impairments: designing and creating audio-tactile content from existing objects. In: Miesenberger, K., Kouroupetroglou, G. (eds.) ICCHP 2018. LNCS, vol. 10897, pp. 193–200. Springer, Cham (2018). https://doi.org/10.1007/978-3-319-94274-2_26

An Indoor Navigation App Using Computer Vision and Sign Recognition

Giovanni Fusco[1] , Seyed Ali Cheraghi[1] , Leo Neat[2],
and James M. Coughlan[1(✉)]

[1] The Smith-Kettlewell Eye Research Institute, San Francisco, CA, USA
{giofusco,ali.cheraghi,coughlan}@ski.org
[2] Department of Computer Science and Engineering, University of California,
Santa Cruz, CA, USA
leosneat@gmail.com

Abstract. Indoor navigation is a major challenge for people with visual impairments, who often lack access to visual cues such as informational signs, landmarks and structural features that people with normal vision rely on for wayfinding. Building on our recent work on a computer vision-based localization approach that runs in real time on a smartphone, we describe an accessible wayfinding iOS app we have created that provides turn-by-turn directions to a desired destination. The localization approach combines dead reckoning obtained using visual-inertial odometry (VIO) with information about the user's location in the environment from informational sign detections and map constraints. We explain how we estimate the user's distance from Exit signs appearing in the image, describe new improvements in the sign detection and range estimation algorithms, and outline our algorithm for determining appropriate turn-by-turn directions.

Keywords: Navigation · Wayfinding · Accessibility · Visual impairment · Blindness · Low vision

1 State of the Art and Related Technology

The key to wayfinding tools is localization – a means of estimating and tracking a person's location as they travel in an environment. The most widespread localization approach is GPS, which enables a variety of wayfinding tools such as Google Maps and BlindSquare, but it is only accurate outdoors. There are a range of indoor localization approaches, including Bluetooth beacons [1], Wi-Fi triangulation[1] and RFIDs [7]. However, all of these approaches incur the cost of installing and maintaining physical infrastructure, or of updating the system as the existing infrastructure changes (e.g., whenever Wi-Fi access points change). Dead reckoning approaches such as step counting using inertial navigation [3] can estimate relative movements without any

---

[1] https://techcrunch.com/2017/12/14/apple-maps-gets-indoor-mapping-for-more-than-30-airports/.

© Springer Nature Switzerland AG 2020
K. Miesenberger et al. (Eds.): ICCHP 2020, LNCS 12376, pp. 485–494, 2020.
https://doi.org/10.1007/978-3-030-58796-3_56

physical infrastructure, but this tracking estimate drifts over time unless it is augmented by absolute location estimates.

Computer vision is a promising localization approach, but most past work in this area has either required special hardware [9] or the use of detailed 3D models of the environment [8] that are time-consuming to generate and make the approach vulnerable to superficial environmental changes (e.g., new carpeting or moved shelves). The iOS app Clew [15] uses visual-inertial odometry (VIO) [10], a function built into modern smartphones, to perform dead reckoning, which requires no model of the environment. However, while dead reckoning allows a blind user to retrace their steps from a destination they have already reached back to their starting point, on its own it doesn't provide guidance to a new destination, and does not provide absolute localization. To overcome these limitations we developed an indoor localization system [4] that combines computer vision-based recognition of barcodes posted on walls of the environment for absolute location information with VIO to track movements between barcode detections. The new version of our localization system [5] is a self-contained iOS app that recognizes standard Exit signs, eliminating the need for barcodes. In this paper we describe enhancements to this system, including the development of an accessible navigation function that provides turn-by-turn directions to guide the user to a desired destination.

2 Overall Approach

This section summarizes our localization approach. The sections that follow it describe the specific contributions of this paper: improved sign recognition, improved range estimation from a sign detection, and turn-by-turn navigation directions.

Our localization approach is described in detail in [5]. It combines three main ingredients to estimate the user's location in an indoor environment and track it over time: (a) A 2D floor plan (map), annotated with the locations of walls and other impassable barriers, locations of interest such as rooms, elevators and stairwells, and the locations of informational signs such as Exit signs. (b) A sign recognition algorithm, such as the one we have implemented [6] for standard Exit signs, combined with an algorithm that estimates the distance to the sign from its appearance in the image and its known physical size. (c) A dead reckoning algorithm that estimates the user's relative movements, even when no signs are visible. We use the iOS ARKit's[2] built-in visual-inertial odometry (VIO) function, which combines computer vision and inertial sensing, to perform dead reckoning.

Our localization algorithm combines the three ingredients as follows. It uses a particle filter (a standard tool used in robotics [14]) to maintain multiple hypotheses ("particles") of location and bearing (i.e., the direction the smartphone camera is facing relative to the map) over time. The particle filter integrates multiple sources of information, and after some time it converges to an estimate of the location and bearing – even if the algorithm is initialized with no knowledge other than the specific floor the

---

[2] https://developer.apple.com/augmented-reality/.

user is on. These information sources include distance estimates obtained from sign detections, VIO estimates of the user's movements (available even when no signs are visible), and two constraints: traversability (the fact that the smartphone can't move through walls) and visibility (the smartphone camera can't see a sign through a wall).

We implemented our localization algorithm as a real-time app running on an iPhone 8. Studies with blind participants [5] show that the app is accessible to blind users, who need only hold the smartphone camera straight ahead while walking, rather than having to aim the camera at specific signs (which would be challenging for people with low or no vision). Alternatively, the user can "wear" the smartphone to point the camera straight ahead, using a lanyard, shirt pocket or other means. The median localization error in our studies was shown to be approximately 1 m or less, which is more than adequate for typical wayfinding applications.

3 Sign Recognition and Range Estimation Algorithms

The localization algorithm [5] currently used in our iOS app uses an Exit sign recognition algorithm that we developed previously [6]. This algorithm is a fast AdaBoost [12] (short for "Adaptive Boosting", a machine learning technique for combining multiple forms of evidence into a single more reliable decision) cascade-based approach that processes a single VGA frame on the smartphone in about 7 ms, and returns an approximate bounding box (Fig. 1a) for each detected Exit sign. While our previous algorithm for estimating the distance to the Exit sign (see below) requires only knowledge of the Exit sign centroid in the image (which can be obtained from even an approximate bounding box), our new algorithm depends on having at least a rough segmentation of the Exit sign – in other words, knowledge of the Exit sign boundaries in the image.

Accordingly, we have explored other sign recognition algorithms that return detailed segmentations instead of a rough bounding box. The algorithm that has proved most promising so far is a deep learning one called U-Net [11], using MobileNet 2 as a backbone to facilitate a mobile implementation[3,4]. Since the standard U-Net implementation processes small images of resolution 224×224, we have devised a multi-scale procedure that first detects any Exit signs at coarse scale, zooms in on the part of the image centered on the detected Exit sign and then applies U-Net again on that part of the image to segment it accurately. We are in the process of integrating the U-Net algorithm with our iOS app, which will require efforts to optimize its speed for real-time iOS performance.

Previously [5] we estimated the distance to the Exit sign using a simple calculation that assumes knowledge of camera height above the ground and the height of the Exit sign above the ground. The range (distance to the Exit sign) was estimated using the apparent elevation of the detected sign in the image: the closer the sign appears to the horizon, the farther away it is. While this approach is effective, it is inconvenient to

---

[3] https://medium.com/vitalify-asia/real-time-deep-learning-in-mobile-application-25cf601a8976.

[4] https://github.com/akirasosa/mobile-semantic-segmentation.

have to obtain the camera and Exit sign heights above the ground. The camera height depends not only on the user's height but on how they hold the smartphone, which also varies over time; moreover, the Exit sign heights may vary from sign to sign, even within the same floor of a building.

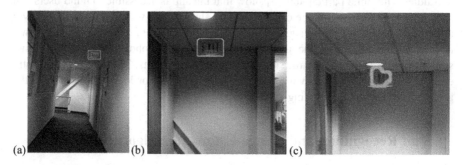

Fig. 1. Sign recognition algorithms. (a) Original Adaboost approach [6] returns a rough bounding box around the Exit sign. (b) U-Net algorithm shows an accurate segmentation border (red pixels). (c) More distant view of Exit sign, zoomed in for clarity, shows a noisy segmentation by U-Net. (Color figure online)

Instead we decided to estimate the range using the apparent size of the sign in the image, which eliminates the need for knowledge of the camera or sign height above the ground. A standard computer vision approach is to use a pose estimation algorithm such as PnP [13]. For a rectangular sign, this requires knowledge of the physical height and width of the sign, and the pixel locations of all four sign corners in the image. However, getting accurate location estimates of the sign corners is difficult without a precise segmentation (Fig. 1b) – and segmentations are often noisy in images acquired under real-world conditions, such as when the sign is viewed at a distance (Fig. 1c) or when the image quality is degraded by motion blur.

Thus, we have devised a range estimation algorithm that is effective even when the segmentation is approximate. Our approach relies on three key assumptions:

1. The sign is rectangular, with a known physical height (e.g., in cm).
2. It is mounted so that the sign lies in a vertical plane, with the borders of the sign horizontal or vertical with respect to gravity.
3. The camera pitch (angle that the camera line of sight makes with respect to the horizontal plane) and roll (the angle the camera is rotated about its line of sight, with $0°$ and $90°$ corresponding to portrait and landscape orientations, respectively) are known. This enables us to estimate the horizon line and the apparent angle of the sign above the horizon, which is a key measurement in our range estimate.

Fortunately, these assumptions are satisfied for our application. Exit signs are rectangular, with a standard size, and they are almost always mounted in a way that satisfies assumption 2. Moreover, the camera pitch and roll are estimated in real time on modern smartphones using the built-in inertial measurement unit (IMU).

We have derived a simple formula for calculating the sign range in terms of known and measured quantities. Briefly, instead of requiring the pixel coordinates of the four corners of the sign in the image, the formula requires only an estimate of the apparent height of the sign in pixels and its location in the image. This is an important advantage over the PnP approach, since it is possible to estimate the apparent height even when the segmentation is too blurry to clearly identify the four sign corners.

Next we describe this formula in detail. Given our assumptions, we can transform the raw image acquired by the camera into an *unrolled* image, which is an image that is rotated to undo the effects of any non-zero roll (i.e., rotation about the camera line of sight). This means that the horizon line appears horizontal in the unrolled image. Then we can analyze the scene geometry of the sign relative to the camera in 2D (Fig. 2), in which the Y axis represents the vertical axis (with respect to gravity) and the Z axis represents the horizontal axis. Given a column of pixels in the image plane, this sweeps out a vertical plane (shown in the figure) that intersects the camera center and a vertical slice of the sign. (Different image columns give rise to different slices of the sign, and thus slightly different ranges Z, but this discrepancy is minimal at typical sign viewing distances).

We denote the camera pitch by γ, the angle between the bottom pixel of the sign and the center row of the image (the camera line of sight direction corresponds to the pixel in the center of the image) by α, and the angle subtended by the sign (from its bottom pixel to top pixel) by δ. (It is straightforward to estimate α and δ from the pixel locations of the corresponding image features using the camera focal length and a simple pinhole model). The bottom of the sign is height H above the ground (assumed unknown), and the physical height of the sign is h_0 (known). From trigonometry we have:

$$\tan(\gamma + \alpha) = H/Z \tag{1}$$

and

$$\tan(\gamma + \alpha + \delta) = (H + h_0)/Z \tag{2}$$

Combining both equations allows us to solve directly for Z and H in terms of known quantities, leading to this range estimate equation:

$$Z = h_0/[\tan(\gamma + \alpha + \delta) - \tan(\gamma + \alpha)] \tag{3}$$

Given a segmented sign (e.g., Fig. 1c), which is obtained for an unrolled image, we analyze multiple vertical slices of the segmented sign to arrive at a single robust estimate of α and another of δ. This is done by calculating the height (top row – bottom row) of each slice, and calculating the median height over all the slices; calculating the median of the bottom row over all the slices; and then converting the median height and bottom values into an overall estimate of α and δ.

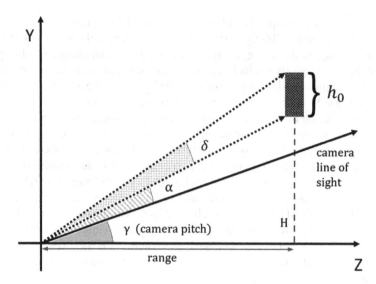

Fig. 2. We can estimate the range Z to the sign in terms of easily measured quantities: the camera pitch γ, the angle α between the bottom pixel of the sign and the center of the image (which corresponds to the camera line of sight), the angle δ subtended by the sign (from its bottom pixel to top pixel) and the physical height h_0 of the sign. (The height of the sign H above the ground is assumed unknown.)

Table 1 presents experimental results describing the accuracy of various range estimation algorithms, obtained using 852 Exit sign images taken in the Smith-Kettlewell building. The top row indicates the actual range of the Exit sign (measured with a tape measure) and the next three rows show results for each of three methods for detecting and segmenting the sign: VGA uses the approximate bounding box reported in [5], HR refers to the same approach applied to a higher resolution image (1920 × 1440) and U-Net refers to the new multi-scale approach detailed above. The accuracy is reported as the median percent range estimation error, where the median is taken across all detected signs in a distance category, and the percent range estimation error is defined as $|e - a|/a$ (expressed as a percentage), where e = estimated distance and a = actual distance. N/A indicates that no Exit signs were detectable for that algorithm and distance. (Of the 852 Exit sign images, there are 74 false negatives, in which the U-Net recognition algorithm fails to detect an Exit sign and for which no range estimate is available; these cases, most of which occur at distances of 7 m and greater, are excluded from this error analysis). Note that the U-Net approach almost always yields the smallest median errors, even at distances as far as 9 m.

We expect that our new range estimation algorithm will improve our localization results, both in terms of accuracy and the time needed to arrive at an accurate localization after the wayfinding app is first launched. These improvements will be augmented in the future as we continue to improve the underlying Exit sign recognition algorithm, and extend this algorithm to other types of signs.

Table 1. Median percent range estimation error, categorized by actual distance to sign. See text for details.

Actual	2 m	3 m	4 m	5 m	6 m	7 m	8 m	9 m
VGA	9.1%	14.7%	20.8%	11.0%	11.8%	25.0%	31.5%	N/A
HR	9.2%	13.8%	14.1%	11.4%	10.7%	15.5%	17.7%	13.3%
U-Net	9.2%	7.7%	9.3%	8.9%	5.6%	8.0%	8.5%	9.1%

4 Turn-by-Turn Navigation Directions

This section describes the turn-by-turn navigation directions that build on our localization algorithm, which are verbal directions that guide a visually impaired traveler in real time to a desired destination. Navigation directions are necessary for transforming a localization algorithm into a fully accessible wayfinding app.

These turn-by-turn directions assume that the walkable area of an indoor environment is described by a graph (Fig. 3) whose nodes are either (a) points of interest (POIs) or (b) *control points* where the traveler either must turn or has multiple turning directions to choose from. The graph, including nodes and edges connecting neighboring nodes, is embedded in the (x, y) coordinate system used by the localization algorithm to identify locations on the map. Given a destination node and current location estimate (x, y), we first "snap" the location (x, y) to the closest point (x', y') on the graph; note that this point (x', y') lies either on a graph edge or (in rare cases) a graph node. Next we use a standard Dijkstra shortest-path algorithm [2] to determine the shortest path in the graph to the destination. Our app issues directions such as "turn left" shortly before the suggested action should be executed, for instance, when the snapped location (x', y') is 0.75 m before the control nodes where a left turn should be taken.

The app allows the user to specify their starting location from a pull-down menu, or to indicate the current floor if the starting location is unknown. The desired destination is selected from a second pull-down menu. Note that the app issues no directions other than "start walking" until it is able to estimate the user's location. If the user begins heading in the wrong direction (e.g., the wrong direction down a corridor), the app signals this path deviation with haptic feedback. The app continuously updates the shortest path to the destination, which means that re-routing is automatically performed as needed. Guidance is provided until the destination is reached, including directions announcing where the destination is relative to the user as they approach within 1 m and also announcing whether the desired destination is behind a door.

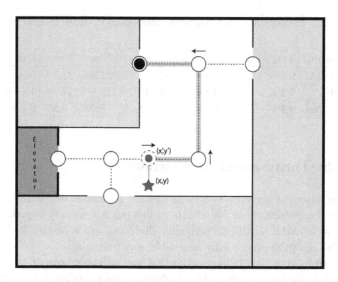

Fig. 3. 2D floor plan (map) of indoor area showing a graph of the walkable area defined by nodes and vertices. In this example, the destination node is filled in black, and the user's current location (x, y), indicated by a star icon, is snapped to the nearest location (x', y') along the graph. The shortest path to the destination is shaded in gray, with arrows indicating the directions to turn at each node on the path.

The graph representation we are currently using is optimized for environments dominated by corridors and other narrow paths; in the future we will explore appropriate ways of representing walkable areas in large open spaces, such as shopping centers or airports, and of communicating appropriate verbal or non-verbal directions in these spaces.

5   Conclusions and Future Work

We have described enhancements to our previous indoor localization approach, including improved Exit sign segmentation, a more effective method for estimating the range of a sign, and a navigation app that provides turn-by-turn directions to a desired destination. We have begun informal testing on the navigation app by two visually impaired participants, which demonstrates the app's accessibility.

We will conduct systematic tests of the app with more visually impaired participants as soon as this is possible, and will expand our testing to include multiple buildings. Future work will focus on optimizing the user interface to communicate information in a timely fashion without overwhelming the user with unnecessary feedback. We will also test and refine an algorithm that uses the built-in smartphone barometer to estimate floor changes, allowing the app to provide guidance in an entire building. Our sign recognition algorithm will need to be optimized for real-time use in the app, and we will explore ways of recognizing multiple sign types (such as restroom signs and room number signs) of any shape, size or appearance. Finally, we will experiment with the persistent Augmented Reality capabilities that have recently been added to ARKit[5] and ARCore, which allow an app to create and save a 3D model of an environment and use it later for localizing the camera (effectively a SLAM-based approach), and which may be useful for handling wide open spaces.

Acknowledgments. GF and JMC were supported by NIH grant 1R01EY029033 and NIDILRR grant 90RE5024-01-00. LN was supported by NIH grant 1R01EY029033 and SAC was supported by Smith-Kettlewell's CV Starr Fellowship. We thank Dr. Roberto Manduchi at UC Santa Cruz for helpful discussions about sign recognition.

References

1. Ahmetovic, D., Gleason, C., Kitani, K., Takagi, H., Asakawa, C.: NavCog: turn-by-turn smartphone navigation assistant for people with visual impairments or blindness. In: Web for All Conference. ACM (2016)
2. Dijkstra, E.W.: A note on two problems in connexion with graphs. Numer. Math. **1**, 269–271 (1959)
3. Flores, G., Manduchi, R.: Easy return: an app for indoor backtracking assistance. In: CHI 2018 (2018)
4. Fusco, G., Coughlan, J.M.: Indoor localization using computer vision and visual-inertial odometry. In: Miesenberger, K., Kouroupetroglou, G. (eds.) ICCHP 2018. LNCS, vol. 10897, pp. 86–93. Springer, Cham (2018). https://doi.org/10.1007/978-3-319-94274-2_13
5. Fusco, G., Coughlan, J.: Indoor localization for visually impaired travelers using computer vision on a smartphone. In: 17th International Web for All Conference, Taipei, Taiwan (2020)
6. Fusco, G., Tekin, E., Coughlan, J.: Sign Finder Application-Technical Report (2016). https://www.ski.org/sign-finder-application-technical-report
7. Ganz, A., Gandhi, S.R., Wilson, C., Mullett, G.: INSIGHT: RFID and Bluetooth enabled automated space for the blind and visually impaired. In: 2010 International Conference of the IEEE Engineering in Medicine and Biology (2010)
8. Gleason, C., Guo, A., Laput, G., Kitani, K., Bigham, J.P.: VizMap: accessible visual information through crowdsourced map reconstruction. In: ASSETS 2016 (2016)
9. Hu, F., Zhu, Z., Zhang, J.: Mobile panoramic vision for assisting the blind via indexing and localization. In: Agapito, L., Bronstein, M.M., Rother, C. (eds.) ECCV 2014. LNCS, vol. 8927, pp. 600–614. Springer, Cham (2015). https://doi.org/10.1007/978-3-319-16199-0_42
10. Kelly, J., Sukhatme, G.S.: Visual-inertial sensor fusion: Localization, mapping and sensor-to-sensor self-calibration. Int. J. Robot. Res. **30**(1), 56–79 (2011)
11. Ronneberger, O., Fischer, P., Brox, T.: U-net: convolutional networks for biomedical image segmentation. In: Navab, N., Hornegger, J., Wells, W.M., Frangi, A.F. (eds.) MICCAI 2015. LNCS, vol. 9351, pp. 234–241. Springer, Cham (2015). https://doi.org/10.1007/978-3-319-24574-4_28
12. Schapire, R.E., Singer, Y.: Improved boosting algorithms using confidence-rated predictions. Mach. Learn. **37**(3), 297–336 (1999)

---

[5] https://developer.apple.com/documentation/arkit/saving_and_loading_world_data.

13. Szeliski, R.: Computer Vision: Algorithms and Applications. Springer, London (2010). https://doi.org/10.1007/978-1-84882-935-0
14. Thrun, S., Burgard, W., Fox, D.: Probabilistic Robotics. Massachusetts Institute of Technology, Cambridge (2005)
15. Yoon, C., et al.: Leveraging augmented reality to create apps for people with visual disabilities: a case study in indoor navigation. In: ASSETS 2019 (2019)

Suitable Camera and Rotation Navigation for People with Visual Impairment on Looking for Something Using Object Detection Technique

Masakazu Iwamura[1]([⊠]) [iD], Yoshihiko Inoue[1], Kazunori Minatani[2] [iD], and Koichi Kise[1] [iD]

[1] Graduate School of Engineering, Osaka Prefecture University, Sakai, Japan
{masa,kise}@cs.osakafu-u.ac.jp
[2] National Entrance Examination Center, Tokyo, Japan
minatani@rd.dnc.ac.jp

Abstract. For people with visual impairment, smartphone apps that use computer vision techniques to provide visual information have played important roles in supporting their daily lives. However, they can be used under a specific condition only. That is, only when the user knows *where the object of interest is*. In this paper, we first point out the fact mentioned above by categorizing the tasks that obtain visual information using computer vision techniques. Then, in *looking for something* as a representative task in a category, we argue suitable camera systems and rotation navigation methods. In the latter, we propose novel voice navigation methods. As a result of a user study comprised of seven people with visual impairment, we found that (1) a camera with a wide field of view such as an omnidirectional camera was preferred, and (2) users have different preferences in navigation methods.

Keywords: Omnidirectional camera · Rotation navigation · Object detection.

1 Introduction

For people with visual impairment, the lack of access to visual information can cause difficulty in their daily lives and decrease independence. To mitigate it, smartphone apps that can tell the user visual information have been developed. VizWiz [5] and Be My Eyes [4] are apps that enable people with visual impairment to ask remote sighted workers or volunteers in supporting them. EnVision AI [6], TapTapSee [12] and Seeing AI [11] are apps that use computer vision techniques [8] to obtain visual information. As of the time of writing this paper,

This work was supported by JSPS Kakenhi Grant Number 17H01803.

The original version of this chapter was revised: the introduction was updated. The correction to this chapter is available at https://doi.org/10.1007/978-3-030-58796-3_61

K. Miesenberger et al. (Eds.): ICCHP 2020, LNCS 12376, pp. 495–509, 2020.
https://doi.org/10.1007/978-3-030-58796-3_57

Table 1. Categorization of visual information obtained by computer vision techniques. "What" and "where" indicate *"what it is"* and *"where it is,"* respectively.

	Condition	Representative task	Required tools and techniques
(i)	"What" is <u>unknown</u>. "Where" is <u>known</u>.	Obtaining the visual information on the object that the user photographs	Current smartphone apps that use computer vision techniques such as [6,11,12] can be used.
(ii)	"What" is <u>known</u>. "Where" is <u>unknown</u>.	Looking for something	It is better to use a camera with a wide FoV such as a fisheye camera and an omnidirectional camera.
(iii)	"What" is <u>unknown</u>. "Where" is <u>unknown</u>.	Finding something valuable and unexpected to the user	It is better to use a camera with a wide FoV, and the information provided to the user should be selected.

these apps except VizWiz are used by many people with visual impairment and play important roles.

This paper focuses on the latter approach, i.e., the apps that use computer vision techniques. While it has not been argued before, they can be used under a specific condition only. It is only when *the user can photograph the object of interest by oneself.* Let us confirm this. To take a photo of an object, the user has to know where it is. Of course, the purpose of using the apps is to know what it is. Hence, these apps are used only when "what (it is)" is unknown and "where (it is)" is known. Extending this idea, we find the following three types of visual information exist, as summarized in Table 1.

Category (i)—*what is unknown and where is known.*
   In this category, the user can photograph the object of interest by oneself. This type of visual information can be obtained by the current smartphone apps that use computer vision techniques such as [6,11,12].

Category (ii)—*what is known and where is unknown.*
   A representative task of this category is *looking for something.* That is, the user knows *what the user is looking for*, but does not know *where it is.* As the user does not know where the object of interest is, the user cannot use the current smartphone apps in the same way as category (i). It is because the user needs to move the smartphone here and there to take a photo of the object. Hence, it is expected that using a camera with a wide field of view (FoV), such as a fisheye camera and an omnidirectional camera, is better. As the user already knows *what it is*, differently from category (i), the app is expected to tell only *where it is* if found.

Category (iii)—*both what and where are unknown.*
In this category, the user does not expect that the app will provide any visual information to the user. However, if provided, the information is expected to be valuable to the user. Concept-wise, it is similar to the recommendation system used in e-commerce websites such as Amazon.com, because it is expected to introduce products that are potentially interesting and unexpected to the user. Thus, a representative task is finding something valuable and unexpected to the user. In the real world scenario, the app is required to obtain as much visual information all around the user as possible. Hence, similar to category (ii), it is expected that using a camera with a wide FoV is better. A big difference from other categories is that the amount of visual information potentially provided by the app can be much. In other words, the app may find multiple objects valuable to the user simultaneously. However, too much information is just annoying. Hence, the amount of visual information to be provided to the user must be controlled.

Among them, we focus on category (ii) and argue *looking for something*, which is a representative task of the category, in the following two issues.

The first issue is about cameras. In the task, we assume the user looks for a designated object around the user using an app that uses a computer vision technique to detect the object and guides the user to reach the target object. As the system needs to capture the object with the camera, the task is expected to become easier by using a camera with a wide FoV, such as a fisheye camera and an omnidirectional camera. Hence, in a user study, we investigate if our expectation regarding the cameras is correct.

The second issue is about rotation navigation methods. In turn-by-turn navigation, Ahmetovic et al. [3] have studied rotation errors and found that the participants tend to over-rotate the turns, on average, 17° more than instructed. They have concluded that simply notifying the user when the user reaches the target orientation, like they did in the research, is error prone, and a different interaction, such as continuous feedback, is required. As a follow up, Ahmetovic et al. [1] have investigated three sonification techniques to provide continuous guidance during rotation. However, it is not necessary to instruct by sound. Hence, we introduce three voice instructions and investigate the users' preferences in the user study.

2   Method

2.1   Prototype System

In *looking for something*, we implement a computer-vision-based prototype system that guides the user to reach the target object in a step-by-step manner.

- **Step 1: Object detection**
  The system detects an object of the designated category in the captured image. In the user study, we designated easy-to-detect object categories, but

only one instance existed in the room, such as a *laptop* and a *bottle*. Once the object detection method outputs the bounding box of the target object, the direction of the target object from the user is recorded.

- **Step 2: Rotation navigation**
  The user rotates on the spot until the target object comes in front. By comparing the output direction of the electronic compass with the direction of the target object, the system guides the user to rotate using a rotation navigation method.
- **Step 3: Forward navigation**
  With the guidance of the system, the user advances toward the target object and stops in front of the object. It uses the depth camera to measure the distance to the target object, and speaks the distance periodically, like "1.5 m, 1.3 m, ..." It ends when the user reaches a distance of 0.8 m.

The implemented prototype system consisted of a laptop computer (MacBook Pro) and a camera system in Fig. 1. As shown in Fig. 1(a), one consisted of an omnidirectional camera (Ricoh Theta Z1) used in Step 1 of the above procedure, an electronic compass (Freescale MAG3110 installed on BBC micro:bit), and a depth camera (Intel RealSense D435). The electronic compass was used in Step 2 to quickly sense the user's direction and promptly give the user feedback. The depth camera was used in Step 3 to measure the distance to the target object. The other was a pseudo smartphone shown in Fig. 1(b). Instead of the smartphone's embedded camera, we used a web camera (Logicool HD Webcam C615) in Step 1. We used the same electronic compass and depth camera for a fair comparison. To detect the target object, we ran a PyTorch implementation [13] of *you only look once* (YOLO) version 3 [10], which is a representative object detection method, on the laptop computer. It was trained on COCO dataset [9] consisting of 80 object categories. As the object detection method assumes to input a perspective image, the image captured with the omnidirectional camera was converted to eight perspective images in the same manner as [7]. The prototype system speaks its current state, like "Searching an object. Please stay and wait." "Detected." "Measuring the distance." and "The object exists near you."

2.2   Existing Rotation Navigation

Ahmetovic et al. [1] have introduced the following three sonification techniques that provide continuous guidance during rotation.

Intermittent sound (IS) triggers impulsive "beeping" sounds at a variable rate, which is inversely proportional to the angular distance, like a Geiger-Müller counter.

Amplitude modulation (AM) employs a sinusoidal sound, modulated in amplitude by a low frequency (sub-audio) sinusoidal signal. The frequency of the modulating signal is inversely proportional to the angular distance, producing a slowly pulsing sound at large angular distances, which becomes stationary when the target is reached.

(a) Omnidirectional camera (810 g)   (b) Pseudo smartphone (550 g)

Fig. 1. Camera systems used in the user study. They were comprised of a depth camera and an electronic compass, in addition to (a) an omnidirectional camera or (b) a web camera attached to a smartphone.

Musical scale (MS) plays eight ascending notes at fixed angular distances while approaching the target angle.

They concluded that IS and MS when combined with Ping (impulsive sound feedback emitted when the target angle is reached) were the best with regard to rotation error and rotation time.

2.3   Proposed Rotation Navigation

We examine the following five (three voice and two sound) navigation methods.

Left or Right (LR) repeatedly (approximately 1.5 times per second) tells the direction toward the target object, i.e., "Left" or "Right." When the target object comes within 15° in front of the user, it tells "In front of you."

Angle (AG) repeatedly tells the relative rotation angle to the target object, followed by "Left" or "Right." The front of the user is always regarded as 0°. For example, if the target object exists at an angular distance of 60° on the right-hand side of the user, the system speaks "60°, right." After the user rotates by 15°, it speaks "45°, right." In front of the target object (within 15°), it tells "In front of you."

Clock Position (CP) is similar to AG but uses the clock position. Taking the same example as AG, it speaks "2 o'clock." In front of the target object (within 15°), it tells "In front of you."

Intermittent Beep (IB) is similar to IS of [1]. It triggers impulsive "beeping" sounds at a variable rate, which is inversely proportional to the angular distance. The rates in the front (15°) and back (180°) were approximately 5 Hz and 1.2 Hz, respectively. IB is designed to use earphones; beeps are played on only the left or right earphone to indicate the rotation direction. When the target object comes within 15° in front of the user, it plays beeps sounds at a rate of approximately 8 Hz on both earphones.

Pitch (PT) plays sounds with a variable pitch. In our implementation, the front and back pitches were 1570 Hz and 785 Hz (six and three times of C4 in scientific pitch notation), respectively. In contrast with MS of [1] that plays eight discrete notes, PT plays continuous notes. Same as IB, PT plays sounds on only the left or right earphone to indicate the rotation direction. In front of the target object, PT behaves in the same manner as IB.

3   User Study

We performed a user study comprised of seven people with visual impairment. As summarized in Table 2, the participants consisted of four males and three females, ages 23 to 48. Six were totally blind, and one had low vision. The user study consisted of the following four parts.

Table 2. Participants' demographic information. "OA" denotes "Onset age."

ID	Age	Sex	Visual impairment	OA
A	23	F	Totally blind	2
B	27	M	Totally blind	5
C	27	F	Totally blind	7
D	48	M	Low vision (left: blind, right: 0.03, narrowing of visual field)	10
E	48	M	Totally blind	6
F	27	M	Totally blind	10
G	34	F	Totally blind	13

1. Instruction of the experiments
We told the participants that our research topic was *looking for something* and gave a brief overview of the experiments.

2. Pre-study interview: Survey on looking for something
We asked the participants about looking for something. This interview was performed for every two persons except A. That is, the interview groups were [A], [B and C], [D and E], and [F and G]. The questions and answers are summarized in Table 3. Answers of Q7 and Q9 are shown in Tables 4 and 5.

The answers of the participants are summarized as follows. Five out of seven participants lived together with someone (Q1). Among them, two lived with sighted persons (Q2). While they all looked for something every day (Q3), they did not encounter trouble every day (Q4). They all looked for something at home, and three did it in other places (office or school, and outside) (Q5). They all groped to look for something, expecting to find it in arm's reach, while four asked a sighted person if available (Q6). Five mostly looked for a smartphone,

Table 3. Questions and answers of pre-study interview.

Question	A	B	C	D	E	F	G
Q1. Do you live together with someone?	Yes	No	Yes	No	Yes	Yes	Yes
Q2. If yes in Q1, is the person(s) sighted?	Yes	–	No	–	Yes	No	No
Q3. How often do you look for something? (1: Every day, 2: 3–4 days per week, 3: once a week, 4: once a month, 5: several times per year)	1	1	1	1	1	1	1
Q4. How often do you encounter trouble in looking for something? (1: Every day, 2: 3–4 days per week, 3: once a week, 4: once a month, 5: several times per year)	2	3	4	3	2	2	5
Q5. Where do you mostly look for something? ([multiple choice] 1: home, 2: office or school, 3: store, 4: other)	1,2	1	1	1,4 (outside)	1,4 (outside)	1	1
Q6. How do you look for something? (1: grope, 2: ask a sighted person, 3: use a smartphone app, 4: other)	1,2	1,2	1	1,2	1,2	1	1
Q7. What item do you mostly look for?	See Table 4						
Q8. How long does it take to find lost stuff? (1: within 1 min., 2: 1–5 min., 3: more than 5 min.)	3	1,2	1	3	3	2	2
Q9. Where do you find lost stuff?	See Table 5						
Q10. What causes you to look for something? (1: wrongly remember where the lost stuff is placed, 2: do not remember where the lost stuff is placed, 3: the stuff is moved without knowing it, 4: other)	2	1,2	2	1,2	1,3	1	4
Q11. Do you have any idea of how to avoid looking for something? ([multiple choice] 1: keep the room clean, 2: fix the place, 3: use an IC tag, 4: other)	2	2	2	2	2	1,2	1,2

while earphones and other stuff were also often looked for (Q7). Required time to look for lost stuff was of variety (Q8). Some answered that they gave up looking for if it took more than 5 min. (Q8). The lost stuff was found in the pocket of a jacket and a bag, and on a chair and a table (Q9). Losing stuff was mostly caused by wrongly remembering and forgetting where it was placed (Q10). They all answered that their remedy to avoid losing stuff was to fix the place, while two answered to keep the room clean (Q11).

Table 4. [Pre-study Interview] Answers to Q7 "What do you mostly look for?"

ID	Answers
A	Smartphone, and braille notetaker. I always give up looking for hairpins and hair rubber bands.
B	Smartphone, earphones, charger, and credit card.
C	Smartphone.
D	Smartphone for work.
E	Something dropped. Remote controller for TV.
F	Prepaid transportation card, and earphones.
G	Smartphone, keys, and slipper.

Table 5. [Pre-study Interview] Answers to Q9 "Where do you find lost stuff?"

ID	Answers
A	On a chair or table. Sometimes on the floor. Lost stuff is merely covered by something.
B	In the pocket of a jacket which is not usually worn. In a bag pocket.
C	In many cases, within arm's reach. I often encounter difficulty in finding stuff that is neatly placed on the table.
D	In the pocket of a jacket or bag.
E	As the person living together moves stuff, I find where it is moved.
F	On the table or in a bag. Otherwise, in the pocket of a jacket.
G	In many cases, on the floor.

Fig. 2. A snapshot during the experiment. The experimenter holding the laptop computer stands behind the participant to prevent the camera from capturing him. In this case, the laptop computer at the bottom was the target object.

Table 6. Evaluation of navigation methods on a 5-point scale.

Navigation method		A	B	C	D	E	F	G	Average
Voice	Left or right (LR)	4	2	3	2	1	4	2	2.6
	Angle (AG)	4	4	3	5	3	4	5	**4.0**
	Clock position (CP)	5	2	5	3	4	5	3	3.9
Sound	Intermittent beep (IB)	3	5	4	4	4	3	5	**4.0**
	Pitch (PT)	2	4	4	4	5	2	4	3.6

3. Experiment 1: Comparison of five rotation navigation methods

Differently from the pre-study interview, the following two experiments were performed for each participant. In this experiment, we asked participants to use five rotation navigation methods one by one through Steps 1 (object detection using the omnidirectional camera) and 2 (rotation navigation) in Sect. 2.1. As IB and PT were designed to use earphones, for a fair comparison, participants used earphones for all navigation methods. Figure 2 shows how the experiment was performed. Table 6 shows their preferences on a 5-point scale, in which a large number means better. Besides, their comments on the five navigation methods and ideas about easy-to-use navigation methods are shown in Tables 7, 8, 9, 10, 11 and 12.

Table 7. [Experiment 1] Feedback on Left or Right (LR).

ID	Answers
A	Though I could not see how much I should rotate, I could try to rotate much.
B	Simple but not intuitive. As I could not see how much I should rotate, I over-rotated.
C	I could get the rotation direction, but could not see how much I should rotate.
D	The most primitive.
E	I felt anxious, as I could not see how much I should rotate. I needed to concentrate on listening.
F	Simple and intuitive. Though I could not see how much I should rotate, this way is easy to use.
G	I thought this way was simple and easy to get in the instruction. However, as I could not see how much I should rotate, I felt it was unreliable. I think it can get better with improvement.

Table 8. [Experiment 1] Feedback on Angle (AG).

ID	Answers
A	The resolution in angle was too detailed. I prefer CP.
B	While the resolution was too detailed, this way was easy to get, as the angle is absolute.
C	Though it seemed not to cause trouble and easy to get, it was not easy for me to imagine how much I should rotate.
D	If I get used to this way, it would be the safest choice.
E	I needed to be strategic. It took some time to think about how much I should rotate after hearing the angle.
F	Simple. Though I could get the angle, I could not immediately imagine how much I should rotate. I may need to get used to it.
G	It was easy to get when I needed to stop, as spoken angles were decreasing.

Table 9. [Experiment 1] Feedback on Clock Position (CP).

ID	Answers
A	This way was the easiest to get.
B	Once it says "5 o'clock," it should keep saying "5 o'clock" even if I rotate. Or, it is easier for me to get if (by fixing the target at the 12 o'clock position) it says "you are now at the 5 o'clock position." Maybe I need to get used to it.
C	This way was easy to imagine both rotation direction and angle.
D	I need to get used to this way.
E	As I am used to this way, I could imagine how much I should rotate. But, the resolution in angle maybe too rough.
F	As I am used to the clock position, this way was very easy to understand, so that I could reach the target direction immediately.
G	I needed to think about which direction 5 o'clock is. It is because I am not used to it.

Table 6 shows that the participants' preferences were of variety. That is, all navigation methods except LR were selected as the best by at least one participant. Related results are reported in two papers; musical experience affects the users' behavior [1]; expertise affects interaction preferences in navigation assistance [2]. In our experiment, while we did not ask their expertise, from their comments[1], we can see that the participants have their compatibility with

---

[1] Let us highlight some comments. **Participant B on CP:** He preferred to put the target, instead of himself, at the 12 o'clock position. **Participants C, E, and G:** C and E were not good at AG but good at CP, while G was the opposite. **Participant A on IB:** As he imagined a 3D audio effect, hearing the sound played on only left or right, he felt the target object was on the side.

Table 10. [Experiment 1] Feedback on Intermittent beep (IB).

ID	Answers
A	Different from what I imagined. Using a 3D audio effect, hearing the sound from the target direction is more intuitive. I felt the target always existed on the side.
B	Intuitively, this way was the easiest for me. It was easy to rotate toward the direction I could hear the sound. This way is close to an audio game for the blind. Using both ears is negative.
C	Intuitively, it was easier to get, compared to LR.
D	Everyone would be able to get this way.
E	Though this way was intuitive, it took time to sense the time difference between two beeps, which would negatively affect when I rotate fast.
F	As hearing the sound in either of my ears made me confused, voice navigation was better. Though I could not get how much I should rotate, I could notice that I rotate too much when I heard the sound in the other ear.
G	I had the impression that I was approaching the target. I felt it was trustable.

Table 11. [Experiment 1] Feedback on Pitch (PT).

ID	Answers
A	The pitch of the first sound was too low. To me, the high pitch did not link to getting close to the target.
B	The pitch of the last sound was too high. Compared to IB, it was not easier to expect the target angle. Using both ears is negative.
C	Intuitively, it was easy to get, even without hearing a voice. It would be usable in a noisy place.
D	I like this way, while I think this way requires a sense of pitch. This way is used in a screen reader (NVDA).
E	This way was the best among the five methods. I could get feedback immediately. I could find the target sensuously.
F	As hearing the sound in either of my ears made me confused, voice navigation was better. I could not imagine how much I should rotate, as I could not see how the pitch became when I approached the target. I could notice that I rotated too much when I heard the sound in the other ear.
G	Though this way was easy to get, I could not distinguish sounds in detail. If it takes long to find the target object, my ears will hurt.

navigation methods. These imply that no single best method for everyone exists, and personalization of user interfaces is vital. We also asked the participants if they hesitate to wear earphones on both ears, and found that one (D) did not hesitate, four (A, C, F, and G) did not if they are at home, two (B and E) did.

Table 12. [Experiment 1] Idea about easy-to-use navigation methods.

ID	Answers
A, D	I have no idea.
B	Use of sound volume, 3D audio effect, and the interval of vibration.
C	The vibration of the camera, which makes earphones unnecessary, while telling left or right maybe not easy.
E	To be strategic, it is better to tell the angle first. Then, using a sensuous method such as the duration or interval of vibration. It is also ok that a band wrapped around the belly tells the direction by vibrating the target direction part.
F	While vibration is a possible solution, I think CP is the best.
G	Voice with vibration would be able to be used in a noisy place.

4. Experiment 2: Selection of camera

We asked participants to use each of the two camera systems and complete the 3-step finding process in Sect. 2.1. They used the best navigation method selected in experiment 1 for each participant but had the freedom to use or not to use earphones. Table 13 shows an omnidirectional camera was preferred by six, while the pseudo smartphone by one. Tables 14 and 15 show the participants' comments on the camera systems. Six (all but C) commented on the difficulty of using the pseudo smartphone in *looking for something*. In contrast, they all, including participant C who preferred the pseudo smartphone, found advantages of the omnidirectional camera, while three (A, C, and F) commented its heaviness. Hence, we conclude the omnidirectional camera has advantages in the task.

4   Conclusions

In this paper, we focused on apps that use computer vision techniques to provide visual information. We pointed out that the current smartphone apps can only be used under a specific condition, and categorized the tasks of obtaining visual information into three. As a representative task of a category, we focused on

Table 13. Evaluation of a camera on a 5-point scale.

Camera	A	B	C	D	E	F	G	Average
Omnidirectional camera	4	4	4	5	5	3	5	4.3
Pseudo smartphone	3	2	5	3	3	1	2	2.7

Table 14. [Experiment 2] Comments on the omnidirectional camera.

ID	Answers
A	It was a bit heavy. If it was not heavy, it was the most convenient.
B	To find the object, I did not have to rotate. Even so, I would buy the smartphone.
C	While it seems convenient and I think it can find the stuff quicker, requiring a particular device (i.e., omnidirectional) and its heaviness were negative points.
D	It was unexpectedly good, as it told me how far in the angular distance to the object, and found the object earlier than the smartphone.
E	It was good, as it told me the direction of the target object.
F	It was heavy. Finding the bottle took time more than I expected. While it found the laptop computer quickly, the "front" the system said was slightly different from my real front.
G	It was convenient, as I did not have to rotate. It was more accurate and quicker than I expected. I want to use this. The distance to the object was not important.

Table 15. [Experiment 2] Comments on the pseudo smartphone.

ID	Answers
A	If I have to find the object by moving the smartphone, I prefer to grope. The response was slow. Quicker is better.
B	I had to rotate to find the object. Even if the system did not find the object, I could not judge if it exists in the room (the omnidirectional camera is the same).
C	An advantage is easy to introduce, as I can use my smartphone. Easy to hold.
D	I expected the smartphone was better. However, I needed to adjust the angle.
E	The system could not find the object unless it captures it, which frustrated me. As I could not see how quickly the system processed an image, I could not see how fast I could rotate. While it was faster than groping, it took time.
F	While the camera was not heavy, it is not suitable for looking for something. In real use, if I can roughly guess the direction of the object, I may be able to use this. If not, groping is better.
G	It was hard to capture the target object, as I needed to take care of horizontal rotation and vertical rotation. I prefer to grope.

looking for something. In the task, we proposed a prototype system that used an omnidirectional camera and the use of voice in rotation navigation. A user study comprised of seven people with visual impairment confirmed that (1) a camera with a wide FoV is better in such a task, and (2) users have different preferences in rotation navigation. The latter implies that no single best method for everyone exists, and it is vital to personalize user interfaces.

References

1. Ahmetovic, D., et al.: Sonification of rotation instructions to support navigation of people with visual impairment. In: Proceedings of the PerCom (2019)
2. Ahmetovic, D., Guerreiro, J., Ohn-Bar, E., Kitani, K.M., Asakawa, C.: Impact of expertise on interaction preferences for navigation assistance of visually impaired individuals. In: Proceedings of the W4A (2019)
3. Ahmetovic, D., Oh, U., Mascetti, S., Asakawa, C.: Turn right: analysis of rotation errors in turn-by-turn navigation for individuals with visual impairments. In: Proceedings of the ASSETS (2018)
4. https://www.bemyeyes.com/
5. Bigham, J.P., et al.: VizWiz: nearly real-time answers to visual questions. In: Proceedings of the UIST (2010)
6. https://www.letsenvision.com/
7. Iwamura, M., Hirabayashi, N., Cheng, Z., Minatani, K., Kise, K.: VisPhoto: photography for people with visual impairment as post-production of omni-directional camera image. In: Proceedings of the CHI Extended Abstracts (2020)
8. Leo, M., Medioni, G., Trivedi, M., Kanade, T., Farinella, G.: Computer vision for assistive technologies. Comput. Vis. Image Underst. **154**, 1–15 (2017)
9. Lin, T.Y., et al.: Microsoft COCO: common objects in context. arXiv preprint arXiv:1405.0312 (2014)
10. Redmon, J., Farhadi, A.: YOLOv3: an incremental improvement. arXiv preprint arXiv:1804.02767 (2018)
11. https://www.microsoft.com/en-us/ai/seeing-ai
12. https://taptapseeapp.com/
13. https://github.com/ayooshkathuria/pytorch-yolo-v3

Expiry-Date Recognition System Using Combination of Deep Neural Networks for Visually Impaired

Megumi Ashino and Yoshinori Takeuchi$^{(\boxtimes)}$ (iD)

Department of Information Systems, School of Informatics, Daido University,
10-3 Takiharu-cho, Minami-ku, Nagoya 457-0530, Japan
ytake@daido-it.ac.jp

Abstract. Many drink packages have expiry dates written in dot matrix characters (digits and non-digits, e.g., slashes or dots). We collected images of these packages and trained two existing deep neural networks (DNNs) to combine and form a system for detecting and recognizing expiry dates on drink packages. One of the DNNs is an object-detection DNN and the other is a character-recognition DNN. The object-detection DNN alone can localize the characters written on a drink package but its recognition accuracy is not sufficient. The character-recognition DNN alone cannot localize characters but has good recognition accuracy. Because the system is a combination of these two DNNs, it improves the recognition accuracy. The object-detection DNN is first used to detect and recognize the expiry date by localizing and obtaining the size of the character. It then scans the expiry-date region and clips the image. The character-recognition DNN then recognizes the characters from the clipped images. Finally, the system uses both DNNs to obtain the most accurate recognition result based on the spacing of the digits. We conducted an experiment to recognize the expiry dates written on the drink package. The experimental results indicate that the recognition accuracy of the object-detection DNN alone was 90%, that of the character-recognition DNN alone was also 90%, and that combining the results of both DNNs was 97%.

1 Introduction

There are various inconveniences for the visually impaired. One such inconvenience is shopping. When shopping, it is essential to obtain product information. However, the visually impaired cannot easily obtain this information. From the results of an interview of 14 visually impaired individuals regarding shopping [1], they can go to the front of the product shelves of the shop where they often visit, because they remember the arrangement of the shelves in the shop. However, they cannot obtain the name, price, or expiry date of perishable foods. In this paper, we focus on automatic recognition of expiry dates.

Tanaka *et al.* proposed a system for recognizing expiry dates [2]. They used a commercial optical character-recognition software to recognize expiry dates.

© Springer Nature Switzerland AG 2020
K. Miesenberger et al. (Eds.): ICCHP 2020, LNCS 12376, pp. 510–516, 2020.
https://doi.org/10.1007/978-3-030-58796-3_58

Fig. 1. Example of dot matrix characters

They used dilation image processing to recognize dot matrix characters. Such characters are represented by a set of dots, as shown in Fig. 1. Their experimental results indicated that the accuracy of their method for recognizing dot matrix characters was only 43%. Hosozawa *et al.* proposed an erosion and dilation procedure for dot matrix characters [3]. However, they did not give the recognition accuracy for this procedure. Zaafouri *et al.* proposed an automated vision approach for recognizing expiry dates using a multilayer NN [4]. Gong *et al.* proposed a DNN for localizing the expiry date in an image [5]. The last two studies did not consider dot matrix characters.

We propose a system for detecting and recognizing the expiry dates written on drink packages. Many drink packages have expiry dates written in dot matrix characters (digits and non-digits, e.g., slashes or dots). We collected images of such dates and trained two existing DNNs to combine to form our system. With this system, the visually impaired can read expiry dates without the need for assistance. They can also read the expiry date of products they previously bought at home. Our system is not only useful for the visually impaired but also for applications where sighted people manage perishable foods by expiry dates.

2 Expiry-Date Recognition System

2.1 Overview

As mentioned above, our system is a combination of the two DNNs that are object-detection and character-recognition. The object-detection DNN can localize and recognize the characters written on drink packages, but the recognition accuracy is not sufficient. The character-recognition DNN cannot localize the characters but has good recognition accuracy. In our preliminary experiment, the recognition rate of our system was 99%. Figure 2 shows the comparison between the object-detection and character-recognition DNNs.

In our system, the object-detection DNN first detects and recognizes the expiry date by localizing and obtaining the size of the characters. The system then scans the expiry-date region with a raster scan method and clips the image. The character-recognition DNN then recognizes the characters for the clipped image. Finally, the system combines the results of both DNNs to obtain the final result based on the spacing of the digits.

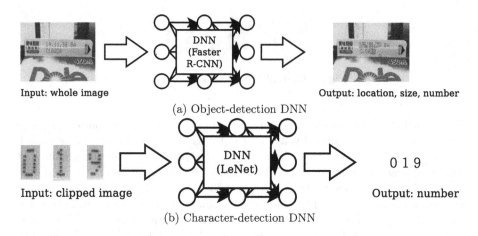

(a) Object-detection DNN

(b) Character-detection DNN

Fig. 2. Comparison between object-detection and character-detection DNNs

2.2   Object-Detection DNN

We use the Faster R-CNN as the object-detection DNN to localize and recognize the expiry date [6]. We collected 108 images of drink package. Then, we obtained the location and number of digits and dots in the images and created training data. We distorted the images randomly to increase the amount of data. The images were collected in 2011–2019. There was a bias in the frequency of certain digits, i.e. the digit '1' was more common than the others. To make the amount of the digits almost same, we painted more frequent digits white. We increased the amount of the training data to 9,996 and trained the object-detection DNN by using these data.

2.3   Character-Recognition DNN

To create the input data to input to the character-recognition DNN, the system scans the input image and clips a small rectangle of the image. If the system scans and clips the entire image, there will be a huge number of clipped images. The system first limits the scanning area. It scans only the area where the digits were detected with the object-detection DNN. To reduce the number of clipped images, the system first binarizes the image and clips it after satisfying the following criteria.

1. The image edges are white pixels,
2. The center of gravity of the black pixels is at or slightly above the center of the image.

The reason for including above the center of the image is that the center of gravity of digit '7' is slightly higher than that of the image. The system can estimate the size of the digit from the object-detection DNN. However, the size may not match the actual digit size. Therefore, the system repeats clipping by

Fig. 3. Examples of clipped images

changing the size of the digit. It adds −2 to 2 pixels to the size of the digits and repeats scanning and clipping five times. Figure 3 shows examples of clipped images from the image of a drink package shown in Fig. 4(e). The system clips digits as well as non-digits.

We use the same training data as those mentioned in Sect. 2.2 and clip the images. Then, we select a total of 1838 clipped images as training data. We use LeNet as the character-recognition DNN [7], which was developed for handwritten digit recognition. We trained this DNN by using the training data.

2.4 Combination of Two DNNs

If the two DNNs output the same expiry date, the system can output the date with high reliability. Due to the errors in recognition, the outputs of two DNNs may differ. In such case, the system needs to select the output from two obtained expiry dates based on the spacing of the digits. For example, when the output of the object-detection DNN was '1.11.30' and that of the character-recognition DNN was '19.11.30,' the system selects '19.11.30' as the final recognition output. When the outputs from two DNNs are inconsistent like '20.01.18' and '20.01.13,' the system determines that recognition failed. In this case, it asks the user to take the image again.

3 Experimental Results

3.1 Object-Detection DNN Alone

We trained the object-detection DNN by using 108 images of drink package and conducted an experiment to localize and recognize the digits in the images. We used 30 other images of drink packages as test images. Figure 4 shows some of the recognition results. We calculated the following recall and precision as the performance index of recognition accuracy.

$$\text{Recall} = \frac{\text{Number of correct recognitions}}{\text{Number of digits in the image}}, \tag{1}$$

$$\text{Precision} = \frac{\text{Number of correct recognitions}}{\text{Number of recognized digits}}. \tag{2}$$

Table 1 lists the results of recognizing each character.

input   output

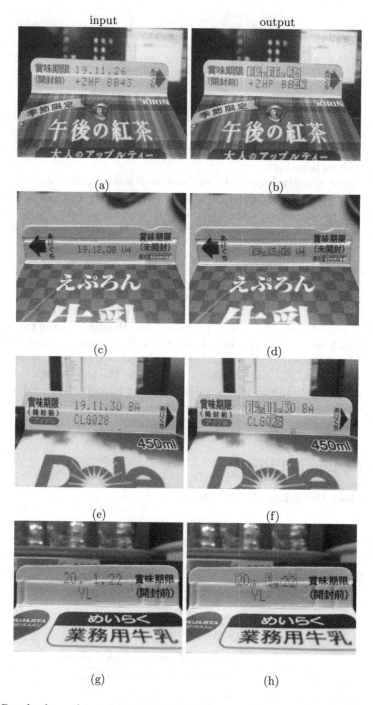

(a)   (b)

(c)   (d)

(e)   (f)

(g)   (h)

Fig. 4. Results from object-detection DNN. Red rectangles in output image show recognized digits. (Color figure online)

Table 1. Recognition results from object-detection DNN

Character	1	2	3	4	5	6	7	8	9	0	Dot	Total
Recall	0.988	1.000	0.900	1.000	0.875	1.000	1.000	0.857	1.000	0.895	0.933	0.961
Precision	0.963	0.979	0.818	1.000	0.875	1.000	1.000	1.000	1.000	1.000	0.982	0.974

The system estimated the expiry date by the format "yy.mm.dd." For example, the results of input images (a), (c), (e), and (g) in Fig. 4 were '19.11.26,' '19.12.08,' '19.11.3,' and '2.1.22,' respectively. The last digit '0' in Fig. 4(f) and the digit '0' in Fig. 4(h) were not detected. Expiry dates were correctly estimated for 27 out of the 30 images; thus, the recognition accuracy was 90%.

3.2 Character-Recognition DNN Alone

We used the same test images mentioned in the Sect. 3.1 and obtained recognition results. The results of input images (a), (c), (e), and (g) in Fig. 4 were '19.11.26,' '19.12.0,' '19.11.30,' and '20. .22,' respectively. The last digit '8' in Fig. 4(c) and digit '1' in Fig. 4(g) were not recognized. Expiry dates were correctly estimated for 27 of the 30 images; thus, the recognition accuracy was 90%.

3.3 Combination of Two DNNs

The system combined the results of both DNNs based on the spacing of the digits. Expiry dates were correctly estimated for 29 of the 30 images; thus, the recognition accuracy was 97%. The only example for which the expiry date could not be estimated was that in Fig. 4(g).

4 Discussion

From the experimental results of the object-detection DNN, 96% of characters were correctly recognized. However, looking at Table 1, precision of 1, 3, and 5 is not sufficient. The digit '8' was recognized as '3'. Characters other than the expiry date were also nearby. The character 'S' was recognized as '5' and 'I' as '1' because the character shapes were similar. This will improve by increasing the amount of training data.

The recognition accuracy of the character-recognition DNN was the same as that of object-detection DNN. The last digit '8' in Fig. 4(c) was recognized as a non-digit. The digit '1' in Fig. 4(g) was not clipped. The reason may be the lack of training data.

Three of the 30 images were not recognized with the object-detection DNN alone. However, two of them were recognized with the character-recognition DNN. Similarly, three of the 30 images were not recognized with the character-recognition DNN alone. However, two of them were recognized with the object-detection DNN. Therefore, the two DNNs complement each other, improving the final recognition accuracy.

5 Conclusion

We proposed a system for recognizing the expiry dates written on drink packages. The system uses two DNNs, one is an object-detection DNN and the other is a character-recognition DNN. The system improved the recognition accuracy by using both DNNs. The experimental results indicate that the recognition accuracy of the object-detection DNN was 90%, that of the character-recognition DNN was 90%, and by using both DNN, the system's recognition accuracy was 97%.

For a future work, it is necessary to consider a method for improving recognition accuracy by increasing the amount of training data, including the digits that have been incorrectly recognized. It is also necessary for visually impaired people to use the system and give feedback on it. We plan to implement the proposed system in a smartphone application.

References

1. Doi, Y., Matsumoto, T., Takeuchi, Y., Kudo, H., Ohnishi, N.: A merchandise information acquisition system for the blind. IEICE Tech. Rep. WIT **110**(164), 47–52 (2010). (in Japanese)
2. Tanaka, N., Doi, Y., Matsumoto, T., Takeuchi, Y., Kudo, H., Ohnishi, N.: A system helping the blind to get merchandise information. In: Miesenberger, K., Karshmer, A., Penaz, P., Zagler, W. (eds.) ICCHP 2012. LNCS, vol. 7383, pp. 596–598. Springer, Heidelberg (2012). https://doi.org/10.1007/978-3-642-31534-3_87
3. Hosozawa, K., et al.: Recognition of expiration dates written on food packages with open source OCR. Int. J. Comput. Theory Eng. **10**(5), 170–174 (2018)
4. Zaafouri, A., Sayadi, M., Fnaiech, F.: A vision approach for expiry date recognition using stretched Gabor features. Int. Arab J. Inf. Technol. **12**(5), 448–455 (2015)
5. Gong, L., Yu, M., Duan, W., Ye, X., Gudmundsson, K., Swainson, M.: A novel camera based approach for automatic expiry date detection and recognition on food packages. In: Iliadis, L., Maglogiannis, I., Plagianakos, V. (eds.) AIAI 2018. IAICT, vol. 519, pp. 133–142. Springer, Cham (2018). https://doi.org/10.1007/978-3-319-92007-8_12
6. Ren, S., He, K., Girshick, R., Sun, J.: Faster R-CNN: towards real-time object detection with region proposal networks. In: Cortes, C., Lawrence, N.D., Lee, D.D., Sugiyama, M., Garnett, R. (eds.) Advances in Neural Information Processing Systems 28 (NIPS 2015), pp. 91–99. Curran Associates, Inc. (2015)
7. Lecun, Y., Bottou, L., Bengio, Y., Haffner, P.: Gradient-based learning applied to document recognition. Proc. IEEE **86**(11), 2278–2324 (1998)

Indoor Query System
for the Visually Impaired

Lizhi Yang[ORCID], Ilian Herzi, Avideh Zakhor$^{(\boxtimes)}$, Anup Hiremath, Sahm Bazargan,
and Robert Tames-Gadam

University of California, Berkeley, Berkeley, USA
{lzyang,ilianherzi,avz,anup.h,sahm.bazargan,robert_gadams}@berkeley.edu

Abstract. Scene query is an important problem for the visually impaired population. While existing systems are able to recognize objects surrounding a person, one of their significant shortcomings is that they typically rely on the phone camera with a finite field of view. Therefore, if the object is situated behind the user, it will go undetected unless the user spins around and takes a series of pictures. The recent introduction of affordable, panoramic cameras solves this problem. In addition, most existing systems report all "significant" objects in a given scene to the user, rather than respond to a specific user-generated query as to where an object located. The recent introduction of text-to-speech and speech recognition capabilities on mobile phones paves the way for such user-generated queries, and for audio response generation to the user. In this paper, we exploit the above advancements to develop a query system for the visually impaired utilizing a panoramic camera and a smartphone. We propose three designs for such a system: the first is a handheld device, and the second and third are wearable backpack and ring. In all three cases, the user interacts with our systems verbally regarding whereabouts of objects of interest. We exploit deep learning methods to train our system to recognize objects of interest. Accuracy of our system for the disjoint test data from the same buildings in the training set is 99%, and for test data from new buildings not present in the training data set is 53%.

Keywords: Non-visual query system · Object detection · RGB-D · Panoramic camera system

1 Introduction

According to the 2019 WHO World Report on Vision, at least 2.2 billion people have a vision impairment globally [17]. Thus, it is no surprise that there has been consistent interest in providing non-visual descriptions of the environment to this population. Existing methods use GPS and RFID [23], or multiple cameras around the user [24] requiring pre-configured environments. Others draw

This project was funded by Microsoft AI for Accessibility program.

K. Miesenberger et al. (Eds.): ICCHP 2020, LNCS 12376, pp. 517–525, 2020.
https://doi.org/10.1007/978-3-030-58796-3_59

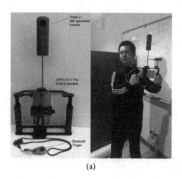

Fig. 1. Three designs: (a) Handheld design consisting of a panoramic and a mobile phone with a time-of-flight camera. (b) Wearable design, backpack with depth sensor, panoramic camera and mobile phone. (c) Wearable custom 3-D printed ring with panoramic camera, depth sensor and mobile phone.

inspiration from biomimetics and use a dual-camera setup [11] to detect the object and its distance from the user. Recently, methods using RGB-D cameras have gained traction due to a simpler hardware setup. Some combine the aforementioned methods with state-of-the-art computer vision techniques [5], using a RGB-D camera for object detection and distance sensing [1]. A few commercial apps include the Be My Eyes phone app [6], a platform connecting the visually impaired person with sighted volunteers for assistance, and the TapTapSee [4] app utilizing the CloudSight Image Recognition API to identify objects. A recent advancement in commercial apps is the Microsoft Seeing AI [15], which carries out numerous tasks such as describing the scene around the user and identifying currency bills when paying.

While these existing systems are able to recognize objects surrounding a person, one of their significant shortcomings is that they typically rely on the phone camera with a finite field of view (FoV) to take a picture of the scene before objects are detected and reported to the user. As such, if the object is situated behind the user, it will go undetected unless the user spins around and takes a series of pictures or a video of the scene. Recent introduction of affordable, easy to use panoramic cameras, can easily solve the "spin around" problem by taking one image which can be used to detect objects of interest surrounding a person, thus obviating the need for the user to look or spin around. In addition, most existing systems merely report all "significant" objects in a given scene to the user, rather than respond to a specific user-generated query. In practice, the user might want to inquire whether or not a specific object is in his/her environment, and if so, approximately where it is located. Along these lines, our informal survey of the visually impaired population shows particular interest in navigation-related objects such as doors, exit signs, staircases, elevators, restrooms, as well as utilitarian objects such as electric plugs on the walls. The recent introduction of text-to-speech and speech recognition capabilities on mobile phones paves the way for such user generated queries, and for audio response generation to the user.

In this paper, we propose a wearable query system for the visually impaired utilizing a panoramic camera and a mobile phone. The concept of operation of our system is as follows: the user pushes a button on a Bluetooth device to connect to the phone to activate the app and asks for a specific object. The phone then triggers the panoramic camera to take a picture of the surroundings and runs the recorded audio signal on a speech recognition engine. Once the phone receives the captured 360° picture from the panoramic camera, it runs a pre-trained object recognition model with the requested object as input, in order to identify it in the panoramic image; it then reports the direction of the object back to the user via the text-to-speech engine. An optional commercially available inexpensive depth-sensing camera can also identify the distance of the object from the user, if the object is within the FoV of the depth camera.

2 System Overview

2.1 Hardware Design

Figure 1 shows the evolution of three designs of our proposed system, all consisting of a mobile phone as well as a panoramic camera. Figure 1(a) shows our first design which is a handheld device with two handles. Upon informal survey of the visually impaired community, we migrated to our second design shown in Fig. 1(b) which is a wearable backpack and hands-free. Specifically, we found the user community to have a strong preference for a hands-free versus a handheld system since their hands are already occupied by a cane. In the backpack system of Fig. 1(b) the panoramic camera is connected to a rod which is then secured inside the backpack with additional hardware; in addition, a mobile phone and a depth-sensing camera is attached to the backpack in front of the user. Figure 1(c) shows our third design inspired by Project BLAID at Toyota [21], consisting of a ring that the user wears on his/her shoulder. Here, a depth camera and a mobile phone is attached to the front and the panoramic camera on a rod is attached to the back of the ring. In all three designs the panoramic camera is high above the user's head, enabling it to capture 360° images surrounding the user without much occlusion. While from a technical point of view, this approach results in non-occluded panoramic imagery and improves object detection, we readily acknowledge that from an aesthetic point of view, this might not be the best choice. In particular, we have received feedback from the visually impaired community regarding the stigma attached to wearable devices that draw attention to them. As such, in our latest design in Fig. 1(c), we have included two mounting screws on the two shoulders to accommodate future designs with two panoramic cameras pointing sideways. This obviates the need for having a camera high above the users head, since the two panoramic cameras can capture the entire surroundings of the user, to the right, left, up and down.

As seen, the designs in Fig. 1(b) and 1(c) include a front facing depth camera, which can relay the distance of the object to the user as long as the object is in front of the object, i.e. within the FoV of the depth camera. Since there are no panoramic depth cameras currently on the market, to find distances to objects in all directions, our future design might need to have multiple depth cameras pointing at different directions. For the design shown in Fig. 1(a) we have used a depth-sensing mobile phone, namely Oppo R17 Pro, rather than using a separate depth-sensing device. Clearly, in all three designs, it is possible to either use a depth-sensor enabled mobile phone or a regular mobile phone with an additional depth sensor. The advantage of the former over the latter is fewer components and therefore increased robustness to failure. For the experiments in this paper, we use the RGB-D depth-sensing camera Realsense D415 from Intel [9], Android mobile phones such as the Google Pixel 2 or the Samsung Galaxy S8, and the panoramic camera Theta V from Ricoh [19]. The Bluetooth trigger is hung around the neck of the user for safekeeping and easy access purposes.

2.2 System Operation

We now describe the details of the operations of our proposed system: Upon a single click of the Bluetooth trigger, the user talks to the app to ask for a specific object of interest. We use the Kaldi speech recognition toolkit [18] for transcribing the user speech. At the same time the phone signals the panoramic camera via WiFi connection to capture a picture with resolution $5,376 \times 2,688$. The mobile phone then downloads, splits and recti-linearizes the image into 4 pictures of size $1,344 \times 2,688$ using OpenMVG [16], which corresponds to the front, right, left and back quadrants around the user respectively. The 4 images are then passed into our TensorFlow Lite model trained on our custom dataset to localize the object of interest. It then reports the results through a text-to-speech engine, where the objects are described in a clock coordinate system with the user's front corresponding to 12:00, right to 3:00, left to 9:00 etc. Figure 2 showcases the visual output of object detection in one of the recti-linear pictures created from a panoramic capture.

By clicking the Bluetooth trigger twice, the user again talks to the app to ask for a specific object of interest, but this time the depth detection pipeline will be invoked, capturing a recti-linear RGB image and its associated depth map. For the handheld device in Fig. 1(a) we use the Oppo phone depth sensor, while for the wearable backpack and ring systems in Fig. 1(b) and 1(c) we use the Intel Realsense D415 depth device. In both cases, there is a need to align the RGB image and depth map by mapping each point in the depth map to a point in the RGB image. This is achieved by using the intrinsic camera matrices for both the RGB camera and the depth camera, taking into account focal length and optical center in x and y. Figure 2(a) shows the ground truth and 2(b) the result of detected objects. The TensorFlow Lite model trained on RGB images detects the queried object in front of the user, calculates and reports back its distance through the text-to-speech engine. If the confidence level of the recognized object is too low, the panoramic camera is invoked to locate the desired object in the 360° surrounding of the user. In this case, if the detected object via the panoramic camera is found to be within the FoV of the depth camera with high confidence, then the distance to the user will be reported via the text-to-speech engine on the phone.

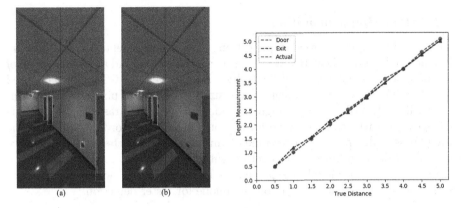

Fig. 2. Detection example. (a) Ground-truth (b) Results from recognition model

Fig. 3. Measurements of object depth vs. actual distance.

In order to calculate the distance of the object to the user, we average over the depth values near the center of the detected bounding box for the object. The size of the region is taken proportional to the size of the bounding box. The depth to RGB point mapping is stored in a two dimensional K-d tree [3] to provide fast look up of the points near the center of the detected object.

The accuracy of the depth detection is tested by taking measurements of 2 representative classes, namely doors and exits, at $0.5\,\mathrm{m}$ steps from $0.5\,\mathrm{m}$ to $5\,\mathrm{m}$ with objects being fronto-parallel to the camera. The result is shown in Fig. 3, indicating a close match between measured and ground truth distance.

3   Object Detection Model

3.1   Dataset Collection

We manually collect panoramic pictures using the setup in Fig. 1(a), with the panoramic camera held above the head as to emulate the height of the final design. We then recti-linearize the panoramic pictures into 4 pictures of equal resolution for the front, right, back and left of the person respectively using OpenMVG [16]. We use LabelImg [22] to create the ground truth bounding boxes. Fast inference time is a crucial requirement of a real-time query system; thus we choose SSD with MobileNetV2 [20] as the object detection model architecture in our system [8]. Specifically MobileNetV2 is used as the feature extractor and 6 additional SSD layers are used for bounding box regression and object classification. To compare the performance of the model against better feature extractors, we also trained the model with ResNet-50 FPN [7,12] as the backbone. The models are pretrained on the Microsoft COCO dataset [14] and then finetuned on our collected dataset.

3.2 Model Implementation

The training pipelines are adapted from [8], an implementation of SSD w/ MobileNetV2 and SSD w/ResNet-50 FPN in TensorFlow, and a machine setup of an Intel Core i7-6850K CPU @ 3.60 GHz with one GeForce GTX 1080Ti is used in the training process. All images are resized to 400 × 800 pixels per the memory limit of the GPU. Twelve augmentations including contrast, brightness, hue changes and various crops are performed on the dataset in order to improve the robustness of the model. To overcome the imbalance of objects in the dataset, we used the Adam optimizer [10] together with focal loss [13] to train the model. After training, the model is exported to TensorFlow Lite, which allows us to store the trained model directly on the phone for faster detection.

Table 1. The confusion matrix with "same" and "different" tests of SSD w/MobileNetV2 with 12 augmentations. Nothing means that either an object of a class of interest is not detected, or an object detected is not in the ground-truth.

SSD w/MobileNetV2 @0.5 IOU ("same" test)		Prediction					
		exit	elevator	door	bathroom	plug	nothing
	exit	204	0	0	0	0	8
	elevator	1	95	3	5	0	5
Ground	door	0	1	341	5	0	24
Truth	bathroom	0	0	2	46	0	3
	plug	0	0	2	0	109	20
	nothing	18	29	57	13	19	0

SSD w/MobileNetV2 @0.5 IOU ("different" test)		Prediction					
		exit	elevator	door	bathroom	plug	nothing
	exit	64	0	2	0	0	2
	elevator	0	19	9	0	0	7
Ground	door	0	10	193	13	0	8
Truth	bathroom	0	4	8	12	0	12
	plug	0	0	1	0	2	0
	nothing	24	22	124	21	7	0

Table 2. Precision and recall for each class.

SSD w/MobileNetV2 @0.5 IOU ("same" test)			SSD w/MobileNetV2 @0.5 IOU ("different" test)		
Class	Precision	Recall	Class	Precision	Recall
Exit	0.92	0.96	Exit	0.73	0.94
Elevator	0.76	0.87	Elevator	0.35	0.542
Door	0.84	0.92	Door	0.572	0.861
Bathroom	0.67	0.90	Bathroom	0.261	0.333
Plug	0.85	0.83	Plug	0.222	0.667

3.3   Experimental Results

We train the model with batch size of 8. The initial learning rate was chosen in the range of [0.001, 0.0008, 0.0004, 0.0002, 0.0001], with 0.0002 performing the best in the first 3000 steps. We use logarithmic decreasing learning rate and train for a total step number of 250K steps chosen empirically to perform best. We train the model on 518 pictures from Cory, Soda and Stanly Halls on U.C. Berkeley campus with a train/test split of 0.8/0.2. We refer to the results from this test as "same", indicating that training and test data were disjoint but from the same buildings. In addition, we test the model on 228 pictures taken from new buildings not in the training set, namely Dwinelle and Evans Halls. We refer to this test as "different" since the test data was from different buildings than the training data. The confusion matrix of the SSD w/MobileNetV2 model, along with precision and recall of each of the classes are also shown in Tables 1 and 2. As seen, for both tests the precision and recall values are best for exits, followed by doors. This is not surprising as they have the largest number of training examples. As expected, there is a drop in precision and recall from "same" to "different" test. We also trained the models with fewer augmentations, without random cropping as a comparison. The accuracy of all the models can be seen in Table 3. The accuracy drop from same to nfew test buildings is in agreement with [2], as it is difficult for the model to generalize to the objects of interest not in the training set. As seen, increased augmentation from 5 to 12 improves accuracy and generalization for new test buildings from 44.8% to 53.6%.

Table 3. Accuracy of different models measured by mAP @0.5 IOU

Models	Augmentations	"Same" test	"Different" test
SSD w/MobileNetV2	12	90.9	52.9
SSD w/MobileNetV2	5	99.6	51.7
SSD w/ResNet-50 FPN	12	86.2	53.6
SSD w/ResNet-50 FPN	5	99.8	44.8

From the results in Table 3 we observe that SSD w/ResNet-50 FPN performs marginally better than MobileNetV2 with 12 augmentations. However the latency of ResNet-50 FPN as the backbone to be higher than MobileNetV2 [8]. The ResNet-50 FPN feature extractor is also worse at detecting small objects such as plugs. Thus we choose SSD w/MobileNetV2 as our model, allowing a very slight accuracy drop for faster and more usable detection.

Future work involves improving accuracy for new buildings, new hardware designs with less conspicuous cameras, and extensive user studies.

References

1. Bai, J., Liu, Z., Lin, Y., Li, Y., Lian, S., Liu, D.: Wearable travel aid for environment perception and navigation of visually impaired people. CoRR abs/1904.13037 (2019). http://arxiv.org/abs/1904.13037
2. Balamurugan, A., Zakhor, A.: Online learning for indoor asset detection. In: 2019 IEEE 29th International Workshop on Machine Learning for Signal Processing (MLSP), pp. 1–6 (2019)
3. Bentley, J.L.: Multidimensional binary search trees used for associative searching. Commun. ACM **18**(9), 509–517 (1975). https://doi.org/10.1145/361002.361007
4. CloudSight: Taptapsee (2012)
5. Dai, J., Li, Y., He, K., Sun, J.: R-FCN: object detection via region-based fully convolutional networks. CoRR abs/1605.06409 (2016). http://arxiv.org/abs/1605.06409
6. Eyes, B.M.: Be my eyes (2015)
7. He, K., Zhang, X., Ren, S., Sun, J.: Deep residual learning for image recognition. CoRR abs/1512.03385 (2015). http://arxiv.org/abs/1512.03385
8. Huang, J., et al.: Speed/accuracy trade-offs for modern convolutional object detectors. In: 2017 IEEE Conference on Computer Vision and Pattern Recognition (CVPR), pp. 3296–3297 (2016)
9. Intel: Realsense d415 (2018)
10. Kingma, D.P., Ba, J.: Adam: a method for stochastic optimization. arXiv e-prints arXiv:1412.6980, December 2014
11. Kotyan, S., Kumar, N., Sahu, P.K., Udutalapally, V.: Drishtikon: an advanced navigational aid system for visually impaired people. CoRR abs/1904.10351 (2019). http://arxiv.org/abs/1904.10351
12. Lin, T., Dollár, P., Girshick, R.B., He, K., Hariharan, B., Belongie, S.J.: Feature pyramid networks for object detection. CoRR abs/1612.03144 (2016). http://arxiv.org/abs/1612.03144
13. Lin, T.Y., Goyal, P., Girshick, R., He, K., Dollár, P.: Focal loss for dense object detection. arXiv e-prints arXiv:1708.02002, August 2017
14. Lin, T., et al.: Microsoft COCO: common objects in context. CoRR abs/1405.0312 (2014). http://arxiv.org/abs/1405.0312
15. Microsoft: Seeing AI (2017)
16. Moulon, P., Monasse, P., Perrot, R., Marlet, R.: OpenMVG: open multiple view geometry. In: Kerautret, B., Colom, M., Monasse, P. (eds.) RRPR 2016. LNCS, vol. 10214, pp. 60–74. Springer, Cham (2017). https://doi.org/10.1007/978-3-319-56414-2_5
17. World Health Organization: World report on vision. World Health Organization (2019)
18. Povey, D., et al.: The Kaldi speech recognition toolkit (2011)
19. Ricoh: Theta v (2017)
20. Sandler, M., Howard, A.G., Zhu, M., Zhmoginov, A., Chen, L.: Inverted residuals and linear bottlenecks: mobile networks for classification, detection and segmentation. CoRR abs/1801.04381 (2018). http://arxiv.org/abs/1801.04381

21. Toyota: Project blaid (2016)
22. Tzutalin: Labelimg (2015)
23. Yelamarthi, K., Haas, D., Nielsen, D., Mothersell, S.: RFID and GPS integrated navigation system for the visually impaired, pp. 1149–1152, August 2010. https://doi.org/10.1109/MWSCAS.2010.5548863
24. Yi, C., Flores, R., Chincha, R., Tian, Y.: Finding objects for assisting blind people. Netw. Model. Anal. Health Inform. Bioinform. **2**, 71–79 (2013). https://doi.org/10.1007/s13721-013-0026-x

SelfLens: A Personal Assistive Technology to Support the Independence of People with Special Needs in Reading Information on Food Items

Giulio Galesi[1], Luciano Giunipero[2], Barbara Leporini[1,3(✉)],
Franco Pagliucoli[3], Antonio Quatraro[3], and Gianni Verdi[2]

[1] ISTI-CNR, Via G. Moruzzi 1, 56124 Pisa, Italy
{giulio.galesi,barbara.leporini}@isti.cnr.it
[2] EDI GROUP s.r.l., Via G. La Pira 1/A, 52011 Bibbiena, Italy
{luciano.giunipero,gianni.verdi}@edigroup.it
[3] I.Ri.Fo.R. Toscana, Via L. Fibonacci 5, 50131 Florence, Italy
irifor@irifortoscana.it

Abstract. Grocery shopping or handling food items (e.g. packets, boxes, etc.) can be a very difficult task for people with special needs. Object labels may contain much information that can be difficult to read because the data shown is a lot, and the text is difficult to read by many people. Blind people are unable to get that information autonomously, and many sighted persons (e.g. elderly people and visually-impaired) may have a lot of difficulty in reading labels. Several tools or applications are available on the market or have been proposed in the literature to support this type of activity (e.g. barcode or QR code reading), but they are limited and may require specific skills by the user. Moreover, repeatedly using an application to read label contents or to get additional information on a product can require numerous actions on a touch-screen device. This can make their use inaccessible or unusable for many users, especially while shopping or cooking. In this work, a portable tool is proposed to support people in simply reading the contents of labels and getting additional information, while they are at home or at the shop. Our study aims to propose a portable assistive technology which can be used by everyone both at home and in the shopping, independently from the personal skills and without requiring no smartphone or complex device, and that is a low-cost solution for the user. Such a product could be very useful for the people independence in a period like that one we are living due to the lockdown required by the Covid-19 situation.

Keywords: Interactive device · Accessibility · Shopping · Smart home

1 Introduction

People with special needs may face numerous difficulties in performing many everyday activities. Blind people, for instance, encounter many obstacles in carrying out tasks, such as shopping [14], managing products at home [8], and cooking [5] amongst others. Partially sighted people may also have problems reading labels or a large

© Springer Nature Switzerland AG 2020
K. Miesenberger et al. (Eds.): ICCHP 2020, LNCS 12376, pp. 526–533, 2020.
https://doi.org/10.1007/978-3-030-58796-3_60

amount of content information printed on numerous products. This difficulty is due to the inadequate use of colors, inappropriate color contrast, the type and size of the text fonts, etc. [13]. Consequently, several issues are encountered when performing everyday activities, such as using products at home and at the shop.

In this context, some tools have been proposed to aid the visually-impaired to get information on products. At home, for instance, it is currently possible to use tools like the PenFriend labeler (www.rnib.org.uk/rnibconnect/technology/penfriend-3-audio-labeller), which can be bought on the market to allow people with visual impairments to label products (e.g. food items) themselves using their voice. For example, when placing a product in the pantry, a blind person has to record in braille or voice-based format the name, expiration date, as well as other additional information like important ingredients or key cooking instructions. This type of activity, however, is time-consuming and requires support from a sighted person to obtain the information from the product label. The tool ORCam (www.orcam.com) is also available on the market to read written text or identify products, but it is very expensive. On the other hand, some recent mobile applications like 'Seeing AI' proposed by Microsoft (www.microsoft.com/en-us/seeing-ai) can offer functions designed to read on the fly a written text or a barcode via a smartphone. Other studies have proposed alternative mobile-based technologies [10], however, they may require specific skills in order to use them. Elderly or disabled people might not like using touch-screen devices, because it can require technical skills or it can be very complicated [2]. Furthermore, using those applications while shopping or cooking can become a very arduous task for a blind person, especially to get information on elements like name and brand, expiration date, and so on. In addition, elderly or partially-sighted people will likely need to use glasses or a magnifying lens to be able to read that information. For these reasons, we propose a standalone tool, which does not require a smartphone and is very simple to use for both sighted and blind users.

In this work, we present a potential portable tool named SelfLens designed to support anyone in using autonomously products and items both at home and in the shop, especially in getting specific information on the product itself. The tool we propose is aimed at (1) making people with special needs autonomous in reading information on a product, (2) offering a device which is easy to use by anyone at any time without requiring advanced skills, and (3) proposing a portable and low-cost solution.

The proposed solution might be particularly useful in a context like the one caused by issues due to Covid-19. Lockdown does not allow the visually-impaired and elderly people to receive adequate assistance from other sighted people. Autonomy is particularly useful, especially to check the name and expiration date of home-delivered food items purchased online.

2 Related Work

Numerous studies have been investigating possible tools and services designed to support visually-impaired people with shopping [4, 7] and [15]. However, the technologies proposed are mainly intended to assist navigation, and others to locate the products in the shop [3, 9, 11].

Our study is particularly focused on the accessibility of the information written on product labels, in order to allow people with special needs to be able to read them autonomously. This can be very useful both at home [8, 14], and at the shop [15]. Unfortunately, this feature risks being undervalued when considering the main needs and numerous actions to carry out in autonomy at home and when shopping [6]. The main issue is related to the difficulties in reading textual contents written on the labels. This is a problem encountered not only by the visually-impaired, but also by the sighted. In fact, the study reported in [13] suggests personalizing eBook visualization to adapt the rendering for sighted, visually-impaired and blind people. These results reveal the need for text customization functionalities in reading tools, as well as the opportunity to provide the information in an alternative way in specific contexts, such as shopping.

Our solution is based on a QR code approach, with some changes. Results reported by the study [1] indicate that a QR code solution can be used for visually-impaired users when shopping. However, in this case a smartphone is needed in order to use this application, as is also the case for the solution proposed in [12]. In fact, several proposed tools to support blind people in recognizing products at the shop are based on touch-screen devices, such as [10]. This requires certain digital skills by the user. On the contrary, our solution is aimed at offering a tool which can be used also by those people who are not familiar with smartphones. In addition, using an app on a smart-phone may require numerous steps (e.g. taking the smartphone, unlocking the screen, finding the app, interacting with the user interface, etc.) to be performed when getting information about a product. This is not so practical when performed frequently and on a daily basis, such as when shopping. Our approach is to gain access to the information quickly by pointing the device at a product and just pressing a button This should be easier also for those who are less experienced with technology.

3   The Proposed Tool

In this section, the proposed tool is introduced by providing a description, the main features, as well as the necessary architecture.

3.1   Description

A portable tool named SelfLens has been proposed as a personal assistive technology which can be used by everyone, including elderly, partially-sighted, blind and hearing-impaired people to get information on a product, which is usually available on its label. The device is able to provide information on the (a) name and brand, (b) components such as ingredients, allergens, etc., (c) prices and discounts, and (d) instructions or other information about the product usage.

The device looks like a remote control that can be easily held in one hand. The tool is designed to be used by any person, by simply (1) pointing at the product and (2) pressing a button to get information on it or to buy it. The information is provided on demand and presented both via voice messages and on a small screen. In Fig. 1 how the tool can be used by a user to get information on a product is shown. The tool is also designed to be used for purchasing the desired products, but this function will be better designed in the next version of the prototype.

To sum up, the tool SelfLens has been built to provide:

1. Product recognition: thanks to a special coding system used to mark each product, Self-Lens is able to recognize it by using a video camera;
2. Product information: for each product, Self-Lens is able to provide information on the name, prices, expiration date, components and ingredients, etc.
3. Product purchasing: the user will be able to buy the product immediately, or add it to the shopping cart to place the order at a later time.

Fig. 1. A customer collecting information about a product using the SelfLens device.

3.2   Prototype Features

The tool has been designed so that it can become a practical assistive tool that can be on hand and used by everyone at any time without the need for specific skills or mobile smartphones. The user can use it to get the product information very quickly and (if required) buy it in just one click. It could be useful both in the home and in the shop. Therefore, its usage should be very practical and immediate.

The tool has been designed so that it has the following features:

- Simple and practical interaction: thanks to a minimal User Interface (UI) composed of only two buttons, one display, and a speaker, The tool can be easily and practically used by everyone;
- Portable and lightweight: the tool looks like a small remote control which can be held in one hand;
- Multi-purpose functions: the tool is able to provide (1) text information and (2) purchasing functions;
- Audio and visual feedback: in order to ensure full inclusion for people with different types of disability, information as well as the dialogue messages are provided to the user via both audio and visual perception.

3.3   Tool Architecture

SelfLens is a tool based on a system which is composed of three main components: (1) the portable device, (2) the marker code for each product identification, and (3) a products database. The connection between the device and the database is based on a SIM card. The user relies on the portable device as the main component of the system. More specifically:

Portable Device: it is used by the user to identify each product through a video camera, and to get information via vocal messages (through the speaker or earphones), or written messages (through a display). A SIM card is installed to connect the device with the database on the net.

Marker Code: it is used to mark each product. It is based on a QR code solution, with some differences in the shape and size of the printed code. This is because the needed information for each product requires a lot of space, which cannot be guaranteed by an everyday QR code.

Products Database: it is used to store and retrieve information on each product. The content of the product labels is structured and stored in this database, which is located on the net. The link between the product and its data is based on the marker code ID. Since some issues on the connection between the device and the database can occur, a local instance of the database is stored in the device memory. In this case updated and context-dependent data like the prices and offers (which are shopping store-dependent) could not be provided to the user. The device regularly updates the local database with the content of the database on the network.

4   Design Requirements

When designing the prototype (see Fig. 2), some specifics and functions have been defined sections. The specifics regarded the following aspects:

- Recognition via a properly-designed code to mark any product and also to overcome some limitations of existing QR codes or barcodes; Shape and size were designed to adapt the marker code to the item and its contents. The code is a label which can be attached onto the product. A blind user can identify it by touch and its position, which is the same for each similar product (e.g. on the stopper or on the corner of boxes and packets). In addition, the tool supports the identification of the code through audio feedback.
- Functions are triggered by the two buttons according to the type and number of presses.
- Feedback messages are defined according to the current function and the output modality (voice or screen).

4.1   User Interface and Components

The tool has been designed as a device with a rectangular shape, a display on the front, two buttons (circular and square), and a video camera located on the back (see Fig. 2). The speaker on the front, located below the two buttons, has been added to provide information via voice messages and short sounds. The two buttons have been designed with a different shape and label ('I' for information, and 'A' for purchasing) to make them easily distinguishable by touch.

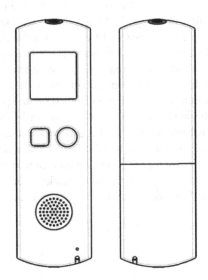

Fig. 2. Prototype with the camera on the top.

4.2   Functions Triggered by the Buttons

The device is designed to receive 9 commands triggered through the two buttons (circular and square), which can be pressed separately or simultaneously. For each function, the button pressure, function name and description as well as both audio and visual feedback are explained. With reference to each button, the type of pressure on the button (how many times and seconds) is reported as a command to use to trigger the related function. The square button ('i') and circle button ('A') can be pressed separately or simultaneously.

Table 1 reports an example of how three functions have been assigned to a single (square) button. A similar approach can be used for the circle button.

Table 1. Functions assigned to the square button (labelled with 'i').

Action	Function	Description
1 press 1 s	**Product info**	Name, expiry date
2 presses 1 s	**Product details**	Name, exp. date, price, allergens, ingredients
1 press 3 s	**Switch on**	The device is turned On It is turned Off after 5 min of inactivity

5 Pilot Evaluation

A first version of the prototype was analyzed with the support of 3 sighted users and 3 blind users. The aim was to use the feedback to design and refine (1) the interaction mode and (2) the functions assigned to the two buttons of the device. Other user interface components have been considered in the life-cycle of the product. Specifically, various aspects were evaluated with the end-users, such as (a) the position of the video camera installed on the device to detect the product from the special marker code, (b) the number, shape and size of the buttons, and (c) the main functions to consider in the first prototype. The first prototype had two buttons with the same shape and size. The evaluation with the users revealed that two very similar buttons can be confusing for the user, resulting in a poor natural interaction while using the tool. In addition, based on the fact that the second button will be dedicated to purchasing, the users commented that the purchasing operations need to be done safely, without the risk of mistakenly pressing the button which immediately starts the purchase. They observed that "one-click" certainly may facilitate the purchasing tasks, but the device should be able to avoid unintentional purchases. Another aspect considered in the evaluation was the camera position. The first prototype had the video camera on the top; regarding this, the users commented that pointing the product with a camera located at the bottom, as if the device were a smartphone, might be more practical since the user interacts in this way for other activities. This aspect will be considered in a second version of the prototype.

6 Conclusions

In this work, a portable personal device has been presented as a potential assistive technology to get information on items and products. The SelfLens tool has been proposed to be (1) easy to use for everyone, (2) portable and practical, (3) suitable for various types of needs thanks to the audio and visual feedback. The tool is able to provide information on (a) names and brands, (b) prices, (c) ingredients and components, and (d) additional information such as instructions and so on. The proposed tool differs from the existing solutions due to the fact that no digital skills are required to use it, and it can be used by everyone, not just a single category of users. SelfLens can thus offer the elderly and people with disabilities the opportunity to become more autonomous both at home and at the shop in just one click. SelfLens could be a personal assistive technology useful to support the autonomy of people with special needs in the critical situation caused by the Covid-19 lockdown, thanks to the opportunity to check product information or send a purchase order to the favourite store. Future work includes user testing conducted with end-users to evaluate the proposed functionalities and building a new version of the prototype to develop the purchasing function assigned to the circle button.

References

1. Al-Khalifa, H.S.: Utilizing QR code and mobile phones for blinds and visually impaired people. In: Miesenberger, K., Klaus, J., Zagler, W., Karshmer, A. (eds.) ICCHP 2008. LNCS, vol. 5105, pp. 1065–1069. Springer, Heidelberg (2008). https://doi.org/10.1007/978-3-540-70540-6_159

2. Chiti, S., Leporini, B.: Accessibility of android-based mobile devices: a prototype to investigate interaction with blind users. In: Miesenberger, K., Karshmer, A., Penaz, P., Zagler, W. (eds.) ICCHP 2012. LNCS, vol. 7383, pp. 607–614. Springer, Heidelberg (2012). https://doi.org/10.1007/978-3-642-31534-3_89

3. Duarte, K., Cecílio, J., Furtado, P.: Overview of assistive technologies for the blind: navigation and shopping. In: ICARCV, pp. 1929–1934. IEEE (2014)

4. Gharpure, C.P., Kulyukin, V.A.: Robot-assisted shopping for the blind: issues in spatial cognition and product selection. Intell. Serv. Robot. 1(3), 237–251 (2008). https://doi.org/10.1007/s11370-008-0020-9

5. Kostyra, E., Żakowska-Biemans, S., Śniegocka, K., Piotrowska, A.: Food shopping, sensory determinants of food choice and meal preparation by visually impaired people. Obstacles and expectations in daily food experiences. Appetite 113(5), 14–22 (2017)

6. Kulyukin, V., Kutiyanawala, A.: Accessible shopping systems for blind and visually impaired individuals: Design requirements and the state of the art. Open Rehabil. J. 3(1) (2010)

7. Lanigan, P.E., Paulos, A.M., Williams, A.W., Rossi, D., Narasimhan, P.: Trinetra: assistive technologies for grocery shopping for the blind. In ISWC, pp. 147–148. IEEE (2006)

8. Leporini, B., Buzzi, M.: Home automation for an independent living: investigating the needs of visually impaired people. In: IAT, pp. 1–9. ACM, New York (2018)

9. López-de-Ipiña, D., Lorido, T., López, U.: Indoor navigation and product recognition for blind people assisted shopping. In: Bravo, J., Hervás, R., Villarreal, V. (eds.) IWAAL 2011. LNCS, vol. 6693, pp. 33–40. Springer, Heidelberg (2011). https://doi.org/10.1007/978-3-642-21303-8_5

10. López-de-Ipiña, D., Lorido, T., López, U.: BlindShopping: enabling accessible shopping for visually impaired people through mobile technologies. In: Abdulrazak, B., Giroux, S., Bouchard, B., Pigot, H., Mokhtari, M. (eds.) ICOST 2011. LNCS, vol. 6719, pp. 266–270. Springer, Heidelberg (2011). https://doi.org/10.1007/978-3-642-21535-3_39

11. Nicholson, J., Kulyukin, V., Coster, D.: ShopTalk: independent blind shopping through verbal route directions and barcode scans. Open Rehabil. J. 2(1) (2009)

12. Sahasrabudhe, S., Singh, R., Heath, D.: Innovative affordances for blind smartphone users: a qualitative study. In: The 31st Annual International Technology and Persons with Disabilities Conference Proceedings, San Diego (2016)

13. Schwarz, T., Rajgopal, S., Stiefelhagen, R.: Accessible EPUB: making EPUB 3 documents universal accessible. In: Miesenberger, K., Kouroupetroglou, G. (eds.) ICCHP 2018. LNCS, vol. 10896, pp. 85–92. Springer, Cham (2018). https://doi.org/10.1007/978-3-319-94277-3_16

14. Yuan, C.W., Hanrahan, B.V., Lee, S., Rosson, M.B., Carroll, J.M.: Constructing a holistic view of shopping with people with visual impairment: a participatory design approach. Univ. Access Inf. Soc. 18(1), 127–140 (2017). https://doi.org/10.1007/s10209-017-0577-1

15. Zientara, P.A., et al.: Third eye: a shopping assistant for the visually impaired. Computer 50(2), 16–24 (2017)

Correction to: Suitable Camera and Rotation Navigation for People with Visual Impairment on Looking for Something Using Object Detection Technique

Masakazu Iwamura⊙, Yoshihiko Inoue, Kazunori Minatani⊙, and Koichi Kise⊙

Correction to:
Chapter "Suitable Camera and Rotation Navigation for People with Visual Impairment on Looking for Something Using Object Detection Technique" in: K. Miesenberger et al. (Eds.): *Computers Helping People with Special Needs*, LNCS 12376, https://doi.org/10.1007/978-3-030-58796-3_57

The original version of this chapter was revised. The introduction was updated because important information, such as a reference, was missing.

The updated version of this chapter can be found at
https://doi.org/10.1007/978-3-030-58796-3_57

Author Index

Printed in the United States
By Bookmasters